THE COST OF
GLOBALIZATION

THE COST OF GLOBALIZATION

Dangers to the Earth and Its People

Julian E. Kunnie

McFarland & Company, Inc., Publishers

Jefferson, North Carolina

LIBRARY OF CONGRESS CATALOGUING-IN-PUBLICATION DATA

Kunnie, Julian.
    The cost of globalization : dangers to the earth and its people /
Julian E. Kunnie.
        p.   cm.
    Includes bibliographical references and index.

    ISBN 978-0-7864-9608-2 (softcover : acid free paper) ∞
    ISBN 978-1-4766-1977-4 (ebook)

    1. Globalization—Economic aspects.   2. Globalization—Social
aspects.   3. Externalities (Economics)   4. Anti-globalization
movement.   5. Poverty.   6. Social justice.   I. Title.

HF1365.K786 2015
303.48′2—dc23   2015004267

BRITISH LIBRARY CATALOGUING DATA ARE AVAILABLE

On the cover: *clockwise from top left* Smokey Mountain, Manila,
Philippines (Stockbyte/Thinkstock); Barbed wire fence (iStock/
Thinkstock); Masai warrior at sunset (iStock/Thinkstock); Global
Warming (iStock/Thinkstock)

Printed in the United States of America

McFarland & Company, Inc., Publishers
  Box 611, Jefferson, North Carolina 28640
    www.mcfarlandpub.com

To Mother Earth and All
of Her Struggling Children
and to
Magdalin and Matthew Kunnie,
beloved Parents, and Grandmother Ayah
and to
Hataali Jones Benally,
my ever-wise Teacher and Mentor

Table of Contents

Acknowledgments

This project is conceived as an acknowledgment of a central ethos in traditional indigenous cultures. This ethos emphasizes the interconnectedness of all life and relationships on this Earth. Even though I am the principal author whose name appears on the cover, I offer this book as exemplar of the rewarding insights many great and wonderful people shared with me in a genuine knowing of us all belonging to the Earth and the universe.

First, thanks go to the Creator, *Usen, Bik'ehgo'ihi'nan, Wakan Tanka, Mdali, Modimo*, the Great Mystery, who has no beginning and no end and whose mysteriousness in the Universe continues to amaze us as human beings. Thanks go to ancestors of the Indigenous peoples of this sacred land, *Abya Yala* or Turtle Island, generally known as North America, and the ancestors of Africa, Asia, and the rest of the Indigenous world for inspiration and courage to be able to pen so many words.

My primary teacher and mentor and to whom this book is also dedicated, Hataali Jones Benally, from Big Mountain/Black Mesa, Arizona, receives special mention for being a paragon of humility and assisting me in understanding the *real* power of the Universe. The Benally family in Flagstaff, particularly Berta, Jeneda, Clayson, and their children, Dahi and Daschils, has been a decisive part of this literary and spiritual journey. So has Michael Paul Hill from our San Carlos Chi Endeh community, Sister Ofelia Rivas, our spiritual elder from the Tohono' O'odham community in Ali-Chuk, on the Arizona-Mexico border, Anthony Van Dunk and Edward from the Indigenous Lenape community in the northeast, who has hosted me each May during the UN Permanent Forum on Indigenous Peoples, Elder Mala Spotted Eagle Pope and Sky who hosted me at Nanish Shontie in 2011 and who have been spiritual guides to our family, and Colleen Hicks, of the Cherokee community and Executive Director of the Museum of the American Indian in Novato, California, who welcomed me and reminded me of the vast and diverse histories and cultures of Indigenous peoples in California.

The relatives from Indigenous communities around the world who hosted me in so many different times and places over the past thirty years need to be mentioned too because of their generosity and kindness that made such protracted book-writing possible: Thandi and Patrick Mkhize Lybon Mabasa, Alwiya Omar and family, the Mathys, Geoffries, Hoyi, Kunnies, Kurasha, Munavu, Kehinde, Laguda, and Gamal families, in various parts of Africa, as well as Bahru Zewde and the Mohammed family in Addis Ababa, Gondar, Axum, and friends in Lalibela, Ethiopia, who hosted us in 2005; friends from the Imazighen community in Ifrane, Morocco, who took me around in 2006; Jianping Yi, colleagues and friends from the Chinese Academy of Social Sciences in Beijing, Chenyang Li from Yunnan University, colleagues from Shaanxi Normal University in X'ian, and so many members of the staff and students from Renmin University in Beijing who made my stay in China so enjoyable in 2011, 2013 and 2014 like Wei Dedong, Yuna Lee, Jialu Zheng, and Akida Yerken from the Uygur community, Dennis Khoibur from Papua who showered me with so many spiritual gifts, along with Septer, Socrates, Roberth, Neles, Fien, Johannes, and Petronella from Papua, and Elias and Bata who traveled with me in Papua and Papua New Guinea; Umakanta Meitei and Soyam Lokendrajit and their families and colleagues in Manipur, northeast India; Laxmi Gurung, Mani, and the sisters from the Nepalese Indigenous Womens' Federation who warmly welcomed me during my research in Nepal in 2012; Niloh Ason and Igat Biju in Sarawak, Malaysia; Ellen Dictaan-Bang-Oa, Mila Singson, Windel Bolinget, Bestang Dekdeken, Wilfredo Alangui, and Pau Pamintuan-Riva from Baguio City, Pya from KAMP, Cynthia Deduro, Jay, and friends in Iloilo, and Norma, Joel and friends in Cotabato in the Philippines; Lapic (Debbie Lin) and Unga Kalay Joy Lin in Taiwan, Roger Thomas, Khadija, Veronica Arbon, Dennis O'Brien, Nathan Pabai, and Jennifer Caruso from the University of Adelaide, Jubba and Tom in Mossman Gorge, Felecia Watkins Lui from the Indigenous Australian Center at James Cook University in Cairns, and Willy Gordon and Trish in Hopevale, Queensland, Australia; Linda Tuhiwai Smith, Sandy Morrisen, Keely Smith, Hannah, and colleagues at the University of Waikato in Hamilton, Aotearoa (New Zealand); Ghazi Nahar and family in Jordan; John Hairo and Anita and elders in Cacarica, Colombia, during the *Encuentro para la vida, la paz y la dignidad* in 2002; Oscar Santillan in Ecuador; Felipe Toledo and Leticia Espiño's family in Veracruz, Mexico; Paul Baker and friends from the Alliance for Global Justice in Nicaragua; friends from Santiago de Cuba, Cuba, who hosted the

Atlantic Research Team of which I was a member led by Jualynne Dodson in 2000; former Haitian president Jean-Bertrand Aristide and his wife, Mildred Trouillot, whose spirit of resistance to oppression is indomitable and who honored me by attending my lecture in Tshwane, Azania (South Africa), in 2005 and whose persevering spirit is reflected in the courageous people of Haiti who hosted me there in 1992; Randall Robinson in St. Kitts, whom I hosted in Tucson in 2004 and whose work on behalf of the oppressed is commendable; the Quecha-speaking elders from Cuzco, Peru, who hosted me in 1990 during our wonderful visit in the Andes Mountains there; and the family of Eunja Lee in Osaka, Japan, where I had the opportunity to visit with Indigenous Ainu communities in the late 1980s. What joy and peace to have so many wonderful relatives who are part of my global community circle!

I would be remiss if I did not acknowledge the thoughtfulness and compassion of people behind bars whom I met, spoke with, and whose lives have touched me beyond imagination: Mumia Abu-Jamal at SCI Mahanoy, Pennsylvania, whose speaking truth to power continues behind the walls and fences, and at San Quentin State Prison, California: Troy Williams (released in summer 2014) and Lonnie Morris from the San Quentin Film School, Rafael Calixo, Forrest Jones, Charles Ross, Fanon Figgers, Sam Johnson, Sam Kearnes, Abdul Wahid, Curtis Roberts, James Metters, James Jenkins, John Leroy, Troy Smith, Curtis Carroll, and "Chief" Douglas Stankewitz, who continues to struggle for his freedom from unjust incarceration after 37 years on death row. Sam Robinson and Chris Siino in Public Information at San Quentin deserve thanks for their interest in my work.

For the research and editing of the book, I need to extend thanks to my research assistants from 2008 through 2012, Amanda Holmes, Noelle Miesfeld, and Adriana Zuniga-Terran at the University of Arizona. For constant critical and scholarly discussions, thanks go to Percy Hintzen, my longtime academic mentor from the University of California, Berkeley, and now at Florida International University, to Phoebe Ferris, mentor and friend, and to Chuck Tatum, for their constructive input through my writing and scholarship over the years. Celestino Fernandez, my colleague at the University of Arizona whose review of the original book proposal encouraged me forward, warrants special mention. I am grateful to Sharon Streater, longtime friend, supporter, and an activist whose dedication to keeping hope alive for the oppressed for the past three decades reflects the best of the human spirit.

For the final editing and revisions in the book, particular recognition needs to go to my dear colleague, Yuxuf Abana, who has been a true brother, and made all the difference in the final polished product. Collegial support from Jiang Wu who facilitated my visits to China and the Africana circle in Tucson, Praise Zenenga, Bayo Ijagbemi, Teles Machibya, and Baba Eno Washington, whose tireless and iconic work in Pan African dance for five decades, need special mention. I am thankful too to Casey Ontivero and Veronica Rodriguez from the Office of Instructional Assessment at the University of Arizona whose respective work on compiling graphs and tables in the book and advice on pictures and input on my DVD productions related to the book made my work so much easier. I am appreciative of efforts and the time invested by Will Slattery from the College of Humanities at the University of Arizona to find appropriate high-quality pictures used in this book.

If I have omitted anyone who assisted me during the past two and a half decades of global research in this section, I earnestly apologize and assure you that it was wholeheartedly unintentional and I echo my thanks. Ultimately, the oversights and shortcomings are my responsibility and I am humbled by the limits of my own intellectual knowledge in a world of inexhaustible knowledge.

Finally, acknowledgment of support go to Kim, Mandla, and Sibu for their love and generosity in providing the supportive space for me to engage in this massive writing project over so many years.

Asante Sana to all!

Abbreviations

ACP—African Caribbean Pacific initiative
ADX—Administrative Maximum Facility
AEI—American Heritage-Enterprise
AFP—Americans for Prosperity Foundation
AFRICOM—Africa High Command
AIDS—Acquired Immune Deficiency Syndrome
AIO—Americans for Indian Opportunity
ALEC—American Legislative Exchange Council
APEC—Asian-Pacific Economic Cooperation
ARI—Ayn Rand Institute
BJS—Bureau of Justice Statistics
BRICS—Brazil, Russia, India, China and South Africa
CARE—Citizens Against Ruining our Environment
CBD—Center for Biological Diversity
CCA—Corrections Corporation of America
CCAP—Climate Change Adaptation Project
CCCSN—Canadian Climate Change Scenarios Network
CDC—Centers for Disease Control and Prevention
CFCs—Chlorofluorocarbons
CIA—Central Intelligence Agency
CNY—Chinese Yuan
CONAIE—Confederation of Indigenous Nationalities of Ecuador
DARE—Drug Abuse Resistance Through Education
DBCP—Dibromochloropropane
DEA—Drug Enforcement Agency

DIA—Defense Intelligence Agency
ECCB—East Caribbean Central Bank
ECLAC—Economic Commission for Latin America and the Caribbean
ECOWAS—Economic Community of West African States
EPA—Environmental Protection Agency
EPI—Economic Policy Institute
EPZs—Economic Processing Zones
EU—European Union
FBI—Federal Bureau of Investigation
FDI—Foreign Direct Investment
FMLN—Farabundo Martí National Liberation Front
FSLN—The Sandinista National Liberation Front
GDP—Gross Domestic Product
GEO—Group on Earth Observations
GM—Genetically Modified
GWP—Global Warming Potential
HANDS—Humans Against Nuclear Dumping
HIPC—Heavily Indebted Poor Countries
HUGO—Human Genome Organization
ICA—International Coffee Agreement
ICE—Immigration and Customs Enforcement
IDP—Internally Displaced Person
IMF—International Monetary Fund
IPCC—Intergovernmental Panel on Climate Change
IPR—International Property Right
ISCST—International Support Center for Sustainable Tourism
IUCN—International Union for the Conservation of Nature
LGBT—Lesbian Gay Bisexual Transgender
LWOP—Life Without the Possibility of Parole
MAI—Multilateral Agreement on Investment
MTV—Music Televison
NAACP—National Association for the Advancement of Colored People
NAFTA—North American Free Trade Agreement
NASA—National Aeronautics and Space Administration
NATO—North Atlantic Treaty Organization
NSW—New South Wales (Province of Australia)

NYCLU—New York Civil Liberties Union

OECD—Organization for Economic Cooperation and Development

OPEC—Oil Producing and Exporting Countries

PLO—Palestine Liberation Organization

PRD—Party of the Democratic Revolution (political party in Mexico)

SACTWU—South African Clothing and Textiles Workers Union

SARDC—Southern Africa Research and Documentation Centre

SHU—Special Housing Unit

TASSC—The Advancement of Sound Science Coalition

TBI—Traumatic Brain Injury

TEK—Traditional Environmental Knowledge

TEPCO—Tokyo Electric Power Company

TGNP—Tanzania Gender Networking Programme

TNC—Transnational Corporation

TRIPS—Trade Related Aspects of Intellectual Property Rights

UNCTAD—United Nations Conference on Trade and Development

UNFCCC—UN Framework Convention on Climate Change

URNG—Unidad Revolucionaria Nacional Guatemalteca

WCC—Wackenhut Corrections Corporation

WIC—Women, Infants, and Children

WIEGO—Women in Informal Employment: Globalizing and Organizing

WIMSA—Working Group of Indigenous Minorities in Southern Africa

WTO—World Trade Organization

Preface

The Earth on which we live is beautiful. The sky, with its endless celestial bodies with constellations, galaxies, suns, stars, planets, satellites, comets, and other distant forms that can only be measured in terms of the speed of light bespeak a universe of mystery and wonder that human language is unable to adequately capture. On the Earth and in the seas, the mountains, landscapes, four-leggeds, birds, insects, plants, bugs, sea-creatures, and organisms too tiny to see with the human eye remind us that we are surrounded by beauty and incredible diversity. The universe is so immense that we cannot begin to imagine the incredible power that she is and wields. During extensive research and study travels over the past 37 years, I have been moved by the divine beauty of the universe, from the beauty of Crater Lake in Oregon, to the sacred *Dook'oos'liid* (the San Francisco Peaks) in Northern Arizona, to observing the beautiful red liquid erupting from the Kilauea volcano in the Big Island of Hawaii, to trekking in view of Annapurna and the Machhapuchhre mountain ranges in Nepal, to the majestic spray from *Mosi-Oa-Tunya* (Victoria Falls) in Zimbabwe, to boating on the world's longest river, the Nile, to beholding the spiritual site of *Uluru*, the sacred rock in Central Australia that has a perimeter of 9.4 kilometers, and to climbing to the glacier almost 4,600 meters high in Yulong Snow Mountain in Yulongxueshan in Yunnan, in southern China, the Earth is One and awesome.

Yet the irreplaceable beauty of Earth and the Universe is being shattered by a human system that refuses to understand, accept, and respect the divine beauty for all life to enjoy: a destructive economic and social system that has accelerated and is unable to change course to "come down to Earth." Human beings, along with most of the rest of the natural world, are faced with the dilemma that human civilizations have not had to face for tens of millennia: the possible *extinction* of the human race and the continued extinction of other forms of life on the Earth. Human beings are compelled to come to grips with an unassailable fact of existence: we do not wield *real power* in determining the present nor the future of the world even though some elements of human cultures may have falsely assumed so, with now portentous lethal consequences. We have *some* capacity to undo the damage, but never the power to *control* how the Earth and her children live. How do we attempt to address, redress, and undo the irreparable ecological, environmental, social, and economic damage on Earth now boiling in all quarters so that life is hardly sustainable in the ever hotter and drier Sonoran desert of Arizona and the southwest of the U.S., known as Turtle Island to many of the nation's Indigenous people according to the Iroquois creation story? This book is an attempt to illuminate the pain of a globalized world and provide vistas for action to address the crisis and deadly effects of globalization.

The introduction explains in detail why globalization is lethal for the Earth, the ecology, Indigenous peoples, women, the poor, and other vulnerable communities and sectors of the world. It lays out the rationale for the plan of the book that focuses on globalization's devastating impact on global ecological systems, global warming and climate change, Indigenous people, impoverished women, and those members of the poor and working classes in the United States who find themselves trapped within the growing prison industrial complex.

Globalization has evoked untold poverty and suffering of the world's working classes with billions marginalized by globalized capitalism's obsession with profits, a subject discussed in Chapter 1. The rhetoric of economic prosperity for all within the globalized "free market" is hardly free for the overwhelming majority, the virtual "99 percent" in the U.S. and the world. Chapter 1 highlights some of the diverse viewpoints of scholars on the globalization phenomenon, discusses global trade unevenness and commodity price instability and situations of globalization's "achievements" and pitfalls in Asia, Africa, Latin America, the Caribbean, and the BRICS countries (Brazil, Russia, India, China, and South Africa), culminating with the entrenchment of global financial and social instability as witnessed especially in the U.S. in 2008 and whose lingering effects can never be undone.

Chapter 2 focuses on the impact of globalization on Indigenous peoples in the first decade and recent years of the new millennium and the lethal threats facing the world's Indigenous peoples as they struggle for reclamation of ancestral lands, protection of sacred sites, cultural rights, and language rights, and resist the hegemonic power of nation states that refuse to implement policies according human rights to Indigenous peoples in the lands of their ancestors. The chapter documents Indigenous peoples' resistance to globalized colonization and illuminates issues of globalization and ecocide, as species extinction has accelerated moreso in the era of globalization than in the past 65 million years of the Earth. The very traditional practitioners among the world's Indigenous peoples like the San peoples of Southern Africa, the Maasai, Ogiek, and Samburu of East Africa, the Indigenous peoples of Australia, the Indigenous Ramu peoples of Papua New Guinea, and the Indigenous Yanomami and Guarani peoples of the South American Amazon, who have been warning the world's powerbrokers about the lethal effects of disrespecting the Earth by pursuing rapacious industrialism, are the ones whose voices need to be amplified today, and this chapter gives voice to such traditional peoples.

Chapter 3 engages in a discussion of globalization processes that have intensified the social and economic subjugation of women around the world, especially working class and poor women who are grossly underpaid as they work for large transnational (TNC) corporations in Asia, Latin America, and Africa. Though women constitute over half of the world's human population, they still reap only a tiny percentage of the world's wealth. This chapter details the roles played by global financial and commercial institutions like the World Bank and the International Monetary Fund in furthering globalized exploitation of women. The question of AIDS and the manner that women are especially susceptible through globalized capitalism is raised in this chapter. The chapter illuminates the socio-economic experiences and struggles of women in the U.S., particularly working class women, and demonstrates that the connections between war and globalization are interwoven where women and children are generally the most adversely affected. It concludes with elucidating women's resistance to globalization in various contexts and highlights the need for the expansion of alternative and collective women's cultures that provide constructive redress to the deep problems of gender and economic injustice as the consequence of globalization.

Chapter 4 is the longest and most substantial chapter of the book because of the confluence of race, class, capitalism, and criminal justice as endemic to the globalization regime in the 21st century. The startling fact that the U.S. today has one-quarter of all prison inmates in the world even though we are only 5 percent of the world's human population warrants a discursive analysis of prisons and globalization. This chapter provides a concise history of the roots of the incarceration system in chattel slavery and the manner that Black people and other persons of color and the poor are specifically targeted for imprisonment in a globalized world in the early 21st century. It delineates a range of issues pertaining to the criminal justice system and globalization, including race theory, drugs, crime, punishment and the national security state, the "war on drugs," political prisoners and violence against women and those considered sexually deviant, police brutality, racism and harsh prison sentences, solitary confinement and prison torture, capital punishment, expansion of prison construction, and the private prisons industry in the U.S. and other Western nations that requires the massive incarceration of men and women for profit, including through political legislation like SB 1070 in the state of Arizona.

The final chapter of the book discusses the most pressing issue of our time, *global warming and climate change*, and the role that globalization plays in the perpetuation of the warming of the Earth at levels unparalleled in the history of the Earth. The emission of carbon dioxide and other green house gases principally by automobile and automation at levels of 30–32 gigatons into the atmosphere when Earth can only recycle half this amount is graphically and painstakingly illustrated in the chapter. The lethal impact of global warming and climate change all over the world, including the U.S., where over 60 percent of the country continues to experience some form of adverse drought and now threatens viable food production, is detailed in this chapter. The catastrophic effects of climate change where prolonged dry summers and shortened intensive cold winter spells interspersed by unprecedented tornadoes, lightning storms, hurricanes, tsunamis, typhoons, and freezing weather are experienced constitute key sections of the chapter. The submerging of island countries in the Pacific, the forced migration of peoples due to unprecedented climate changes, the crisis of food shortages in Asia and Africa, the shortened growth seasons for all kinds of species of plants and animals, the melting of polar ice caps and glaciers in the Arctic and the Himalayas that threatens to raise sea levels, and the reconfiguration of geographical contexts around the globe, raise the subject of globalization and global warming and climate change to a new level and warrant extensive action by educators, governments, farmers, scientists, Indigenous people, civil sector organizations, corporations, and the world. In the final analysis, the chapter calls for a radical shift away from global capitalism and dependence on fossil fuels, mining, and material extraction from the Earth as the basis of a viable global economy and challenges the reader to decide between abandoning capitalism or accelerating the extinction of species of life, including human beings, perhaps in the next century.

The somber outlook from Chapter 5 makes a transition into an epilogue of optimism and transformation by reclaiming our essential humanity, in the words of Tadadaho elder Leon Shenandoah, "Becoming a Human Being." The epilogue points out ironically that for humans to move forward, we will need to delve deeply into the wellspring of human ancestral wisdom to be the best human beings we can be and to struggle to find sustainable and Earth-friendly ways of living as Indigenous peoples have always lived and to return to the *circle of life* of which we are all an integral part. *We are part of nature and can never improve on nature*, a lesson communicated in the film *Sugar Cane Alley*. Practicing Indigenous knowledge in tandem with those who understand the environmental destruction of the Earth and all life is thus indispensable. We will all need to return to our ancestral roots to reclaim those ways of mutual respect and reciprocity of living with one another and the rest of the natural world in the 21st century and to preserve precious resources so that the next seven generations can live in dignity and replace exploitation of women with mutual respect, imprisonment with genuine programs of intervention and rehabilitation, and ecocide with new forms of economic life that accord respect to all life. Human beings are not indispensable and if humans disregard the Earth, their Original Mother, they do so with dire consequences and great peril to the future of the human race. Mother Earth will defend her children who are fast becoming extinct by all means at her disposal ... and she has power to do that, *real power*, unlike us as human beings...

The Cost of Globalization invites you, dear reader, to a dialogue about our future as human beings and as essentially *spiritual* beings, about how we need to chart a way forward to preserve the future for our great-grandchildren's great-grandchildren. The Epilogue provides concrete data on issues discussed in each chapter. Wishing you a thoughtful reading!

Introduction

The glaring effects of globalization particularly over the past two decades have been visible for all to see: growing chasms between the few superwealthy and the majority poor who have become further impoverished and experience consistent turbulence and instability in the global capitalist economies of the world; intensified ecological destruction to the point that anywhere between 50 and 200 species become extinct or permanently disappear every day according to the Center for Biological Diversity, reflecting the reality that humans have caused more species of life to disappear in recent history than over the previous 65 million years of the Earth, with rates of extinction between 1,000 and 10,000 times previous rates[1]; continued violation of Indigenous peoples' lands and sacred sites and erosion of their languages and cultures in most parts of the world; increased hardships for women especially in working class communities and underdeveloped countries; and a rapid and explosive expansion of the prison industrial complex especially in the U.S. where close to 3 million people are incarcerated and over 5 million people are involved in some capacity with the criminal justice system either on parole or probation, the inevitable result of poverty and marginalization from the disappearance of millions of manufacturing jobs in the 1990s, during the recession in the early 2000s, and most recently following the great recession of December 2007 through 2009 when 8.4 million jobs were lost in the overall U.S. labor market, the bulk of which has never recovered even after October 2010 sixteen months after the recession had officially ended when the job market had 5.4 percent less jobs than before 2008.[2] Even though 4.5 million jobs were created since Barack Obama was first elected in 2008, the rate and the quality of job creation has hardly been commensurate with the growth within the U.S. working-age population of 213,000 each month since most of these new jobs have generally been entry-level, service sector, and low-paying. Two hundred thousand new jobs over 29 months is neither real job growth nor robust in line with an economic recovery as the White House claimed in 2012 since it only represents a net gain of 47,000 once population increase over that time period is considered.[3] The loss of manufacturing jobs escalated from the 1990s and peaked in the 2000s when 5.7 million jobs were lost and when transnational corporations and manufacturing and textile industries relocated to places in Asia, Latin America, and Africa where labor costs are a fraction of those in the U.S.[4]

The U.S. has the largest prison population in the world. Though the U.S. is 5 percent of the world's human population, it has 25 percent of the world's prisoners. The U.S. has 500,000 more prison inmates than China, which has a population five times that of the U.S.[5] It also has the largest private prison industrial system in the world, generating hundreds of millions of dollars in profits for corporations like Corrections Corporation of America (CCA), the GEO Group, and Federal Prison Industries (FPI). Private prisons that have particularly expanded under globalization due to greed for unbridled profits and the teetering U.S. economy generate about $3 billion each year, using prison inmates as cheap labor for corporations like Starbucks, Boeing, Victoria's Secret, and McDonalds. Private prisons now house 10 percent of all prison inmates in the country and grew exponentially 1,600 percent from 1990 through 2010.[6] In 1998, there were five private prisons housing 2,000 people. By 2008, there were 100 private prisons incarcerating some 62,000 inmates.[7] Incarceration at all levels cost the U.S. government some $55 billion annually.[8]

The military industrial complex in the United States has been yet another demarcating trait of globalization, with trillions of dollars spent on wars in Asia and Africa that have left millions dead and homeless and hundreds of thousands of U.S. military personnel suffering from post-traumatic stress syndrome and severe body injuries. The United States spends about $1.2 trillion on the military each year, more than the defense budgets of the rest of the 189 countries of the world combined, and has spent over $13 trillion on wars abroad since 2001. Some 253,330 military personnel suffered from Traumatic Brain Injury (TBI) from 2002 through 2013 and almost 400,000 U.S. military personnel have suffered from post-traumatic stress syndrome and other physical and mental injuries since 1991.[9]

The ecological destruction and natural devastation witnessed in the first years of the new millennium attest to the vicissitudes of the ongoing crisis— global warming has become the norm and floods, drought, earthquakes, hurricanes, and tornadoes have become daily global events. The shocking reach of Hurricane Sandy in the northeastern part of the United States that erased hundreds of houses, flooded major coastlines and disrupted shipping and commerce in New Jersey and parts of New York for a week in 2012, while leaving millions without power and thousands homeless, is a sobering reminder of the impact of global warming and climate change on one of the most important financial centers of the world. The Philippines, a nation of 96 million people, experienced one of the worst typhoons ever recorded in November 2013 with the central part of the island country totally devastated, thousands dead and missing, and millions left homeless. Globalization with its obsession with optimal profit and maximization of mass production with the minimum injection of financial capital has much to do with this situation of unprecedented heating of the Earth and the turbulence of weather patterns that has never been witnessed over the past century. The pulverization of the Earth, a living Being and Mother to us all, through mining, oil-drilling, fracking, and other violent industrial processes, has had lethal side effects on all human societies and ecologies around the globe, and as opposed to globalizing civilization, has globalized the accelerating destruction of natural life.

That rubber plantations in Thailand and Indonesia were besieged by droughts in 2011 and floods later resulted in wide-spread rubber plantations being destroyed, triggering the most serious shortages since 2007 and sending the price of rubber in September 2010 higher, is just one example of climate change side effects.[10] Yet another is the crisis of drought in Kwazulu-Natal in South Africa (Azania) that has seen the devastation of sugar cane plantations and the radical reduction of sugar cane production, long the mainstay of the agricultural industry in the country, with a drop of 2.2 million tons of cane for mill delivery in 2010 and over 300,000 sugar cane worker jobs under threat of loss.[11] In March 2011, the world was stunned to witness the catastrophic effects of the 9.0 earthquake and accompanying tsunami that pulverized Japan, followed by progressive leaking and excessive levels of radiation emitted from some of the nuclear reactors in northeast Tokyo, whose lingering effects on people's lives, animal and plant life, and the environment will be around for some time. In October 2013, Typhoon Wipha struck the area around Fukushima and resulted in 17 people losing their lives, 50 people missing, and floodwaters overflowing 12 radioactive water tanks at the Daiichi nuclear plant and leaking radiation into the groundwater supply. Workers at the Tokyo Electric Power Company (TEPCO) had to pump rainwater from 1,000 radioactive water tanks, and officials noted that "400,000 becquerels per liter of beta-emitting radioactive substances—including strontium" were found at a nearby well. Radioactive levels were 6,500 times higher than that a week before Wipha hit.[12]

Nuclear power, after all, is a military technology that involves splitting atoms and is lethal in effect: The Manhattan project that led to the atomic bomb and bombing of Hiroshima and Nagasaki when 200,000 people were incinerated, is being played out ironically today with the Japanese government determined to shield the public from the lethal effects of the leaking Fukushima Nuclear Plant that have resulted in dangerously high radiation levels which have effected all surrounding earth and marine life and will take their toll on the health of millions of Japanese people, especially young people, over the next two decades.[13]

What about advancing the principles of democracy, fairness, and justice that the Western capitalist world extols in its daily calls for "progress" on "human rights" and "economic opportunity for all" and "openness" to governments and peoples around the world? These are all obscured under the regime of globalization, particularly in that a tiny minority of nations of the world benefit. Considering that there are 189 countries in the world, the benefits of globalization patently accrue to a few with just twelve countries—China, India, Singapore, Indonesia, South Korea, Malaysia, Taiwan, Thailand, Hong Kong, Argentina, Brazil, and Mexico—accounting for 70 percent of exports and 75 percent of manufactured exports from Africa, Asia, and Latin America while receiving 90 percent of capital inflows to this sector of the world.[14]

We have begun to see the deprived peoples in West Asia in places like India, Pakistan, and in nations around the Caspian Sea rejecting their victimization by globalization and state domination and thus agitating for secession in regions like Kashmir in India and Chechnya in Russia.[15] Globalization quintessentially benefits a few countries at the cost of the majority, and ironically reinforces minority rule and privilege, a *global apartheid system*, where the vast marginalized majority remains confined to conditions of economic and material poverty in many instances, most of Africa, Asia, and Latin America and the Caribbean being cases in point. Globalization's benefits can only accrue to those countries in the underdeveloped world (formerly colonized countries of Africa, Asia, and Latin America) that have an entrenched infrastructure of industrial and technological success, namely the twelve identified in the preceding paragraph. The good news is that globalization is *not* the final world, and neither is capitalism, as the rapidly declining and collapsing economies of the capitalist world evince.[16]

To add to this analysis of the gravity of human suffering wrought from globalization, we need to highlight the pain of the creatures of the natural world that are an integral part of the global ecological system within which we as human beings participate. For the poor and the four-leggeds, birds,

Globalization has generated dilapidated slum housing in many urban metropolises, like the one depicted in Ahmedabad, Gujarat, India, where rural migrants travel long distances to reside in cities with hopes of higher income and a decent living (Emmanuel Dyan).

insects, trees, forests, rivers, mountains, sea life and oceans, the effects of globalization have been lethal, documented in the almost daily news about oil spills, floods, torrential downpours, landslides, earthquakes, heatwaves, and other effects of an excessively heated globe, the subject matter in the second chapter of this book. The June 2011 finding by scientists from the International Program on the State of the Ocean and the International Union for the Conservation of Nature (IUCN) that "the world's oceans are faced with an unprecedented loss of species comparable to the great mass extinctions of prehistory," that a single mass coral bleaching event in 1998 eliminated 16 percent of all the world's corral reefs, and that increasing hypoxia (low oxygen levels) and anoxia (absence of oxygen which are ocean dead zones) coupled with ocean warming is destroying marine life, is sound reason for a reversal of globalization's economic system grounded in industrialism, materialism, and consumption.[17] In September 2012, climate change scientists lamented the fact that only 24 percent of the glacial ice sheets are evident in the Arctic Ocean, some 1.32 million square miles, down from 29 percent in 2007.[18]

The reality of globalization has begun to take deadly effect on the beautiful, but fragile planet on which we live, Earth, and indeed, all of life.[19] The radical political economist, Samir Amin, excoriates the champions of globalization for their compliance in prolonging the problem of what he calls the TINA syndrome, the "There is no Alternative syndrome." He argues that "their attempt to legitimate their choices by the state ideology of the 'self-regulating' market, by affirming that 'there is no alternative,' or by pure and simple cynicism, is not the solution but in fact part of the problem."[20] As George Casalis wrote, ideas just do not fall from the sky; instead, they are manufactured, concocted, fabricated, and constructed as ways of communicating certain messages, and in the context of oppression, are designed to keep oppressors in power and the oppressed in their places of subjugation.[21] Ideological advocates of globalization function in this capacity of defenders of oppressor classes.

This book will discuss how globalization in the 21st century has extended itself into every quarter of the globe and permeated every grain of our society, including our thinking, so that we become enslaved to its ideological tentacles and are stymied in our very thought processes and in our imagining of a reality different from that of the current global order. It will demonstrate how structures of monopoly capital, Eurocentric epistemology, sexism, class privilege, cultural imperialism, military hegemony, religious ideology, and technological scientism, have ravaged the Earth and all life in-between, gutting the humanities in the process, leaving genocide, ecocide, and what I refer to as "mentacide"—a pervasive sense of social insouciance, political unconsciousness, and mimicking of the superficial and cosmetic that pass easily for substantive and ground-breaking among the world's middle classes—in its wake.[22] It will discuss the devastating effects that globalization has had on vital sectors of the globe: the poor and working classes, Indigenous people and their continued loss of languages, cultures, and lands; poor women in the underdeveloped world; incarcerated people, particularly in the United States where the prison industrial complex and military industrial complex (to quote the words of former U.S. president Dwight Eisenhower in the latter) persists; and the reality of global warming and climate change. It will conclude with proposing alternative educational and social ways of living so that we might simply live ... and live in ways which harmonize with the rhythm and cycle of the Earth, as Mother, as Teacher, as all Indigenous peoples refer to the Earth.

This book is distinctive in that it echoes the cries of the poor and amplifies the perspectives of the oppressed peoples. It reflects the views of peoples whose experiences have been suppressed by the successes and excesses of globalization. It signifies *a pedagogy from and for the oppressed*, echoing some of the issues raised in the *Pedagogy of the Oppressed* by Brazilian educator Paulo Freire, over four decades ago.[23] It also speaks on behalf of the voiceless Earth and the rest of the natural world whose voices have been equally suppressed and ignored in the globalization onslaught. In a real manner, the book is concerned with enlightening the middle classes in the world in particular on the righteous and just cause not only of the globe's oppressed people but also the rest of the natural world in their quest for refusing to be ongoing *victims* of the regime of globalization. The book is singularly different in that it challenges the dominant patriarchal epistemological assumptions of the "progress" of human civilization and the cosmological cornerstones of Western cultures that elevate human scientism as the key principle to the problems of the human and global condition. It utilizes an Indigenous cultural and philosophical framework to discuss the question of globalization and the problems of global suffering in the 21st century. Further indigenous cosmologies unlike Western worldviews do not subscribe to a linear view of time and do not view the universe as limited but rather as infinite with no center.[24] *Similarly, Indigenous peoples do not view human beings as enjoying elevated or privileged status above nature and other creatures; instead, human beings are part of and are "nature" like all other forms of life on earth and contiguous with the animals, birds, insects, fish, plants, and other terrestrial life.*[25] The book offers a perspective toward deepening our understanding of what it means to be *human* and part of the natural world, understanding full well that Indigenous peoples of Europe like the Saami and the people of Lapland and Greenland and most working class people who live within Western societies are themselves victims of globalization's duplicity and elitist expropriation and manipulation of resources for enrichment of the few at the cost of the many.

While Western science has made relevant discoveries in medicine and technology, the iconic character of scientism has in the main served to bolster the interests of the ruling elites of the world and functioned to legitimate hegemonic discourses on the future direction of the world because of the obsession with technological and mechanistic progress that has stripped the Earth of her resources and disrupted the natural ecological system.[26] The torture of all kinds of mammals, animals, birds, and insects by medical science for purposes of finding cures to human ailments is an index of human arrogance that views all other life as expendable for sole human survival, a scientific impossibility. Hamsters tortured with laced viruses in the medical scientific quest to discern the cause of the AIDS virus as conceded by discoverer of the AIDS virus, Robert Gallo, in the late 1970s, underscores the fundamental violation of Indigenous medical ethics. The hypothesis by dentist researcher Leonard Horowitz that "simian virus 40 (SV40) infected polio vaccines may be linked to the evolution of acquired immunodeficiency disorder (AIDS), and certain cancers" as the result of such viral experimentation by medical scientists, may require further investigation and research owing to Western medical science totally discounting other forms of life as having proportionate sacred value as humans.[27] The reason why Western medicine's effectiveness is limited is because of its resorting to testing and experimenting on animals (and humans like people incarcerated and poor persons of color) that has resulted in premature death or excessive pain for those in such experiments and tests. We are all relatives within the fragile web of nature and destroying one element or subjecting it to unnatural pain to cure another is bogus science.[28]

The deification of human technology in Western scientism where the problems generated by capitalist cultures of greed and consumption are resolved by technological skill and invention is precisely the fundamental flaw in Western bases of knowledge, and this fatal myopia has wrought the uncontrollable environmental, ecological, economic and social crisis in the world today where the commodification of the Earth has resulted in perilous conditions facing all life globally.[29] The solutions to the problematic of globalization reside in spiritual and cultural practices in which the Earth and all terrestrial life work together to live in sustainable ways as harmonious communities.[30] The fact that the contemporary industrialist path is unsustainable with the intensity of warming of the Earth compels Indigenous people to ask: Why does "civilization" lie to the world about the future residing in technologies that cause ecological destruction denying humans and all life a future? Indeed, if we are all "civilized," why do we continue to use plastic that comes from oil and that industry acknowledges is "cancer-causing"?[31] Similarly, why does society promote the expansion of automobiles that are the leading cause of carbon emissions that are principally responsible for greenhouse gases that intensify the heating of the Earth? *Are the architects of the "progress of industrial civilization" secretly harbouring a death wish?! Is their megalomania so obsessive and addictive that it is incorrigible? As I jogged in my neighborhood in Tucson, Arizona, I looked at the massive road construction taking place for the widening of existing roads. The construction of destruction, I thought. Why do we build more roads that will carry more automobiles that cause more climatic and ecological devastation? Is it similar to the convoluted reasoning that suggests using more air-conditioners in Arizona and other extremely hot places is the solution to global warming, while the use of increased air-conditioners damages the environment and exacerbates the crisis of the Earth becoming hotter?[32]*

How is it possible for humans to survive if the rest of the ecologies of the Earth are destroyed, as we are witnessing with species extinction? It is no wonder then that well-known biologist E. O. Wilson indicated that after the publishing of his 27th book, *The Social Conquest of Earth*, and engaging in academic and discursive intellectual debates on biological evolution over many decades, he is dedicating the rest of his life to preserving the threatened ecology of the Earth, including further study and understanding of the cooperative nature of ants![33] Hints of Indigenous knowledge by a globally renowned Harvard biologist!

In this book, we critique both neo-liberalism and the general role and function of state governments around the world because most governments preside over states deriving from the colonial period and demand allegiance and uniformity from diverse citizens whose cultural and social citizenship may transcend state boundaries, as with Indigenous peoples in Central and South America and the southwestern United States, Africa, Asia, and the Pacific. Indigenous peoples do not recognize colonially defined boundaries and nations. The Tohono O'odham of Arizona and northern Mexico and the Maasai of East Africa do not recognize the legitimacy of the borders of Mexico and the United States and Kenya and Tanzania, respectively, because their communities' existences in these places preceded the nation states of Africa and the Americas by many millennia. The Achuar of the Amazon who live across Ecuador and Brazil in the Amazon where territorial boundaries are alien to their culture and way of live, derive their identities from cultures that existed for innumerable generations. Indigenous peoples thus do not subscribe to xenophobic policies and tendencies in so many parts of the world, in places like South Africa which saw hundreds die in 2008 and flee their homes in places like Kya Sands in July 2010 due to attacks on Black migrants from outside the country or in Arizona and Texas where "illegal aliens" are targeted by U.S. citizens' groups like the Minuteman vigilantes and the Border Patrol as criminals. In some sense, the book echoes Nikita Khrushchev's cynicism about governments when he remarked, "Politicians are the same all over.... They promise to build bridges even when there are no rivers."[34]

Unequivocally, there has been change in the world over the past sixty years, in particular through the history of colonization in which new identities, cultures, and social languages have evolved; however, the more fundamental question in this book is the *substance of change* when it comes to the worldview of hegemonic materialistic cultures. Have these cultures abolished their view of Indigenous peoples who honor the Earth and practice land-based religio-cultures as being "primitive"? Are the leaders of these dominant cultures willing to acknowledge that the plunder of the Earth through mining, oil drilling, and extraction has in fact destroyed much of the fragile ecosystems and delicate web of relations among all of the creatures of the world and that a different manner of living is essential for us to live as beings where we can respect each community and being's right to be here? *Hardly.*[35] The paradox is that in actuality all of the world's people are *Indigenous* by virtue of being children of the Earth regardless of whether many recognize this or not; we all come from the Earth and return to the Earth regardless of our economic status, culture, religious affiliation, gender, education, or any other attribute. The denial by modern industrialized societies steeped in technological accomplishment does not alter this fact. The differences that exist between Indigenous peoples who still practice Earth-based religions and cultures and those who do not—citizens of the industrialized societies—are rather more reflections of *perceptions* of the world than in *substance*.

The catastrophe in the Gulf of Mexico wrought through the oil leak from BP's drilling of the coast in April 2010 where anywhere between 30,000 and 60,000 gallons of oil have leaked each day and which devastated the coast line of the south eastern region of the U.S., killed thousands of fish and other marine life, and permanently and irreparably contaminated beaches and sea water, did not halt all off-shore oil drilling operations in the U.S. or around the world. A federal judge ruled in June 2010 that offshore oil drilling would not be terminated or placed on hold because of the impact on BP and the

---

local economy.[36] BP and the oil industry have not in any manner begun dismantling their operations for ecological preservation. In fact, even in the wake of what is now indisputably the world's worst oil spill in the Gulf of Mexico with over 5 million barrels of oil that gushed into the Gulf as BP prepared to seal the leak with mud and cement in the first week of August 2010, Douglas Shuttles, BP chief operations officer, commented that BP could return to deepwater oil drilling in the future at the same spot where the rupture occurred since oil was still evident, and sure enough, in March 2012, BP returned to deepwater drilling in the Gulf after national concerns about lethal effects of oil spills gradually dissipated.[37] BP will begin offshore oil drilling on the Libyan coast in the near future at depths far greater than the Gulf of Mexico oil well as part of its penetration of global resources particularly in Africa.[38] The invasion, bombing, destruction, and occupation of Libya by NATO, led by the U.S. in 2011 under the pretext of supporting "freedom-loving rebels" and the installation of a pro–U.S. dictatorship (ironically with Al Qaeda elements that the U.S. supposedly views as anathema and public enemy number one) paved the way for the looting of Libya's vast oil resources by U.S. corporations.[39]

The relentless exploitation of the Earth for fossil fuels and "natural gas" by the oil conglomerates, which are accountable to nobody else except to powerful corporate shareholders, continues unabated. As Antonia Juhasz from Global Exchange eloquently describes the power from 1918 onwards of the cartel of the world's seven largest oil companies or the "Seven Sisters," Standard Oil of New Jersey, Standard Oil of New York, Standard Oil of California, Texaco, Gulf, British Petroleum, and Royal Dutch Shell, that today have become Exxon Mobil, Chevron, BP (Beyond Petroleum!), and Shell, she notes that "World War I was the first large scale oil war ... oil was the source of victory and its reward." She contends that these wars have continued into the present in Iraq and through military aggression directed against or within countries like Iran, Afghanistan, Ecuador, Indonesia, Angola, and Oman.[40] The economic and political power wielded by these oil giants penetrates all levels of governments, the military, trade, and commerce all over the world. Juhasz argues that Big Oil constitutes the most powerful sector of the global economy and that "The largest oil companies operating in the United States took in $133 billion in profits in 2007, making ExxonMobil, BP, Shell, Chevron, Conoco-Philips, Valero, and Marathon together the fiftieth largest economy in the world" so that "their combined profits were larger than the individual gross domestic products of New Zealand (Aotearoa), Egypt, Kuwait, Peru, Morocco, and Bulgaria, among 129 additional countries."[41] It is indeed incredible that each company is also dramatically increasing its profits. For example, "between 2003 and 2007, Chevron's profits increased by an astounding 158 percent, ConocoPhillips by 153 percent, and ExxonMobil's by 89 percent" even while consumers around the world have been forced to pay exorbitant prices for gasoline because oil companies have claimed that oil prices have sky-rocketed.[42] The granting of merger permissions by the U.S. Trade Commission has resulted in these explosions of oil companies' profits.[43]

Juhasz makes a passionate plea for collective peoples' action against Big Oil, cogently explaining that there is a direct connection between war and global warming through oil, noting the irony that the United States is an "oili-garchy." She explains that the Washington, D.C.–based Oil Change Interna-tional, Greenpeace, and twenty other organizations have called for a "separation between Oil and State (SOS) so that the United States can be steered clear from the clutches of Big Oil and "petrol-imperialism."[44] She warns about the cost of passivity in the face of the impending ecological catastrophe and lethal planetary cost generated by Big Oil's obsession with drilling for oil through every available avenue on Earth and the Sea, including the very costly extrac-tion of oil from the tar sands of Alberta in Canada and the shale regions of Colorado.[45] Indigenous communities from the Oglala Lakota in South Dakota and Nebraska, involving activist and grandmother, Deborah White Plume, among others, blocked roads travelled by trucks carrying massive oil extracting equipment from Texas to Alberta in 2012 and continue to protest against the destruction of the boreal forest in Alberta for tar sands oil-from-shale extrac-tion.[46] It is an outrage in an era where water is now the most precious water needed for the sustenance of all life on Earth in the driest ever aeon in history, three barrels of water and four tons of sand will be drained for every barrel of oil removed, presaging an unprecedented ecological and hydrological catas-trophe since the boreal forests hold some of the largest freshwater reserves on Earth. The pumped water, some 400 million gallons per day, will be dumped as toxic waste in huge pools containing poisonous substances such as cyanide.[47]

Small wonder then when a person living in oil-rich Nigeria lamented that Nigeria was cursed with the riches of oil. The ongoing violent conflict between guerrilla groups and the Nigerian authorities especially in the Niger Delta of Nigeria and the accompanying ecological and cultural devastation of Indige-nous peoples there attests to the problem of obsession with fossil-fuels and energy production for industrialism. Millions of people living in the Niger Delta can no longer engage in fishing and farming because all of the waterways have been contaminated with oil residues and all regional forests and agricul-tural lands have been decimated by forest fires and underground water poisoning. Similarly, millions of Iraqis today ponder the deaths of loved ones, almost 2 million of them over the past decade, all because of wars over oil in their country.

This book distinctively subscribes to an Indigenous philosophical framework and challenges the mythic universality and "objectivity" of Western sociological and political theory and underscores that all knowledge is particular and shaped by the extant ethos of social values and specific historical contexts. Indigenous perspectives do not merely adjust or modify existing Western concepts in social science, for example, but look to multiple Indigenous cultures for understanding and deriving key concepts and understanding of the universe.[48] This book will discuss the impact that globalization has had with the growing impoverishment of the already poor; the destruction of Indigenous people's lands and cultures along with ecocide; the subjugation of poor women who are the primary human victims of globalization since in "Africa and southern Asia, 80 percent of all women are self-employed or unpaid family workers"[49]; the rapid growth of the prison industrial complex, mass incarceration, and capital punishment in the United States; and the pressing issue of global warming and climate change that is now threatening the very existence of life on Earth.

1

21st Century Globalization: Illusions of Global Economic Prosperity Yet the Reality of Poverty

There was a time in which the economic decisions corresponded to the needs of the concerned social groups. This happened when communities showing solidarity were the rule instead of the exception. This decision process, founded on the imperative of social needs, has been progressively replaced by a cold and blind efficiency guided by an economic system in which the essential value is financial benefit.[1]

Introduction

Though globalization was the word used to describe the status of the world becoming a "global village" by politicians, economists, and educators alike in the last twenty years of the 20th century, it continues to be a force in the second decade of the 21st century and is still generally associated with the escalation of exchange and interaction of cultures and interwovenness of open market economies around the world and the forging of a borderless and multicultural globe unrestrained by geographical and territorial boundaries.[2] For many, it is concerned primarily with economic expansion and international social "progress" on poverty reduction, women's rights, human rights, political democratization, and cultural hybridization.[3] Paul Bowles and Henry Veltmeyer are correct when they argue that the literature on globalization "has been largely monopolized by scholars of Western academia…. It is their interpretations of globalization that have been the dominant ones; it is they who set the agenda and established the parameters of the discussion" and that "the vast literature on globalization is not itself global but heavily skewed in favor of the core countries."[4] Some political economy theorists like Immanuel Wallerstein, for example, view globalization as an extension of the global capitalist system based on the centering of Europe and North America over the past six centuries with the principal focus on maximizing profit accumulation through trade and all avenues of global commerce.[5] This chapter will discuss the ideology of globalization that claims economic and financial prosperity, while in actuality, effecting impoverishment of the world's vast majority, reflecting a classic case of the few benefitting at the cost of the many.

Some Examples of Globalization and Uneven Trade and Development

FOREIGN DIRECT INVESTMENT AND COMMODITY PRICE INSTABILITY

Globalization in the underdeveloped world (note that I use this term, as opposed to "developing," to establish that the independent courses of evolution and socio-economic development of peoples of color globally were arrested by colonization and slavery) has meant concentration of wealth in the hands of a few within certain nations successful in international trade.[6] The World Bank reported in 1996 that between 1985 and 1995, the overall ratio of trade to Gross Domestic Product rose 1.2 percentage points a year, yet this increase was concentrated in a small cluster of countries in East Asia, Latin America, and the Caribbean.[7] Just ten countries benefited from three-quarters of the increase. The trade ratios actually fell in forty-four countries out of ninety-three underdeveloped countries studied by the World Bank. On the Foreign Direct Investment (FDI) ratio, just eight, mostly Asian countries garnered two thirds of overall foreign invest inflows in 1990–1993. Most other countries experienced a drop in ratios of foreign investment to Gross Domestic Product (GDP). Twenty of the thirty-seven countries where this occurred were in Africa, nine in Latin America and the Caribbean, and seven were in the Middle East.[8] Interregional trade now constitutes the bulk of total trade in goods, with 61 percent for the European Community, 41 percent for Asia, and 35 percent for North America.[9] Africa's intra-regional trade is much smaller than of its overall international trade, most of which is done with countries outside Africa. While the Bretton Woods institutions lavish praise on the efficacy of Foreign Direct Investment as the principal medium for jump-starting economic growth among underdeveloped nations, they conveniently neglect to mention that the European Union (EU), Japan, and the United States receive over 60 percent of all investment inflows, and FDI to the Western powers rose from $481 billion in 1998 to $636 billion in 1999, whereas for underdeveloped countries, FDI increased from $179 billion in 1998 to $208 billion in 1999.[10] Seventy-five percent of all accumulated stock in the global economy resides in the G3 Triad—North America, Europe, and Japan—which dominate as both the source and recipient of global investment.[11] These statistics clearly demonstrate that the capitalist infusion model proposed by agencies like the World Bank and the International Monetary Fund (IMF) are designed to assist a few beneficiary countries, underdevelop the vast majority of the rest, and to concentrate wealth in the hands of fewer as globalization intensifies its pace. Patently, participants in the capitalist system only stand to benefit when they possess capital or are able to gain access to capital. Underdeveloped and formerly colonized countries cannot generally benefit from capitalism because they were undermined by colonialism and slavery, intrinsic precursors to the spawning of capitalism. Globalization ensures a speedy race to the bottom since workers are forced to work much harder for lower wages (inflation pressures significantly reduced the value of local currencies over the past 20 years) and compete with low-wage earners employed by transnational corporations who invest heavily in low-wage zones as the result of enticement by governments to attract capital-intensive investment in these areas. The transnational corporations constantly use their capital-wielding leverage to remind governments and workers that they need to comply with capital's designs and be appreciative of the fact that they are in paid employment as opposed to being unemployed. These corporations generally have no obligations to workers or countries; they maximize profits in one location and move on to a cheaper one when it is more profitable to do so.[12]

Most countries in Africa, Asia, and Latin America are more stringently held to IMF and World Bank conditionalities, such as devaluing of local currencies, dismantling of food and educational subsidies, privatization of public utilities and services, deregulation of banks and financial systems, and opening of domestic markets to cheaper imports, producing economic catastrophe as in the cases of many countries in Africa and Central America.[13] The unjust global economic policies that impoverished the many countries of the underdeveloped world are crystallized in an internal World Bank memo by Lawrence Summers, leading economist of the World Bank in 1991 who subsequently was appointed U.S. Treasury Secretary under the Clinton administration, followed by president of Harvard University, and then Director of the

The privatization of fundamental natural resources like water and land under globalization has had destructive effects on the livelihood of all people, especially indigenous peoples. Here, First Nations people are joined by other protesters outside a G20 Summit in Toronto, Canada, in 2010 (Loozrboy/Flickr).

National Economic Council under the Obama administration from 2009 to 2011:

> Just between you and me, shouldn't the World Bank be encouraging more migration of the dirty industries to the LDCs (least developed countries)? I think the economic logic behind dumping a load of toxic waste in the lowest wage country is impeccable and we should face up to that.... I've always thought that underpopulated countries in Africa are vastly under-polluted, their air quality is probably vastly inefficiently low compared to Los Angeles or Mexico City.... The concern over an agent that causes a one in a million change in the odds of prostate cancer is obviously going to be much higher in a country where people survive to get prostate cancer than in a country where under 5 mortality is 200 per thousand.... The problem with the arguments against all these proposals for more pollution in LDCs (intrinsic rights to certain goods, moral reasons, social concerns, lack of adequate markets, etc.) could be turned around and used more or less effectively against every Bank proposal for liberalization.[14]

The same ideology of globalized capitalism, privatization, and deregulation was foisted by the World Bank and the IMF on the former Soviet Union and the Socialist bloc countries in the early 1990s. With the adoption of the market system, Russia, for example, has seen the vast majority of its population become poorer and subject to massive unemployment, forcing many to flee to Western Europe to support Russian families economically.[15] Energy companies like Gazprom have boomed with giant profit margins, while the conditions of educational outlays, social security for the elderly, and affordable food previously available under the Soviet state, quickly vanished with the intensification of globalization and privatization, as official poverty rates grew 2.3 million from 20.6 million in early 2010 to 22.9 million in 2011.[16]

Another severely debilitating factor has been the radical drop in the prices of major commodities on the world market, particularly agricultural products in Africa, Asia, and Latin America, for export to the core countries of the North. "Substitutionist" technologies in the core rich countries have had a major negative effect on workers and producers in the underdeveloped countries. This is the case in which commodities produced in the underdeveloped countries are no longer viewed as essential for consumers in the core Northern countries, such as caffeinated beverages replacing coffee, agricultural and chemical substitutes like sweeteners for sugar, non-cocoa vegetable fats for cocoa, and soybean oil replacing palm oil in the main.[17] In some instances, the World Bank and other lending agencies weakened commodity cartels by financing new producers among underdeveloped countries. In Vietnam, for example, the World Bank financed the expansion of land for coffee cultivation from 20,000 hectares in 1980 to 300,000 hectares in 1998, so that Vietnam produced 13 million bags of coffee in 2000, replacing Colombia as the second largest coffee producer in the world after Brazil. Vietnam, where poverty levels hovered at 29 percent in 2004, was required to accept 41 World Bank conditionalities for the receipt of financial aid in the form of loans, including privatization of major state enterprises and banking reform.[18] Vietnam ended its lending program with the IMF in 2004 since the IMF demanded foreign audits of the State Bank of Vietnam that were prohibited under Vietnamese law.[19]

Since 1980, prices of commodities have dramatically fallen, so that coffee which is the mainstay of economies like Uganda, Kenya, and Colombia, is now 30 percent of its 1980 value, sugar is 30 percent of its 1980 price, cocoa is 40 percent of its 1980 prices, and soybean production has replaced groundnut production, since soy-based ethanol has been in high demand for energy use in the U.S. and soy oil is viewed as having lower levels of cholesterol.[20] The results for farmers around the world have been devastating, dragging hundreds of thousands of farmers deeper into poverty. In Thailand, thousands of farmers have been driven deeper into debt and poverty as higher-than-market prices for food production promised by the government remained unfilled in February 2014, compounding difficulties for farmers purchasing fertilizers and agricultural equipment, and many farmers had received no payments for three months.[21] In India, over 125,000 farmers have committed suicide over a ten-year period extending into 2008, after being dragged into debt and financial ruin after being compelled to purchase genetically modified (GM) seeds sold by Monsanto, the U.S. company that is the largest GM seed corporation in the world, that cost 1,000 times the price of traditional seeds. The former sold at $15 for 100 grams and the latter at the same price for 1000 grams.[22] When GM crops failed, farmers were unable to re-plant the GM seeds since the seeds have a "terminator technology" component where crops do not produce any viable seeds for the following year. Instead, farmers are required to purchase new GM seeds each year. The result has been economic devastation for hundreds of thousands of farmers due to failed GM crops and unpayable debt that has driven thousands into suicide, with the Ministry of Agriculture in the northern state of Maharastra acknowledging that 1,000 farmers take their lives each month due to this growing GM seed crisis and financial indebtedness. India has 17 million acres of land under GM seed cultivation as part of its agreement with Monsanto that promised higher production and lucrative profits. Tens of thousands of farmer families have been dragged into deeper poverty, begging, and in many instances, suicide, what a journalist described as "GM genocide." Monsanto has refused to assume responsibility for this wave of death in India's vast agricultural sector.

The imposition of genetically modified corn, for example, has decimated indigenous corn production in places like Mexico, so that today, genetically modified corn constitutes one-quarter of the Mexican market where 15 million Mexicans depend on corn for their livelihood. The skyrocketing oil prices triggered increases in prices of corn, wheat, and soybeans that in turn sparked food riots in Indonesia, Guinea, Mauritania, Yemen, Uzbekistan, Senegal, Ivory Coast, Burkina Faso, Morocco, Egypt, Cameroon, Haiti, and Mexico in 2008. In Egypt, a corrupt and misplaced bread subsidy program enabled flour merchants to sell subsidized wheat for a profit while the policy of globalization was operational and one to which Egypt has adhered. Egypt imports 6 million tons of wheat from the U.S., financed by U.S. "aid" money and in line with WTO mandates, even though Egypt and Sudan jointly could produce enough wheat domestically to feed their countries and the rest of the African continent.[23] Such is the stringent nature of the globalization regime and its inequitable trade policies as foisted on impoverished countries like Egypt by the

WTO.[24] The combination of mismanagement by regimes, like the former Mubarak regime in Egypt, and the embracement of globalization that shifted focus from public investment to privatization and from manufacturing to service industries and eschewed protectionist measures for local production in favor of cheap food imports, has resulted in the present crisis of impoverishment and anger. It manifests among the already poor who constitute half of Egypt's people and earn $2 a day or less. Since 2002 global food prices rose 65 percent and in 2007 dairy prices increased 80 percent and grain, 42 percent.[25]

Asia

In 2013, the part of the underdeveloped world previously and now speeding ahead to become industrially developed, southeast Asia, is where the bulk of economic growth in terms of trade and export of manufactured goods, particularly ships, telecommunications equipment, computer equipment, and technical parts like valves, tubes, diodes, transistors, circuit boards, etc., has occurred. In 2011, these countries that still signified a handful of industrial powers in Asia and the world, namely, China, Korea, Taiwan, and Singapore, saw their portion of manufactured goods within the world economy rise to 40.2 percent. Ships and floating products manufactured in Korea, China, and India increased by 64.7 percent of the world total, exponentially growing by 37.4 percent from 1995 to 1996 (**Fig. 1a**).

Fig. 1a
Developing economies' market share increased the most between
1995-1996 and 2010-2011 for the following export products:

Products	2010-2011 average of developing economies ($ millions)	Share of developing economies into world exports %			Principal net exporters 2011
		1995-1996	2010-2011	Share Gain	
Ships, boats, floating structures	114,689	27.3	64.7	37.4	Republic of Korea, China, India
Computer equipment	234,233	35.3	70.0	34.7	China, Hong Kong (China), Singapore
Telecommunications equipment, parts	311,493	31.5	65.5	34.0	China, Republic of Korea, Taiwan Province of China
Valves, tubes, diodes, transistors	389,381	41.4	70.5	29.1	Singapore, Taiwan Province of China, Republic of Korea
Office equipment parts and accessories	119,680	35.7	60.1	24.4	China, Singapore, Taiwan Province of China

Source: UNCTAD Handbook of Statistics 2012.[26]

However, it needs to be emphasized that within the context of globalization, it's a tiny minority of elites within these industrialized Asian countries and the underdeveloped world that benefit economically. For most countries in Asia, Africa, and the Caribbean, the reality of economic dependence, impoverishment, and reduced health quality of the vast majority of people is stark and painful as currency devaluation and economic hardship persists.

Though inequality in health and education may be declining in some areas, the tenacious fact of income inequality persists (**Fig. 1b**).

In South Asia, the island nation of Sri Lanka illustrates the gravity of the problem of globalization's rising inequality and skewed economic growth favoring the wealthy. Given the astronomically high bank interest rates in most countries of the underdeveloped world, like Sri Lanka, where they hovered between 10 percent and 24 percent per year in 2000, along with the forced conditions of foreign exchange deregulation, financial liberalization, and elevation of private sector finance and banking, Sri Lanka entered a critical credit crisis and was forced to turn to the IMF for loans and a structural adjustment package. During this period at the turn of the millennium, international credit card debt became available, largely accessible though to only urban individuals

Fig 1b

Most regions show declining inequality in health and education and rising inequality in income

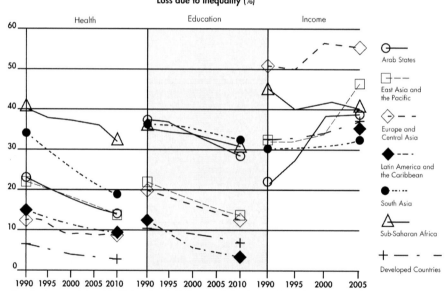

Note: Based on a population-weighted balanced panel of 182 countries for loss due to health inequality, 144 countries for loss due to education inequ and 66 countries for loss due to income inequality. Data on income inequality from Milanovic ⊠ (2010) are available through 2005.
Source: HDRO calculations using health data from United Nations Department of Economic and Social Affairs life tables, education data from Barro and Lee (2010) and income inequality data from Milanovi (2010).

Human Development Report 2013: The Rise of the South: Human Progress in a Diverse World (New York: United Nations Development Program, 2013), p. 32, at http://hdr.undp.org/sites/default/files/reports/14/hdr2013_en_complete.pdf accessed on June 8, 2014. Used with permissions from the United Nations Development Program, licensed by Creative Commons 3.0 IGO at http://creativecommons.org/licenses/by/3.0/igo/legalcode

who were lower to upper middle-class. The net result was that the "poorest 40 percent of households had received just 16 percent of the income and 10 percent of the bank credit during the year 1996/7."[27] Distribution of bank credit was even more skewed than income, both overwhelmingly marginalizing the already poor.

As to the view that certain regions of the South performed better than others during the 1980s and 1990s, globalization's defenders have claimed that countries like China and India did so because they rigidly adhered to prescriptions from international financial institutions like the World Bank and the IMF. This is certainly not the case. As Giovanni Arrighi explains, China and India experienced substantial growth of their economies because both have huge human populations of 1.3 billion and 1.1 billion respectively, and both have been able to sell cheap manufactured products abroad as a result of their membership within the World Trade Organization (WTO), in the case of China since 2001.[28] China's rate of economic growth has unequivocally slowed since 2007, when it was an impressive 13 percent, to 9.2 percent in 2011 and plummeted to 7.6 percent in the first quarter of 2012, reflecting its weakest economic performance since the global financial crisis of 2008–09.[29] Second, countries in East Asia benefited from the increase in demand for cheap industrial products and the ballooning U.S. trade deficit with countries like China. The result was a growth in China's balance of payments and a redirecting of its vast surpluses to finance the U.S. debt crisis and borrowing through purchase of government treasury bonds that totaled almost $900 billion in 2007.[30] As of November 2013, China held $1.317 trillion in U.S. debt, after off-loading $37.6 billion in U.S. debt over the previous two years.[31] By February 2014, China had reduced its U.S. foreign debt holdings by $47.8 billion.[32] China is patently aware of the unreliability of the U.S. dollar and is increasingly uncomfortable with its huge debt holdings in dollars. It is considering reverting to the gold standard or to another viable exchangeable unit currency for trading in commodities as discussed within the BRICS bloc (Brazil, Russia, India, China, and South Africa) and expanding its banking interests in Europe. Correspondingly, China has reduced its demand for metals like iron ore and minerals like coal and copper, driving down global prices in 2012.[33] It has begun to reduce finished product exports to cut down deficits, startled by the massive $31 billion trade deficit between January and February 2012 that signified a radical interruption of the regular global trade surpluses it had previously enjoyed from manufactured product exports especially to the U.S.[34] China's banking sector is also extremely fragile, with loans in 2009 that were three times those of loans in 2008, with half of these financing property acquisitions and speculation that is fueling a skyrocketing property and stock bubble.[35] The incidence of labor unrest given the strenuous condition under which Chinese workers are forced to work and the rising discontent with wages and corporate labor policies has not helped either. Farmers and peasants losing land to large corporations in mining and industrial areas has been a serious problem in many parts of China. Ninety-four thousand citizen's actions against state housing, land, and social policies were recorded in 2006, followed by 120,000 in 2008 and 58,000 in the first three months of 2009, compounding state-citizen tensions.[36]

India's advantage for instance, resides in the fact that it has had a history of diversified production and possesses a large supply of skilled labor with an infrastructure in transportation and communication. However, India's economic growth has also slowed from preceding highs of 9 percent to 6.7 percent in 2009 and an anemic 5.3 percent in the first quarter of 2012.[37] Further, the country has faced huge power outages like the one that crippled industry and transportation in North India during the summer of 2012 prior to my visit there in late July, along with labor strikes and deleterious effects from global warming and climate change that has reduced rainfall for agricultural production by as much as 40 percent in June 2014.

Africa

Though Africa represents close to 15 percent of the world's population, she only accounts for under 2 percent of the total global Gross Domestic Product, and though Africa attracted up to 9 percent of total private capital flows to the underdeveloped world in the 1970s and 1980s, that figure dropped to a trickle of 2 percent in the 1990s.[38] While it is true that Africa's GDP is $1.6 trillion, and consumers spend $860 billion annually,[39] the bulk of this economic wealth is based in a few countries: South Africa (whose GDP is almost one-quarter of the rest of the African continent), and oil-producers like Nigeria, Algeria, Libya, and Angola constituting the bulk of the remaining wealth outside of Egypt, which has the second largest African population after Nigeria. The impoverishment of Africa has been ensured with Africa being entangled within the concatenation of the international commercial capitalist system. Robert Cummings, a political scientist at Howard University, notes:

> Much of Africa's financial losses have taken place under the rubric of international commerce and exchange. It is not an overstatement, to claim that the trade has been between, first, unequal trading partners, and secondly, via a global economic framework that seemed more adept at sucking capital out of the continent than it did at fostering economic growth and security for Africa and its people.[40]

Though Africa received $568 billion between 1960 and 2003 to end the cycle of poverty, the ranks of the impoverished steadily climbed over the same period.[41] The duplicitous manner with which global financial institutions like the World Bank, the International Monetary Fund, and other banks, have held African countries economic hostage, demanding that they service "the debt" that accrued from loans to corrupt neo-colonial African regimes in the 1970s and 1980s since the prices of African commodities fell precipitously, reveals the inherent and tangible dangers of Africa's continued dependence on Western capitalism. Thanks to the hegemonic role of the global financial institutions, 153 countries around the world owed $2.5 trillion in debt and debt servicing to them in 2005. By the end of 2010, even after supposed cancellation of billions of dollars in "debt," underdeveloped countries owed an astronomical $4 trillion in "debt."[42] African countries in particular have assured the wealthy Western powers of reaping lucrative gains in interest revenues from debt-strapped Africa.[43] *Why should African countries continue to be pay "debts" to Western financial institutions when these institutions and their governments benefitted from the raping of African resources and enslavement of her people for four centuries? The question is germane: Who really owes Whom?!* Regarding this condition of economic subjugation in the early 1990s, Cummings asserts that after the oil crisis of 1973, Africa became trapped in debt servicing so that by 1987, Africa

> transferred out considerably more of its financial revenues than it has been able to hold in reserves or to receive from trade in the decade of the 1980s via its exorbitant interest payments and capital flight to western institutions ... at the end of the first year of the special UN Recovery Program (1987), the world economy actually took $14 billion more out of Africa in the form of debt servicing and lowered commodity prices than it returned in the form of development assistance and private lending.[44]

Since 1980, Africa's "external debt" grew several score-fold from $6 billion to close to $400 billion in 2014, with South Africa alone having a gross external debt of $137.09 billion at the end of 2013.[45] Even with debt relief for 33 Heavily Indebted Poor Countries (HIPC) from Africa as the World Bank defines them, these countries still owed over $300 billion in 2013. Bretton Woods institutions resorted to what has been described as "casino capitalism," where they awarded loans to African governments for the sole purpose of ensuring that old loans were repaid.[46] Between 1990 and 1997, for instance, African countries spent between $24 billion and $33.4 billion in debt service to Western banks and financial institutions.[47] By 2005, Africa had paid out an astounding $550 billion in loan payments on the original loans of $540 billion, but due to high interest rates, some $245 billion was still outstanding. Each year, the countries of the South lose between $30 billion and $50 billion to the North in net capital transfers, resulting in compounded socio-economic hardship and escalating ineradicable poverty for the underdeveloped nations. Private wealth transfers from wealthy African individuals invested over $700 billion abroad between 1970 and 2008, earning high rates of interest on personal wealth, but draining the continent's financial coffers.[48] The Gleneagles, Scotland agreement by the G8 countries to cancel this interest on debt of the 20 most impoverished countries in Africa amounted to a mere $1.5 billion per year, equivalent to an hour of economic activity in the G8 countries![49] Africa's debt service payments grew from $12 billion in 1980 to $23 billion in 1997.

Between 1993 and 1995 for instance, Foreign Direct Investment (FDI) flows and other private capital investment totaled a mere 1 percent of Africa's Gross Domestic Product, in contrast to Latin America, where it was 3 percent, and Asia, where it was 6 percent of GDP.[50] Africa is the continent where the lowest Foreign Direct Investment in ratio to Gross Domestic Product exists, and in the case of twenty African countries, actually decreased between 1990 and 2000. The only area where Africa attracts foreign investment inflows and portfolios is in the area of petroleum and mineral mining, both essential for Western industrial capitalist expansion and indicative of the predatory nature of Western corporations and financial institutions, especially in their relationships with Africa.[51] FDI in Africa totaled $59 billion in 2009, down from $72 billion in 2008, with most of these investments directed toward countries with hydrocarbon and mining resources, principally Angola, Nigeria, Algeria, Sudan, and Libya for fossil fuels and South Africa and the Democratic Republic of the Congo for mining.[52] Three-quarters of FDI went to 24 African countries richly resourced in oil, gas, and minerals.[53] This FDI concentration in those African countries with energy and mineral resources serves as a reminder that foreign investments, be they from Western capitalist countries or corporations from China or India, are only interested in Africa for extractive values that serve to industrialize their respective economies.

Outside of South Africa, Africa's stock markets are capitalized at 0.6 percent of all global emerging stock markets, while concomitantly other stock portfolios were rapidly expanding in some Asian and Latin American countries. In the area of telecommunications, another pivotal area in which globalization's success is determined, Africa is at an abysmal disadvantage, falling outside the purview of comparison with other parts of the underdeveloped world. Only 1 in 8 fixed telephone subscribers was in Africa. Africa had only

1 in 60 of the world's mobile cellular phones in 2000 and constitutes just 1 percent of the world's Internet users.[54]

Though the ten largest economies of Africa, named in scale from largest to smallest, South Africa, Egypt, Algeria, Nigeria, Morocco, Libya, Tunisia, Sudan, Kenya, and Cote d'Ivoire, experienced a drop in economic growth from 3.0 percent in 2001 to 2.2 percent in 2002, these economies constitute 80 percent of Africa's GDP and cater to 55 percent of the continent's population.[55] Another factor demonstrating the skewed character of the African economies, again a product of the hegemony of the Western imperialist needs-oriented economy, is that oil-exporting countries, though about one-ninth of the continent's countries, contribute about 15 percent of Africa's GDP.[56] In other words, those African countries that possess energy resources upon which the Western capitalist economies depend, are viewed as essentially significant and warranting attention from the stalwarts of globalization. The U.S. spent $17.8 billion on oil imports from Africa in 2003, and 70 percent of all purchases by the U.S. from Africa was oil.[57] In 2005, the U.S. imported some $40.1 billion worth of oil from African countries excluding Algeria and Libya, principally from Nigeria, Equatorial Guinea, Chad, Angola, and Gabon, accounting for 79.8 percent of all U.S. purchases from Africa.[58] African oil imports now constitute 20 percent of total U.S. oil imports so that African imports exceed those of U.S. oil imports from the Persian Gulf oil producers. The remaining African countries are expected to be hangers onto the periphery, virtually totally dependent on the benevolence and charitable goodwill of the Western powers. It comes as no surprise then to learn that the finance minister of Malawi received his salary in U.S. dollars as part of an agreement with the World Bank and the government of Benin to receive approval for its budget from the IMF prior to submitting it to parliament![59]

The hegemonic power of food, a weapon during the era of late colonialism, continues unabated in the modern era of globalization, underscoring that *globalization in fact is a form of neo-colonialism.*[60] The same principle of controlling the food supply of the peoples of Asia and Africa was promulgated during the "Green Revolution" of the 1960s and 1970s. During that period, Euro-American agricultural methods that employed chemical fertilizers, engineered seeds, and pesticides were foisted on traditional Indigenous farmers in Africa and Asia who engaged in conservative agricultural practices that spared land from overcultivation and overgrazing.[61] With the offer of free seeds and artificial fertilizers for two years and the promise of expanded grain yields under the auspices of organizations like the World Bank and the Ford Foundation, farmers in Africa and Asia were deceived into abandoning traditional farming practices that conserved and preserved the Indigenous and natural fertility of the land and seduced into engaging in agricultural methods that favored large Western agribusiness corporations.[62] The net result was poorer grain yields, over-exhausted and infertile land, and deep levels of financial indebtedness. These policies and practices were progenitors to the onslaught of Monsanto and Dow Chemical today in the control of Indigenous seeds and widespread use of pesticides on food crops like corn, wheat, and rice all over the world, under the pretext of enhancing food yields. The "Green Revolution" was a convoluted mechanism that essentially ensured that farmers in Asia and Africa would be slavishly dependent on agribusiness corporations from the West. Under the auspices of global financial agencies like the World Bank, the Ford Foundation, and other "aid" agencies, it was designed to perpetuate impoverishment of otherwise generally healthy and self-sustaining agricultural farmlands maintained through centuries of Indigenous traditional farming modes of operation.

One of globalization's marked measures has been the spate of agreements signed between governments of impoverished countries in Africa, for instance. Large transnational corporations from more powerful countries lease land for food production for export to the countries from which the transnational corporations originate. South Korea's Daewoo Logistics leased half of Madagascar's arable land in an agreement signed in 2008 for the cultivation of food for export, where the company would lease the land rent-free, and local farmers were to go uncompensated. Least to say, this land-colonialism triggered intensive opposition from the majority of Madagascar's people, and the ruling government was toppled.[63] Similar agreements are being pursued by arable-land-hungry middle-income countries like Saudi Arabia, which is planning on leasing land for food production from the Sudan.

The UN Human Development Report 2013 substantiates the significantly lower life expectancy and reduced income levels per capita for most countries in Africa, South Asia and East Asia and the Pacific, all of which cumulatively still receive the lowest portion of gross income among world regions (**Table 1**).

Latin America

Agriculture constitutes about 65 percent of the global economy, and corporate centralization is unsurprising. In 1998, the top ten agrochemical companies controlled 81 percent of the $29 billion global agrochemical market.[64] Ten transnational food and drink companies had combined sales of $211 billion in 1995.[65] Deborah Barndt, a researcher on the tomato, described her research

Table 1: UN Human Development Report 2013

HDI and components, by region and HDI group, 2012

Region and HDI group	HDI	Life expectancy at birth (years)	Mean years of schooling (years)	Expected years of schooling (years)	Gross national income per capita (2005 PPP $)
Region					
Arab States	0.652	71.0	6.0	10.6	8,317
East Asia and the Pacific	0.683	72.7	7.2	11.8	6,874
Europe and Central Asia	0.771	71.5	10.4	13.7	12,243
Latin America and the Caribbean	0.741	74.7	7.8	13.7	10,300
South Asia	0.558	66.2	4.7	10.2	3,343
Sub-Saharan Africa	0.475	54.9	4.7	9.3	2,010
HDI group					
Very high human development	0.905	80.1	11.5	16.3	33,391
High human development	0.758	73.4	8.8	13.9	11,501
Medium human development	0.640	69.9	6.3	11.4	5,428
Low human development	0.466	59.1	4.2	8.5	1,633
World	0.694	70.1	7.5	11.6	10,184

Note: Data are weighted by population and calculated based on HDI values for 187 countries. PPP is purchasing power parity.
Source: HDRO calculations. See statistical table 1 for detailed data sources.

Human Development Report 2013: The Rise of the South: Human Progress in a Diverse World (New York: United Nations Development Program, 2013), p. 25, at http://hdr.undp.org/sites/default/files/reports/14/hdr2013_en_complete.pdf accessed on June 8, 2014. Used with permissions from the United Nations Development Program, licensed by Creative Commons 3.0 IGO at http://creativecommons.org/licenses/by/3.0/igo/legalcode

on how Santa Anita pickers, one of the biggest agro-exporters in Mexico with over 2,000 pickers, sells hybrid seeds that originated in Mexico, but were developed and patented by the U.S. or Israel.[66] At the Sayula plant, Santa Anita engaged in lethal spraying of tomato fields with pesticides by giant trucks, with some workers being exposed to these poisons since the company did not provide protective materials or health education against pesticides for all workers.

In Mexico, over 70,000 coffee farmers lost their farms and primary source of living as a result of the drop in the prices of coffee on world markets. Today, coffee farmers earn an absurd five U.S. cents per pound for coffee sold at Starbucks chain stores around the United States, where the average cup of coffee sells for two dollars per cup! Farmers on coffee farms from Kenya to Colombia have been either forced to abandon their farms or lay off thousands of workers, thanks to globalization's tentacles and its deification of market forces. Globalization has had a devastating effect on the Mexican economy and its ability to sustain its indigenous productivity. For instance, the manufacturing industry suffered a deficit of $22.6 billion in 1998 with the two principal exporting sectors, chemicals and metal products along with machinery and equipment, accounting for 71 percent of all manufacturing exports and generating 65 percent of the deficit in manufactures. Rice production has been hit particularly hard with the imposition of the North American Free Trade Agreement (NAFTA) with Canada and the United States, and today Mexico is the second largest rice importer from the United States, even exceeding Canada. Potato imports grew by 77 percent in four years, and while Mexico used to be a major cotton exporter prior to NAFTA, it imported 1.4 million bales of cotton from the U.S. in 1998.[67] For the first decade of the 21st century, Mexican corn farmers who are the descendants of corn growers for millennia have suffered tremendously because they are unable to compete with cheap corn imports from the U.S.[68] As an extension of the regime of globalization, NAFTA ensures Mexico's economic dependency on its "trading partners," Canada and the United States. Ironically, NAFTA does not facilitate the easy movement of people across the borders from Canada through Mexico and "only improves conditions of entry (into the United States and Canada) for business people and highly specialized professionals with competency in computer and media technology."[69] Further, Chapter 11 of NAFTA has been used by some large corporations to skirt environmental protection provisions, including court decisions protecting the environment, to the tune of $4 billion.[70] Transnational corporations are insisting that the right to protect investments by corporate investors as stipulated in Chapter 11 trumps environmental laws and decisions by communities to protect their water and lands from toxic industrial poisons.

The U.S.–Mexico border has now become a war zone with Department of Homeland Security, the U.S. Border Patrol, the Drug Enforcement Agency, and other security agencies constantly harassing, threatening, and in many instances, brutally assaulting Indigenous peoples especially from the Tohono O'odham Nation whose families live both in Mexico and the U.S. Many poor Mexicans cross the 2000 mile-border between the U.S. and Mexico, including an electrified section around Nogales, hoping to gain entry into the U.S. to seek employment and a livelihood following the massive job displacements in Mexico in the 1980s and 1990s as a result of NAFTA and globalization policies that dismantled protective trade barriers and undermined local Mexican agricultural producers and industries. Many border crossers have either been shot by Border Patrol agents for being drug smugglers or violent criminals or died in the steaming 100+ degree Fahrenheit summer heat of the Sonora desert over the past two decades.[71] Between 1990 and 2012, 2,238 migrant bodies were found in the region, tightened border securitization and policing being a major factor that forced people to desperately resort to cross at distant unmanned border points where summer conditions are dangerous and cause rapid dehydration resulting in eventual death.[72] In April 2014, three Tohono O'odham men were shot by Border Patrol agents in Arizona, including one who was shot badly in the face. In 2012, 16-year-old José Antonio Elena Rodriguez was killed after Border Patrol agents fired 14 shots at him at the Arizona-Mexican border after border agents claimed that Rodriguez threw stones at them over the border wall. Anastasio Hernandez Rojas was killed by Border Patrol agents in San Diego after agents claimed that Rojas was aggressive even though PBS video footage showed Rojas being tasered by the agents while he lay screaming on the ground.[73] The Department of Homeland Security awarded a $140 million border security contract to Elbit systems, an Israeli company responsible for building the high wall around the West Bank in occupied Palestinian territories, including constructing large surveillance towers facing O'odham lands.[74] O'odham residents in southern Arizona have documented evidence of the Border Patrol invading sacred sites and harassing elders going on mundane trips to the grocery store.[75] An environment of fear and intimidation has become the norm for these Indigenous peoples in their ancestral homeland.

In Latin America, some positive news emerges, not because of globalization forces, but despite them. Poverty rates have dropped significantly as reported by Economic Commission for Latin America and the Caribbean, falling by 17 percent from 1990 to 2010, from 48.4 percent to 31.4 percent and the rates for the extremely poor falling by 10.3 percent from 22.6 percent to 12.3 percent over that period.[76] The drop in poverty rates was evident especially in Peru, Ecuador, Argentina, Venezuela, Uruguay, and Colombia and largely attributable to heavy infusion of government spending on social programs targeting the poor, especially food production and supports in a global climate where food prices and the global recession increased pressure on national budgets elsewhere in the world. In Venezuela, for instance, extreme poverty has been cut by 70 percent and 250,000 new houses have been constructed in the past five years, with education from kindergarten through university freely accessible by all Venezuelan citizens.[77] Overall, poverty in Venezuela was reduced from 49 percent in 1998 to 25.4 percent in 2012 and universal health care is available to all.[78] The country is now reputed to have the lowest income inequality in Latin America. Venezuela of course has embarked on a Bolivarian revolutionary strategy based on a governmental policy of 21st century socialism as late president Hugo Chavez proclaimed, being a fierce opponent of the neo-liberalist policies imposed by globalization. As much as all progressive forces endorse the Bolivarian revolution in Venezuela, including most Indigenous people in the country, compelling me to visit the country in 2007, I was reminded of the challenges even a country like Venezuela faces. It depends on oil as the basis for its positive economic accomplishments, and the representatives from the Indigenous parliament with whom we met in 2007 (including from the Karina people) explained that they had some tensions with the government over oil drilling in the Orinoco basin where Indigenous people live. Even with these factors of poverty alleviation, the fact is that 177 million lived in poverty in Latin America in 2010, of which 70 million were extremely poor, only four of every ten people employed make social security contributions, and in 12 of 17 Latin American and Caribbean countries, social security and retirement beneficiaries were less than half of senior citizens.[79] Female-headed households in rural communities in Latin America generally still bear the brunt of economic hardship. This fact was starkly evident for the majority of village women in Nicaragua, for instance, during my visit there with the Alliance for Global Justice in the fall of 2012, although the Nicaraguan government has worked industriously to address rural poverty, especially the experiences of women, through its *zero-ambré* (zero hunger) program and *zero-usuria* (zero usury) program, where 100,000 women receive low interest loans to purchase individual cows for engagement in community milk production.[80] However, though many Indigenous communities are supportive of the Sandinista government, similar to Indigenous peoples in Venezuela, tensions over destruction of the ecology and impacts on Indigenous cultures of the Nicaraguan Caribbean coast persist. The Nicaraguan government is planning construction of a deep-water port at Monkey Point and a dry canal that would connect the Caribbean and Pacific coasts where many Indigenous Rama, Sumo, and Miskito people live, raising significant opposition from Indigenous peoples in the region as I heard during my visit in September 2012.[81]

Global financial institutions like the World Bank and the International Monetary Fund celebrate the fact that the number of people living on less than $1 per day dropped from 1.5 billion in 1981 to 1.1 billion in 2001 and that global poverty rates have halved over that twenty year period, much of this alleviation in Asia and Latin America. The reality is that while some levels of poverty may have fallen in some parts of the world like in Latin America, the reality of those living in extreme poverty is still entrenched, as in Africa and South Asia (**Table 2**).

Table 2: UN Human Development Report 2013

Number of people in extreme poverty by region and selected countries, base case and accelerated progress scenarios, 2010–2050 (millions)

Region or country	2010	2020	2030	2040	2050, base case	2050, accelerated progress
Arab States	25	19	17	16	17	1
East Asia and the Pacific	211	74	42	29	29	9
China	94	13	5	1	1	0
Europe and Central Asia	14	2	3	3	4	1
Latin America and the Caribbean	34	29	26	27	32	13
South Asia	557	382	243	135	81	13
India	416	270	134	53	21	2
Sub-Saharan Africa	371	333	297	275	267	60
World	1,212	841	627	485	430	96

Note: Extreme poverty is defined as $1.25 a day in purchasing power parity terms. See *Technical appendix* for a discussion of the base case and fast track scenarios.
Source: HDRO calculations based on Pardee Center for International Futures (2013).

Human Development Report 2013: The Rise of the South: Human Progress in a Diverse World (New York: United Nations Development Program, 2013), p. 25, at http://hdr.undp.org/sites/default/files/reports/14/hdr2013_en_complete.pdf accessed on June 8, 2014. Used with permissions from the United Nations Development Program, licensed by Creative Commons 3.0 IGO at http://creativecommons.org/licenses/by/3.0/igo/legalcode

The Caribbean

In this part of the world that witnessed the genocidal annihilation of major Indigenous nations like the Caribs, Arawaks, and Tainos by various European colonial and slave-based powers and the subsequent importation of forced free African labor via the institution of chattel slavery, globalization is viewed by some scholars as a subset of colonialism, imperialism and capitalism.[82] In the view of the Caribbean scholar, Hilbourne Watson, the economies of that region have been structured to serve essentially in the interest of U.S. transnational conglomerates at the heart of the capitalist system. Watson argues:

Caribbean workers, like other workers around the world, have to compete with machines and other smart tools for jobs as they deal with the strategic power of the World Bank, the IMF, the WTO and the U.S. state. The U.S. subsumes its doctrine of free trade and open regionalism under its structured national security doctrine.... Resolution 1080 of the OAS (Organization of American States—mine)—the Santiago Commitment—commits the OAS and its member states to defend against "threats" to capitalism, state sovereignty and market democracy in any American republic.[83]

Watson emphasizes that Resolution 1080 ensures that the economies in the Western hemisphere are subject to the hegemonic dictates of the U.S. economy in areas of production, investment, finance, transportation, all commercial activity, and military relations. This statute "redefines reciprocal collective security" by requiring that Latin American and Caribbean states become havens for capitalist market security with focus on global private property rights as the key index of state sovereignty.[84]

Nations that have refused to adhere to the politico-economic recipe dictated by Washington, have in the past experienced the full brunt of U.S. political and economic intervention. For instance, the CIA destabilized the Manley government of the 1970s when it attempted to introduce a more egalitarian economy with social justice provisions that led to the pro–Washington Seaga regime winning elections in 1980 with the full endorsement of the IMF.[85] U.S. military intervention in Grenada occurred in 1983 following the assassination of socialist-leaning Prime Minister Maurice Bishop in a military coup. U.S. troops invaded Grenada on the pretext that U.S. medical students in Grenada had to be protected and the Cuban presence in Grenada was a threat to the island and U.S. national security.[86] The second overthrow of the democratically elected government of Jean-Bertrand Aristide in February 2004 signified a repeat of the 1991 coup that forced Aristide into exile. The then–U.S. Secretary of State, Colin Powell, was a leading figure responsible for ousting Aristide, kidnapping him, and forcing him into a closed-window plane that flew Aristide to the Central African Republic and eventually to exile in South Africa.[87] Haiti is now been reduced to a colony of the United Nations with the United Nations Stabilization Mission in Haiti (MINUSTAH) still present some four years after the massive January 12, 2010, 7.0 earthquake devastated the country, leaving thousands dead and over 1.5 million homeless. In 2014, 200,000 people remained homeless and lived in tents, only 7,515 new houses had been built, 27,000 houses were repaired, and 55,000 families received one-time payments of $500 to live outside the temporary housing camps.[88] The largest beneficiaries of the $6.4 billion disbursed by international donors have been large foreign corporations.[89] When the military regime replaced tyrannical ruler Jean-Claude Duvalier in February 1986, it promoted policies that dismantled local trade protection barriers, subsidies for the agricultural sector, and privatized public industries to satisfy U.S. capitalist investment demands, all reversed in the victory of the Lavalas party under Jean-Bertrand Aristide in September 1991, who himself was subsequently overthrown in another military coup. Aristide was conditionally returned to the presidency in 1994 with the intervention of U.S. troops in the same year, but not after trade tariffs on rice and other food imports were radically reduced to 3 percent. In the current era, Haiti imports most of its food, including 80 percent of its rice and most of its other basics foodstuffs from the U.S., profiting rice farmers from Arkansas, home state of former president Bill Clinton who has been involved in ostensible U.S. aid programs to Haiti.[90] Haiti has been reduced to an economically and socially dependent neo-colony of the U.S., after being self-sufficient in sugar, rice, poultry, and pork production for decades. Today, Haiti is also a source of cheap labor for U.S transnational corporations in areas of textile production like Fruit of the Loom and Hanes. Quotas require that a portion of apparel imports into the U.S. use U.S. materials that benefit U.S. textile manufacturers.[91] In 2009, WikiLeaks cables revealed that the U.S. Embassy in Haiti and USAID worked closely with Levis, Hanes, and Fruit of the Loom to block a minimal increase of daily wages to $5 per day mandated by the Haitian parliament.[92] Small wonder why Haiti is the most impoverished country in the Western hemisphere! Haiti is paying a dear price for being the first independent and liberated Black republic in the world in 1804 after over-throwing French slavery on the island. In mid–April 2014, tens of thousands of people marched in Port-au-Prince, Haiti's capital, demanding that President Martelly leave the presidency and that MINUSTAH depart from Haiti and end its occupation of the country.[93] Clearly, Haitians view the UN as an occupying force that serves the interests of Western globalized powers like the U.S. and have not benefitted from the UN presence, particularly in the wake of a cholera outbreak caused by UN peacekeepers in mid–2010.

Quintessentially, the U.S. views the Caribbean as a haven for cheap labor and as a tourist paradise for pleasure-seeking white U.S. tourists, with the imposition of Free Trade Zones, where U.S. transnationals make goods ranging from clothes to electronics and food products made by cheap Caribbean labor, often women. Given the reduced prices of raw materials that are found preponderantly within the underdeveloped parts of the world (Africa, Asia and Latin America, the "periphery nations" of yesteryear) and the elevated and inflated prices of manufactured goods generally in Western industrialized countries (the "core" nations of yesteryear and now receiving challenging competition from the BRICS nations—Brazil, Russia, India, China, and South Africa), the Caribbean has found itself heavily dependent on tourism from North America and Europe, making the region extremely vulnerable to the economic and political vicissitudes of the Western industrialized world.[94]

Globalization's advocates laud the increased income of people in the

Caribbean in general compared to other parts of the underdeveloped world, in Latin America, for example. However, the reality is that

> the distribution of income is highly uneven. A large share of the gains from trade is siphoned off by foreign investors with the rest going into paying the wages of the labor force. A major share of this wage income goes to pay for consumption and capital goods imports. When most of the gains from trade get recycled abroad, the impact of trade openness on growth is diminished. This large leakage reflected the high dependence of the region on foreign investment. It also indicates that the impact of foreign investment on the local economy is much smaller than it could be.[95]

Over the past twenty-five years, Caribbean countries have enjoyed special nation status in their exports to the countries of Western Europe, most recently, the EU on the basis of the Lomé Convention and its four protocols over this period that accorded preferential treatment to African, Caribbean, and Pacific (ACP) countries as part of the attempt to redress the historical colonial economic imbalances between the European powers and the colonies of the Caribbean, Africa, and the Pacific. This arrangement provided for higher prices for Caribbean goods such as bananas and sugar than on the world market, and the products benefited from price supports to European farmers. On the other hand, however, there is growing concern about the EU consideration of a flat tariff on Latin American bananas being exported to the EU that proposed a flat fee of $300 (200 Euros) in 2008. This is in accordance with a WTO agreement in November 2001 that requires a new tariff on EU banana imports from countries outside the ACP, since Ecuador, which would be directly affected by this new regime, is the largest exporter of bananas in the world, exporting some 700,000 tons to the EU annually.[96] Ecuador's bananas, like Nicaragua's, derive from plantations owned by U.S. transnational corporations like Dole and Chiquita, so U.S. commercial interest is again primary in these considerations. To add insult to injury, banana workers in Nicaragua are required to use pesticides like Nemagon and Fumazone containing dioxins that cause reproductive illnesses, infertility, cancer, and deformed babies, recounted in poignant testimony that I recorded from banana workers in Managua, Nicaragua, in August 2012. Banana workers filed a suit against the Dole Corporation in U.S. District in 2003 for this situation of grievous bodily harm by the corporation's persistence in forcing its employees to use toxic chemicals as documented in the 2009 film by Frederick Gertten, *Bananas*. Dole Food Company settled with 4,000 former Nicaraguan Dole workers for damages in August 2011.[97]

To contain the perceived threat of Cuban and "communist ideologies" in the aftermath of the Cold War, the U.S. introduced its own Caribbean Basin initiative that included special quotas for rice and sugar. The Uruguay Round of Talks under the auspices of the former General Agreement on Trade and Tariffs that became the World Trade Organization at the Marrakech meeting in 1994, changed the global trading environment substantially, and the Caribbean was directly affected by the emerging policies of liberalization, deregulation, and privatization. Non-agricultural exports from the Caribbean to the EU dropped from 50 percent in 1990 to 33 percent in 2001.[98]

Globalization and the liberalization regime on the Caribbean foisted by the WTO protocol and conditioned through structural adjustment policies imposed by the World Bank and the IMF forced Caribbean governments to desist from intervention in their respective agricultural sectors and quickly resulted in the flooding of markets with cheaper imported goods. The net consequence was the decimation of agricultural farmers (domestic milk production suffered severely for instance), and banana and sugar production saw losses unparalleled in recent Caribbean history. The pressure from U.S. commercial interest on the EU in the area of banana imports shattered the previous preferential trade agreement since the U.S. insisted on EU purchase quotas from its banana plantations in Latin America, owned by corporations like Dole and Chiquita. Though the U.S. was fully aware that island countries like St. Kitts depended preponderantly on sugar for exports (in 2001 St. Kitts' sugar production was 26.4 percent of the agricultural contribution to its GDP), and St. Lucia depended heavily on bananas (33.6 percent and 33.9 percent of the agricultural share to GDP, respectively), it nevertheless insisted on such revisions of trade practices. The aftermath of this insertion of globalization intervention was immediate:

> In the Eastern Caribbean banana production fell by 7.7 percent between 1998 and 1999 and by 41.1 percent in 2001 (ECCB, 2001, 2002). Production decreased by 51.6 percent in 2001 in St. Lucia alone, which accounted for 50 percent of the total Eastern Caribbean production in that year.
> These developments in the banana industry contributed significantly to the decline in the agricultural sector generally (ECCB, 2002) from almost 60 percent of total EU imports from the region in 1991 to 32 percent in 2001.... This, combined with the trials being experienced in the sugar industry where production fell from 98,879,732 tonnes in 1991 to 50,406,027 tonnes in 2001 [FAO, 2002a].[99]

The concomitant problem of liberalization implied the forced removal of subsidies from food crops, raising the prices of agricultural commodities for residents of the region, and the dismantling of import controls. Imports of food items into the Caribbean from the wealthy countries of the EU multiplied, even while the EU increased farmer subsidies in the same breath. So much for fair trade under the rubric of globalization of the new millennium championed by advocates within the WTO, World Bank, IMF, the EU, and the U.S. government. The policies of these organizations constitute a rigid colonial imperialism in which capitalism's obsession with profit by any means necessary saw farmers and agricultural producers supporting millions of people in the Caribbean being driven into bankruptcy and directed into poverty. It is for this reason that many Caribbean countries were forced into further dependence on tourism as revenue earners, compelled to sell the culture of oppressed people of African descent in the islands as a commodity for consumption by wealthy tourists from the north. This was poignantly illustrated in the film *Life and Debt*, where U.S. citizens are able to enter many Caribbean countries with U.S. drivers' licenses even though these are supposedly sovereign nations.[100] It was only in 2008 that this policy was changed for reasons of U.S. "national security," and electronic passports issued by the U.S. State Department for all U.S. citizen travel has been required for all U.S. travel abroad.

Globalization has shattered the ability of countries of the Caribbean to compete in international markets, inducing many countries to rely on loans and transfers from international aid agencies to finance basic national services, and drawing them deeper into a spiraling quagmire of indebtedness.[101] The weak infrastructure of many of these countries is unconducive for expanded industrial production. Countries like Bermuda and the Cayman Islands essentially function as havens for off-shore banking operations for wealthy individuals from Europe and the United States and their local populations eke out a meager existence from being service workers in this distorted casino economy maintained by speculation and foreign-owned real estate. I still recall the painful accounts of the struggle to survive by a taxi driver in the Cayman Islands in the early 1990s as he described the unmanageable cost of living due to the astronomical price of gasoline and exorbitant cost of food. Globalization has very assuredly entrenched a colonial-beneficiary economy where wealthy white landlords and commercial "developers" benefit lucratively, all the while waited upon by the local Black people, reduced to service slaves just to live from day to day.

Even in the Arab world, oil-rich countries may have received large revenues from booming oil prices, but many are still beset by debt. Saudi Arabia, which earned some $170 billion from oil in 2005, has government debt that is equivalent to almost 100 percent of its GNP and has suffered serious budget and trade deficits over the past two decades, as its population doubled and the structure of its mono-product capitalist economy did not generate positive

economic production owing to a severe lack of investment in non-oil producing sectors of the economy.[102] Similarly, industrial production and investment
in infrastructure in the major oil producing nations like Algeria, which earned
$40 billion from oil exports, Iran ($49 billion) and Libya ($30 billion) in
2005 were static for the most part. Libya may have been one of the few major
oil-producing countries that used its lucrative oil revenues for investment in
public services with free education, health care, subsidized housing and transportation, and a massive water transportation pipeline for agricultural production in the arid Sahara desert.[103] Since 2011, Libya's infrastructure has been
thoroughly destroyed by the U.S. and NATO bombing of the country and a
U.S. client-regime sympathetic to oil-conglomerate interests has been installed,
shattering any semblance of Libyan national independence attained over the
previous four decades.[104] Venezuela is another example of productive use of
oil revenues. Yet, generally, large revenues within a capitalist dispensation that
is essentially driven by an imperialist-defined global economy do not translate
into tangible benefits for the overwhelming majority of the people. The Arab
Human Development Report of 2002 declared, "traditional culture and values, including Arab culture and values, can be at odds with those of the globalizing world."[105] Patently, globalization's colonial economic foundations, the
presence of imperialist oil corporations from the West, and its accompanying
culture of consumerism and expediency does not sit well with the masses of
people across the Arab-speaking world who are still traditional in their value
systems in the main.

The Oil Producing and Exporting Countries (OPEC) was founded by
Venezuela, along with Iran, Saudi Arabia, Iraq, and Kuwait in 1960, as a way
of protecting national interests of these oil-producing nations and to function in concert as a global energy cartel. Venezuela, which has reaped tens of
billions of dollars from oil revenues and has pumped these monies into infra-
structural development and community projects under the banner of building an indigenous socialism in the twenty-first century led by the principles
of the Bolivarian revolution presided over by the late-president, Hugo Chavez,
is the exception to all oil-producing nations. The Bolivarian revolution continues in Venezuela, presided by Nicolas Maduro. However, Indigenous peoples
in Venezuela like the Karinâ people are still concerned about the devastating
environmental impact of oil production in areas like the Orinoco Basin, and
during my visit there in 2007, this subject was widely discussed. The government is currently involved in serious discussions with the more than 70 Indigenous nations on exploring alternative energy sources, a challenge for a system
predicated on oil revenues as its mainstay.

The "BRICS" Countries (Brazil, Russia, India, China, and South Africa)

Globalization has been viewed by numerous political and economic stalwarts in the West, and even by some putative critics, such as Nelson Mandela, the first and late president of post-apartheid South Africa/Azania, as inevitable in the global scheme of cultural and economic evolution. The distinctive ethos of globalization is evinced too by the expanding capitalist economies of the "BRIC" countries, Brazil, Russia, India, and China, which have seen their gross economic products grow phenomenally from 1980 to the present. South Africa/Azania aspires too to become part of this band of "booming" economies as part of BRICS even though its economic growth in 2009 and 2010 slowed dramatically to 3 percent due to the global financial recession. The country experienced deep economic stress and even stagnation following the continued strikes by hundreds of thousands of miners in the country's platinum and gold mines following the shocking killing of 34 striking miners in Marikana by police on August 17, 2012.[106] It appears that South Africa/Azania will never be the same again after that gunning down of Black miners, a horrific act recalling the bloody Sharpeville and Soweto apartheid-era massacres in 1960 and 1976 respectively and highlighting the very tenuous situation of South Africa's/Azania's mining-based economy that still thrives on the exploitation of cheap Black labor even in a post-apartheid "democracy." In October 2012, over 100,000 workers, including 75,000 in the mining sector, continued expanded strikes in the freight, transport, tire manufacturing, and other areas of Africa's largest economy, resulting in weekly losses of $150 million per week in the freight sector alone.[107] In early 2014, South Africa/Azania was faced by its longest platinum workers strike involving over 70,000 workers that resulted in $2.2 billion in production losses over a five-month period.[108] Workers lost millions of dollars in pay and were forced to accept a settlement on June 23, 2014, because workers hadn't been paid for months and were unable to support their families any longer. Their demand was twelve thousand South African rands ($1,250) per month, hardly a livable wage in a high-cost country like South Africa/Azania. The tragedy was that these Indigenous workers had to sacrifice their family livelihoods to demand a livable wage, while the CEOs of platinum mining companies like Anglo American Platinum, Impala Platinum, and Lonmin earn millions of rands in annual compensation requiring no striking to meet salary demands! Notwithstanding the global economic recession from 2007 to late 2009, South Africa/Azania saw its revenue grow by 4.5 percent for two years from 2008 to April 2010, and its GDP totaled

$288 billion in 2008, demonstrating the resilience of the country's economy even while the United States saw its economy contract by 14 percent over the same period.[109] Yet South Africa's/Azania national debt in March 2014 stood at $136.6 billion and is 38.2 percent of the country's GDP, much of it accruing from the apartheid era.[110] Private sector loans in the country increased by 225 percent and external debt grew by an astronomical 250 percent in the past decade, with debt levels increasing by about 87 percent since the financial crisis of 2008.[111] Given that within the ruling African National Congress Party (ANC) in South Africa/Azania, "72 percent of ANC National Executive Committee members own shares, 50 percent own shares in more than one company and 18 percent own shares in more than five companies and fifteen members of the Zuma presidential family are involved in a staggering 134 companies" it comes as no surprise that some 16 million eligible voters either did not register to vote or, if registered, did not cast their votes on election day on May 7, 2014.[112] Essentially, 32 percent of the voting population have voted the ruling party into power, hardly reflective of a participatory post-apartheid democracy.

Brazil's Gross Domestic Product (GDP) doubled from 1984 to 1985 from over $300 billion to $604 billion in 2004–05 with a growth of 5.2 percent in the same year.[113] China's GDP in 2000 was $1.1 trillion, ten times levels in 1970, and by 2004 it rose to $1.9 trillion, making it the sixth largest economy of the world.[114] Today, it is the second largest economy after the U.S., surpassing that of Japan and Germany. Neighboring India, which witnessed a snails-pace economic growth level of 3.5 percent from independence in 1947 to 1970, saw its economy grow by 5.6 percent from 1980 to 2000 and more recently by almost 7 percent so that, by 2004, India had the eighth-largest economy in the world with a GDP worth $691 billion.[115] India enjoyed an annual growth of over 7 percent from 1997 to 2007, and its GDP in April 2010 almost doubled from that in 2004 to $1.217 trillion.[116] Russia quadrupled its per-capita GDP from 2000 to 2007 to almost $7,000 per year.[117] Do these GDP figures reveal the substance of the quality of life of humans and the ecology in these respective countries and are they accurate indices of *value* of the labor of the producers and workers in each country? Are they artificially inflated figures to convey economic might, particularly when many of these figures reflect wealth, either based on treasury bonds carried in other countries' debt portfolios or concealing actual indebtedness of the lending countries themselves? China for example carries $1.4 trillion worth of U.S. debt bonds denominated in U.S. dollars and counts this figure as part of its sovereign wealth funds.

While the financial magnates of the world give plaudits to the wonders of globalization in the explosion of profits from the corridors of finance and trade in the capitals and stock exchanges of the world's economic powers, the growing chasm between rich and poor in the very same countries like Brazil, India, South Africa, Russia, and China have intensified, and the poor continue to suffer lower real wages mostly from temporary employment and casual labor, unemployment, and lack of nutrition, decent public education, and access to previously provided public health care and social services. Notwithstanding Brazil's massive economic growth, for instance, the situation of poverty and inequality is staggering. The top 1 percent received 15 percent of all income, the top 10 percent received half of all income, and the bottom 50 percent received 10 percent of the nation's income in 2000.[118] Twenty thousand families control 46 percent of the country's wealth and 1 percent of the landowners in Brazil possess 44 percent of the land.[119] The infant mortality rate for the northeastern part of Brazil, which is predominantly Black, is shocking at 47.79 deaths per 1,000 births to age 1 compared to 18.3 deaths per 1,000 births in the southern part of the country.[120]

Globalization: Financial Crises, Debacles, and Instability Ad Infinitum

The picture is not as rosy as it appears even for the rapidly growing Asian capitalist "tiger" economies. The 1996–1997 financial crisis that shook these "tigers"—South Korea, Taiwan, Malaysia, and Singapore—for example, still lingers as external debt ratios remain high, manufacturing has been modest, exports in certain industrial sectors have been sluggish, and dependence on irregular foreign investment has been excessive, making long-term financial growth unsustainable.[121] Foreign investment inflows in underdeveloped countries or expanding industrial economies have not always been favorable. One of the hallmarks of globalization was its relaxation of market controls and financial deregulation that caused financial upheaval in economies of poor and middle-income countries, with banking crises in Brazil, Mexico and other Latin American countries in the early 1980s and "in Venezuela (1993–95), Mexico (1994–95), Hungary (1995), the Asian 5 (1997–99), Czech Republic (1997), Brazil (1998–99) and Russia (1998–2000) during the closing decade of the millennium," all of which produced a contagion effect on other countries' economies.[122]

The role of international banking in the global financial and commercial system over the past twenty years is unprecedented in the history of banking and world economic output. Net international bank loans grew from 42.6 percent world trade to 66.9 percent of such trade and across border inter-bank liabilities increased astronomically from $5.56 trillion in 1990 to $8.99 trillion in 2000.[123] Yet few mainstream economists predicted the financial collapse within the capitalist world of 2008 as Samir Amin (who together with critical political economists like Francois Morin, Frédéric Lordon, Elmar Altyvater, Peter Gowan and a few others) had analyzed and prognosticated prior to the September debacle that year.[124] The explosive expansion of monetary and financial markets from the 1980s and its subsequent implosion in 2008 signified the crisis of oligopolistic capitalism and its hyper-concentration and accumulation of financial resources within a small segment of the globe, represented by banks and financial conglomerates based on insurance, pension and hedge funds, property investment, and the like. These were the principal beneficiaries. The financial crisis of September 2008 was thus triggered not by the sub-prime mortgage crisis as we were all led to believe by the media-conglomerate establishment, but rather by the internal contradictions endemic to financial capital and the capitalist system itself. The crisis prompted editors in the *Financial Times* to declare in March 2009 that "the world of the past three decades is gone."[125] It is thus unsurprising that banks are now returning to the pre–2008 practice of providing money to hedge funds and financing purchases of complex debt securities that accelerated the debt boom and was a major spark in the financial debacle of 2008.[126] The capitalist system thrives on exorbitant borrowing and debt accumulation, making it constantly unstable and globally unsustainable, experienced in successive economic and financial crises over the past century.

In 2008, the confidence of financial capital was shaken to its core. Stock markets around the world, which symbolized the power of financial capital, lost almost 50 percent of their value, some $35 trillion.[127] Five Wall Street investment banks disappeared. Banks around the world—in Ireland, Britain, Germany, Iceland, Spain, Italy, and several other European and Asian countries—saw their wealth melting within weeks and then days. General Motors (GM) and Chrysler, hitherto iconic symbols of United States motoring might, collapsed and were ironically rescued by the U.S. government, which laid the burdens of such salvaging on the country's loyal taxpayers. General Motors has since repaid most of its $50 billion bailout and Chrysler repaid $11.2 billion. The cost to taxpayers is still $11.2 billion for the GM bailout and $1.3 billion for Chrysler. Italian car giant, Fiat, purchased the 6 percent of the government interest in Chrysler for $500 million.[128] Though most establishment spokespersons rave about the bailout as successful since over a million jobs were saved and tens of billions of dollars were saved from the cost of the U.S. government expenditures on unemployment benefits and other services, there are looming questions that one needs to raise concerning the bailout of the auto industry by the U.S. government.[129] Why do auto companies wield such powerful economic and political influence in U.S. society to the point that they can muster such governmental bailouts from the tax-paying public, rights that are denied to tens of millions of individuals who are in debt to large banks and the government for mortgages, credit cards, student loans, etc., and yet cannot claim bankruptcy except under very rigorous conditions? For instance, average student debt stood at $29,400 for 70 percent of all college graduates in 2012.[130] Forty million people owe thousands of dollars in loans from college debt for a record total of $1.2 trillion. Barack Obama's plan to cap loan payments to 10 percent of monthly income in no way absolves loan debtors of their loans; it merely prolongs the duration of payment.[131] Over 13 percent of all U.S. mortgages are under water, affecting some 6.4 million homes, where mortgage holders are struggling to pay for their mortgages even though such mortgages are worth more than the real market value of their houses.[132] No bailouts for such indebtedness of desperate people are in sight. Millions of people lost their homes because they were unable to keep up on mortgage payments during and after 2008. Why were GM and Chrysler bailed out and why do they continue to make billions through corporate mergers, buyouts, and profits while their executives and board members continue to receive lucrative compensation packages hundreds of times the earnings of these companies' employees? Where was GM's loyalty to the tax-paying public that bailed it out when it refused to immediately investigate the faulty ignition switches on over 2.6 million cars that were recalled in 2014 and have caused the deaths of at least 13 people through 2014, even though GM CEO Mary Barra received an email indicating that the ignitions were potentially faulty in 2011?[133] Most importantly, why were giant auto companies being bailed out by U.S. government taxpayer-funded money when auto emissions are the single most lethal cause of greenhouse gases that are causing global warming and climate change, which threatens the Earth and all life? A May 2014 scientist panel climate report found that the "U.S. Climate Has Already Changed...Citing Heat and Floods," reinforcing the case that such bailout funds of auto companies ought to be invested in non-fossil fuels and alternative energies that are ecologically sustainable, rather than in expanded fossil-fuel-dependent automobile production.[134]

Between 2007 and 2010, over 3.3 million jobs were lost in the U.S. in various sectors, including finance, construction, auto assembly, and the service sector. This consistent pattern of job losses has continued relentlessly since the 1970s into the present. Large transnational corporations have moved their principle bases of operation from the U.S. to places like India, China, and Taiwan or to Latin America thousands of miles away where labor costs are a fraction of what corporations would need to pay comparable workers locally, especially in the high-tech and information technology sectors. By the peak of the financial crisis in 2008, 48 percent of all products made by the Standard & Poor's top 500 corporations were made abroad.[135] For instance, IBM had many more workers employed abroad from the early 1990s. Apple, the largest corporation in the world today, worked hard to have most of its operations staffed by people overseas, so that by 2008, Apple had 25,000 domestic employees and 250,000 in China.[136] Due to expanded off-shoring from the 1970s and 1980s that culminated in an unprecedented financial and unemployment crisis in 2007–2008, high-tech employment peaked at 3.8 million jobs and flattened out during that period. Even more ominous was the reduced need for college-level trained employees, so that by 2014, only 21 percent of all jobs in the U.S. required college degrees.[137]

Millions of mortgage borrowers lost their homes or continued to walk away from homes that were driven under water, where the amount owed on their homes exceeded by far the market value of their homes. In states like California, Florida, Nevada, and Arizona, houses lost up to 50 percent of their market values over that period prior to 2008. The financial crisis in Greece in May 2010 after Greece defaulted on its massive $120 billion debt to large financial banks, followed by the imposition of severe austerity measures including reduced social security allocations for Greek workers that triggered intensified social protests, sent tremors across European, Asian and U.S. stock markets and financial houses to the point that the Dow Jones Industrial Average dropped close to 600 points in one day.[138] Latvia fired one third of its teachers, Ireland reduced government employees' salaries by 22 percent, and California cut its health insurance programs for 900,000 children and laid off over 20,000 teachers.[139] In 2012, Greece's unemployment rate was 25 percent and for youth, an astounding 50 percent. Unemployment in Spain, the Eurozone's fourth largest economy, grew to 24.4 percent in September 2012. The situation of desperation by 600,000 people in Spain who have no form of income forced many to scavenging for food from Madrid's trash cans, leading the city to install locks on the trash cans![140] Over 5 million people engaged in self-employment jobs in Britain since 2008 now earn incomes that are 40 percent of those engaged in other productive employment. Half of middle-income earners in Britain can no longer afford home purchases.[141] Small wonder then that in 2011, on the other side of the Atlantic, the British government announced that the country was in the worst ever financial crisis since the 1930s and would print 75 billion British pounds as part of a "quantitative easing" monetary policy.[142] This measure will certainly not cure the cancer of indebtedness sown by capitalist bankers in Britain or anywhere else and perhaps not even function as a palliative to the critically ill British and other global economies since living with mountains of debt well into the future is simply unsustainable. Such is the insouciance of globalization at work in industrialized Europe, where globalization of the modern era ironically has its roots. Retirement ages for women have been raised to 65 in Italy. In many countries of the Eurozone and in the U.S. similar policies of raised retirement ages for women and men are being discussed broadly.

The bubble of rising values of stocks and real estate that funded the economic boom of the post–2001 recession was short-lived and quickly arrested in 2008, harking back to the depression days of 1929 in its severity and suddenness and dwarfing the recessions of the early 1980s and those of the early 1990s and the early 2000s. The bounce-back expected from previous recessions with this deep capitalist crisis is not forthcoming since "creative destruction," the term coined by Joseph Schrumpeter to describe capitalism's volatility of growth and contraction and the fallout from such dissonance, is now essentially "permanent destruction," with the depletion of the non-replenishable natural resources of the Earth.[143] It is no secret too that while the stock market has boomed with the Dow Jones Industrial Average closing on to 17,000 in June 2014, the lot for 99 percent of people in the U.S. is hardly a financial boon. While the top 7 percent of the U.S. population saw an increase of mean net household wealth by 28 percent, the lower 93 percent of households experienced a mean net loss of 4 percent.[144] The mean net worth for families declined by 12 percent from 2005 to 2009, except for those whose mean net household worth was $500,000 or more.[145] This pattern has continued consistently from 1979 to 2007 during which the upper 1 percent received 53.9 percent of all increases in income. From 2011, most states reflected similar income distribution levels with the top 1 percent receiving anywhere from half to 84 percent of all growth in incomes. The top 1 percent in New York and Connecticut received more than 40 times the increase of the bottom 99 percent. Figure 2 shows the breakdown for the states.

The grossly skewed income disparities between the top 1 percent and the remaining 99 percent in many of the states in the U.S. in figure 1 reflect the obscene greed inherent in the globalized capitalist system even in the wake of the deepest financial, economic, and social crisis of the past century. Wall

Fig. 2

State	Percentage of Income Growth Received by Top 1 percent
Arizona	84.2
Oregon	83.8
New Mexico	72.6
Hawaii	70.9
Florida	68.9
New York	67.6
Illinois	64.9
Connecticut	63.9
California	63.9
Washington	59.1
Texas	55.3
Montana	55.3
Utah	54.1
South Carolina	54.0
West Virginia	53.3
North Dakota	34.2
Arkansas	34.0
Maryland	33.6
Mississippi	29.8
Iowa	29.8
Virginia	29.5
Louisiana	25.6

Based on data from the report "The Increasingly Unequal States of America: Income Inequality by State, 1917–2011," by Estelle Sommeiller and Mark Price, *Economic Policy Institute,* **February 19, 2014.**[146]

Street executives and CEO's of large transnational corporations continue to reward themselves with unearned mammoth salaries where the median CEO compensation rose 13 percent to $10.5 million in 2013 while the median earnings for 104.8 million U.S. workers grew by a mere 1.4 percent in the same year.[147] Table 3 demonstrates this fundamental violation by globalized capitalism of the principles of economic democracy and fairness that has intensified since the global financial crisis of 2008 with the chunk of the increases in wealth appropriated by the top 1 percent.

The fact of the capitalist system basing its accumulation of wealth on speculation, with derivatives, "a financial contract whose price is supposed to derive from some underlying asset" and ostensibly "reduced financial risk" as the cornerstone, no longer holds financial water.[148] Underlying prices are based on future values of such assets and thus follow the principle of speculation. The fundamental problem is that the humiliation experienced by bankers and investors in 2008 was swiftly replaced by the customary capitalist arrogance of claiming a year later that the recovery was on track and gargantuan profits

Table 3

Income growth from 1979 to 2007, overall and for the top 1% and bottom 99%, U.S. and by state
and region

Rank (by top 1% income growth)	State/region	Average real income growth			Share of total growth (or loss) captured by top 1%
		Overall	Top 1%	Bottom 99%	
1	Connecticut	72.6%	414.6%	29.5%	63.9%
2	Massachusetts	82.1%	366.0%	51.7%	43.1%
3	New York	60.5%	355.1%	22.2%	67.6%
4	Wyoming	31.5%	354.3%	-0.8%	102.3%
5	New Jersey	62.6%	264.7%	41.3%	40.3%
6	Washington	31.2%	222.3%	13.9%	59.1%
7	Florida	38.8%	218.8%	13.8%	68.9%
8	Vermont	42.4%	217.0%	27.8%	39.5%
9	South Dakota	44.8%	216.0%	30.5%	37.2%
10	New Hampshire	53.2%	215.9%	37.6%	35.5%
11	Utah	31.0%	214.9%	15.4%	54.1%
12	Virginia	58.2%	214.8%	44.6%	29.5%
13	Illinois	31.4%	211.6%	12.2%	64.9%
14	Maryland	51.0%	202.1%	37.0%	33.6%
15	Colorado	37.4%	200.8%	21.2%	48.3%
16	Idaho	30.1%	197.6%	16.3%	49.9%
17	California	31.5%	191.8%	13.2%	62.4%
18	Pennsylvania	40.0%	184.9%	25.2%	42.8%
19	Tennessee	35.3%	178.0%	20.2%	48.4%
20	Minnesota	44.4%	175.9%	30.9%	36.8%
21	North Carolina	44.8%	172.0%	32.1%	34.8%
22	Georgia	37.5%	170.9%	23.5%	43.3%
23	Rhode Island	53.8%	170.3%	40.4%	32.6%
24	Nevada	8.6%	164.0%	-11.6%	218.5%
25	South Carolina	25.4%	163.5%	12.8%	54.0%
26	Nebraska	43.5%	160.3%	31.8%	33.5%
27	Alabama	33.7%	158.8%	20.5%	44.9%
28	Arizona	17.0%	157.8%	3.0%	84.2%
29	Wisconsin	28.5%	150.4%	17.4%	44.0%
30	Oklahoma	33.9%	149.6%	20.3%	46.6%
31	Maine	39.9%	149.4%	30.2%	30.5%
32	North Dakota	33.7%	147.8%	24.0%	34.2%
33	Montana	22.3%	146.8%	10.9%	55.2%
34	Missouri	31.9%	140.5%	20.3%	42.5%
35	Kansas	37.0%	132.3%	26.6%	35.0%
36	Oregon	13.5%	127.2%	2.7%	81.8%

Rank (by top 1% income growth)	State/region	Overall	Top 1%	Bottom 99%	Share of total growth (or loss) captured by top 1%
37	Texas	26.6%	124.1%	13.5%	55.3%
38	Delaware	31.5%	122.6%	21.2%	39.7%
39	Arkansas	35.0%	121.6%	25.6%	34.0%
40	New Mexico	14.0%	119.3%	4.2%	72.6%
41	Alaska	-10.3%	118.6%	-17.5%	ⱦ
42	Hawaii	12.4%	118.0%	3.9%	70.9%
43	Indiana	21.4%	115.3%	12.6%	46.5%
44	Ohio	20.4%	111.2%	11.3%	49.4%
45	Iowa	30.9%	110.5%	23.7%	29.8%
46	Kentucky	19.9%	105.1%	11.2%	48.8%
47	Michigan	8.9%	100.0%	-0.2%	101.7%
48	Mississippi	31.8%	93.4%	24.8%	29.8%
49	Louisiana	35.4%	84.6%	29.5%	25.6%
50	West Virginia	12.9%	74.1%	6.6%	53.3%
6*	District of Columbia	88.1%	239.4%	65.8%	34.8%
	United States	36.9%	200.5%	18.9%	53.9%
	Northeast	59.0%	301.2%	31.0%	52.9%
	Midwest	26.5%	147.1%	14.4%	50.7%
	South	37.6%	167.5%	22.6%	46.1%
	West	27.3%	186.2%	10.5%	65.2%

* Rank of the District of Columbia if it were ranked with the 50 states

ⱦ Only the incomes of the top 1% grew over this period.

Note: Data are for tax units.

Source: Authors' analysis of state-level tax data from Sommeiller (2006) extended to 2007 using state-lev data from the Internal Revenue Service SOI Tax Stats (various years), and Piketty and Saez (2012)

Ratio of top 1% income to bottom 99% income, U.S. by state and region, 2011 (based on Emmanuel Saez's August 2013 Excel file, accessible at http://elsa.berkeley.edu/~saez/TabFig2012prel.xls.) and cited in Estelle Sommeiller and Mark Price, "The Increasingly Unequal States of America: Income Inequality by State, 1917 to 2011," *Economic Policy Institute*, February 19, 2014 at http://www.epi.org/publication/unequal-states/, accessed on June 9, 2014.

would continue to grow unchecked and unrestrained. All while the working class poor and the creatures of the Earth suffer in silence.

The entire capitalist system is predicated on credit extensions and debt accumulation, presupposing stability in an inherently unstable system that enriches a few at the cost of the many through unbridled profit accumulation. Just as Western banks extended high-interest loans to regimes of the underdeveloped countries in the 1970s and 1980s, so that what came to be known as "Third World External Debt" jumped from $47.5 billion in 1968 to $560 billion in 1980, followed by default or close to default on loans by countries like Chile, Mexico, Brazil, Poland, Nigeria, and Venezuela, so too the same banks subsequently turned on domestic populations and extended credit to needy citizens while assuring wealthy creditors that they would receive the highest returns.[149] Thus, securitization entered the capitalist financial stage, where all outstanding debt was re-packaged and sold as a "security that can be purchased."[150] Essentially, the incredible but real irony was that the liability of debt was sold under the absurd and deluded assumption that such debt can be listed as assets on the record accounting books. This was how poor and working class homeowners, especially vulnerable Black and Latino people in the U.S. (in 2008 one third of those who suffered financial losses from the housing bubble was Black and one fifth was Latino) were lured into the sub-prime mortgage trap with promises of low-interest fluctuating rates by lending companies like Countrywide Financial that reaped billions from such loan scams to these financially unstable clients. Countrywide was then conveniently taken over by Bank of America since it was viewed as unviable.[151]

The Enron debacle in 2001, which saw $60 billion erased in days followed by the failure of WorldCom shortly thereafter, was minuscule compared to that of Lehman Brothers that lost $635 billion in five days. These crises are typical of the instability of the capitalist system. The untold suffering of poor and working class women, youth, children, and the elderly in the U.S. and in other capitalist countries along with the destruction of the creatures of the Earth and vitiation of water and air from globalized violence that views *wealth creation as synonymous with accumulation of toxic financial assets and uses the arbitrary value of "fictional capital" to dictate the quantity and terms of citizens' indebtedness and which determine whether they starve or live, are able to support their families or not, are homeless or accorded the right of a home, unemployed or not,* is unjust and unfair to the previous generations of working class peoples of the U.S. who have sacrificed much for the well-being of all who live in our nation today.

The U.S. governmental sequestration policy that became effective in January 2013 will result in $1.2 trillion in budget cuts over the next decade at the rate of about $109 billion per year and will scale back payments to Medicare providers, elementary and secondary education, and rehabilitation and disability research programs that serve tens of millions of people. The government shutdown in October 2013 that saw close to 800,000 federal workers being furloughed has already had a negative ripple impact on various segments of the economy. Programs that are vital to the health of the nation, like the Women, Infants, and Children (WIC) nutrition programs for the poor and needy, were seriously affected. Agencies that are involved in environmental protection, parks and forests protection, and monitoring of contaminated food like the Center for Disease Control and Prevention (CDC), all suffered cutbacks in programs.[152] Many small business operations that depend constantly on government contracts closed. Thousands of people lost their jobs in sectors like air travel and tourism as a result, and families were subject to conditions of further economic hardship and poverty.

The practices of finance capital over the past three decades signifies nothing other than modern-day economic slavery as the poor and working classes of the world become mired in and enslaved to debt. While our children are brainwashed into believing that the American Dream is real and will materialize in the not so distant future, we are all trapped into living in the nightmarish world of debt, lies, violence, deception, and the destruction of humanity and the rest of creation for the next seven generations—with the foisting of financial indebtedness to citizens of the "free world"—so long as we continue to live under the tyranny of the capitalist system. Damon Vickers, the investment manager who personally lived through the repeated global financial crises from 1987, reminds us in his didactic and prophetic book, *The Day After the Dollar Crashes*, of the impending nightmare in the U.S., with the nation strangulated by $136 trillion in debt, of which $13.1 trillion is the official national debt, while "unfunded federal obligations of Social Security, Medicare, government pensions, and more equal $107.8 trillion."[153] Future generations of people living in the U.S. have been mortgaged on the altar of globalization's culture of permanent financial indebtedness just to live. Social security recipients today may have seen the best of the U.S. welfare state if it can be called that at all! The number of people working in ratio to persons receiving social security has been reduced from 4:1 to 2:1, presaging a social security shortfall crisis in the near future. This is one of the reasons that consideration of raising benefits-eligible-retirement-ages above 65 years for many sectors in the U.S. is being vetted by policy makers.

Yet globalization in its arrogance trumpets its laurels of the trillions capitalism has generated for the prosperity of all. What of the vast trillions of dollars in foreign exchange reserves that the Chinese ($2 trillion in 2010) and Japanese, Russian, and Middle Eastern oil-economies possess that are lauded as indicators of globalization's financial success stories? These foreign reserves are essentially in foreign *debt* bonds. Most of these are held in treasury bonds of U.S. debt so that even though the United States is the largest debtor nation in the world, it is still able to ensure levels of capital accumulation.[154] Given the frightful case of the financial meltdown and virtual economic collapse of many countries in 2008, Chinese colleagues amusingly wondered during my visit to the Chinese Academy of Social Sciences in Beijing in August 2011: "Will the United States be able to repay us what we have loaned them or will they default?" The prospects for a default in debt payments by the United States appeared frightfully real during the government shutdown in October 2013. It thus does not require economic and financial genius capabilities to figure why the powerful U.S. and other Western financial powerhouses and their instruments would insist on the positives of globalization in the world, akin to "What's good for GM is good for America!" or Coca Cola adverts in Africa that declare, "What's good for Coke is good for Africa!" During the 2010 World Cup in South Africa, which was primarily sponsored by Coca Cola, fans were confined to buying Coke products, including water, at exorbitant prices at all World Cup soccer games.[155]

It's estimated that some 60 million people around the world lost their jobs as a result of the 2008 financial crisis, over 10 million in the Eurozone alone. Why did Wall Street compensation grow by 4 percent in 2012 a staggering $60 billion, higher than any year with the exception of 2007 and 2008, while millions of people in the U.S. and in other parts of the world are still unable to find gainful employment or experience massive underemployment?[156] Why are national budgets that have historically funded public services in the U.S., Europe, and other places around the world being slashed while CEOs of corporations reap billions in cumulative annual compensation? How is it that individual oligarchs make billions overnight in speculative financial deals with no corresponding fundamental exercise of labor, increase in material production essential for the generation of wealth, or buying and selling goods for profit, upon which capitalist principles were founded, while we are constantly fed the lie that it's the market that runs the world? *Market of what or in what?* Wealth generation through electronic wheeling and dealing is but an *idea* that is used as the basis to dispossess the vast majority of impoverished and marginalized people in the world and to confine them to a life of perpetual misery. There is no tangible human reason for such pathological behavior on the part of human beings except the *illusion* of personal gratification through megalomaniac practices. Perhaps there's much more to it than meets the eye or what we have been conditioned to hear and accept. As Lakota medicine person, Black Elk, described it in the classic, *Black Elk Speaks,* after the *Wasichus* (colonialists) who invaded the Black Hills in South Dakota in the 1880s, promised food to the hungry Lakota, but slaughtered the bison relentlessly for no reason and then sent only a portion of the promised cattle to the starving and besieged Lakota, "I felt like crying for the sacred hoop was broken and scattered."[157] Globalization's lies have broken the sacred hoop of the Earth too and cannot feed the impoverished and marginalized masses of the world in the 21st century either.

The lingering downside of globalization from the perspective of Indigenous and other colonized peoples, of course, is the "politics of hegemony or dominance ... to the economics of globalization."[158] Following the collapse of the Soviet Union in 1991, a monopolar world emerged with formidable transnational corporations imposing globalization and "cultural standardization" or "cultural Mcdonaldization."[159] Neoliberalism provided the ideological foundations for globalization after World War II both in Western Europe and the United States based on Frederick August von Hayek's publication of *The Road to Serfdom* in 1944 so that the state would be impeded from imposing any restrictions on the operation of "free markets."[160] During contemporary financial globalization, the introduction of novel derivatives that involve debt swaps, futures trading, and stock options, was heavily responsible for the crippling financial and housing mortgage crisis witnessed in the U.S. and Europe in 2008.[161] The derivatives practice that was designed to reduce financial risk in lending and investment paradoxically turned out to be the riskiest venture for many large financial corporations in these countries.

So too, the movement of immigrant labor has been severely stanched, the case of the south western part of the U.S. being a classic case in point with new legal immigrant restrictions imposed by the Arizona state government, particularly on Mexican and Latin American migrant laborers to the U.S., such as the signing into law of Senate Bill 1070 by Arizona governor Jan Brewer in April 2010, which was challenged by various civil rights groups and the U.S. Department of Justice as unconstitutional.[162] The reason for this curtailing of international migration not only revolves around issues of race and ethnicity (since most of the migrants to the U.S. and Europe are people of color from Asia, Latin America, and Africa), but also the importing of manufactured goods by industrialized countries, which now reflects reduced dependence on physical human labor since most of manufacturing has become mechanized. On the other hand, the Western industrialized powers export capital for profit to countries with cheap labor laws in the underdeveloped world that do not involve labor-intensive operations. Radical unevenness of globalization, with benefits contingent upon "gender, age, race, and other social relations," is enshrined in these global structural arrangements.[163] The border restrictions and stringent visa requirements for migrant labor in the U.S., which now target especially Latinos and, most recently, imposes fines and penalties on U.S. corporations that hire East Indian technicians, is one indicator of the unfreedom of the labor movement in this phase of globalization.[164]

Unlike the role of gunboat diplomacy employed in the colonial period in the case of the British occupation of Ghana in the late 19th century, for instance, or direct U.S. intervention and even occupation of parts of Latin America in the early 19th century, for example, today global financial instruments like the World Bank, the IMF, and the WTO represent essentially the same financial and commercial interests of the industrial capitalist nations that were former colonial countries. The militarized role of the U.S. in West and Central Africa constituted as the Africa High Command (AFRICOM) and in areas around the Caspian, strategic regions of the world where fossil fuels and energy resources are in abundance, however, is a continuation of the old colonial policy of exercising of military might for economic hegemony ends.

It is in this vein today that giant transnational corporations protected by military powers monopolize international trade, commerce, and profit accumulation, and mammoth financial banks control global financial transactions.[165] Globalization ensures the vast chasm in economic and social well-being and financial wealth between the Western industrialized countries and the majority of underdeveloped countries.[166] It comes as no surprise then to learn that major banks in the U.S. like Wachovia, which was shut down in 2008 due to illegal money-laundering (and subsequently acquired by Wells Fargo), was cited for transferring some $374.4 billion (one third of Mexico's gross national product) from *casas de cambios* (money changing houses) in Mexico to the U.S.[167] The incredible irony is that no bank officials were imprisoned for flagrant violation of U.S. federal banking and drug laws. This is the core corruption of globalization exploding across the global economy in the first decade of the new millennium, with banks receiving public taxpayer monies (Wells Fargo for instance received $25 billion as a bailout during the height of the 2008 financial crisis) and still engaging in illegal transactions involving illicit drug monies. Wells Fargo is the largest bank in the world today by market capitalization (it surpassed the Industrial and Commercial bank of China in July 2013) and yet depended fully on trade in drugs as the "only liquid investment capital" during the 2008 crisis. It is the same bank too that paid $175 million in a court settlement in 2012 where its mortgage brokers were found to have charged Black and Latino mortgage borrowers 30 percent more in loan fees than white borrowers who "posed the same credit risk."[168] Wells Fargo continues to profit lucratively from investments in the private prison industrial complex in the United States, with major investments in the GEO Group, the second largest private prison corporation in the country. Many of those incarcerated in private prisons are imprisoned for non-violent drug-related crimes, another scandalous fact about the world's largest bank, the subject of which is discussed further in Chapter 4 of this book.

The ideology of globalization that insists that states are by nature inefficient and incapable of addressing public need and therefore need to resort to privatization as an antidote to inefficiency, is bifurcated and does not apply to all governments in the world; the rhetoric is directed toward those vulnerable states in the underdeveloped world, while the states in the industrialized countries are not given the same dictum from global capital (Greece being an exception since its virtual economic collapse was a boon for German capital). The IMF and World Bank do not impose austerity measures on powerful Western countries when they need to borrow from global multilateral institutions. For example, when indebted countries like Ireland or Portugal need to secure international bank loans, the conditions are not as devastating as say those imposed on Mexico, Tanzania, or countries in the underdeveloped world, so that "Bretton Woods institutions seek to harmonize policies and institutions across countries which is in consonance with the needs of globalization."[169] Globalization fosters disequilibrium in economic growth and output and still overwhelmingly favors already wealthy or cash-flush economies.[170] The net result is economic hardship even for those working class women and men in industrialized countries, as witnessed in Britain, for instance. The former colonial power is in the financial doldrums as workers brace for 600,000 job cuts, massive layoffs and salary freezes, downsizing of school facilities and public and social services, astronomical tuition increases at all public universities, and an ushering in of an era of economic and social uncertainty unlike any other for the past century.[171]

The United Nations Economic Projections for 2015 are not very sanguine considering that a second recession following that of 2008 may be in the offing. The fact of a deficit of 71 million jobs around the world, 17 million of which are in Western countries, is a lingering thorn in the side of the social security of the world's human beings.[172] The economic growth increase of 5.1 from 2013 (a 0.4 percentage point drop from 2012) does not address the fundamental condition of the vulnerability of hundreds of millions of workers in informal employment and lacking access to decent and adequate public education and health care due to globalization's private educational and health care emphasis with "user pays" and "market choice" models.[173] Even though $575 billion in capital flows landed in the countries of the underdeveloped world in 2011, 45 percent of this amount went to already booming Asian economies, followed by some nations of Latin America where energy resources and industrial expansion were normative, like Brazil.[174] Foreign Direct Investment was not directed toward the most impoverished countries in Africa like Somalia, Ethiopia, Niger, Mauritania, and Chad or to Asian countries like Bangladesh and Nepal or to desperate Latin American and Caribbean countries like Bolivia and Haiti respectively. Globalization unequivocally persists in enriching the already well-to-do while further impoverishing the already long-term poor.

Conclusion

One of the fundamental assumptions of globalization is that economic growth implies prosperity, "progress," and enhanced living for all people on the planet. Its myopic vision overlooks the phenomenon of uneven development among and within nations and peoples. "Growth" does not translate into positive transformation for all people, certainly not for the Indigenous peoples and majority of the world's workers. Growth, which indicates "increase of real output of an economy over time," does not imply the quality of all peoples' lives changing under the capitalist system because "growth does not necessarily imply structural change" and *"can result simply from doing more of the same things rather than better than before"*[175] (italics mine). *Economic growth is thus not synonymous with "economic development,"* and it is "possible to have 'growth without development.'"[176] This chapter painstakingly illustrates that the larger the economy and the more incremental the growth does not translate into economic empowerment for the majority of the world's people, but actually enhances control of that majority by the elitist few. Globalization signifies the pinnacle of uneven and unjust development and as opposed to expanding participatory democracy and enhancing the livelihood of the most vulnerable, squeezes them into a tighter economic straitjacket because it insists on standardization and uniformity of the ideology of capital accumulation and materialistic acquisition as core global principles of the new millennium, disregarding diversity of culture, religion, language, and background. Intensifying existing modes of production can increase the gross national product, but qualifiedly so, since once population growth exceeds economic growth indices, the possibility of economic contraction overall becomes greater. This is precisely what has been occurring with the global capitalist economy since the 1970s, with cycles of protracted growth and contraction, instigating recurring crises and portending perpetual social and environmental instability to the point that the principle of unbridled growth and natural resource extraction and exploitation became unviable and unsustainable.

Under the globalization regime, what has been the lot of Indigenous peoples or the First Nations peoples in their ancestral lands and the condition of the majority of the working classes and rural villagers? Most importantly, what have the consequences of globalization been for the Earth and all of the forms of ecological life on the planet? In the following chapter we will discuss the impact of globalization on the original human peoples of the world, those peoples who have refused to accept globalization as the last word and paid a dear price for tenaciously adhering to their cultural ancestors and sacred respect for the Mother Earth: Indigenous peoples.

2

Globalization, Ecocide and the Lethal Threats Against Indigenous Peoples

What treaty that have whites kept has the red man broken? Not one. What treaty that the white man ever made with us have they kept? Not one. When I was a boy the Sioux owned the world; the sun rose and set on their land; they sent ten thousand men to battle. Where are the warriors today? Who slew them? Where are our lands? Who owns them? What white man can say I ever stole his land or a penny of his money? Yet, they say I am a thief. What white woman, however lonely, was ever captive or insulted by me? Yet they say I am a bad Indian. What white man has ever seen me drunk? Who has ever come to me hungry and unfed? Who has ever seen me beat my wives or abuse my children? What law have I broken? Is it wrong for me to love my own? Is it wicked for me because my skin is red? Because I am a Sioux; because I was born where my father lived; because I would die for my people and my country? —*Sitting Bull*

We belong to the Earth. The Earth does not belong to us...—*Jones Benally*, Haatali *(traditional Dineh healer), Northern Arizona*

Uncritical belief in Western science and technology as the only valid approach to resolving environmental problems has fallen by the wayside. In fact, science and technology are believed to be the cause of many of the problems we now face (Mander, 1991). Realizing the faults in its own system and recognizing the value of other knowledge in addressing environmental concerns is a significant step for dominant Western society. Science and technology, at least on their own, cannot get us out of the situation that we are in now. Other approaches are required, especially ones with long successful track records like Traditional Environmental Knowledge (TEK).[1]

Introduction

History is living because its legacy still lives with us in the 21st century. Of any segment of the human population that has suffered the worst form of

64

annihilation of their cultures and lands, it is the Indigenous or First Nations people of the world. Indigenous people living on all six continents continue to experience the ravages of globalization and view it essentially as an extension of early Western European conquest of their lands, dispossession of their resources, and the despoliation of their natural environments. As the Indigenous nations of Brazil affirmed over 40 years ago, a struggle continuing well into the second decade of the 21st century:

> Today, the 19th of April is the day dedicated to the Indians all over Brazil. We know neither when nor why the Day of the Indian was created, but we wish to take advantage of the opportunity to make public our message of the Day of the Indian.
> First, we want to say that the 22nd of April, 1500, when Pedro Alvares Cabral stepped for the first time on these lands, was the beginning of the expansion of western civilisation and the beginning of the end of the indigenous societies.
> With the passage of the years, our destruction was intensified, carried out by western civilisation. The most diverse instruments of degradation were used in the massacre of indigenous groups. Factors contributing to this process were sicknesses brought by the white man which had until then been unknown to us, the plundering of our lands, and the application of colonialist and ethnocentric educational methods which did not respect our political, economic and religious structure.
> So much so that in the 16th century the Indians were considered irrational animals, and it was necessary for Pope Paul III to declare to the public of the time that we were human beings, with body and soul. But in spite of this, the destruction of the indigenous people continued [from Message of the Day of the Indian, April 19, 1977, signed by representatives of the Xavante, Bororo, Pareci, Apiaka, Guarany, Kaingang, Kayabi, and Terena and Kaiowa nations].[2]

Indigenous peoples along with the rest of the natural world, struggle to resist the real effects of genocide and ecocide, where species of animals, birds, insects and plants have become extinct, much of it wrought by globalization and industrialism. A Brazilian doctor aptly captured the gravity of the problem of globalization in an interview with a newspaper, *O Estrada de Sao Paulo*, when he stated, "Globalization is the modern name for colonialism."[3] In the words of Konai Helu Thaman from Tonga, globalization is another propagation of the particularity of Western aristocratic culture that is concerned with propagating "Anglo-American knowledge, values, and practices, rather than indigenous knowledge and wisdom practices."[4] Thaman laments the fact that globalization as imposed by the industrialized world has been foundational in foisting Western languages, culture, and consumerism on peoples of Oceania that has led to a radical cultural self-deprecation and reduction of self-esteem among Indigenous peoples. Young people feel embarrassed by their origins, traditions and way of life.

According to Vine Deloria, the Indigenous American Indian scholar, the

New Global Order announced by George H.W. Bush, symbolic of the ethos of globalization, "looks startlingly similar to medieval feudalism in that the elites of each country have devised ways to keep political and economic power while the mass of humankind is unable to muster any sense of national or planetary will" and "the social sciences of academia have been revealed as the hobbies of the affluent class ... molding the personalities capable of accommodating the business world."[5] Deloria argues that globalization is yet another manifestation of the dysfunction of European medievalism. While globalization advocates claim that globalization culture fosters instant communication of peoples and communities, including Indigenous communities, across the globe, the contradictory side of globalization is evident. Erica-Irene Daes, former UN Special Rapporteur of the Sub-Committee on Promotion and Protection of Human Rights, notes in her illumination of issues pertaining to the protection of Intellectual Property Rights of Indigenous peoples (even while states make claims on Indigenous Intellectual Property Rights through the World Intellectual Property Organization that violate the rights of self-determination of Indigenous Peoples), that globalization is "creating a global market for the dissemination of fresh ideas and new voices, while making it easier for one voice to drown out all the others ... it is making it possible for even the smallest society to earn a livelihood by selling its ideas, rather than selling its lands or forests.... But it is also threatening the confidentiality of indigenous peoples' most private and sacred knowledge."[6]

One of the most critical issues facing all Indigenous peoples is the inalienable right to utilizing resources on their lands, especially those that possess vital water, energy, and forest resources. For instance, though the Indigenous Saami people of Norway, have their own parliament, the right to use their own natural resources in Norway (and in neighboring Sweden) has "not been clarified."[7] Similarly, even though the 1840 Treaty of Waitangi established fishing rights for the Indigenous Maori people of New Zealand (Aotearoa), Tom te Weehi, a member of the Ngati Porou community was still arrested by a fisheries officer on Montanau Beach, even after asserting his rights to fishing for abalone for food after securing permission from the local guardian (kaitiaki) for fishing earlier. The case was remanded to the courts, which later affirmed Weehi's right to fish in traditional Maori waters.[8]

This chapter will delve into the questions of the impact of globalization on the Indigenous peoples of the world, and the manner in which ecological devastation has become intensified, and describe the resistance of Indigenous peoples to a total onslaught by the forces of globalization. Western colonialism and now capitalism is responsible for much of the genocide experienced by the

Indigenous peoples of the world. Genocide is encapsulated in the moving account of Truganini, daughter of a leader from Tasmania, who saw her mother stabbed, her sister kidnapped, her uncle shot dead, and her partner drowned by colonists. Truganini was not cremated according to Aboriginal custom; instead her skeleton was exhibited for decades on show at the Hobart Museum in Hobart, Tasmania, until 1976, when her remains were cremated and her ashes disbursed in the sea.[9]

Definitions of Indigenous Peoples and Resistance to Globalization

All peoples of the world are Indigenous or autochthonous in that they belong to some part of the Earth. For the purpose of contemporary discourse, however, "Indigenous" refers to those peoples around the world who have been colonized by the military powers of Western Europe and Asia for the past five centuries and continue to experience ethnic cleansing in that their nations have been decimated, their lands dispossessed, their resources pillaged, and their cultures still trampled by capitalist industrialism. Further, most Indigenous peoples, like the San of Southern Africa, Maasai, Ogiek, and Samburu of East Africa, Tuareg of North Africa, Yamomami of Brazil, Achuar of the Amazon, Dayak of Sarawak, Malaysia, Saami of Norway, Pitanjarra of Australia, for example, have refused to be assimilated into the capitalist system and have resisted the cultural onslaught, insisting on retaining their languages, cultures, and lands in the wake of this hegemony. Dineh leader and Chief Justice of the Navajo Nation, Robert Yazzie, eloquently and accurately observes of North American colonization of Indigenous peoples, when he asserts that "the word *democracy* comes from the Greek and it means 'rule by the people'" but "in the United States and Canada, we have 'kakistocracy,' which means 'rule by the worst.'"[10] He cites *The Congressional Record* or *Hansard* for substantiation of this contention.[11]

The description developed by Jose Martinez Cobo, an Ecuadorian diplomat, during his work with the United Nations subcommittee on Indigenous peoples' rights during the 1970s, is appropriate here: "Indigenous communities, peoples and nations are those which, having a historical continuity with pre-invasion and pre-colonial societies that developed on their territories, consider themselves distinct from other sectors of the societies now" and who are determined to transmit their ancestral territories, cultures, and languages to successive generations.[12]

At the 1992 UN Conference on Environment and Development in Rio de Janeiro, Brazil, the inextricable interwovenness of cultural distinctiveness and territory with the concept of "indigeneity" was affirmed in paragraph 26.1 of Agenda 21, and adopted consensually by member states present, stating that "Indigenous people and their communities have a historical relationship with their lands and are generally descendants of the original inhabitants of those lands," and that "the centrality of land tenure systems and ecological knowledge to the knowledge and heritages of indigenous peoples was reaffirmed, again by consensus at the International Conference on Population and Development at Cairo."[13] In 2007, the United Nations formally declared and adopted the UN Declaration on the Rights of Indigenous Peoples, having inaugurated the UN Permanent Forum on Indigenous Issues in May 2002 where Indigenous peoples took their place at the UN as bona fide representatives of Indigenous nations as other national governments represented national states.[14]

Indigenous peoples are those who have never surrendered their birthright, landright, and their ancestral ways; they are determined to preserve their historical ways of being, as Deborah White Plume Owe Oku from the Oglala Lakota nation of North America notes in her community's resistance to the tar sands oil-from-shale project in Alberta, Canada, that the struggle is to "Bring Back the Way" of Indigenous peoples living in respect of and in harmony with the Earth.[15]

Indigenous Peoples and the State

Consequently, in resisting such Europeanized imperialism for five centuries, it would be fair to declare that Indigenous people are tireless revolutionary defenders of the Earth and their ancestral lands. It is imperative that we discard the pejorative term "minorities" to refer to those Indigenous peoples in European colonial-settler republics in the Americas, Oceania, and Africa, and in Asian, African, and European countries. "Minority" is often used to describe peoples who are smaller in number and social significance in many lands but is also laden with political undertones. Many national governments, for instance, often relegate peoples whose languages are not dominant to a marginalized role under the justification that the numerical and cultural import of such peoples is not "decisive" for the success of essentially majoritarian societies. The Indigenous Ainu peoples of Japan are a good example of this kind of marginalization by a society claiming to be culturally homogenous compared to the "minority Ainu" who generally view themselves as inferior to the dominant Japanese culture.[16]

Indigenous peoples cannot by any extension of logic become "minorities," reduced to "less than" in the lands of their ancestors. For instance, calling Indigenous people of North America "minorities" in their ancestral land is ethno-centric and blatantly ignores the fact that the legacy of European colonization and settlement of what is called the United States today decimated 85 percent of the Indigenous people out of a total population of between 14 and 20 million people within the first one hundred years of the Indigenous-European encounter.[17] In this sense, the organization, the Working Group of Indigenous Minorities in Southern Africa (WIMSA), which advocates for the rights of Indigenous people there, needs to erase the term "minorities" from its organizational name. Jorge Calbucura concurs with this explanation when he states that indigenous organizations reject the association with "minorities" and "populations" but opt to be defined as *people* since that juridically accords them recognition as *people entitled to self-determination* and thus appeals to the first article of the International Covenant on Economic, Social and Cultural Rights: "All people have the right of self determination…. By virtue of that right they freely determine their political status and freely pursue their economic, social and cultural development."[18]

It is on this global basis of human rights that Indigenous struggles for self-determination are waged. National constitutional provisions of protection of Indigenous peoples' rights by nation-states, which emerged in the wake of the colonial partition and structuring of the peoples of the world, are not adequate in most countries and are hardly enforceable by international law. The elevation of Indigenous people to the presidency of the governments of Bolivia, like Evo Morales of Venezuela, like current president Nicolás Maduro and the late Hugo Chavez of Indigenous, African, and Spanish ancestry, is worth noting. Further, the prominent role that Indigenous people have played in the political process in Ecuador that resulted in progressive president Rafael Correa emerging as leader, is indicative of the growing significance of Indigenous peoples in political transformation in Latin American countries in recent years. However, it is important to underscore that these are exceptions to the norm of political and social disenfranchisement of Indigenous peoples in the rest of Latin America and the world. Political parties on either the right or the left, are generally inadequate in their advocacy of the right of self-determination of Indigenous peoples, with left-wing political parties in Latin America often disappointing Indigenous peoples in their expectations of support of Indigenous peoples' rights, whether by the Sandinistas in their relationship to the Miskito Indians in Nicaragua or the Party of the Democratic Revolution (PRD) in Mexico at the beginning of the new millennium. In

Nicaragua in April 2013, for example, Elias Charly Taylor, a member of the Indigenous Mayangna community, was killed in a confrontation with *mestizo* colonial settlers who engage in logging and burning lands for cattle grazing in the Bosawas Biosphere Reserve, angering the Indigenous communities of the North Atlantic Autonomous Region of the country.[19] The Mayangna people have demanded that the Nicaraguan government act immediately to remove the 2,000 illegal settlers in Indigenous areas and indicated that they would take the issue of settler occupations of their lands to the Inter-American Human Rights Commission if no government action is forthcoming. Though the Nicaraguan government has instituted legal protections for the land and cultural rights of Indigenous people through the Law on Communal Property of the Indigenous and Ethnic Communities of the Autonomous Regions of the Atlantic Coast and of the Bocay, Coco, Indio and Maiz Rivers, it has been reluctant to engage in swift action to remove settlers from invading Indigenous lands.

Margarito Ruiz Hernandes, a member of the Maya-Tojolab'al people of Mexico, a federal deputy in the LIVth Legislature of the Congress of the Union for the Party of the Democratic Revolution (PRD) from 1988 to 1991 and a member of the Executive Board of the Secretariat of Indian Peoples of the PRD, and Aracely Burguete Cal y Mayor, a Mexican sociological researcher, contend that generally during the 20th century most political parties ignored Indigenous peoples' rights and claims to sovereignty and land. Political parties more often than not used Indigenous peoples to secure votes for political advancement within the dominant cultures found in individual countries while opening few spaces for Indigenous peoples and their own institutions.[20] This is precisely why electoral politics within "democratic" societies built on Western European cultures and institutions have in the main been irrelevant to the decolonizing struggles of Indigenous peoples for reclamation of dispossessed lands and for self-determination.

Globalization and Destruction of Lands and Sacred Spaces of Indigenous Peoples

For most Indigenous peoples, their sacred sites and places have rarely been recognized within national boundaries and states. A closer look at the impact of globalism's colonializing effects on the Amazon rainforest provides a classic point of departure. The Amazon region, located mainly in Brazil, covers 8 million square kilometers, and even though it is just 3.5 percent of the

Indigenous protestors protest outside the courthouse against regional government's treatment of rural villages in Cuzco, Peru (powless/Flickr).

earth's surface, it has 50 percent of all the living species on the planet and provides invaluable benefits to the earth's natural systems. Under the pretext of "developing" the Amazon in line with the obsessive Western colonialist ideology of "human progress," the Amazon has been penetrated by commercial elitist groups and corporations involved in logging, gold mining, cattle ranching, fishing, and hunting, essentially vocations of scavenging that continue to deplete the natural resources of the precious Amazon rainforest. This point hits poignantly home when we realize that 12 percent of the land cover of the Amazon has been destroyed, that an acre of Brazilian rainforest is decimated every nine seconds, and that 13,000 acres are erased every day, the equivalent of eight football fields each minute.[21] At the current rate of deforestation, the European environmental protection organization, Greenpeace, predicts that nearly all tropical rainforests could be destroyed by 2030. A 2011 report by British and Brazilian scientists noted that the Amazon rainforest, long an absorber of carbon dioxide, earning its title "the lungs of the planet," has become a net emitter of carbon gases, some 8 billion tons in 2010, more than that emitted by the U.S., because of extraordinary drought conditions that were characterized as the worst in one hundred years.[22] This is the second occurrence in a decade. Horrifying indeed! Tragically, it does not end there. The Belo Monte Dam is under construction in the Amazon today as part of the Brazilian government's plan to erect the third largest dam in the world. Under the guise of supplying power while considering Indigenous peoples' cultural and environmental concerns and promising the creation of 40,000 jobs (of which only 2,000 would be long-term), this power-hungry project will flood 668 square kilometers of land, of which close to two-thirds would be forest and over 20,000 Indigenous people would be displaced from their traditional lands.[23]

Ninety Indigenous nations have been erased from the Amazon forest region as a result of the encroachment by Western industrial colonialism, and the over half-a-million Indigenous people who live in the Amazon are constantly under threat by the practices of the logging and mining extractionist multi-national corporations whose sole motivation is the agglomeration of monetary profit. The "highways to progress," like the Cuiaba to Porto Velho highway in Brazil, for example, may facilitate Western communication and the movement of commercial traffic, but for the Nambiquara people of the region, it signified a knife that ripped out the heart of the community, akin to Chinua Achebe's description of colonization in Africa in *Things Fall Apart*.[24] In 2011, according to official reports, 51 Indigenous people were killed all over Brazil, with almost half of these killings related to land struggles, especially by gold miners against Yanomami people and non–Indigenous farmers invading Indigenous lands of some 20,000 Macuxi people. In Mato Grosso do Sul, a large state in southwest Brazil, 75,000 Indigenous Guarani people are resisting land invasions of sacred sites and ceremonies, including the French commodities corporation, Louis Dreyfus.[25] The Guarani people continue to be subject to high suicide rates, astronomical poverty levels, and severe child malnutrition, living in small land lots in Dourados. Indigenous people from Brazil issued a statement at the World Social Forum in Porto Alegre to this effect:

> Despite having been submitted to a continuous process of violence and extermination, we are alive and are looking forward to the construction of a new Brazil and a new world, with peace, equality, and justice. From an original population of 6 million 500 years ago, we have been reduced to approximately 550,000 individuals, belonging to 235 different peoples who speak 180 different languages. We occupy 741 pieces of land, most of them still occupied by non–Indigenous people or non-demarcated.
>
> Central America today is experiencing globalization, a more devastating pillage than what its people underwent 500 years ago. With the conquest and colonization

... [the dominant force is not the market but rather] a strong transnational state that dictates economic policy and plans resource allocation.[26]

In 2009, Indigenous peoples in Peru suffered death and injury by police and government forces for resisting oil, gas, and gold prospecting and mining on their ancestral lands. Thirty-three people were killed in Bagua for demanding an end to such encroachment on their lands and the signing of the Peru–United States Trade Promotion Agreement.[27] Equally devastating is the insistence by the forces of globalization that in the twenty-first century, Indigenous and other colored peoples conform to a Western colonialist mode of thought and apprehension of knowledge and *modus operandi,* particularly in relating to economic, material, and cultural concerns. Indigenous Maori scholar, Makere Stewart-Harawira, confirms the lethal effects of this form of globalization with no sense of reprieve when she asserts, "In the face of increasing globalization,

Under globalization, Indigenous peoples' lands have been subject to further dispossession and Indigenous cultures have been undermined by political repression and corporate exploitation. An Indigenous injured protestor is detained by police in Bagua, Peru, in April 2009 (powless/ Flickr).

indigenous cultures and identities are being increasingly threatened by the commodification of indigenous culture that is occurring at multiple levels."[28]

Concretely, Western forms of imposed industrialized "development" under the banner of globalization, especially in harnessing energy resources, have fragmented Indigenous communities and fractured historical relationships, like the Foe and the Fasu peoples in Kutubu, Papua New Guinea, who were deliberately pitted against each other by the U.S. oil company, Chevron. The dispute between the two closely knit peoples resulted from the issue of royalties from oil revenues, and has created internecine animosity between these peoples, all to the benefit of the Chevron oil company, which has a history of "commercial ruthlessness," be it in Papua New Guinea, Angola or Nigeria.[29] The net end-result is impoverishment of the Indigenous people, their social stability destabilized, their cultures ravaged, and their lands despoiled with the construction of golf courses for white expatriates at Lake Kutubu. The struggles of the Ramu people of Boson, Papua New Guinea, to protect their sacred lands and ancestral sites against a nickel mining company, Chinese NiCo, has resulted in wide-spread relocation of people's homes and deaths of people removed from ancestral lands.[30] At Barrick's Porgera mine in Papua mining security personnel have been responsible for shooting at local residents and forced evictions of Indigenous community members by Barrick have occurred in flagrant contravention of international law.[31]

In the Asian context where Indigenous peoples continue to be subject to the ravages of land dispossession, resource depletion, economic exploitation, and cultural commoditization, Dev Nathan, economist and Senior Visiting Fellow at the Institute for Human Development, and Govind Kelkar, Coordinator at the International Fund for Agricultural Development-United Nations Development Fund for Women, argue that "it is not only environment services, but also indigenous peoples' cultural products and knowledge (of medicinal plants and herbs) that are being extracted from them free of charge."[32] Indigenous peoples knowledge of medicine and healing is expropriated from their lands and cultures and sold as pharmaceutical products at great profit, underscoring the lethal economic point at which Indigenous peoples encounter the globalized capitalist economy as victims of rapacious corporations' practices.

Under the devious pretext of enhancing cultural diversity and working for the collective health welfare of the peoples of the world, Western pharmaceutical companies have been involved in launching projects around health and science with euphemistic names like the Human Genome Diversity Project which is ostensibly about finding cures for incurable illnesses like cancer by extracting blood samples from Indigenous peoples to study their DNA structures. Further, these companies have penetrated Indigenous communities by manipulating, coercing or bribing governments in the underdeveloped countries under the rubric of "economic development" to sign agreements that grant such companies unrestrained access to medicinal plants on Indigenous peoples' lands, and then insisting that they are the primary patent holders for medicinal cures based on extracting medicines from Indigenous plants. In 1996, for example, the International Plant Medicine Corporation, a U.S. multinational, patented *Ayahuasca,* a plant sacred to the Indigenous people of the Amazon, without prior free and informed consent. The corporation's action sparked intense anger among the Indigenous people there.[33] Indigenous people refer to this perverse practice of Western pharmaceutical patenting as "biopiracy." "Biopiracy" or "bioprospecting" is a lucrative industry, prototypical of the motivation of *all* Western capitalist enterprises making billion of dollars in profits for avaricious Western multi-national corporations based on annual world-wide sales of $43 billion of nature-based healing remedies and pharmaceuticals.[34] The seeds that are extracted from traditional crop varieties are worth $50 billion per year to the agricultural and pharmaceutical industries. While the United Nations Convention on Biological Diversity affirms the "need to respect, preserve and maintain" the ecological knowledge of Indigenous peoples around the world, the convention has no teeth in that it is unable to enforce its provisions among national governments.[35]

A similar situation applies to the Intellectual Property's Agreement discourse at the United Nations. Indigenous peoples have little power to protect their Indigenous knowledge and plant genetic resources from the economic predators of the world, especially the mammoth commercial and industrial corporations in the industrialized countries. Indigenous peoples are very suspicious of these international agreements supposedly protecting their knowledge and ecologies. They generally "regard it as little more than a sovereignty grab by nation states, who want to take over all biological and ecological resources existing on their land and territories ... they are hardly convinced that their governments that have so often tried to annihilate them, take away their lands and destroy their habitats are now suddenly going to defend their rights."[36] It is for this reason that Indigenous delegates from North America at the 11th Permanent Forum on Indigenous Peoples held at the UN in New York in May 2012 wore t-shirts that read "World Intellectual Piracy Organization" in reference to the dubious actions of the World Intellectual Property Organization.[37]

Given the history of parasitic extraction of both vital Indigenous knowledge and medicinal plants for commercial profit by Western corporations, such suspicions on the part of Indigenous peoples are well founded. The mapping of the human genome through the multi-billion Human Genome Organization (HUGO) and the attempt to collect blood-samples from 700 different Indigenous nations are viewed with hostility by most Indigenous peoples because of the commoditizing of Indigenous identity: Makere Stewart Harawira, a Maori educator, explains that there is a marked "racialization of the genomic industry, citing experiments on pregnant women in Africa, Thailand, and the Dominican Republic, as a result of which 'over 1,000 infants who could have been saved will contract the AIDS virus needlessly.'"[38] Experimentation with peoples of color that has resulted in premature death in cases where antidotes to lethal viruses have been deliberately withheld is well documented in the U.S. and South Africa, for example.[39] In Libya in 2004, five Bulgarian nurses and a Palestinian doctor were convicted for intentionally infecting over 400 children with the AIDS virus ostensibly to find a cure, resulting in the deaths of 23 children.[40]

Indigenous peoples rightfully and legitimately ask: Why *us* always as the experimental sacrificial lambs and guinea pigs in this "modern age of Western civilization?" While we acknowledge that the eugenics ideology that viewed the underclasses of society of Europe in the early 20th century as incapable of ever becoming "productive" members of society led to involuntary sterilizations, for example, of some 63,000 Swedes between 1935 and 1975, and was even championed by both liberal theorists like Alva and Gunnar Myrdal that viewed the poor, the mentally ill, gypsies, and the like as a "threat" to the norm of "Swedish cultural heritage," the persistence of using Indigenous people as medical guinea pigs in this age of late capitalism is extraordinary and indicative of the *ethnocidal* nature of Western medical experimentation when it comes to Indigenous people.[41] Further, why with the tens of billions of dollars spent on HIV/AIDS research, are Africans and other Indigenous and poor peoples still dying in such large numbers? It is important to understand that the history of the relationship between European powers and Indigenous peoples particularly over the last two centuries has been fraught with suspicion and hostility often due to malicious intent in the Indigenous-colonial encounter. Delivery of smallpox blankets to Indigenous peoples in North America,[42] poisoned water by apartheid forces of African villagers in Zimbabwe and Namibia in the 1970s and 1980s,[43] and the U.S. government-funded medical research from the Public Health Service and National Institute of Health that deliberately infected over 700 Guatemala inmates (of which Indigenous people were included given that 70 percent of Guatemala is Indigenous) with gonorrhea and syphilis without their permission (similar to the Tuskegee experiments) in the 1940s, are just some of the stark examples.[44] Failure to honor ancestral land, cultural, and religious rights of the world's Indigenous peoples has irreparably vitiated relationships between the respective sides. Western medical science has much to do to restore trust in these badly perforated social relationships with Indigenous peoples, given ill intentions and practices of the past and present.[45] The words of Rose Ominayak, from the Lubicon Cree Nation of Turtle Island, at a Lubicon Lake Nation Women's Circle, underscores lucidly the basis for suspicion and skepticism of the intentions of non–Indigenous corporations and entities that claim they are interested in the welfare of Indigenous peoples:

> We, the Lubicon Lake Nation, are tired. We are frustrated and angry. We feel we cannot wait another minute to have our land claim settled. Fifty years is too long. In those fifty years we have watched our land and lives be destroyed by Canadian governments and corporations.... We ask why? Why us? What have we done to deserve such treatment? Why can't the government settle with the Lubicon? Why

have they spent so much time and energy trying to destroy us rather than deal fairly with us? What have we done, our children, our people? What wrong have we done to the outside?

We demand an end to the genocide. Hear our voice and our message—we don't know if we'll be here tomorrow.[46]

As the youth of Soweto, South Africa, sang, *Senzenina, Senzenina* (What have we done?) after the violent police shooting down of over 1,000 in Soweto in June 1976, the same cry is echoed by Indigenous peoples globally. *If the scientists want to support us, why don't they have their governments restore our land, they ask, instead of asking for our DNA and blood samples to cure us from disease caused by industrialism?!* It is high time that Western societies realized their own Indigenous roots like all other societies and thus honor the lives of all Indigenous peoples by restoring the lands that Western colonialism violated and dispossessed in recent human history.[47]

Natural resources and human guinea pigs for experiments are not the only assets that industrialism seeks from the Indigenous peoples; traditional knowledge is also highly valued yet denied ownership rights by Indigenous peoples themselves. It is virtually impossible for Indigenous peoples to protect their Indigenous knowledge systems since they do not possess the economic and political power to counteract the hegemonic role of capitalist market forces, coupled with the fact that intellectual property rights address individual ownership while Indigenous peoples are collectively defined and Indigenous knowledge is trans-generational, communally utilized, and ineluctably transmitted into the public sphere.[48] It should come as no surprise to learn then that most Indigenous people actually view the designs of "ethno-researchers" today as part and parcel of the same old problem of Western colonialism and extractive exploitation because "Universities and scientific researchers increasingly utilize IPRs (Intellectual Property Rights) to protect the results of their research that, in turn, provide much of the intellectual and informational underpinnings of international trade and development" and thus Indigenous peoples view scientists, ethno-botanists, and anthropologists as "bio-prospectors" who are greedy for the extraction of Indigenous knowledge.[49] Erica Irene Daes, a UN diplomat who has worked on the Working Group on Indigenous Populations since 1982, notes that while poor peoples are struggling to gain access to the Internet to promote their perspectives and issues, "for indigenous peoples, the major problem of the future would not be gaining access to the Internet, but keeping their most private and sacred knowledge *out* (italics mine) of the Internet."[50] She observes correctly too that Indigenous peoples "challenge the fundamental assumptions of globalization" and "do not accept the assumption that humanity will benefit from the construction of a world culture of consumerism."[51] Indigenous peoples know that consumerism is not sustainable and their future generations will not survive under this way of life.

What is evident is that the legacy of the state apparatus assuming complete authority and ownership of Indigenous peoples' forests has severely eroded Indigenous peoples' land and cultural rights under the regime of globalization. Western industrialized powers and most state governments bear some culpability for being accomplices in the crime of dispossession and usurpation of Indigenous sovereignty. Nathan and Kelkar accentuate the magnitude of this problem today when they contend that "if the livelihoods of the indigenous peoples were earlier historically ignored in extracting timber and other forest products for the purpose of first colonial and then national accumulation, they are thus largely ignored in current global-cum-national environmental goods."[52]

The increasing control over Indigenous peoples' lands, forests, and sacred sites in contemporary globalization by governments is a direct carry-over from the colonial period. In Chile, in South America, for example, the colonial state expropriated 81 percent of the Indigenous Mapuche people's land in 1881, using it for wheat cultivation and cattle breeding, leading to some 300,000 hectares of deforestation during the second half of the 19th century. Expropriation of the Mapuche land also occurred in the Argentinean Patagonia during the Desert Campaign favoring foreign settlers that raised millions of sheep, overgrazing the vast prairies in just a few decades. By the beginning of the 20th century, 580,000 hectares of deforestation occurred, so that in 2003, the total amount of deforested land in Argentina was 4,300,000 hectares.[53] What Europe catastrophically did with its forests between the 9th and 15th centuries, colonialism did with the forests of Chile. The construction of the Pangue hydroelectric dam funded by the World Bank resulted in the flooding of 500 hectares of Mapuche land and forests, and inflicted social, cultural, and economic damage on the Indigenous Peheunche community, causing at least 6,000 Indigenous people to suffer irreparable harm to their cultural and social survival. This is a form of *ethnocide* in the words of Jorge Calbucura, a researcher at the University of Uppsala in Sweden.[54]

African Indigenous peoples have also seen their natural resources being stolen and destroyed by systems of Western industrialist expansion. In Tanzania, in East Africa, processes promoting privatization of agriculture and land cultivation and liberalization of commercial policies in conformity to the dictates of globalization has particularly affected Indigenous peoples who are pastoralist and hunter-gatherers and who have seen their traditional land rights progressively eroded by government policies that favor large private transnational ranching corporations.[55] According to a report by the Oakland Institute, Ivy League universities like Harvard and Vanderbilt have endowments invested in hedge funds that are engaged in land purchases in Africa for private profit, dispossessing thousands of Indigenous farmers from 60 million hectares of farmland in Mozambique, Mali, Sierra Leone, Tanzania, Zambia, Ethiopia and South Sudan.[56]

Communal lands are increasingly under threat as regimes like that of Tanzania and Kenya continue to modify national land protections and allow unbridled access to such lands by land-hungry conglomerates bent on exploiting forested areas and woodlands for optimal profit. African communal lands are thus mortgaged off to the highest bidder, ironically by African governments that claim that they exist to protect the health and well-being of their citizens. If most Africans are poor and considered third-class world citizens, Indigenous communities within Africa are clearly fourth-class citizens in the lands of their birth. The Indigenous San, Tuareg, Maasai, Ogiek, Bambhuti, and Samburu peoples of Africa continue to struggle for protection of traditional forests and sustainable grazing lands that are under constant threat of invasion and expropriation by governmental agencies in partnership with large private corporations. The Ogiek people of East Africa have formed the Ogiek Peoples' Development Program (OPDP) to shield their lands from encroachment by urban "developers," mining companies, agricultural and deforestation interests, and dam construction. The Kengen Hydroelectric Project in Kenya is being opposed by the OPDP since it undermines the traditional lands, livelihood, and cultures of the Ogiek people.[57]

In Nigeria, West Africa, the Ogoni people in the Niger Delta region continue to struggle for protection of their ancestral lands and rivers against toxic environmental damage by oil companies such as Shell and Chevron. After soldiers seriously wounded a woman whose land was being expropriated for oil extraction in 1993, the Ogoni community rose in protest and forced Shell to withdraw. Ongoing resistance by the Ogoni resulted in the execution of 9 Ogoni activists from the Movement for the Survival of the Ogoni people in 1995 by the military regime of Nigeria at that time.[58] The protests and resistance continues into the second decade of this millennium, with no resolution in sight. The Nigerian authorities continue to protect the giant oil companies like Shell and Chevron that are engaged in extracting oil and responsible for the toxic contamination of the Niger Delta on which Ogoni people have depended for fishing and their livelihood for many generations. The Royal Dutch Shell Oil Company has been an inveterate polluter and destroyer of the fragile Niger Delta area for the past 60 years.[59]

In countries like Thailand, India, and Nepal, Indigenous peoples today are subject to arrest for violating trespassing laws such as the 1865 Forest Act in India and the 1993 Nepal Forest Act, modeled on British colonial law, which in turn had its roots in the German colonial administrative system in Tanzania and Namibia in Africa, for example, where Indigenous peoples were barred from living on their traditional ancestral lands.[60] In Malaysia, the Indigenous peoples of Sarawak continue to resist the impact of globalization on their lives through the forced construction of the Bakun hydroelectric power plant that will displace over 10,000 people and the decimation of the tropical rainforest in their lands, one of the most deforested regions in the world.[61] The Indigenous Dayak people outside Kuching, Sarawak, continue to resist the encroachment of their ancestral lands by palm oil companies and forestry corporations that are shielded by governmental authorities.[62]

Similarly, in the Cordillera region of the Northern Luzon in the Philippines, the collective group of Indigenous peoples called the Igorots continue to resist the mining of gold and copper by mining companies. From the 1970s, Indigenous peoples, especially women, have fought against the Chico Dam and Cellophil logging in Kalinga, Abra, and Mountain provinces and have been successful in staving off the encroachment by corporations on their ancestral lands, often with many casualties and violence by military forces. In April 2014, a large global Indigenous peoples conference was held on the banks of the Chico River to highlight ongoing struggles against the mining and logging companies. The Cordillera region contains up to one-quarter of all gold reserves and 39 percent of copper reserves in the Philippines and is constantly targeted by plundering mining interests in the face of the 1995 Philippine Mining Act that opened up such areas to corporate mining and extraction.[63] In Benguet province where Indigenous Ibaloi and Kankana-ey Indigenous peoples live, mammoth mining corporations like Benguet Corporation, Lepanto Consolidated Mining Corporation, and Philex Mining penetrated the ancestral lands of Indigenous peoples in their pursuit of large profits.[64] The presence of transnational corporations like Anvil Mining and Royalco from Australia, Phelps Dodge from the U.S., Tiger International from Canada, Zijn Mining Group from China, and Metals Exploration and Anglo American from Britain and South Africa, underscore the intensity of mineral greed and desperation on the part of mining capital. Globalization's policies of liberalization and privatization, which are facilitated by governments like the Philippines compound the difficulties experienced by Indigenous peoples in defense of their ancestral lands and sacred sites since they need to resist both governmental authorities and money-hungry corporations.

Indigenous people around the world, like these protestors in Davao City, Mindanao, in the Philippines, have demanded the inalienable right of cultural and territorial self-determination (Keith Bacongco).

In Burma, the military government has opened up Indigenous lands to mining concessions. Eighteen percent of the Hugawng Valley in Kachin State is subject to mining projects and since 2006, eight mining companies have started over 31 different mining sites in the valley.[65] The presence of some 26 battalions of military forces has made it extremely dangerous for Indigenous residents of the Hugawng Valley to move freely since their freedoms are curtailed and their attempts to voice their cultural grievances are often brutally suppressed. The military forces provide protection to the mining corporations in violation of the rights of Indigenous peoples to ancestral lands and sacred sites.

Indigenous communities in the U.S. have been exploited by the U.S. government though violation of historic treaties and dumping of hazardous waste from all over country. The Forestry Service, Parks Board, Department of Energy, Department of the Interior, and other national administrative structures have been granted full authority by the Federal government to administer forests and even sacred sites, causing the erosion of Indigenous nations' rights to sacred places and Indigenous lands, in complete violation of the various treaties signed between First Nations and the U.S. government. The Western

Shoshone nation has persisted in challenging the illegal take-over of lands within the western state of Nevada in flagrant violation of the 1823 Treaty of Peace and Friendship at Ruby Valley, and wages an ongoing court battle to protect Western Shoshone Territorial Integrity and their sovereign status as an Indigenous nation because the U.S. Supreme Court dubiously ruled in 1985 in *United States v. Dann, 470 U.S. 39* that the Shoshone extinguished their land rights when they accepted money for Shoshone territory.[66] This was a distortion of facts since the U.S. government presumed to accept the money on behalf of the Shoshone when the Shoshone refused such monetary payments for their land.[67] Around the town of Mercury, 50 miles outside Las Vegas, Nevada, the U.S. military continues to practice underground atomic tests, 650 in all. The U.S. Department of Energy has declared that it plans on storing 77,000 tons of nuclear waste in Nevada in 2017. The lethal impact of this waste storage and transportation of such radioactive waste in 4,000 trucks across the United States each year is incalculable.

For Indigenous people and other people of color in North America, environmental racism is living hell. Eighty percent of all toxic waste sites in the country are located close to communities of color.[68] For Indigenous people,

Indigenous communities are often places close to where landfills are located and environmental waste is dumped, like this cleanaway landfill in Tullarmine, Victoria, Australia (Mugley/Flickr).

the effects are particularly severe. Andrea Smith, a Cherokee women's rights and environmental activist with the *Women of All Red Nations*, explain that Indigenous women experience miscarriages at six times the national average and that uranium tailings in Arizona may be the cause of children having ovarian and testicular cancer at fifteen times the national average. Because 60 percent of the nation's energy resources of coal, oil and uranium sit on Indian land, such lands are most susceptible to environmental devastation, like the Black Hills in South Dakota and the Four Corners region at the confluence of the states of Utah, Colorado, New Mexico, and Arizona where coal mining's effects have been lethal to Dineh (Navajo) people over the past six decades.[69] In New Mexico, the planned Mt. Taylor uranium mine will have a destructive impact on the religious practices of all of the Indigenous nations in the region, including the Dineh (Navajo), Hopi, Zuni, Puebla, and Acoma.[70]

In Oklahoma, the Kerr-McGee uranium processing plant was stopped following protests and resistance by groups like Native Americans for a Clean Environment in the 1990s, where Jessie DeerInWater, an organizer with the group, discovered that Kerr-McGee used radioactive wastes to make fertilizers. The Nuclear Regulatory Commission granted permission to Kerr-McGee to use this toxic fertilizer on 15,000 acres of grass fields in Oklahoma where cattle grazed and were later sold. Ten percent of the cattle developed cancerous growths, which the EPA declared was "normal."[71] This is precisely where one realizes that federal governmental authorities, in Western settler-societies in particular, merely pay lip service to policies that foster a clean environment; ultimately they are beholden to large transnational corporations and are willing to overlook the illegal conduct of industrial corporations that dump or use toxic waste for profit. A 2006 report on National Public Radio in Chicago indicated that the U.S. military on coasts as far off as Australia and as close as New Jersey has dumped unexploded toxic chemical bombshells for the past fifty years, and that the toxic waste products from these shells have been used in driveways in the state of New Jersey.[72]

In Arizona, a fierce struggle continues for the protection of the sacred *Dook'o'osliid* (San Francisco Peaks), the highest mountain in the state. Various Indigenous nations have come together, including the Dineh, Supai, Hualapai, Hopi, Ndee (White Mountain, Yavapai Apache, Chirachua Apache), Yoeme (Yaqui), Zuni, and the Tohono' O'odham, in challenging the U.S. Parks Service permitting the piping of sewage water to the sacred mountain for the purpose of snow-making by the Arizona Snowbowl resort. The Ninth Circuit Court ruling of 2008 ruled that the spiritual violation of the Peaks is acceptable and does not constitute a violation of Indigenous peoples' religious rights.[73] In the

U.S. legal case, *Fools Crow v Gullet* (1982), when the Lakota (Sioux) elders complained that tourists were desecrating their most sacred site, Bear Butte mountain in South Dakota, and that this violated the Lakota's religious rights, a federal judge ruled against the Lakota plaintiffs, declaring that tourism would not be an "insurmountable obstacle" to the Lakota practicing their ceremonies at Bear Butte.[74] Both the 1982 and 2008 cases substantiate that the U.S. legal system is unreliable and inadequate since it does not recognize the fundamental human and religious rights of Indigenous people. Actions toward redress for violation of Indigenous peoples' religious and cultural rights are warranted at an international legal level like the World Court.

On Dragoon Mountain outside Superior, Arizona and close to the Ndeé Neé (Chiricahua Apache) community in San Carlos, Arizona, Resolution Copper, a mining operation owned by Rio Tinto Zinc (RTC) and BHP Billiton, two of the largest mining corporations in the world, is engaged in developing the largest underground copper mining operation in the world, in violation of the sacredness of Dragoon Mountain where Ndeé Neé members regularly pick plants and herbs for traditional ceremonies. The mountain overlooking San Carlos is also the location where Agent Orange, an herbicide used to clear forest cover, crops and vegetation, was first tested prior to it being used by the U.S. military against the people of Vietnam in the 1960s and

The San Francisco Peaks (*Dooko'oosliid*) in Flagstaff, Arizona, is sacred to all Indigenous peoples of the southwest. Indigenous peoples view the piping of sewage effluent to create artificial snow for skiing by the Arizona Snowbowl from 2012 as a spiritual and cultural desecration (author's photograph).

1970s.[75] The lethal herbicide was sprayed on vegetation across Ndeé Neé and adjoining lands in Arizona as a way of eradicating invasive species of plants and vegetation.[76] In October 2012, at a hospital in Globe, a town neighboring San Carlos, there were reports of 10 Indigenous people diagnosed with cancer, a continuation of the lethal effects of Agent Orange contaminating water supplies and vegetation from the late 1950s no doubt, that has triggered.[77] On May 31, 2014, the San Carlos Chamber of Commerce held a meeting to hear from people who suffer from lethal effects of exposure to Agent Orange and other herbicides that may have caused the following diseases: Amyloidosis, Chronic B-cell Leukemias, Chloracne, Diabetes Mellitus Type 2, Hodgkins Disease, Ischemic Heart Disease, Multiple Myeloma, Non-Hodgkins Lymphoma, Parkinson's Disease, Peripheral Neuropathy, Porphyria Cutanea Tarda, Prostate Cancer, Respiratory Cancers (includes lung cancer), and Soft Tissue Sarcomas.[78] Dow Chemical is currently awaiting approval of use of the herbicide, 2,4-D, that was used in Agent Orange, to be sprayed on genetically modified crops for killing weeds, even after lethal effects of the herbicide are well known.[79] The combination of the active ingredients in Agent Orange, dichlorophenoxyacetic acid, 2,4-D and trichlorophenoxyacetic acid, 2,4,5-T, contains an unwanted byproduct of herbicide production, 2,3,7,8-tetrachlorodibenzo-p-dioxin, which is the most toxic dioxin and is classified as a dangerous carcinogen by the Environmental Protection Agency (EPA).[80] Contrary to the widespread ideology propagated by the genetically modified (GM) food lobby that GM food is particularly resistant to natural weeds and thus reduces pesticide use, glyphosate-resistant weeds have been growing exponentially in "herbicide-resistant weed management systems," resulting in a 527 million pound increase in herbicide use in the United States between 1996 and 2011, and pesticide use increased by 404 million pounds during the same period.[81] If Dow Chemical receives approval to use the 2,4-D herbicide, increases in herbicide use, particularly for corn, soybeans, and cotton will approach another 50 percent. Herbicide-laced crops that are staple for most people in the U.S., like corn and soy, are used to make all kinds of processed food which would eventually result in a cancer epidemic of frightening proportions. According to the American Cancer Society and the Centers for Disease Control and Prevention, over 1.6 million people are diagnosed with cancer in the U.S. and tens of thousands die from cancer-related conditions each year.[82] Around the world, over 14 million people learn that they have cancer annually, and some 8 million die each year, more than twice the numbers of people dying from AIDS, malaria, and tuberculosis combined.[83] Though the causes of cancer are multifarious according to medical scientists, it is unequivocal that the combi-

AGENT ORANGE:
HELPING APACHERIA HEAL

Presumptive diseases associated with exposure to Agent Orange or other herbicides

AL Amyloidosis
A rare disease caused when an abnormal protein, amyloid, enters tissues or organs

Chronic B-cell Leukemias
A type of cancer which affects white blood cells

Chloracne (or similar acneform disease)
A skin condition that occurs soon after exposure to chemicals and looks like common forms of acne seen in teenagers. Under VA's rating regulations, it must be at least 10 percent disabling within one year of exposure to herbicides.

Diabetes Mellitus Type 2
A disease characterized by high blood sugar levels resulting from the body's inability to respond properly to the hormone insulin

Hodgkin's Disease
A malignant lymphoma (cancer) characterized by progressive enlargement of the lymph nodes, liver, and spleen, and by progressive anemia

Ischemic Heart Disease
A disease characterized by a reduced supply of blood to the heart, that leads to chest pain

Multiple Myeloma
A cancer of plasma cells, a type of white blood cell in bone marrow

Non-Hodgkin's Lymphoma
A group of cancers that affect the lymph glands and other lymphatic tissue

Parkinson's Disease
A progressive disorder of the nervous system that affects muscle movement

Peripheral Neuropathy, Early-Onset
A nervous system condition that causes numbness, tingling, and motor weakness. Under VA's rating regulations, it must be at least 10 percent disabling within one year of herbicide exposure.

Porphyria Cutanea Tarda
A disorder characterized by liver dysfunction and by thinning and blistering of the skin in sun-exposed areas. Under VA's rating regulations, it must be at least 10 percent disabling within one year of exposure to herbicides.

Prostate Cancer
Cancer of the prostate; one of the most common cancers among men

Respiratory Cancers (includes lung cancer)
Cancers of the lung, larynx, trachea, and bronchus

Soft Tissue Sarcomas (other than osteosarcoma, chondrosarcoma, Kaposi's sarcoma, or mesothelioma)
A group of different types of cancers in body tissues such as muscle, fat, blood and lymph vessels, and connective tissues.

A community meeting and discussion will be held on the subject of Agent Orange Outreach Programs in San Carlos for the health and well-being of our people. All interested persons are welcome and invited to attend. If you or anyone you know has become a subject to any of the illnesses listed in association with the area, your input will be well recieved.

Agent Orange

was used and tested in the United States.

Where: San Carlos Apache Tribal Council Hall # 1 San Carlos Avenue, Main Building on east side of the street

When: Saturday, May 31st 2pm- 4pm

For more information contact the Chamber of Commerce at: **928-475-2579**

Advertisement for Agent Orange meeting in San Carlos, Arizona, May 31, 2014.

nation of pesticides, radiation of meat, genetically modified food, and spiritual disharmony are major factors in the perpetuation of cancer, a view strongly held by traditional Indigenous healers in Turtle Island like Hataali Jones Benally from Flagstaff, Arizona.[84] The unusually high levels of cancer and diabetes of Indigenous communities in San Carlos and Gila River, Arizona (the highest in the country) following the spraying of poisonous herbicides like 2,4-D and 2,4,5-T certainly lend credence to this assertion. Vietnam-era Agent Orange use and spraying has been acknowledged by the Department of Defense during the 1960s and 1970s in various locations around the U.S. and Canada, Puerto Rico, Hawaii, and in Laos, Cambodia, and Thailand in southeast Asia, underscoring the pervasive deployment of these very toxic chemicals that were used as defoliants and are known to cause serious illnesses.[85]

Further, U.S. soldiers who were deployed in Vietnam and other parts of Southeast Asia were themselves exposed to serious poisons like Agent Orange that may have resulted in proliferation of various kinds of cancers, psychological trauma, emotional instability, and suicidal tendencies. U.S. soldiers are guinea pigs for the military industrial complex and even the medical establishment too since they generally hail from working class and poor socioeconomic backgrounds, have less economic mobility than many from the upper and lower middle classes, and are compelled to accept the dictates of governmental authorities that promote war and conquest of lands of Indigenous peoples in other parts of the world. U.S. military personnel are often most vulnerable to projects that involve psychiatric experiments that date back to World War II, as depicted in the documentary, *The Hidden Enemy*, produced by the Citizens Commission on Human Rights International. The documentary notes for example the extraordinarily high rates of U.S. military suicides:

> Since 2002, the U.S. military suicide rates have almost doubled. From 2010 to 2012, more U.S. soldiers died by suicide than from traffic accidents, heart disease, cancer and homicide. In 2012 alone, more U.S. active duty service men and women committed suicide than died in combat, and veterans are killing themselves at the rate of 22 per day.[86]

Ironically, globalized powers have used both Indigenous peoples and military personnel employed for self-serving hegemonic economic, political, and social ends.

In southern Arizona, Indigenous Tohono O'odham people continue to be subject to violent intimidation and harassment by the U.S. Border Patrol in Nogales and on the U.S.–Mexico border from Sells, Arizona as they struggle to cross the colonially-defined border that breaches their ancestral lands to practice ancestral ceremonies. Quitovac, in Sonora, northern Mexico, an ancestral site for the Tohono O'odham people, is subject to continued dumping of toxic waste. The organization, *O'odham Voice Against the Wall,* started by Ofelia Rivas, a traditional elder, mounts ongoing challenges to the imposition of surveillance towers and a massive security fence by the U.S. Department of Homeland Security and Border Patrol at the U.S.–Mexico border outside Ali-Chuk, an O'odham village. An Israeli company that is one of the largest security corporations in the world and was responsible for providing electronic detection for the high-rise security wall around Palestinians living in the West Bank, Elbit Systems, received a $145 million contract from the Department of Homeland Security in early 2014 to build the security apparatus at the U.S.–Mexico border, part of a booming eight-year project that could grow to $1 billion in cost.[87] Elbit has recommended that Homeland Security beef up border monitoring and security and "adopt a more complete border security system, which combines radar and electro-optical sensors, unattended ground sensors, unmanned air systems, and manned or unmanned ground vehicles to enhance agents' flexibility and responsiveness."[88]

In Australia, identical stories are told. When Indigenous Ngarrindjeri women claimed that the planned Kumarangk/Hindmarsh Island bridge would violate the sacred sites of Indigenous people, the Australian government challenged the veracity of the women's claims, specifically because they were women and Indigenous at that.[89] When the Jawoyn people from northern Australia confronted the BHP mining company about its mining on Coronation Hill in the Northern Territory in Australia in 1991 because Coronation Hill is located within the area associated with *Bula,* a principal creation figure, the white Australian establishment, mocked them, and Australian television humiliated the Indigenous people by parading twenty five youngsters pleading for employment at the mine. It was only through the personal intervention of then Prime Minister, Bob Hawke, who banned subsequent mining at the site, that this desecration was halted.[90]

European missionaries have long disrespected sacred sites all over the world. The Christian missionary system that claimed that there was a great God in the sky now assumes the role of God in assessing the value of Indigenous peoples' ceremonies and sacred practices! It was small wonder that the Cherokee in North America balked at the thought of being forced to convert to Christianity by itinerant European missionaries in the 18th century, symbolized by Old Tasse's response in 1777:

> Much has been said of the want of what you term "Civilization" among the Indians. Many proposals have been made to us to adopt your law, your religion, your manners and your customs. We do not see the propriety of such a reformation. We should

be better pleased with beholding the good effects of these doctrines in your own practices than with hearing you talk about them or of reading your newspapers on such subjects.[91]

Similarly, the struggles by Mohawk people and other Indigenous nations for protection of Sun Mountain in British Columbia, persists. Globalization has witnessed an intensification of the violation of Indigenous peoples' religious and cultural rights as the insatiable lust for profit assumes uncontrollable proportions. Under globalization's ostensible "diversity" initiative, as proposed by leading advocates like former U.S. president Bill Clinton, who apologized to the *Kanaka Maoli* (Indigenous Hawaiian people) in 1993 for the criminal overthrow of the Hawaiian monarchy and Queen Lilikuolani in 1893 by the U.S. government in collusion with the Dole fruit company, there has been no move to break the cycle of perfidy on the part of the U.S. government and restore the validity of the 371 treaties made with Indigenous nations that were all broken by the same government.[92] This threat to Indigenous life constitutes acts of genocide, and Indigenous peoples are forced to resort to the jurisprudence system of the settler state to reclaim their original rights and lands, knowing that the system of justice established by these settler-colonial states has been anything but just when it comes to the rights and returns of lands stolen from Indigenous peoples.[93] Indigenous scholars Marie Battiste (Mi'kmaq) and James (Sa'ke'j) Youngblood Henderson (Chickasaw) explain the veracity of this historical and contemporary injustice against Indigenous peoples in settler-colonial states:

> Despite many calls for the universalization of human rights, the nation-states fail to understand the necessity of the equal application of existing human rights to Indigenous peoples. In particular, the nation-states reject the right of Indigenous peoples to self-determination, since this might lead to unacceptable freedoms for them.... They ignore the requirement laid out in the Principles on Friendly Relations Among States in Accordance with the Charter (1970) that they grant such ideas only to those states that conduct themselves in conformity with the principles of equality and self-determination of all peoples.
>
> The daily existence of Indigenous peoples in the nation-states also reflects the debates and intellectual violence of the working group.... Eurocentric legal doctrine makes it possible to represent and discuss civilization and its institutions, and thus to sustain and develop the privileges of the colonists.[94]

Depending on the Supreme Court in the U.S. or the U.S. government or the High Court in South Africa to practice justice for Indigenous peoples, is like "running from the wolf to the fox," in the parlance of Malcolm X, the Black freedom fighter in the U.S. from the 1960s.[95]

In terms of economic hardship, if most peoples in Asia and the rest of the underdeveloped world are poor, the socio-economic conditions for Indigenous people have been dire. In India, for example, while the poverty rate for the general population in 1993–94 was around 40 percent, for the Indigenous people, the "Scheduled Tribes," it was 54 percent. Though the Indigenous peoples of India, many of whom are from forest communities and mountain people, constitute 8 percent of the total population, they are 40 percent of the nation's internally displaced people. In Vietnam, Indigenous peoples like the Thai, Day, Hmong, Nung, Dao, Degar, and Koho (among the poorest), who are part of 54 different communities living in the Northern Mountains and Central Highlands, experience poverty at the rates between 66 percent and 100 percent, compared to the rest of the population where the average rate was 51 percent in 1999.[96] While the per capita income of the average Vietnamese person was $290 in that year, for Indigenous people it was only $100. Most startling are the conditions facing the 54 Indigenous communities in China like the Achang, Yao, Hui, Miao, Yi, Shui, Lhoba, Manchu, Tujia, Akha, Maonan, Quiang, Kazakh, Uygur, Tibetan, and various other Indigenous peoples in China where incomes have generally been very low and access to land has become more difficult with increased pursuit of mining and factory construction by globalized industrialism.[97] In the Wulin mountain area of China, where 80 percent of the population is Indigenous, the per capita income was CNY (Chinese Yuan) 521 in 1996, compared to CNY 1,792 for the rest of the province of Hunan and CNY 1,277 for the rest of the province of Guizhou, wherein the Wulin Mountains are found.[98] In addition, Indigenous peoples find themselves consistently disadvantaged and victimized by large hydroelectric power projects and dam construction, as when a mine-related landslide killed 83 people in the Gyama Valley in Tibet in April 2013.[99] China's race toward attaining industrial supremacy in Asia and the world inevitably results in Indigenous communities having their lands and communities overrun by factory construction. Water extraction for industry in urban areas has been devastating for Indigenous rural dwellers in China. The underground aquifer in Beijing and on the North China Plan that provides half of the country's wheat and a third of the corn is virtually depleted (deep wells around Beijing have to be drilled 1,000 meters or 3.300 feet to reach underground water), and the city is being forced to consider piping water from the Yangtze River Basin in the south, a tedious and financially prohibitive project that would cost tens of billions of dollars.[100]

In Japan, it was only in 1997 that the government conceded recognition of the Indigenous Ainu people, mostly found in Hokkaido, with the promulgation of the law concerning Promotion of the Ainu Culture and Dissemination and Enlightenment of Knowledge About Ainu Traditions.[101] Prior to 1997, the Japanese government systematically pursued an assimilationist policy vis-à-vis the Ainu people, relegating them to the status of a national minority group.[102] The most devastating development against the Ainu people was the construction of the Nibudani dam in the late 1990s as part of the plan of hydro-electric power to advance Japanese industrial expansion, a process now radically and perhaps permanently disrupted by the 2011 earthquake, tsunami, and radiation leaks from the Fukushima nuclear power plant. In the process 80 percent of the 500 residents of the area in Hokkaido had their lands directly affected by the dam construction and 85 Ainu residents had their lands forcibly bought by the Japanese government. Two Ainu residents who refused to sell their land, Tadashi Kaizawa and Kayano Shigeru, had their land confiscated by the government.[103]

The Western-style capitalist industrial economy of Japan also followed the West's practices of expropriation of Indigenous peoples' lands, particularly when valuable mineral or energy resources were found on such lands. The relegation of the Ainu to the margins of Japanese society and the colonization of their communities was a model derived from the Dawes Act of 1887 in the United States following a visit by a Japanese politician Kato Masanosuke to the U.S.[104] The Dawes Act accorded the United States government the right to assume responsibility of welfare over Indigenous people after having dispossessed them of their lands and resources. Similarly, the 1899 Hokkaido Former Aborigine Act in Japan offered to allocate lands to the Ainu for agriculture, even though the same lands had been confiscated by the Japanese government. This act kept the Indigenous people oppressed because the exchange of land was heavily regulated and their cultural status was relegated to "former aborigine."

Exploitation of Indigenous People by Ecotourism

One of the most lethal issues facing Indigenous peoples in this climate of economic impoverishment induced by the enveloping system of globalization is that of *eco-tourism*, where Indigenous cultures are being commoditized and marketed by governments of countries as if Indigenous peoples are the property of such governments, be they in places in the U.S., Canada, Peru, India, Australia, New Zealand (Aotearoa), Kenya, Tanzania, and Thailand. While the environmentalist movement claims that it is concerned with "preserving nature" in pristine form, little is said about the fact that 80 percent of all nature conservation parks around the world were established through the dispossession and forced relocation of Indigenous peoples, be it Yosemite in California (established in 1864), Yellowstone in Wyoming (established in 1872), Grand Canyon in Arizona, Amboseli, Maasai Mara, Ngorongoro, and Serengeti in Tanzania, Laikipia East Park, Nairobi National Park and Tsavo (Queen's) National Park in Kenya, the Bwindi Impenetrable and Mgahinga Gorilla National Parks in Uganda, the Kahuzi Biega Park in the Democratic Republic of the Congo, the Kruger National Park in South Africa/Azania, and the Kaeng Krachan National Park in Thailand, to name some of the prominent ones. Yellowstone and Yosemite became the model for nature parks that were established globally and dispossessed Indigenous peoples accordingly, presupposing a Eurocentric cosmology that arrogated the right to human beings to designate certain areas of "nature" for pristine or recreation purposes in contradistinction to Indigenous cosmologies that view humans as an integral part of the natural world and living within the web of nature and all life. The Kahuzi Biega Park has marginalized and threatened the very survival of the Indigenous Batwa and Bambhuti peoples of East and Central Africa respectively since these peoples depend on the resources of the Kahuzi forest for food and cultural ceremonies.[105] The Samburu have lodged a formal grievance complaint against the African Worldlife Foundation and the Kenya Wildlife Conservancy to protest the dispossession of 17,000 acres for "conservation."[106] The Ogiek people in Kenya face destruction of the Mara Forest, upon which they depend for food like honey and fruit, due to global warming and governmental intervention forcing their eviction. An Ogiek elder defiantly declared, "We don't know where to go.... Our grandfathers and fathers lived here.... They can kill us, but we cannot move from the forest."[107]

In the Australian state of New South Wales, the Indigenous people of that state have claims to aboriginal ancestral lands by virtue of the New South Wales (NSW) Aboriginal Land Rights Act of 1993. However, in over 2,000 instances of the 7,000 claims lodged through the year 2000, the lands that were restored were all considered residue lands that Australia decreed nobody desires and are of no essential public interest.[108] In other words, Indigenous peoples of Australia are entitled to ancestral lands so long as such lands have no productive value in the national Australian economic interest. Similar policies prevail in most situations in North and South America, Africa, and Asia, where Indigenous peoples are awarded lands that are considered residual and the least productive.

Uluru, the sacred site of the Anangu people in Australia, and Machu Picchu in Peru are classic examples where governments use Indigenous peoples' cultures for economic and financial gain. Australia is being publicized as a "spiritual" tourism destination because tourists can come to view the spirituality of "exotic" Indigenous people and even climb the sacred ancestral rock in violation of the Indigenous people's requests not to. In Peru, where Machu Picchu is heralded as a national treasure based on the exoticism of the "barbaric" and dead Inca Empire, Indigenous people have been essentially disconnected from the role of spiritual guardian of the area. Western eco-tourists hardly notice the desert settlement of impoverished Indigenous children who are poisoned daily from sniffing gasoline just over a hundred yards from the huge monolith at Uluru, in the tourists' eagerness to climb the sacred rock, just as tourists at Machu Picchu fail to see the Indigenous children virtually collapsing under the heavy weight of carrying luggage of wealthy "sensitive" Western tourists.[109] Today, every major international tourist outfit in the West markets Machu Picchu, grossing $6 million a year in gate receipts at the site in 2004 and contributing mightily to the $1 billion tourism industry in Peru, from which few Indigenous people benefit.[110] At Uluru, the Anangu people receive one quarter of all visitor receipts to the park and engage in their own commercial activities, yet still experience racial discrimination when they are excluded from using the facilities at the neighboring resort town of Yulara, prompting a series of lawsuits in 2002. Additionally, Uluru is considered public property by the tourism industry, fuelled by the entrenched racism of Australian society against Indigenous people who are denied the inalienable right of self-determination in their own land and unrestrained access to and control of their sacred ancestral lands and sites. Ecotourism, like commercial mining for precious minerals like uranium and gold by multi-national corporations in Australia, continues to exploit the Aboriginal people in this age of rampant globalization.

In Kenya, Maasai Mara is considered the world's most popular wildlife game park, generating millions of dollars in revenue for the Kenyan government. Yet, the Kenyan government has consistently refused to honor 100-year treaty obligations from the old British colonial regime that accord the Maasai self-determination and rights to occupation of their traditional ancestral lands, causing Maasai activists to protest in 2004, which resulted in one being shot dead and many others injured by Kenyan police.[111] The Maasai are currently engaged in a fierce struggle to preserve their last ceremonial ground in neighboring Tanzania, the Naimina Enkiyio Forest, battling the designs of the World Conservation Union (IUCN), which is funded by the European Union, to keep the forest open for tourism.[112] Samwel Naikada, an Indigenous activist from the Dupoto community in Transmara, Kenya, and the author are currently involved in promoting the Nyakweri Cultural Restoration and Ecological Preservation Project, which entails building the Dupoto Community Center and inviting students and educators especially to visit and live in the forest to understand the diversity and struggle of the forest, the peoples, and the ecology under the leadership of Maasai traditional practitioners.[113] The privatization of traditional Maasai lands for ownership by wealthy white companies has continued steadily during this eon of globalization. Miyere Miyandazi, an activist from the Maasai community, walked in protest from Kenya to the east coast of South Africa/Azania to highlight the Maasai's struggle for rights to their ancestral lands, and was arrested by border authorities at various points for not having a passport. He now works with homeless "street children" in iThwekwini, South Africa/Azania, Africa's wealthiest country. Miyandazi encapsulates Maasai culture, with two rudimentary principles: To be free and enjoy life, and to live by the philosophy that land can only be used, never owned.[114]

In post-apartheid South Africa, globalization's defenders continue to violate the rights of the sacred sites of the First Nations San people, Southern Africa's original people, by permitting unfettered tourism and construction of cable cars at sites like Table Mountain in Cape Town and the Ukuhlamba Drakensberg Park in Kwazulu, where tourists still desecrate rock paintings and petroglyphs with soft-drinks and even urine, prompting the San Council to insist that it become the primary guardian of the Ukuhlamba site. Similar desecrations have occurred around historical Tohono O'odham sites in Arizona in Turtle Island, where visitors have drawn chalk around petroglyphs and left litter at such sacred sites.[115]

Essentially, Indigenous peoples are forced to sell the sacredness of their cultures to economically survive in a system of Euro-capitalism that forced them into conditions of poverty through dispossession of their lands and thus to depend on and be subservient to the prevailing globalized order. Alison Johnston, director of the International Support Center for Sustainable Tourism (ISCST), brings the contradictions of eco-tourism into stark relief when she contends that while ecotourism accounts for only 5 percent of the annual $25 billion tourism industry, it is expanding at four times the rate of other kinds of tourism and is predicated on exoticizing Indigenous cultures that were ravaged by the very cultures from which tourists originate.[116]

Though eco-tourism is being promoted by "progressive" tour companies in the West as ethical and responsible tourism that benefits Indigenous people, Johnston's point is well taken: ecotourism is principally about the icon of the Western capitalist and is being marketed in the supposed philanthropic style of "cultural sensitivity to the natives" solely because it is the best form of money-making in tourism today and accrues lucrative profits to Western tour companies. In Nepal, for instance, tourism revenues from the Chitwan Park, the country's principal tourist site along with the Everest Park, generally accrue to large tourism companies based in countries from which tourists originate and to large tourism operators in the capital, Kathmandu. Indigenous peoples living in these areas receive only around 2 percent of such revenues.[117] Eco-tourism is practiced at the expense of Indigenous peoples' dispossessed lands, ravaged cultures, and economically depressed status in global societies. It is yet another instance where the West *has its cake and eats it too—while the Indigenous people go hungry at the table.* Eco-tourism does not "help" Indigenous people get their dispossessed lands back; it essentially is another social practice that makes Westerners feel good about their ostensible "charity" to impoverished Indigenous people while making mammoth profits simultaneously, akin to the West offering "aid" to the underdeveloped world. Eco-tourists are no more than 21st century Western missionary and touring colonists, penetrating exotic lands for their own egotistical self-aggrandizement with little concern for the rights and lands of Indigenous peoples. It is similar to the recent acts of "philanthropy" of billionaire figures like Bill Gates, Rupert Murdoch, and Richard Branson, who are giving billions to the impoverished peoples of Africa, Asia, and Latin America, to fight diseases such as AIDS and malaria. In addition to these being huge tax-write offs and hardly dents to the billions that these supremely wealthy individuals possess (the 356 billionaires in the world possess more wealth than half of the world's population), Westerners hardly ponder the question: Why do many people of color need to depend on Western "charity" for their health care or education for that matter? Or the question: How did these corporate tycoons make their billions in the first place? Was it perhaps through their profit-hungry corporations raping the resources and exploiting the already impoverished workers of the underdeveloped world in Asian, African, and Latin American countries? Alison Johnston's comments of the duplicity of Western "giving" are apropos here, when she notes that "when funding and other corporate 'giving' stems from industrial activities which capitalize on colonialism or damage life systems, it is inaccurate and misleading to call this philanthropy, corporate citizenship or corporate social responsibility.... It is takers who do such 'giving.'"[118] It should come as no great surprise, then, to read that an investigative team sent by the *Financial Times* in early 2006 discovered that Fair Trade coffee was being harvested and sold by companies that underpaid coffee workers in Peru in violation of fair labor practices.[119] Such is the nature of the globalized capitalist system: its soul is tainted so badly that everything it initiates reeks of the stench of *greed*.

Indigenous peoples have been the primary victims of globalization's violent penetration and are now determined to resist this onslaught on all continents, from the Saami in Norway, to the Inuit people of Alaska and the Aymara of South America, to the Indigenous people of Australia and Indigenous peoples of the South Pacific, to the peoples of Africa, like the San of Southern Africa, the Maasai of East Africa, and the Tuareg of North Africa.

Loss of Language and Indigenous Cultural Rights Under Globalization

One of the most painful issues facing Indigenous peoples globally is the loss of Indigenous languages occurring in especially European settler-colonial societies in North and South America, Oceania, and Southern Africa, where English or French assume primacy and Indigenous children are miseducated into believing that their mother-tongues are valueless and aspire toward becoming fluent European language speakers. Felipe Molina, a traditional Yoeme (Yaqui) teacher in Tucson, Arizona, laments this crisis among young people in the Yoeme nation when he observes that "in Arizona many young Yoeme people do not speak the Yoeme language anymore so this makes it more difficult to learn about the Yoeme truth."[120] Richard Grounds, an Indigenous Yuchie scholar and a colleague formerly at the University of Oklahoma, has been involved in Indigenous language teaching and training among college students in the persevering movement to reclaim and retain Indigenous Indian languages.

In post-apartheid South Africa/Azania, for example, many parents of Indigenous African children are demanding that their children be instructed in the English language since they view European languages as the languages of the future and the key to economic success, a belief that is reinforced by the post-apartheid African National Congress government's embracing of the ideology of globalization and foreign investment.[121] Though Indigenous African languages are encouraged within all curricula in schools where non–Indigenous languages take precedence, the former are not required as mandatory for all students. This policy of voluntary schooling in Indigenous African languages inevitably marginalizes Indigenous cultures since it presupposes that dominant European languages like English or Afrikaans (from the Dutch settler-colonialist legacy) are primary *lingua franca* for South Africa/Azania.

The lethal side effects of colonization of Indigenous peoples in Africa and the world has compelled the internalization of negative values about and deprecation of their languages and cultures. Though there are elements within government circles that are seriously committed to the instruction and training of children in African languages, the rhetoric of the Western market capitalist system holds sway in the minds of parents as they reflect upon needs for economic security in the future. I was shaken too during a visit to a travel agent in Fez, Morocco, in June 2006, when the Moroccan travel agent whose mother tongue was Arabic opted to communicate in French with her fellow Moroccan who was also Arabic-speaking. The hegemonic role that English (and other European languages like French play) is destructive for the preservation of Indigenous languages. Today, there are only about 20 speakers of the Indigenous Kara/Mapuche language in Chile's Patagonia region left and the struggle is to continue such language lines by teaching children in their Indigenous mother tongues. One of the fundamental pitfalls of globalization, as with colonialism in the past, is the rush toward maintaining the supremacy of languages like English even though it is not the first language or mother tongue of most people in the world. Indigenous languages preserve the profound and subtle nuances of their cultures, and translation into English from these languages does not capture the cultural distinctiveness of such languages in which deep meanings are embedded. Tsitsi Dangerembga articulates this point in her classic work, *Nervous Conditions*, when she describes villagers communicating in Shona in Zimbabwe as opposed to English, the language of formal education in the country.[122]

On the rest of the African continent, where about 2,500 languages of the world's 7,000 languages are spoken, most languages of Indigenous communities are endangered by the imposition of European colonial languages like French, English, and Portuguese and in some instances, African *lingua franca*. For example, though Kiswahili in East Africa bridges cultural divides across East Africa, it simultaneously obscures the more than 230 languages in the region, and Setswana in Botswana overshadows the Khoisan languages like ! Xoo, #Hua, Khute, Naro,/Gwi//Gana. Kxoe,//Ani, Ju/'hoan,#Kx'au ll'ei, Deti (Teti), Kua, Tshwa, Tshasi, Buga, /Xaisa, Ts'ixa, Danisi, and Cara (Tshara), confining the Khoesan communities to the society's margins.[123] Herman Batibo, a linguistics professor at the University of Botswana in Southern Africa, warns about the severe ripple effects of linguistic erosion on ecological and cultural systems since "the loss of linguistic and cultural diversity in Africa is occurring with the loss of biodiversity.... Africa is now experiencing critical desertification, hostile climatic conditions, such as continued droughts, unavailability of clean water, and disappearance of certain species, including the white rhinos and elephants" and "the younger generations are rapidly losing their competence in the knowledge of their ecosystem, such as names of plants and wild animals and their characteristics or uses, at the same time that they are losing interest in their folklore and traditions."[124] Loss of language implies loss of culture and ultimately loss of identity in this period of encroaching globalization, and thus inevitable cultural extinction.

Globalization and Ecocide

The Genesis creation story in the Hebrew Judeo-Christian scriptures portrayed human beings as the pinnacle of all creation where the natural world is expected to subordinate itself to human domination. Western Judeo-Christian based societies over the past eight centuries have progressively demonstrated that they are determined to live by this principle of human dominance within the web of the natural world. Indigenous peoples on the other hand view human beings as an integral component of the diversity of nature, adhering to principles of harmonious co-existence as opposed to those of domination and subjugation. While Rachel Carson's ground-breaking work, *Silent Spring,* was a critical element in the 20th century's environmental movement call for the banning of insecticide and pesticides and other chemicals that kill animal, insects, birds, and plant life and the book's view that humans are an integral part of the natural world is commendable, it concomitantly needs to be borne in mind that Indigenous peoples of Turtle Island (North America) and the rest of the world have been rooted in such worldviews from time immemorial.[125] Since the colonization of the world via technology and the military, specifically the European development of gunpowder for conquest invented by the Chinese, the Earth has suffered profusely.[126]

Today, bees are among the most threatened of species and the consequences of such ecocide are portentous for all of life on the Earth. During the winter of 2012, a third of all bee colonies died in the U.S.[127] Forty percent of all bees in California, the "breadbasket" of the nation, are dying each year.[128] In the winter of 2013, half of California bees died and in the first week of July 2013, 50,000 bees were found dead in an Oregon park.[129] In the same month and year, 37 million bees were found dead in Elmwood, Ontario, in Canada, with more than 600 beehives lost, attributable to neonicotinoid pesticides, according to apiarist Dave Schuit.[130] In Rheintal in the western region of Germany, between 330 and 500 million bees were killed by clothianidin, a pesticide made by Bayer AG in 2008.[131] Over a third of all food and probably much more, depend on bee pollination, part of a $30 billion food economy. Apples, broccoli, melons, onions, cherries, and over a hundred fruits and vegetables depend on bee pollination.[132] U.S. scientists found over 12 pesticides in samples of bees, pollen, and wax, contributing to the radically declining bee populations in the U.S. each year over the past eight consecutive years.[133] Monsanto, the world's largest genetically modified corporation, which makes 60 percent of pesticides that are toxic for the environment and all humans, along with Dow Chemical, which manufactured Agent Orange, used on lands of the Chi Endeh (Chiricahua Apache) people in San Carlos, Arizona, Vietnam, Laos, and Cambodia, are leading manufacturers of neonicotinoid pesticides.[134] Pharmaceutical giant Bayer AG, a German company, Syngenta, Du Pont, and BASF are other corporations engaged in the manufacture of these very lethal poisons exterminating the bulk of the bee population in the world and threatening all life as we know it, including that of human beings.[135] Pesticides that kill bees inevitably kill human beings since we are part of the same web of the natural world!

Polar bears, walruses, and narwhal in the Arctic are facing possible extinction due to the melting of polar ice caps and glaciers in the Arctic and Antarctic regions. The most well known creature vulnerable to global warming and melting ice is the polar bear, numbering about 20,000–25,000 today. Though numbers of the Pacific Walrus are unclear, they are known to be declining rapidly according to the International Union for Conservation of Nature (IUCN). Other Arctic and Antarctic vertebrates either facing extinction or extremely vulnerable to climate change are the narwhal, which number about 80,000, and the ivory gull, which is estimated to be between 15,000 and 25,000.[136] Much of the coral reefs on Caribbean coasts, the Great Barrier Reef in Australia, and Karimunjawa Reef in Indonesia, have been thoroughly devastated from bleaching over the past five decades and now reflect dead coral.[137] In 2005, half of the coral reefs on the coasts of Puerto Rico and near the Virgin Islands suffered bleaching, stressing coral seriously and making them more vulnerable to permanent elimination.[138] Ofu Island off the coast of American Samoa has experienced coral stress and death due to warming temperatures.[139]

The IUCN has estimated that of the 1.5 million named species (the unnamed could number in the tens of millions of a high of over 100 million), a systematic ecocide and biocide is underway. A quarter of all mammals, 1 of every 8 birds, one third of all amphibians, conifers, and gymnosperms are facing extinction, and over a half of all reptiles, 52 percent of all insects, and 73 percent of all flowering plants are under serious threat.[140] A landmark 2010 study, *The Sampled Red List Index for Plants*, has indicated that a fifth of the world's plants stand a real risk of extinction.[141] E. O. Wilson, the world-renowned biologist, who noted that we know so little of the vastness of the organisms found on the Earth, with over 1.5 million such organisms in one gram of sand, predicted that half of all known species of life will become extinct by 2100 at the rate of between 2.7 and 270 species erased each day.[142] According to the Royal Society for the Protection of Birds, forty species of birds in Britain will not survive unless they receive special protection.[143] The African lion, long a symbol of the African plains, is currently under threat, with lion numbers dwindling by 30 percent in the past twenty years and with Kenya alone losing 100 lions each year from its pride of 2000 in the country, principally because lions are killed for medicinal value by Far East traders. If this trend continues, conservationists contend that there's a 10 percent chance that lions could become extinct in 20 years.[144] Over 1,700 plant, animal, and insect species have moved towards the North Pole at a rate of 6 kilometers per decade during the last half of the 20th century, undermining their ability to adapt to non-tropical habitats and thus jeopardizing their future existence. It has now been confirmed that the black rhino of West Africa is extinct.[145]

Diverse species of animals are rapidly becoming extinct because they are intra-breeding due to being crowded out by human industrialization, defor-estation, urbanization, and sprawling residential expansion, making human activity the greatest threat to the rest of the natural world. Most disturbing is the fact that in this modern era "the normal trickle of extinction has become a gushing hemorrhage as 100 species or more disappear every day."[146] As people celebrated the quincentennial of the Columbian "discovery" of the Americas in 1992, little was said about the discovery that most of the cod fishing resources, which were the pillar of the northwest Atlantic coastal economies, were virtually depleted in 1991.[147]

What of the horrors of dumping nuclear waste from the Western indus-trial countries in impoverished nations of the underdeveloped world, partic-ularly in west Africa, like waste from Italy being dumped in the Ivory Coast, which killed several people and poisoned tens of thousands of people in Sep-tember 2006?[148] Though there are international laws like the Organization for Economic Cooperation and Development (OECD) Initiatives Concerning Transfrontier Movements of Hazardous Waste of 1984 and 1985, the UN Basel Convention on Control of Transboundary Movements of Hazardous Waste and Their Disposal (Basel Convention), the European Union/African Caribbean and Pacific Initiative (EU/ACP initiative), and the 1988 Economic

Community of West African States (ECOWAS) resolutions against transboundary waste, cash-strapped Guinea Bissau was willing to accept $600 million for storing hazardous waste from abroad.[149] The dumping of toxic waste on Kassa island in Guinea in the 1980s and the location of hazardous waste landfills close to the water table in Dakar, Senegal, are all in violation of international environmental laws protecting people against contamination by toxic waste. One of the reasons for ship piracy off the coast of Somalia has been the dumping of nuclear waste off the northeast coast of Africa and the depletion of fishing supplies by foreign fishing trawlers. The virtually weekly stories about oil slicks on the coastlines of the earth's ocean and from leaks in tankers transporting oil around the world, all signify the instability of the globalized maritime and fossil fuels industry. The Gulf of Mexico spill in 1979, the catastrophic Exxon Valdez spill of 1993, the oil slick from a Serbian port that destroyed 100 km of the Danube River waterway in October 2006, and the worst spill in history with over 5 million barrels of oil spilled into the Gulf of Mexico and the south eastern Gulf Coast as a result of the explosion of the BP oil well on April 20, 2010, that left 125 human beings and thousands of other bird, fish, and plant life dead and where dispersants used to scatter the oil intensified fish kills, caused dolphins hemorrhaging and poisoned people living on the Gulf Coast. These are just some of the glaring environmental

The tragedy of bird and sea life being decimated by oil spills is reflected in this somber picture of a bird covered in oil in the Black Sea (Igor Golubenkov).

and ecological catastrophes in the era of globalization.[150] One hundred forty thousand European factories dump industrial waste in the Mediterranean Sea each year, killing fish and poisoning marine life that are intrinsic to the global food chain.[151] Each year, 400 million electronic products from the United States, including exhausted computer circuit boards, are dumped on underdeveloped countries like China, India, and Nigeria, causing dangerous levels of toxicity to communities of these nations.[152] In 2011, 20 million recycled batteries were shipped to Mexico and exposed plant workers and residents, especially children, to high levels of lead contained in such batteries.[153] When 350 tons of oil leaked from the Rena off the port of Tauranga in New Zealand (Aotearoa) on October 10, it was described as the country's "worst environmental disaster in decades."[154] Western technology's dispersants were unsuccessful in occluding the spread of oil in that historic Pacific oil leak from a ship that was carrying hazardous substances.[155]

Even more troubling for some 5.2 billion people in the world who are cell phone users and part of what may be called "the world's largest human experiment," the effects of radiation emitted by cell phone towers may be causing cancer, resulting in the World Health Organization (WHO) classifying cell phones as a "carcinogenic" in 2011, even though it quickly asserted that there was no conclusive evidence to substantiate that cell phone use was a cause of cancer. Yet neither did the WHO conclude that cell phones are absolutely non-cancer causing. When cell phone companies fund such research on cell phone use and radiation effects, we need to remain suspicious! A May 2014 report in the British journal, Occupational and Environmental Medicine, noted that many scientists contend that repeated use of cellphones for 15 hours each month over five years could cause brain cancers like glioma and meningioma tumors in the brain.[156] The case of the Rail family farming in Mansfield, Ohio and animals there contracting tumors, ducks laying eggs that refused to hatch, and children born with defects, losing hair and whirling in waves of hyperactivity accompanied by neurological problems, is one worth analyzing, particularly since the Rails lived 800 feet from a cell phone tower. An EPA scientist informed the family that the official EPA position was that the family was totally safe being so close to the cell phone tower, yet he personally urged that the family move for their own well-being. All of these gruesome side effects of ill health disappeared when the Rail family moved to Michigan.[157] Numerous other stories of effects of cell phone use and possible cancer from radiation abound, as Christopher Ketcham explains.[158] Wireless activities that depend on certain wave frequencies may have deleterious effects on bee, butterfly, bird, and other insect populations since they interfere with these creatures' abilities to migrate in ways that Nature has endowed them, disrupting critical migrations in the fragile ecological system. One fact is abundantly clear: There is no such thing as a safe dose of radiation, since the Nuclear Information and Resource Center has accurately demonstrated that "permissible" does not mean "safe" and, drawing from Donnell Boardman's research on medical observation of nuclear workers, pointed out that

> no two radiation exposures are ever the same, even to the same individual and that a single alpha particle, acting on a single cell, may damage that cell to the same degree as if a thousand x-rays had hit it ... one radiation particle can cause great damage to a single cell ... that damage can even lead to a person's death, while registering a dose to the total body of zero![159]

Capitalism as a system developed off colonization, slavery, and the destruction of bio-diversity *is now the most lethal enemy of all life*. The European colonial system that enslaved between 25 and 50 million Africans in the Americas for over two and a half centuries and which exterminated 100 million Indigenous people in the Western hemisphere, also annihilated significant sectors of this region's ecological life. Fifty million buffalo were decimated by the European colonization of North America.[160] Fur trade between Europeans and Russia continued when the Europeans invaded North America in the 17th century and, during the peak of the squirrel trade, half a million skins were being exported each year from the 14th through the 16th centuries. Commercial whaling has resulted in gutting of the whale population, so that just about 400 right whales live in the North Atlantic and 250 in the North Pacific oceans today.[161] The California gray whale was almost hunted to extinction in the latter part of the 19th century, but has since recovered in small numbers. Though Indigenous people like the Makah in Washington State hunted whales for food, such practices never threatened the continuation of the species as Euro-capitalist practices did and do.

Globalization has caused impoverished and heavily indebted underdeveloped countries in Africa and Asia to mortgage their forests so as to generate revenue. The Philippines has exported $50 billion worth of forested products between 1981 and 1989, so that only 18 percent of wooded forests remain today. Only 30,000 hectares from an original half a million hectares of mangroves are left. In Indonesia, where some of the most distinctive diversity of natural species are found, over 1 million hectares of the nation's tropical forests were erased between 1980 and 2000. Wood products generate more than $3 billion annually in foreign exchange. More forests fires raged around the world in the 1990s than in all of human history. The United States, though possessing 5 percent of the world's population and 6 percent of the forest cover, consumes 40 percent of the world's resources and one third of the world's paper.[162] Eighty percent of the Earth's rivers are no longer safe for swimming or washing due to toxic pollutants.[163]

Conclusion: Resistance by Indigenous Peoples to the Ongoing Genocide and Ecocide Under Globalization

All over the world, Indigenous peoples are organizing themselves into coalitions, from the Indigenous Environmental Network, the Dineh Citizens Against Ruining our Environment (CARE), Native Resource Coalition, the Good Road Coalition, and Humans Against Nuclear Dumping (HANDS) in Turtle Island (North America), to the Aboriginal Rights organizations in Australia and Maori resistance to the Multilateral Agreement on Investment (MAI) and the Asian-Pacific Economic Cooperation (APEC) initiative in New Zealand (Aotearoa) and the Pacific.[164] There are global organizations like the International Work Group for Indigenous Affairs (IWGIA) and WIMSA in Southern Africa that are engaged in struggles for the unconditional return of stolen Indigenous lands and the restoration of Indigenous sovereignty and autonomy. In May 2010, activists and leaders from over 120 nations gathered in Tiquipaya, on the outskirts of Cochabamba, Bolivia, for the World People's Conference on Climate Change and the Rights of Mother Earth.[165] Evo Morales, Indigenous president of Bolivia, was highly dissatisfied with the commitment of world governments to address issues of climate change from a fundamental respect for Earth principle, and sought to create a place where voices of Indigenous people and other activists could gather to address the crisis of global climate change from the perspectives of those most adversely effected. Elder Ofelia Rivas, traditional Tohono O'odham elder and spiritual leader from Arizona, was in attendance and noted that this was a historic moment for the world's Indigenous peoples because it signified a new movement of collective action by Indigenous peoples to address global concerns from their land-based cultural viewpoints.[166] The Pachakutik Movement of Bolivia was responsible for the election of Evo Morales, an Indigenous coca grower, and for the ousting of the previous Bolivian president, Mesa, who was firmly aligned with the minority wealthy European-descended elites.[167]

In Ecuador, similarly, the Pachakutik Movement, which is the political arm of the Confederation of Indigenous Nationalities of Ecuador, or CONAIE, was responsible for the ousting of two previous presidents and the return of president Rafael Correa whose role was threatened in an attempted coup in

2010, possibly sponsored by the U.S.[168] Ecuador is a major oil producer and though Correa had initially been strongly disposed toward championing the interests of the Indigenous people of the country, garnering significant support from the Ecuador's large Indigenous communities at the time that he was first elected in 2006, he has since turned course, citing economic growth reasons, and is now embarking on opening up a $1.77 billion open-pit mine at El Mirador, owned by the Chinese company, Ecuacorriente. The mine would devastate up to 450,000 acres of deep forest that for millennia has been the home to the Achuar people. Thousands of Indigenous people marched in protest for 700 kilometers, from El Pangui in the Amazon forest to the capital, Quito, in March 2012, demanding that the government end its mining contracts because of the destruction of Indigenous cultures and rainforest areas.[169] In Bolivia, Indigenous protesters against construction of a road through a national park and the Isibore-Secure Indigenous area outside the presidential palace in La Paz was met with tear gas and water-cannon sprays by Bolivian police.[170]

Indigenous peoples are fighting for their rights everywhere. From Flagstaff, Arizona, where the Save the Peaks coalition, with Dineh leaders like Jones and Klee Benally, to Canada, where the Mohawk people have erected barricades and even taken up arms in Ontario to stave off construction of golf courses on ancestral lands and Athabascan Chipewyan and Mikisew Cree people still resist the dangerous Keystone Pipeline that rapes the Earth for tar sands oil in Alberta, to Mexico, where the Indigenous peoples of Chiapas took up arms against the Mexican government to demand their lands and rights in the 1990s, Indigenous people resist neo-colonization. Throughout South America resistance can be seen in places like Bolivia, where Indigenous Aymara leader, Evo Morales, as the first Indigenous elected president, is having to live up to his promise to protect Indigenous peoples' ancestral lands, rights, and cultures amid economic pressure from global corporations greedy for extracting the country's vast natural gas resources. In Venezuela, Indigenous people are involved in liberation struggles to have sacred ancestral lands returned to them, as in 2005 when landless peasants occupied the foreign-owned Vestey landed estate demanding access to their own land.[171] In Ecuador, Indigenous people have taken over oil fields from U.S. and Canadian oil companies and struggle to "keep oil in the ground" and are demanding UN compensation for this practice since it mitigates the deleterious effects of global warming. In Brazil, Indigenous Yanomami and twelve other Indigenous communities are resisting the planned construction of the Belo Monte Hydro-electric Dam that along with other designated dams in the region would flood some 22,000 square kilometers in the Xingu basin for the generating of a projected 14,700 megawatts of power to meet Brazil's rising industrial energy needs.[172] The Xingu River will be diverted for 80 percent of its flow, causing a permanent drought in the river's "Big Bend," directly affecting the livelihoods of Indigenous Juruna and Arara peoples and resulting in the forced flooding of over 20,000 Indigenous peoples who will no longer be able to fish and engage in traditional cultural practices in the Paquicamba and Arara land areas.[173] The Yanomami, who are prominent among the 232 Indigenous nations in the Amazon, continue to struggle against the encroachment of their lands in Roraima by *garimpeiros* (gold diggers) since 1987 and the invasion by lethal diseases such as flu and malaria.[174]

Resistance continues across the globe and Mother Earth shakes all colonial foundations to the core, as in New Zealand (Aotearoa) where the Indigenous people are growing in significant numbers to the point of finally becoming a majority in their own land so that their land can be reclaimed. In neighboring Australia, a judge ruled in 2010 that 200,000 square kilometers around the city of Perth belongs to the Indigenous people and for their ceremonial use and livelihood access. The Indigenous peoples of the hills of the Philippines, Malaysia, India, Nepal, and Bangladesh continue to resist the encroachment of their lands by hungry timber and energy companies and the construction of dams in their ancestral lands.[175] In October 2011, the Inter-American Commission on Human Rights of the Organization of American States charged Canada with the injustice of failing to compensate the Indigenous Hul'qumi'num six First nations comprising of the Chemainus First Nation, Cowichan, Halalt First Nation, Lake Cowichan First Nation, Lyackson First Nation, and Penelakut for dispossessing these nations of their ancestral lands in a landmark case brought to the Commission by the Hul'qumi'num Treaty Group.[176] Further examples of Indigenous resistance are evident among the people of Palestine, who are resisting Israeli colonial occupation and militarism, the Maasai people of East Africa who are determined to protect the Nyakweri Forest in Transmara, Kenya, and the San people of Southern Africa, who resist the lascivious hand of the predatory corporations and the liberalized free-market system of globalized capitalism.[177] The struggle is never-ending.

It is in the same spirit of *Goyathlay*, whom the Spanish called Geronimo, and Black Elk, who were able to stave off the bullets of the U.S. colonial armies, that lives on in the movements for self-determination and return of confiscated and occupied lands five hundred years later.[178] The theme of the 13th UN Permanent Forum on Indigenous Issues (UNPFII) in New York City in May 2014 focused on Articles 3–6 and 36 on the principles of "self-determination and good governance" in the UN Declaration on the Rights of Indigenous People. The focus was very timely, yet lacked the substantive backing of most governments in the world, particularly the U.S, Canada, Australia, Brazil, New Zealand (Aotearoa), South Africa, and Kenya to name some of the principal places where Indigenous peoples continue to be disregarded and their rights trampled over by governmental structures.[179] The distinctive cultural histories and matrices that have defined Indigenous peoples' identities and lives from time immemorial are still ignored by leading governments since Indigenous peoples are generally expected to conform to federal and national laws that reflect parochial Eurocentric cultural and economic histories and experiences. Sites like *Dook'oos'liid* (the San Francisco Peaks) that are sacred to all Indigenous peoples of the southwest in Turtle Island and sacred grounds like the Superstition Mountains that are revered by the Chi Endeh (Chiricahua Apache) nation are still viewed as commercial and financial opportunities for tourism and mining corporations respectively, with little protection of the inalienable rights of Indigenous peoples. La Donna Harris, founder of Americans for Indian Opportunity (AIO), recalls all people to the vocation of relentless and eternal struggle against globalization and colonialist-styled-capitalism:

> The current form of globalization ... is a threat to cultural and political autonomy.... Many times those who resist the negative forces of globalization and of economic, political and cultural domination are labelled terrorists...
>
> My grandfather could have been considered a "terrorist" at the end of the last century. He was one of the last "wild" Indians to be brought in for "pacification" at Fort Sill, Oklahoma.... As we look at the world around us, we have to recognize that existing systems based on Western models of governance are not working. The imposition model continues to cause us great pain. We need to establish respectful, caring relationships of responsibility with each other.
>
> This is what is wrong with the present "free market" system. It is devoid of care. It is devoid of responsibility mechanisms. It has no such mechanisms at all vis-à-vis communities, whether they exist on the local, regional or even the national level. The present economic system does not care if any of these communities, or if the Earth itself, exists into the future.[180]

Wise words from an Indigenous woman elder to which we all need to pay heed!

The generally amoral demeanor of globalized corporations that allow them to destroy the earth without any legal, economic or social consequence, with the sole pursuit of profit, is the fundamental cause of this severe devastation of Earth and all life in a globalized world. In the next chapter, we will discuss the peculiar impact that globalization has had on the carriers of tradition and bearers of life, the *women* of the world, particularly women within impoverished contexts.

3

Unjust Globalization and the Acute Marginalization of Poor Women in the World

> Women experience globalization daily when they go in search of water at the hydrants in poor neighborhoods, or when they busy themselves in thousands of other ways to fulfill the needs of their families. These are needs that men are no longer able to meet, or needs arising from the cutting of state provision for education or health services, under the constraints of structural adjustment policies. It is primarily women who pay the actual costs of the privatization of the economy.[1]—*Fatou Sow, Senegalese sociologist*

Introduction

Of any segment of human society that has been most devastated by the colonializing effect of globalization, it is women. Largely ostracized and subjugated through centuries of patriarchal feudalism and tradition, colonialism, and Western modernism, the contemporary evolution of women's marginalization by capitalism and its surrogate insignia, the transnational corporation, has become more pervasively institutionalized and entrenched than ever before. Under the auspices of global colonization launched five centuries ago, Indigenous women all over the world have been forced to bear the brunt of the perversity of sexual violence imposed on them while glorifying the Puritan morality of the European "Christian" male, where "the sexualization of social relations—with short term liaisons, rape, and the birth of mixed-race children being key features of indigenous-colonial relations—drove a firm wedge between the groups."[2]

Though women constitute over half of the world's human population, they reap about 1 percent of the world's wealth.[3] Women receive about 10 percent of the world's income, the bulk of these women being numerically women of color and deeply impoverished in Africa, Asia, the Pacific, Latin America and the Caribbean, and among Indigenous, African, and Latino communities in North America.[4] In 1995, women contributed $11 trillion of the $16 trillion global economic output, according to the Human Development Report for that year.[5] In 2000, women were 60 percent of the world's poor of over 1.3 billion people according to official United Nations indices, and of the 350 million formally classified as absolutely poor, the vast majority were women.[6] Over 6 million women, 99 percent of whom live in the underdeveloped world, died from complications relating to giving birth in 1999. Of the 1 billion people living in abject poverty in the world today, most are women.[7] Almost 43 percent of the agricultural labor force is women and women are the bulk of the 600 million poor livestock keepers.[8] In Africa almost half of all agricultural labor in 2010 was female.[9] Women constitute two-thirds of the almost 1 billion illiterate people in the world.[10] The empirical studies done by researchers such as D. Thomas and S. Handa in the mid–1990s for instance indicate that the rise in women's incomes in family households globally tend to become invested in children's education, health, and nutrition, more than their male counterparts.[11] Clearly, gender and economic viability for families and community is a defining dynamic in capitalist societies, particularly in the underdeveloped world.[12] Table 1 underscores the high under-five mortality rate as a consequence of the absence of formal education of mothers in the economically vulnerable countries of Africa and Asia.

It is unequivocal that with the onset of the modern technological age and the eruption of electronic communication and cheap labor regimes installed in most capitalist countries of Africa, Asia, Latin America and the Caribbean, the burden on women has been most adverse. In 2006, the International Labor Office reported that "excluding North Africa where women account for just 40 percent of informal workers, 60 percent or more of the developing world's [*sic*] working women are in informal employment (self-employment—mine) outside agriculture" and "in Africa, women's participation in this form of informal employment is nearly 85 percent; in Latin America the share is nearly 60 percent; and in Asia the figure is 65 percent, compared with 63 percent, 48 percent, and 65 percent of men, respectively."[13] In Bolivia, for example, women comprise 71 percent of the informal labor sector compared to 54 percent of men. Informal employment refers to that sector of the population that uses independent initiative to work as street vendors, traders, salespeople, etc., to support their families.

In the globalized Caribbean, a region long viewed as the "economic and

Under-five mortality rate and total fertility rate by mother's education level

In selected countries, most recent year available since 2005

Country	Survey year	Under-five mortality rate (per 1,000 live births)				Total fertility rate (births per woman)			
		No education	Primary	Secondary or higher	Overall	No education	Primary	Secondary or higher	Overall
Bangladesh	2007	93	73	52	74	3.0	2.9	2.5	2.7
Egypt	2008	44	38	26	33	3.4	3.2	3.0	3.0
Ethiopia	2005	139	111	54	132	6.1	5.1	2.0	5.4
Ghana	2008	103	88	67	85	6.0	4.9	3.0	4.0
India	2005/2006	106	78	49	85	3.6	2.6	2.1	2.7
Indonesia	2007	94	60	38	51	2.4	2.8	2.6	2.6
Liberia	2009	164	162	131	158	7.1	6.2	3.9	5.9
Mali	2006	223	176	102	215	7.0	6.3	3.8	6.6
Niger	2006	222	209	92	218	7.2	7.0	4.8	7.0
Nigeria	2008	210	159	107	171	7.3	6.5	4.2	5.7
Rwanda	2007/2008	174	127	43	135	6.1	5.7	3.8	5.5
Uganda	2006	164	145	91	144	7.7	7.2	4.4	6.7
Zambia	2007	144	146	105	137	8.2	7.1	3.9	6.2

Note: Data refer to the period 10 years before the survey year.
Source: Lutz and KC 2013.

Table 1: UN Development Report 2013

social backyard" by the U.S, while male unemployment has risen dramatically, women are coerced into the labor force and "become preferred employees" where they can be exploited further with non-unionized status, reduced wages, fewer benefits and part-time employment in line with the structures of the global economy. These conditions underscore that "the gendered aspects of labor are very much a part of economic globalization today."[14] Though the level of female participation in the labor force has jumped from 35 percent in 1980 to over 53 percent in the Caribbean in 2007, the bulk of these jobs have been low-paying and are often within the informal sector.[15] Over one-quarter of urban women employed in the Caribbean work in the service sector, making them very vulnerable to exploitative practices and low wages by transnational and local corporations.[16]

Economies of the Caribbean, like those of the rest of the Americas, were rooted in the forced depopulation and genocide of Indigenous Caribs, Arawaks and Taino peoples and the enslavement of Africans from the early 1500s. That legacy continues today in a system of globalized capitalist dependency on exports and the tourism industry that has had devastating effects on women's economic wherewithal since women are viewed as cheaper exploitable labor than their male counterparts. Since a small sector of farmers produced the bulk of agricultural exports, domestic agricultural and food production was left often to women. Many agricultural producers were single mothers who were forced into subsistence production to support their families, while higher prices for imported commodities "increased opportunities for petty commodity production and small-scale producers serving domestic markets."[17]

This chapter will delve into the dynamic of women's impoverishment, subjugation and marginalization by the forces of globalization, and include research on unionized workers in South Africa that I conducted from 2005 through 2010, specifically focusing on women's struggles in post-apartheid society.

The Economic and Social Exploitation of Women in the Underdeveloped World Intensified Through Globalization

One of the most critical areas in which globalization has taken a devastating toll on the lives of women has been that of global migration, as the demand for cheap labor by transnational corporations and the avarice for profit pursued by these entities has peaked. In a study on female migration of Asian women, Mana Oishi, a Japanese academic, avers that "the forces of globalization are increasing the demand for cheap and docile female labor in all regions," and from "1960 and 2000, the number of migrant women around the world increased more than twofold, from 35 million to 85 million; by 2000, women constituted 48.6 percent of the world's migrants," underscoring that global migration is no longer principally a male dynamic as in the past.[18]

Oishi describes this obsession on the part of capital as a globalized "race to the bottom," where countries in Asia, Africa, and Latin America are competing to offer large corporations the most genial conditions for exploitation of cheap female labor: unlimited repatriation of profits, ban on union organizing, non-permanent status for workers, and the protection of the interests of the corporations by the state.[19] Globalization has unleashed the forces of economic strangulation of women of color by compelling a climate of migration where families become fragmented and the mentality of the "survival of the fittest" reigns supreme. The demand for migrant women is also fueled by the globalized sex industry, which constitutes 1 percent of the Japanese Gross National Product for example, coercing hundreds of thousands of women, especially from Thailand, the Philippines, other Asian nations, Latin America, and Eastern Europe, into sex-related occupations. In Thekwini (Durban) in South Africa, while sports and entertainment corporations were gearing up for making lucrative profits from the World Cup being hosted in the country in 2010, the sex industry and trafficking in human flesh experienced an accompanying boom. One thousand neighboring Mozambican women were being smuggled into the country annually during the years leading to the World Cup for forced labor as sex slaves, and thousands more women from Thailand ended up being trapped in brothels around South Africa, all under the watchful eye of the South African authorities.[20] The sex industry in Thailand is one of the most notorious in the world, with over 35,000 young women and girls subjugated by debt bondage and controlled by prostitution syndicates like Always Prospering. This globalized sex-sale industry netted an estimated 42 billion baht ($1.7 billion) in income for Thailand in 2004.[21]

In Japan, the principal category for migration is "entertainment," a euphemism for the legalized enslavement of Asian migrant women, particularly serving the sexual needs of male corporate and business elites from all over the world. For instance, in 2003, 133,103 "entertainers" were admitted to Japan, the majority of whom were single women from the Philippines.[22] Most of these women are part of the trafficking in human sex slaves, a notorious industry from which globalization has derived billions of dollars in the intensification of the objectification and commodification of women. Though Japan has signed the UN Protocol to Prevent, Suppress and Punish Trafficking in Persons in 2002, the trade in young Asian women has grown.[23] Local Japanese authorities have also been involved in securing "foreign wives" for middle-aged rural farmers who have been rejected by younger Japanese women, akin to the "mail-order bride" system popular in North America and Europe.

Today, women and children are the largest grouping of migrants from Mexico into the U.S.[24] Migrant women are particularly susceptible to the vicissitudes of globalization's restructuring, which produces impoverishment of migrant women workers in the host country, concomitant with the erosion of the middle class in the same country. Rhacel Salazar Parreñas, who studied migrant Filipina domestic workers in Italy and Los Angeles, concluded that though these were different national contexts, there were significant parallels in the experiences of these migrant female workers. She notes that "parallels ... emerge from a particular process of globalization—global restructuring and its corresponding macroprocesses, which include but are not limited to the formation of the economic bloc of post-industrial nations, the feminization of labor, the unequal development of regions, the heightening of commodification in late capitalism, and the opposite turns of nationalism."[25] Women from the Cape Verde, an island off the coast of Senegal in West Africa, travel as far as Brazil, Portugal, and other countries in Africa to purchase goods and then sell them locally to enable families to economically survive, given globalization's scope across Africa and the world.[26] Globalization demands a pool of cheap urban labor and female migrant workers are the most susceptible targets since they desperately need to support their families and accept the subminimum wages.

Equally foreboding is the rapid commodification of migrant families so that the employer family can maintain its own family intimacy at the cost of the fragmentation of migrant families. This is implicit in the assumptions of globalization's countenance of migrant female workers for service work, where "the heightening of commodification is keenly illustrated by the global commodification of caretaking, which is a process that refers to the hierarchical chain of reproductive labor in globalization."[27]

In the rest of Asia, the anecdotes recounting the horrors of the exploitation of women's labor by transnational corporations from North America and Europe abound. Radhika Balakrishnan, a researcher on economic developments in Asia, recounts:

> In Thailand ... The woman we met ran a small shop in her backyard and all the workers were her neighbors. This was one of the rare instances where we were able to actually identify the retailer of the product. There was a price tag for a shop in the United States that sold plastic flowers. Each stem sold for $3.99 per stem in the United States (about 160 Thai Bhat at the time). The women got paid 1 bhat per stem. They worked long hours for a piece rate.... One of the women we met had been a weaver but had to stop weaving because it was strenuous, took too long, and she could not make a living.... It was interesting to observe the extent of the penetration of transnational capitalism. Far away from any urban center, a group of women sat in their backyards and made plastic flowers for a shop in the United States because weaving was no longer a viable way of making a living.[28]

Similarly, in the Philippines, mostly female garment workers work in poorly ventilated shops and factories with few benefits and social security, making designer labels for products sold in the United States. Most Filipino emigrants are now women and are often professional nurses, engineers, teachers, skilled managers, and administrators who are forced to migrate to seek employment abroad because the government urges such emigration to ensure lucrative repatriation of foreign worker earnings into the country. Eighty-seven percent of all remittances, some $5.9 billion in 1999, went to servicing the Filipino government's national debt through taxation of remittances.[29] For instance, in the health care sector, though the Filipino government spends millions in training nurses and other professional health care workers, 70 percent of nurses end up migrating for overseas jobs, with some large hospitals losing 10–12 nurses per month since 2001 because in recent years over 200 hospitals have been closed and another 800 are slotted for closure.[30] The predominance of female domestic Filipino labor for foreign lands, especially the U.S. and Europe, reinforces the exploitation of Filipino women based on gender and nationality.

In Gujarat, India, workers worked in factories that resembled assembly lines and were checked before they entered and as they left the work premises to ensure that they were not stealing. In Bangladesh, women were killed in a garment factory due to hazardous conditions and because doors were locked during an emergency.[31]

For a woman in Thailand to earn the equivalent of 2 U.S. pennies for making a stem for plastic flowers that's sold for $3.99 in the U.S, is the worst form of wage slavery! Daily, consumers in the U.S., Canada, Europe, and Japan particularly, spend billions of dollars in mammoth shopping malls, purchasing anything from underwear to jeans and electronic products like stereos, DVD and CD players, computers and iPods, all made by Asian or Latin American workers earning poverty slave-wages and operating under the most inhumane of working conditions, including no guarantee of wages and denial of maternity leave in many instances. It is hardly comforting to know that those among us owning Apple iPods, iPads, and iPhones purchased these products from Apple contracting with FoxConn in Chengdu, China, where 137 workers were injured in 2010 following use of a chemical to clean iPhone screens and in 2011, two explosions at iPad factories killed four people and injured 22, even though Apple had been warned of hazardous conditions at the plant by a Chinese human rights group earlier.[32] In January 2012, more than 150 workers in Shanghai threatened to commit suicide if they didn't received decent earnings for their labor at Apple, Hewlett-Packard, and Microsoft product factories, part of an inflammatory labor dispute that saw 45 workers resign in protest.[33] All of these obscene labor practices by Apple occurred as the electronics giant saw its market value climb to $500 billion in February 2012, the most valuable market-determined corporation in the world.[34]

These workers, like millions of others in Asia, Latin America, and Africa are enslaved by the profit-obsession syndrome of gargantuan transnational corporations like Nike, Reebok, Sony, Hanes, Liz Claiborne, Revlon, Levis, General Electric, Motorola, and countless others. The absurdity of this assembly line slavery is that the sub-contractors do not know in all situations where something is made. I purchased a Revlon nail-clipper from a grocery store in

Chicago in 2005 in which the plastic wrapping indicated "Made in China or Korea." Profit accumulation from poor women's exploitation on the part of these corporate exploiters is unconscionable. Like the pilots on U.S. fighter-bombers that dropped 15,000-pound bombs on "targets" that include women and children in Iraq and Afghanistan beginning in 2001 without viewing the carnage at close sight and then celebrating their military successes, corporate executives are far removed by thousands of miles and psychologically anesthetized to the slave conditions in the underdeveloped world that produce billions of dollars for their companies. The global system of capitalism makes billions from forced and enslaved labor, with the beneficiaries being the large corporations and the exploited being the people of color in Latin America, Asia, and Africa, and workers around the world. The consumers are middle-class citizens mostly in the wealthy Western metropole countries, many of whom justify this horror of enslavement as "economic opportunity" for poor and employed people. I witnessed this first-hand in the suburb of Wembley in the city of Pietermaritzburg in 2010 in Kwazulu, South Africa, where wealthy white householders employ Black women, including elderly women, as "domestic labor" and in many instances underpay and cheat these workers of their benefits.[35] During the chattel enslavement of Africans in the Americas for over three centuries, the enslaved Africans were assured of jobs ... as slaves. The same principle applies to the poor living in the 21st century.

In the Islamic world, especially in the Arab world, education for women is a right that many women do not enjoy. Haifaa Jawad, a lecturer in Middle East and Islamic Studies at Westhill College in Birmingham, England notes:

> Nothing substantial has been achieved, despite the fact that all Muslim countries have encouraged the spread of female education.... In 1991, the illiteracy rates among females in Afghanistan was 8 percent, in Pakistan 7 percent, in Egypt 66 percent and in Iran 56 percent. Although women's literacy varies enormously from country to country and also from area to area in any particular country, women in the Arab world are still a small minority among the student population.[36]

In Palestine, for instance, Shaddia el Sarraj asserts that "the percentage of women being educated at the elementary level is 44 percent that of men ... at the preparatory stage it is 38 percent, and at the secondary stage, 34 percent" and "between 33 and 56 percent of Palestinian women from fourteen to forty-four years of age are illiterate" (*Al Quds,* September 4, 1995).[37] In 2009, though literacy rates for adults aged 15 years and over were still high in the occupied Palestinian territories, women's literacy rates in 2009 were around 92 percent and those for men, 97 percent. To make matters worse, Palestinian women are the highest unemployed, up to 88 percent.

Women engage in challenging manual construction work in many parts of Africa, Asia, and Latin America, a labor sector that has intensified under the globalization regime. Women work in construction at a pilgrimage site in Gondar, Ethiopia (author's photograph).

In the Maghreb region of Africa, which includes Algeria, Tunisia, and Morocco, where ongoing anti-government unrest simmered in 2011, the illiteracy rate for women in 1990 was 64 percent, 43 percent, and 54 percent respectively.[38] In 1995, the rates of illiteracy for women were 51 percent in Algeria, 45.4 percent in Tunisia, and 69 percent, worsening in the case of Morocco.[39] In Algeria, a major oil producer, while the literacy of men was 81 percent for adults aged 15 years and over, for women the literacy rate was 64 percent in 2006. In Egypt, the literacy rate for the same group of adults was 75 percent for men and 58 percent for women in the same year. Though literacy rates for adults aged 15 years and over are relatively high in Iran, the literacy rate in 2009 was 81 percent for women and 89 percent for men. In Iraq, the differences were even more substantial in 2009, with literacy rates for the same group at 86 percent for men and 70 percent for women. In Jordan, male adult literacy rates for men at 95 percent were higher than those for women in 2007, which stood at 89 percent. In Lebanon in 2007, women's adult literacy rates stood at 86 percent, while those for adult men was 93 percent. Even in Libya, a country with the highest literacy on the African continent, women's literacy rates lagged behind that of men at 82 percent and 95 percent respectively in 2009.[40] In Syria, beset by a rebel movement funded and supported by the U.S. and other Western powers, the literacy rate for adult women was significantly lower than for men in 2009, 78 percent and 90 percent respectively. In Tunisia, the literacy rates for adults aged 15 years and over were 86 percent for men and 71 percent for women in 2008, while in Turkey, which prides itself on being a secular state with a predominant Muslim population, the lot for women is still generally below that of men, with literacy rates for women standing at 85 percent and 96 percent for men in 2009.[41]

In the Arab world "with the exception of the urban poor, rural women have historically been the most disadvantaged group of women in socio-economic terns."[42] The regimes of the Maghreb have generally reflected little concern for the rights of workers, let alone those of women workers, since the ruling establishments in each of these countries governs each country with an iron fist, with no attention to either participatory democracy or justice. Gender disparities in a key area of life quality like literacy run rampant throughout the Arab world and in most parts of Africa and Asia, and globalization has not undermined that patriarchal cultural trend either.

In the Egyptian context, Noha El Mikawy, like Mohau Pheko in South Africa, criticizes those stalwarts of globalization who claim that it will "connect an economy to the international market, bring in capital and increase employment" and repudiates those economists who sanguinely reify the experiences of women in the informal sector as "signs of economic vitality and capital formation/accumulation."[43] She argues that research has demonstrated that this sense of economic empowerment is mythic because such informal sectors are publicly unregulated and can actually exacerbate the fragmentation of women's work and value and compound their political marginalization.[44]

Egypt was forced to accept the bitter pill of structural adjustment, where it was required to radically scale down the public sector from the 1980s and early 1990s, so that in 1995, just 43.2 percent of women were employed. Today, that figure has now fallen drastically, forcing women to seek employment in the private sector where educational qualifications are not always the determining factor in employment, unlike in the state sector. Female unemployment has thus skyrocketed in Egypt, creating significant hardships for families. In the area of agriculture, one-quarter are unpaid workers, rendering them even more vulnerable to socio-economic changes.[45] The massive uprisings against the Mubarak regime that unfolded early in 2011 were sparked by growing impoverishment of rural people and the economic vacuum precipitated by increased urban unemployment and skyrocketing prices of food and essential goods.[46] It is indeed ironic within the Islamic world that "civilized" Europe from the presence of the Moors in Spain from the 8th century CE, where "'Europe' (itself a problematic category) absorbed all manner of ideas from 'other' cultural complexes, notably from predominantly Islamic societies," is now recasting these "European" traditions into its contemporary social and political institutions.[47] Globalization may end in self-destruction anyway, because there is no cultural core to it and it depends on an extractionist economics and snippets of world cultures. Western Europe, after all, has produced nothing of lasting historical significance save its 500-year imperialist colonization of the world that is now fast drawing to a close.

In much of Africa, women bear the brunt of poverty, illiteracy, and war. Forty-four percent of Africa is poor, mostly women, living below the poverty datum line of $39 per month.[48] The majority of those who are illiterate in Africa are women, in a continent where the overall literacy rate is an astoundingly low 50 percent.[49] The impact of globalization, especially forced privatization of vital public sector services and particularly on African women, is astounding:

> The economic and social costs of liquidation, rehabilitation and privatization of the public sector in Africa are immeasurable. They are all associated with a contraction of output; massive job losses and falling incomes. This is particularly true for women and other low-skilled workers who are mostly government and public

sector employees. This explains, among other things, why women in the labor force have decreased from 57 percent in 1970 to 53 percent in 1990.[50]

While the Scandinavian countries continue to maintain state-run industries, the same Western powers, in a paternalistic stroke, insist that African industries and institutions are unproductive and problematic because they are administered by the state and must therefore be privatized. The net result has been the essential opening up of all protected national industries in Africa to powerful transnational corporations with roots mostly in Western Europe, North America or East Asia, further disempowering working class women.[51] Most women lack access to basic facilities in health care, credit opportunities, clean drinking water, adequate sanitation provisions, food, land, and transportation, since they are most often located in rural areas. Most of Africa, like most of Asia and significant portions of rural Latin America, lacks adequate sanitation, part of the 2.5 billion people suffering such deprivation in the world. African women, like their counterparts in other parts of the world, are often subject to sexual harassment and assault as the result of seeking toilet facilities away from the security of their homes, where they are often nonexistent. The rape of two young women in India in May 2014, highlighted this excruciating reality for impoverished women in particular, part of the 1 billion people who have no toilet facilities in a world of globalized "civilization."[52] Neo-liberalist regimes in the underdeveloped world generally ignore the rural sector in their overall programs of "development," exacerbating conditions of violence against rural women.

Mohau Pheko, a South African/Azania activist and analyst, laments the cooperative stance that African regimes have adopted vis-à-vis globalization, describing the heavy toll that liberalization has taken on all poor people, especially women, as "a site of Terrorism and Violence Against Women":

> Our country's response has been to apply export-led economies, cut budget deficits, so that the bulk of national budgets is spent in paying debt, an increase in monetary policies, lifting of exchange controls, lifting of trade tariffs, and a creation of free-trade zones.
> This era of trade liberalization promotes gender-blind policies that undermine the socio-economic rights of women. In South Africa, there appears to be a township romance, where women's lives have been used to show how resilient they are to poverty, and because of this, policies are made that glorify women selling meat in boxes on the sidewalks of our streets, calling this empowerment.[53]

During my field work interviewing workers from the South African Clothing and Textile Workers Union in Port Elizabeth and Cape Town, South Africa, in July 2006, especially women, the message was unequivocal: globalization has been the principal factor that has impoverished workers in general and women in particular.

With the flooding of the South African textile markets with cheaper imports from countries like China and Korea, over 120,000 textile workers in Cape Town, mostly women, lost their jobs from 1998 through 2006, producing a steady social disintegration that took its deadliest toll on working class Black families in the Western Cape. Interviews with trade unionists revealed a virtual collapse of vital public services such as health care and education, so that ill persons who did not possess private health insurance were forced to assemble at 4:00 a.m. outside public hospitals in Cape Town to be seen the same day.[54] Public schools were routinely underfunded, undersupplied and overcrowded, with dropout rates in the thousands around South Africa. Workers who could not afford to send their children to "Model C schools" (formerly white-only schools) were forced to have their children attend dilapidated and fast deteriorating public schools. Academic success in impoverished public schools was generally remote and part of an economic downward spiral for young Black people.

Mauritius, an island nation off the southeastern coast of Africa, has long been seen as a stable country influenced heavily by Western metropolitan culture and characterized by Export-oriented Free Trade Zones since the late 1970s. While women see work outside the home as a liberating experience, considering the strong patriarchal traditions of the country, they nevertheless find themselves at the bottom-most rung of the socio-economic ladder, holding mostly unskilled and the lowest paid jobs in the large textile and garment workers sector.[55] During the Asian economic crisis in 1997–1998, women workers in the textile industry were the first to be laid off. The unemployment of women in Mauritius grew from 9.2 percent in 2000 to 14.4 percent in 2007 as a result of factories and assembly plants in Mauritius hiring cheaper workers from China and Bangladesh and laborsaving technologies institutionalized during the globalization era.[56]

Globalization is thus viewed by Africans as the "supreme stage of Western imperialism," argues Yassine Fall, the Executive Secretary of the African Association of Women for Research and Development, and "another state of the process of capital accumulation and expansion and concentration in the hands of a few."[57] Notwithstanding the cornucopia of works on globalization's benefits, the core function for impoverished people is unassailable: the accumulation of capital through coerced and exploitative labor, using neo-liberal ideology and deceptive corporate terminologies like "prosperity," "economic boom," and "industrial expansion." It comes as no surprise, then, when African womanist activists view the spread of the HIV virus and the AIDS pandemic in Africa, and now increasingly in Asia, as part of the designs of global capitalism in its designs and effects that decimate impoverished communities while preserving the extraction of vital resources needed for the engines of Western industrialism. *Why do all African regimes earmark little funding for health care and AIDS treatment when AIDS is a continent-wide pandemic along with malaria, tuberculosis, and, now increasingly, cancer?* Sisonke Msimang, a South African activist involved in gender justice issues and in HIV/AIDS prevention, caustically elaborates on the scheme that perpetuates the AIDS pandemic, warranting the detailed citation:

> If there was a recipe for creating an AIDS epidemic in Southern Africa, it would read as follows: Steal some land and subjugate its people. Take some men from rural areas and put them in hostels far away from home, in different countries, if need be. Build excellent roads. Ensure that the communities surrounding the men are impoverished so that a ring of sex workers develops around each mining town. Add HIV. Now take some miners and send them for holidays to their rural, uninfected wives. Add a few girlfriends in communities along the road home.
>
> Add liberal amounts of patriarchy, both home-grown and of the colonial variety. Ensure that women have no right to determine the conditions under which sex will take place. Make sure that they have no access to credit, education, or any of the measures that would give them options to leave unhappy unions, or dream of lives in which men are not the centre of their activities. Shake well and watch an epidemic explode.
>
> There's an optional part of the recipe, which adds an extra spice to the pot: African countries on average spend four times more on debt servicing than they do on health. Throw in a bit of World Bank propaganda, some loans from the IMF and beat well. Voila. We have icing on the cake.[58]

There is no question that the explosion of the sex worker industry, attributable largely to exacerbated conditions of impoverishment of women due to globalization's impact on rural economies, is another major factor in the spread of the AIDS virus in Africa and other parts of the underdeveloped world. Marjorie Mbilinyi, a Tanzanian educator, observes in her study on the effects of globalization and structural adjustment policies, and on so-called debt cancellation of the Heavily Indebted Poor Countries (HIPC), that

> increased poverty and rural-urban migration have also led to increased sex work among women and men and children, which is partly associated with the rise of sex tourism and expatriate workers in most countries.... Many others turn to sex work as an escape from low pay, harsh working conditions and sexual harassment experienced in domestic service, the other main job "opportunity" available for young rural girls in town.[59]

It is not a conundrum when it comes to understanding the AIDS pandemic, especially in Africa. In South Africa, Africa's wealthiest country, the Women's

Health Project reported that in 1998, "20 percent of African households live[d] in a single room and 46 percent live[d] in three or fewer rooms, while half of these households lacked proper sanitation facilities, adequate water and indoor toilets."[60] The propagation of the AIDS virus is clearly facilitated under such poverty-stricken conditions, ironic in a land where gold, copper, diamond, platinum, and coal mining is the mainstay of the capitalist economy. Fifty-eight percent of all AIDS cases in Africa are women and half of those infected in other parts of the world are female.[61] Black people who are rooted in collective Africana cultures globally are particularly susceptible to HIV/ AIDS in a globalized world where unhealthy side orty-fourendeveloping world's (effects of industrialism, stress from unemployment and economic depression, pervasively poor diets from processed genetically-modified food, sedentary lifestyles, and overcrowded urban conditions facilitate the radical weakening of human immune systems. Half of those suffering from HIV/ AIDS in the U.S., for example, are Black women. According to the Phoenix Birthing Project, Black women in Maricopa County in the state of Arizona experience 16.1 times the rate of HIV infection compared to white women.[62]

Western financial institutions, corporations, and governments are fully aware of the dynamic transpiring around globalization, intensified poverty, and the spread of AIDS as the result of the expanding sex worker industry and the crippling effect particularly on women. Many still insist that African women and men are promiscuous by culture, as part of a racist rationalization, and demand that African governments reduce public health care services in order to pay for "debts" incurred to the West, knowing quite well that African women and children are the most vulnerable to illness and death in this scenario. Western governments and corporations are fully aware of the decimating nature of the HIV/AIDS pandemic on the African continent, particularly in the manner that it has affected millions of women, so that children are now being orphaned routinely with deaths of parents from AIDS in places like South Africa, Zambia, Zimbabwe, Uganda, and Kenya. This is precisely why AIDS is sometimes viewed as a form of *socio-biological* warfare waged by the forces of globalization against African people, a legacy of the system of colonialism that willfully gave smallpox infected blankets to Indigenous people in North America in the 19th century knowing that it would annihilate a people who lacked immunity against viruses stemming and transmitted from the unhygienic conditions in Europe in the 18th and 19th centuries.[63] In the U.S. in 1801, Thomas Jefferson exposed hundreds of enslaved Africans to an unused smallpox vaccine before it was administered to whites, medical researchers deliberately infected Black male sharecroppers with syphilis in the southern

U.S. in the 1930s through the Tuskegee experiments, involuntarily sterilized Indigenous Indian, Black, and Puerto Rican women in the 1960s and 1970s, experimented on Black prisoners and military personnel, used African American and Black Dominican boys for drug experiments that investigated disruptive behavior, and infected over 700 Guatemalan prisoners with gonorrhea and syphilis in the late 1940s.[64] If Western corporations and governments are so concerned about the humanitarian catastrophe resulting from the AIDS crisis, why is it that anti-retroviral drugs that have successfully slowed the disease in many Western nations have not been provided free or at low-cost to a continent that is economically ravaged and deeply impoverished? Why did Western pharmaceutical corporations and the U.S. government under former president Bill Clinton threaten the South African government with legal sanctions for potentially violating pharmaceutical patent law if South Africa proceeded to purchase anti-retroviral drugs at much cheaper rates from India and Brazil in the late 1990s? Would the same treatment and level of insouciant engagement be accorded to nations or peoples in Europe where people are literally humiliated and forced into begging for antidotes and medicines to save them from premature death? These occurrences make one wonder too about the reasons that individuals within the U.S. medical research sector resurrected the flu virus in June 2014 after receiving approval from the federal government following a year-long moratorium on such research because of fears that the virus could spread uncontrollably.[65] The flu virus killed 50 million people in 1918 and contains strains similar to that of the H5N1 virus or Avian flu that has killed 386 people since 2003 and seriously threatened people's lives in Asia and Africa in recent years.[66] The eruption of the Ebola virus at the Kekema Hospital first in Sierra Leone in August 2014, where researchers from Tulane University and the U.S. Army Medical Research Institute of Infectious Diseases (USAMRIID) were conducting tests on patients and then immediately asked by the Sierra Leonian government to stop after patients started dying, raises many questions about bio-weapons research in densely populated areas of the world like West Africa.[67]

What is palpable in the dynamic of capitalist coercion in the eon of globalization is the corporations whose homes reside in the U.S., Europe, or Japan, but outsource their production in countries that are ruled by regimes controlled by and subservient to global capitalist forces, particularly found in Asia, Latin America, and Africa.[68] Female labor assures the maximization of profits on the basis of gender, race, and class. Valentine Moghadam observes that due to economic restructuring of the global economy, unemployment rates for women soared in Malaysia in the mid 1980s, "Vietnam in the late

1980s, Poland, Bulgaria, and Russia in the early 1990s, and Morocco, Tunisia, and Turkey in the latter part of the 1990s."[69] In the late 1990s, women workers in South Korea, Thailand and Indonesia experienced job erosion more severely than men, and in the case of Korea, twice that of men.[70]

Moghadam concludes that the "feminization of unemployment, therefore, is as much a characteristic of the global economy as is the feminization of labor."[71] What Moghadam implies, but does not accentuate, is the fact that women are the preferred labor force by capital because they are the most exploitable on the grounds of gender, an exploitation that is compounded many times when they are Black or Brown women. Under globalization, women's levels of employment have dropped, as unemployment of workers has grown round the world, owing to the hegemonic role of industrial, commercial, and financial automation in late capitalism. Capitalism's sole purpose is agglomeration of profits, and cutting labor costs often becomes the easiest route in the age of globalized automation. The same principle applied to the rationale for Ford Motor Company, for instance, eliminating 32,800 employees at its North American plants as a "cost-cutting" measure from 2006 through 2012 principally to make "operations profitable," even though other reasons may be cited by corporate executives.[72] Capitalism views humans essentially as workers and profit-makers for the ruling classes of the world.

Capital financiers claim that micro-finance has been effective in addressing under-financing of impoverished farmers, businesses, and organizations in the underdeveloped world, where small loans are given to certain women entrepreneurs from the working classes to begin small businesses that could grow eventually into economically viable larger ones based on the assistance of start-up capital. However, there are lingering questions about the actual effectiveness of these micro-finance schemes. Finance liberalization that entails deregulation of interest rates, removal of subsidies, privatization of government-owned banks, and use of market-based instruments to determine monetary policy, empowers the market to decide who receives credit and how much. Yet such liberalization has hardly resulted in the working classes and poor becoming more prosperous and economically independent. Instead, poverty conditions have become aggravated as globalized financial forces have favored the powerful and disregarded the poor, making life much more difficult for the latter through accruing of debt. Microfinancing involves extending loans to millions of poor people. In Bangladesh, 6 million received loans through the Grameen Bank in 2006, and most are now drowning in debt as a result of the sputtering national and global economy with little financial ability to repay such debit without incurring exorbitant rates of interest.[73] This level of strangulating debt exists in the U.S., with a crippling $1.1 trillion of student loan debt and U.S. credit card holders finding themselves mired in $854.2 billion as of April 2014.[74]

Kavaljit Singh, a researcher who is the Founder and Director of the Public Interest Research Centre in New Delhi, India, argues, "the paradox of globalization is that it unifies and integrates the rich and affluent classes while marginalizing the poor masses who lack requisite skills and resources to profit from world markets."[75] For women who are supposedly beneficiaries of microfinancing since the onset of globalization, the results have been anything but successful. Singh's research on microfinance's programs in Bangladesh is palpable, underscoring the contradictory financial and political assumptions of the programs with the objective of economically empowering poor women. He explains that the programs run by the Grameen Bank (world renowned for its supposed success in microfinancing small business enterprise) not only do not reach the poorest of the poor, but place undue stress on borrowers by increasing debt liability several-fold. Most of the loan monies are often used to pay for essential items of food and education as opposed to investment in business since cash availability for borrowers is extremely low.[76]

So much for the World Bank's and the IMF's ostensible philanthropic concern for poor women! The contradiction lies in these financial institutions' insistence that the state remove itself from economic and financial decisions and leave such matters to the directives of the market. Concomitantly, these institutions demand that states reduce allocations for vital public service sectors such as food subsidies, health, education, and housing. The irony is that poor women are forced to spend the loans received under microfinance schemes to pay for these vital services that are non-existent or severely impaired in many instances due to underfunding as a result of globalization's liberalization requirements for such loans.

In Latin America in the mid–1990s, the World Bank was compelled to acknowledge that globalization's tendencies, endemic to the capitalist system, have induced high rates of poverty, particularly for women, where women are 34 percent more likely to find them themselves trapped in the lower 20 percent of income levels, compared to a 15 percent probability for men.[77] In Honduras and Venezuela in 1990 for example, urban poverty rates for female-headed households were 79.7 percent and 42.6 percent respectively, compared to rural poverty rates for female-headed households of 42.6 percent and 51.2 percent respectively.[78] By 2009, few radical changes in terms of female poverty were evidenced. Poverty for women was 1.15 times greater than for men and 1.7 times higher for children under 15 than adults. In its November 2009 report, the UN Economic Commission for Latin America and the Caribbean noted that

> exposure to poverty among women is higher than for men in the entire region and is significantly greater in Panama (1.37 times higher), Costa Rica (1.30 times), the Dominican Republic (1.25 times), Chile (1.24 times) and Uruguay (1.21 times greater). In 13 out of 18 countries this pattern worsened between 2002 and 2008.[79]

The ECLAC report observed that unpaid women's labor at home and on child-care, along with a stratified paid workforce that generally favors men over women, were the biggest factors responsible for women's higher level of poverty. In Uruguay, for example, women spent an average of 5 hours per day on unpaid domestic work, while in Guatemala, women worked an average of 7 hours daily and received no compensation.[80]

In Latin American rural areas, with the exception of socialist Cuba,

> Illiteracy rates in rural areas, an indirect indicator of vulnerability to poverty, are generally higher for women than for men, and are considerably higher for rural women than for their urban counterparts. The hours worked and number of women working seems to have intensified in rural areas and within domestic units themselves, without a commensurate increase in access to education.[81]

In revolutionary and socialist Cuba, "women workers are guaranteed equal pay for equal work, paid vacations and maternity benefits, and a much wider array of support is found than in capitalist societies."[82]

The U.S.–based Dole corporation, which makes its profits off the sweat and labor of workers of color all over Latin America and in Hawaii, continues to force mostly women workers among the 100,000 Colombian flower plantation workers to work overtime to produce thousands of flowers for Valentine's Day for grocery stores and flower vendors across the U.S., even while requiring those same workers to spray pesticides on the flowers. Women workers in these plantations resultantly suffer disproportionately high miscarriages, headaches, nausea, congenital abnormality and neurological complications.[83] It is no coincidence that Dole has been cited for using the hormone-harming pesticide dibromochloropropane (DBCP) on its Nicaraguan banana plantations and exposing workers to poisonous effects including sterility in males, refusing to provide safety equipment for workers or medical treatment for those effected.[84] In September 2012, the author and members of the Global Alliance for Justice heard moving testimonies from female banana workers who worked for the Dole Food Company (the largest fresh fruit and vegetables producer in the world with $6.9 billion in revenues in 2010), Chiquita, Dow Chemical, and the Standard Fruit Company. Anecdotes recounted gruesome experiences of families of workers suffering from abnormal growths and documented cases of children of workers born deaf, blind, sterile, or deformed as a result of working in the fields sprayed by toxic chemicals like Roundup and Nemagon, the latter which has been banned in the U.S.[85] Other corporations like Chevron and Shell also used such lethal chemicals and along with the fruit companies attempted to force workers to sign liability waivers by bribing worker leaders. Also, 2,520 workers have died from toxic chemical effects, according to Cecilia Leonardo from the Nicaraguan Union of Banana Workers.[86] This is corporate globalization at work in Latin America! Anti-exploitation activists have advocated a boycott of Dole Flowers and all products made by the Dole Food Company, morally appropriate action that U.S. consumers can take to undermine globalization's violence against women workers as perpetrated by the Dole Food Company and in solidarity with Nicaraguan banana workers.

In the Caribbean, the most important development in globalization's drive has been the activation of the Economic Processing Zones, originally put in place in 1970 in the policy called the Caribbean Basin Initiative in 1983 and subsequently in 1990 under the Caribbean Basin Initiative II, instituted under Ronald Reagan and George H. Bush respectively. It was not for philanthropic reasons, to "diversify and expand the economic lease, increase employment, and increase the foreign exchange earnings," but simply because the U.S. received a favorable trade surplus of $2.6 billion over the period 1985–1995, compared to massive U.S. trade deficits with other nations during that time, specifically China.[87]

Research conducted by the Centre for Gender and Development at the University of the West Indies in Mona, Jamaica, reveals that micro-business undertaken by women generally tend to be smaller in Jamaica, for instance, both with regard to start-up capital and employment size. Women consequently generally operate in the least-profitable micro-business enterprises and receive meager incomes, exacerbating economic dependence and vulnerability.[88] The 1985 Economic and Social Survey of Jamaica noted that women were particularly affected by structural adjustment and privatization policies (SAPs). From 1972 through 1989, almost one-third of all employed women in the country were self-employed.[89] This was largely the result of SAP's, since the state sector was required to scale down employment, the manufacturing sector was hit, prices of export commodities dropped, and private capital investments did not create wide scale employment opportunities for women and men. The reality of the suffering of women has worsened since the late 1990s and into the new millennium:

In late 1998, Jamaica's booming financial sector, which represented the major engine of growth during the decade, almost totally collapsed.... Although women now achieve higher educational levels than men, they remain relatively underpaid and underemployed ... the crisis in the financial sector and the widespread downsizing of companies have resulted in massive layoffs, leaving many women unemployed, including those in supervisory and middle management positions.[90]

The view that Economic Processing Zones (EPZs) have been good for countries like the Dominican Republic where they employed 170,000 in 2000, mostly in textiles for the U.S. market, with Dominican workers, including many women, still earning one sixth of what U.S. workers make in the textiles sector because the zones contributed toward "job creation, export increase, and foreign currency generation" as some "experts" have argued, is not persuasive nor ethically viable.[91] In actuality, the real hourly minimum wage in the Dominican Republic dropped by 62.3 percent between 1984 and 1990, and unemployment continues to be higher for women than for men, hovering around 26 percent.[92]

Caribbean nations were particularly affected by the passage of the North American Free Trade Agreement (NAFTA) since it "undermined the Caribbean Basin initiative of trade preferences for Caribbean countries" as agreed to by the U.S.[93] Caribbean textile workers were unable to compete with competition from Mexico for instance. Textile and garment workers in Jamaica and the Dominican Republic were the hardest hit, and 9,000 textile jobs were lost in Jamaica in 1994 as a result. Female banana plantation workers in the Windward Islands of the Caribbean experienced hardship during the dismantling of preferential trade agreements on bananas for Caribbean growers since they faced stiff competition from U.S.–based banana exporting companies like Chiquita and Dole in Latin America in the early part of the millennium. The net result was that Caribbean agricultural women workers in particular were unable to challenge the supremacy of the large agribusiness companies from the U.S. and many lost their jobs, saw significantly reduced incomes, and struggled even harder to support their families when they were the sole breadwinners.[94]

The 2001 film documentary, *Life and Debt*, powerfully demonstrated in its depiction of globalized Jamaica that the EPZs are directed toward one objective alone: maximizing profits at the cost of the exploitation of workers, mostly female, with little benefit to the indigenous Jamaican producers and the Jamaican economy.[95] The beneficiaries of foreign currency revenues in such situations, be they in the Dominican Republic or Jamaica or any other country in the Caribbean for that matter, are mainly U.S. corporations and local bureaucrats who function to maintain these countries' dependence on export services and tourism that provide little basis to develop the resources of Caribbean countries for national economic benefit and sustainability. These EPZs confine Caribbean workers to service roles; essentially slaves who produce goods for the powerful North, with no power and dignity to produce goods that meet their local need and build their home nations. The conditions of long working hours, few breaks, and overcrowding of workers in assembly line settings who are subject to searches at the end of each day, are particularly humiliating for workers, especially women. EPZs reflect essentially racist and sexist policies by U.S. policy makers working for profit-greedy transnationals who view the Caribbean as a backyard where slave labor and paltry wages for Black people are acceptable and where surplus U.S. goods can be dumped, graphically illustrated in *Life and Debt.*

It is important to highlight too that women are generally disadvantaged and victimized by breakthroughs in biotechnology and other computer-aided technology in manufacturing and information technology in the service sector, principally because these technologies are male-biased and oriented. Cyber-culture is generally male-biased and oriented because far fewer women have access to computers and the Internet due to having to work in household settings (cooking, addressing children's needs, etc.) and thus comparatively have less exposure to benefits from these technological mediums.[96]

Women in the underdeveloped world, particularly rural and tradition-practicing women, face increased marginalization as the result of the WTO agreement on Trade Related Aspects of Intellectual Property Rights (TRIPS). Women's knowledge on biodiversity, Indigenous health and medical knowledge are subjugated by piracy practices by the large pharmaceutical corporations. Women are unable to pay royalties to large corporations like Monsanto, Dow, Du Pont and other biotech corporations for improved biogenetic seeds since they have lost rights over their traditional medicinal knowledge to large corporations, although they are the original seed keepers on earth. These biotech corporations now claim that such seeds are their exclusive property after they had pirated this traditional knowledge.[97] Similarly, the depletion of forests and other natural resources intensifies the suffering of women, including in areas of fishing and aquaculture in places like India. Vandana Shiva, an environmental feminist activist from India, declares that "GNP and growth in international trade is becoming increasingly a measure of how real wealth— the wealth of nature and the life-sustaining wealth produced by women—is rapidly decreasing" since "when trade in commodities is treated as the only economic activity, it destroys the potential of nature and women to produce life, goods, and services for basic needs."[98]

Globalization's Impact on Women in the U.S.

Within the U.S., working class women generally and women of color in particular experience comparable levels of disempowerment and exploitation to their sisters in the underdeveloped world. The statistics are disturbing and serve as a reminder of the pathological effects of globalization in areas of race, class, and gender. In the 1990s

> almost 30 percent of all African Americans and Latinos and Latinas live in poverty, whereas only 10 percent of whites do. This number includes almost half of all African American children and more than one-third of Latino and Latina children. The poverty rates calculated for children living in households headed by women are even more dramatic. Two-thirds of African American and Latino and Latina children in families headed by single mothers live in poverty (compared with 20 percent of white children in such families).[99]

The expansion of the services sector of the U.S. economy that began in the 1980s and stagnated in the 1990s with the onset of globalization had dire implications for Black women, where "by the 1990s, some predicted changes with negative impacts for Black women had already occurred," and job losses in manufacturing, bankruptcy in real estate, insurance, and transportation intensified job layoffs in the thousands.[100] The 2008 recession has made it particularly difficult for all sectors of workers, including blue-collar workers across the spectrum, with job losses of 8.4 million between 2007 and 2010. Black female mortgage holders were the most susceptible to the sub-prime mortgage lending crisis of 2008.[101]

For Indigenous women in the U.S. who face increased marginalization on scattered "reservations" around the country, economic hardship is akin to that of women in the underdeveloped world. Unemployment in communities like Rosebud and Pine Ridge in South Dakota is a staggering 70 percent. The average family income in these communities is under $3,000 per year, with women bearing the brunt of poverty-stricken conditions, lack of access to health care, and unemployment.[102] Women shockingly have a life expectancy of 52 years and men 48 years. Elderly women are subject to the vagaries of climate change, especially in frigid winters in South Dakota where temperatures drop to 30 below zero and many women suffer or die from hypothermia. In the Indigenous community of 24,000 families at Pine Ridge, poverty runs rampant. Ninety-seven percent of the families fall below the U.S. Department of Health and Human Services definition of poverty, where tuberculosis rates for the Lakota are 533 percent higher than non–Indian people for tuberculosis, 249 percent for diabetes, and 71 percent for influenza.[103] These Indigenous people, the Original Caretakers of this land, live at levels similar to the impoverished people of Haiti, the poorest country in the Western hemisphere.

Today, the equation of womanhood with poverty in the world, including the U.S., is not hyperbolic. While the ruling class euphorically claims that *the land of the free and home of the brave is the land of opportunity for all*, women, especially poor women of color, experience the brunt of the absence of opportunity, economic deprivation, and social degradation. Of the 36 million U.S. citizens, 13 percent of the population, living below the poverty line in 2004, 80 percent of the adult poor were women.[104]

> Poverty is not equally distributed across the U.S. population: 9 percent of white Americans, 23 percent of African Americans, 21 percent of Latino/as, 10 percent of Asian Americans and 30 percent of Native Americans live in poverty (U.S. Census Bureau, 2002). Poverty is particularly concentrated among single-women heads-of-household, that is among women who are raising their children alone: 22 percent white, 35 percent Black, 37 percent Latina, and 15 percent Asian American women heads-of-household live on incomes below the poverty line, which the federal government set at U.S.$8,890 for a single individual and U.S.$18,400 for a family of four in 2004. The kind of poverty experienced by women household heads is acute: more than half are living with income less than 50 percent of the official poverty level.[105]

Poverty exists not merely because of the absence of employment or insufficient wages. According to the minimum wage in the U.S. for 2004, $5.15 per hour, a person working full-time would earn an annual salary of U.S.$10,700. The minimum wage workforce in the U.S. is made up of 61 percent women and more than 50 percent of these women have children. A person who works 40 hours per week for one year with two weeks unpaid vacation and is paid the minimum wage of U.S.$5.15 per hour will earn U.S.$1,400 less than the governmental established poverty line if she has one child to support. If the same woman had three children instead of one, her salary would be U.S.$7,700 less than the poverty line.[106] Though the minimum wage was raised to $7.25 from July 2009, the minuscule increase in no way accounts for the steady increase in inflation, particularly the growth of the price of food. Food prices rose 0.1 percent in February 2014 and again by a whopping 1.1 percent in March, marking the largest increase in the first half of the year, particularly because of the entrenched drought in Western food-producing states like California.[107] Boxed meat prices experienced their greatest jump since August 1980.

What is most deceptive about official U.S. Census figures in this regard, of course, is the manner that official poverty levels are determined. It is indeed absurd to expect a family of four to survive on $18,400 per year. How many U.S. congresspersons or senators would be prepared to live on such meager annual salaries? Yet the same political ruling class slashed social welfare programs that benefit the working poor and all impoverished people, particularly women and children, by over $36 billion in early 2006.

Half of all the poor population in the U.S. are children. The Economic Policy Institute (EPI) that studies the effects of U.S. government policy on economy and society indicated in 2004 that it would require an annual income of $27,000 per year to afford a two-bedroom apartment and meet basic living needs in a rural community, and $52,000 per year to receive the same minimal standard of living in an urban area in that year.[108] For 2013, the EPI budget calculator estimated that a basic family budget for a modest standard of living for a two-parent family with two children varies from $48,166 in Marshall County, Mississippi to $94,676 for New York City.[109] For a median income area like Topeka, Kansas, a similar family needs about $63,364 to live at a decent social level, well above the $23,283 determined as the 2012 poverty level for a two-parent, two-children family in that area.[110] The governmental poverty level for families in 2013 was well below the actual income needed to maintain a stable family household, considering fundamental costs of housing, food, transportation, children's education, health care, utilities, and other basic services. Working class women particularly are most adversely affected since they generally fall at the bottom end of socio-economic ladders and income levels given strictures of class and gender.

Almost one-quarter of U.S. workers earn less than $8.23 per hour, or $16,640 per year, many of them women with children. Globalization's underlying philosophy and its discourse of neo-liberalism claims that the poor "sponge off" the system and need to work hard to realize the American dream, and are thus undeserving of any safety net that may prevent them from falling deeper into or remaining within the ranks of poverty. The poor are punished because they are mostly female and children, many being persons of color. When then liberal Democratic president Bill Clinton promised to reform "welfare as we know it," he did exactly that, reforming it so that it penalized poor, working women in its "reform." According to Pamela Loprest, a researcher with the Urban Institute, welfare leavers are often

> concentrated in low-wage entry level work; work night hours; often have multiple jobs; and struggle with child care.... Most lack health insurance and the median hourly wage of welfare leavers is $6.61. Although this was substantially higher than the minimum wage at that time (1997–mine) ($4.75) ... it is in the twentieth percentile of hourly wages for all workers ... on an annualized basis, the median earnings of leavers, in 1997, was $13,778, which was roughly the line for a family of three. This does not take into account other sources of income, such as child support or the Earned Income Tax Credit. Substantial numbers of leavers report serious

problems providing food and rent. The poorest 20 percent of these families lost more in welfare benefits—almost $1,400 per family—than they gained in earnings.[111]

What is also disconcerting is the manner in which globalization and the changing nature of capital in the U.S. have caused tremendous shifts in families, particularly families with children. In 1970, while married families with children were 40.3 percent of all families, the percentage of families with children today has halved to 24.1 percent. For couples without children, the rate of working wives rose from 42 percent in 1970 to 60 percent in 2000. From 1969 through 2000, single parent households increased from 6 percent to 31 percent of families, and single-parent households increased from 17 percent to 25 percent.[112] These are average statistics for the national U.S. population of families; statistics for Indigenous, African American, Latino/a, and Asian American families slightly differ, with Indigenous, Black and Latino/a families having higher rates of single-parent households overall.

When illuminating the subject of poverty, one would be remiss to overlook the question of the intensification of women's incarceration in the U.S. With the onset of globalization and the U.S. "War on Drugs," essentially a smokescreen for the "War on the Poor" from the 1980s through the present, many people of color, disproportionately female, were targeted by law enforcement for arrest for petty non-violent crimes. From 1982 to 1991, the number of women arrested for drug offenses increased by 89 percent and those who were incarcerated grew 43 percent, from 24,180 to 130,430 between 1980 and 1996.[113] In 1991, most women who were imprisoned were poor and of color, with 5 percent unemployed and 32 percent separated or divorced. Most women in prison have suffered a history of physical or sexual abuse, mental illness, or substance abuse, with the average age around thirty-one years.[114]

It is germane to note that violence against and objectification of women is heavily promoted by dominant globalized media corporations through television programs on MTV and Black Entertainment Television (BET). The distorted image of women reduced to beings for male sexual gratification is intrinsic to the culture of profit maximization under globalization and perpetuates the subjugation of women on grounds of gender, race, and class. Pancho McFarland, a teacher of Chicano/a culture, expresses the scandalous character of the contemporary music and entertainment industry that is determined to prostitute Black, Latina/o culture for monetary accumulation:

> Rap lyrics and videos often present women as mere sex objects. For evidence of this problem in rap, one need only tune into Black Entertainment Television (BET) on any weekday afternoon to see images of scantily clad black women dancing as

"video'hos." Rarely are women depicted as protagonists in rap videos. Rather they exist in the videos as titillation and to further aggrandize the male rappers who demonstrate their prowess through their association with these unrealistically sexualized women. As rap has become more corporatized (transitions from ghetto streets to Wall Street) and an increasingly important part of the global entertainment industry, these images of women become increasingly devoid of substance and unidimensional. Once again, globalization has taken deeply entrenched notions of race and sex and turned them into a profit.[115]

Such is the desperation on the part of globalization for profit by any means necessary: using variables of culture, gender, race or class to promote an amorphous and vacuous notion of "diversity" that will be embraced by the uninformed people of the world.

Women and War: An Intrinsic Element in Globalization

In the early 1990s, as the capitalist world marveled at the collapse of the Soviet Union, many people overlooked the horrors of ethnic and nationalistic wars that emerged in the former Soviet-bloc countries of Eastern Europe, all to the joy of the lascivious transnational corporations that saw yet another consumer market for their commodities. In Serbia, there were "559,000 registered and 150,000 unregistered refugees in the territory of the Federal Republic of Yugoslavia," mostly women and children.[116] Eastern Ukraine in 2014 was yet another political opportunity for Western globalization forces to foment instability and ethnic conflict to justify intervention in the affairs of the peoples of the Eastern Bloc, all to maintain the countries of this sector within the orbit of capitalism even if it was not in their best social and economic interest.[117] During this era of globalization, it's interesting to see how "balkanization" has become part of normative language, used to describe peoples and cultures outside that of Western Europe as the "other, and as in the case of the Balkans, as places rooted in 'ancient hatreds,'" that warrant Western military intervention to bring sense out of ethnic madness and social order out of chaotic barbarism. This was exemplified when NATO began bombing Kosovo in 1999, led by the U.S. air force. Listen to British TV journalist, Michael Nicholson's account of the Balkans conflict shortly after he adopted a girl from Sarajevo in his book, *Natasha's Story:*

> The ferocity of the Balkans people has at times been so primitive that anthropologists have likened them to the Amazon's Yanamamo, one of the world's most savage and primitive tribes. Up until the turn of the present century, when the rest of Europe was concerned as much with social etiquette as with social reform, there

were still reports from the Balkans of decapitated enemy heads presented as trophies on silver plates at victory dinners. Nor was it unknown for the winners to eat the loser's heart and liver ... the history books show it as a land of murder and revenge before the Turks arrived and long after they departed.[118]

Vesna Goldsworthy, a literature academic, warns about the obsession with conquest violence in this era of globalization, not unlike that of the early colonial period, but preponderantly pathological in its embrace of sadistic forms of violence to the point that killing is perceived as pleasure, using the case of the Balkans as a real-life illustration:

> The defamiliarizing of accounts of Balkan conflicts in the Western media—describing ethnic wars as unthinkable elsewhere in Europe while supplying gory details of singularly "Balkan" butcher to an eager audience—contribute to the perception of the peninsula's ambiguous, "not-yet" or "never-quite" Europeanness. They also, however, reveal an ambiguous attitude toward war itself. Editorials profess horror at bloodspilling and yet an enormous, and frequently voyeuristic, media output (newspapers, TV, publishing, and film industries have all developed their own "Balkan" production-lines during the 1990s) offers daily testimony to a fascination with war and killing about which we have as many taboos as the Victorians did pornography.[119]

This perverse excitability in things violent and in blood-letting in the U.S. has been heightened in contemporary globalization, as fictional movies and comedies alike glorify war, and children and youth are urged to participate in the orgiastic and graphic depictions of war and violence in the comfort of their own living rooms, through X-box games that evoke the killing of "savage Apaches" to other caricatures of violence that assault and "neutralize" people in "exotic" lands. The promotion of movies like *King Kong* and *Tarzan*, which grossed tens of millions of dollars at the box office, serve as a stark reminder that Hollywood is a firm adherent of globalization as constructed by U.S. imperialism, heavily invested in colonial racism that justifies conquest and pre-emptive military strikes against colored nations. What most U.S. audiences don't realize is that the dramatic depictions of violence on television and in the movies, is the real-life experience for peoples around the world, from Colombia to Iraq, Kosovo to the Philippines.

The U.S. pulverization of the nation of Iraq in 1991, shamefully under the auspices of the United Nations, a supposed humanitarian peace-fostering agency, resulted in close to 200,000 deaths. Over 500,000 children died in Iraq since the imposition of United Nations sanctions, spearheaded by the U.S.[120] Since the U.S. invasion and beginning of the occupation of Iraq in 2003, almost a million people have been killed and seriously wounded. Close

Globalization's economic and social impoverishment of peoples in the underdeveloped world exacerbates community and ethnic tensions that degenerate often into military conflict and civil war particularly in Africa and Asia, affecting women and children most adversely who are often forced to leave their ancestral homes because of ongoing violence and become refugees, as in this camp in refugee camp in Ethiopia (Cate Tuton, UK Department for International Development).

to 2 million people were made homeless. The U.S. government has spent $330 billion on its wars against the peoples of Afghanistan and Iraq since October 2001, and is projected to have spent a total of $3 trillion on the invasion and occupation of Iraq by 2015![121] War especially victimizes women and children, who are always the most vulnerable to conditions of violence. Sadly, the U.S. is adamant on pursuing a scorched-earth policy in the underdeveloped world, particularly around regions holding vast oil resources like the Arab countries, the Caspian Sea, and other areas that have vital natural resources for insatiable energy transnational corporations. Ralph Peters, a former intelligence officer who specialized in war planning, provides a candid, cold-hearted, and sadistic view of the future, as envisioned by the stalwarts of U.S. imperialist intervention:

> We are entering a new American century, in which we will become still wealthier, culturally more lethal, and increasingly powerful. We will excite hatreds without

precedent…. The de facto rule of the U.S. armed forces will be to keep the world safe for our economy and open to our cultural assault. To those ends, we will do a fair amount of killing.[122]

The killing urged by Peters is essentially of poor people of color, including mostly women and children in the underdeveloped world.

In Guatemala, in Central America, over 200,000 people died in the 1980s and one million people were forced to flee from their homes or to Mexico as refugees. Most were Indigenous Mayan and suffered such persecution as a result of U.S. support of the military regime of Efrain Rios Montt, a so-called "born-again Christian." The U.S. complicity in these genocidal crimes was documented by the UN Commission on Human Rights.[123] Women who resisted Guatemalan military repression were often brutalized, sexually assaulted, and murdered by death squads.[124] The results of Indigenous peoples' struggle against policies of military genocidal violence forced the Guatemalan government in 1995 to institutionalize constitutional protection for Indigenous culture and identity.[125] While the U.S. claimed that the era of the 1990s was one of ushering in post-military democracies, places like Guatemala actually experienced further impoverishment of her already poor people through free-trade policies under the leadership of ideologues like Alvaro Arzu, who intensified privatization policies that made Guatemala a haven for cheap labor for transnational corporations and the joy of wealthy white landowners.[126] Globalization's tentacles in Guatemala were portrayed as the "victory of democracy over militarism," both supported and maintained by U.S. imperialism. Women have successfully formed, albeit under conditions of severe social repression and the gaze of capitalist hegemony, a variety of women's organizations like the Council of Mayan Women and the Coordination of Mayan Women's Organizations that have become powerful advocates of the rights of poor women against discrimination in the workplace and society and against domestic violence.[127] Women guerrillas from the URNG (Unidad Revolucionaria Nacional Guatemalteca) are still struggling to become a formidable force for poor women's rights in Guatemala, as a political party formation.

In El Salvador, over one million people, especially many women and children, were displaced as refugees as the result of the cumulative military violence by the juntas led by Napoleon Duarte and Robert D'Abuisson, all fiercely supported and propped by the U.S. government through infusion of billions of dollars of military aid in the 1980s and early 1990s. Today, thanks to globalization, military repression has retreated, only to be replaced by large U.S. transnational corporations who make lucrative profits from slave labor of the Salvadoran people, including many women textile and garment workers. El

Salvador was forced to embrace the ideology of liberalization imposed from the North. The women's movement in El Salvador through the FMLN (Farabundo Martí National Liberation Front) has been actively organizing for women's rights after this guerrilla organization first participated in elections in 1997, albeit beset by internal conflicts.[128]

In Nicaragua, the FSLN (Sandinista National Liberation Front) did not pay adequate attention to the advocacy of women's rights and the need to organize the revolutionary women's sector in successfully toppling the repressive Somoza dictatorship in 1979. Yet the women freedom fighters' organizations have worked industriously to organize themselves as a formidable radical force since the Sandinistas lost the elections of 1990. At that time Violeta Barrios de Chamorro became president with 54.7 percent of the vote, campaigning as the "mother of the country" and a "traditional good wife," ironically on an anti-feminist and anti-revolutionary platform.[129] The context of the U.S. war on the Sandinistas played a major role in the population spurning the Sandinistas in favor of Chamorro. The ascendance of the Sandinistas to political leadership of Nicaragua under current president Daniel Ortega in 2006 and again in 2011 has opened avenues for the restoration of social justice for the impoverished people of Nicaragua. In August and September 2012, the author was able to witness first-hand successful anti-poverty programs that focused on women in rural communities outside Esteli, Nicaragua, particularly female-headed households, through the *Zero-Ambré* (Zero Hunger) and *Zero-Usuria* (Zero Usury) programs that provided individual cows and water pumps to destitute households repayable at very low rates of interest. Such governmental assistance was vital in developing small-scale rural milk and agricultural production to earn sustainable incomes.[130] The successful resistance to globalization by the Sandinista leadership and the Nicaraguan masses in this decade will depend on the organization and mobilization of working class women and respect for Indigenous peoples' rights, who jointly constitute the majority of the rural and agricultural communities in Nicaragua.

In Mexico, the world was awakened to the true revolutionaries of history, during the height of the globalization period, when the Indigenous women and the Indigenous people of Chiapas, southern Mexico, rose up in a fierce guerrilla insurrection, symbolized by the events in the town of San Cristobal in 1994. Sylvia Marcos, a well-known Latina scholar from Mexico noted that everyone at the Mexican parliament was amazed when they discovered that the real leader of the *Ejército Zapatista de Liberación Nacional*, was not Subcommandante Marcos, as was widely propagated by the ruling class media and its global affiliates, but Commandanta Esther, from the *Comite Central Rev-*

olucionario Indigena, who spoke to the Mexican Chamber of Deputies on March 28, 2001. Commandanta Esther declared to the assembly that she, along with the *Comite Central Revolucionario Indigena*, gave orders to Subcommandante Marcos, the head of the armed militia.[131] Commandante Esther's words rang sharp and clear that morning of March 28: "Here I am. I am a woman and an Indian and through my voice speaks the *Ejército Zapatista de Liberación Nacional*."[132] The revolutionary fervor of the Indigenous uprising in southern Mexico lies in the women of the region, who staved off the Mexican military which attempted to impose martial law in Chiapas. The resistors to globalization and colonization in Mexico had spoken and acted through the culture of Indigenous women. The resistance of Indigenous women provides inspiration to the struggles of Mexican woman workers in U.S.–owned *maquiladoras*, export-processing factories, that make everything from underwear to electronic components and automobile parts for consumption by Mexico's northern neighbor, where exploitation, prostitution, and violence against women is rife. In Ciudad Juarez, the fifth largest city in Mexico, almost 250,000 workers were employed in these factories in 2000, mostly female. The horror of over 300 women and girls having been murdered in Juarez since the beginning of the 1990s and their unresolved murders, is another sinister indicator of the violence and brutality of globalization and cheap labor among the poor, facilitated by profit-hungry corporations who view women as yet another appendage of the assembly plant.[133]

On the African continent, wars have raged in many regions, particularly with the onslaught of globalization as transnational corporations incessantly pursue profits from mining and oil extraction particularly. In the Democratic Republic of the Congo (DRC) in Central Africa, four million people, mostly women and children, have been killed between 1997 and 2006, as Western transnational corporations like De Beers from South Africa and diamond and gold-extracting companies loot the DRC, along with Sierra Leone in West Africa and Angola in Southern Africa.[134] In many of these places where war and poverty plague the population, globalization's hand in war is evident. Marjorie Mbilinyi succinctly states:

> Deepening war and military conflict are actively promoted by "northern" states by means of massive arms exports, on the one hand, and continued donor support for defensive activities on another.[135]

Soldiers who have been responsible for rape of women and other atrocities against civilians in the Democratic Republic of the Congo have been trained by the U.S. Africa Command (AFRICOM), which is now involved in training "Elite Antiterror Troops" in Mali, Niger, Mauritania, and Libya, intensifying levels of violence in these impoverished countries.[136] In Rwanda and Burundi in 1994, over a million persons were killed from the political conflict that was rooted both in the Belgian colonial legacy of dividing Hutu and Tutsi people though they are from the same community and from a deteriorating economic situation with depressed global prices of coffee, the country's main export crop.[137]

War inevitably creates millions of refugees, particularly now in West Asia and Africa, where a country like Tanzania, though peaceful and safe from war, has been the recipient of a million refugees from wars in Burundi, Rwanda, Uganda, Mozambique, and Somalia. The victims are often women:

> Refugee women arrived in Tanzania with memories of hardship and atrocities—hunger, rape, sexual harassment, and other maltreatment done to them by soldiers. Some have walked barefoot for long distances, pregnant, hungry and with little children on their backs.[138]

The lot for women and internally displaced persons (IDPs) is excruciating. In 2000, 300,000 Angolans were uprooted by ongoing civil war, 150,000 Burundians fled from atrocities and civil war in their country, and 1 million fled from the Democratic Republic of the Congo, where military conflict has intensified. In the same year, 60,000 Guineans fled cross-border attacks by rebels from Sierra Leone, 50,000 Liberians fled insurgent attacks and retaliation from Liberian troops, 210,000 Sierra Leonians fled renewed war and rebel violence, 100,000 Sudanese were forced from their homes due to serial bombings by the Sudanese military and conflict between northern and southern armed groups, and 120,000 Ugandans were uprooted by insurgents waging war against the government.[139] The tragedy is that

> it is estimated that 75 percent to 80 percent of refugees and IDP's are women and their children. Women usually become titular head-of-household because the men either have been killed, conscripted into the army, or stay behind to care for their herds of animals. And because women are occupied with providing food, shelter, and water for their children, reproductive health of women is often neglected. In a recent study of pregnancy outcomes in the Mtendeli refugee camp in Tanzania, it was found that reproductive-health-related deaths were the most common cause of death among women in the camp; maternal and neonatal deaths accounted for 16 percent of all death among these refugees.[140]

Rape of young girls around 12 is commonplace in such war-torn situations, like in the Congo and in refugee camps throughout Africa.

In Lebanon, a beautiful country often called the "Switzerland of the Middle East," war has been the lot for the Lebanese people in this modern

Globalization's economic scope is far-reaching in its destructive social effects, and military conflict and war become inevitable as the result of such pressures, particularly in places in the arid Sahel region of Africa. Women and children are the predominant victims of displacement and forced to leave their homes and families. This is the Farchana Refugee Camp in Chad (SuSanA Secretariat/Flickr).

period from 1975 through 1991, heightened by the Israeli invasion of Lebanon in 1982 to rout the Palestine Liberation Organization (PLO), when 20,000 people were killed by Israeli bombing and soldiers, followed by the war between different Christian and Muslim factional elements. Lamia Rustum Shehadeh, a professor of cultural studies at American University in Beirut, recalls this tragic phase of Lebanese history when women once more were particularly afflicted by the effects of the war in which over 700,000 people were either made homeless or forced to flee the country: "Women suffered greatly in their traditional roles as homemakers, mothers and caregivers during the Lebanese conflict ... they lost the support of their husbands and sons who had joined the fighting or were taken hostage or kidnapped or migrated for greener pastures or, worst yet, killed."[141]

War is big business for globalization's profit-making machine. Pre-emptive strikes by the U.S. government as part of official foreign policy, accompanied by NATO military intervention in Afghanistan, Ukraine, the Caspian region, and most recently in places like Libya, Yemen, Pakistan, Syria, and Somalia, assure the military industrial complex and its mammoth corporations of mega-profits. Lockheed-Martin, Boeing, Northrop Grumman, Raytheon, and General Dynamics receive one-third of all Pentagon contracts, followed by the Carlyle Group (on whose board the former president George H. Bush sits), Honeywell, General Electric, and Halliburton.[142] These corporations have received $400 billion in contracts as the result of the wars in Afghanistan and Iraq, part of the over $1 trillion earmarked for U.S. defense and security in recent years in the aftermath of the bombing of the World Trade Center on September 11, 2001.[143] It is mind-boggling to realize that the U.S. spends more on armaments and security than the rest of the world combined, some $2.2 million per minute! The American Friends Service Committee has now for a few years documented the abnormal structure of discretionary spending proposed by the White House in an emboldened multi-colored broad sticker for all to see. In 2012, president Barack Obama presented his discretionary budget, which read as follows:

President Obama's Discretionary Budget Item	Percentage of Budget (rounded)
Military: (Department of Defense, War, Veterans Affairs, and Nuclear Weapons Programs):	60 percent
Health and Human Services	6 percent
Education	6 percent
State:	5 percent
Other programs	4.5 percent
Department of Homeland Security	4 percent
Housing and Urban Development:	3 percent
Agriculture:	2 percent
Justice	1.5 percent
NASA	1.5 percent
Energy	1.5 percent (excludes nuclear weapons programs)
Labor:	1 percent
Treasury	1 percent
Interior	1 percent
Environmental Protection Agency	1 percent
Transportation	1 percent

Hardly a liberal budget, to say the least, when 60 cents of every tax dollar is earmarked for military expenditures and war![144]

The manufacture of weapons of mass destruction by military industrial corporations most pointedly affects women and children in U.S. military invasion and occupation campaigns as evident in Afghanistan, Pakistan, Yemen, and Somalia and other parts of the world where the U.S. military has a formidable occupying presence.[145]

Today, globalization's penetration of the world by large transnational corporations protected by powerful imperialist powers like NATO under the leadership of the U.S., represents the most lethal threat to all existence, especially women, as it prepares for ongoing invasion of Indigenous peoples' lands and territories around the world. The use of the U.S. military to both police and administer relief operations in hurricane-ravaged New Orleans in 2005, has raised the specter of the military being authorized by the U.S. government to administer law and order in cases of disruption of basic services following a natural catastrophe or some human-caused disaster.[146] Globalization's war architects were preparing for such aggression already in the late 1970s following the oil-embargo imposed by OPEC in the early 1970s. If the bombing of the World Trade Center in New York on September 11, 2001, was a carefully planned Al Qaeda operation, which many skeptics legitimately question, then those CIA operatives who trained the Muhajadeen guerrillas fighting the Soviet-backed Afghanistan government in 1979 that became Al Qaeda, later leading to the emergence of the Taliban government, bear full responsibility for such heinous actions.[147] The Taliban was subsequently overthrown by the full-blown U.S. military invasion of Afghanistan in October 2001. The invasion of Afghanistan and Iraq was orchestrated well before September 2001.[148] The globalized onslaught as dictated by U.S. intervention in the underdeveloped world behooves perennial wars and fabrication of ethnic and social conflicts with deployment of military force in the guise of peacekeeping and civilian administration. Gerhard Kummel, a German researcher, describes the scenario of the globalized soldier in no uncertain terms:

> The nontraditional soldier is an armed street worker and constable or policeman. This non-traditional element of the military, however, does not replace its traditional tasks of deterrence and self-defense as can be notably inferred from September 11, 2001, but is complementary to them. In military operations, other than war, in particular, traditional and nontraditional roles cannot be neatly separated. Soldiers, then, will be required to know how to fight, how to establish local security, how to deal with the local adversaries, and how to cooperate with local partners and civilian international relief organizations.[149]

It is horrifying to read about researchers in the 21st century writing in such callous and nonchalant terms of the role of soldiers in this era of globalization, in specializing in "non-traditional" ways that augment soldiers' primary specialty of *killing*. Yet, as Samir Amin reminds us, in the era of globalization, Washington is ruled by imperial-thinkers whose designs are akin to those of World War II Europe, and therefore, one ought not be soundly astonished![150] Note that Kummel designates the role of soldier in strictly male terms, presupposing that these soldiers will be predominantly male. The torturous atrocities at Abu Ghraib prison in Iraq that involved U.S. female soldiers and the role of Israeli female soldiers in interrogation of Palestinians remind us that women too will be used in the execution of imperialist violence against other peoples, including defenseless women. The fires of war ignited in the previous century know no gender bounds, hence our attention to women and war in 21st century globalization.

Conclusion

Globalization's victimization of migrant women around the world, female workers in sweat shops around the world, in the sex industry around the globe, and now in imperialist wars of invasion, occupation, and aggression, recalls all peace-loving people, especially women, to reclaim their rightful roles in history, not as 21st century economic slaves of the transnational corporation, but as agents of fundamental socio-cultural, economic, and political transformation that evoke justice, mutuality, reciprocity, and collectivity in sharing resources responsibly. Indigenous women's cultures need to be reclaimed everywhere so that we can all live respectfully and harmoniously on and with Mother Earth, in balance with her spirit and gyration, as opposed to resisting Earth's culture. Globalization, as the transmogrification of human relationships with each other and the rest of the natural world experienced in late and dying capitalism, will be dissipated by Indigenous women's culture and radical praxis, an arduous process in which all men must participate so that their spirits and cultures can be radically renewed and reshaped. Indigenous Sto:Loh author and activist from Turtle Island, Lee Maracle, describes this power of womanhood aptly:

> Grasses know stillness. Women know the grasses. Grasses feel this knowing. They exchange pleasantries with these women every day. In their modest desire to know these women the grasses listen, learn songs as the women create melodies that urge them along pathways that would help them to ally themselves with the natural world. The sounds are familiar; they engage each other, attending to the need for comfort as the earth transforms. This knowing between them is mature, comfortable. Plant people know something about the living. Any alteration of human breath causes them to stir. Today, the cadence of voice, the rhythm, seemed out of the ordinary. Breath caught unwittingly in the throats of the women. Plants begin to whisper to one another: "Something is up. The humans don't feel the same today. There is a pall in the air. Do you feel it?"[151]

Beyond the experiences of women and war, globalization has wrought destructive effects on the poor peoples of the U.S. through another industrial complex: *prisons*. The U.S., which has 5 percent of the world's human beings and claims to be the "land of the free and home of the brave," can hardly be free when the nation houses the largest prison population in the world. Globalization and the insatiable lust for profit and power has much to do with the development and expansion of the prison industrial complex, including the phenomenon of private prisons. Globalization and incarceration in all of its manifestations and ramifications is the subject of the next chapter.

4

Unjust Globalization and Unfair Justice Against the Poor: Lethal Racism, Expanded Incarceration, Law Enforcement Violence and Punishment Over Education

This political, economic and social system of America was produced from the enslavement of the Black man and that particular system is capable only of reproducing that out of which itself was produced. The only way a chicken can produce a duck egg [is] you have to revolutionize the system.—*Malcolm X*[1]

In the last 20 years the United States has built more prisons than any country during any period in history. The cost of the U.S. criminal justice system now runs $147 billion per year. But the financial costs are only part of the story. There are other costs not so easily seen, costs passed on to those least able to pay them—the poor rural towns in which most prisons are built and the poor urban communities from which most prisoners are sent. Because the costs of the current prison expansion are being passed to people of color, we say that prisons are examples of economic injustice and environmental racism.—*The 2005 Report of the Critical Resistance and California Moratorium Project*[2]

On any given day, about one in every ten young male high school dropouts is in jail or juvenile detention, compared with one in thirty five young male high school graduates, according to a new study of the dropping out of school in an America where demand for low-skill workers is plunging. The picture is even bleaker for African-Americans, with nearly one in four young black male dropouts incarcerated or otherwise institutionalized on an average day, the study said. That compares with about one in 14 young, male, White, Asian or Hispanic.

The report puts the collective cost to the nation over the working life of each high school dropout at $292,000.—*Center for Labor Market Studies Report Northeastern University, October 2009*[3]

Introduction

The astounding fact that the United States has 25 percent of the world's prison population even though it only has 5 percent of the world's people, with some 743 people incarcerated per 100,000 people, followed by Israel (325 prisoners per 100,000 people), and Chile (317 prisoners per 100,000 people) in 2011, reminds all of the role of incarceration in a globalized U.S. society and world.[4] These shocking statistics are in stark contrast to Japan (75 prisoners per 100,000 people), Greece (101 prisoners per 100,000 people), and China (120 prisoners per 100,000), for example, and underscores the serious human toll globalization has taken in areas of crime and punishment especially in the U.S.[5] The U.S. has the highest incarceration rate among 34 of the wealthy Organization of Economic Cooperation and Development (OECD) countries.[6] Its prison rate is five times that of OECD countries.[7] *New York Times* columnist Eduardo Porter captures the gravity of this crisis of punishment and economics in the era of globalization:

> Few things are better at conveying what a nation really cares than how it spends its money. On that measure, Americans like to punish.
> The United States spent about $80 billion on its system of jails and prisons in 2010—about $260 for every resident of the nation. By contrast, its budget for food stamps was $227 a person.[8]

According to the Hamilton Project, which did a two-year study on "The Economic Facts about Crime and Incarceration in the United States," the total cost of police protection and judicial and legal services reaches an astronomical $261 billion each year.[9] Equally startling is the statistic that all Black men without high school diplomas have a 70 percent chance that they will spend some time incarcerated by their mid-thirties.[10] One of every nine persons incarcerated, some 159,000 people, are serving life sentences, with one-third having no possibility of parole.[11] While the crime rates have dropped since the 1960s, the prison incarceration rates have multiplied four-fold and though criminal offences have actually decreased by about half since 1990, the rates of punishment and imprisonment have grown significantly.[12] The politics and economics of race, class, globalized restructuring of the U.S. economy where millions of manufacturing jobs disappeared over the past two decades, and the injection of drugs into impoverished Black and Brown communities by drug syndicates under the watchful eyes of the U.S. Drug Enforcement Agency (DEA), the CIA, and other law enforcement agencies are interwoven into the expansion of the prison industrial complex (PIC) in recent years. Anti-racism and anti-globalization activists are correct when they note:

There is a very direct link between corporate globalization and the prison industrial complex. The same corporations that benefit from mass incarceration domestically benefit from economic domination in the "Third World" (*quotation marks mine*). Some prison companies benefit even more directly from globalization, like Wackenhut (headquartered in South Florida), which opened a super maximum prison in South Africa in 2002. Both the PIC and corporate globalization predominantly impact and target the same classes of people: poor or working class people of color. This is as true in Argentina as it is in Alabama, in Kenya and in Kansas. MCI, Halliburton, the Carlyle Group, IBM, General Electric, and many other corporations are leading the way in this corporate domination of the world.[13]

Prisons function as the domestic arm of the U.S. military that polices and controls colonized and impoverished people in the underdeveloped world like Iraq, Afghanistan, Somalia, Yemen, and Pakistan, with racism and classism as operating principles and practices:

> Prison, along with an increase in militarized policing, are the way the United States controls its domestic poor/working class people and people of color. (Abroad, globalization is enforced through military might, often backed with training and weapons supplied by the United States.) In this way, the prison industrial complex constitutes a form of "internal globalization."[14]

The CIA for example has a history of dealing with drug cartels from as far back as 1949 when it supported the Nationalist Chinese Army fighting against Communist China. It countenanced and funded anti-communist groups deeply involved in the smuggling of opium in the Golden Triangle (Burma, Laos, and Thailand) and transported drugs on the CIA airline, Air America.[15] These actions escalated during the U.S. wars in Southeast Asia in the 1960s and 1970s and into the 1980s through the U.S.-funded Nicaraguan Contra wars, which involved selling drugs and using profits to fund the Contras fighting the Sandinista government in Nicaragua.[16] One of the lingering effects of both militarization and a de-industrialized U.S. manufacturing economy is the booming prison industrial complex where almost half of all persons incarcerated in the nations' jails and prisons today are Black, over 1 million people, and the rest overwhelmingly poor and disproportionately other persons of color.[17] Jails are even being constructed at high cost for the first time in large Indigenous Dineh (Navajo) communities in Northern Arizona, ensuring that Indigenous people will continue to become grist for the prison industrial mill.[18]

According to a Bureau of Justice Statistics Special Report from 2003, "Prevalence of Imprisonment in the U.S. Population, 1974–2001," if trends continue at the present rate, 32.2 percent of 13-year-old Black male and 5.6

percent of Black female children today can expect to spend part of their lives in jail.[19] Of all U.S. residents born in 2001, 6.6 percent will spend some time in prison if incarceration rates remain virtually the same as those from 1974 to 2001.[20] **Tables 1–4** substantiate the growing levels of incarceration of people in local jails from 2000 to 2013, for instance, with White inmates increasing from 260,500 in 2000 to 344,900 in 2013 (**Table 2**) and persons of color like African Americans and Mexican Americans being imprisoned at unprecedented high rates exceeding their proportions in the U.S. population, with African Americans constituting 41.3 percent of the local prison population in 2000 (**Table 3**).

Most Black and Latino people in prisons are jailed for non-violent crimes related to illegal drugs. It's troubling that in the aftermath of basketball star Len Bias' tragic death from a cocaine overdose in 1986, the U.S. Congress rushed to pass the Anti-Drug Abuse Act of 1986, including the Narcotics Penalties and Enforcement Act, which resulted in hundreds of thousands of drug offenders subsequently receiving mandatory minimums of nine years in prison without parole for possessing 52 grams of cocaine.[21] Why has this tragedy been used as the basis to incarcerate almost one million women and men for non-violent drug-related crimes since 1986 and as political football by racist politicians whose careers catapulted after supporting harsh anti-drug laws and generally criminalizing Black people? Does the economics of globalization have something to do with the interlocking dynamics of race, class, and incarceration?

TABLE 1
Inmates confined in local jails at midyear, average daily population, and incarceration rates, 2000–2013

Year	Inmates confined at midyear[a]			Average daily population[b]			
		Year-to-year change			Year-to-year change		
	Total	Number	Percent	Total	Number	Percent	Jail incarceration rate[c]
2000	621,149	15,206	2.5%	618,319	10,341	1.7%	220
2001	631,240	10,091	1.6	625,966	7,647	1.2	222
2002	665,475	34,235	5.4	652,082	26,116	4.2	231
2003	691,301	25,826	3.9	680,760	28,678	4.4	238
2004	713,990	22,689	3.3	706,242	25,482	3.7	243
2005	747,529	33,539	4.7	733,442	27,200	3.9	252
2006	765,819	18,290	2.4	755,320	21,878	3.0	256
2007	780,174	14,355	1.9	773,138	17,818	2.4	259
2008	785,533	5,359	0.7	776,573	3,435	0.4	258
2009	767,434	-18,099	-2.3	768,135	-8,438	-1.1	250
2010	748,728	-18,706	-2.4	748,553	-19,582	-2.5	242
2011	735,601	-13,127	-1.8	735,565	-12,988	-1.7	236
2012	744,524	8,923	1.2	737,369	1,804	0.2	237
2013	731,208	-13,316	-1.8	731,352	-6,017	-0.8	231
Average annual change							
2000–2012			1.5%			1.5%	
2012–2013			-1.8			-0.8	

[a]Number of inmates held on the last weekday in June.
[b]Sum of all inmates in jail each day for a year, divided by the number of days in the year. Based on revised data for 2012.
[c]Number of inmates confined at midyear per 100,000 U.S. residents.
Sources: Bureau of Justice Statistics, Annual Survey of Jails, midyear 2000–2004 and midyear 2006–2013, and the 2005 Census of Jail Inmates.

TABLE 2
Number of inmates in local jails, by characteristics, midyear 2000 and 2005–2013

Characteristic	2000	2005	2006	2007	2008	2009	2010	2011[a]	2012[a]	2013[a]
Total[b]	621,149	747,529	765,819	780,174	785,533	767,434	748,728	735,601	744,524	731,208
Sex										
Male	550,162	652,958	666,819	679,654	685,862	673,728	656,360	642,300	645,900	628,900
Female	70,987	94,571	99,000	100,520	99,670	93,706	92,368	93,300	98,600	102,400
Adult	613,534	740,770	759,717	773,341	777,829	760,216	741,168	729,700	739,100	726,600
Male	543,120	646,807	661,164	673,346	678,657	667,039	649,284	636,900	640,900	624,700
Female	70,414	93,963	98,552	99,995	99,172	93,176	91,884	92,800	98,100	101,900
Juvenile[c]	7,615	6,759	6,102	6,833	7,703	7,218	7,560	5,900	5,400	4,600
Held as adult[d]	6,126	5,750	4,835	5,649	6,410	5,846	5,647	4,600	4,600	3,500
Held as juvenile	1,489	1,009	1,268	1,184	1,294	1,373	1,912	1,400	900	1,100
Race/Hispanic origin[e]										
White[f]	260,500	331,000	336,500	338,200	333,300	326,400	331,600	329,400	341,100	344,900
Black/African American[f]	256,300	290,500	295,900	301,700	308,000	300,500	283,200	276,400	274,600	261,500
Hispanic/Latino	94,100	111,900	119,200	125,500	128,500	124,000	118,100	113,900	112,700	107,900
American Indian/Alaska Native[f,g]	5,500	7,600	8,400	8,600	9,000	9,400	9,900	9,400	9,300	10,200
Asian/Native Hawaiian/ Other Pacific Islander[f,g]	4,700	5,400	5,100	5,300	5,500	5,400	5,100	5,300	5,400	5,100
Two or more races[f]	...	1,000	700	800	1,300	1,800	800	1,200	1,500	1,600

Note: Detail may not sum to total due to rounding.
...Not collected.
[a]Data for 2011–2013 are adjusted for nonresponse and rounded to the nearest 100.
[b]Midyear count is the number of inmates held on the last weekday in June.
[c]Persons age 17 or younger at midyear.
[d]Includes juveniles who were tried or awaiting trial as adults.
[e]Data adjusted for nonresponse and rounded to the nearest 100. See *Methodology*.
[f]Excludes persons of Hispanic or Latino origin.
[g]Previous reports combined American Indians and Alaska Natives and Asians, Native Hawaiians, and other Pacific Islanders into an Other race category.
Sources: Bureau of Justice Statistics, Annual Survey of Jails, 2000 and midyear 2006–2013, and the 2005 Census of Jail Inmates.

TABLE 3
Percent of inmates in local jails, by characteristics, midyear 2000 and 2005–2013

Characteristic	2000	2005	2006	2007	2008	2009	2010	2011	2012	2013
Sex										
Male	88.6%	87.3%	87.1%	87.1%	87.3%	87.8%	87.7%	87.3%	86.8%	86.0%
Female	11.4	12.7	12.9	12.9	12.7	12.2	12.3	12.7	13.2	14.0
Adult	98.8%	99.1%	99.2%	99.1%	99.0%	99.1%	99.0%	99.2%	99.3%	99.4%
Male	87.4	86.5	86.3	86.3	86.4	86.9	86.7	86.6	86.1	85.4
Female	11.3	12.6	12.9	12.8	12.6	12.1	12.3	12.6	13.2	13.9
Juvenile[a]	1.2%	0.9%	0.8%	0.9%	1.0%	0.9%	1.0%	0.8%	0.7%	0.6%
Held as adult[b]	1.0	0.8	0.6	0.7	0.8	0.8	0.8	0.6	0.6	0.5
Held as juvenile	0.2	0.1	0.2	0.2	0.2	0.2	0.3	0.2	0.1	0.1
Race/Hispanic origin[c]										
White[d]	41.9%	44.3%	43.9%	43.3%	42.5%	42.5%	44.3%	44.8%	45.8%	47.2%
Black/African American[d]	41.3	38.9	38.6	38.7	39.2	39.2	37.8	37.6	36.9	35.8
Hispanic/Latino	15.2	15.0	15.6	16.1	16.4	16.2	15.8	15.5	15.1	14.8
American Indian/ Alaska Native[d,e]	0.9	1.0	1.1	1.1	1.1	1.2	1.3	1.3	1.2	1.4
Asian/Native Hawaiian/ Other Pacific Islander[d,e]	0.8	0.7	0.7	0.7	0.7	0.7	0.7	0.7	0.7	0.7
Two or more races[d]	...	0.1	0.1	0.1	0.2	0.2	0.1	0.2	0.2	0.2
Conviction status[b,c]										
Convicted	44.0%	38.0%	37.9%	38.0%	37.1%	37.8%	38.9%	39.4%	39.4%	38.0%
Male	39.0	33.2	32.8	32.9	32.3	33.0	...	...	...	...
Female	5.0	4.9	5.0	5.2	4.8	4.8	...	...	...	...
Unconvicted	56.0%	62.0%	62.1%	62.0%	62.9%	62.2%	61.1%	60.6%	60.6%	62.0%
Male	50.0	54.2	54.3	54.3	55.2	54.8	...	...	...	...
Female	6.0	7.7	7.8	7.7	7.8	7.4	...	...	...	...

Note: Percentages are based on the total number of inmates held on the last weekday in June. Detail may not sum to total due to rounding.
...Not collected. Starting in 2010, the Annual Survey of Jails did not collect data on conviction status by sex.
[a]Persons age 17 or younger at midyear.
[b]Includes juveniles who were tried or awaiting trial as adults.
[c]Data adjusted for nonresponse. See *Methodology*.
[d]Excludes persons of Hispanic or Latino origin.
[e]Previous reports combined American Indians and Alaska Natives and Asians, Native Hawaiians, and other Pacific Islanders into an Other race category.
Sources: Bureau of Justice Statistics, Annual Survey of Jails, 2000 and midyear 2006–2013, and the 2005 Census of Jail Inmates.

TABLE 4
Inmates confined in local jails at midyear, by size of jurisdiction, 2012–2013

Jurisdiction size[b]	Inmates confined at midyear[a]				Percent of all inmates	
	2012	2013	Difference	Percent change	2012	2013
Total	744,524	731,208	-13,316	-1.8%	100%	100%
Fewer than 50 inmates	25,091	23,545	-1,546	-6.2%	3.4%	3.2%
50 to 99	41,630	38,970	-2,660	-6.4	5.6	5.3
100 to 249	93,085	95,031	1,946	2.1	12.5	13.0
250 to 499	102,640	102,362	-278	-0.3	13.8	14.0
500 to 999	123,512	123,155	-357	-0.3	16.6	16.8
1,000 or more	358,567	348,145	-10,422	-2.9	48.2	47.6

Note: Detail may not sum to total due to rounding.
[a]Number of inmates held on the last weekday in June.
[b]Based on the average daily population (ADP) during the 12-month period ending June 30, 2006, the first year in the current Annual Survey of Jails series. ADP is the sum of all inmates in jail each day for a year, divided by the number of days in the year.
Source: Bureau of Justice Statistics, Annual Survey of Jails, 2012–2013.

In 2007, there were 3.5 million Black people under some form of criminal justice administrative supervision or incarcerated, compared to 1850 when 3.2 million Black people were still "legally" enslaved.[22] Why is it that after the passage of the Fourteenth Amendment to the U.S. Constitution in 1868, which expanded citizenship rights to Black people and nullified the *Dred Scott v. Sandford* ruling of 1857, which declared that the rights of Black people were not protected by the Constitution; the Due Process Clause of the Fifth and Fourteenth Amendments that all persons are entitled to procedural due process in civil and criminal proceedings, substantive due process; the Equal Protection Clause, part of the Fourteenth Amendment that prohibits the deprivation of life, liberty, and property without due process of law and ensures equal protection by the law; the Civil Rights Act of 1964; and even after the video-taped brutal beating of Rodney King by police in 1992 that was screened around the world, racial profiling by police and law enforcement persists and the grossly unfair application of the law in sentencing mostly people of color and poor people to prison continues unabated? Why does the persistence of pervasive incarceration of Black and Brown people in the U.S. continue at such high levels in the 21st century so that almost 3,074 Black people per 100,000 residents are confined behind bars and Black men in their 20s and 30s experience incarceration at six times the national average, while Latinos are one-third of all inmates in federal prisons ands are seven times more likely to be imprisoned than Whites in states like Connecticut and Pennsylvania and six times more likely to be imprisoned than Whites in Massachusetts and North Dakota?[23] Further, why do images of Black and Brown people as criminals or potential criminals to be feared continue to pervade the minds of the average person living in the U.S., so that in a 1995 conducted survey, when asked about their image of a typical drug user, 95 percent of respondents described somebody Black?[24] Do globalization discourses on "race" and Blackness/Brownness feature within this continued criminalization of Black and Brown people?

This chapter will discuss the manner in which the prison industrial complex in the U.S, with its roots in the slave system of the South, has continued to function as an instrument of oppression in the contemporary capitalist system, particularly of young Black and Brown women and men, other poor people, poor White women, and those who are considered sexual minorities in society, and is particularly exacerbated during the era of economic globalization where issues of race, class, and economics all intersect to intensify levels of incarceration.[25] It's important to note too that there has been a consistent growth in the incarceration of Asian Americans, especially those of Southeast Asian descent, a phenomenon that is often obscured in the mainstream U.S. media.[26] The fact of 10 million people being processed through the criminal justice system each year serves as a stark reminder of the severely punitive character of the state.[27] This chapter will illuminate the role that penal punishment plays in U.S. society with emphasis on race and class, particularly on people of color who are incarcerated at rates disproportionate to their numerical composition within the nation. It will highlight the intensification of the privatization of incarceration under globalization so that prisons have become havens for profit accumulation by corporations specializing in "Corrections." The stress on Blackness within the system of incarceration and globalization in the U.S. does not imply an exclusivist posture and analysis in this chapter; Blackness is simply the most salient factor in terms of race, imprisonment, and globalization. However, the dynamics of anti–Black racism are directly and clearly connected to and interwoven with the incarceration of Native Americans, Latinos, women, and all poor people. Racism, classism, and incarceration all conjunctively function within the contemporary globalized economy. The war on drugs and crime, the national security state, police brutality, capital punishment, private prisons and starved public service budgets, and the "war on terror," are all auxiliary policies and practices that function to bolster the globalized profit-making prison industrial complex, recalling the history of enslavement and emancipation in the U.S.[28]

19th Century Slavery, Racist Codes, and Early U.S. Prisons

In his 1903 classic, *The Souls of Black Folk*, W.E.B. Du Bois notes that "(1) ... the inevitable result of Emancipation was to increase crime and criminals, and (2) that the police system of the South was primarily designed to control slaves."[29] He avers that the courts functioned as an instrument of re-enslaving freed Black people when free labor became impossible following emancipation. In the North, the penitentiary system of the early 18th century was a carry-over from the old English system that punished people through death for a host of crimes and was designed to control the lower classes and emerging urban poor who were perceived as threats to the property of the ruling elites—the gentry.[30] Class stratification and isolation of the marginalized were foundational dynamics in the European prison system imported into the American colonies. This legacy is visible in 21st century globalization and is perpetuated by the prison industrial complex. The purpose of incarceration from almost three centuries ago continues into the present, and anybody who has been incarcerated will testify to the truth of this intention. Elam Lynds, a "deputy keeper" of Auburn penitentiary in New York in the early 1800s summarized it aptly: "Break the spirit and you will have a better maintained prison. Make him kneel, make him fear you and break his spirit. Dominate him."[31]

John Hope Franklin notes that "various methods were used to keep blacks on Southern plantations—the enforcement of vagrancy and labor contract laws, the enactment of legislation imposing penalties for enticing laborers away, and the establishment of systems of peonage by which blacks were hired out by the county in order to pay the fine for a crime or to pay a debt" and in some instances, former slavemasters "sought to persuade blacks to remain by promising them good treatment and high wages."[32]

Following Emancipation, Southern states like Louisiana and Mississippi instituted the Black Codes, which placed restrictions on the mobility of freed Black people and on Black workers employed by Whites. For instance, in the Black Codes passed by Louisiana in 1865, it was declared that, under section 9, "Failing to obey reasonable orders, neglect of duty, and leaving home without permission will be deemed disobedience; impudence, swearing, or indecent language to or in the presence of the employer, his family, or agent, or quarreling and fighting with one another, shall be deemed disobedience."[33] Section 5 of the Mississippi Penal Law decreed that should freed persons be unable or refuse to pay a fine and associated costs, they would be leased as convict labor to the sheriff or a similar office to any White person who was willing to pay the fine.[34]

Clearly, the intention of these racist Black Codes was to make things maximally difficult for the people freed from slavery and to institutionalize a system of law that meted out the harshest punishment to those who were found guilty of petty offenses that were officially classified as misdemeanor crimes. This harsh punitive legal apparatus targeted Black people whether they were "freedman, free negro or mulatto." Katheryn Russell confirms this essential criminalization of Blackness when she explains that "Blackness itself was a crime" and that "the codes permitted Blacks to be punished for a wide range of social actions" so that Black people could even be punished for walking down the street if they did not move out of the way quickly enough to accommodate White people who passed by and even for speaking to Whites.[35] These laws were the precursors to the emergence of the Black chain gangs throughout the Jim Crow South, yet another convoluted manner in which freed Black people became re-enslaved as leased and free labor.

Lest anyone operates with the illusion that the obscenely disproportionate number of Black people in U.S. prisons is a relatively recent phenomenon, the statistics from 1918 are revealing about the historical criminalization and incarceration of Black people way beyond their composition in the national population. Jerome Miller, who has conducted extensive studies in his work, *Search and Destroy: African American Males in the Criminal Justice System*, explains that "in its 1918 report Negro Population: 1790–1915, the Bureau of the Census noted that while Blacks made up about 11 percent of the general population they constituted about one-fifth (21.9 percent) of the inmates in the prisons, penitentiaries, jails, reform schools, and workhouses of the states" and "they represented 56 percent of those held for 'grade homicide' and about half of those held for 'lesser homicide,' and contributed slightly less than one-third of the commitments for robbery, burglary, and larceny."[36] Of course, there was a general tendency among legal experts then, and even now, to contend that Black people perpetrated criminal offenses in proportions far in excess of their composition within the population, and thus were rightly deserving of the punishment for their criminality.[37]

What is evident from the Bureau of Justice data on the ethnic breakdown of inmates incarcerated is that the rate of African Americans had steadily increased with a more than doubling between 1926 and 1993, so that the chart is as follows.

	White (percent)	Black (percent)	Other (percent)
1926	79	21	1
1930	77	22	1
1935	74	25	1
1940	71	28	1
1945	68	31	1
1950	69	30	1
1960	66	32	2
1964	65	33	2

	White (percent)	Black (percent)	Other (percent)
1974	59	38	3
1978	58	41	1
1981	57	42	2
1986	40	45	15
1993	27	55	18[38]

Miller observes that from 1986, the percentage of White inmates dropped sharply as the number of inmates of color correspondingly increased in significant numbers. The number of people in U.S. prisons doubled from 1980 to 1989, with half of all inmates being people of color.[39] Public expenditures for corrections and law enforcement efforts and private security outlays totaled $165 billion in 1995, almost as much as the U.S. military budget in that period.[40] Corrections alone received over $31 billion in 1994, a sharp 359 percent increase since 1980.

Globalization is concerned with reinforcing structures of race while using the ironic language of "diversity" and ostensibly proclaiming freedom for all while disproportionately confining poor people of color. While the federal government has been prominent in its rhetoric on racial and social equality, it constantly appears totally powerless to enforce its own laws that accord protection of the civil rights of all people. Globalization's designs of profit using race and class and the political economy of the anti-drug war from the early 1980s features centrally in the expansion of 21st century globalized capitalism.

Critical Race Theory and Incarceration

Scholars like Cornel West have reiterated from the early 1990s that still *Race Matters,* and in 2015, poverty matters.[41] Manning Marable, the late political historian, described the painful experiences of people incarcerated at Sing Sing Correctional Center in New York as nothing but "evil" because of the "whole oppressive environment—the pungent smells of sweat and human waste, the absence of fresh air, the lack of privacy, the close quarters of men who have been condemned to live much of their natural lives in tiny steel cages" and pointedly asks, "How can Americans who still believe in racial equality and social justice stand silently while millions of our fellow citizens are being destroyed all around us?"[42] Marable concurs with the view that we are living in a nation that is steeped in a prison industrial complex where federal and state budgets are heavily invested in prisons and punishment for crimes, particularly of the poor and marginalized, illiterate and vulnerable, while state educational budgets suffer from radical cuts at all levels.[43] Other activist scholars like Joy James and Angela Davis who have conducted substantive research on prisons in the U.S. describe the system of incarceration quite accurately as "neo-slavery" and an extension of the plantation system from the days of chattel slavery.[44] Their views were confirmed by an incarcerated person who was interviewed in 2012 who described the history of slavery as being the fundamental cause of his familial dysfunction and disintegration that resulted in him landing on the streets, joining a gang, and being sentenced to 35 years for killing someone.[45] A recent book by Khalid Gibran Muhammed contends that the tenacity of incarceration of Black people in the U.S. stems from the northern practice of widespread imprisonment of Black people in the 19th century and is rooted in a racist ideological view of Black people as inherently dangerous and innately criminal in nature.[46]

Derrick Bell, a former Harvard University legal scholar considered a pioneer of critical race theory, suggests that race is at the foundation of the makings of U.S. society, defines the social existence of all persons. He argues that the goals of desegregation and racial equality are illusory and will never be attained because racism is so entrenched.[47] Instead, Bell maintains, Black people should relentlessly struggle to free themselves through Black solidarity without dependence on the nation's courts and civil rights since these emanations from the dominant White ruling propertied class will never recognize the legitimacy of Black humanity.[48] Angela Davis, a longtime advocate of the rights of those confined behind bars, integrates issues of race, class, gender, sexuality, and, unlike some other critical scholars, *empire*, in her critique of the prison industrial complex, which is reflective of the deeply rooted slave system from the 17th century. She contends that prisons have become an integral and "natural" part of U.S. society and global capitalist societies due to historical domestic factors and the reconfiguration of globalized capital in the world.[49]

Patricia Collins, another renowned legal scholar, reminds us that the racist violence meted out to Black men via the instruments of law enforcement and the prison industrial complex cannot be viewed in isolation from the U.S. history of violence from chattel slavery. The pervasive practices of the rape of Black women during slavery by White men produced a "new racism" that is interwoven with the politics of gender and sexuality. She asserts that the levels of violence induced through the prison industrial complex have reached such astronomical proportions that on a regular day one quarter of all Black men aged 20–40 are in jail, on parole, or involved on some level with the criminal justice system and that the national state itself could be viewed as performing the function of lynching hitherto practiced in Southern formerly slave states. She explains that capital punishment is an inevitable controlling mechanism over a rising urban poor Black population and that institutional practices for controlling women are transferred to bureaucratic incarceration of Black men.[50] This segment of the society is viewed as redundant labor by a high-tech capitalist economy under globalization, particularly since "the problem that poor black people face is that they live in an economic world that has little use for their labor and in a country whose commitment to free markets includes a high tolerance for economic inequality."[51]

Critical race theory, while important for comprehending the tenacious character of racism at the heart of U.S. society and the world, as A. Leon Higginbotham, Jr., Aderson Bellegarde François, and Linda Y. Yueh very persuasively argue in their analysis of the O.J. Simpson trial in their article, "The O.J. Simpson Trial: Who Was Improperly 'Playing the Race Card?,'"[52] is still inadequate when it comes to analyzing the organic nature of oppression where elements of race, class, gender, culture, sexuality, and capitalized imperialism all collectively constitute the machination of oppression. In the case of Black people and other oppressed and marginalized peoples, the theoretical framework analyzing both the tenacity of social incarceration in the U.S. requires a deep understanding of the historical foundations of the country, particularly with regard to the intentional genocide of Indigenous peoples and the enslavement of Black peoples and the manner that interlocking dimensions of race, class, gender, culture, and sexuality feature centrally in the configuration of capitalist accumulation and oppression of all marginalized people in the nation. Straight-White male middle class culture is viewed as the general norm and all other social categories of experience are viewed as potential aberrations.[53] Critical race theory, expounded even by historical icons like Frantz Fanon on White supremacy, and colonized Black identity needs to recognize, as Howard Winant points out, that though White supremacy is foundational in the systemic functioning of U.S. society (and the world), "the politics of White identity is undergoing a profound political crisis" where "undoubtedly while still a minority among Whites" there are "millions who have resisted the siren song of neo-conservatism, recognizing that the claim of 'color blindness' masks a continuing current of White supremacy and racism."[54] Winant argues that this "'color-blind' White supremacy ... embodies the racial duality of contemporary White identity."[55] The *Campaign to End the Death Penalty* is a positive example of this inter-racial agitation demanding justice for those being subject to capital punishment due to victimization by structures of race and class. In Fanon's critique of race, the acknowledgment that he was ignorant about Black women blunted his incisive critique of race.[56]

Drugs, Crime, Punishment, Prisons, and the National Security State in the Globalized U.S.

The normative criminalization of Black and Latino social groupings such as gangs and moieties warrants probing issues of economic deprivation, poorly equipped and funded schools, high rates of unemployment, saturation of urban communities by drug lords as part of national and international crime syndicates integral to the U.S. political economy, and familial disintegration as the result of segregation and impoverishment. These ills feed directly into state law mechanisms that emphasize punishment rather than treatment and ensure incarceration of poor youth, especially Black and Brown people. Prisons are an exaggerated reflection of the persistence by the capitalist ruling class to both insist on conformity to dominant White Anglo-Saxon views of law and morality and to utilize the conviction of persons considered offenders as grist for the profit mill from the expansion of the prison industrial complex. The punishment meted to persons incarcerated even for non-violent crimes such as illegal drug use, for instance, is rooted in a contradictory morality that criminalizes sectors of the population like Indigenous people, impoverished people of all groups, particularly Black and Latino, segments of the unemployed, the homeless, those considered politically subversive, gays, lesbians, bi-sexual, and trans-gendered people, and others considered "deviant" by Western Judeo-Christian "moral standards."[57]

The word "contradictory" is used because various members of the U.S. ruling class have resorted to occasional drug use at one time or another, not just some presidents like Bill Clinton and Barack Obama who have acknowledged such; use among Wall Street executives is pervasively documented from the early 1990s through the present.[58] How is it that this class of wealthy people isn't harassed by law enforcement and aren't convicted and condemned to long prison terms for illicit and habitual drug use? Worse still, why aren't drug-laundering banks and wealthy executives whose financial operations benefit from drug monies charged and imprisoned? As globalization research writer Dylan Murphy writes:

> If any member of the public is caught in possession of a few grammes of coke or heroin you can bet your bottom dollar they will be going down to serve some hard time. However, if you are a bankster caught laundering billions of dollars for some of the most murderous people on the planet you get off with a slap on the wrist in the form of some puny fine and a deferred prosecution deal.[59]

The high-profile role of presidential figures and national security agency executive staff in drug smuggling is directly interwoven with issues of racism, poverty, drug-sales and profits, drug-infested neighborhoods, corporate take-overs of such neighborhoods, prisons, and prison bonds.

During the 1980s, while the U.S. government was involved in funding the Contras fighting the Sandinista government in Nicaragua which overthrew the U.S.–sponsored Somoza dictatorship, Barry Seal, a government agent was delivering billions of dollars worth of narcotics from Latin America to an airport in Mena, Arkansas, home state of subsequent Democratic president, Bill Clinton.[60] Seal was subsequently assassinated in February 1986, yet the smuggling in drugs and contraband continued. Later that year, a plane carrying arms for the Contras was shot down in Nicaragua and the only survivor, Eugene Hassenfuss, confessed to funding the Contras from the operations at Mena airport. The revelations led to an independent counsel investigation and a congressional committee examination chaired by then Senator John Kerry that found that executive members of the National Security Council headed by George H.W. Bush and at least 14 members of the Council and others including the Secretary of Defense were culpable in covering up serious government activity in drug smuggling and narco-trafficking. These members were indicted (including Harvard-trained lawyer and former Bechtel General Counsel, Caspar Weinberger, who served as Secretary of Defense under president George H.W. Bush) and subsequently pardoned by president George H.W. Bush who initially served as Director of the CIA, then as Vice President, and finally as President. Investigative journalists have uncovered relationships to narco-trafficking of agencies at the highest levels of the government, including the National Security Agency, the Department of Justice, and the CIA.

Bill Clinton, Governor of Arkansas from 1978 to 1991, and the Arkansas Development Finance Agency (ADFA), a local distributor of U.S. Department of Housing and Urban Development programs responsible for issuing municipal housing bonds, were also involved in the cover-up of these illegal drug-trafficking activities and drug money laundering involving billions, operated by Barry Seal, a former pilot of the U.S. Army Special Forces Division and a leading CIA operative.[61] The ADFA, a Bill Clinton creation, had Hillary Clinton at one of its law firms and partnered with other members of Bill Clinton's administration. An advanced software program, PROMIS, originally developed to track comprehensive legal data on individuals was stolen from Inslaw Incorporated, the computer firm that had developed the software, and became the possession of Jackson Stephens, an Arkansas company. Jackson Stephens Investment bank, Stephens Incorporated, subsequently became the largest issuer of prison municipal bonds in Arkansas, underscoring the intricate and complex, but nevertheless real, relationship of government drug smuggling, law enforcement, and prison construction, particularly targeting poor Black people in drug-infested neighborhoods.[62] The first company ADFA funded was Park on Meter Incorporated (POM), a parking meter company, that was eventually "enlisted in a project with the Stormont Labs of Woodland, California, and Wackenhut Corporation to develop chemical and biological weapons that could be deployed in guerrilla warfare," particularly to attack the Nicaraguan government, underscoring how important Clinton's state of Arkansas was in the Contra war against Nicaragua during a time when support of the Contras was prohibited under U.S. law.[63] Of relevance to our prisons discourse is the fact that the Wackenhut Corrections Corporation, a division of the Wackenhut Corporation, which was formed in 1984 and partnered with POM, developed into a leading private prisons corporation known as G4S Secure Solutions today. The Wackenhut Corporation was founded by three former FBI agents.

One of the most disturbing elements about this intriguing story of drugs, politics, and prisons is the revelation of a legal document, a *Memorandum of Understanding (MOU) Between the CIA and the Department of Justice*, of February 11, 1982, and enforced till August 1995 that essentially provided the Justice Department legal cover to the CIA to engage in illegal narcotics and arms smuggling so that the CIA would be "relieved ... of any legal obligation to report information of drug trafficking and drug law violations whether with respect to CIA agents, assets, non-staff employees, or contractors."[64] When California Congresswoman Maxine Waters held hearings in November 1996 about the CIA being involved in trafficking drugs into South Central Los Angeles, many in the middle class were shocked. In 1996, Gary Webb, a journalist with the *San José Mercury News*, wrote a powerful article following a year-long investigation that revealed that the CIA was involved in drug-trafficking in Los Angeles and diverting the profits to fund the CIA-backed Contras in Nicaragua.[65] He was asked to retract the article, demoted, forced to quit the newspaper, and was subsequently found dead in 2004, apparently of a suicide, even though questions about his death linger given that he constantly received death threats and was followed. The *New York Times* finally conceded in October 2014 that Webb's investigative journalism that exposed the role of the CIA in funneling drugs into south-central Los Angeles in the 1980s was legitimate and "real," following the release of the movie *Kill the Messenger*.[66]

If the CIA was involved with opium-smuggling gangs and the drug trade for fifteen years in Laos, Cambodia, Vietnam and Thailand in the late 1960s that expanded the marketing and distribution of heroin, including to U.S. troops in the region, and if the CIA was funding the Contras battling the

Nicaraguan Sandinista government in the 1980s while the Contras were established drug smugglers, these drugs had to find their way to the largest drug-consumer market in the world: the United States.[67] The targeted areas would primarily be impoverished communities of the inner cities of the nation where the particularly desperate socio-economic plight of people in these over-crowded "ghettoes" is well known. Many Black and Brown people residing in the sprawling urban metropolises of the country knew clearly from their experiences, including those who fought in south-east Asia, that the drug influx into the impoverished urban communities was deliberate and systemic. As Catherine Austin Pitts who unearthed much of the information from the Department of Justice–CIA Memorandum of Understanding on protection of the CIA-cover-up of illegal drug activity in effect from February 1982 to August 1995, noted:

> A crack cocaine epidemic ravaged the poorer communities of America and disen-franchised hundreds of thousands of poor people into prison who, now classified as felons, were safely off of the voting roles. Meantime, the U.S. financial system gorged on what had grown to an estimated $500 billion–$1 trillion a year of money laundering by the end of the 1990s. Not surprisingly, the rich got richer as corporate power and the concentration of investment capital skyrocketed on the rich margins of state sanctioned criminal enterprise.[68]

The concatenation of the governmental-corporate role in drug trafficking and the drug trade, inner city impoverishment, law enforcement, and incarceration, are all integral to globalization's designs of unbridled profit from both poverty and punishment.

It is no coincidence too that following the U.S. invasion and occupation of Afghanistan in 2001 to rout out the Taliban, Afghanistan has become the world's largest opium producer and exporter with 90 percent of world production, according to the UN's 56th Session of the Commission on Narcotic drugs held in Vienna in March 2013.[69] Poppy production and heroin export consumption is now the cornerstone of the Afghan economy. Prices of low-quality heroin in the U.S. are around $172 per gram and of pure heroin much higher.[70] It is a most lucrative cash crop, a "cash cow" of sorts, facilitated by the U.S.–sponsored Karzai regime in Afghanistan (Karzai was a former employee of the U.S. oil corporation, UNOCAL) under which production jumped from 181 tons in 2001 to 3,400 tons in 2002 and prices skyrocketed ten times the level from 2000. The British-funded opium eradication program working with the U.S. Drug Enforcement Agency under "Operation Containment" in Afghanistan following the U.S. invasion in 2001, ironically stimulated the further explosion of poppy production and a resurgence of international opium consumption. The efforts of these "drug eradication" programs were thus highly suspect, particularly in the wake of the opium trade and sales as an international commodity worth billions, estimated at $70 billion in 2012.[71] In 2013, Afghanistan produced a massive 5,500 metric tons of opium, 49 percent higher than 2012 and more than the opium production in the rest of the world put together. It is indeed mind-boggling that with thousands of U.S. troops stationed in Afghanistan and with the most sophisticated surveillance and monitoring equipment in the world, the U.S. military and auxiliary anti-drug agencies like the CIA and the DEA, the poppy farms that these troops are guarding are invincible from security detection.[72] The only explanation is the cover-up of such poppy cultivation for the facilitation of the multi-billion opium trade that funds the U.S. military operations in the country and that makes billions for opium merchants and international drug cartels and syndicates, conveyed in 2009 by a former Russian commander who served during the Russian occupation of Afghanistan in the 1980s.[73] The CIA wouldn't be suspect if it had a clean record in the international political and economic arena; the history of its activities in southeast Asia in the 1960s and 1970s and its working with drug cartels in Central America to fund the Nicaraguan Contras in the 1980s, along with a disclosure from a Mexican government official that the CIA and other anti-drug agencies simply "manage" the drug trade as opposed to fighting it since it is so lucrative job-wise, places the agency in a very culpable role when it comes to the drug trade.[74] An Indigenous elder from the Tohono O'odham nation recounted how he took pictures of U.S. Border Patrol agents escorting drug dealers across the Mexico-Arizona border and showed them to his supervisor, only to have his employment as a ranger terminated.[75]

Author and former Los Angeles Police Department narcotics investigator Michael Ruppert explains in the chapter "The CIA Is Wall Street and Drug Money Is King" in his book *Crossing the Rubicon: The Decline of the American Empire at the End of the Age of Oil* that the CIA has always been involved with Wall Street.[76] Wall Street lawyer and banker Clark Clifford, a former Secretary of Defense, who wrote the National Security Act of 1947, for example, was successful in having the Bank of Credit and Commerce International (BCCI) operate in the U.S. BCCI was a corrupt CIA-bank founded by Pakistani financier Agha Hassan Abedi, and it laundered drug money and financed the Afghan rebels under the leadership of the CIA fighting the Soviets in the late 1970s. John Foster Dulles was an executive with Standard Oil in the 1950s and eventually became Secretary of State under Dwight Eisenhower. His brother, Allen, a business lawyer with the powerful corporate law firm Sullivan and Cromwell, was Director of the CIA under Eisenhower and was fired by John F. Kennedy following the 1962 Bay of Pigs invasion of Cuba. Both brothers jointly were key in the CIA-led overthrow of Jacobo Arbenz, the democratically elected president of Guatemala in 1954, since Arbenz legislated land reform where unused land of large banana plantations like the United Fruit Company (Chiquita today), where the Dulles brothers were major shareholders, was to be redistributed among landless Guatemalan peasants. Arbenz had offered to compensate the United Fruit Company that owned 42 percent of Guatemala's land area and yet paid no taxes.[77]

Enron, the energy company that went bankrupt and destroyed the retirement funds of thousands of employees worth billions, was a leading client of Sullivan and Cromwell and had several CIA officers in its employment prior to its collapse. Other prominent clients of the law firm were American International Group (AIG), Global Crossing, ImCline, Martha Stewart, and the Harvard Endowment, with AIG having been linked to the heroin trade and Martha Stewart having been charged and imprisoned for insider trading and financial conspiracy.[78] Bill Casey, the director of the CIA under Ronald Reagan, was a Wall Street lawyer and stock trader. Stanley Sporkin, Casey's general counsel, was close to Oliver North, a member of the National Security Council and a central figure in the Iran-Contra scandal who was convicted on several felony charges for lying to Congress in the 1980s. Sporkin worked for 20 years at the Securities and Exchange Commission. Following his tenure at the CIA, he joined the Wall Street law firm Weill, Gottschall, and Manges, which worked as Enron's counsel. David Doherty, who followed as CIA general counsel in 1987, returned to Wall Street as the executive vice president of the New York Stock Exchange on Enforcement. A.B. "Buzzy" Krongard, who joined the CIA in 1998, was the CEO of the investment bank Alex Brown. John Deutch, director of the CIA who met with congressional representatives in south central Los Angeles in 1996 to discuss the CIA role in injecting drugs into the Black community, retired shortly thereafter and became a board member of Citigroup, notorious for laundering drug money, particularly through its Mexican subsidiary, Banamex. Maurice "Hank" Greenberg, the CEO of AIG, oversaw the breaking of federal laws by an Arkansas subsidiary of AIG in collaboration with the Arkansas Development Financial Authority (ADFA), which was cited for money-laundering operations for drug funds from CIA-smuggled cocaine from Latin America into Mena, Arkansas, in the 1980s.[79] Quite a revolving door between the CIA, government officials, and Wall Street, with the globalized economy of illegal drug trafficking featuring pivotally at various levels.

It's relevant too to look at the manner in which the CIA, Capricorn Holdings, Dyncorp, Enron, and the Harvard Endowment Fund were all interlocked in the impoverishment of Black and Brown communities in major metropolitan areas like south-central Los Angeles, the District of Columbia, and New Orleans' predominantly Black communities. Herbert "Pug" Winokur, a Wall Street "insider," was one of the seven Fellows on Harvard's governing board, while serving on Enron's board and the board of Capricorn Holdings. A member of the Council on Foreign Relations, Winokur was the CEO of Capricorn Holdings, which was the leading investor in Dyncorp, a military company that has received $600 million in U.S. government monies for the defoliation of Colombia, Peru, and Bolivia as part of the U.S.-drug war program, Plan-Colombia, underscoring the interwovenness of corporate executives, political powerbrokers, the CIA, and the drug economy and drug war particularly in a globalized world. Winokur was a "facilitator" at Enron that laundered billions in drug money. Harvard Endowment Fund and Enron often invested alongside each other and Harvard sold Enron stock for high profits prior to the Enron debacle.

A more careful examination of the manner in which the CIA pumped Central American drugs into Black and Brown neighborhoods in south-central Los Angeles from 1982 through 1995 and subsequent developments reveal an insidious picture of globalization and racist oppression. Austin Fitts, a former Under-Secretary at the Department of Housing and Urban Renewal (HUD) and a former partner with the Wall Street firm Dillon & Read, started her own company, Hamilton Securities, that developed a software program called Community Wizard that provided information on governmental expenditures for local community programs. Community Wizard discovered that a large sector of the HUD properties in south central Los Angeles, where the cocaine epidemic and narcotics trafficking were rampant, were moving into foreclosure due to falling real estate values in the area during the 1980s and 1990s. Thousands of middle-class Black families were walking away from their properties due to the crack cocaine epidemic and pervasive violence from drive-by shootings and drug-related violence. These houses were then loaded for sale on the property market at a fraction of their real value, at ten to twenty cents of the dollar in many instances. Wealthy investors then came in and purchased thousands of these properties, one of the investors being the Harvard Endowment Fund. It is no exaggeration then to conclude that such investors were "beefing up a very large tax-free investment portfolio for short-term capital gains from the destruction of African American communities and asset forfeiture brought on by the drug trade."[80] The drug war and the impoverishment of Black and

Brown urban communities tie directly into the globalized profit system and subsequently into the politics of race and class that feed into the prison industrial complex.

The $400 billion global illegal drug economy (estimated at $600 billion by Michael Ruppert), in which banks benefit lucratively from laundering drugmoney, certainly features prominently in the persistence of the production and consumption of illicit drugs, much of which finds its way inevitably to cash-strapped and employment-deprived urban communities in Russia, Europe, and the U.S.[81] The connections of the global drug trade to the U.S. economy and banking system are stark: mammoth banks like HSBC, Western Union, Bank of America, JP Morgan Chase & Company, Citigroup, and formerly Wachovia (taken over by Wells Fargo in 2010 after being exposed for illegal drug money-laundering) that are among the world's largest banks and possess trillions in assets have all violated U.S. federal anti-money laundering laws, yet not a single bank has been prosecuted and not a single bank official has been jailed to date. Wachovia paid a fine of $160 million for its involvement in money laundering in Mexico worth $374 billion and was taken over by Wells Fargo, the largest bank in terms of capitalization worth in the world.[82] In December 2012, the U.S. Department of Justice negotiated a deal with HSBC, levying a fine of $1.9 billion fine for its active role in assisting the Mexican drug cartels through laundering drug money through HMEX, the subsidiary of HSBC in Mexico. A *small price* to pay for a bank that made profits of $22 billion in 2011! The horrific reality of this global drug war and trade, where banks make hundreds of billions of dollars from drug money laundering, is the *lethal and harsh price* paid by the poor: over 150,000 people have been killed in Mexico since 2006 and half a million poor people, mostly Black and Latino, have been sentenced to long terms in prison for selling illegal drugs.[83] Meanwhile the *real* beneficiaries, managers of these heinous drug crimes, remain unpunished and ensconced in corporate boardrooms and skyscraper banking and investment offices in 2015.

Given the stark reality of abysmally low family incomes, run-down schools due to low tax revenues, widespread unemployment particularly for youth, and very few decent social recreational amenities and outlets for youth, the essential ingredients for an impoverished economic and social ethos were created in U.S. urban metropolises. These anomalous social conditions provided fertile ground for many in these communities becoming susceptible to the drug dealer and drug pusher who signified extensions of the drug syndicates that really controlled the drug economy, which were in some instances, facilitated by law enforcement and security agencies like the CIA and even police departments in inner cities like Chicago, New York, and Los Angeles, where the aforedescribed conditions are rife. So long as "crime" is inevitable due to lack of resources engineered by a heartless capitalist system and its selective monitoring application makes mega-profits for the ruling class and provides a plethora of vocations connected to prisons—politicians running for office on "tough on crime" platforms; Department of Justice and subsidiary offices; judges and court personnel; security agencies like the National Security Agency, CIA, FBI, Defense Intelligence Agency, Drug Enforcement Agency, and Customs and Border Patrol; police and sheriff's departments at city, county, and state levels; and various direct and indirect sectors of incarceration employees like construction company personnel, bond investors and brokers, psychologists and counselors, guards, lawyers, food companies supplying prisons with food supplies, medical doctors working in prisons, pharmaceutical companies selling medication to prisons, social workers, and telephone companies that charge higher rates for incarcerated persons' calls—the prison industrial complex is assured of booming, especially under globalization, where the interlocking dimensions of crime, punishment, national security, and the economy assume decisive proportions.

The published 1996 Report of the National Criminal Justice Commission, *The Real War on Crime*, systematically documents the manner in which the U.S. Justice Department deliberately distorted factual information so as to mislead the public into believing that the solution to violent crime is tougher prison sentences and enhanced prison construction. For instance, to convey the view that all persons trapped within the criminal justice system are dangerous, a 1991 analysis report by the department noted that "94 percent of inmates had been convicted of a violent crime *or* had a previous sentence to probation or incarceration," permitting the government to "consolidate two different classifications into a single claim," and exaggerate the levels of violence by people incarcerated.[84] In 1992, the Department of Justice published *The Case for More Incarceration*, part of a systematic effort by then Attorney General William Barr to urge states and cities to construct more prisons. The publication claimed that every inmate behind bars saved the country $430,000 per year, assuming that each person incarcerated would commit 187 street crimes per year that cost victims $2,300 per crime as the result of property damage or medical bills. The researchers who originally compiled the data retracted their conclusions. Franklin Zimring and Gordon Hawkins systematically examined the claim of $430,000 in savings and found that even if it were assumed that each released prisoner committed 187 crimes per year, law enforcement would need to imprison 230,000 additional criminals to erase some 42.5 million national crimes. Persons incarcerated increased significantly more than that number since the collection of the data and the published report of the Department of Justice. By 1996, there were 1.5 million people held in prisons even while the national crime rate still remained high—between 30 and 40 million crimes per year.

Similarly, the Justice Department inaccurately stated that the incarceration rate of state prisoners "doubled for both black and White inmates" from 1984 to 1994 to 1 million people, deliberately obscuring racial discrepancies between African Americans and European Americans whose incarceration rates increased at the rate of 98 percent and 78 percent respectively. The Justice Department cooked figures to include Latinos (or Hispanics) within the White prison population so that the racial divide in imprisonment (African Americans were incarcerated at six times the rates for Whites) would appear benign.[85]

Even more revealing is the DARE (Drug Abuse Resistance Education) program that started in the Los Angeles Police Department (itself tainted by a history of illicit drug involvement, violence, and corruption during the Ramparts scandal of the late 1990s) and has spread to almost half of all school districts in the country. Even though this Department of Justice program cost taxpayers some $700 million in the 1990s, research by the department found that it did not deter drug use among children. The department withheld the report showing failure of the program.[86] Some scholars criticized the program for creating family dissension because it casts children in the role of "informant," and they question the long-term effectiveness of the currently $1 billion drug education program.[87] Studies have consistently demonstrated that DARE is ineffective and, in some instances, causes children to engage in activity of profiling persons and family members in ways that are destructive.[88] Yet through aggressive political lobbying and as a result of law enforcement's influence in attracting hundreds of millions of federal and state tax dollars, globalization's policy of profit from punishment continues to keep this wasteful program in place.

Crime and punishment are political code-words within the dominant national discourse used for economic and political self-serving purposes especially in the age of globalization. The issue of the safety of the public is loaded with propagandistic ideas about the "dangerous" condition of living in the U.S. given the pervasiveness of "criminal" behavior. It is thus no coincidence that the notion of "Homeland Security" was invoked in 2001 and a multi-billion dollar department instituted following the events of September 11, 2001. "Homeland Security" is a reflection of globalization's ideology of containing the growing socio-economic conflicts generated in many parts of Latin America, Asia, and Africa as a result of globalization processes like deregulation, privatization, and dismantling of public services provided by state governments, which saw hundreds of millions become unemployed and quickly enter the ranks of poverty. The National Security state went into full gear with an open declaration by then president George W. Bush of a "War on Terror" and, once again, wars against the people of Asia, this time Afghanistan and, subsequently, Iraq, were declared, with intolerable human, environmental, and financial cost—millions were killed, wounded, and made homeless (5 million orphans and 600,000 homeless children live in Iraq today!), hundreds of thousands of U.S. soldiers suffer from Gulf-War syndrome, broken or destroyed limbs, and mental illness, and a $1.3 trillion war bill has been foisted on the U.S. public taxpayer, with interest.[89]

The promulgation of the U.S.A. Patriot Act of 2001, which was extended and ratified by President Barack Obama in 2010, implies the stripping of fundamental liberties and abolition of rights to privacy enshrined in the U.S. Constitution. Philip Giraldi, a former CIA-official, likened the Patriot Act to laws of Nazi Germany because it implies the nullification of citizenship rights under the pretext of waging a ceaseless "War on Terror."[90] All of these dehumanizing laws are part and parcel of the globalized restructuring of the world into "good" and "evil" by powerful governments, which has resulted in the deaths and incarceration of millions in overcrowded prisons in many parts of the world. The poor and defenseless are increasingly criminalized by the forces controlling globalization so that they can be discarded by wars or confined behind bars for long periods of time. The "Three Strikes" law that has been legislated in a few states within the U.S. and which was promoted by Bill Clinton during his State of the Union address on January 25, 1994, confines even non-violent offenders to life imprisonment and is essential to globalization's practice of punishing the poor while making money off their imprisonment for decades. Ironically, Clinton's state of Arkansas was a key location for the illegal smuggling of drugs from Latin America in the 1980s, germane to the three-strikes law that has seen persons receiving life sentences for committing three consecutive non-violent crimes, including crimes like illegal drug possession or drug sales.

Following George W. Bush's pronouncements in 2001, the War on Terror continues its work of harassing and terrorizing people of all backgrounds, especially people of color who continue to be profiled racially by national security agencies like the U.S. Border Patrol and the Department of Homeland Security. Many people are denied access to proper legal aid and defense and kept in detention centers that are unclean and subject to humiliating conditions, as with many in U.S. prisons. The detention of more than 255 people considered "enemy combatants" since 2008, some of whom have been held for six years without a trial or being formally charged, continues till today.

George W. Bush claimed in his recent memoirs, *Decision Points*, that water-boarding was not torture and that it thwarted two attacks on London, even though these torturous acts did not prevent the bombings on London on July 7, 2005.[91] When Bush was asked if waterboarding was ever used on the captured Al Qaeda leader Khalid Sheikh Mohammed, his response to *The Times* was "Damn right!"[92] When human rights activists within the U.S. and around the world charged that the U.S. government and the CIA engaged in torture of detainees apprehended as terrorism suspects when waterboarding was deployed, actions that constituted a violation of the Geneva Convention and the UN Convention on Human Rights, George W. Bush strenuously defended the governmental position by declaring that the U.S. does not engage in torture.[93] What he did not acknowledge was that torture has always been a part of the internal prison system in the U.S. President Barack Obama insisted that he would end such torture, ban inhuman interrogation techniques and even close Guantanamo Bay in early 2009. What he did not explain was that there were many loopholes and contradictions within his "new" policies that ostensibly distanced him from his predecessor. Gregory B. Craig, the White House Chief Counsel during Obama's first term in office, assured John A. Rizzo, the CIA's top lawyer then, that Obama had no intention of doing away with torture altogether, but simply "ending its abuse."[94]

Rendition policies and other short-term torture practices continue to this day and Guantanamo remains open for imprisonment and punishment business under Obama's administration. In a speech, he only conceded that the U.S. "tortured some folks" in August 2014, obscuring the fact that U.S. torture of terrorism suspects was pervasive and systemic, as at Abu Ghraib prison in Iraq.[95] To date, nobody has been prosecuted at the highest levels of the CIA and other military agencies for torture, rendition policies, and killing of innocent civilians by national security agencies as part of the U.S. "war on terror." In September 2014, it was revealed that some Al Qaeda suspects held at Guantanamo in Cuba were excessively tortured to the point that a medical doctor's presence was necessary to ensure that the detainees did not die, far more dangerous and excruciating than what the CIA had acknowledged previously regarding its interrogation techniques.[96] Hundreds of suspected terrorists from around the world have been subject to gruesome forms of torture, have never been formally charged in an international court of law, are still being held indefinitely and, in some cases, transferred to repressive regimes in other parts of the world for interrogation and torture under the U.S. government's rendition program. Since the Obama administration came to office in in 2009, 390 covert drone strikes have killed almost 2,400 people, including innocent civilians in Pakistan, Yemen, and Somalia.[97] Drone strikes under Obama were used eight times more than when George H. Bush was president. This is the ugly character of U.S. globalized security policies and practices that have caused suffering and death to millions, while imprisoning and torturing hundreds of thousands of people in Iraq, like at Abu Ghraib prison, and other detention facilities in countries with which the U.S. has a strategic military relationship, especially in West Asia and North Africa.[98] The War on Terror, like the prison industrial complex in the U.S., is big business under globalization.

In 1994, the average daily detention population of legal and undocumented immigrants was 5,532. By 2001, this number increased to 19,533 and, in 2007, it was 30,000. Almost 2 million legal and undocumented people were deported, mostly for non-violent violations. Ironically, president Barack Obama, the first president of color who promised Latinos whose vote helped him win the states of New Mexico, Colorado, Nevada, and Florida in 2012 that he would support immigrant rights, deported 400,000 people in his first year in office, more than George W. Bush did in his last year in office. Obama authorized the deportation of some 150,000 mothers and fathers of children who were U.S. citizens each year in office.[99] At the end of 2002, according to the U.S. Bureau of Immigration and Customs Enforcement (ICE), there were "21, 065 detainees specifically being held under ICE jurisdiction by the Office of Detention and Removal."[100] Almost 25 percent of those detained or held in federal prisons are not U.S. citizens, some 33,873 people. Under the auspices and protection of Section 215 of the USA Patriot Act, the FBI and other national security agencies can monitor both citizens and non-citizens regardless of whether they are criminals or not, nullifying basic protection of peoples' rights guaranteed under the U.S. Constitution and raising the ire of rights groups like the American Civil Liberties Union, which views such laws as a foundational assault on human liberties in the U.S.[101] This injustice is compounded with the fact of 5,500 immigrant detainees working each day for as low as a dollar a day, 13 cents an hour, or for nothing in the country's immigration detention centers. Government and private prisons save about $40 million each year through this exploitative practice since the federal minimum wage of $7.25 per hour does not apply to federal detainees.[102] In 2013, some 60,000 immigrants worked in federal government and private detention centers in Washington, California, Arizona, Texas, New Mexico, Colorado, Indiana, Illinois, Wisconsin, New York, New Jersey, Florida, Louisiana, Georgia, Virginia, Missouri, and Nebraska.[103]

Immigration bill SB 1070 signed by Arizona governor Jan Brewer in April 2010 was motivated and engineered by a group of state legislators and corporate executives called the American Legislative Exchange Council that included the billion dollar Corrections Company of America along with Exxon Mobil, Reynolds American Inc., and the National Rifle Association. The bill, initially drafted by State Senator Russell Pearce with the explicit intention of detaining and imprisoning thousands of Mexicans and other "illegal aliens" to be housed in for-profit private prisons in Arizona, is a stark reminder of globalization and incarceration at work together.[104]

Globalization's ideological design, which upholds the doctrine of national security as a core patriotic principle within late capitalism, ensures that torture and capital punishment continue in line with the Bush-initiated War on Terrorism and the Project for the New American Century. The result is violence and terror of poor people within the U.S. and those from other parts of the globe where resource-fought wars are waged so that all are forcefully brought into conformity and allegiance to the national security state—the homeland as described in the Department of Homeland Security.[105] The 1997 document, *United States Space Command: Vision for 2020,* is now in full swing as wars in the Arab world in Syria, Iraq, Yemen, and around the Caspian like Afghanistan, rage. This blueprint of the U.S. national security state in the 21st century explicitly states that, "although unlikely to be challenged by a global peer competitor, the United States will continue to be challenged regionally.... The globalization of the world economy will continue, with a widening between the 'haves' and 'have-nots.'"[106] In this manner, the infusion of hundreds of billions of dollars into the coffers of military industrial contractors and correctional apparatuses to hold the "have-nots" in check can be justified to a gullible and economically depressed U.S. public.

Incarceration of Political Prisoners, Women, and Violence Against People Considered Sexually Deviant

The continued incarceration during this globalized era of almost 150 Black, Indigenous, Chicano-Mexicano, and Puerto Rican *political* prisoners in the U.S., for over three decades in many instances, is an affront to any sense of justice because it confines some of the leading spokespersons and human rights activists from these communities to a life of irrevocable punishment and isolation. The names and figures are internationally renowned. Journalist and author Mumia Abu Jamal, on death row for 29 years and sentenced in 2011 to life in prison without parole; Jamil Abdullah Al-Amin (formerly Student Non-Violent Coordinating Committee chair and Black freedom fighter H. Rap Brown), in a supermax Special Management Unit (SMU) for life at ADX-Florence Correctional Facility, Colorado; Black Panther activists Jalil Abdul Muntaqim, Herman Bell, and Marshall Eddie Conway (released in early March 2014 after being imprisoned for almost 44 years after being framed by COINTELPRO infiltrators within the Black Panther Party), who have each spent over 35 years in jail after being falsely charged by the FBI[107]; Sundiata Acoli, Albert Woodfox (incarcerated 40 years at Angola Prison and now at Homer, Louisiana); American Indian Movement leader Leonard Peltier for 30 years, framed for the killing of members of the FBI and other persons at the Pine Ridge Indian reservation in 1975; Hugo Pinell, who is the world's longest incarcerated person and has been held in jail for over 49 years, 44 of which have been in solitary confinement, and was denied parole nine times; Cinque McGee, a radical activist of the "August 7th Rebellion" that called for the release of Black political prisoners George Jackson, John Cluchette, and Fleeta Drumgo in 1970, who was sentenced to life imprisonment in that year; and Puerto Rican independence advocates like Oscar López Rivera who has been jailed for almost 33 years, are persons whose continued confinement indeed constitute "cruel and unusual punishment" in violation of the United Nations Convention on Human Rights.[108] Globalization's long-term and irrevocable prison cruelty is part of the ideological framework that punishes any resistors to oppression with the harshest penalties, especially radical civil rights activists from the 1960s and 1970s or anti-colonial justice activists from the early 1980s and 1990s.

Two-thirds of women in prison are persons of color.[109] Though the composition of women in prison is diverse, most are "dark-skinned, poor, unskilled mothers who are incarcerated for low-level drug involvement."[110] Black women represent the largest increase of all women being incarcerated in the U.S. with rates of 185 per 100,000 women, twice that of Latino women, and five times that of White women, so that Black women are now three-quarters of the number of females in state and local prisons, according to a 2005 released criminal justice report.[111] Black women have experienced a 78 percent increase in incarceration since 1989.[112] They are also most likely to suffer ill-health afflicted by conditions of hypertension, asthma, sickle cell anemia, and breast and cervical cancer. More than three-quarters of women in prison who have HIV/AIDS are women of color and half of all new HIV infections among women prisoners are Black.[113] The female prison population increased dramatically from 12,300 in 1980 to 96,000 in 2002 even though crime rates dropped during that period.[114] Black women in gangs is another rapidly growing phenomenon during this phase of globalization considering that in some instances, between 10 and 30 percent of gangs are female, resulting in sequential imprisonment of female gang members since they inevitably become targets of law enforcement like their male counterparts.[115]

The system of patriarchal and capitalist violence of the broader society that continues in male prisons is reproduced in female prisons. As Faith Lutze, a criminal justice researcher, notes, while the effect of incarceration on men is often the stripping away of their masculinity and sense of personhood through abuse and punishment policies like solitary isolation, for example, for women's prisons, the ideological "ultramasculine environment" and accompanying policies are "extrapolated to women's prisons, so that women yet again are subject to abusive policies and treatment that make them submissive, weak, and dependent."[116] The incidence of rape of women in prisons, often by male corrections officers and sometimes by female officers with threats against victims of retaliation if disclosed to authorities or family members, is an integral part of the prison industrial complex.[117]

Equally disconcerting is the violence against persons who are lesbian, gay, bi-sexual, or trans-gendered (LGBT) within the prison industrial complex, who are often targeted by anti–LGBT societal prejudices. Violence against transgendered people constituted "17 percent of the violence enacted against LGBT persons nationally."[118] It was only in 2009 with the passage of the Matthew Shepard and James Byrd Hate Crimes Prevention Act that federal hate crimes were expanded to include a victim's perceived gender, sexual orientation, sexual identity, or disability. Yet the problem of violence against LGBT communities that results in conviction of individuals perpetrating such violence feeds into the prison industrial complex, which signifies another form of institutionalized violence in its system of punishment, deprivation, and confinement: individuals are simply imprisoned and uneducated about the nature and causes of such violence and the need for reparations to victims of this violence.[119] In a globalized society, LGBT Rights groups thus need to adopt a system-wide analysis that interrogates interlocking dimensions of race and class in their defense of victims of violence against LGBT persons since the prison system generally ignores the distinctive experiences of LGBT persons and their being subject to violence even within prisons themselves.

People of Color, Poor People and the Prison System in the Globalized Late 20th and Early 21st Centuries

Ruling class political code words, especially from the 1970s, following the struggles for social justice, the civil rights movement, the Black Power Movement, the Indigenous Peoples Movement, the Women's Movement, and the Peace Movement, were widely disseminated by corporate media and the political establishment to justify enhanced incarceration policies. Then president Richard Nixon initiated a "law-and-order campaign" and "getting tough" policy that translated into an ostensible "war on crime" for subsequent decades to the present, in line with his assertion that drug use was "public enemy No. 1."[120] Vijay Prashad writes that, "in 1968, as the world despaired over the U.S. bombardment of Vietnam and Cambodia, President Richard Nixon declared war on drugs." "Within the last decade," he told Congress, "the abuse of drugs has grown from essentially a local police problem into a serious national threat to the personal health and safety of millions of Americans."[121] This war on drugs has persisted for over four decades into the contemporary globalized era.

Incarceration rates skyrocketed from approximately 100 state and federal prisoners per 100,000 people during the mid-seventies to 509 per 100,000 in 2008.[122] In 2010, in state, federal, and local jails, for instance, these numbers multiplied three to four-fold. Black men aged 35–39 years old were imprisoned at the rate of 2,813 per 100,000 residents, and Whites from the same age group were imprisoned at the rate of 1,581 per 100,000 residents, among the highest confinement rates in the world (**Table 5**).

With the election of Ronald Reagan as U.S. president in 1980, the War on Drugs that Reagan promised assumed an ugly intensification with arrests of hundreds of thousands of Black and Brown youth for drug possession so that, in some instances, Black people constituted 80 to 90 percent of those sent to prison for drug offenses even though White youth used illegal drugs in proportion to their composition within the population: about 60 percent.[123] The War on Drugs of the early 1980s was a particularly hideous assault on poor people of color who clearly had few economic options given the recession of that decade and the high levels of unemployment that plagued Black youth, as high as 35 percent during that period. The militarization of the campaign to stamp out drug use was particularly foreboding, underscoring the dynamics of race and class in the criminalization of Black and Brown people. Michelle Alexander asserts that "the drug war has been brutal—complete SWAT teams, tanks, bazookas, grenade launchers, and sweeps of entire neighborhoods—

Table 5

Bureau of Justice Statistics
Filename: cpus10at03.csv

Report title: Correctional Populations in the United States, 2010 NCJ236319
Data source(s): Annual Probation Survey, Annual Parole Survey, National Prisoner Statistics Program,
Annual Survey of Jails, and Census of Jails
Author(s): Lauren E. Glaze
Refer questions to: askbjs@usdoj.gov or 202-307-0765
Date of version: 12/13/2011

Estimated number of inmates held in custody in state or federal prisons or in local jails
per 100,000 U.S. residents, by sex, race and Hispanic/Latino origin, and age, June 30, 2010

Year	White/a	Black/b
Total/c	732	1,352
18-19	829	1,508
20-24	1,538	2,728
25-29	1,696	3,018
30-34	1,798	3,215
35-39	1,581	2,813
40-44	1,355	2,435
45-49	1,000	1,848
50-54	642	1,213
55-59	386	750
60-64	212	420
65 or older	70	155

Note: Based on the total incarcerated population on June 30, 2010, and the U.S. resident population
estimates for July 1, 2010, by sex, race and Hispanic/Latino origin, and age. Rates may be different than
those reported in appendix table 2 due to different reference dates. Detailed categories exclude persons
who reported two or more races.
a/Includes American Indians, Alaska Natives, Asians, Native Hawaiians, other Pacific Islanders, and
persons identifying two or more races.
b/Excludes persons of Hispanic or Latino origin.
c/Includes persons under age 18.

but those who live in middle-class White communities have little clue to the
devastation wrought."[124] The militarization of anti-drug campaigns by law
enforcement that often leads to arrest, conviction, and incarceration of mostly
poor Black and Latino people substantiates the interwovenness of militarization, incarceration, and globalization, the "get tough" and "show them who's
boss" rhetoric that is conveyed to a generally pliable and gullible U.S. public.
Alexander explains that though Whites and people of color use illicit drugs
in general proportion to their composition within the U.S. population and in
some instances, White youth are three times more likely to be serious drug
users, African American youth are criminalized the most and often comprise

80–90 percent of those imprisoned for drug offenses.[125] A Humans Right Watch report of 2001 disclosed that most people in the U.S. continue to envision a "Black man slouching in an alleyway, not a White man in his home" when it comes to conceiving of a typical drug user, even though significantly higher numbers of Whites use powder and crack cocaine than Blacks.[126]

The manner in which racist incarceration policies feature in political leadership and especially presidential campaigns underscores the politics of race and punishment in the globalization era of the early 21st century. When 18-year-old high school student, Keith Jackson, was arrested for selling cocaine a block from the White House in 1989, then president George H.W. Bush immediately seized the opportunity to proclaim a national policy of harsh punishment for illicit drug use. Jackson was a young Black man with no prior arrest record for drug use, yet his arrest case became a *cause celebré* in Bush's convoluted administering of justice that singled out poor Black youth as the primary culprits for such offenses. Though Jackson was a responsible student who rarely sold drugs for pocket money and had to be lured by Drug Enforcement Agency (DEA) agents to the area around the White House to make the sale because he had little idea where the White House was, he received the maximum ten-year sentence without parole for the offense in accordance with mandatory drug time for crack cocaine-related crimes. Bush did not commute the sentence and the media once again projected the picture of a young Black man in handcuffs for drug use, goading Washington politicians to demand tougher penalties for crack cocaine use and sales. Little mention was made of the fact that while most crack users and sellers are White, Jackson was a law-abiding Black citizen working to complete high school, yet economically disempowered by the loss of jobs due to "deindustrialization and globalization" of the late 1980s.[127]

Globalization's right-wing political harshness against the poor of color is reflected in the promulgation of federal crack cocaine laws from 2003 that saw Black defendants constituting 80 percent of those sentenced under such laws, compared to White defendants who were 7.8 percent of those sentenced for cocaine convictions.[128] A federal Substance Abuse and Mental Health Services Administration 2004 survey revealed that in fact 66 percent of the nation's crack cocaine users were White or Latino, underscoring again the insidious anti–Black racism of the criminal justice system.[129] Federal mandatory sentencing laws have affected poor Black women in particular since Black women's incarceration rates rose 800 percent since 1986 compared to 400 percent for women from other ethnic groups.[130] Federal law is heavily stacked against crack cocaine users, often Black, and relatively lenient on powder cocaine users, mostly White, since 5 grams of crack triggers the mandatory five-year sentence while it takes 500 grams of powdered cocaine to invoke the same mandatory sentence.[131]

In 1991, Black youth were twice as likely to end up being detained for drug use as Whites were, and Black youth were four times as likely as White youth to be tried in adult court.[132] The effects of mandatory sentencing have taken a devastating toll on Black people, as Barbara Meierhoefer's study of 267,278 offenders sentenced in federal courts between January 1984 and June 1990 demonstrated, with Whites being "consistently more likely than blacks to be sentenced to less than the minimum sentence."[133] Black defendants in court were twice as likely to be incarcerated for larceny and weapons offenses as Whites.[134] In 1998, Black people were 35 percent of the close to 3.5 million people on probation, and while White men were "incarcerated at a rate of 491 per 100,000," Black men were "incarcerated at a rate more than six times that figure—3,235 per 100,000."[135] According to the Center for Disease Control in 2000, even though White high school students were four times more likely to use cocaine than their Black classmates, the Black students were one and a half times more likely to end up in prison.[136]

Incarceration for drug convictions rose by two thirds in federal prisons and by 50 percent in state prisons over the past three decades.[137] The growth in the "punishment industrial complex" is phenomenal to the point that no other country in the world has seen such an intensification of confinement of its people from 1980, when 1,842,100 people fell under some form of correctional system adjudication, to 6,592,800 in 2001 and those in prison grew from 503,586 to 1,962,220 during that period, much of it resulting from drug convictions and giving the U.S. the dubious distinction of having the most persons per capita imprisoned in the world.[138]

The patent racist and unjust character of the criminal justice system is observed in the manner that drug use and race are deployed in the execution of apprehensions, arrests, and convictions of suspects sought for illegal drug possession. Manning Marable notes that in New York, while "African Americans and Latinos make up 25 percent of the total population" by "1999 they represented 83 percent of all state prisoners and 94 percent of all individuals convicted on drug offenses" and that "while African Americans ... constitute only 14 percent of all drug users nationally, they account for 35 percent of all drug arrests, 55 percent of all drug convictions, and 75 percent of all prison admissions for drug offenses ... the racial proportions of those under some type of correctional supervision, including parole and probation, are one in fifteen for young White males, one in ten for young Latino males, and one in three for young African American males."[139] It comes as no surprise then to learn that "more than eight out of every ten African American males will be arrested at some point in their lifetime."[140]

For young people charged with drug offenses, Black youth are forty eight times more likely than Whites to be sent to juvenile prisons.[141] This kind of inordinately cruel punishment underscores the gravity of a deeply racist society and signifies an economic extension of slavery from the 17th through the 19th centuries. For instance, 90 percent of those arrested for drug possession also have their assets confiscated by police and most are people of color.[142] Reports out of Chicago have described corrupt police officers that were expropriating the property of drug dealers for their own financial enrichment.[143]

The War on Drugs from the 1980s translated into a War on Black and Brown people, just as the War on Terrorism today translates into a War on Muslims here and abroad (even though there is now compelling evidence to suggest that the government explanation of events of September 11, 2001, and its attempt to blame Muslims is not trustworthy).[144] The fundamental question of why the "United States has 5 percent of the world's population but consumes 60 percent of its illicit drugs" has never been radically addressed by the ruling class establishment because this class's interest lies in benefitting from a drug-economy that exceeds over half a trillion dollars, a significant portion of the U.S. gross domestic product.[145] As Dirk Chase Eldredge, a conservative White Republican businessman, thoughtfully lamented "in the name of 'winning the war on drugs' ... the United States has allowed expediency to trump constitutional principle.... Rather than trying to heal the unwell, we have caused the reordering of many of the precious priorities we call 'civil liberties.'"[146] He cautions that while the drug abuser has made foolish life choices, it's just as myopic that the nation resorts to the option of punishment instead of treatment of those abusing drugs. Simply confining people away from society in prisons to make them invisible rather than preventing such abuse does not resolve the drug problem, Eldredge contends.[147] What sensible analysis and sensitivity coming from a conservative Republican businessman that many liberal thinkers would dismiss in a heartbeat! The political divide in the U.S. is apparently not between Democrats and Republicans and liberals and conservatives, but between people who understand and care about the trampled ones of society who are the most vulnerable, and those who do not. As Mumia Abu-Jamal and I discussed during our historic meeting in Waynesburg Correctional Center in May 2009, we must judiciously shy away from viewing the world with Manichean lenses where the lines between right and wrong are rigidly and inaccurately drawn. Eldredge's point about the wrong choice of a drug abuser recalls the poignant scene of a man who I interviewed in a prison in October 2012 who broke down and wept while telling me that there was nothing more painful in his life than realizing that his best friend whom he had shot died from the inflicted wound, all because of a feud in which rival gang members poisoned information about him and his friend so that both would kill each other. Here was a human being who had made the wrong choice and killed his best friend and later regretted his deadly deed, but was offered little opportunity to rehabilitate himself, being sentenced to 25 years to life for a crime that he viscerally regrets.

David Cole, a legal scholar, stresses the racial and class-tiered nature of criminal activity and the punishment meted out for crimes by the "justice" system. He writes that "the vast majority of those behind bars are poor; 40 percent of state prisoners can't even read; and 67 percent of prison inmates did not have full-time employment when they were arrested" and "the per capita incarceration rate among Blacks is seven times that among Whites.... Nationally, for every one Black man who graduates from college, 100 are arrested."[148] Cole reminds us that it's the impoverished who suffer more than middle-class folks from the effects from violent crimes because they live in poor neighborhoods and do not receive adequate protection from law enforcement and that Black people are victims of robbery at a rate 150 percent higher than Whites, are subject to rape and aggravated assault 25 percent more times than Whites, and that intraracial crime is most pervasive in impoverished communities, making homicide the leading cause of the deaths of young Black men.[149] For crimes in general, while middle-class and upper-class White society generally call for laws made more stringent for non-violent crimes, the fact of the matter is that families earning less than $7,000 per year are 1.6 times more likely to suffer property theft than families earning more than $75,000 per year and three times more prone to burglaries than families earning the latter figure annually.[150]

Coramae Richey Mann observes with regard to issues of race and crime that "the race/ethnicity of the stereotyped offender usually varies depending upon the specific concentration of African Americans, Asian Americans, Hispanic Americans, or Native Americans in an area, but the notion persists that members of these American sub-populations are more criminal or dangerous than the Euro-American majority group.... White Americans typically stereotype (and often caricature) other Americans who happen to be of a different skin color by, for example, viewing the classic rapist as a 'black man,' the representative opium user as a 'yellow man,' the archetypal knife wielder as a 'brown man,' the 'red man' as a drunken Indian, and each of these peoples of color, individually and collectively, as constituting the 'crime problem.'"[151] These racist images have been compounded under globalization and are reproduced widely within media and social circles with the objective of gaining popular endorsement from the dominant White culture, all in the interest of currency for the prison industrial complex and pursuit of profits from punishment. Though judges like U.S. District Judge, Reggie B. Walton, the leading drug policy advisor to George H.W. Bush in the 1980s, and U.S. District Judge Mark W. Bennett (featured in the 2012 documentary *The House I Live In*), lawmakers, and civil rights leaders have all called for swift corrective changes to federal mandatory drug sentencing laws that they assert disproportionately victimizes Black drug defendants, no policy shift towards racial justice has been made to date.[152]

A common practice now has become the relocation of incarcerated persons to states and towns far from their places of residence, so that familial visits are made difficult, and these places of residence are weakened economically since they represent one more potential wage-earner who no longer functions within his or her original place of residence. A young Indigenous Tohono O'odham woman in Tucson painfully described to me how her family had to come up with the $25 visiting fee plus transportation costs from Tucson to visit her two incarcerated brothers in Yuma and Florence, both towns some three hours and thirty minutes away respectively.[153] Hundreds of Hawaiians serving prison time have been transferred to private prisons in Arizona, making it impossible for family visits considering the exorbitant cost of family members traveling from Hawaii to Arizona.

Further, the economic impoverishment and political disenfranchisement that prison inmates suffer is an essential by-product of the globalized prison system. Few employers are willing to hire former prisoners, particularly in inner-city environs, and former inmates are often hired at low-wage levels and are generally confined to conditions of poverty or just above. According to the Sentencing Project, a non-governmental research center based in Washington, D.C., about 3.9 million U.S. citizens, or one of every fifty adults, have either permanently or recently lost their voting rights; 1.4 million Black men or the equivalent of 13 percent of all Black men are disfranchised, seven times the national average; over half a million women have become voteless; and in seven states where felons have lost their voting rights, one-quarter of Black men are permanently disfranchised. In 2002 there were more Black people in prison (close to 1 million women and men) than there were in college, and in New York State, there were more Black people (34,809) and more Latinos (22,421) in prison in the late 1990s than there were Black and Latino students enrolled at the State University of New York.[154] The U.S. political economy of globalization, in which incarceration of poor people is intrinsic, and the continued and rapidly expanding long-term incarceration of people of color ensures that millions of the poor will become permanently disenfranchised and thus constitute a dispensable segment of the U.S. human population.

From 1980 through 2005, the prison population grew more than four-fold, so that by the end of December 2004, there were nearly 7 million people involved with the corrections system, including 2,135,901 persons in state and federal prisons and jails (state- and privately-owned) and almost five million on probation or parole.[155] In mid–2004, city, state, federal, and community prisons in the U.S. held over 2.1 million people, with 123 female inmates per 100,000 women, compared to 1,348 per 100,000 men.[156] Forty percent of 182,101 inmates held in federal prisons in March 2005 were Black.[157] What is disturbing is that former "liberal" president Bill Clinton passed legislation in 1995 that makes it virtually impossible for incarcerated inmates to qualify for Pell grant funding to complete their college education, even though it has been substantively documented that college-educated inmates have much lower recidivism rates, of 5–10 percent, compared to non-college federal parolees whose recidivism rates are around 40 percent.[158] Clinton's legislation punished drug felons, even for petty offenses, by prohibiting them from living in public housing and denying them food stamps and other basic benefits. Under Clinton's presidency, the prison population in state and federal facilities saw the largest increase under any sitting U.S. president.[159] It is ironic that Democratically-elected "liberal" Bill Clinton, hailed as the first "Black" president in the White House by Nobel Laureate Toni Morrison, assumed narrow Republican platform positions on crime, supporting capital punishment, expanding private prisons, advancing the "three-strikes law" and mandatory unusually harsh sentencing, and funding the expansion of 100,000 more law enforcement officers in the late 1990s as part of his "tough on crime" policy even as crime rates were dropping. Clinton was also the president who interrupted his campaign for president in 1992 to return to Arkansas to oversee the execution of a mentally retarded inmate, anticipating the supportive votes of pro-death penalty voters.[160]

In 2013, the situation for all poor youth, particularly Black and Latino, revealed that issues of class and social stratification particularly compounded under globalization were pivotal in the escalation of imprisonment and the expansion of the prison industrial complex. For most of middle class society in the U.S., the invisibility of this underclass segment of society may be comforting, yet inevitably destabilizes any sense of a stable society since priorities become skewed as the result of globalization's obsessions with punishment and prisons. The massive investment in corrections, as in the military, exerted direct negative impact on the starved education and higher education budgets in states across the nation. Globalization's neo-liberal promotion of the national security state has left higher education in particular and education in general in the U.S. in tatters as states scrounge for public tax dollars to fund higher education, now seen as largely the responsibility of the private corporate sector and not worthy of public funding.[161] In the state of Arizona, for example, while the University of Arizona budget was cut by close to $100 million from 2008 to 2010 and while tuition rates increased 96 percent from 2006 through 2012, the budget allocation for Corrections was not radically dented. The budget allocation for corrections in Arizona for fiscal year 2011 was $1 billion, about one and a half times what the state spends on higher education. Arizona has the highest prison per capita population among Western states in the U.S., some 40,000 people behind bars.[162] Poor and under-resourced schools in impoverished neighborhoods ineluctably produce high levels of school dropouts, especially among communities of color. Researchers Bruce Western and Becky Pitt note that

> the influence of the penal system on social and economic disadvantage can be seen in the economic and family lives of the formerly incarcerated. The social inequality produced by mass incarceration is sizable and enduring for three main reasons: it is invisible, it is cumulative, and it is intergenerational.[163]

About 70 percent of state inmates have not completed high school and even among those with school diplomas, one in ten is incarcerated. Globalization's effects of punishment on the poor is reflected in the phenomenal growth of African American high school drop-outs who wound up in jail, from 10 percent in 1980 to 37 percent in 2008. For White dropouts, imprisonment rates also skyrocketed so that one in eight was behind bars in 2008. Intensification of class inequality during the rapidly moving economic downturn has produced opportunities for further oppression of young people based on race and class through the expansion of the prison system to unprecedented new levels in the U.S.

Social, racial, and economic stratification via the prison industrial complex under the globalization regime continues at the end of the first millennium of the 21st century, taking a painful toll on the lives of all poor people in prison, especially families. Some 200,000 children (1.75 percent of White children, 3.5 percent of Latino children, and 11 percent of Black children) had one parent in prison in 2008.[164] These figures quadrupled for Black and White children from 1980 to 2008 and doubled for Latino children over the same period. As prisoner rights advocate Angela Davis notes, "Mass incarceration is not a solution to unemployment, nor is it a solution to the vast array of social problems that are hidden away in a rapidly growing network of prisons and jails.... Racism has undermined our ability to create a popular critical discourse to contest the ideological trickery that posits imprisonment as key to public safety.... The focus of state policy is rapidly shifting from social welfare to social control."[165] Under globalization, such social control is both draconian and broadly institutionalized within the perimeters of a national security state, the globalized empire that imposes a deceptive ideology of "leader of the free world" and claims U.S. exceptionalism in the credo of "one nation under God."

Police Brutality, Harsh Sentencing, and Communities of Color in a Globalized U.S.

In his informative book, *Race, Crime, and the Law,* Harvard legal expert Randall Kennedy has provided excellent documentation of the historical injustices meted out to Black people.[166] He recounts for example how in 1934 three innocent Black farmhands, Ed Brown, Henry Shields, and Arthur Ellinger, were sentenced to death for the killing of White farmer Raymond Stewart. The three men were forced to accept a compromise "no contest" plea in lieu of a death sentence being re-imposed or the possibility of being lynched, after the Supreme Court in *Brown v. Mississippi* declared that the Mississippi court trial was unconstitutional and reversed the court decision.[167] Brown, Shield, and Ellinger were thus jailed for 10 years, 5 years, and 3 years respectively. Between 1976 and 1982, 16 people were killed by chokeholds by police in Los Angeles, 12 of them Black even though Black people were just 9 percent of the city's human population then.[168]

Under the system of globalization, police brutality and violence by SWAT teams and other para-military law enforcement and security agencies against poor Black and Latino people in particular has become widespread. Numerous police departments have acquired sophisticated military equipment as part of this enveloping militarization of law enforcement. The brutal 1992 beating of Rodney King by White police officers in Los Angeles, which was videotaped and broadcast around the world, basically captured the violent nature of law enforcement particularly when it comes to relating to people of color. The savage beating of King was certainly not the first of its kind in the last five decades. In August 1970, well-known *Los Angeles Times* journalist

Rubén Salazar, who documented police brutality against people of color, was killed by police during the National Chicano Moratorium Against the Vietnam War, along with 15-year-old Brown Beret Lynn Ward and Angel Diaz. In 1973, Luis "Junior" Martinez, a Chicano rights activist, was slain by police in Denver, Colorado.[169]

The deaths and brutalization of men and women of color at the hands of law enforcement is one of the most urgent socio-political problems facing the U.S. in this globalized era. In fall 1998, Tiyesha Miller was fatally shot in California after police pumped fifteen bullets into her body as she sat traumatized from a diabetic disorder in her car. In October of that year, Donta Davison, a teenager sitting in his car, was shot to death by police in Philadelphia. In January 1999, a municipal court judge dropped the manslaughter charge against DiPasquale, the officer who killed Davison, based on the judge's view that the shooting was not unwarranted since five other police officers testified that they would have responded with equal force under the circumstances. Mumia Abu-Jamal, himself on death row for a crime that he did not commit, wrote of Davison's assassination by police:

> Donta's life was cheap to the police.... Donta's life was cheap to the judiciary ... for both cheated him, and by extension, his family and community ... when one looks at the roots of the state's police, we can see clearly the historical traces of what we see today: police as agents of state corporate power, organized to protect their interests, and to oppose the interests of the poor and the Black.[170]

One of the most notorious and horrifying incidents was the death of Amadou Diallo, who was shot 46 times while he stood in a stairway of an apartment complex in New York City on the night of February 4, 1999. In April 2001, nineteen-year-old Timothy Thomas was shot dead by police officers in Cincinnati, sparking major demonstrations against police violence in the Black community in that city.[171] In early summer 2003, the town of Benton Arbor in Michigan erupted into waves of Black fury with cars overturned and police reinforcements called in to quell a potential uprising, following the shooting of a young Black male by police. In February 2005, a fourteen-year-old high school student was shot dead by LA police for stealing a car. On November 29, 2011, the world was horrified to read about the firing of 137 rounds into a car being pursued by Cleveland, Ohio, police in a high-speed chase resulting in Timothy Russell, 42, and Malissa Williams, 30, dying from 24 and 23 gun shot wounds, respectively.[172]

John Burris, an Oakland civil rights attorney, documents the systematic atrocities of law enforcement when it comes to policing the Black community in his informative work, *Blue vs Black: Let's End the Conflict Between Cops and*

Minorities. He notes that police officers were neither disciplined nor prosecuted for unjustified police shootings of civilians and the City of San Francisco paid out exorbitant awards in civil lawsuits for officer-involved shootings and that between 1990 and 1995, "police involvement in shooting deaths averaged 4.1 people per every 100 murders committed" and "75 percent of the people shot at or killed by the police between 1993 and 1996 were minorities or people of color, or people living in low-income neighborhoods."[173]

What is abundantly clear from the systematic nature of police violence against Black and Brown people during the globalization era is the ideology of racial criminalization of people of color sown into the minds of law enforcement nationally, so that the first suspect in criminal activity is often a Black person or a person of color, and upon the identification of a potential suspect who happens to be Black, the over-reactive response of violence, harassment, and terror, is quickly triggered. The shooting death of Michael Brown by Ferguson, Missouri, police in August 2014 led to serious riots and a national focus on Ferguson and on the injustice of lethal police force against unarmed youth of color.[174] The fact of Brown's body being left on the street uncovered for four hours after being shot several times raised the ire of the local Black community.[175] The instant unprovoked shooting of a Black motorist attempting to show his driver's license to a white policeman at a gas station in South Carolina in September 2014 is another indication of racist violence by law enforcement widely accepted in a globalized society.[176] Such is the politics of race and law enforcement in this globalized era. Police departments in most cities and towns do very poor jobs of providing cultural and racial sensitivity training to their officers, notwithstanding the historical legacy of continued alienation between law enforcement and communities of color that led to the Kerner Commission Report in 1968 recommending such corrective actions following the urban riots of the 1960s.[177] Madison Mobley, arrested and tortured by four Chicago police officers, who later testified that Mobley had started a fire that killed his wife, son and five others, resulting in him being convicted and sentenced to death for the fire, explains:

> It is sad that we put our trust in police who would sacrifice a person like me for the color of my skin and execute me for a crime I did not commit. If you had experienced what I did, I don't think that you would be pro-death penalty. There is no doubt that we need prison, because many inmates were guilty of crimes, but I also learned that they are human beings.[178]

Mobley spent three years on death row until former Illinois governor Jim Ryan granted him a pardon in 2003.

Human Rights Watch, a division of Amnesty International, issued a detailed report *Shielded from Justice* on police brutality in fourteen U.S. cities—Atlanta, Boston, Chicago, Detroit, Indianapolis, Los Angeles, Minneapolis, New Orleans, New York, Philadelphia, Portland (Oregon), Providence, San Francisco, and Washington, D.C.—in June 1998, and determined that "excessive use of force was primarily directed against Blacks and Latinos," including engaging in "unjustified shootings, severe beatings, fatal chokings, and unnecessarily rough physical treatment."

How does one explain the continued existence of Angola prison in Louisiana, so named after the slave plantation in the 18th century, when Africans from Angola in Africa were forcibly brought to work for White slavemasters in the same location? Seventy-seven percent of the 5,000 inmates in this slave prison are Black and 85 percent of all inmates never leave the prison alive, kindling pictures of chattel slavery on this 18,000-acre plantation. Inmates earn an average of 4 cents a day and a maximum of 20 cents per day, and are often moved in shackles so that they have little chance of escape.[179] For example, Vincent Simmons, 45, has spent 37 years in Angola Prison as part of a 100-year sentence for two rapes of White women that he claims he did not commit based on exculpatory evidence that he compiled in the prison's law library, including the fact that one of the victim's statements that she could not confidently identify the rapist because all Black men looked alike to her. In a photo line-up, Simmons was the only person in handcuffs. Simmons produced further evidence of a medical practitioner's statement that verified that the two girls supposedly raped were in fact virgins after the rape. All of this evidence was dismissed by a three-man parole board in 1997, and Simmons is still in jail at the time of this publication.

A second egregious case is that of 65-year-old Eugene "Bishop" Tannehill, who was sentenced to life for murder and who became ordained as a minister while in prison. He has now spent forty-two years in Angola prison. He has hoped and prayed for a governor's pardon even though no sitting governor in the state of Louisiana has ever granted such a pardon. Ashanti Weatherspoon, who served 27 and a half years of a 75 year sentence for armed robbery, was finally paroled in 1999 after several prior appeals for parole were denied. Angola Prison in Louisiana, along with the Arizona prison system that continues to legally retain racist anti–Latino Maricopa County sheriff Joe Arpallo, who was investigated for human rights violations by the U.S. Department of Justice, highlights the tenacity of cruelty under the globalization prison system.[180]

Following the detailed explication of the pattern of racist abuse and violence at the hands of police, in a normal democratic society one would expect that the perpetrators be brought to justice. The acquittal of the officers who brutalized Rodney King that led to the Los Angeles uprising in 1992, the dismissal of a lawsuit by lawyers for a homeless man who had been beaten by police in the early 1990s in New York City even after the man was awarded $200,000 in damages,[181] and the jury award of $1.6 million to Officer Jeremy Morse where the jury declared that the officer had been unfairly disciplined after being fired from the Inglewood Police force following a 2002 incident in which he slammed a 16-year-old into a squad car and punched him on the jaw during a routine car stop (all caught on videotape), are just some of the cases that substantiate the fact of racial injustice within the U.S. criminal justice system.[182] So much of U.S. society refuses to acknowledge that brutalization of people of color is normatively acceptable and that law enforcement and other security public and private agencies that perpetrate acts of violence and abuse of such people are generally shielded by the law.[183]

The killing of 22-year-old Oscar Grant in Oakland, California, on New Years Day 2009, by Bay Area Rapid Transit police officer Johannes Mehserle and the subsequent conviction and sentencing of Mehserle to two years imprisonment on involuntary manslaughter charges, outraged many residents of California and people of color around the U.S. precisely because of the unjust double standards used in the administration of justice, particularly when the victims are Black and the perpetrators are White law enforcement officers. Hundreds of people marched and protested in Los Angeles and the San Francisco Bay Area after the court decision on Mehserle was announced on November 5, 2010.[184] While Mehserle appeared remorseful at his trial, was given a light two-year sentence, and was released after 11 months in prison, most Black offenders don't get off so lightly. They are generally punished to the fullest extent of the law and given harsh sentences in prison, like 10 years in jail for non-violent drug offenses, and often receive 35 years to life or death sentences for capital crimes.[185] Globalization's rhetoric of "tough on crime" penalties is part of the ruling class's tactics in selling prisons as a stimulus for economic growth. Unusually long and stiff prison sentences for poor Black, Indigenous, and Latino women and men, which garner scarce state dollars are the means by which the prison industrial complex assumes decisive significance in social discourses around crime, punishment, and community security in the face of an increasingly volatile financial and economic national ethos.

In 2014, it is troubling to note that under the Obama administration, the flagrant militarization of police departments around the country has grown to become a national phenomenon. Police departments have stepped up purchases of outright military gear, acquiring 432 Mine-Resistant Ambush Protected Armored Vehicles (MWRAPs), 435 other armored vehicles including cars and trucks, 533 planes and helicopters, 44,900 binoculars, goggles, lights and night gear accessories, 93,763 machine guns that include 5.56 mm and 7.62 mm rifles, and 180,718 magazines.[186] During public demonstrations by protesters in Ferguson, Missouri, in August 2014, in Oakland, California, in October 2011, and in Anaheim, California, in July 2012, police used "tear gas grenades, 'triple chaser' gas canisters and stun guns" made by Combined Systems Inc., and Defense Technology Corporation, weapons used by Israeli security forces against Palestinian protestors.[187] Of deep concern is the acquisition of surplus military equipment from the Iraq and Afghanistan wars at low-cost by police departments in over 30 states and at over a dozen schools, 30 colleges, and 40 universities from the Department of Defense through the 1033 program, such as 900 M-14 and M-16 rifles, 191 pistols, 41 shot-guns, grenade launchers, and MWRAPS.[188] Overall, more than 100 colleges and universities have received Department of Defense equipment since 1998.[189] The Los Angeles School Police Department received 61 M-16 rifles, 3 grenade launchers, and 1 MWRAP, and the San Diego Unified Police Department received one MWRAP. Central Florida University acquired 8 M-16 rifles in 2011 and Arizona State University has purchased 70 M-16 rifles thus far, followed by Florida International University and the University of Maryland which each received 50 M-16s. This militarization of civilian educational institutions under globalization has generated controversy and opposition from groups like the National Association for the Advancement of Colored People (NAACP), where education policy counsel Janel A. George noted that "inserting these weapons into school climates that are already fraught with tension and hostility between students of color and school police" will only exacerbate racial and social tensions. Such is the racial insensitivity and growing militarization of law enforcement in this age of globalization, with students of color being potentially targeted unnecessarily by law enforcement, which often leads to incarceration and in lethal incidents like in the case of Michael Brown in Ferguson, Missouri, death.

Police departments that often describe themselves as "community protectors" in many places are now being turned into "military defenders," all funded by taxpayer monies. Is there great potential that *excessive military force may be deployed and abused* particularly when either innocent bystanders are caught in the cross-fire of police-armed suspect(s) shootouts or the wrong people are apprehended as has occurred in many instances especially among poorer communities of color? Again, one is struck by the concatenation of militarism, racism, criminalization of poor Blacks and Latinos, and the globalized economic system of incarceration that benefits from such aggression.

The militarization of domestic law enforcement in the U.S. reaches across U.S. boundaries, underscoring the globalized concatenation of law enforcement. For instance, over "300 high-ranking sheriffs and police from agencies large and small—from New York and Maine to Orange County and Oakland, California—have traveled to Israel for privately funded seminars in what is described as counterterrorism techniques," and the former St. Louis Chief of Police received a sponsored trip to Israel as part of law enforcement's globalized integration.[190] Against who are these proliferations of militarized police departments declaring *war*? Israeli military personnel have trained Mexican police and military officers in Chiapas, Mexico, since the 1994 Indigenous Zapatista uprising.

Poor Black People and "Human Sacrifice": Capital Punishment and Criminal Justice

The U.S. prides itself on being an enlightened and civilized society, especially as the leader of the "free" and "globalized" world. It is not uncommon to hear anthropologists often excoriate Indigenous peoples of the ancient world, like the Mayan, Inca, and Aztecs for their barbarism in practicing human sacrifice. Yet, in 2013, the U.S. shamelessly continued to sacrifice human beings and call for their deaths, 3,700 in total, 50 percent of whom are Black. Even though it has been historically documented that the death penalty is innately racist since a Black person is more likely to receive the death penalty than a White person for the same crime, and particularly when the victim is White, the injustice of capital punishment persists. Capital punishment is directly interwoven with the politics of racism and the economics of globalization, hence its extensive discussion here.

It is a sense of vindictiveness and racial animosity that fuels the movement calling for the death penalty of individuals, half of whom are Black, and in most instances where the victims are White. The April 29, 2014, botched execution of Clayton D. Lockett, a Black man charged with kidnapping, rape, and murder, sent chills down the spines of many in the U.S. who view capital punishment as unjust and inhuman, similar to the member countries of the European Union that all outlawed capital punishment. Lockett experienced torture for 43 minutes as he writhed in agony, moaned, and attempted to sit up on the execution gurney because the lethal injection drugs did not instantaneously kill him, whimpering, "Man...."[191] Lockett attempted to cut his wrists and was later Tasered by prison authorities before the execution, compounding the horrific scenario of his botched execution.[192] In the aftermath of the torturous execution, Oklahoma governor Mary Fallin said that she hoped that the family of the victim of the Lockett's murder crime, Stephanie Neiman, had found "some measure of closure and peace."[193] Can there be real familial peace following such gruesome *torture* of murderers by state justice officials? Even the White House found that the botched execution "fell short" of humane standards, although Barack Obama qualified the White House statement by indicating that he still supported the death penalty in Clayton Lockett's case.[194]

The shocking fact is that this was not the first botched execution in the U.S. Austin Salat, a jurisprudence academic, who, along with his students, studied executions of 9,000 people in the U.S. from 1890 to 2010, noted that the botched execution of Clayton Lockett was not an exception but rather a pattern that revealed that 3 percent of all executions went awry, resulting in burned flesh, failed strangulation, and electric shocks that did not execute condemned persons.[195] This pattern of torture preceding executions resulting from the obsession with the criminal justice system to administer "retributive justice" raises pointed questions about morality within the justice system and within the U.S. as a whole. If kidnapping, rape, and murder are viewed as morally repugnant by the U.S. justice and legal system, how does the U.S. justify its killing and torture of people in other countries like Iraq (where the Abu Ghraib torture scandal was exposed in 2003–2004), assassinating civilians with drones in Afghanistan, Pakistan, Yemen, and Somalia, or allowing the wide-scale brutality and torture of incarcerated persons within the U.S., at Guantanamo Bay, for instance? How is it that these killings by the U.S. of civilians on a regular basis do not provoke moral outrage among most residents in the U.S., yet the killing of a woman by Clayton D. Lockett does, warranting execution of the murderer? Why are there double standards in the adjudication of justice when it comes to capital offenses, one defending the action of the state when it claims to seek retributive justice for victims of murder, but no moral arbiter to determine the morality of state-sanctioned murder and human sacrifice when it comes to killing innocent people in wars of occupation like in Iraq, Afghanistan, or Vietnam? Oklahoma delayed the execution of Charles Warner, another Black man who was scheduled to be executed immediately after Clayton D. Lockett, pending an investigative review. Yet the foundational review of race and class in capital punishment cases in the U.S. and the unfairly high systematic execution of mostly Black men has not been promulgated at the highest levels of the criminal justice system. Many within the anti-capital punishment segment of the nation have reason to believe that poor Black life is expendable and that Black men are "open season," especially in a globalized political economy where a rapid high-tech electronic and automated economy has made low-skilled Black labor value redundant.[196]

Though capital punishment has become obsolete in many parts of the industrialized world, like in the European Union (EU), it continues to be practiced by most states in the U.S., as part of the enforcement of justice even in the 21st century when such practices are considered "uncivilized" and anachronistic by "advanced" societies. Again, globalized economic considerations play a role since anyone on death row normally entails the investment of hundreds of millions of dollars in prison maintenance, legal appeals, defense costs, and judicial administration, often over a 10–20-year period during which legal battles are waged between defendants and the prosecution. Kevin Cooper at San Quentin prison in California was spared execution at the last minute in February 2004, after lawyers successfully claimed that the material evidence supporting his guilt had been tampered with, and he continues to fight for his freedom. Vernon Evans, a Black man who was convicted in 1984 of the contract murder of a federal witness and a bystander, was sentenced to die by lethal injection in the week before April 18, 2005.[197] His victims were two Whites.

Stanley "Tookie" Williams was executed on December 13, 2005, for the killing of a 7-Eleven clerk in 1979, in a trial where none of those on the jury that convicted him was Black. Williams was a founder of the Cripps gang in California and was denied a pardon from Governor Arnold Schwarzenegger (known for his film role as the *Terminator*) in his appeal for a re-trial at the U.S. Supreme Court in April 2005 and a last-minute reprieve from the same court. He was subsequently executed even though he was a model prisoner who rehabilitated himself, a nominee for the Nobel Peace Prize, an author, and a peacemaker who inspired other prison inmates to direct themselves toward constructive roles in society.[198] Williams' execution demonstrated that the endemic racism entrenched in capital punishment has no provision for rehabilitation, repentance, and transformation as so foundationally articulated in Judeo-Christian principles that are extolled often by Christian evangelicals who champion the right to life of unborn fetuses but are aggressive defenders of the death penalty.[199] Schwarzenegger also campaigned vigorously against Proposition 66 in California in November 2005, defeating the measure that would have weakened the three-strikes law.[200] Of the 42,000 persons imprisoned under the three-strikes law, "45 percent are Black, 26 percent are Latino, and 25 percent are White," underscoring the deep racism in the application of this law. Capital punishment does not just affect Black inmates, however. Donald Beardslee, a 61-year-old White man, was executed in California in 2005 even though warders described him as a model prisoner who suffered from a brain defect since birth.

In October 2012, I had the opportunity to speak with an incarcerated person who was convicted under the three-strikes law even though he had committed one of the crimes in another state. This person was sentenced to life imprisonment; his crimes did not involve murder or death. He shared the gravity of his pain at receiving such a harsh sentence and expressed deep remorse for his deeds of selling drugs and robbing people for money. The system, however, had little compassion and capacity to rehabilitate and reform him since it was so steeped in stiff and inhumane punishment of life sentencing for non-capital crimes. Fortunately, he was released on parole in the spring of 2013.[201]

Globalization's economic designs ensure that in the event capital punishment sentences are abandoned, life without parole is a substitute, where funds for housing life prisoners continue until the death of the incarcerated inmate. The case of Mumia Abu-Jamal, on death row until December 9, 2011, when his death sentence was changed to life without parole following a U.S. Supreme Court decision that required a re-sentencing hearing in light of egregious flaws in his original sentencing process, deserves special attention in this regard. Nobel Peace Laureate Desmond Tutu, Nobel Literature Laureate Wole Soyinka, and the French Parliament have all called for Mumia's unconditional and immediate release.[202] Mumia is the United States' most famous political prisoner, who languished on death row for 29 years, framed for the shooting that led to the death of White police officer Larry Faulkner. In his case, he was denied *habeas corpus*, prosecutorial witnesses were coerced, confessions were fabricated, and African American jurors were excluded solely on the basis of race. Daniel Williams, though a problematic writer when it comes to the unequivocal defense of Mumia's innocence, contends that "racism, while most visible in the jury selection process, is a virus that permeates the entire machinery of death ... and feeds on discretion." He notes that "racism has always existed in the nineteenth and twentieth century death penalty jurisprudence in the United States ... the death penalty ... is a relic of slavery and racial violence in the United States" and as "Justice Thurgood Marshall expressed ... in one of his capital punishment opinions: 'The criminal law expressly differentiated crimes committed by and against Blacks and Whites, distinctions whose lineage traced back to the time of slavery.'"[203]

In the mid 1980s, the NAACP Legal Defense Fund took on the case of Warren McCleskey, a Black man who was sentenced to die in Fulton County Superior Court in Georgia for killing a White policeman. Lawyers for McCleskey compiled statistical evidence to substantiate the pattern of racial discrimination in the over 2,000 murder cases examined in Georgia, what had come to be known as the Cornell Law Review study, an investigation of the process of legal sentencing between 1983 and 1993 by David Baldus and Gary Woodworth. This study established that "race and racism played a powerful role in how juries meted out the ultimate sanction."[204] The study verified that between 1976 and 1980, persons convicted of killing Whites were 4.3 times more likely to receive the death penalty than those charged with killing Black people. It also concluded that Blacks accused of killing Whites were more likely to receive the death penalty than any other racial combination. When the victim was White and the person charged was Black, the death penalty was most often sought. McCleskey's review and appeal went all the way to the U.S. Supreme Court, where many legal experts anticipated that their positive ruling would finally end the death penalty that was approved in 1976 after being abolished by the Supreme Court in 1972. Astonishingly, the Supreme Court ruled by 5–4 against McCleskey, arguing that McCleskey had failed to demonstrate that those who had sentenced him to death did so with racial malice. Discriminatory impact was inadequate in the minds of the majority of the Court justices, and the majority justices insisted that clear demonstration of discriminatory intent must be established, and therefore there was insufficient evidence to establish a constitutional violation. The Court majority also ruled that the death penalty did not violate the Eighth Amendment because of unusually harsh and painful punishment. The same majority wrote that though there was racism in the death penalty process, it was acceptable under the constitution! Justice Brennan, one of the four dissenters, wrote that the court ignored the permeation of racism in death penalty decisions at its own peril and stated that the majority of the court justices did not want to rule in McCleskey's favor because such decision could throw "into serious question the principles that underlie our criminal justice system." Brennan then unabashedly declared that the majority court decision in the McCleskey case reflected a fear of "too much justice."

In the case of Mumia Abu-Jamal, the ruling judge that heard Mumia's legal appeal in the mid-1990s, William Yohn, refused to accord Mumia the right of *habeas corpus*, by insisting that the Supreme Court had ruled against McCleskey even though it had scrutinized the elements of the Cornell Review study on the death penalty. Yohn argued that Mumia's trial in 1982 fell outside the parameters of the study that spanned the 1983–1993 period. He failed to acknowledge that Mumia was sentenced to death in 1983, the year in which the study began. He also ruled that since Mumia's defense had failed to put then prosecutor Joe McGill on the stand in 1982, it could not raise the issue of *habeas corpus* since it had already missed the opportunity. What is striking here is that the judge was not at all concerned with the question of justice and the fact that Mumia had received an unfair trial that landed him on death row, but rather with the technicalities of the legal system. On November 9, 2010, as crowds of people from all over the world gathered in protest to demand justice for Mumia Abu-Jamal in Philadelphia, the Third Circuit Court of Appeals there heard arguments as to whether Judge Yohn's ruling on life without parole would be sustained or whether the case should move forward toward execution of Mumia.

The historic case of Mumia Abu-Jamal is emblematic of the racism against Black men within capital punishment in the globalized U.S. Mumia is a prolific author of six books and numerous newspaper columns and has been a tireless voice from death row against globalization, war, and oppression, formerly from death row and now from prison where he was sentenced to life without parole in 2011.

Life without parole is horrible and torturous punishment and the U.S. continues to insist that this is more "humane" than the death penalty. But is it? Darrell Lomax, an innocent person on California's death row, responds to the question as to whether life without parole can be considered a more lenient and humane sentence:

> NOT LONG ago, I was invited to answer a question posed by someone out in the free world. The question was: "Is life without the possibility of parole (LWOP) a legitimate replacement for the death penalty, even if the only justification offered is to stop pending executions?"
>
> My answer is a resounding "no." A sentence of LWOP is, in essence, the very same sentence as the death penalty. The purpose of both of these sentences is to ensure that the fate of the prisoner is to be murdered—by lethal injection or by incarceration.[205]

Once one is sentenced to life without parole, one loses all appeals to the courts and is destined to die in prison. For many who are innocent, living is a slow and torturous process. Again, life without parole maintains a prison industrial complex that is intrinsic to a globalized punishment industry with extension and enlargement of profits so long as more people are incarcerated and for longer terms than actually necessary in overwhelming cases, particularly in situations of Black and Brown convictions.

Mumia Abu-Jamal greeted me warmly in his deep staccato voice when we first met in Greene State Prison in Waynesburg, Pennsylvania, in May 2009, "Welcome to hell!" As I visited with Mumia for over four hours, thanks to Pittsburgh attorney and Free Mumia activist Martha Conley, I wondered how it was possible that so much energy, time, and money could be invested by the state of Pennsylvania in the death of a brilliant person such as Abu-Jamal. How could a person who is innocent of the crime of murder, who has written six books that are very well researched and could easily be used by all college students in the U.S., even after 27 years on death row languish in a tiny prison smaller than a regular bathroom?[206] Mumia Abu-Jamal and I discussed how death row is symptomatic of the obsession with a selective and perverted morality on the part of the U.S. status quo that insists on upholding a convoluted Manichean morality that divides the "just" from the "unjust," the "redeemed" from the "damned," and the "good" from the "evil." Of course, capital punishment provides grist for the U.S. political machinery where politicians are elected on the basis of being tough on crime and supportive of the death penalty and it ingests billions of dollars in prison construction and administration staff, court and legal costs, lawyer fees, and through retirement funds for all those employed within and associated with corrections and the meting out of "justice." The U.S. Supreme Court refused to issue a ruling in favor of Mumia's death sentence as requested by Philadelphia prosecutors in November 2011. Instead, the Supreme Court referred the sentencing issue back to the federal appeals court that had ordered a new sentencing hearing for Mumia following the fact that the death-penalty instructions given to jurors in 1982 were "potentially misleading." Prosecutors were then given a choice to either agree to a life sentence for Mumia or attempt to re-sentence him to death.[207] They opted for the former due to the deep inconsistences and fabrication of evidence in the case. Yet, Mumia is now a victim of the notoriously inhumane criminal justice policy that disregards the fact that he has spent 29 years behind bars on death row (and in shackles when visitors like me visited with him behind a thick plexi-glass window) with the conviction of life without parole and desires that he die in prison. Justice can only be served with a new trial and his immediate release. The continued incarceration of an innocent man who fell prey to a racist justice system is unacceptable under the International Convention of Human Rights that decreed that the solitary confinement of individuals beyond 15 years is inhumane punishment.

Racism has been accepted as part of the normative functioning of the death penalty sentencing process by the nation's highest court, and Black people are its primary victims. In early 2004, 3,374 persons were on death row in 37 states, of whom 42 percent were Black, and 47 women were under sentence of death in 2003, marking an increase from 38 women in 1993.[208] In 2011, of the 3,300 people on death row, more than half of them were people of color, with Black people constituting 42 percent of this number.[209] Incredibly, in the state of Alabama, where even though 65 percent of all murder victims are Black, 80 percent of the people awaiting execution today were convicted for murder crimes in which the victims were White. Though 6 percent of murders in Alabama were committed by Black defendants and White victims, over 60 percent of Black people on death row were sentenced to death for killing someone White.[210]

Justice delayed is indeed justice denied. After Bill Clinton's signing of the Anti-Terrorism and Effective Death Penalty Act in 1996 following the Oklahoma City bombing, his action "imposed the most rigorous constraints on the constitutional right to seek Federal review of convictions since Lincoln suspended the writ of habeas corpus in the Civil War." *Habeas corpus*, which technically refers to the empowerment accorded a judge to "inquire into the legitimacy of any form of loss of personal liberty," was responsible for over-turning 40 to 60 percent of all capital cases presented for habeas review by federal courts.[211] Today, the system of "human sacrifice," via what is called the *criminal justice system*, persists. In California alone, seven people who have been convicted of murder were sentenced to death in 2011, skyrocketing those on death row to 640, half of them Black.[212] Though the courts acknowledge the racist application of the death penalty, they have ruled that it is accept-able—racism is thus an acceptable part of justice in the U.S., especially in an era of globalized economics!

The result has been protection of those within law enforcement who perpetrate racist and criminal acts, as recounted earlier in this book. In Chicago, it was learned that 40 Black men were tortured by police commander Jon Burge in Chicago Area II Violent Crimes Detective Unit over the past 20 years, receiving praises and promotions from Mayor Richard Daley, even though 10 of the men were unjustly convicted and sentenced to death. Burge has since retired in Florida at tax-payer cost and has not faced criminal charges for torture and falsely sending 10 Black men to death row. Former governor Jim Ryan, who made history and commuted the sentences of 167 men on death row to life without parole, pardoned four of the 10 who were tortured, while the remaining 6 sought new trials. Since 1976, 13 innocent people were released from death row in Illinois, and 12 were executed, the sixth highest rate of executions in the nation. Yet, as Mumia Abu Jamal asked in his article, *Gov. Ryan's Song*, what about the innocent people on *life-row?* Many agree that the system is broken and fundamentally racist and unjust as documented in the 2012 film documentary, *Broken on All Sides*, but who or what will correct it, and release the potentially thousands of innocent men and women, many people of color, who have either been wrongly criminalized or received long-term sentences solely for non-violent drug-use, is the begging question.

Did former president George W. Bush have anything to do with death row and with torture? Absolutely. Under his watch as governor of Texas, 153 men were executed, half of them Black. He has since claimed that he is positive that all of the executions he authorized under his governorship were correct. Is this his *weapon of mass destruction*? What does overseeing so many executions, including of possibly innocent people, and then winning the presidency illegally as a result of the injustice of the U.S. Supreme Court tell us about justice? In 2011, it was a case of unbelievable déjà vu. Texas governor Rick Perry who sought the Republican Party presidential nomination cited the fact of his presiding over 234 executions as governor to appeal to pro-capital punishment voters during candidate debates. The "tough on crime" rhetoric and, in many instances, record of executions of people on death row, serve as significant political capital for persons running for the highest office in the land, as reflected in the campaigns of Richard Nixon, Ronald Reagan, George H.W. Bush, Bill Clinton, George W. Bush, and current U.S. president Barack Obama. Under globalization, political expediency that appeals to racist sentiment, especially among politicians clamoring for higher positions in government, is at an all-time high.

The death penalty signifies a pathological continuation of the lynching of Black men in the South, where between 1882 to 1927, some 3,513 Black people were lynched by racist White mobs. Somehow, the death penalty serves as a reminder of the ferocious injustice of the U.S. when it comes to race, and the insistence on the part of the White power-structure to demonstrate to Black men and women that this system still despises them from slavery to the present to the point of wishing them away, execution style. This elimination of Black men through capital punishment is integral to the design of the globalized economy since poor Black men are considered a burden to an unbridled capitalist system in which Black physical labor has become redundant. Like poverty and war that decimates poor Black life for people living in many parts of west and north Africa, where incessant wars over resources continue to be waged, capital punishment fragments Black social life by permanently removing yet another potential bread-winner from family and community life, eviscerating already marginalized Black communities.

Globalization, "Supermax" Solitary Confinement, and Sexual Violence in U.S. Prisons

Under globalization, the U.S. has been at the forefront of promoting tough law and order and punishment, propagating a "culture of fear, the growing awareness of risk management, and the control of surplus populations originating in neoliberal governance," the "efficiency" principle of the globalization status quo.[213] Of deep concern under the security apparatus of globalization culture is the proliferation of super-maximum security prisons or Security Housing Units (SHUs) where the supposedly "most dangerous of American criminals" are housed, confined for 24 hours a day, seven days a week with a brief exercise time in a "dog-run" wire cage. Britain, New Zealand (Aotearoa), and Australia have followed in step with the supermax model of imprisonment, albeit in modified versions. The roots of supermax lie in excruciating prison punishment of 19th century Europe and the U.S. when prisoners were flogged, shackled to walls, held in swat boxes, and the like, part of the Puritan ethic of eviscerating the "evil" ones from the "good" ones of society. The Federal Bureau of Prisons administers a supermax prison in ADX-Florence, Colorado, and most prisons in the U.S. have a supermax section.[214] There are six of these dehumanizing facilities across the country, the first of which was simulated in Marion, Illinois, in 1983 when two correctional officers were killed by a member of the Aryan Brotherhood and Marion became a "control unit."[215]

California has more people in solitary confinement than any other state. The Pelican Bay Special Housing Unit (SHU) in California with over 1,200 inmates saw a massive hunger strike in October 2011 to protest inhumane conditions such as inedible food and the denial of religious materials such as Bibles.[216] In the *60 Minutes* segment that ran on June 21, 2009, entitled, "Supermax: A Clean Version of Hell," reporters filmed scenes from the ADX-Florence Supermax where Imam Jamil Abdullah Al-Amin (formerly Student Nonviolent Coordinating Committee leader H. Rap Brown) and other Black liberation leaders are confined. It is in such facilities that the highest rates of suicides have been recorded—two of every three in U.S. prisons are in these supermax facilities. In 2005, 70 percent of the 44 suicides in California prisons occurred in such hellish prisons.[217] At least 25,000 persons are held in SHU's with another estimated 50,000–80,000 in segregation units.[218] In Florida, the number of persons held in such supermax prisons grew three-fold from the 1,009 in the mid 1990s to 3,176 in 1999, nothing "short of hell" according to inmates who were subject to the experience of isolation and cruel punishment.[219] While such repressive punishment of crime policies have intensified, the rates of violent crime and gang violence has actually decreased.

In December 2012, the New York Civil Liberties Union (NYCLU) filed a suit in federal court challenging the widespread practice of solitary confinement on the basis of the 8th and 14th amendments on behalf of Leroy Peoples, a Black man, who was sentenced to 36 months of isolation for intentionally filing false documents in 2009, a non-violent crime, and to six-months of isolation for possessing multi-vitamins and amino acids in his prison cell while such vitamins were available at the prison commissary. The lawsuit filed against New York state charges that "the system-wide policies and practices governing solitary confinement ... are responsible for the arbitrary and unjustified use of extreme isolation on thousands of individuals incarcerated in New York's prisons every year."[220] Between 2007 and 2011, more than 68,000 cases of solitary isolation sentences were issued in the justice system, followed by 4,500 in 2012 or 8 percent of all prison inmates' sentencing. The NYCLU further alleges that Black people are heavily disproportionately over-represented in the solitary isolation units of New York's prisons and subject to isolation sentencing far more than the rest of the prison population.

The notion of a "prison industrial complex" looms at the center of the supermax prison paradigm. For instance, it costs on average $75,000 to house a person in a supermax prison facility and $25,000 in a regular state prison. Construction of complex maze-like supermax prisons attract large investments from architectural firms, large construction companies, banks, and other financial investment organizations, functioning as an economic boon to either stagnant or depressed community economies, particularly in the wake of successive recessions over the past twenty to twenty-five years. State supermax prisons far exceed those of federal governmental facilities and are expanding in 36 states, with plans to house well over one hundred thousand inmates, approaching 8 to 10 percent of all persons held in state prisons.[221] Some of the facilities opened over the past decade include Minnesota Correctional Facility-Oak Park Heights (MCF-OPH), Stillwater, Minnesota, from 1983, Maryland Correctional Adjustment center in Baltimore from 1988, Tamms Correctional Center in Tamms, Illinois, from March 1998, Wallens Ridge State Prison, Big Stone Gap, Virginia, which opened in April 1999, and Varner Supermax in Grady, Arkansas, built in 2000.[222] Texas has 16 supermax prison facilities in line with the state's tough crime and punishment policies. Supermax is part of globalization's push by powerful class and interest groups that consider prison construction and expansion to be an essential cog in the profit-making machine. Citing Eric Schlosser's coining of the term, "prison industrial complex,"[223] Jeffrey Ian Ross observes that "if Schlosser is correct, a whole panoply of non-profit and for-profit businesses capitalizes on a seemingly insatiable need to incarcerate individuals and build prisons, ultimately making money from the pain and suffering of others behind bars."[224] This is precisely what the hyper-profit motive nature of globalization is all about, and with careers of local prison administrators at stake and advanced through emulating expanded and comparable well-resourced prison facilities at state and federal levels, the rush for more supermax facilities grows. These steps signify extensions of the demise of rehabilitation approaches urged by the Reagan-Bush era of the 1980s and fulfill globalization's desire for those deemed "incorrigible" and "depraved" by the ruling classes to be punished to the maximum, hence the term "supermax."

Tellingly and in line with globalization's trajectories, post-apartheid South Africa has constructed two supermax facilities, C-Max in Tshwane (Pretoria) and Ebongweni in Kokstad, Kwazulu-Natal, the latter modeled on the supermax prison in Marion, Illinois, following the visits of South African prison officials to the U.S.[225] Supermax facilities have arisen in Mexico, Brazil, the Netherlands, New Zealand (Aotearoa), Australia, Britain, Canada, and Iraq, all differing from the U.S. model in some manner, yet reflecting a similar globalized ideology of profits from the prison industry and harsh and irreversible penalties and punishment for severe or repeated criminal offenses in allegedly "incorrigible" cases. In most of these countries, supermax prisons are under filled. The U.S. is the only country to operate two supermax facilities outside its borders: the notorious Abu Ghraib facility in Iraq and equally torturous Guantanamo facility in Cuba. The future of supermax facilities remains to be seen considering the growing international opposition to these unusual penal institutions and the fact of it violating global statutes on human rights that prohibit unusual and cruel punishment and torture of people, including prisoners.[226]

Another element of violence obscured by mainstream media is the pervasiveness of sexual assault and rape within the prison system. The culture of wide-scale rape of men and women in prisons that is consistently denied by prison administrators is an institutional means of demasculinizing incarcerated men, especially men of color and subjugating women for further humiliation. Evidence of the degradation of men of color is demonstrated when they are stopped by police and asked to "assume the position" and "spreadeagle over a car hood" akin to a female rape victim. The strip searches of Black men in prisons and experience of humiliation of having their private parts searched by guards and corrections officials constitutes an extension of the form of sadistic violence of rape and gender degradation experienced under slavery and is indicative of the systemic globalized violence of racism.

Prison rape of men and women is not an aberration of the U.S. penal system; it is endemic to the culture of control and punishment of offenders of any stripe. In a telling report entitled *Prison Rape and the Government*, authors David Kaiser and Lovisa Stannow recount how the Bureau of Justice Statistics (BJS), a unit of the U.S. Department of Justice, initially declared that of 7,444 reported allegations of sexual abuse in prisons, only 931 were substantiated, but later retracted these figures and stated that 90,000 people had been abused in 2007.[227] Finally in January 2011, the Justice Department owned up and acknowledged that more than 216,000 people were sexually abused in prisons and jails across the country in 2008, including 17,100 in juvenile detention facilities, and in cases of women, often by prison guards and officials. The inference here is that about 600 people were sexually abused in a day, about 25 per hour on average, making the U.S. perhaps the only country in the world where more men are raped than women considering that most prison inmates are male.[228]

It is deeply ironic too that in 2003, the Congress and Senate passed the Prison Rape Elimination Act, a law that produced a commission to devise standards and codes of conduct for corrections institutions to detect and prevent prison rape. Six years later, the commission's recommendations were submitted to Attorney General Eric Holder who had twelve months to review them and approve of standards that would be nationally binding. Holder missed the deadline, resulting in 100,000 sexual abuse cases in prisons in 2009. Such is the concern by the Justice Department for victims of sexual abuse within its own institutions of justice! In an interview with a person incarcerated in a Corrections facility in October 2012, he informed me how he was threatened with sexual assault after borrowing a can of rice from an inmate who expected to be paid "in kind" and described the excruciating reality of pervasive prison rape in New York prisons and the violence of such experience being either ignored or downplayed by prison authorities since such victims of sexual assault were often viewed as "deserving" of such violence because of their perceived "incorrigible misbehavior."

The violent contours of U.S. society reflected in institutions like law enforcement and the military are played out in pathological practices of rape of women and men with race, class, gender, and sexuality being foundational points of reference for such traumatic and destructive experiences. To add complexity to the pathology of rape in prisons is the interwovenness of race and power where incidents involving rape of vulnerable White male inmates by Black men are often justified by the latter as "revenge" for the pain of Black man under White slavery.[229] The prison industrial complex that fosters such a violent sexual culture is harmful for all races of women and men incarcerated and poisons race and personal relations in an already toxic social disciplinary environment. Further, prison rape distorts and perverts the practices of sexuality and culture of gay inmates in particular since homosexuality is generally viewed by most prison authorities as deviant and in some cases even as causes of rioting and intra-personal violence.[230] The engendering of such dehumanization by the prison industrial complex is neither accidental nor inadvertent; rather it signifies an exaggeration of the flagrant disregard of individual's fundamental human rights particularly on the grounds of race, class, social background and sexuality.

Prison Construction and Starved Education and Public Services Budgets Under Globalization

The marked increase from an already inflated federal and state outlay for Corrections was launched in 1994 as ideologies of globalization and security assumed monumental proportions when public expenditures for law enforcement efforts and private expenditures for security totaled $165 billion, almost as much as the U.S. spent on the military that year. It's mind-boggling to realize that in that year, $31 billion was spent on corrections, an increase of 359 percent on punishment since 1980.[231] In 1995, the total cost of state-issued bonds to finance prison construction exceeded that to finance colleges, underscoring the obsessive state push to invest in punishment of people in the U.S. rather than in education.[232] California constructed prisons in the 1980s and 1990s but not one college or university over those decades. In 2002, the then-governor of that state, Gray Davis, insisted that he was a tough leader on crime and awarded salary increases of 39 percent to prison warders while inflicting budget cuts on education and health care, since he was beholden to the large financial contributions and powerful lobbying role of the California Corrections and Peace Officers Association.[233]

According to the Pew Center on the States, in fiscal year 2005, "U.S. states allocated an average of 7.2 percent of their general fund expenditures on corrections" and Federal, state and local governments spent approximately $62 billion per year on corrections and were projected to spend another $27 billion on corrections over the five years following, including $15 billion for operations and $12 billion for capital projects.[234] In 2008, corrections in the U.S. was a $70 billion enterprise.[235] In 2011, $50 billion of the annual $70 billion spent on prisons came out of starved state budgets. Nine of every $10 in state prison funding comes out of the same budget that finances higher education. Inevitably, state spending on prisons has grown six times the rate of spending on higher education. In 2009, the year after the global financial crisis of 2008, 33 states spent more on prisons than in the previous year.[236] On the other hand, tuition at state colleges and universities grew by an average of 6 percent and in many states to double-digit levels.[237] Small wonder then that 71 percent of college students graduated with an average debt of $30,000 per student and over three-quarters have been in arrears in student debt payment since 2012.[238]

The state of Arizona raised tuition levels by 98 percent from 2006 through 2012. Fred Duval, a former Arizona Board of Regents member who ran for the office of governor in 2014, was on the board in 2007 just before the 2008 recession and, though Duval was a Democrat and outvoted by a Republic-dominated legislature, he nevertheless voted for tuition increases for each year from 2006 and proposed a freeze on tuition increases only in 2011.[239] From 2007 through 2012, tuition and fees at Arizona State University rose a shocking 97 percent to $9,700. Student graduation debt climbed 6 percent each year from 2008 through 2012. Though Article 11, Section 6, of Arizona's constitution declares that "the university and all other state educational institutions shall be open to students of both sexes, and the instruction shall be as nearly free as possible," the Arizona Board of Regents administering the state's three universities insist that this means that the each of the state's universities tuitions' costs should be at the lower third of public universities, a very subjective interpretation indeed. The courts have claimed that the issue is political and not judicial, maintaining the status quo at the cost of financially strapped college students, the majority of students in the state.[240]

The disturbingly punitive and militaristic trend of the role of the state during the past two decades of globalization is patently reflected in the startling fact that the cost of incarcerating one prisoner for a year in California is equivalent to the cost of educating ten community college students and one University of California student.[241] The lacerating budget cuts suffered by education in California (some $3.5 billion in 2010–2011) begs the question of the human priorities of that state (and most other states) as millions of poor people in particular are hurried through the criminal justice system for mostly non-violent (drug-related) offenses.[242] California, the "Golden State," now has the dubious distinction of having the largest and costliest prison industrial complex in the world. In 1982, California spent 10 percent of its budget on education and 3 percent on corrections.[243] In 2012, the state allocated 11 percent of its budget for prisons and 7.5 percent for higher education.

Similarly, in Michigan, which used to pride itself on being a leading state promoting and supporting higher education, state budgetary priorities have shifted radically over the past decade. The state spends 51 percent more on prisons than neighboring states and has progressively cut its public funding of higher education so that in 2012 only 40 percent of workers in the state possessed a degree or diploma, whereas 62 percent of jobs in this decade require an undergraduate college qualification.[244] Michigan has tough prison laws in line with globalization's law and order ideology that keeps people in prisons for longer terms for comparable crimes in 35 other states. While the state spent $34,000 for every person it imprisoned, it spent only $11,000 on every college student, forcing college tuition levels to rise phenomenally and making it increasingly difficult for most students to afford attending college.[245] The state of Georgia like most other states spends three or more times per capita on prisons than on education, so that the state allocation for prisons was $18,000 per inmate while that allocated for a child in the public education system was about $6,000. Decreased funding for public education inevitably produced a poorer educational system, resulting in Georgia's high school dropout rate growing to 30 percent, making this youth sector potentially prone to crime and incarceration given limited employment options particularly for low-income students.[246] In New York state too, the state earmarks a substantial $56,000 per incarcerated inmate and $11,000 per college student. The message is clear: Universities and prisons are fiercely competing for sparse state revenues in this globalized age, and prisons are winning hands-down!

How do the dynamics of globalization relate to the prisons boom and shrinking budgets for education, higher education in particular? The dimensions of race, class, and capital accumulation feature centrally within the globalized paradigm. Higher education is increasingly considered a privilege and no longer a right and hence is being made unaffordable at all levels, particularly decimating impoverished and lower-classed families who struggle to send their children to college hoping that future economic success will be the result. These working class and lower-middle class families are now saddled with debt to the tune of $1.2 trillion in 2014, even surpassing consumer credit card debt levels. The federal government has refused to forgive any levels of student debt, although president Barack Obama signed a freeze on debt payment *interest* to 3.4 percent in 2013. These palliatives still keep students and their families generally mired in student debt. In the wake of a "jobless recovery" following the deep recession of 2008, high-paying jobs and long-term employment, particularly for college graduates, is but a dream.

The ruling class in the U.S. has determined in an era of insatiable lust for profits in a globalized world economy that people in the U.S. no longer warrant employment with higher levels of compensation since such privileges are reserved for the tiny elite and their upper-middle class associates. The message is patently clear: the general U.S. workforce should expect to remain at socio-economic levels just barely above poverty, while maintaining lifelong debt in areas of housing, education, and health care, for example. Essentially, then, the U.S. labor force becomes an expanded underclass of cheap labor. For persons of color, particularly the majority who live in overcrowded and under-resourced urban communities where job creation is at a virtual standstill, the conditions for crime are riper than ever before. A recessionary economic ethos ensures poverty levels and compels particularly young people with little education and often high school or college dropouts to resort to extra-legal modes of subsisting, especially siphoning them into the entrenched mega-billion illegal drug economy where they eventually become grist for the globalized prison industrial mill.

Law enforcement and corrections budgets thus assume swollen budget status, to the detriment of public education, particularly higher education. Well-informed graduates who are capable of understanding the dynamics of economic globalization are remote because most are forced to work long hours to pay for the cost of attending college and then to eke out a low-paying job to service debts, leaving little time for substantive study and reading. The coerced financial and economic environment that conditions working class women and men into lives of illegal drug selling and petty crime, particularly people of color, inevitably produces a bloated criminal class who are confined to the nations' prisons for unusually long terms. Prison construction expands through corporate investment in prison bonds, as with Lehman Brothers, Goldman Sachs, Merrill Lynch, and Fidelity Management and Research, for example. In line with expanded prisons, politicians use the code words of "law and order" to criminalize principally persons of color and all poor working class people so that such persons fill the beds being constructed rapidly around the nation. Billions of dollars invested in retirement portfolios of prison staff around the country serves as a financial insurance for those who have worked within the prisons system for decades and motivates harsh and long prison sentences with little opportunity for parole. The longer a person remains incarcerated, the more lucrative the retirement package of prison administrators and staff. In a globalized economy where financial insecurity and instability is the norm for most service sector businesses, law enforcement and corrections becomes the *one* place where one's economic future is guaranteed through the confinement of the incarcerated, whose incarceration is funded by public tax monies that are allocated by greedy politicians working in cahoots with prison corporations and investors in prison bonds. Globalization's success resides in its manipulative ability to deceive a gullible and economically vulnerable public that is steeped in debt to become pliable and accept the rhetoric of crime and punishment and colonialist-capitalist ideology of race, class, and culture of White supremacy discussed at the beginning of this chapter. The ideologues of globalization who are now bureaucratic administrators at colleges and universities, hospitals and clinics, schools and social agencies, halls of congress and state legislatures, investment banks and law firms, aid agencies, philanthropy organizations, non-profit corporations, and the like, all converge on implementing the globalized ideology of the wealthy elite fringe remaining in economic and political power, and the vast working and underclasses serving the elite powerstructure—the 1 percent as the Occupy Wall Street Movement described it. It can be described as a form of *slow genocide* when one includes dimensions of race, class, gender, and culture because marginalized and vulnerable communities become depopulated of vital women and men, children become parentless, and familial disintegration becomes normative when imprisonment is pervasive, since families cannot visit imprisoned loved ones who may be behind bars hundreds or thousands of miles away. Again, permanent underclass status of both the incarcerated and the families of the incarcerated is assured through the prison system.

Very importantly, the national security state, which is now fully computerized and has the entire citizenry under surveillance so that privacy rights and constitutional protections no longer apply, is able to monitor the activities of the poor and vulnerable at all levels. The poor committing crimes generates a criminal record that cannot be removed in the federal system of law enforcement; instead, once one is arrested, convicted, sentenced, and imprisoned, even for non-violent offenses, one has an unerasable stain on one's record that ensures that one is permanently relegated to the margins of society: the right of voting in elections, the right of receiving public housing, the right of receiving student aid, the right of receiving loans or bank credit, and the right to gainful employment are all denied for the rest of one's life in most instances. Essentially, incarceration under globalization disables the incarcerated from being able to reclaim their humanity and return to the life of "normal" citizenry as others. Racism, classism, anti–Black, anti–Latino, anti-immigrant, and anti-poor ideologies and cultures are bred, nourished, nurtured, and institutionalized by the tiny 1 percent ruling class, so that the interests of the ruling class are foisted upon and become championed by the rest of the society. This behavior is akin to the manner in which we are made to believe that U.S. firms trading on Wall Street like Goldman Sachs or General Electric or Walmart are engaged in business practices that protect *our* national economic interest, whereas in actuality they are gluttonous, self-serving, profit-hungry corporations making billions in profits at the cost of the lives of U.S. workers by outsourcing most of their investments and viable jobs to those parts of the underdeveloped world where labor is cheapest and profit margins are highest.

The Private Prisons Industry and Poor People

Private prisons have their origins in the "convict lease" system at the end of the 19th century and the beginning of the 20th century, principally located in the South. Due to high rates of fatalities, they were abolished by governmental corrections agencies. It is not coincidental that most private prisons are founds in the South and in many Western states of the country like California, Arizona, and Texas. The role of deep-seated racism from the slavery epoch combined with right-wing ruling class economic and social ideology resurfaced with the onset of globalization in the 1980s. The privatization of prisons has become the leading growth industry in the U.S., generating $5 billion in 2011.[247] The prison industrial complex as a whole is booming today and worth over $50 billion.[248]

In 2005, 7 percent of 1.5 million people incarcerated in U.S. prisons were confined in a privately owned prison.[249] Seven thousand six hundred eighty-eight federal inmates were housed in privately managed facilities in the same year.[250] In 2006, there were 64,867 state prisoners and 27,108 inmates in private prisons, a 10 percent increase from the previous year. Private prisons have grown from 350 prison beds in the early 1980s to 80,000 beds in 1997. The number of private-for-profit prisons grew three-fold between 1987 and 2007. Companies like Corrections Corporation of America (CCA), the GEO Group, and Community Education Centers benefit lucratively from private prison operations. CCA's stock skyrocketed from a dollar to $23.13 in 2000, all accruing from the company successfully securing contracts for immigrant detention and attracting investors like William Ackman's Pershing Square Capital Management.[251] In Houston, for example, the Immigration and Customs Enforcement department (ICE) pays CCA to house 1,000 alleged illegal immigrants prior to processing for possible deportation.[252] If states need growing private prison labor, inmates are shipped out of state to work in such states so that profit maximization is assured. As with slavery, the sole motive of prisons is the agglomeration of profit at the cost of decimating especially Black and poor humanity.

The state of New Mexico has overpaid millions of dollars to private corrections companies that were responsible for housing 40 percent of the state's prison inmates.[253] Arizona's political agenda on "immigration reform" is driven by the greed for profits through private prison construction and expansion and the governor, Jan Brewer, who signed SB 1070 in April 2010 that authorizes arrest of "illegal aliens" and has been legally and politically challenged, has been influenced in her governorship by two of her top advisors, Paul Senseman and Chuck Coughlin, former lobbyists with private prison companies.[254] Thanks to George W. Bush's policy of major national security clampdowns on "illegal aliens," immigrant detention has become a lucrative business in the U.S. By the end of 2007, it was estimated that about 27,500 "illegal immigrants" were locked in detention facilities at the cost of about $95 per night, costing almost $1 billion per year.[255]

In 2008, 8 percent of state and federal prisoners were held in privately owned facilities with over 126,000 people.[256] Staffing costs consumed 80 percent of private prison budgets and staff turnover rates were as high as 53 percent in 2000 compared with a 16 percent staff turnover rate at public corrections facilities. Numerous studies, including one published in the *Federal Probation Journal* in 2004, have shown that assaults among inmates in private prisons were twice those in public facilities and there were almost 50 percent more inmate-on-staff assaults in private prisons than in public prisons.[257] Private prisons are also problematic because they are not covered by the Freedom of Information Act and corporations like CCA do not provide audit reports to government agencies since they are accountable principally to their shareholders. Cost-savings of private prisons compared to public prisons are negligible. Ironically, while the states of Kentucky, Texas, Idaho, and Mississippi terminated contracts with CCA because of conditions of violence, brutality, premature inmate death, financial cost, and understaffing at the corporation's facilities in these states, California's governor Jerry Brown is still planning on moving thousands of incarcerated persons into private prison facilities owned by CCA to address overcrowding problems at the cost of $1 billion for the next three years.[258]

The intensification of the privatization of prisons is part of *the shifts of globalization* that have occurred within capitalist and imperialist circles in the past decade and have resulted in industrial operations being subcontracted, the incarceration of people being one of these sectors. Donna Selman and Paul Leighton explain that as the 2008 financial crisis bit deeply into urban and rural communities where unemployment peaked, as in the Midwest, for example, private prisons boomed, so that "many other communities had similar dreams of replacing lost jobs with prisons," and while "processes of globalization threaten manufacturing and some service jobs ... prison construction and guard jobs cannot be easily moved overseas." Resultantly, "areas with high unemployment and unstable job bases offered tax breaks and other subsidies to have a prison built, be it public or private."[259] Economic depression in the rural U.S. is ironically being redressed with injection of private prison construction and promises of employment from guarding and housing prison inmates.[260]

Victor Hassine, a law graduate who has been in prison in Pennsylvania for a capital crime for thirty years without parole, explains that present-day prisons have become combinations of correction and disabling programs within single detention facilities and thus the supposed original goal of producing law-abiding citizens and "corrected" individuals has largely been abandoned and supplanted with a prison program that produces "a compliant convict who remains stable enough to adapt to indefinite incarceration without causing a disturbance—in other words, a 'warehouse stable inmate,' or more cynically, a 'warehouse friendly inmate.'"[261] The reduced dependence on forced prison labor has been replaced with business incentives from the process of incarceration, Hassine contends, so that "prisons are now operated to provide government-funded job opportunities to unemployed blue-collar workers who have been displaced by our nation's shift from an industrial to a service-based economy."[262] He explains that states benefit economically from deploying the unemployed in prison jobs because tax-coffers are replenished and, consequently, "prisons are now built in high unemployment areas where they are greatly desired, appreciated, and encouraged to expand."[263]

Hassine observes that communities and private companies generate further income through providing services to prisons and persons incarcerated. Prisons themselves receive additional revenues from taxing such services. It is now commonplace for many services provided in prisons such as catering, counseling, health care, transportation, telephone communication, and even security to be outsourced, creating a boon for private corporations. Labor contacts between public and private prisons with large corporations like IBM, MCI, Motorola, TWA (merged with American Airlines in 2001), Victoria's Secret, Compaq Computers and numerous other companies are an integral part of the U.S. globalized economy.[264] Mammoth Wall Street corporations like Merrill Lynch, Allstate, Lehman Brothers (which collapsed after going bankrupt in 2008), Smith Barney, and Goldman Sachs function as underwriters of prison construction by selling "tax-exempt, high-interest, non-voter approved, lease-revenue, a.k.a. lease-payment, bonds to institutional and individual investors" as part of a booming $2.3 billion prison "bond" industry.[265] The indirect effect of this booming prison industrial complex is that growing segments of the U.S. population become dependent and inevitably advocates of tougher crime laws and punishment so that communities can benefit from expanded prison construction that leads to more job opportunities and increased revenues. Hassine notes that between 2003 and 2004, there were 13 million people in state or federal prison, with 760,000 prison guards employed and projects that "by 2014, the incarceration revolution promises to disenfranchise, through incarceration, at least an additional 6 million Americans while employing 325,000 more prison guards to keep these people removed from the benefits of the Constitution and full citizenship."[266]

Angela Davis, whose ongoing work around resistance to the prison industrial complex is well-known, describes the extractive character of the privatized prison industry eloquently when she writes that, in 2002, "the Corrections Company of America (CCA), the largest private U.S. prison company, claimed 54,955 beds in 68 facilities under contract or development in the U.S., Puerto Rico, the United Kingdom, and Australia," and "CCA opened a women's prison outside Melbourne, Australia," given the lucrative nature of imprisonment of women.[267] G4S Government Solutions Incorporated (formerly Wackenhut Corrections Corporation—WCC) was started by four former FBI agents and is the second largest U.S. prison company. CCA and WCC saw revenues rise 58 percent from $293 to $462 million and from $138 million to $210 million, respectively, from 1996 to 1997. Net profits of CCA almost doubled during that period, from $30.9 million to $53. 9 million.[268]

Pricor was the third largest private prison company of the 1980s that operated out of Texas and, though it received $30 million in revenues in 1991, it was unable to sustain its operations in that state by late 1992.[269] In 2003, CCA generated over $268.9 million in revenue, and in 2004, the company's political action committee *generously* donated $59,000 to candidates running for federal office.[270] In addition to CCA stock being traded on Wall Street under the symbols CXW, in 1994 CCA acquired TransCor America Unit, responsible for transporting inmates across the 2,000 correctional facilities around the country.[271] TransCor America Unit offers career opportunities in transportation of the incarcerated, claiming to have transported 1.2 million detainees over the past 23 years and be the largest detainee-prisoner transportation company in the country.[272] CCA faces stiff competition from another private prison company whose stock is traded on Wall Street, Cornell Companies, trading on the New York Stock Exchange under CRN. Cornell Companies earned $291 million in 2004, and enjoyed profit of $7.4 million. It administers more than 80 adult and juvenile facilities in 15 states and has 18,500 beds. The G4S Government Solutions Corporation is even larger, earning $614.5 million in 2004 and receiving $16.4 million in net returns.[273] Both CCA and G4S Government Solutions Incorporated, two of the nation's largest private prison corporations, house less than 20 percent of immigrants in detention, but are expecting to see this number rise phenomenally. They administer 8 of the 16 federal detention centers.[274] G4S Government Solutions has prison beds in Canada, Australia, New Zealand (Aoteroa), and South Africa, all European settler-colonial republics. In 2006, these countries with the exception of Canada had 21 private prisons with 17,000 inmates.[275] South Africa's Department of Correctional Services was involved in putting out tenders for four large private prisons, with an estimated cost of 9 billion South African rands (almost $1.25 billion) in 2010.[276] California, Texas, and Florida, in addition to the U.S. government, are G4S Government Solutions' largest clients.

Angela Davis underscores the point that the entire national security industrial complex is intimately interwoven with the private prisons industry, with architectural design finding a new niche in advanced prison design, so that companies like Westinghouse that have military contracts with the U.S. government have branched out into developing new prison technologies that can be used by law enforcement and prisons.[277] U.S.–based corporations like IBM, Honeywell, Motorola, Compaq, Texas Instruments, Microsoft and Boeing regularly use prison labor. Inmates in Maryland regularly inspect jars and bottles made by Revlon and Pierre Cardin, and "prisoners do data entry for Chevron, make telephone reservations for TWA (now out of business—mine), raise hogs, shovel manure, make circuit boards, limousines, waterbeds, and lingerie for Victoria's Secret—all at a fraction of the cost of 'free labor.'"[278] Computer circuit boards are made by Texas prison inmates for IBM, Texas Instruments, and Dell. JCPenney and Kmart benefit from jeans sown by Tennessee inmates. McDonalds employs tens of thousands of lowly paid employees who wear uniforms made by prisoners earning a pittance as part of coerced prison labor.[279] The number of people in prison who have worked as exploited labor increased phenomenally from 169,000 in 1972 to 523,000 in 1992, a whopping 300 percent, giving prisons the dubious distinction of hiring more people than any Fortune 500 company except for General Motors.[280]

Private prisons ultimately have nothing to do with social rehabilitation or reform of "criminals"; a CCA prospectus describes its mission not as addressing a social ill, but rather as a business opportunity, underlining the fact that private prisons exist to maximize profits in line with the convergence of goals of globalization of the privatization of industry like punishment and expansion of the national security state in its pursuit of justice against "injustice."[281] CCA has 90,000 prison beds in 20 states. It has promised to alleviate overcrowding of state-run and federal prisons and generate income for debt-ridden state governments by buying state prisons. State contracts require that CCA prisons are 90 percent occupied for the next 20 years; hence the rush to introduce legislation like SB 1070 in Arizona promoted by organizations like the American Legislative Executive Council (ALEC) that funds state politicians who urge tough crime and sentencing laws.

Private prisons were found to be an excessive waste of taxpayer monies and much more costly than public prison facilities in a 2010 Arizona State audit.[282] Even health care companies are cashing in on the prison bonanza. Corizon Prison Health Management makes $1.4 billion each year from supposedly providing health care to sick inmates with contracts to provide such care to 29 states.[283] In late October 2013, Corizon signed a lucrative five-year contract with the state of Florida worth $1.2 billion. The company was sued 660 times over a five-year period from 2008 to 2013 for its woefully inadequate and insouciant health care practices when it came to treating the sick behind bars. In the words of Corizon nurse Diane Jackson, "We save money by skipping the ambulance and taking prisoners directly to the morgue."[284]

Jalil Abdul Muntaqim, a political prisoner in the U.S. since 1971, reflects on the incredible escalation of the construction of prisons to the point that marginalized communities lobby their congressional representatives for support of prison construction in their communities so as to reap the economic benefits of punishment. Muntaqim describes it as a "slice of the bounty," where giant corporations are making huge profits.[285] He asserts that "Goldman Sachs & Co., Prudential Insurance Co. of America, Smith Barney & Shearson Inc., and Merrill Lynch & Co., are among those competing to underwrite prison construction with private, tax-exempt bonds—where no voter approval is required" and "in essence, big business is investing in the prison system."[286]

Private imprisonment is big business. As Phil Smith asserts, punishment is a huge money-making enterprise and while private prisons house a small portion of inmates, they are becoming increasingly powerful in shaping punishment policies and progressively securing more substantial contracts from state and federal justice agencies with the corrections budgets for state, local, and federal governments rising to more than $20 billion a year in the early 1990s.[287] Prison construction is rapidly expanding to be congruous with the high influx of persons incarcerated and jailed and is fast approaching $6 billion a year. Such construction provides employment for over 50,000 guards and tens of thousands of administrators, health care providers, educational personnel, food producing, and vending companies.[288]

In 2014, the state of California alone is expected to spend up to $5 billion in construction of new prisons in the next ten years at the rate of $500 million per year.[289] For 2014-2015, California's allocation for prisons was $10 billion, even as the state struggles to pay off past fiscal debt and come to grips with a shortage of $217 billion in public-employee pension and health care costs that includes an $80 billion shortfall in the California State Teachers Retirement System which is projected to be bankrupt within 30 years. As California Con-

Under globalization, prison overcrowding in the United States and around the world, including in the underdeveloped world where societal violence is widespread, has become a chronic problem. Political repression, expanded wars, and severity of economic hardship have resulted in millions breaking national crime laws and being imprisoned. This overcrowded prison in Bunia in the Democratic Republic of the Congo has 1,000 inmates even though the prison was constructed to house 200 people. Inmates have suffered cholera and typhoid outbreaks in Bunia prisons (powless/Flickr).

gresswoman Barbara Lee pointed out in 2002, California was constructing prisons then for those who are today's kindergartners, particularly the poor.[290]

As the U.S. recession (during which globalization's off-shore capital and plant relocation to places where cheap labor is abundant intensified) continues its caustic after-effects into 2014, 13 of 15 cash-strapped states in the U.S. that have high prison populations, including California, Arizona, Alabama, and Michigan, have resorted to reviving "debtors prisons" where "a growing number of impoverished people are jailed for being unable to pay their legal fees— including charges for use of public defenders, a guaranteed right in the United States."[291] These practices violate the Equal Protection Clause of the 14th Amendment, but are being used in places like New Orleans, Louisiana, where up to two-thirds of such fines defray court costs in the wake of rising budget deficits and reduced state allocations for court operation costs. In its report, "In for a Penny: The Rise of America's New Debtors Prisons," the American Civil Liberties Union noted that this was ultimately a waste of vital state budgets since the states were responsible for financing the incarceration of people confined in prisons while they struggled to pay legal fees.[292]

Another area where globalized economic dynamics of profit from the prison industrial complex is in bond companies that make lucrative profits from posting bail for unsentenced inmates who are awaiting trial and can't afford to post bond, often due to living within the ranks of poverty. Some 500,000 persons are confined in U.S. jails even though they haven't been formally sentenced, costing taxpayers some $9 billion in jail housing costs. Most are awaiting trial for petty theft or non-violent offenses like being involved in a scuffle. Due to the onset of globalization where small rural towns across the U.S. lost vital industrial jobs over the past three decades, no longer are petty crime offenders released "on their own recognizance." Instead county jails emerged in recent years with a minimum of 10 counties around the country each year building jails to provide relief to an overcrowded prison system in places like Baltimore County in Maryland, Philadelphia City in Pennsylvania, and Davidson County in Tennessee all experiencing overcrowding of 116 percent, 102 percent, and 107 percent of capacity.[293] The pre-trial phase of prison sentencing has earned millions of dollars for hundreds of counties in the U.S. through the bail bond business. Lubbock, a city of 250,000 people in Texas has 12 bond companies, accompanied by plans to build a massive $110 million county jail. One company alone, Trammel's Lubbock Bail Bond, has between 2,500 and 3,000 active accounts, seeing at least six cases daily.[294]

Unsurprisingly, capitalist economics permeates the judicial system with bond companies benefitting heavily from high bail bonds set by judges particularly for people who can't pay. Someone who can afford to pay his or her bail bond $1,000 in cash is given a $10,000 bail bond, for example, ensuring that the person posting bond has to go to a bail bond company that charges a non-refundable 10 percent fee to post the $10,000 bond. Should those posting bail not show up for trial, the bond companies are generally required to pay 5 percent of the non-refundable fee they received to the county so that they make a 5 percent profit. Bond companies never lose even when trial defendants are absent at their hearings. In places like Erie, Pennsylvania, bond companies are no longer pursued by county officials for outstanding bail monies because of the tedious efforts required to get bond companies to pay on their debts. As part of the brokering of bonds, persons awaiting trial are generally discouraged from paying cash since it takes many more hours to post cash bail and few defendants have knowledge of this option anyway. The bond bail business sector is intrinsic to the prison industrial complex and reflects the contours of globalized economics where poor people awaiting trial are coerced into further debt for being unable to post bail and are grist for the bond bail companies that receive non-refundable fees from these already desperate indigent persons.

It should thus come as no serious surprise too that the Black bourgeois class is also cashing in on profits from private prisons. Some Black companies have entered into commercial ventures involving private prisons, including one that is now a multi-billion dollar enterprise.[295] In the late 1990s, Adelaide Tambo, the widow of the African National Congress leader Oliver Tambo, of Azania/South Africa, embarked on a private enterprise opportunity with the Lindela Accommodation Center, part of the Dyambu Trust that entailed imprisoning people convicted of crimes of "illegal migration" in that country.[296] Globalization's stretch is evidenced too in national legislation targeting international residents in places like South Africa, where millions of neighboring Zimbabweans resident in the country legally and illegally were required, as of January 1, 2011, to produce valid immigration documentation or face deportation to Zimbabwe or imprisonment. Similar kinds of xenophobic political legislation are being considered in France, Germany, Italy, and Spain. Thanks to globalization, the U.S. "global prison economy" has extended beyond our shores to places like Turkey and South Africa.[297]

Though some academics may be skeptical about the exponential growth of private prisons in the near future since they have been uneven in many southern states, with North Carolina deciding against them after a brief spell from the late 1990s through 2000 and South Carolina and Alabama only turning toward private prisons in 2002, the fact of the matter is that the politics of tenacious racism as championed by the right-wing political brokers of the last two decades combined with the economic volatility of globalization compels countries like the U.S., where the prison population is unusually large, toward private prisons for optimal profit.[298] Private prisons, which are especially prominent in former slave-holding states of the South and in some western states, will continue to be an integral feature of globalized economies in varying degrees along with the globalization of harsh penalties for non-violent crimes, justified by strong "law and order" regimes.[299]

Prison as *Punishment or* for *Punishment?*

The confusion between prison *as* punishment and prison *for* punishment persists in the obduracy of prisons like Special Housing Units (SHUs), Maximum Security, and Supermax. Most prison systems are places of cruelty, including torture and rape, witnessed with the policies of *extraordinary rendition* of those accused of crimes of terrorism by the U.S. government and within prisons in the U.S. and around the world. Prisons or "Corrections" are supposedly about administration of justice and rehabilitation of those whose lives have been convicted for criminal and illegal offenses against others. The conditions in prisons in many parts of the world where dictatorial, even military, regimes rule are too horrific to recount. Accounts of torture by police and prison authorities have been extensively documented by organizations like Amnesty International over the years. *What are prisons really for*? Lukas Muntingh from the University of the Western Cape in South Africa, explains that "people are sent to prison *as* punishment, not *for* punishment" (italics mine) and "the state is therefore obliged to develop and put in place such measures that (sentenced) prisoners are able to receive the necessary assistance to fulfill their human potential."[300] What Muntingh emphasizes is that prisons were never meant to *cause* suffering in the first place and were originally conceived to *rehabilitate* persons who commit societal crimes, but have now essentially become places of perpetual physical, emotional, and sexual violence.

The recurring question for all persons interested in justice and desiring rehabilitation of those behind bars is: why is it that the overwhelming majority of people imprisoned are poor, illiterate, and often people of color? Why have not wealthy criminals like Martha Stewart, Kenneth Lay, Ivan Boesky, Leona Helmsley, Paris Hilton, and Lindsay Lohan, all of whom have either been arrested and convicted for stealing or defrauding the government of millions of dollars or repeated illegal drug offenses, been sent to jail for long terms? Martha Stewart, for instance, spent five months in prison from October 8, 2004, to March 4, 2005, and was then given a "gorgeous home prison" for a five-month sentence even though she was found guilty of conspiracy, obstruction of an agency proceeding, and making false statements to federal investigators after being indicted on nine counts, including charges of securities fraud.[301] She is now a national "media moghul" back on the business circuit, reaping millions from sales of brand-labeled bed, bath, and cookware products at leading department stores in the country. Why is it that many of those convicted of petty theft and non-violent drug crimes are not granted "equal opportunity" to both rehabilitate themselves and engage in productive economic activity? Most of those who are incarcerated for such crimes have their names permanently stained so that they are generally denied access to public housing, student and bank loans, voting rights, and the like. Most people arrested and convicted for felonies in 13 states in the U.S. are prohibited from exercising the right to vote in elections.

Neill Franklin, a former undercover narcotics agent who turned against the war on drugs, stated it clearly:

> You want safer communities? Sending people to prison won't do it. Think about it—if you put a man in prison, you put his whole family in prison too. You've just put that family into financial dire straits. Prisons are not institutions of higher learning. They are institutions of corruption, institutions of violence. People come back to their communities worse off than when they went in. They've got a record, so they're unemployable for the most part except for the drug trade. The drug trade will hire you no matter what. It's a vicious cycle.[302]

What is clear is that the real color of crime in the U.S. is not "Black, Brown, Red, or Asian or poor White"... but green. Those who wield real money like the bank fraudsters at Wachovia are part of the corporate elite and are generally not subject to the harsh strictures of justice and law enforcement as the poor are. This is the reason that nobody did prison time for flagrant violation of the country's banking laws during Wachovia's indictment, and the Justice Department was willing to "go easy" on persons responsible for laundering drug money from Mexico in the hundreds of billions of dollars. The real enemies of justice and society are not the impoverished drug dealing youth of the inner cities of the United States; they are merely the puny little pawns coerced into living lives of perpetual crime (most non-violent) because structures of race, class, and culture entrap them in ways in which they cannot envisage a world free from coercion, manipulation, hustling for survival, and constantly preying on others equally vulnerable as themselves (the poor are still the largest segment of crime victims in the country).

Globalization's role in siphoning millions of jobs out of the U.S. and in inducing economic vacuums in desperate urban communities for the unbridled generation of hundreds of billions in profits for the wealthy ruling elites both in the U.S. and abroad, including through the prison industrial complex, needs to be exposed for the crimes of dispossession and impoverishment of people who already live at the precipice of economic vulnerability and fragility. The 2008 economic downturn saw hundreds of thousands of Black and Latino households lose their homes, and in vast disproportion to white householders losing their homes, because of racist banking practices that viewed mortgage holders of color as less likely to pay off their mortgages and thus subject to higher interest rates than Whites.[303]

Conclusion

Globalization has institutionalized the cruelty and punishment of poor peoples in its insatiable appetite for profits, causing unprecedented suffering and death through the prison industrial and military industrial complexes, mediated through prisons and wars of aggression and occupation of poor peoples' lands. For true democracy to emerge, wars against the poor domestically and globally must cease and the pervasive incarceration of poverty-stricken women and men especially in the U.S. must end through tireless resistance to globalization and its ugly tentacles manifest in violent prisons. Making profits from criminal activity, prisons, punishment, and torture is no way for any society to live in peace and thrive in prosperity since such profit-making is in itself criminal and inhuman. No person is really free until the wrongfully imprisoned, overwhelming poor, are free.

This chapter has demonstrated that the intrinsic nature of violence and torture within the prison industrial complex during this phase of late globalized capitalism persists in confining the underclasses of society to lives behind bars for extended periods, regardless of the kind of crimes committed. The majority of people incarcerated today are jailed for non-violent drug offenses. Classism and racism continue to rear their ugly heads within the political economy of the prison industrial complex. With the vanishing of millions of semi-skilled jobs during the periodic economic downturns over the past two and a half decades, like that of the early 1990s, the early 2000s, and the most recent financial crisis of 2008, many policy makers around the country have turned to toughening sentencing laws for non-violent and repeated offenders, including legislating three-strikes laws that mandate life imprisonment for offenders, to stimulate economic growth for financially depressed states. Arizona, Arkansas, California, Colorado, Connecticut, Florida, Georgia, Indiana, Kansas, Louisiana, Maryland, Massachusetts, Montana, Nevada, New Hampshire, New Jersey, New Mexico, North Carolina, North Dakota, Pennsylvania, South Carolina, Tennessee, Texas, Utah, Vermont, Virginia, Washington, and Wisconsin all have three-strikes laws.[304]

The dire financial situation that has unfolded over the past decade with the accompanying element of lower labor force participation of less-skilled people has resulted in an overall desperate situation for economically and financially vulnerable people. Many of these impoverished people are inevitably sucked into cycles of crime since employment opportunities for semi-skilled and unskilled workers have devolved to a trickle over the past two decades. The fact of 55 percent of Black college graduates being *underemployed* in 2014 underscores the gravity of the globalized employment crisis.[305] Such conditions in turn provoke a propensity toward unconventional and illegal methods for securing livable earnings and supplementing meager incomes since gainful employment is so hard to come by. Contrary to popular opinion, young people are not instinctively inclined to lives of crime. Steven Raphael and Michael A. Stoll confirm this assertion when they explain that "there is now considerable evidence that economically motivated crime increases with unemployment and decreases with average wages, especially the average wages of lower-skilled workers."[306] Lower levels of education compound unemployability in formal employment sectors, compelling especially young people to seek incomes outside legal avenues. Interwoven with the dynamics of race and class, globalization's impact of diminished employment in the U.S. for all sectors, including manufacturing and erstwhile factory employment, has evoked a condition of long-term structural unemployment, driving those with "low earnings ... toward criminal activity."[307]

The top 1 percent of the ruling capitalist class in the U.S. ensures that the bottom 20 percent is trapped in an ongoing spiral of economic and material deprivation and reduced self-worth as the ruling class engages in the unbridled pursuit of profits and material accumulation, elaborated in the introduction and in Chapter 1 of this book. Incarceration is an integral component of this entrapment. So long as structural poverty compels people into lives of desperate crime and prisons make lucrative profits from crime and punishment policies that favor the wealthy elites and further marginalize the already impoverished, the prison industrial complex will remain an important cornerstone in the U.S. capitalist system. Globalized corporations' shift from employment within the U.S. to much more profitable enterprises in the underdeveloped cash-strapped countries of the world where labor costs are at a bare minimum ensures that the starved employment and ensuing crime culture in the U.S. will continue for some time since prisons are a growing multi-billion dollar public and private enterprise. For persons of color, especially Black people, the prison underclass is part of a racial caste, as Michelle Alexander explains in her instructive work, *The New Jim Crow: Mass Incarceration in an Age of Color Blindness*, where the criminal justice system feeds into a "much larger system of racial stigmatization and permanent marginalization."[308] This same system, under the pretext of globalized color blindness, has propelled the U.S. into having the dubious distinction of imprisoning three times as many Black people as South Africa did during the height of apartheid, shocking both Republican and Democrat lawmakers.[309] As Harvard Law expert Randall Kennedy argues, the endemic anti–Black racism of U.S. society is indicated in the probability that if poor Whites were incarcerated at such high levels as Blacks, there would be a national outrage that demanded sweeping policy changes against such unjust incarceration.[310]

In a broader sense, the ruling classes of globalization, especially in the

U.S., have enslaved all others so that everyone functions in a subservient manner and is compelled to obey the dictates of globalization ideology, which demand allegiance to the national security corporate capitalist state that rules through the politics of instilling *fear* in the general populace. Everybody is expected to know her or his particular place within the economic and social hierarchy generated by the rulers of globalization and be content with their lot in fear of the situation changing for the worse in the widespread corporatization of all work places. Prisons are just one manifestation of such corporatization under the globalization regime, along with hospitals, school districts, universities, and other work places, especially with most public universities in the U.S. coming to depend heavily on private corporate funding.

In the final chapter, we will discuss the most critical issue facing us as life on the Earth, which recalls us to the grim truth that globalized capitalism is the *enemy* of the Earth because it is imprisoned within the culture of profit accumulation and materialistic acquisition with little consideration of the lethal consequences of its actions of perpetual plunder: *global warming and climate change.*

5

Globalization's Intensification of Global Warming and Climate Change

Much of the controversy that now surrounds global warming is not whether global warming will occur but just how sensitive the climate is to increases in carbon dioxide levels.[1]

Mountain glaciers are melting, along with ice at the poles. The oceans are getting warmer and expanding ... sea levels are rising ... sea levels will rise so fast in the next 50 years that some low-lying island nations may disappear altogether. In the unprotected river deltas of Bangladesh, Egypt, and Vietnam there are a total of 30 million people living within 1m (3.3 feet) of the high-tide mark. They have no safeguard.[2]

Global Warming is already upon us.... The impacts of global warming are such that I have no hesitation in describing it as a weapon of mass destruction.[3]

Introduction

During my travel and research in various countries of Asia, Africa, and Latin America over the past 37 years into the present, one glaring fact has been consistently visible throughout: the world's most precious resource and now in critical short supply is not oil but water! Even in the 1970s, water taps with running water were accessible only twice a day in India, Nepal, and many countries in East Africa. During my visit to Haiti in 1992 shortly after the illegal ousting of democratically-elected president Jean-Bertrand Aristide, a personal friend, it was water that was in scarce supply in the communities around Port Au Prince, the capital, and surrounding towns like Citi Soleil and Gonaives. Clean drinking water was impossible to acquire from taps and one was forced to purchase drinking water. In Ibadan, Nigeria, water for bathing trickled from taps and one had to use it sparingly for washing and bathing. During a visit to Dakar, Senegal, in the summer of 2008, water from taps in the apartment where I stayed came on at 3:00 a.m. each day and we all scrambled to fill many buckets for washing and bathing. The same story applies to places like Lijiang, China, which I visited in 2013, where fresh water was clearly the most valuable resource, yet found in short supply. In 2012, I recall our hosts in Nicaragua urging us to avoid flushing toilets after urination and only after defecation.

Though we live in a world that is surrounded by water, only 2.53 percent of the Earth's water is fresh, with two-thirds of this fresh water confined to glaciers and permanent snow cover.[4] Water is indeed the "bread of life." Even within the European Union, where many may incorrectly assume that Western capitalist countries are immune from global warming's effects because of possession of monetary and industrial resources, the facts bespeak a different reality. Droughts have increased markedly over the past three decades and destructive effects have increased 20 percent. The combined cost of damages has been over $100 billion. Eleven percent of the human population of Europe and 17 percent of the landmass is now suffering from water shortages, with Malta and Cyprus, followed by Spain and Italy experiencing the most adverse effects of water scarcity.[5] Northern China which has about 43 percent of China's human population has just 14 percent of the country's water resources and China's per capita water. Asia has over 60 percent of the world's human population while possessing only 36 percent of the world's water resources.[6] Given that China and India together have almost one-third of the human beings in the world, the shortage of water in these countries is certainly the most pressing issue of the 21st century, particularly given the continued heating of the planet. According to the UN Water Development Report of 2012, groundwater abstraction has tripled over the past 50 years and more than 1.5 billion rural and economically vulnerable people in Africa and Asia and other parts of the world depend on groundwater for their water needs.[7] Much of the water is lost through waste and pollution. Results of findings from the Comprehensive Assessment of Water Management in Agriculture at World Water Week in Stockholm, Sweden, revealed that in 2005, over one-third of all human beings in the world experienced water scarcity, close to 2.5 billion people.[8] Africa is more fortunate than other regions of the world in that she has 13 percent of the world's human beings and possesses 11 percent of the world's water.[9] The El Niño effect from 1997 to 1998 is already back with the intense warming of the Pacific Ocean. In June 2014, the regular monsoon rains in India were delayed and the first rains were 40 percent below averages for the monsoon season.[10] In Malaysia, the country is preparing for an 18-month dry spell and residents in Cebu in the Central Philippines have been asked to engage in radical water conservation measures. Australians are bracing for an even drier and hotter spell in 2014 with low rainfalls expected, all in the aftermath of 2013 being the hottest year on record.[11]

The very future of life on Earth depends on a planet that is balanced in temperature around its circumference on all sides and within. While the Earth has experienced heating spells over hundreds of millions of years, what is evident is the escalation of heating of the Earth's surface since the European industrial revolution of the 1700s that saw fossil fuels combustion grow astronomically and that unleashed massive emissions of carbon dioxide.[12] The effects from the irruption of human industrial and technological activity with the invention of diesel and fossil-fuel engines three centuries ago, along with subsequent intensification of agriculture and land-use change and the use of aerosols that contain microscopic airborne particles that cool the atmosphere, were transmitted into the 20th and now 21st centuries according to the reports of the Intergovernmental Panel on Climate Change (IPCC) from 1995 and 2001, with temperatures increasing by an average of 0.6 degrees centigrade in the 20th century.[13] The combustion of fossil fuels has destabilized the balance of heat-retaining gases in the atmosphere, raising the levels of carbon dioxide levels from about 280 parts per million (ppm) to 380 ppm.[14] The glaring reality is that in 2004 temperatures related to fossil fuel combustion are similar to those of 1960 when fossil fuel consumption was much lower than the 2000s.[15] The reason is that feedback loops are tremendous: carbon emissions from the 1960s lingers in the atmosphere for 50 years. Human industrial activity in 2014 will have effects for the next 50 years as part of the feedback loop cycle, threatening the very potential for life of future generations. Even if emission levels of 2000 were to remain by the year 2100, the Earth will still warm by at least 0.6 degrees centigrade, making life everywhere practically unbearable.[16]

The globalization regime over the past few decades must be held culpable for the global warming and climate change crisis because its obsession with unbridled profit and relentless pursuit of vital energy and material resources for intensified and unregulated industrial production have conjointly functioned to deplete the Earth of precious forest cover, stripped away the tops of mountains and hills for mining gold, platinum, copper, coal, uranium, diamonds, columbite-tantalite (coltan), and other minerals, and depleted non-renewable water supplies from rivers, wells, streams, ponds, and underground aquifers so that extremely low-level water-tables are pervasive in many parts of the world.

This chapter will describe the very lethal situation the world finds itself in with the dynamics of global warming and climate change in various capacities and demonstrate how globalization, which was ostensibly designed to enhance human well-being, now ironically constitutes the most severe threat to life as we know it and how the initiatives of the ruling classes and governments of the major industrial nations are more fluff than substance and are ultimately feckless in the need to redress global warming's annihilation effects on the world. Global warming is "primarily a problem ... of global capitalism" that is obsessed with incessant agglomeration of profits through "increasing production and consumption."[17] The urgency of addressing and redressing global warming compels new ways of human living in which industrial production expansion and profit maximization as institutionalized by the hegemony of globalization are no longer held sacred; rather, the idolatry of global capitalism is replaced by lifestyles of living in harmony with the Earth and not being at war with Earth, a leadoff from this final chapter into the epilogue.

Climate Warming, Greenhouse Gases, Pollution, and Contamination

The unprecedented levels of temperature increases over the past two decades, with the past ten years being the hottest on record (since records have been kept from the early 19th century), and the fact that global temperatures have risen and the decades of the 1990s and 2000s being warmest before the past ten years clearly are reason for deep concern. Present carbon dioxide levels have been the highest in the past 420,000 years and most likely over the past 20 million years.[18] The steady and intensified emissions of carbon from 1750 through 2010 is evident from Figure 1, indicating a growth of zero in 1715 prior to the 19th century's industrial revolution to a high of almost 8 billion tons in 2010.[19]

Three-quarters of carbon dioxide over the past few decades are attributable to human activities of fossil fuel burning like coal, oil, and "natural" gas, with processes like deforestation being responsible for the remaining quarter.[20] The combined effects of carbon dioxide and methane gas are generating a new greenhouse gas, chlorofluorocarbons (CFCs), which were banned in the 1970s because of damage to the ozone layer by aerosols, air conditioners, refrigerators, paints, perfumes and the like, and the net result is that 200,000 gigawatts of power is trapped by carbon dioxide in the atmosphere, causing serious heating of the Earth.[21]

Fig. 1

Emissions of Carbon Dioxide from 1750-2010

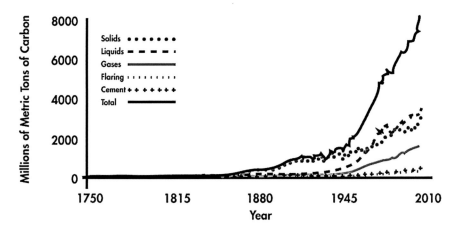

Carbon dioxide by itself is not a negative product since it is part of the natural cycle of respiratory life processes. The Earth has her own natural manner of both storing carbon dioxide in the atmosphere and of eliminating it when it becomes excessive called *carbon cycles*. Cycles storing and removing water are called *hydrological cycles* and cycles that balance storing and removal of nitrogen are called *nitrogen cycles*. The Earth balances carbon dioxide and other gases in the atmosphere constantly so that life itself can survive as demonstrated in Figure 2.[22] However, the excessive emissions of greenhouse gases from deforestation and burning, fossil fuel burning, and other industrial activity in combination with volcanic and other Earth and Ocean natural processes is now out of balance: Earth can absorb only 14–16 gigatons of carbon dioxide annually while our human activity generates 36–38 gigatons per year in this globalized industrialized era.

The low concentrations of the Freons in the CFCs like CFC-11 and CFC-12 compound their radiative capacity so that they are 20,000 times more potent per molecule than carbon dioxide and have the fastest release into the atmosphere.[23] Carbon dioxide is increasing at the rate of 1 percent annually. In May 2013, scientists reporting from a research facility at the top of Mauna Loa volcano on the Big Island of Hawaii declared that the threshold of daily carbon dioxide levels in the atmosphere had been reached with 400 parts per million, higher than any level for the past three million years, a reminder of the gravity of the global warming crisis.[24]

Fig. 2

Biospheric-related Carbon Dioxide Cycle Illustrating the manner that the Earth stores and recycles carbon and maintains atmospheric gases balance.

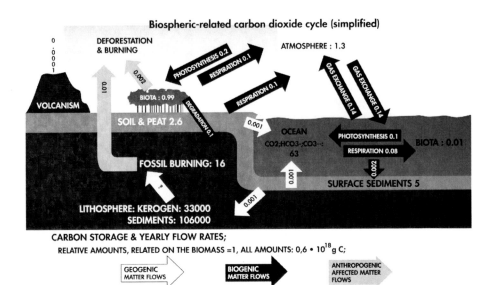

In the U.S., transportation, particularly automobiles and light trucks, produce 30 percent of all the country's global warming emissions.[25] Sadly, China, which has the second largest economy of the world, has now displaced the U.S. as the leading emitter of carbon dioxide in the world, depending on coal production for three-quarter of its power needs even while coal burning produces twice the emissions of carbon dioxide as "natural" gas and oil.[26] The fact that South Africa, the wealthiest country on the African continent, for instance, is expanding coal production even while it is the world's sixth-largest coal exporter, the seventh-largest coal producer, and the 13th largest carbon dioxide emitter, is planning on expanding coal production by constructing two of the four largest 4,800 megawatt coal-fired power plants in the world at Medupi and Kusile, is troubling.[27] The reason cited by Pravin Gordhan, South Africa's mining minister, that "to sustain the growth rates we need to create jobs, we have no choice but to build new generating capacity—relying on what, for now, remains our most abundant and affordable energy source: coal" is unconvincing considering that the bulk of power utilized in South Africa is utilized by powerful mining and industrial corporations and in far heavier proportions by the elite minority than by the vast impoverished majority.[28] Further, it is the black working class poor who work in the most dangerous of conditions in South Africa's deep coal mines to extract this black stone, suffering from serious respiratory diseases and other ailments in the process. The long-term effects of coal mining are reflected in the very people who extract this power-source since their life spans are shortened so that the engine of economic growth can be advanced, accompanied by the devastating ecological and environmental impact on the Earth and the intensified and unsustainable warming of the globe. Tycoon families from India connected to the president, Jacob Zuma, and his son, Duduzane, the Guptas, have stakes in two large coal companies, Idwala Coal and Tegeta Resources, that are mining coal in hitherto unexploited coal resource areas in South Africa. These facts underscore the deeply political and economic dimensions of global warming's causes, with globalization firmly in the driver's seat of this catastrophe.

The highly probable scientific prediction that greenhouse gases, principally carbon dioxide, will double sometime later this century, perhaps before 2050, raising mean temperatures on Earth by an average 2–3 degrees Centigrade (3–5 degrees Fahrenheit), is alarming indeed.[29] The principle causes of this meteoric temperature increase are anthropogenic. While the various global organizations and UN agencies that monitor and assess the effects of global warming around the world and host meeting after meeting with thousands of climate scientists and researchers participating at these global forums, little tangible change is evident and, if anything, things have grown progressively hotter notwithstanding Al Gore's 2006 award-winning documentary, *An Inconvenient Truth*, or James Orlowsski's 2012 National Geographic documentary, *Chasing Ice*.

In the main, though many in the U.S. and in other parts of the world, particularly those effected in regions of Africa, Asia, and Latin America where global warming effects are most pronounced, would like to do something constructive about stopping the tide of global warming in its tracks, the overwhelming majority feel powerless to engineer any radical alternative changes in their lifestyles because they are forced to live within the parameters of economic globalization and eke out an existence under this unjust and unviable system. These economically vulnerable people are forced to accept the dictates of the architects and beneficiaries of globalization: the transnational conglomerates who demand the denuding of forests and the mining of hills and valleys for minerals or the imposition of genetically modified organisms (GMOs) that are harmful and destructive to the fragile balance and cycles of all elements of the natural world, the Monsanto corporation being a leading player in this violation of the beings of the natural world. Globalization is the system that uses the ideology of economic prosperity and materialistic pro-gress as its mantra and it is this obsession with economic and financial growth through industrialism that is now pitted against the Earth, a Mother to all of us who breathe, plant and four and two-legged alike. Globalization's protag-onists insist that the driver of the world is *economic growth* and that the Earth can be manipulated to meet expansion of human materialistic pursuits, refus-ing to realize, as Indigenous people have explained, that the Earth is a living being who cannot be manipulated by human beings for the benefit of commod-ities and agglomeration of profit. After all, Earth has been here for millions, even billions of years, without the presence of human beings. Globalization in its arrogance towards the Earth, thus, signifies in actuality "wars against the Mother Earth," precipitating the current lethal crisis of global warming and climate change.

Of equal concern, though not receiving the equivalent attention as car-bon and methane, is nitrous oxide that has been increasing at the rate of 0.7 ppb or 0.26 percent each year for the past few decades.[30] Microbial production of nitrous oxide from expanded use of chemical fertilizers in industrialized agriculture are held to be the principal cause for this increase as determined by the IPCC Third Assessment Report of 2001 and the IPCC Fourth Assess-ment Report of 2007 respectively.[31] While nitrogen oxide is found in natural terrestrial ecosystems such as wet tropical forests, scientific research on global emissions of nitrous oxide from 1990 through 2001 concurs with the assess-ment that emissions from agriculture constitute the most formidable source of such emissions attributable to synthetic agricultural fertilizers and animal waste, from 0.01-2.2 Tg N 2 O-N yr-1 in 1990 to 4.2 (0.6-14.8) Tg N 2 O-N yr-1 in 1998.[32] With the expansion of global cereal production by 20 percent and meat production by 26 percent and the manufacture of synthetic fertilizers through the Haber-Bosch industrial process from 1995 through 2005, reactive nitrogen Nr creation increased dramatically. The proportions of Nr that's not used for synthetic fertilizers for agricultural production is used for the man-ufacture of nylon, other plastics, resins, fish food supplements, and explosives.

The "nitrogen cascade" phenomenon is now of deep concern to all cli-matologists for a few significant reasons. Nitrogen has a direct impact on ozone depletion, loss of biodiversity, warming of the Earth, acidification of soils and water, and groundwater pollution. The troubling and complex element about reactive nitrogen Nr in gaseous forms (NH_3 and NO_x) is that its effects are felt thousands of miles away from its original source through runoff from rivers to marine systems that is diminishing all aquatic life. Its presence in the environment is most acute with the intensification of agricultural industrial activity.[33] While British climatologists might disproportionately blame Saharan dust, other dust particles and ozone for the extremely high pollution levels in Britain in the first week of April 2014 that caused breathing problems for the elderly especially, the fact of global warming and climate change due to increased levels of nitrous oxide and other greenhouse gases by auto emissions within Europe itself can never be understated in the instability and volatility of weather patterns, wind movements, and air flow.[34]

The impact of fossil fuels and combustion engines too can never be downplayed in the discourse on global warming. Marine transportation that uses large freighter ships, for example, emit significant air pollutants through use of combustion engines to power their movement through river and ocean waters. Inland waterways and oceans are all heavily polluted as a result of shipping, with discarding of oily bilge and ballast water, dumping of non-biodegradable solid wastes into oceans, oil spills, and transportation of non–Native species of plants and animals that damage local ecosystems. Ballast water is used to fill empty tanks of oil freighters, for example, since all ships need to have significant weight to enable them to sail through ocean water. Before loading of oil and petroleum products cargo into the holds of such ships at ports, ballast water containing wastes and oil needs to be discarded, resultantly causing heavy pollution in waterways and adding to water and air pollution.[35]

Even alternative fuel use presents its own problems, part of the contradiction of all Western industrial systems. Though there may be zero emissions of greenhouse gases from electric powered vehicles, the electricity needed for an electric vehicle battery is generally produced from a coal-fired power plant, resulting in net carbon dioxide emissions being higher than that of conventional fuel.[36] Though biofuels like biodiesel and ethanol that are often promoted by the alternative energy lobby may have the potential for offsetting and reducing carbon dioxide emissions as in Brazil, where ethanol and bagasse substitution from fossil fuels have been used, the global warming potential (GWP) of nitrogen oxide (N20) is 320 times that of carbon dioxide, influenced by questions of temperature, operating conditions, excess air level, and catalytic activity.[37]

Globalization's boasting about the claim that more humans are consumers of food, especially meat, at levels far exceeding those of any period of human history, does not consider the unhealthy fact that more than one billion human beings in the world are overweight and 300 million are officially classified as "obese," attributable to the fossil fuel revolution since humans in industrialized societies are now more sedentary, walk much less, and depend on automobiles for transporting themselves.[38] One third of human beings in the U.S. are obese and almost half are overweight, followed by Britain where the obese human population is expected to rise to 50 percent by 2050.[39] People in Canada, Australia, Argentina, China, and many other industrialized societies are eating excessively poor quality food laden with fats and sugars excessively and becoming overweight. These facts not only underscore increased human weight on the planet but the escalating pressure on ecosystems as the result of expanded agricultural production using synthetic fertilizers with nitrogen composition that inevitably decimates marine and other natural ecosystems. English health practitioner and researcher Ian Roberts explains that "the human race is getting fatter and the planet is getting hotter, and fossil fuels are the cause of both," the principal causes being sunlight, petroleum, food, and fat, underpinned by money and greed.[40]

Sea level rise is one of the most catastrophic effects of global warming and climate change. Since 1870 and during the height of European industrialism to the present, sea levels rose 20 centimeters.[41] The sea is rising at the rate of 3.2 millimeters each year and steadily increasing in various regions of the world.[42] Around island nation countries like Tuvalu and Kiribati in the South Pacific, sea levels have already risen to the point of virtually extinguishing the existence of these countries. High tides occurring at the end of the summer there cause flooding of low-lying areas like the airport ,and cyclones that are becoming frequent cause the storm dunes to collapse, making life for Tuvalu residents even more difficult.[43] The tiny island of Mauritius off the southeastern coast of Africa is under threat of rising sea levels and many are considering migrating to Australia. The beautiful island of Maldives, a nation of 300,000 people and encompassing some 1,190 islands of about 90,000 square kilometers, is just 2.4 meters above sea level and a foreign tourist paradise. Yet for the Indigenous Maldivians, their island is anything but paradise. The country has been subject to massive flooding and its atolls are subject to constant destruction because of powerful storms in the Indian Ocean. In 2004, the tsunami that hit Indonesia and killed over 240,000 people made its way to the waters of Maldives. Eight-two people drowned, 12,000 were rendered homeless and key tourist resorts were destroyed.[44] Though the government subsequently invested millions of its tourist revenues in 2007 to raise the height of Hulhumale Island by dredging sand and sucking them into a shallow lagoon so that it would be a higher ground refuge for the residents, the lingering impact of global warming and lethal sea level rise has prompted consideration among some circles of suing the U.S. government for being the key cause of global warming.[45] Within the U.S., the aftermath of Hurricane Katrina on the southeast Gulf Coast in 2005 and Hurricane Sandy in 2012, which was the deadliest hurricane of the Atlantic for that year, still reverberates among all communities living close to coastal areas in the country. The deaths of over 1,500 in New Orleans and the forced evacuation of over 300,000 residents, most of whom have been unable to and prevented from returning because they are overwhelmingly Black and poor, serves as a reminder of the incredibly powerful effects of global warming especially on those socially and economically marginalized. The Gulf Coast is particularly vulnerable. With the erosion of 130 square kilometers of marshland each year and the reduced silt from the Mississippi River each year, Louisiana has shrunk by 4 million square kilometers from over 100 years ago.[46] The Everglades in Florida where the Indigenous Seminole nation once thrived and lives today, like all wetlands, was considered the "kidneys of the Earth" because of its massive natural filtering and draining system and covered some 2.9 million acres south of Lake Okeechobee over 150 years ago.[47] It consisted of peatland with tall saw grass in shallow water. In an ecologically balanced manner, when Lake Okeechobee's levels rose, the surplus water flowed slowly over a 50-mile sheet south, about a foot deep. With widespread European American occupation and settlement of the area in the late 1880s, settlers began draining the watershed of the Kissimmee River-Lake Okeechobee-Everglades system.[48] The organic muck soil was subsequently exposed and gradually eroded to the point that just 50 percent of the Everglades are left today, a truly human-caused ecological extinction and environmental disaster, with just 50 panthers left and most alligators under threat of being permanently erased since their habitats are unsustainable in an ever-eroding Everglades wetlands. The ivory-billed woodpecker, indigenous to the Big Cypress Swamp, is extinct, birds have been reduced by one-third, and one-third of all four-leggeds and birds on the U.S. Endangered species list are found in Florida.[49] To compound problems, a nuclear power plant was built on one of the freshwater diversion waterways as a result of the St. Lucie canal, part of a network of canals spanning 1,400 miles that have drained the Everglades. This is the magnitude of the irresponsibility of capitalist "development" of areas like the Everglades, intrinsic to the natural filtration and drainage actions of Earth.

Climate warming is not just a concern of raised temperatures for human life. Food and crop production is directly effected. For instance, animal mortality is a consequence of higher temperatures and has an impact on milk production by cows and fertility. Warm weather resulted in loss of 5,000 head of cattle during heat waves of 1995 and 1999.[50] In the south-central and southeastern parts of the U.S., pig and beef production were most adversely effected, while dairy production suffered in the Midwest and northeast. Research by T. L. Mader, K.L. Frank, J. A. Harrington, Jr., L. Hahn, and J. A. Nienaber from 2009 indicates that temperature increases in the Midwest and northeast will result in lower milk production levels, exerting pressure on both availability of milk products and prices.

The impact of intensified industrialization is very evident around the world, with massive and lingering smog in megacities like Beijing, Mumbai, Jakarta, Taipei, New York, Mexico City, Sao Paulo, and more recently in Paris and French cities, where pollution from a week in mid–March reached dangerous levels due to smog particles, is one of the lethal effects of globalization's obsessive industrialism that views the commodity production as the key to economic prosperity and human culture in the world.[51] The net result is the vitiation of the quality of air that we breathe, particularly for the poor and the working classes of the world, who are forced to live in overcrowded cities after migrating from their rural villages and homes due to either overgrazing of lands, closure of thousands of farms, drought, and lack of infrastructure to sustain village life. Respiratory diseases are now rampant in most cities as the result of industrial smog.

Nuclear power, which is considered an alternative to the global energy crisis is hardly a solution given the aftermath of events like Chernobyl in the Ukraine in 1986 that killed 28 of the 600 workers at the nuclear power plant within four months and affecting another 200,000 cleanup workers who received between 1 and 100 rem (roentgen equivalent man) doses of radiation.[52] Some 5 million people in surrounding areas were also effected to varying degrees and deleterious health effects from cancer are still being studied and analyzed. The real long-term effects of Chernobyl will never be fully known since cancer illness from this disaster has been experienced over decades since 1986.

Depletion of the Ozone Layer and Melting Glaciers

The rape of the Earth continues to escalate in lightning proportions today with the depletion of the ozone layer in the atmosphere so that a hole as large as Antarctica is visible, the icecaps are beginning to gradually melt, and the emissions of carbon dioxide has exacerbated pollution levels, causing cancer and respiratory diseases like asthma affecting millions around the world. The magnitude of the crisis of melting ice hits home when one realizes that just two continental ice sheets, Antarctica and Greenland, constitute over half of all fresh water and almost 99 percent of the freshwater ice on Earth.[53] Hundreds of thousands of years of accumulated ice is now disintegrating in front of our eyes in a few decades. On September 19, 2012, a new low of sea ice covering the Arctic was reached, covering 1.32 million square miles or 24 percent of the surface of the Arctic, down even further from the 2007 low of 2 percent of Arctic surface cover.[54] Arctic ice has disappeared at the rate of 8.9 percent per decade in September and 2.5 percent per decade in March over the past three decades, and the area and thickness of ice is steadily declining so that the Northern Sea route on Russia's Arctic coast is navigable between 20–30 days annually and is expected to attain 80–90 days annually by 2080.[55] At present rates of ice melting, the Arctic is predicted to become a mostly ice-free zone by 2100, threatening to affect the extinction of the polar bear as a species, yet another index of the lethal ecocidal scope of global warming. Greenland is particularly critical in the balance of temperatures globally because it encompasses a total area of 1.7 million square kilometers, constituting a volume of 3 million cubic kilometers of ice sheet. It is especially susceptible to small temperature increases that result in surface melting and rapid direct drainage into the ocean, reducing the level of ice sheet volume. Indirectly, this melting causes the lubrication of the base of the outlet glaciers, destabilizing the existing ice topography further.[56] If the entire Greenland ice sheet were to melt, it would raise sea levels around the world by 7 meters![57] Antarctica has 27 million cubic kilometers of ice and is correspondingly affected radically by the pattern of climate warming with the collapse and removal of foundational ice shelves. Sea levels have risen by about 7 inches over the past century as the result of warmer seawater and glaciers melting and are expected to rise by similar levels in the 21st century. Most acute sea level increases are evident in areas where land loss is severe, like around the U.S. Gulf Coast, with coastal Louisiana experiencing a rise of 8 inches over the past 50 years, twice the global sea rise average.[58] The northeast Chesapeake Bay is also witnessing significant land loss, accompanied by near-future floods and tidal wetland activity that could destroy significant portions of the regional coastline.

The amazing fact about the Earth and the rest of the universe is that the balance within each element and feature is maintained so that life is possible. For instance, the atmosphere is constituted by numerous elements, including gases like water vapor, carbon dioxide, methane, nitrous oxide and ozone, all of which keep Earth warm to the point of sustaining life. The absence of such gases would make Earth so cold that life would not thrive. However, an unsettling balance of these gases results in the opposite effect: Earth becomes too warm so that life in turn begins to diminish and eventually perish, as we are experiencing now with global warming. The ozone is an essential part of the stratosphere layer of the atmosphere, the upward most later that is between 12.9 and 19.3km and increases to 50km above human heads. Ozone is crucial since it absorbs harmful ultra-violet rays of the sun, all part of the electromagnetic radiation along with gamma rays, X-rays, visible light, and infrared radiation. Gamma and X-rays "are absorbed by the upper atmosphere" so that ozone levels are in balance and harm to life on earth is prevented.[59] Anthropogenic activity has now disrupted this very fragile balance of gases within the ozone and heat is now trapped within the atmosphere, generating the results described in the preceding paragraph.

A 2006 report from the Goddard Institute for Space Studies at NASA has confirmed that the Earth is now the hottest that she has ever been, and that warming has occurred at the rate of 0.2 degree Celsius per decade for the past thirty years.[60] The overall temperature is the warmest during this current interglacial period that started 12,000 years ago. The year 2010 has been recorded as the hottest on record since record keeping of climatic conditions began. While NASA scientists like James Hanson urge swift action to arrest carbon greenhouse emissions that could see the ice sheets disappear by 2020, governments like the U.S. and Russia continue to explore drilling for oil in the Arctic.[61]

During my visit via cable-car and then hiking up to the Luyong Snow Mountain glacier outside Lijiang in southern China's Yunnan province in June 2013, I had the opportunity to travel up to 15,000 feet and see the effect of global warming first-hand with the glacier, Eurasia's southernmost and at the tip of the Tibetan Plateau, fast eroding. Baishui, the largest glacier on Luyong Snow Mountain, has retreated 275 yards since 1982.[62] The Tibetan plateau is the source of some of Asia's might, rivers like the Yangtze, the Mekong, and the Ganges and provides water to over a billion people. Temperatures in the plateau have risen markedly and are increasing more rapidly than the rest of China. So too, the world's highest peak, Mount Everest in the Himalayas (*Sagarmartha* in Nepali and *Chomolangma* in Sherpa), is experiencing significant melting with 13 percent of its snow-cover being lost over the past 50 years. The snowline has dropped by 590 feet according to climatologists.[63]

Glacial melting has occurred in Alaska, the Canadian Rockies, Scandinavia, Patagonia, the South American tropics, New Zealand, Austria, where the Vernagtferner glacier has shrunk by 30 percent between 1912 and 2003, Kazhakstan, and in East Africa on the Rwenzori, Kenya, and Kilimanjaro ("Shining Mountain" in Kiswahili) mountains. Most of the glaciers in New Zealand (Aotearoa) are found in the Southern Alps and have experienced a net ice volume loss of 17 percent between 1977 and 2005.[64] Almost half of all the ice in the East African glacial mountains has melted and larger glaciers on Kilimanjaro

Global warming and climate change are direct effects of emission of greenhouse gases that have continued relentlessly under globalized industrialism. Glaciers are melting in many parts of the world, evidenced here at Columbia Glacier in Alaska (Tad Pfeffer).

have become fragmented. From 1906 through 2006, 82 percent of the areas of these glaciers have been lost, from 21 square kilometers to a shocking 3.8 square kilometers today.[65] Between 1962 and 2000, 55 percent of Kilimanjaro's glaciers disappeared.[66] The melting of these East African glaciers will not have a direct impact on water supplies in the region; however, the impact on ecological balance and climate stability will certainly be felt since almost 3,000 plant species are found in Kilimanjaro and over 1 million people depend on the fragile ecosystem and water sources originating in the area. Temperatures in and around Kilimanjaro increased from 1950 to 1960, remained stable from 1960 to 1981, and rose steadily from 1981 to 1995, with average decade temperatures in the adjoining Amboseli region rising by 2 degrees Fahrenheit.[67] Meanwhile, rainfall levels have dropped significantly over the past century and frequently more months with rainfall under 30 millimeters being the pattern. Banana and coffee plantations at the base of Kilimanjaro have been displaced by montane forests at 1,700 meters and subalpine forest at 2,800 meters, indicating that global warming and climate change have forced the upper forest line to move downward and raised the risk of fires several fold owing to the pervasive dryness of the forest cover.[68] Since 1976, over 150 square kilometers of forest has been burned, mostly as the result of human activity. Melting glaciers are a phenomenon that have been observed around the world and signify a troubling issue indeed. The melting of glaciers in the Arctic documented in *Chasing Ice* is just one vivid example.

The Nile River basin is another area of Africa that continues to experience significant water stress as a result of global warming, stretching the resources of the longest river in the world at 6,700 kilometers to the maximum. Since the 1960s, when the levels of Lake Victoria that feeds the White Nile rose by over two meters, there has been a consistent lowering of water flow. Since 1900 there has been a progressive decline in water levels of the Nile entering Egypt, a country that has very sparse rainfall and depends on the Nile for 95 percent of its freshwater needs. Following the completion of the Aswan High Dam in 1972, the annual Blue Nile flood has become non-existent from its preceding quadruple and quintuple flows.[69] The dam eliminated the Nile river silt that functioned as a natural organic fertilizer for food crops, forcing farmers to use non-organic chemical fertilizers.[70] The heating of the climate has raised the evaporation levels further and caused serious hardship for agriculture and rural communities' sustenance in Egypt and Northern Sudan. Almost half of the inflows from the White and Blue Nile entering the Sudd Wetland in Southern Sudan have been lost through evaporation. Average temperature increases in Egypt and the surrounding region are projected to rise

The visible collapse of historic glaciers as the result of warming of the poles is a sore sight for the citizens of the world. This is the calving of Margerie Glacier (Michael Arrighi).

by 1 degree Celsius by 2030, 1.4 degree Celsius by 2050 and 2.4 degrees Celsius by 2100.[71] The effect of reduced agricultural production particularly on food staples like corn and wheat due to higher evaporation levels (10 billion cubic meters annually from the Aswan High Dam itself), reduced Nile flow levels, and sweltering desert temperatures makes this part of the world among the most vulnerable to the devastating implications of global climate change.

Droughts, Food Riots, Heat Strokes and Disease

In the U.S. Midwest where two-thirds of all food is grown, for instance, the region is now susceptible to permanent drought with the progressive depleting of the finite water resources of the Ogallala Aquifer. Aquifers are permeable rock formations that contain groundwater.[72] The mighty 1,450-mile Colorado River that snakes its way through much of the south-western states and from which seven states receive water, is experiencing its driest spell in the past 1,250 years with 14 years of continuous drought and with many of the human-made reservoirs connected to the Colorado sagging to half of their capacities and many water utilities using sewage effluent to compensate for water shortages. Resultantly, federal administration officials will be reducing the quantity of water that flows into Lake Mead, the country's largest reservoir, from Lake Powell, some 180 miles upstream. Cities from Las Vegas in Nevada to Los Angeles in California depend on the water of Lake Mead, including millions of acres of agricultural land. Water administrators are expecting to ration Lake Mead's water to states downstream. The somber reality is that the Colorado is fast drying up and never before are the lives of 40 million people and agricultural producers from Imperial Valley in California to cattle farmers in Wyoming been effected so direly, since three-quarters of Colorado's water flow supports all. Fifteen percent of food supplies in the U.S. depend on the waters of this giant river, now flowing to a trickle from its historical wide blue spread of a couple of decades ago.[73] This is the grim picture of global warming right in our back and front yards.

Visiting California for research in the first weekend of February 2014, the headline news was that California had officially declared that it was in a severe drought period, the worst in the state's history.[74] For the first time in its 54-year history, the State Water Project of California will deliver no water to residents and farmers in the summer of 2014, and regions and towns will need to depend on the scarce water resources of local reservoirs, underground wells, recycled water, and conservation measures. Area, like the industrial hub of Silicon Valley and towns of the East Bay around San Francisco like Livermore, Pleasanton, and Dublin who have been accustomed to receiving 80 percent of their water from the State Water Project will face the hardest of obstacles in acquiring water, particularly over the perennial dry summers in the state. The Board has supplied water to 29 water districts in California, consisting of a labyrinth system of 21 dams and 701 miles of canals and pipelines that pipes water from the northern part of the state to the south, securing melting snow and capturing it for transportation in the pipe grid hundreds of miles across the San Joaquin River Delta down to San Diego, meeting the water needs of some 23 million residents and irrigating 750,000 acres of agricultural farmland. The magnitude of the state's (and by inference the country's since California is the major agricultural and most populous state in the country) water woes is reflected in the fact that in 2012, the State Water Board provided 65 percent of water to cities and farms, 35 percent in 2013, and in November, predicted that it would supply 5 percent in 2014, which turned out to be unrealistic and is now at zero. The ecological devastation of birds and other species of land creatures in California will be unfathomable given the history of recent drought in the state, followed by a deep hole in the state's $40 billion agricultural industry, which will suffer higher costs for cattle-feed and crop irrigation and resultantly higher food and transportation costs, as well as reduced capacity of the state's cheaper hydroelectric power production in the past. The drought will compound further woes for California's forests, which saw raging summer forest fires that destroyed hundreds of thousands of acres of forest and hundreds of homes over the past decade.[75]

Awareness of the lethal effects of global warming and climate change on California has been existent for close to a century. California has experienced serious droughts from 1928 to 1934, successive dry years in the mid–1950s, and a major drought in 1976–77.[76] California's water problems continue to mount, particularly in areas of water supply management where water from the water-rich (previously) northern part of the state need to be piped to drier southern California, maintaining Delta Islands Land Use so that saltwater intrusion into the river system of the Sacramento and San Joaquin rivers is prevented, and ensuring that levees are well maintained in the face of deterioration so that saltwater eastward from San Francisco does not intervene into the river system as a result of wind-surge and sea levels increasing.[77]

Interestingly, the state of Texas, which is larger than many countries in area, is the largest emitter of greenhouse gases in the U.S., on par with Britain and Italy, even though Britain has thrice the human population of Texas. Texas produces almost twice the carbon dioxide of any other state in the country, contributing up to 10 percent of total U.S. carbon dioxide emissions. The bulk of these emissions derive from industry, with oil production being the leading cause and producing almost half of all carbon dioxide emissions.[78] As a leading oil producer in the U.S., Texas extracts, refines, and burns oil, processes that constitute 52 percent of the state's carbon emissions. An indication of the heavy dependence on oil production and extremely poor efficiency of motor vehicles is reflected in the fact that in 1986, the average gas consumption per vehicle was 14 miles per gallon![79] Texas released an amazing 38.8 trillion tons of carbon dioxide in 1988 from use of vehicles, 21 percent of the state's total emissions of greenhouse gas. The bumper sticker that many Texans flaunt, "Don't mess with Texas" is not as revealing as one that should read, "Texas messes with everybody ... especially when it comes to carbon emissions!" Texas is also the state that has experienced drought conditions in various regions, with a serious drought during each decade of the 20th century. Areas of the west like El Paso and San Angelo generally receive very sparse precipitation of an average of 7.8 inches and 18.2 inches per year respectively.[80] The future climate scenario for this wealthy-oil producing state is not very bright given the high incidence of carbon emissions and the fact that 90 percent of the precipitation falling on Texas does not make it to groundwater levels since most is lost to evaporation that returns moisture into the atmosphere, plants, and transpiration.[81] Texas is facing its gravest water crisis in decades, with many small towns in oil and natural gas producing areas experiencing acute water shortages and 29 communities in the state running out of water in the summer of 2014 due to drought conditions, and the effects of fracking and reservoirs in west Texas are only at 25 percent of capacity. Fracking and the drilling of 40,000 oil and natural gas wells since 2011 has resulted in the loss of some 97 billion gallons of water, half of this in Texas alone.[82] Three-quarters of all oil and gas drilling occurred in regions where water was in short supply and 55 percent of the areas experienced drought. There appears to be clear connections between fracking causing the depletion of precious water from aquifers, especially in western states of the U.S. like California, Colorado, Texas, Wyoming, and Oklahoma, and the tenacity of drought-stricken conditions in many of these states today.

In Arizona, the U.S. Department of the Interior has declared that climate change will radically reduce water flow for endangered rivers such as the Colorado, the Rio Grande, and the San Joaquin which provides water for eight western states from Texas to California, and the nation of Mexico, so that rivers will experience an 8 to 20 percent decrease in flow due to drying conditions.[83] Millions of people across the West will face water shortages. In Montana, evergreens have collapsed due to being attacked by beetles who historically have been kept away by the severe cold but who now thrive due to warming temperatures. In Colorado, at last 15 percent of the state's aspen trees have died because of lack of water, and across the northern and central Rockies, millions of pines have become lifeless.

Heatwaves have been scalding in several ways. In 1995, during a heat wave in Chicago, some 700 people were killed, including many from low-income neighborhoods and the elderly.[84] The pattern was similar to that of Europe, later during my sabbatical in 2003, when over 30,000 people died from excessively high and unbearable summer temperatures.

In Canada, the predictions for climate change are quite stark. The Climate Change Adaptation Project (CCAP) reported in 2010 that using a collection of 24 General Circulation Models compiled by the Canadian Climate Change Scenarios Network (CCCSN), winter precipitation was expected to increase in all regions of the country, making many areas prone to intense flooding, particularly in the Winnipeg area.[85] The most radical precipitation decrease is predicted for the southern part of British Columbia and Alberta, leaving the region vulnerable to extremely dry conditions and making forest fire risks rise astronomically. Drying over summer months is expected to hit southern Ontario, Quebec, and Prairie regions, exerting tremendous pressure on drinking water resources and hydroelectric power generation.

In Alaska, the Indigenous Yupik people who have lived there for time immemorial describe the manner in which *Ella Cimissiiyaagtuq* (the weather has changed so much) over the past ten years particularly. The winters and summers are warmer, with temperatures reaching 80 degrees Fahrenheit in the summer and causing food to spoil easily. Snowfall has decreased and the warm south winds have increased, causing warmer weather overall, compared to many elders like Frank Andrew and Paul John recalling very short wind spells of two days as opposed to the fourteen days now.[86] Weather conditions and the observation of mountains and hills could be predicted before; now the high and sudden variability of the weather makes it impossible to predict weather conditions reliably. Ice conditions in the Arctic are becoming milder and the *tuag* (shore fast ice) is thinner and far less than the six miles freeze from the shore from ten to fifteen years ago. Hunting on frozen rivers has thus been limited and dangerous because the ice is thinner, reducing vital food resources. Fewer birds and seals that depend on ice for their livelihoods are the norm for much of Alaska since ice levels have receded significantly.

Russia suffered the worst heat wave in its history during the summer of 2010, which resulted in thousands of people dying from heat stroke and related problems and extending an unprecedented drought that caused the country to freeze grain exports and triggered a 90 percent rise in the price of wheat.[87] Russia, the world's largest grain producer since World War II and now the world's third largest wheat exporter, supplied grain to impoverished countries like Egypt and Mozambique, both of whom raised prices on grain food staples, which in turn provoked rioting and the deaths of at least 11 people in Mozambique in September 2010 and fierce protests in Egypt and India in 2008 and subsequently led to wide scale economic discontent and political anger in February 2011 that saw the Mubarak regime in Egypt dissolve.

Raj Patel from the *Observer* eloquently described the horror of the link between global warming and growing impoverishment in 2010 when he asserted that "Japan had its hottest summer on record, as did South Florida and New York.... But to see how climate change will pan out in the 21st century, you needn't look at the Met Office.... Look instead to the deaths and burning tyres in Mozambique's 'food riots' to see what happens when extreme natural phenomena interact with our unjust economic systems."[88] **Table 1** below highlights the projection of people thrown into the ranks of extreme poverty as environmental disaster escalates, with a general projected increase

Table 1: UN Human Development Report 2013

Population in extreme poverty under the environmental disaster scenario, by region, 2010–2050 (millions)

Region	2010	2020	2030	2040	2050	Increase, 2010–2050	Difference From base case scenario, 2050	From accelerated progress scenario, 2050
Arab States	25	25	39	73	145	120	128	144
East Asia and the Pacific	211	142	211	363	530	319	501	522
Europe and Central Asia	14	6	17	32	45	30	41	44
Latin America and the Caribbean	34	50	90	138	167	134	135	155
South Asia	557	530	738	978	1,207	650	1,126	1,194
Sub-Saharan Africa	371	377	496	709	1,055	685	788	995
World	1,212	1,129	1,592	2,293	3,150	1,938	2,720	3,054

Note: Extreme poverty is defined as $1.25 a day in purchasing power parity terms. See Technical appendix for a discussion of the base case and fast track scenarios. Source: HDRO calculations based on Pardee Center for International Futures (2013).

Human Development Report 2013: The Rise of the South: Human Progress in a Diverse World (New York: United Nations Development Program, 2013), p. 96, at http://hdr. undp.org/sites/default/files/reports/14/hdr2013_en_complete.pdf, accessed on June 8, 2014. Used with permissions from the United Nations Development Program, licensed by Creative Commons 3.0 IGO at http://creativecommons.org/licenses/by/3.0/igo/ legalcode.

of 1.938 billion poorer people from 2010 to 2050. Under current climate change conditions, 2.720 billion more people will be siphoned into extreme poverty while a high of 3.054 billion extremely poor people is projected if climate change conditions steadily worsen over the next 30–40 years.

For Africa south of the Sahara and South Asia, where the most impoverished people of the world live, the UNDP projects about 300 million more people in extreme poverty in the case of the former and about 100 million in the case of the latter should current climate change patterns hold, with these numbers skyrocketing in the event of escalating environmental disasters to a billion in the case of Africa and 1.2 billion in the case of South Asia (**Fig. 1**).

Patel notes that the real causes for Mozambican riots lie in the 30 percent increase in bread prices, the double digit increases for water and energy and the fact that three-quarters of the average household income in Mozambique is earmarked for food, a painful result of the global escalation in oil, wheat, and corn prices in 2008, which saw such staples triple in price.[89]

Fig. 1

Different environmental scenarios have different impacts on extreme poverty

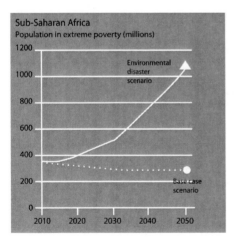 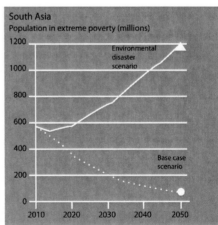

Note: Extreme poverty is defined as $1.25 a day in purchasing power parity terms.
See Technical appendix for a discussion of the base case and fast track scenarios.
Source: HDRO calculations based on Pardee Center for International Futures (2013).

Human Development Report 2013: The Rise of the South: Human Progress in a Diverse World (New York: United Nations Development Program, 2013), p. 25, at http://hdr.undp.org/sites/default/files/reports/14/hdr2013_en_complete.pdf, accessed on June 8, 2014. Used with permissions from the United Nations Development Program, licensed by Creative Commons 3.0 IGO at http://creativecommons.org/licenses/by/3.0/igo/legalcode.

Patel explains that the combination of natural calamities like the drought in Australia, crop disease in central Asia, and floods in south-east Asia, with the effects of unjust social systems and policies that raised oil prices phenomenally in 2007, sparked exorbitant prices for food, and encouraged biofuel policy led by the U.S. that urged ethanol production and forced farmers to divert land for energy production rather than food. The commoditization of food (kindling memories of former U.S. Secretary of Agriculture, Earl Butz, in the 1970s who described food aid as a "weapon ... one of the principle tools in our negotiating kit" following former U.S. president Richard Nixon's threat at the UN General Assembly in 1974 that the U.S. could use food as a weapon as the oil-producing nations did with oil) unleashed riots in Asia, Africa, and Latin America where most people are impoverished in the first place.[90] Thanks to globalization and the oppressive regime of the World Trade Organization (WTO), food production hitherto practiced by small farmers around the world so that domestic needs are met is now the principal monopoly of large transnational corporations such as Cargill, Tyson, Smithfield, Archer Daniels Midland, General Mills, Cenex Harvest States, and Monsanto in the U.S. where for instance, Cargill, Archer Daniels Midland, and Zen Noh alone control 82 percent of corn exporting processes.[91] Food is a profit-making commodity whose profits are lucrative through unjust global trade policies that favor large corporations in the Western metropole countries. The net result of diversion of land for food crops for biofuel production was a further 100 million people driven into deep poverty in 2007 and the explosion of the ranks of undernourished people from 854 million people in 2006 to 1.02 billion in 2009, the highest since records on such details have been kept. The primary victims of this deepening of poverty were women who headed households because of structures of gender bias where they were poorly paid for their labor and were thus disadvantaged economically.[92]

Twenty percent of the Amazon rainforest, the "breathing lungs of the planet," has been decimated.[93] The continuing drought in the Amazon has turned the traditional absorber of carbon dioxide to a net emitter of such gases with scientists predicting eight billion tons of carbon dioxide being released as a result of dying trees and deforestation, which is the equivalent to that annually emitted by the U.S. In 2005, the Amazon drought caused over five billion tons of carbon emissions.[94] The Amazon rainforest has suffered almost 18,000 square kilometers of deforestation and one projected estimate of carbon dioxide emissions, based on deforestation rates that are 15 percent of the forest in the year 2000, would result in 48 Gigatons of carbon dioxide by 2100, or 7 times the rate of current fossil fuel emissions or 30 times the rate of current carbon emissions based on land use.[95] The Congo Basin in Africa is home to the earth's second largest rainforest after the Amazon and, like the Amazon, regulates temperature and rainfall because it absorbs carbon emissions, but is now under constant threat by industrial developers who desire its trees for logging and timber. Though China and the EU have committed themselves to stop illegal logging in the Congo basin, the protection is extremely fragile. China, for instance, is the largest importer of timber from neighboring Gabon, where forests cover 85 percent of the land area.[96] With diminishing revenues from oil reserves, Gabon has turned to exporting its most precious resource, forested wood, especially to China and Europe. From 2000 to 2012, 2.3 million square kilometers of forest have been decimated, releasing millions of tons of carbon into the atmosphere, according to Google map satellite images.[97]

In 2011, a massive cyclone in the Baltics ripped a hole that tore a forest in Finland and stretched over 160 kilometers long. Massive logging, deforestation, and clear-cutting in the upland tropics forests in Sumatra have been extended into lowland areas.[98] The result of such clearing of these forests that are peatland swamps is the release of massive amounts of carbon into the atmosphere. Even the growth of 800,000 square kilometers of forest in Russia does not offset the global annihilation of vital forest cover that functions as a natural medium for holding carbon levels in balance. In 2005, the total emission of carbon dioxide released from deforestation and biomass burning was 5–6 billion tons around the world![99]

The drying of the Earth is pervasive everywhere we look. Euphorbia trees are dying because of water shortage in Southern Africa and Atlas cedars in Algeria are withering due to lack of rainfall.[100] In northeast Africa, water conflicts have taken on proportions of civil war. Darfur in the Sudan is a case in point. Drought conditions in the northern part of Darfur have driven nomadic farmers further south where they encountered the people struggling for land and water in Southern Sudan who are principally of traditional Dinka, Nuer, Shilluk, and other Indigenous descent or members of Christian churches, unlike their northern Muslim neighbors. The result has been eruptive tensions between both areas of Darfur, sparked not by religious affiliation but by the need for access to vital and scarce water resources in the desert since one-third of the Sahel belt has been turned into waterless desert from being semi-desert over the four decades preceding 2006.[101] The ecological, environmental, and demographic changes attributable to global warming and climate change in Africa are radical and sweeping.

Also of deep concern is the rapid spread of insect-borne diseases like

Deforestation (shown in Cameroon) has accelerated under the globalization regime and is responsible for the release of lethal greenhouse gases into the atmosphere (Gordon Ajonina).

Globalization has intensified slash and burn agriculture, as in the Amazon, which has been turned from an absorber of carbon dioxide into a net emitter since 2008 (Matt Zimmerman).

that of dengue, malaria, yellow fever, and encephalitis in many parts of the world generally unaccustomed to such outbreaks and which have warmed in recent decades. For instance, dengue is now a problem in the Andean mountains at heights over 7,200 feet and in high-altitude areas in Indonesia, and malaria has spread to thirteen districts in Kenya from three previously. Outbreaks of encephalitis have been experienced in Sweden and in many southern and western states of the U.S. and dengue has been diagnosed in the Netherlands, while people have suffered from pneumatic plague in India.[102] Cholera has spread in places like Haiti and tropical zones of Africa.

Two-thirds of the continental U.S. is now in moderate to severe drought, the driest in over five and a half decades.[103] William B. Meyer argues that "the net emission of carbon to the atmosphere by human action dates back to at least the origins of agriculture, but half of the total amount released has been released since 1920" and that "Half of the sulphur and half of the lead ever

Water is indeed the most precious resource on Earth today. Global warming and climate change has wreaked ecological and environmental havoc around the world, particularly in arid regions like the southwestern regions of Africa and of the United States. This giraffe died of thirst from the intense drought in Etosha National Park in Namibia in 2003 (author's photograph).

mobilized by humankind have been emitted since 1960; half of the phosphorus since 1975."[104] The net result is that toxic heavy metals emissions are now twenty times that of natural flows from weathering. A June 7, 2012, issue of *Nature* reported that an interdisciplinary group of 22 scientists that included biologists, ecologists, paleontologists, geologists, and complex-system analysis have concluded that the rate of extinctions, climate change and extreme weather, and other natural disasters are occurring at levels unprecedented in world history that threaten the very existence of all life on the planet.[105] The year 2025, when the humans in the world are expected to reach 8 billion, could become a tipping point for the viability of planetary life.

Philip Stephens, a columnist with the *Financial Times*, concurs with this assessment and warns of the consequences of inaction, especially on the part of the Western industrialized world, along with rising industrial Asian giants, China and India, reducing the stark choices for humankind: leaving future generations to face the deleterious and irreversible effects of global warming or making it a leading political issue and compelling human beings to live and work differently.[106]

Earthquakes, Floods, Tsunamis, Typhoons, Landslides and Volcanoes

Warm ocean temperatures have resulted especially in the Indian and Western Pacific oceans, triggering the El Niño phenomenon where intense storms, hurricanes, and floods are the norm for the Earth and sea globally. The mudslides that saw the collapse of four hills and the flooding of several rivers following four days of continuous heavy downpours in the southern Mexican state of Oaxaca and the deaths of numerous Indigenous people, trapping close to 1,000 on September 28, 2010, was one such tragedy unleashed by global warming dynamics.[107]

The devastating earthquake that shook Haiti and left over 240,000 dead and close to 2 million people homeless on January 12, 2010, is another possible effect of global warming and disruption of the natural cycles of the Earth. Haiti has been underdeveloped and impoverished following it becoming the first Black republic to free itself from slavery by the French in 1804, who in turn demanded reparations for its lost property, enslaved Haitians over 120 years, and combined with the U.S. refused to recognize Haiti's sovereign government until sixty years after Haitian independence and historically marginalized Haiti in its foreign policy portfolio. U.S. and Western imperial design

The warming of the Pacific Ocean, for example, has precipitated the El Niñó phenomenon that has caused erratic changes in weather cycles and patterns marked by extremes in rainfall and drought. Mudslides like this one in Pingtung, Taiwan, in 2010 are becoming frequent around the world (author's photograph).

were clearly evinced when in 1990 populist Lavalas Party leader, Jean-Bertrand Aristide, was elected by 65 percent of the vote, only to be overthrown in a military coup in 1991, re-elected in 2000 and subsequently overthrown and exiled to South Africa in 2004. The intervention by the U.S. government to sabotage an already approved Inter-American Development Bank loan of $500 million for Haitian agricultural development and vital infrastructural construction contributed decisively towards Haiti's immiseration and further impoverishment, acknowledged by former U.S. president Bill Clinton in a speech to a Senate Subcommittee where subsidized rice from Arkansas led to 830,000 rural jobs being lost.[108] The massive storm that raged through the Haitian capital, Port-au-Prince, on September 24, 2010, killing five people and destroying almost eight thousand tents, recalls the tremendous power of Nature that whips everything in its path and underscores the manner in which global warming phenomena principally caused by the industrialized countries effects the impoverished countries most deleteriously because the latter have sparse resources to cater to such calamities.[109] Haiti still lies in unrepaired ruin with more than 2 million people living in temporary tent housing.

The effects of the tsunami that hit the Fukushima nuclear plant following the massive earthquake in March 2011 continue to linger three years later with 83,000 residents still living as evacuees and being unable to return to their homes within the 4,500 square mile exclusion zone around the damaged reactors due to the current high radiation levels and the delays in decontamination work.[110] It's chilling to realize that there are 31 reactors similar to the Fukushima one operating in the U.S. and that a fire at a nuclear spent fuel pool could cause serious health damages and displace some 4.1 million humans in an area covering the state of New Hampshire for 30 years.[111] Meanwhile, underscoring the gravity of the nuclear disaster reaching far across the ocean, Cesium 134, a radio active metal released from the Fukushima disaster was detected in the water in the Fraser Valley in the northwestern region of Canada, raising alarming concerns about the effects of radiation from Fukushima on Chun salmon spawning in the nearby Harrison River, on whales and other marine life in the area.[112] Cesium 137, which is more lethal in its long-standing effects, is predicted to have destructive effects in whales off Vancouver Island in 30 years. To top it all, a senior advisor to operations connected to the Fukushima Daiichi nuclear power plant stated that the Tokyo Electric Power Company (TEPCO) may have little choice but to dump hundred of thousands of tons of nuclear contaminated water into the Pacific Ocean, escalating the magnitude of the crisis from the summer of 2013 when 300 tons of poisoned water leaked into the ocean each day.[113] Ongoing spills from storage tanks since the Fukushima disaster have continued for three years, substantiating the porous nature of nuclear spent fuel storage in the first place. Even though we are often informed by operators of nuclear power plants and many scientific researchers that certain levels of radiation are "acceptable," it is unequivocal that radiation effects diverse individuals differently, which translates into unreliable assessments of the safety levels of radiation. Cumulatively, *all* radiation exposure has deleterious effects on all persons' health and exposure to environments where radioactive fuel is present compounds the extent of health hazards experienced.[114]

The South Asian country of Bangladesh, which is surrounded by water and fed by a sprawling delta, experiences major flooding each year. About 30 million Bangladeshis out of 130 million live close to coastal areas that are under significant threat by rising sea levels. Thirty-six percent of Bangladeshis survive on less than U.S. $1 per day, making this economically vulnerable sector of the world even more susceptible to climate change and global warming. A

2 degree centigrade rise will raise water levels by one meter, causing unimaginable devastation to an already majority impoverished people.[115] Bangladesh has suffered the ravages of climate change since it is just 39 feet above sea level, including the most lethal cyclone, Bhola, that left 550,000 dead and Cyclone Aila that killed 300 in 2009.[116] Massive Tropical Cyclone Sidr on November 15, 2007, left thousands dead and missing and scores of thousands homeless.[117] Though Bangladesh emits only 0.3 percent of global toxic emissions, mostly released by the Western capitalist industrialized nations, it is paying a dear price for this state of climate imbalance. The sea levels around Bangladesh is predicted by some climatologists to rise 13 feet by 2100, quadrupling the global average. By 2050, 17 percent of the land area of Bangladesh is expected to be flooded by rising sea levels and 18 million people could be homeless, part of the hundreds of millions who will become the world's future "climate refugees," prompting Atiq Rahman, the country's leading climate scientist, to declare that these "refugees" should be entitled to migrate to the U.S. where much of the greenhouse gases emanate.[118] Somber and tear-jerking anecdotes of children being forced to work in brick factories in Dhaka, the Bangladeshi capital, and of children being forcibly sold to pay for debts from the effects of losing houses and possessions and rebuilding homes abound in the aftermath of the combination of natural and anthropogenic-caused climatic catastrophes, abound.[119]

So too, earthquakes that hit New Zealand (Aotearoa in Maori) in September 2010 and February 2011, widespread floods in Australia in the same period, and the catastrophic 9.0 earthquake followed by a tsunami that generated 500 mile per hour waves under the Pacific Ocean, all serve as a serious life-shaking reminder that the Earth is not to be taken lightly and for granted as Western industrialism persistently and arrogantly assumes. In Australia, where the "Big Dry" began in the 1990s with little rainfall, conditions have steadily worsened, with twelve continuous years of less than average rainfall, drought conditions in the outback, dust storms that at one point reached 1,000 miles long and 250 miles wide, devastating water shortages in the Murray-Darling basin of south-eastern Australia that produces 40 percent of the country's food, depleted reservoirs in Melbourne, cattle dying from water shortages, rice yields declining by 98 percent, soaring temperatures of 115 degrees for three consecutive days in February 2009 that unleashed a thunderstorm possessing energy of 1,500 atomic bombs, and wildfires in the same year that burned a millions acres and killed 173 people.[120] Drought-stricken Australians prayed for water and rain, and it came—in gushing floods so that floods in Queensland in 2011 caused $30 billion in damage. Such horrific results of global warming of Australia led one writer to ponder whether this is the end of Australia, since the mayor of a city in the Murray-Darling Basin lamented, "Australia is drying up, a little bit like a dried apple."[121]

Massive Chinese industrialization projects in Tibet that harness the water source of various rivers in the area have led to deforestation, soil erosion, and land slides, effecting the southern riparian states of Bangladesh and India.[122] In 2000, a landslide in Tibet unleashed catastrophic landslides in the mountain states of northeast India.[123] In 2008, Myanmar was hit by a massive cyclone, Nargis, the first of the year, as a result of the cyclone being churned from storm surges in the Bay of Bengal and traveling across the Irrawaddy River and along the northeast coastline.[124] Over 130,000 people died from the catastrophe and over 1 million human beings were rendered homeless. Pakistan was ravaged by the worst flooding in its history as a nation in late August 2010, with 20 million people affected and 8 million people in urgent need of shelter and supplies and one-fifth of the country—62,000 square miles—in shambles.[125] The destruction of the country's fragile infrastructure—bridges, schools, roads, electrical power lines, and communications—set the country back decades. The incredible irony is that the looming threat of terrorism by Taliban forces and other "Islamic militants" as portrayed by the U.S. government did not shake Pakistan's developmental foundations; it was the force of Nature, with global warming being a key factor. The torrential downpours that caused massive floods which swept eastern Indonesia, Vietnam, and China on October 6, 2010, saw river banks swollen, over 100 dead, and 64,000 people evacuated from the Chinese island of Hainan.[126] Like southern Mexico a week before the east–Asian floods, rains continued unabated for several days. In October 2011, typhoons Pedring and Quiel, which flooded and ravaged Bulacan in the Philippines, saw 15,000 people become homeless.[127] To complicate matters further and add to the devastation, super Typhoon Haiyan (known as Yolanda in the Philippines) struck the central Philippines in November 2013, leaving over 8,000 dead or missing and four million homeless, followed by yet another cyclone in January 2014 that hit the town of Guiuan on Samar Island about 375 miles southeast of Manila, which destroyed the temporary shelters of residents who were reeling from Yolanda's previous strike.[128] On February 14, 2014, Mount Kelud on the island of Java in Indonesia erupted, spewing ash 18 miles into the atmosphere and could be heard 200 kilometers away, causing three deaths, 100,000 people to flee their homes, and three international airports to close.[129] In the same month, a combination of rain, wind, snow, and fire sparked by wind that tore power lines in Britain, left tens of thousands without power with record rainfalls of 1.6 inches (40 mm) in southwest England, and waves 33 ft. (10 meters) high pummeled the coastline, with

208 flood warnings and 320 flood alerts all over England and Wales. More
than 1,000 homes had to be evacuated in Thames Valley and West Country,
bringing the total to 5,800 properties destroyed since December 2013. Britain
has experienced its wettest climate in 250 years.[130] On March 22, 2014, a powerful landslide in the town of Oso, 55 miles northeast of Seattle, rocked the
entire area, burying 30 houses and covering 0.8 miles of State Route 530,
resulting in over 90 people missing. Seventeen human bodies were recovered
as of March 28, 2014. The flow from the landslide dammed and partially choked
the North Fork Stillaguamish River, precipitating a crisis where serious flooding could occur with a pool of water behind the natural dam up to 30 feet in
depth formed.[131] The speed of the landslide was believed by a survivor who
witnessed a 20-foot mudwall moving to be around 150 miles per hour and
caused shaking of the area for an hour.[132] In late March 2014, an earthquake
measuring 5.1 on the Richter scale hit areas around Los Angeles, destroying
scores of houses around Fullerton and dozens of buildings in adjoining areas,
followed by several tremors. Within a few days of the shaking of Southern
California, on April 1, a massive 8.2 earthquake struck the northern Chilean
coast, triggering a tsunami with 8-foot waves, killing six and forcing the evacuation of thousands, especially around the city of Iquique and in Antofa-
gasta.[133] The quake comes in the aftermath of a massive 8.8 earthquake in
Chile in 2006 that precipitated towering waves that killed over 500 people
and destroyed 220,000 homes and significant portions of the Chilean coastline. Seismic experts noted that the tremor from the 2006 quake was so powerful that it shortened each day by half a second due to the disruption of the
Earth's rotation.[134]

South Asia, which consists of close to 1.4 billion people, led by India
(1.1 billion), and followed by Pakistan (180 million), Bangladesh (155 million)
and Nepal (28 million), continues to experience consistent patterns of periodic
droughts and floods. Monsoon seasons have been unpredictable in many seasons, causing direct effects on agricultural production in one of the most populous human settlements in the world. Nepal has suffered from ongoing
landslides from glacier lake outburst floods in recent years, causing further
geographical and social instability as thousands of people lose their homes
from such persistent flooding and land destabilization.[135]

NASA scientist James Hanson and colleagues at the Goddard Institute
of Space Studies concluded in 1981 that scientific evidence was overwhelming
that the single most important factor in the expansion of global warming was
human-made greenhouse gases and were the first to coin the term in the journal, *Science*.[136] His reward for such revelations was a cutting off of funds to

the Goddard Institute by the U.S. Department of Energy under Ronald Reagan shortly thereafter.[137] The warming of the oceans has caused disruption of weather cycles and disruptive floods, storms, and droughts in some of the most arid parts of the world. Fresh drinking water remains the most precious resource known to humanity, for which people in many places are required to pay. The 2006 *United Nations Human Development Report, Beyond Scarcity: Power, Poverty, and the Global Water Crisis* asserts that the water crisis around the world, including for 1.4 billion people living in river-basins whose water use exceeds that of recharge, is not due to physical scarcity per se but is rooted in "poverty, inequality and unequal power relationships, as well as flawed water management policies that exacerbate scarcity."[138] Over 1 billion people suffer acute shortages of drinking and washing water each day, mostly in countries of the South and among Indigenous communities of the North, like the Dineh (Navajo) people of Northern Arizona.

Climate Change Denial and Globalized Capitalist Ideology

Even though the U.S. National Academy of Science sounded a warning in 1979, some 35 years ago, that the Earth was warming and that environmental and climatic changes would not be peripheral, the driving forces of capitalist globalization as late as the early 2000s when George W. Bush ascended to the U.S. presidency insisted in many circles that global warming was a conspiracy and hoax and that it was being fabricated to undermine the lavish materialistic lifestyles of middle-class peoples in the U.S.[139] Jeff Flake, an Arizona congressman running for the U.S. Senate in 2012 described that though he recognized that the climate was warmer, he was opposed to environmental regulations on curbing carbon emissions from coal-fired power plants, and the best solution was through growth of the economy so that people can make decisions about the environment.[140] Flake's congressional vote in favor of opening the continental shelf on the West Coast for oil drilling underscores the lethal effects of climate-denial politicians and bureaucrats within government and the private corporate sector.[141]

It comes as no big surprise to learn that the global warming and climate change-denial lobby is funded by very wealthy corporations who have much vested in propagating deception about the most serious crisis faced by the Earth and all life ever, where the very existence of life on the planet faces extinction. Oil conglomerates like Chevron, BP, and Shell regularly take full-page ads in major newspapers like the *New York Times* touting their concerns about clean energy and environmental preservation. Exxon Mobil, the most profitable corporation in the world, which rakes in $1 billion each day from oil sales, funds some 124 different organizations that are involved in propagating misinformation about global warming and specialize in promoting ideologies of "junk science," myths about deep differences among scientists about global warming, and argue that attempts to change policies and actions that are geared toward addressing global warming and climate change would thwart economic prosperity for all in the world.[142] Groups like the Cato Institute, the Heritage Foundation, TechCentraStation, and the dubious Center for the Study of Carbon Dioxide and Global Change are part of the extensive organizational list designed to sow seeds of confusion about the veracity of global warming's lethal effects among the U.S. public in particular. It is revealing to note that Philip Morris, the mammoth tobacco company that was responsible for hoodwinking the public about the dangers of environmental tobacco smoke for decades until it was forced to abdicate through massive class-action lawsuits in the U.S. in the 1990s, was the main engineer and funder of a fake "citizens" group, the Advancement of Sound Science Coalition (TASSC), whose mission was to portray scientific research about destructive effects of tobacco smoke, nuclear waste, global warming, bio-technology, and the like as "junk science" and ideologically driven by "politically correct" obsessed organizations and individuals. TASSC was the first major "coalition" organization started by Philip Morris, which launched the climate change-denial movement in 1993. Between 2000 and 2002, it received $30,000 from Exxon Mobil to fund its website, JunkScience.com.[143] The amazing fact is that such organizations that are core to the global warming and climate change-denial lobby have infiltrated various sectors of the world including Australia, India, Russia, Britain, and Canada, where issues of global warming are extremely real as explained earlier in the chapter.

Similarly, the Koch brothers have funneled more than $67 million since 1997 to a range of organizations that are involved in challenging any action that regulates corporations' actions vis-à-vis the environment and they have funded groups that oppose clean energy initiatives. The Charles G. Koch Foundation and the David H. Koch Charitable Foundation support all legislative efforts geared toward easing limits on industrial emissions. Groups that constitute the core of the climate-denial establishment like the American Council on Science and Health, the American Enterprise Institute (AEI), the American Legislative Exchange Council (ALEC), Americans for Prosperity Foundation (AFP), Ayn Rand Institute (ARI), Center for Freedom and Prosperity Foundation, Center for the Study of Carbon Dioxide and Global Change, Citizens for a Sound Economy, the George C. Marshall Institute, the Fraser Institute, and the Heritage Foundation are just some of the many organizations funded by the Koch brothers.[144]

Even though one would assume that intelligence would prevail and more people around the world, especially in the Western industrialized countries where so much of information about climate and global warming is available, would become more concerned and consider radical action to stem the course of global warming, the reality is that the numbers of those concerned are dramatically decreasing, thanks to the globalization ideological onslaught. In Australia, the Lowy Institute reported that 56 percent of those surveyed considered global warming a very serious problem, down 10 percentage points from 2008 and 19 percentage points in 2007 and among a survey of 5,000 people, though 83 percent believed that it is a crisis, only about 50 percent believed the causes to be anthropogenic.[145] In generally perceived liberal Norway, the trend of concern about global warming and accompanying environmental catastrophe has eroded over the decade 2000–2010.[146]

U.S. Governmental Initiatives and Global Protocols on Global Warming

In 1992, the UN Framework Convention on Climate Change (UNFCCC) at the Earth Summit in Rio de Janeiro, Brazil, spearheaded the first major international protocol on addressing the urgency of global warming as the result of anthropogenic greenhouse gases emitted in the atmosphere, followed by the 1997 Kyoto Protocol in Kyoto, Japan. The Kyoto Protocol to the United Nations Framework Convention on Climate Change of 1997, which required that greenhouse gas emission countries reduce their emissions by 5 percent below 1990 levels between 2008 and 2012, was never ratified by the U.S. Senate even though the U.S. signed the treaty in 1998. The 5 percent reduction was hardly anywhere the necessary 60–80 percent required by the Intergovernmental Panel on Climate Change (IPCC) to stabilize the global climate system.[147] The allocation was assessed at a 7 percent reduction for the U.S., 6 percent for Japan, and 8 percent for the European Union (EU) countries and an increase of 8 percent for Australia and 10 percent for Iceland. Most underdeveloped and marginalized countries in Africa and Asia were permitted emissions increases since their emissions were significantly lower by contrast to the Western industrialized countries. Ironically, between 1970 and 2000, the global emissions average actually grew by 1.9 percent per year.[148] The Kyoto protocol was finally set in operation in 2005 thanks to Russia's ratification that established the 55 percent threshold following the rejection of the treaty by Australia and the U.S., the world's second largest emitter today and the largest then. When George W. Bush became president in 2004, his administration consistently challenged the veracity of global warming and dismissed it as a hoax, making any national action, even perfunctory, on global warming and climate change policy highly remote.

Subsequently, Barack Obama claimed when he was elected as president in 2008 that he would require that the U.S. reduce carbon emissions by 80 percent by 2050 and fund all kinds of "green initiatives" that would radically lower the U.S. dependence on fossil fuels and other industrial processes like coal production that generate significant amounts of greenhouse gases.[149] In 2009, Obama stated that the U.S. would become a leader in the global effort to address climate change.[150] He declared that the U.S. Department of Transportation would begin implementing the 2007 law that required cars and light trucks to be fuel-efficient by 2020 and that production of such cars would begin in 2011. The U.S. still uses one-quarter of all oil produced in the world even though it has only 5 percent of the world's human beings.[151] The traditional liberal response to global warming that hails such ruling class goals enunciated by the U.S. government as "some action is better than none" does not address the structural dependence of the U.S. and other heavy-energy dependent countries on fossil fuels, coal, and nuclear power for the bulk of their energy needs. While these steps may be considered significant by some in industry, they are largely symbolic within the overall scheme of U.S. fuel and energy consumption since gas-guzzling light trucks and sports utility vehicles continue to be produced, marketed, and sold by the million with little investment in new public transport mechanisms and alternative clean-energies on a national basis. The rhetoric has not been matched by concrete shifts in U.S. energy policy that would disrupt the hegemonic influence of Big Oil in the U.S. economy. For instance, the 2005 U.S. Energy Policy Act mandates that the Department of Interior would conduct research and establish a commercial leasing program that would expand commercialization of oil shale resources so that they can be exploited in Western states like Colorado, Utah, and Wyoming. Oil shale extraction would release toxic gases into the atmosphere, including sulphur dioxide, lead, and nitrogen oxide. The levels of greenhouse gases released from such extraction is ten times that of conventional crude oil. Producing 100,000 barrels of oil shale each day affects visibility for 10 percent of the year and generates 10 million tons of greenhouse gases, along with requiring 2.1 to 5.1 barrels of water for every barrel of oil extracted and needing 1,200 megawatts of power that would reduce the water flow of the Colorado River.[152] Pledging to have 1 million electric plug-in cars on U.S. roads by 2015 and identifying the goal of 25 percent of the nation's electricity coming from other sources by 2025 does not obscure the reality that there are scores of millions of cars and light trucks using fossil fuels, the main source of greenhouse gas emissions, still on the country's roads in 2014.[153] Though the U.S. has only 5 percent of the world's human population, it produces 14 percent of the greenhouse gases in the world and from 1990 through 2011 the U.S. increase of greenhouse gases was 8 percent, at the rate of 0.4 percent per year.[154] In 2004, the U.S. emitted 5,987.98 million metric tons of carbon dioxide at the rate of 20.4 tons per person, exceeding that of China, which released 5010.17 million metric tons at the rate of 3.84 tons per person.[155] In 2006, China's rate of carbon dioxide emissions exceeded that of the U.S., but not in per capita emissions since China has over four times the human population of the U.S. For any sort of stability of climate systems, at least temporarily, the global atmospheric concentration of carbon dioxide should be under 450 parts per million (ppm) by volume, which most critics argue is unrealistic. The reality is that the greenhouse gases concentration is at 380 ppm and inevitably will raise global temperatures by 0.7 degrees centigrade this decade.[156] Though it was reported in June 2014 that some states have already met U.S. government goals of reducing emissions from electricity by 30 percent before 2030, this still falls short of the 80 percent emissions reduction by 2050 needed to maintain tolerable levels of global warming.[157] Further, the question is whether many of these states like Massachusetts, New York, Virginia, Tennessee, Georgia, Nevada, and Washington's emissions cuts will offset the increases of other states like California, Arizona, Wyoming, Nebraska, Iowa, Arkansas, and Louisiana and whether fracking in the states reducing emissions is still permitted.[158]

In late January 2014, U.S. Secretary of State John Kerry received a favorable report from the corporate-leaning environmental review committee, possibly opening the way for the Trans-Canada Keystone Pipeline piping oil from Alberta to Texas. It comes as no surprise that Anita Dunn, a former Communications Director on Obama's staff, ran advertising campaigns for Trans-Canada until 2011, and Brandon Pollak and Broderick Johnson who worked on John Kerry's 2004 presidential campaign were also lobbyists for Trans-Canada.[159] Quite a revolving door between the White House and U.S. and Canadian government offices and corporate oil lobbies still exists even while climate change policy and action is being debated!

Meanwhile, the Keystone Pipeline project rushes full steam ahead with Canadian Prime Minister Stephen Harper and his Conservative Party weakening or abandoning 70 environmental laws so that the drilling into the Alberta boreal forest intensifies. Fisheries, waterways, and precious forest cover are no longer off-limits to the giant oil companies who have had more than 2,733 communications with oil officials from 2008 to 2012.[160] The Keystone Pipeline is only one of 13 massive pipelines either completed already or proposed that will travel 1,200 miles to Texas and 10,000 miles to Asia and the Pacific carrying fossil fuel. The Northern Gateway pipeline crisscrosses thousands of rivers and streams between Alberta and the Pacific, ripping and raping the land as it cuts through the lush forest region. Canada's role in addressing global warming and its lethal effects is hardly laudatory: it is the only country to withdraw from the Kyoto Protocol and it's very far from attaining anything close to the promised reductions of 17 percent of greenhouse gas emissions below 2005 levels. The Alberta boreal forest is one of the largest natural water resources on Earth and it functions as a carbon sink similar to the manner in which the Amazon forest once did. Now that the temperatures have risen phenomenally over the past four decades, the pine beetle has spread all over the region, killing millions of trees and making them a haven for widespread forest fires that once again release tons of carbon dioxide. Stephen Harper's government has been part of the climate-denial clique and has suppressed research and publication of articles on global warming and climate change in peer-reviewed journals, placed limits on the ability of Canada's 23,000 scientists to express their views openly, and consolidated science libraries and slashed funding for such research. Its draconian measures extend to discouraging the medical profession from working in areas where Indigenous people like the Mikisew Cree suffer from cancer and other serious ailments due to poisoning of water and vegetation from the spilloff of toxic waste from tar sands. The national health agency of Canada accused John O'Connor, a medical doctor who worked in Fort Chipewyan some 150 miles from the tar sands, of "professional misconduct" when he reported unusually high rates of rare cancers among Indigenous residents of the area due to environmental poisons, verified by a government review of findings in 2009.[161]

The negotiations on climate change among governments and various non-governmental sector organizations of Copenhagen, Denmark, in 2009, Cancun, Mexico, in 2010 and iThekwini (Durban), South Africa, in 2011 produced little tangible change in terms of any serious commitment especially by the Western industrialized powers who are the leading greenhouse gas emitters in the world. Frustration by the Bolivian delegation headed by Indigenous

President Evo Morales at the Copenhagen summit led to the Bolivians organizing their own Climate Change conference in Cochabamba, Bolivia, in 2010 that declared the Universal Declaration of the Rights of Mother Earth.[162] The Cochabamba conference, drew over 35,000 peoples from all over the Americas and other parts of the world, affirmed the rights of the Earth and all living beings to live in freedom as part of bio-diversity and for all to be accorded the right to enjoy clean air and water, the right to integral health, and the right to be "free from contamination, pollution, and toxic or radioactive waste."[163] The gathering echoed the primacy of Indigenous peoples' cultures as the principal cultural manner of addressing global warming issues since Indigenous peoples have far-reaching histories of living sustainably with the Earth.

In 2014, little tangible effect has been seen in shifting away from fossil fuels dependence and development of alternative and cleaner energy mediums. Huge gas-guzzling automobiles and sports-utility vehicles are still the norm in car usage in the U.S., all symbolic of the hegemonic power of the giant oil companies and the automobile industry. If anything, "green initiatives" are still reflective of obsession with the green ... dollar, as opposed to authentic clean energies! The Trans-Pacific Agreement, for instance, that is being signed between the U.S. and nations of the Pacific like Australia, Brunei, Chile, Japan, Malaysia, New Zealand (Aotearoa), Peru, Singapore, Vietnam, along with Mexico and Canada, does not subscribe to serious environmental protections like prohibition of overfishing, banning on illegal logging and destruction of precious forests, and tight enforceable laws on selling of body parts from threatened species like elephants and tigers, another indicator of the deceptive double-speak of globalization's political and economic protagonists.[164] This globalized trade-agreement would administer 40 percent of the world's GNP and one-third of global trade, once again disregarding any measures to curb global warming from deforestation for example or protect marine ecosystems from overfishing.

Conclusion

The release of the latest report of the Intergovernmental Panel on Climate Change meeting in Yokohama, Japan, in late March 2014 underscores the gravity of the imminent and looming crisis of global warming and climate change and warns that climate change is effecting every part of the world, and the worst is yet to come, with melting icecaps, Arctic sea ice collapsing, water supplies suffering, rising seas, droughts intensifying, heavy rains and storms destroying communities and coastlines, coral reefs disappearing, fish and other creatures migrating toward the poles, and extinction of species accelerating.[165] Dwindling food production is the global norm and food security is direly threatened for billions of humans and other life forms on Earth as the climate changes and water becomes the most precious resource scarcely available in most parts of our drying world. The main causes of this life-death crisis is the emission of greenhouse gases principally from industry and fossil-fuel powered vehicles, all ideas from the Western European industrial revolution that now constitute the cornerstone of the globalized capitalist system. Capitalism and its unbridled obsession with profit through mass industrial production is the root cause of the global warming crisis, and the capitalist world that developed in the aftermath of colonization must bear full responsibility for the suffering of the world and break from their addiction to profit and greed that is plundering the Earth.

Nuclear fission, agro-fuels, bio-technologies, and planetary engineering will not solve the problem of global warming and climate change, but merely prolong it and hasten life's demise. Even alternative energies like wind power, solar power, and hydroelectric power still need stable climates and abundant water supplies, all of which are in scarce supply in the present and in the future. The problem is consumption and convenience for well-to-do human elites at the cost of the rest of the impoverished majority. South Asian scientist and activist Soumya Dutta notes that "false solutions" to the global warming crisis need to be confronted so that the world is not misled and ponders: "If hand-stitched leather footballs were enough for Pele and Garincha to weave their magic on the world stage, why do we need multi-million dollar space-age factories to make the same footballs today? Why do we have to light up our urban nights as if there should be no difference between day and night? Why do we need a 2000 Kg (kilogram) SUV to move a single person weighing less than 100 Kg, from his home to work place, when a convenient bus or rail ride can do the same at one-tenth the energy consumption per person and less than one-twelfth the polluting emission—both from its running and manufacturing energies?"[166] Why indeed?! Dutta poignantly concludes that it's critical for all humans to realize the truth and not bury our heads in the sand or aspire towards a utopian world where materialism and consumerism are permanently enshrined in our cultures: "The root cause of the global warming and climate change crisis ... is the unsustainable and in-equitable extraction and consumption of nature's gifts, of privatization of the commons—global regional and local.... As the capitalist industrialist bulldozer has extracted fossil fuels at ever increasing rates, burned them to produce ever increasing consumables, dumped the wastes (and externalized both the environmental and human costs) into the global common atmosphere and hydrosphere, the Earth's recycling systems are slowly giving in under the enormous extraction/exploitation."[167] Most importantly, Dutta accentuates the fact that *while the total net carbon dioxide-sink capacity of the Earth that includes vegetation, seas, and oceans is about 14–16 billion tons, the total anthropogenic carbon dioxide emissions from fossil fuel burning, deforestation, bio-mass burning, mining, and industrialization in 2005, principally from the Western industrialized countries and the world's elite minority, was about 36–38 billion tons, more than twice what Earth can remove, and this figure is growing each year!*[168] The defeatist attitude by some who contend that all of the nations of the world, rich and poor alike, are committed to the mantra of "economic growth" engineered under globalized capitalism and thus greenhouse gas emissions will inevitably increase in the world and that the solution is "improving energy efficiency of the economy," for example, is myopic because such dispositions fail to recognize the plunder of the Earth and her limited resources by the insatiable kleptocratic forces of globalization and the irreparable ecological and environmental costs of such "efficiency."[169] The cost of all life on Earth cannot be quantified and reduced to economic proportions as Indigenous peoples globally have always insisted from the ancient past into the present. Indigenous Ramu elder, Belchior Ware, from Bosmun, Papua New Guinea, succinctly captures this view in the face of the ongoing resistance of the Ramu people to nickel extraction from ancestral lands and rivers, when he declares: "Life comes from the land ... we are only guardians."[170]

This chapter has illustrated that the global warming and climate change crisis is clearly human-caused and capitalist-driven and a result of political, social, and economic injustice, since the tiny minority of wealthy capitalist nations emits most of the greenhouses per capita in the world, yet the bulk of those who suffer from this toxic vitiation of the Earth are from the world's most impoverished countries. The obsession with economic growth, expressed by politicians and corporate executives who claim that they are unwilling to engage in radical measures that will reduce greenhouse gases by 80 percent, severely curb the use of water for industrial expansion in the light of a drying Earth, and change lifestyles because such steps would jeopardize corporate profits and lower U.S. competitiveness in the globalized economy, is fundamentally flawed.[171] The Earth has spoken and expressed her sweltering anger at the escalating rate of extinction of so many of her children and beckons us to restore our relations with her by respecting life. *There will be no human life, let alone economic growth of any sort, if we persist in repeating the lethal capitalist mistakes of the past. We are compelled now to change course and return to who we were meant to be: human beings with spirits living in co-existence with our relatives on Earth, since we are all from the same Mother.* This chapter demonstrates that the Earth is a Living Being who is unable to take any more of capitalism's violence and destruction of the lives of Earth's children. We as humans are an integral child of Nature and not above her. We must abandon capitalism ... to simply live. It is either *Existence in Respect of the Earth and Shared Life with Her* or *Globalized Industrialized Capitalism and Non-Existence.* There are no in-betweens if we want to live in a world where tomorrow comes. The Epilogue will chart a path for us to reclaim our humanity so that we understand what it means to be and become a human being in a world free of globalized capitalism.[172]

Epilogue: Whither Unjust Globalization? An Open Future Based Neither on Linear Progress Nor Materialist Consumption

The preceding five chapters have painstakingly demonstrated that globalization is a modern form of *neo-colonization*. Intensified exploitation of the Earth, dispossession and further marginalization of Indigenous peoples, subjugation and compounded violence against women, punishment of the working and marginalized classes through incarceration, torture, and capital punishment, and ongoing wars against the people of the underdeveloped world, *the "three-quarters" world*, for vital energy and mineral resources, is *the* globalized system of the late 20th and early 21st centuries.[1] The after-effects of the sub-prime mortgage and housing crisis in the United States, where some of the largest corporate banks in the world have had to write off $95 billion in bad debts by the end of 2007 and begged for loans from Chinese investment agencies and Arab wealth funds to rescue them from financial collapse, is just one indicator of the unbridled accesses of capital coming finally to a head, all exacerbated by the forces of globalization that stressed maximum profits by any means necessary.[2] Bank losses through 2008 and 2009 could total anywhere between $500 billion and $800 billion. Carlyle Capital, part of the Carlyle Group, and one of the largest private equity companies in the world, of which George H.W. Bush is a shareholder, has defaulted on over $16 billion of marginal debt payments.[3] The United States from 2008 through 2010 experienced a full recession with some comparing the current financial crisis to the depression of 1929. Although Wall Street investors and bankers were ecstatic that share values have climbed exponentially to their highest in February 2012 since 2008, the real effects of that recession linger. In 2008 and 2009,

360,000 jobs were lost each month. Jobs growth resumed in March 2010, but they were only at the average rate of 100,000 jobs per month. Even with January 2012's increase of 243,000 new jobs, U.S. payrolls were still "5.6 million below what they were at the start of 2008."[4] The net effect is entrenched unemployment and subsequent poverty and erosion of middle-class positions in the U.S. economy. As former U.S. Federal Reserve chairperson Allan Greenspan wrote:

> Global stock prices peaked at the end of October and then progressively declined for nearly a year into the Lehman crisis. Global losses in publicly traded corporate equities up to that point were $16,000bn (€12,000bn, £11,000bn). Losses more than doubled in the 10 weeks following the Lehman default, bringing cumulative global losses to almost $35,000bn, a decline in stock market value of more than 50 per cent and an effective doubling of the degree of corporate leverage. Added to that are thousands of billions of dollars of losses of equity in homes and losses of non-listed corporate and unincorporated businesses that could easily bring the aggregate equity loss to well over $40,000bn, a staggering two-thirds of last year's global gross domestic product.[5]

During 2008, the net worth of U.S. households lost a total of $11.5 trillion, some 18 percent of their value for the year.[6] While capitalism's ardent defenders insist that there will be a turn-around, the fact of the matter is that the wealth losses will never be recuperated, causing a permanent loss to the capitalist edifice that is incorrigible and irreparable. The economic downturn after all has been generated by the exchange of credit intrinsic to the capitalist system, where banks use deposits of account-holders to lend monies to people who need to live in houses but do not possess the cash resources to pay for such fundamental necessities and are thus forced to take out mortgage loans over two or three decades at phenomenal rates of compounded interest that result in borrowers often paying two or three times the original purchase price of the home. Such is the foundation of the U.S. economy that involves $10 trillion in market value, almost two-thirds of the country's gross domestic product. Although the housing market has generally regained some of the real estate value lost since 2006, the losses are still impossible to regain in entirety. In 2009, housing values dropped by $1 trillion and a further $1.7 trillion in 2010, bringing total losses in housing values to $9 trillion since June 2006.[7] Sooner or later the "American dream" bubble that is rooted in a system of working class and poor people being forced to work as contemporary economic slaves for mammoth transnational corporate banks, was destined to burst, unleashing the well-kept secret crisis of poverty and exposing the unmitigated greed of giant Western banks that constitute the pillars of the Western financial system. In a world where only 8 percent of the people possess bank accounts and where only 5 percent are owners of computers, collapse of the system of monetary accumulation of the wealthy few at the cost of the forced toil and labor of the world's impoverished majority was ineluctable and is now imminent. The middle classes around the world, which are themselves now facing economic hardships are experiencing a little of what the working classes and the impoverished peoples of the world have always suffered: economic, cultural, social, and personal misery as a result of capitalism's blood-thirsty nature and orientation. As Bill Means, a leader of the American Indian Movement put it, "We are all Indian now!" Sad to say, then, the election of Barack Obama as the first Black president of the United States has not ushered in a post-racial United States as some have contended; neither has it institutionalized racial and economic justice within the country or without because all presidents of the United States are beholden to the same capitalist system that installed them in the first place and are required as their office demands: to be the commanders-in chiefs of U.S. imperialist hegemony. It is evident from Obama's over six years in office that the policies and practices of using taxpayer funds, some $2 trillion, to ensure large banking and corporate commercial profits and stability and of maintaining a superpower war budget as from the Reagan-Bush era will continue into the foreseeable future.[8] The early November 2010 decision by the U.S. Federal Reserve to inject some $600 billion dollars into the U.S. economy through purchase of government bonds will not provide the necessary economic corrective because the U.S. economy is based on credit and indebtedness, in which U.S. citizens are urged to purchase homes, cars, and all consumer goods on credit so that the banks earn huge profits from credit interest. Today, the major banks in the U.S. are sitting smug and flush with lots of cash as a result of the U.S. government bailout of failing banks in 2008.

While this economic recession is officially losing steam according to the mainstream media, a recovery is projected with Wall Street gaining trillions in profits from purchase and sale of stocks, but it is still described as a "jobless recovery." What does this mean? In essence, that an economic recovery in the United States has little to do with employing the close to 30 million people who are either unemployed or under-employed, reflective of the over 15 percent unemployment rate that includes people who have exhausted the process of seeking new jobs. It is estimated that at the current rate of job creation, it would take nine more years to regain jobs lost from the recession, which excludes the 5–6 million new jobs needed from the increase in the U.S. population. Given that the median prices of house have fallen by 20 percent since 2005, it would take 13 years for houses to reach their peak, according to Allen

L. Sinai, a leading economist at Decision Economics. In essence, what the United States has had in terms of economic wealth and household and monetary value is never coming back.

What is fundamentally ignored while states slashed budgets in education, health, and basic benefits in 2010 and 2011 and the newly constituted Republican and Tea Party–dominated Congress has promised more radical cuts in public spending to trim yawning budget deficits, is that the escalation of the military budget, about $600 billion, close to a quarter of the federal budget in 2010, has not been radically cut. The U.S. continues to maintain a wartime budget even though the Cold War officially ended in 1989. The preceding chapters painstakingly illustrated the entrenched militarization of the U.S. economy that is now steeped in global wars for resources in the name of the unending "War on Terror." The intensification of this War on Terror, in actuality a *War of Terror*, is a foundational trope in this era of globalization because it is focused on resource acquisition and expropriation as demonstrated in the chapters of this book. One wonders why it is that the U.S. borrows billions of dollars from China to sustain its budget deficits so that it can wage wars in and around Iraq, Afghanistan, Pakistan, and in North Africa. A reasonable-minded person may ask: Why were not chunks of the military budget sliced so that they could be invested in the cleaning of the environment, thus reducing the dependence on oil and fossil fuels to stave off the catastrophic crisis of global warming? Further, why were strategic investments not intensified in education for expansion of schools and universities and quality teacher training, fully funded health care, clean air and energy development and research, public transportation and housing, job creation, child support programs, rehabilitation of the imprisoned and those on drugs, and the renewal and transformation of U.S. society? Sounds quite rational if one thinks about it. The reason that the U.S. is unable to pursue such sensible options is because of the hegemonic role that the oil corporations and the military industrial complex play, as explained in detail in Chapters 1 and 3. So the crisis continues unabated.

The unrelenting devastation of forested regions of the world, massive contamination of marine oceans and fresh water rivers, lakes, and the saturation of our air with pollutants as the result of Western industry, along with the movement of the tropical boundaries toward the poles and the intensification of drought zones resulting in drier summers and winters, have cumulatively been a part of the crisis of globalization in this phase of late capitalism in the world. According to the latest reports, 20 percent of the Amazon rainforest has been deforested and, over the past year alone, a forested area the size of Belgium, has been cleared.[9] If a serious push to immediately terminate deforestation in the Amazon does not occur and does not produce radical changes away from decimation of the forest, an incredulous 40 percent of the forest will be depleted by 2030. The reason for this massive ecocide is the need for soybean cultivation for energy demand in the United States and the greed for timber in Western Europe and North America, executed by loggers in the Amazon. Such felling of the Amazon will result in the emission of anywhere between 55.5 billion and 96.9 billion tons of carbon dioxide gases into the atmosphere, causing a spike in temperatures in areas in North America and as far away as India.[10]

In March 2009, Indigenous communities and the environmental protection movement were horrified to learn that Arizona environmental officials had killed the last remaining wild jaguar in the world through a perverted policy of supposed protection that ended in putting the animal to sleep, falsely assuming that its kidneys had collapsed.[11] The arrogance of positivist strands in Western science and culture that insists that they can recast and remake the world of nature in Western humanity's image causes irreparable suffering and extinction, as with the catastrophic elimination of the southwestern jaguar. Western science insists that it knows how to preserve and save the world without being willing to acknowledge its historical oversight of ecocide.

The nagging question remains: now that we know so much of the disastrous effects of globalization, what can we do or what should we do? The philosophical foundations for economies of the Indigenous peoples of Sabah, Malaysia, which resonate with hundreds of millions of Indigenous people globally recall us to ancestral wisdom that is timeless:

> The traditional economic system, which puts community solidarity as its priority, is being replaced by the dominant capitalist economic system, which puts profit first rather than people.
> Sustaining indigenous systems in the current context where the dominant system continuously imposes itself on the traditional systems and the desire for progress within the community which sees the traditional system as a stumbling block, remains the greatest challenge.[12]

In discussing the subject of the role of the academy and the pursuit of knowledge vis-à-vis the crisis of political governance in Africa, John Morongo writes:

> We have too many academic institutions in the world today that call themselves universities. It may be time for them to stop doing so, for they are not universal or political in the elemental sense. They are simply parochial academic institutions that lack the will and courage to truly be universal. Genuine universities should be

in the business of providing universal political education—the kind of education that is deeply and thoroughly rooted in global justice. They cannot be what they ought to be if they do not practice universal justice. If instead of preparing our students for citizenship in the universe, we continue preparing them for citizenship in an anachronistic, nineteenth-century world of nation-state citizenship, we will continue to reinforce catastrophic governance in the world.[13]

There is no question that the global capitalist system as symbolized by transnational corporations and the Western ruling elites and their ruling class regime allies around the world have no real future because their cosmological foundations are rooted in greed and exploitation of Mother Earth and all life. B. A. Ogot, the noted African scholar, argues:

> It is clear that the liberal world economy as it has existed since 1945 is on its way out. What we have to expect in its place, if present trends are a reliable guide, is something approximating to a world of regional blocks or super blocks ... of exclusive trading areas hedged in by protective tariffs, in which groups of developed [sic] and developing [sic] countries are linked together by mutual interests and stand opposed to other groups of developed [sic] and developing countries linked ... since the free-market economy has failed to provide employment and as a means of distributing the world's wealth, perhaps a regulated, regionally organized world economy, even if it is not perfect, may have tangible advantages to offer, both to the developed [sic] and developing [sic] countries.[14]

The liberal tendency response to globalization has been to call for peaceful settlement of conflicts, whether it is the Indigenous people of the Western hemisphere demanding the return of ancestral lands and barring mining and energy extractionist corporations, or the colonization of Palestine by Western-Israeli colonialism, or the struggles of Indigenous Africans in South Africa and Zimbabwe to have their dispossessed lands returned unconditionally to them, or the struggles of Indigenous people of Australia and New Zealand (Aotearoa) to have access to ancestral lands for ceremonies. Yet this peace is chimerical. Under the auspices of globalization, few historically rooted colonial conflicts have been resolved. Dev Nathan and Govind Kelkar write:

> Peace, however, cannot be simply the absence of conflict or the elimination of fear of physical violence. That would be a "negative" and insecure peace. To be positive, peace must eliminate the structures that support unequal capability fulfillment within or between countries and redress the wrongs done to all those involved in unequal power, including gender relations. Rather than a return to the status quo, a positive peace must include the elimination of unequal power and development relations.[15]

Pakistan was besieged by floods in 2010 that saw up to 14 million people rendered homeless or effected, all while it was being urged to intensify its fights against the Taliban and Al Qaeda "terrorists." It has hardly recovered from the devastation from flooding and hunger and poverty have soared as a result of the flooding, yet another indicator of the lethal effects of global warming, especially on underdeveloped nations who don't possess the resources or infrastructure to redress Earth's anger from global warming. Pakistan, like India, is a nuclear power, yet the bulk of the people in Pakistan and India live in dire poverty, almost a billion people in all. India was ranked 119 in its Human Development Index by the United Nations Development Program, among 169 countries in 2010.

During the 2007 festive season bloodletting continued unabated in Pakistan following the killing of Benazir Bhutto on December 27, with over 42 people killed, 947 vehicles destroyed and 131 banks and 31 petrol stations burned. Bhutto, a former prime minister, had promised genuine democracy in the military-ruled nation, but continued to maintain a family heirloom of wealth and political manipulation beholden to Washington, D.C.[16] Prominent Pakistani-English critic Tariq Ali sums up the situation aptly in his article "Daughter of the West" in the *London Review of Books*, where he explains that both Pervez Musharraf, the former president of Pakistan made so through a military coup in 1999 and the late Benazir Bhutto both functioned as surrogates for U.S. military imperialism, an extensive quote that is warranted here given the obfuscation over Pakistan's "democracy."

> Both parties made concessions. She agreed that he could take off his uniform after his "re-election" by Parliament, but it had to be before the next general election. (He has now done this, leaving himself dependent on the goodwill of his successor as army chief of staff.) He pushed through a legal ruling—yet another sordid first in the country's history—known as the National Reconciliation Ordinance, which withdrew all cases of corruption pending against politicians accused of looting the national treasury.
>
> The "breakthrough" was loudly trumpeted in the West, however, and a whitewashed Benazir Bhutto was presented on U.S. networks and BBC TV news as the champion of Pakistani democracy—reporters loyally referred to her as "the former prime minister" rather than the fugitive politician facing corruption charges in several countries.
>
> She had returned the favour in advance by expressing sympathy for the U.S. wars in Iraq and Afghanistan, lunching with the Israeli ambassador to the UN (a litmus test) and pledging to "wipe out terrorism" in her own country.[17]

In Kenya, presidential elections were held in March 2013 in which Uhuru Kenyatta won a much-contested election against incumbent president Mwai Mbaki. During the December 2007 elections, Mwai Mbaki was returned to the presidency following a patently rigged election. Close to 1,500 people were killed then and 600,000 people were forced to flee their homes from the Rift Valley and around Kenya to live elsewhere by the conflict between the ruling Kenya African National Union Party and Raila Odinga's Orange Democratic Movement. Though the conflict has generally been painted as a "tribal" feud between Kikuyu-speaking Kenyans and Luo-speaking Kenyans and social, political, and economic dominance by the former in Kenya since formal independence from Britain over 40 years ago, the quintessential issue for the upheaval is poverty among the majority of the people in Kenya caused by the Western-capitalist structured and governed economy. As one commentator responded, "There are only two tribes in Kenya ... the haves and the have-nots." The hundreds of thousands of impoverished men and women living in Nairobi's slums like Kibera and Mbare took to the streets in angry protest when they realized that the candidate for whom they had voted and on whom they had pinned their hopes for economic change, Raila Odinga, was not going to be accorded justice in an election controlled by the ruling party. Further, both the Kenyan African National Union Party and the Orange Democratic Movement concurred on the planned invasion of Somalia in line with the political machinations of the U.S. government, which was determined to stamp out the dissident Al-Shabaab organization in Somalia, evoking greater ethnic tensions in the region.

The tragic result of Western-demanded elections in Kenya has been the eruption of colonially-defined ethnic community conflicts that were craftily engineered by elitist groups and from which the latter inevitably benefit, the tearing asunder of a beautiful nation and the forced expulsion of over 200,000 people in the Rift Valley alone. If these elections are patterned on Westminster and Washington recipes for democracy and caused the deaths and dispossession of hundreds of thousands of people in African countries like Kenya, Nigeria, the Democratic Republic of the Congo, and Cote d'Ivoire, for example, then perhaps it is time to re-assess the current political practice of elections every four years, where generally select elite representatives assume the reins of political power to the detriment of Africa's vast impoverished majority. African's political roots are not in Western Europe but in a continent where traditional Indigenous modes of collective participation in decision making prior to colonialism generated positive societal outcomes for diverse peoples for millennia.

African and other colonized peoples need to hearken back to the frameworks of their cultural pasts to understand how to live peacefully and happily in a contemporary world driven by capitalist greed and wars against Mother Earth that continue to heap untold suffering and maintain perpetual social, political, economic, and cultural instability in the world. Libya, the historic intellectual and trade and commercial center of ancient African civilizations, which served as the center of Pan African living and community in the 20th and early 21st centuries, is no more since NATO under the leadership of the U.S. dropped thousands of bombs and shelled the countryside with depleted uranium-laden Cruise missiles to occupy the country and install a surrogate regime that extracts oil from the deep oilfields for Western capitalist consumption and profit by the oil conglomerates. The West finds it so difficult to learn moral lessons from its catastrophic invading wars against Iraq and Vietnam.

The nation state that exists in many parts of the world, particularly in underdeveloped countries, *the "three-quarters" world*, has generally been either irrelevant to the lives of the majority of the people in their respective lands or exploited them through militarization, dispossession from traditional lands, and decimation of forests and coast lines for energy resource extraction. States under the globalization regime have often caused untold family suffering through subjugation of women, particularly in agricultural plantations and industrial assembly plants and factories. Most nation states have protected the wealthy and powerful and impoverished and marginalized the working classes. The colonial roots of these states (since many of these boundaries were officially designated during the Berlin Conference in 1884–1885) have perforated kinship ties and land-based cultures in the Pacific, Africa, Asia, and Latin America. The suffering of the Gypsy communities in Europe is an extension of the callousness of the nation state towards people who come from Indigenous cultures and feel no allegiance to the state, but cherish honoring the Earth. The nation state that demands allegiance, especially under the auspices of globalization through doctrines of national security, is against Indigenous ways of seeing and living on the Earth and thus problematic for human beings living in peace with their relatives, the rest of the natural world. After all, *we are all citizens of the Earth and the Earth does not belong to us, but we belong to the Earth*, the Indigenous Dineh group, *Blackfire*, sings.[18] The Earth knows no colonial, political, territorial, or geographical boundaries as human "civilizations" have demarcated over the millennia. We are her children along with all of our relatives, the four-legged, birds, insects, plants, mountains, rivers, oceans, lakes, and the creatures that walk on their bellies on the face of the Earth.

The wisdom of Indigenous peoples is instructive because of its long-term value and relevance in comparison to the short-term myopic materialist goals sought in Western educational systems. The letter of Chief Seattle, an Indigenous leader in North America in the 19th century, is instructive for our embarkation of paths into the future:

Whatever befalls the earth befalls the sons of the earth. Man did not weave the web of life; he is merely a strand in it. Whatever he does to the web, he does it to himself.

One thing we know, which the white man may one day discover—our God is the same God. You may think that you own him as you wish to own our land: but you cannot. He is the God of man; and his compassion is equal for the red man and the white man. The earth is precious to Him and to harm the earth is to heap contempt on its Creator. The whites too shall pass; perhaps sooner than all other tribes. Continue to contaminate your bed, and you will one night suffocate in your own waste.[19]

Ed McGaa, an Indigenous spiritual leader, contextualizes the critique and call by Seattle for us in the 21st century, referring to the irreparable damage and destruction evoked by human beings obliviously continuously decimating the creatures on Mother Earth and erasing the hopes of future generations of all life, judicious words warranting extensive citation here:

If killing Mother Earth is a sin, as the Indians believe, then avoiding becomes a step on the path of illumination. The theologian Reinhold Niebuhr declared that sin is a separation from the truth. If the truth, as seen in the Native American's holy visions, is the profound interconnectedness of all existence, then sin becomes inevitable when one becomes alienated from nature. Yet has ever there been a time when humanity has been so torn from nature's embrace? Thoreau wrote that "the mass of men lead lives of quiet desperation." People living in the modern age have become alienated, feeling alone, isolated, and separated. Modern myths have created the perception of an atomistic society, where all connections have been cut. Yet nothing is further from the truth. Interdependence is at the center of all things. The separation between us and nature is a mirage. The perception of separation is the result of ignorance. It springs from the arrogant belief that a human being is unlike animal beings and plant beings and rock beings. It is reinforced by the false teaching that technology has lifted us above the web of life. The sin of hubris made modern people believe that human beings are superior to and independent of nature. The Indians knew the meaning of humility when they stood beneath the Great Spirit in ceremony and prayed, "Oh Wakan Tanka (Great Spirit, Great Mystery) make me worthy." We must realize, it is an unbroken flow that runs from humankind to the glory of creation. We do not seek a "back to nature" movement; instead we emphasize the realization that we can never leave nature.[20]

The 2008 research report (*BBC World News*, February 14, 2008) from climate and marine scientists indicates that only 4 percent of the seas and oceans on our planet are undamaged and that sizeable portions of coastlines in northern Europe and southeast Asia have been irreparably damaged by overfishing, commercial shipping and off-shore oil drilling, annihilating thousands of marine species in the process, making the specter that all fish could be erased and sea food diets would become obsolete within fifty years increasingly likely. In March 2008, salmon fishing all along the Pacific West Coast from Mexico to Washington state, was halted due to the critical shortage of Chinook salmon in the cold waters of the northwest.[21] The view by a billionaire businessman at the Davos summit in January 2008 that "water is the oil of the twenty-first century" is a haunting reminder that the expediency of Western industrialism, while satisfying greedy materialistic appetites in the short run, is permanently destructive in the long term. David Loy, a Buddhist scholar teaching in Japan, notes the inordinate power wielded by the transnational corporation, observing that in 1995, "only 49 of the world's largest economies were nations; the other 51 were corporations" and that the "total sales of the top 200 transnational corporations were bigger than the combined Gross Domestic Product (GDP) of all 182 countries except the top nine nations, that is about thirty percent of the world GDP" yet "employed less than one-third of one percent of the world's population."[22] Lamenting the fact that corporations in the United States gradually increased their power following the U.S. Civil War and benefited from the most decisive legal decision in U.S. economic history in 1886 when the U.S. Supreme Court ruled in *Santa Clara County v Southern Pacific Railroad* that a corporation is in fact "a natural person" and enjoys the protection of the Bill of Rights, including free speech akin supposedly to any person, Loy concludes that corporations are morally incorrigible. It is clear though that, since the early part of the 20th century, free speech was radically curtailed for all those citizens who challenged the injustices of society, particularly for African Americans, rights of course which never existed for the Indigenous people since the founding of the United States. Citing the 1984 disaster in Bhopal, India, where a chemical leak from the Union Carbide plant there resulted in 10,000 deaths and over 50,000 permanently injured, Loy balks at the fundamental insouciance of the transnational corporation, the leading pillar of capitalism, because the $400 million in damages that Union Carbide paid for through its insurance has not served as a deterrent to other TNCs, but instead has emboldened them to continue illicit practices that jeopardize both human life and environmental conditions, risking fines for such criminal practice. Loy asserts:

> As the example of Bhopal shows, a corporation is unable to feel sorry for what it has done (it may occasionally apologize, but that is public relations, not sorrow). A corporation cannot laugh or cry; it cannot enjoy the world or suffer with it. Most of all, a corporation cannot love. To love is to realize our interconnectedness with others and live our concern for their well-being. Such love is not an emotion but an engagement with others that includes responsibility for them, a responsibility that if genuine transcends our own selfish interests. If that sense of responsibility is not there, the love is not genuine. Corporations cannot experience such love or

live according to it, not only because they are immaterial but also because of their primary responsibility to the shareholders who own them. A CEO who tries to subordinate his companies' profitability to his love for the world will lose his position, for he is not fulfilling that financial responsibility to its shareholders.[23]

Loy finally underlines the need for the positive abolition of the corporation that he views as the most lethal threat to the future of the world:

> My Buddhist conclusion is that transnational corporations are by their very nature problematic. We cannot solve the problems they create by addressing the conduct of this or that particular corporation; it is the institution that is the problem.... As long as corporations remain the primary instruments of economic globalization, they endanger the future of our children and the world they will live in.[24]

In repudiating the Chinese shift away from socialism towards market capitalism, Samir Amin observes that this "economic revolution" that has stunned the world obscures the fact that the reason for Chinese insertion into prominence on the global world stage is the powerful shake-up generated by the agrarian socialist revolution under Mao Tse-tung in 1949 and lasting until 1976. Amin accentuates the unavoidable truth that "capitalism, by its very nature, is incapable of solving the peasant question, and that the only prospect it offers is a of a 'shantyized' planet with billions of surplus human beings" and that "capitalism is becoming barbarism and directly leading to genocide," necessitating a replacement with a philosophy that is essentially about development and a "higher rationality."[25] Amin surmises that environmental concerns will compel the demise of capitalism and the charting of an alternative path for societies and argues against any deterministic unadulterated economic laws that govern history, but rather views as decisive the "social reactions to the tendencies expressed in them" which in turn shape social relations in the world.[26] He proposes a socialistic order for the future and cautions that "there will be no socialism without democracy, but also democratic advances without social progress," and calls for a pluricentric world where the military designs for control of the Mother Earth by U.S. imperialism are extinguished.[27]

Yet, it is important to move beyond a socialist alternative as Amin so eloquently suggests. Political and economic philosophies, systems, and structures will come and go throughout the unfolding of human history and like human beings and all life will physically become transformed into something other than material body. As much as Marxian thought has provided the most comprehensive and incisive critique of capitalism since the inception of the capitalist system over two centuries ago, it nevertheless is deficient in that it deifies human nature and elevates the realm of humanity over Mother Earth and the rest of the natural world. Human beings cannot be reduced to their materialist proportions and the history of human struggle cannot be couched principally as the struggle to "tame nature" for the well-being of the human species. Human beings are an integral part of the natural world, having originated in Earth. The idolatry of deifying the temporality of human nature as it evolved in medieval Europe has caused enough destruction to the ecology and stability of our very fragile planet. We cannot continue down this path of perennial devolution and self-destruction. This is not in any way to dismiss the noble goals of socialism towards economic and social justice in the world, as employed in the Chinese and Cuban revolutions, for example. The problem is that these socialist experiments are short-term and cannot project themselves into the future, without instruction from the Earth. We need to return to the ways of living with the Earth and not against the Earth as if she were some commodity structured for exploitation and manipulation. The Earth has ways to instruct us on how to engineer economies of scale that can truly develop our societies and ecologies in sustainable and healthy ways. As Dagara spiritual elder, Malidoma Somé notes:

> Indigenous people find their rhythm in nature. Westerners, on the other hand, seem to seek meaning in the realm of the machine, where one finds neither peace nor wholeness, but ceaseless movement. In the West, people are always frenetically rushing somewhere in the countless lanes of the multiple highways of progress.[28]

Western humanity has elevated itself above nature and is now reaping the bitter fruit of such idolatry and narcissism as Westerners find it increasingly impossible to control the processes of Mother Earth, particularly in the manner that weather and ecological systems wreak havoc on artificial human-engineered manipulations of the natural world like rivers and forests. This obsession has produced a permanent restlessness within the contours of Western culture. Vine Deloria, the Indigenous scholar, laments that

> The white man, when viewed in this context (of lack of knowledge about the intricacies of the American landscape-mine), appears as a perennial adolescent. He is continually moving about, and his restless nature cannot seem to find peace. Yet he does not listen to the land and so cannot find a place for himself. He has few relatives and seems to believe that the domestic animals that have always relied upon him constitute his only link with the other peoples of the universe. Yet he does not treat these animals as friends but only as objects to be exploited. While he has destroyed many holy places of the Indians, he does not seem to be able to content himself with his own holy places ... for his most holy places are cemeteries where his forefathers lie under granite slabs, row upon row upon row, strangers lying with strangers.[29]

Human beings are fallible creatures, not immortal, as much as the ancient Greeks aspired in their mythologies to depict humans becoming like eternal gods. We are here for this moment and we need to live in creative and responsible ways that prepare for the next seven generations. Our words and bodies will pass away.

What *will* remain is Mother Earth and the ultimacy and eternity of the spirit world that outlasts all physical life. Spirit is supreme and outlives every materialistic political or economic system constructed by human society. We who have come from Earth, made with Earth, ultimately return to Earth, for burial or as dust when cremated. This is what Indigenous peoples have always exhaustively, even at the cost of peril to ourselves when confronting the edifice of globalization, attempted to teach the master philosophers of the Western world in our simplicity and humble collective village cultures. The Western world has neither seen fit nor possessed the spiritual fortitude to chart a way of life that makes harmonious respect of and living with Mother Earth the ultimate principle of existence. Instead, Western epistemological confusion has elevated the scientism of the human mind to divine proportions, aborted from its spiritual moorings. The result is the pervasive confusion, greed, violence, nihilism, anxiety, fear, oppression, racism, sexism, hatred, social conflict, pollution of air and water, and distortion of spirits, minds, and bodies that ineluctably leads to widespread drug addiction, rootlessness and accompanying ruthlessness, social and diseased epidemics that invade and occupy all communities regardless of electrified gates and high-rise concrete walls and barbed wire fences, preoccupation with probes into space while ignoring the desecration and violation of Earth and the elimination of the right to life of humans and other animal and plant life, and myopia that views the material present as ultimate where genetically modified seedless production terminates our links to the future. In a different world, such would be classified as "insanity." So many call it "progress," "post-modernity," "the pinnacle of civilization," and, yes, "the miracle of globalization." Winona LaDuke, Anishinaabeg activist from Minnesota, emphasizes the gravity of the ecological crisis pointedly:

> According to Harvard biologist Edward O. Wilson, 50,000 species are lost every year. Three-quarters of the world's species of birds are declining and one-quarter of all mammalian species are endangered. Tropical rainforests, freshwater lakes, and coral reefs are at immediate risk, and global warming and climate change will accelerate the rate of biological decline dramatically.[30]

As you complete the final segment of this book, a good question to ask would be: *how many species have been irretrievably erased during the course of my turning the pages? Is it indeed the miracle of life or is it really the horror of destruction?*

The Earth is ultimately the driving force of the world and without us recognizing her sacred and indomitable power, which demands that we as human beings struggle and strive to walk in harmony with her, we will go nowhere, but continue to actively destroy this beloved planet. We need to do more walking on Earth, barefoot as much as possible, to reconnect with the voice of Earth, like the Longest Walk across Turtle Island from Alcatraz Island on the West Coast started in February 2008 and ending in Washington, D.C., in July 2008, like the long walk of Indigenous activists in Australia in July 2007. We need to abandon our automobiles that are powered by the blood of the Arabs, Africans, Latin Americans, and Asians, the poor people of the deserts and the forests of this world. We need to undo the asphalt and the concrete that can never cover the Earth, and become real. We can never remove her since she is the ground upon which we walk, and like the weeds that we attempt to exterminate, she always comes back—sometimes angry enough to cause uncontrollable storms! It needs to be reiterated in this epilogue that the Earth is a living being and like all of the bodies in the celestial sphere, is a live and powerful spirit and by whose natural laws we are required to live, if we are to expect anything meaningful as humans living on Earth. This is precisely the reason that the knowledge possessed and the cultures practiced by Indigenous nations like the Khoi San and the Indigenous people of Australia are so foundational in the discussion of the future of our world. Speaking from the Indigenous nation of Australia, Mary Graham, perspicaciously critiques the endemic individualism, the commoditization of land, and the deification of money in Western industrialism:

> Older Aboriginal people have often stated that white Australians "have no dreaming," that is, they have no collective spiritual identity, no true understanding of what constitutes a correct, "proper," relationship with land/reality.
>
> The spirit of the sacred has been reified as "money." Western behaviour, as we have observed it over the last two hundred years, has elevated money to the status which is normally accorded to the sacred.
>
> By contrast, in Aboriginal society money has the same status as other useful resources, such as food, clothing, transport and housing. These resources are there for the use and benefit of the family group first, and then of the community. Money is therefore subject to the same sort of treatment as other resources—sharing.[31]

Graham emphasizes that particularly in an ethos of globalization where economic production is paramount and resource extraction ultimate, the principles of Indigenous culture are unwavering:

> *The Land is the Law:* The land is a sacred entity, not property or real estate; it is the mother of all humanity. The dreaming is a combination of meaning (about life and all reality, logic) and a guide to living. The two most important relationships in life are between land and people and then between people; the second is always contingent upon the first. Land, and how we treat it, is what determines our

humaneness. Because it is sacred and must be cared for, land ontologically becomes the template for society and social relations. All meaning, then, comes from land.

You are not alone in the world. Aboriginal people have a kinship system that extends to the land. This system was, and still is, organized into clans. *The Western question is: What is the meaning of life? The Aboriginal Question is: Who is it that wants to know?* Aboriginal cultural praxis maintains that one does not need work, money, or possessions to justify one's existence. Over long periods of time, Aboriginal people have invested most of their creative energy in trying to understand what makes it possible for people to act purposively, and experience "events," or to put it another way, *what is it exactly that makes us human?*[32]

The obsession with industrial progress and vulgar individualistic material accumulation is rooted in a culture that has terrorized the Earth and has produced the cultures of impoverishment of Indigenous people all over the world, decimated most beings of the rest of the natural world, subjugated and violated the sacred roles of women as life-givers, underdeveloped the colonized peoples of the world, pursued wars of conquest for possession of economic and political hegemony that have created craters in the Earth and caused animals, birds, insects, and plants to vanish and become instinct, and established regimes of punishment of the poor through the prison industrial complex, all subjects discussed extensively in this book. The resistance movements to globalization around the world, like those at the 1993 WTO meeting in Seattle, the World Social Forum in Porto Alegre in 2003, the protests at Davos in 2008 and in various cities and towns around the world, and the Occupy Wall Street movement, are all positive signs of the spiritual movement towards wholeness and against profit, greed, and colonial imperialist violence. Ultimately, these dissidents around the globe will need to connect with the voices and cultures of Indigenous people who are the oldest caretakers of the Mother Earth as enunciated above.

Finally, it is important to underscore that no singular human being or culture has all of the solutions to the problems of the world. Indigenous peoples have understood two important principles that we all need to earnestly consider: (i) The Earth is not the center of the Universe and (ii) the Universe has no center and is thus timeless and "spaceless." In this sense, Indigenous peoples do not subscribe to the concept of linear time because it is restrictive and unscientific in explaining the manner that the universe functions. The concept of the Earth come into being 15 billion years ago as part of a cosmic explosion of particles as Western science teaches does not expose the fact that 15 billion years is a linear concept of time that is totally abstract because it cannot be imagined. Similar is the concept that declares that the nearest star is 20 light years away, which implies that by traveling at the speed of light, it would take us 20 years to get to such a star. Humans will never be able to accomplish such a feat because it is unachievable and thus totally abstract. It is precisely for these reasons that Indigenous peoples subscribe to the view that we live in a timeless Universe with no center and that we are ultimately all spiritual beings whose spirits manifest themselves in cycles of events that cannot be measured in linear time. This is the reason too that Indigenous peoples are not obsessed with the question of the origin and the time in which the Earth originated because it is a futile exercise with little relevance to the preservation of the spirit that binds every being to the endless universe. In some sense, it is a realization that as human beings are expendable in a timeless universe, so too other forms may emerge in different worlds if it occurs in the future that humans do not exist. In a real manner then, in a cyclical timeless and "spaceless Universe," our physical lives are but a moment of the manifestation of the infinite spiritual manifestation of the universe and that matter in the universe is what Vine Deloria describes as "mind-stuff" that leaves everything open-ended.[33] As he wisely cautions:

> Our expectations in life are that events will occur in a cause-and-effect universe in which it is relatively simple to trace the beginnings and end of any natural phenomenon.... When we experience an event or feeling out of the ordinary, we tend to dismiss it as unreal, a fantasy that somehow broke out into our consciousness. We cannot explain what we have experienced because we have only this narrow materialistic framework to evaluate what has happened.[34]

This book serves as the prophetic call to thoughtful cultural praxis and the abandonment of materialistic capitalist paths and a return to restoring the traumatically violated relationship with the Earth and living in simple ways that ensure harmony with the rest of the natural world since human beings are an intrinsic element of the tapestry of nature, and not extrinsic to her or above her. In a real manner, this epilogue ironically contends and illustrates that for humans to move forward, we will need to delve deeply into the wellspring of Indigenous pasts to be the best human beings can be.[35] It is only through the re-union and the restoration of a harmonious relationship with the Earth that humankind can reclaim some of the positive elements of the global commerce and trade that occurred among the peoples of the world, across Asia as far as China and the Pacific, across north and west Africa all the way from Egypt and the Horn of Africa down the Kiswahili east coast to Senegal and the Congo, with Europe, and with the Western hemisphere, dating back to the early part of the previous millennium that lasted 14 centuries.[36] Paradoxically, it was Asian and African trade with Europe that generated sustainable economies for all peoples, not the kind of slaving predatory inhuman global economies of scale we have today. Those ancient global relations respected the sacred amid serious social and economic contradictions in those industrial societies. Restructured and respectful global relations that are collectively beneficial for all life can only transpire under a supportive Earth. Anything contrary is doomed to self-destruction, as are economic systems or empires themselves. After all, the Earth does not make progress; she rotates relentlessly from season to season in rhythm with the rest of the universe. *If the Earth is indeed our Mother and does not make progress, how could we humans who are her children?!*

Chapter Notes

Introduction

1. "The Extinction Crisis," *Center for Biological Diversity*, Tucson, AZ, at http://www.biological diversity.org/programs/biodiversity/elements_ of_biodiversity/extinction_crisis/, accessed on April 17, 2014.

2. "The Great Recession," *The State of Working America* (Washington, D.C.: Economic Policy Institute, 2012) at http://stateofworkingamerica. org/great-recession/. The complete book is *The State of Working America*, 12th Edition, by Lawrence Mishel, Josh Bivens, Elise Gould, and Heidi Shierholz (Ithaca: Cornell University Press, 2012).

3. John Lott, "President Obama, and the Myth About 4.5 Million New Jobs," *Real Clear Markets*, August 13, 2012, at http://www.realclearmarkets. com/articles/2012/08/13/president_obama_ and_the_myth_about_45_million_new_jobs_ 99816.html, accessed on April 17, 2014.

4. Robert Atkinson, "Why the 2000s Were a Lost Decade for American Manufacturing," *Industry Week*, March 14, 2013, at http://www. industryweek.com/the-2000s, accessed on April 17, 2014.

5. Vicky Pelaez, "The Prison Industry in the United States: Big Business or a New Form of Slavery?" *El Diario-La Prensa, New York* and *Global Research* 10 (March 2008), Montreal, Center for Research on Globalization at http://www. globalresearch.ca/the-prison-industry-in-the- united-states-big-business-or-a-new-form-of- slavery, accessed on December 8, 2013.

6. http://finance.yahoo.com/blogs/daily- ticker/top-5-secrets-private-prison-industry- 163005314.html.

7. Vicky Pelaez, "The Prison Industry in the United States: Big Business or a New Form of Slavery," *El Diario-La Prensa, New York* and *Global Research* 10 (March 2008), Montreal, Center for Research on Globalization at http://www.global research.ca/the-prison-industry-in-the-united- states-big-business-or-a-new-form-of-slavery, accessed on December 8, 2013.

8. Nicole Goodkind, "Top 5 Secrets of the Private Prison Industry," *Daily Ticker*, August 6, 2013, at http://finance.yahoo.com/blogs/daily- ticker/top-5-secrets-private-prison-industry- 163005314.html, accessed on April 17, 2014.

9. http://journalistsresource.org/studies/ government/security-military/us-military- casualty-statistics-costs-war-iraq-afghanistan- post–911.

10. "Rubber shortage drives prices up," *City Press*, Johannesburg, September 26, 2010.

11. *Natal Mercury*, Durban, South Africa, September 27, 2010.

12. *Russian Times*, October 20, 2013. Accessible at http://rt.com/news/fukushima-leak-radio active-overflow-469/.

13. See Michael McCarthy's excellent article on the secrecy surrounding nuclear power and its historical deleterious effects in Europe, North America, Russia, and Asia, "A cloud of nuclear mistrust spreads across the world," *The Independent*, London, March 16, 2011, at http://www. independent.co.uk/news/world/asia/four- explosions-two-fires-and-a-cloud-of-nuclear- mistrust-spreads-around-the-world-2242988. htm, accessed on March 21, 2011. The article "Fukushima's deadly new radiation leak: The worst yet" reveals disturbing trends of nuclear radiation at Fukushima, at http://theweek.com/ article/index/217884/fukushimas-deadly-new- radiation-leak.

14. Deepak Nayyar, "Globalization and Development in the Long Twentieth Century" in *Globalization Under Hegemony: The Changing World Economy*, edited by K. S. Jomo (New York: Oxford University Press, 2006), 91–92.

15. Though such calls for secession in some of the places in South Asia are colored by several historical, economic, socio-political, and cultural dynamics, including those of the roles of global imperialist powers, the reality of ongoing conflict and bloodshed in these regions warrants further scrutiny and redress of social grievances. See, for instance, Jason Sorens, *Secessionism: Identity, Interest, and Strategy* (Montreal: McGill-Queen's University Press, 2012) and *Secession and International Law: Conflict Avoidance: Regional Appraisals*, edited by Julie Dahlitz (The Hague: T.M.C. Asser Press and New York: United Nations Organization, 2003).

16. Deepak Nayyar, "Globalization and Development in the Long Twentieth Century" in *Globalization Under Hegemony: The Changing World Economy*, 93.

17. Michael McCarthy, "Oceans on brink of catastrophe," *The Independent*, London, June 21, 2011.

18. Justin Gillis, "Ending Its Summer Melt, Arctic Sea Ice Sets a New Low that Leads to Warnings," *New York Times*, September 19, 2012, at http://www.nytimes.com/2012/09/20/science/earth/arctic-sea-ice-stops-melting-but-new-record-low-is-set.html?_r=0, accessed on September 20, 2012.

19. See for instance, C. W. L. Hill, *International Business: Competing in the Global Market Places*, Postscript (New York: Unwin-McGraw-Hill, 2001); E. Lee, "Globalization and Labour Standards: A Review of Issues" in *International Labour Review* 136(2), 173–189; M. Waters, *Globalization* (London: Routledge, 1995); and J. Wiseman, *Global Nation: Australia and the Politics of Globalization* (Cambridge: Cambridge University Press), 1995.

20. Samir Amin, "The future of global polarization" in *Globalization and Social Change*, edited by Johannes Dragsbaeck Schmidt and Jacques Hersh (London: Routledge, 2000), 41.

21. Georges Casalis' book, *Correct Ideas Don't Fall from the Skies: Elements for an "Inductive Theology"* (Maryknoll, NY: Orbis Books, 1984), provides a realistic and critical assessment of the confluence of ideas and praxis.

22. Samir Amin, "The future of global polarization" in *Globalization and Social Change*, 41.

23. Paulo Freire, *Pedagogy of the Oppressed* (New York: Continuum, 1970).

24. On the question of cyclical time, see for instance, K.K. Bunseki Fu-Kiau, "Ntangu-Tandu-Kolo: The Bantu-Kondo Concept of Time" in *Time in the Black Experience*, edited by Joseph Adjaye (Westport, CT: Greenwood Press, 1994) and John Mbiti, *Introduction to African Religion,*

Second Edition (London: Heinemann, 1991). The point about the universe having no center and the difference for Africans between "living time" and "living in time" is made by the philosophical scholar Mogobe Ramose in his article "Ecology Through Unbuntu" in *African Ethics: An Anthology of Comparative and Applied Ethics* edited by Munyaradzi Felix Murove (Scottsville, South Africa: University of Kwazulu-Natal Press, 2009), 309, 311.

25. See, for instance, Vine Deloria's *God Is Red: A Native View of Religion, Second Edition* (Golden, CO: Fulcrum, 2003), for a detailed treatment of the Indigenous view of humans on Earth and their status of creature like all others with no special dispensation of power and privilege above others.

26. Vine Deloria's book, *Red Earth, White Lies: Native Americans and the Myth of Scientific Fact* (New York: Scribner, 1995), is an instructive text in this regard.

27. L. G. Horowitz, "Polio, Hepatitis B and AIDS: An integrative theory on a possible vaccine induced pandemic," *Medical Hypothesis*, 56, no. 5 (May 2001), at http://www.medical-hypotheses.com/article/S0306–9877(00)91171-X/abstract. Horowitz raises very pointed questions about the possible spread of the AIDS virus through simian viruses that "likely infected polio-vaccinated blood donors to the initial hepatitis B vaccine" administered to gay men in New York City and Black people in Uganda in the mid–1970s. His book *Emerging Viruses: AIDS and Ebola: Nature, Accident or Intention?* (Healthy World Distributing, 1996) certainly warrants earnest reading on these important issues of Western medical science and the spread of viruses among vulnerable populations and discussed subsequently in this book.

28. See Harriet Washington's excellent book, *Medical Apartheid: The Dark History of Experimentation on Black Americans from Colonial Times to the Present* (New York: Harlem MoonBroadway Books, 2006), which describes the history of racist experiments on unsuspecting and poor Black people, including prison inmates.

29. See for instance Deborah McGregor's chapter "Traditional Ecological Knowledge and Sustainable Development: Toward Coexistence" in *In the Way of Development: Indigenous Peoples, Life Projects and Globalization*, edited by Mario Blaser, Harvey A. Feit and Glenn McRae (London: Zed Books in Association with International Development Research Centre, 2004) for an illumination of the limitations of Western science when it comes to recognizing the problems represented by unbridled technological expansion.

30. Vine Deloria's book, *God Is Red: A Native*

View of Religion, is an excellent book that expands on this view of global ecological community and responsibility.

31. Many plastic-made products, including most automobiles assembled in California, now come with a health warning about the cancerous effects of plastic ingredients.

32. Chapter 5 of the book describes the urgent crisis of climate change and global warming in the 21st century in elaborate descriptive and analytical detail.

33. Jennifer Schuessler, "Lessons from Ants to Grasp Humanity," *New York Times,* April 8, 2012, at http://www.nytimes.com/2012/04/09/books/edward-o-wilsons-new-book-social-conquest-of-earth.html?pagewanted=all. E. O. Wilson's informative book is *The Social Conquest of Earth* (New York: W.W. Norton, 2012).

34. *City Press,* Johannesburg, September 20, 2010.

35. Derrick Jenson's *Endgame: The Problem of Civilization, Vol. 1 and Vol. 2: Resistance* (New York: Seven Stories Press, 2006), is one noted source in this regard. See also the latest DVD release, *END: CIV: Resist or Die,* produced by Franklin Lopez (Oakland: PM Press, 2011).

36. http://www.telegraph.co.uk/finance/newsbysector/energy/oilandgas/7848622/BP-oil-spill-White-House-to-appeal-ruling-ending-deepwater-drilling-freeze.html, June 23, 2010.

37. Clifford Krauss and John M. Broder, "Deepwater Oil Drilling Begins Again as BP Disaster Fades," *New York Times,* March 4, 2012, at http://www.nytimes.com/2012/03/05/business/deepwater-oil-drilling-accelerates-as-bp-disaster-fades.html?pagewanted=all, accessed on June 22, 2014.

38. *City Press,* South Africa, July 18, 2010.

39. See for instance the work of Maximilian Forte, an anthropologist who covers the U.S.–NATO-led invasion and destruction of Libya in his book, *Slouching Towards Sirte* (Montreal: Baraka Books, 2012) and Alexander Mezyaev's pointed article that illuminates the deceptive and fraudulent nature of the U.S.–NATO bombing and colonization of Libya under the pretext of a humanitarian intervention, "Remember Libya: How U.S.–NATO Destroyed an Entire Country Under a Humanitarian Mandate," *Global Research,* March 9, 2013, at http://www.globalresearch.ca/remember-libya-how-us-nato-destroyed-an-entire-country-under-a-humanitarian-mandate/5325776, accessed on April 17, 2014.

40. Antonia Juhasz, *The Tyranny of Oil* (New York: HarperCollins, 2008), 75, 77.

41. Antonia Juhasz, *The Tyranny of Oil,* 372, 274.

42. Antonia Juhasz, *The Tyranny of Oil,* 372, 274.

43. Antonia Juhasz, *The Tyranny of Oil,* 372, 274.

44. Antonia Juhasz, *The Tyranny of Oil,* 371, 376, 385.

45. Antonia Juhasz, *The Tyranny of Oil,* 375.

46. http://bsnorrell.blogspot.com/2012/09/debra-white-plume-sacred-water.html. Deborah White Plume, a Lakota elder and grandmother, is part of a grassroots movement called Owu Oku, "Bringing Back the Way," that is spearheading the opposition to the tar sands oil from shale extraction project.

47. *Friends of the Earth* website, accessible at http://www.foe.org/projects/climate-and-energy/tar-sands.

48. Syed Farid Alatas, "On the indigenization of academic discourse" in *Alternatives,* 18, 307.

49. *City Press,* Johannesburg, September 19, 2010.

Chapter 1

1. L. F. Houtart and F. Polet, Introduction, *L'autre Davos: Mondialisation des resistances et des luttes* (Paris: L'Harmattan, 1999).

2. See, for instance, Avinash Jha, *Background to Globalization* (Mumbai: Centre for Education and Documentation, 2000), 3–4; Deepak Nayyar, "Globalization and Development in the Long Twentieth Century" in *Globalization Under Hegemony: The Changing World Economy,* edited by K.S. Jomo (New York: Oxford University Press, 2006), 70, 71–72; Bruno Amoroso, *On Globalization: Capitalism in the 21st Century* (New York: St. Martin's Press, 1998); John Eade (ed.), *Living the Global City: Globalization as a Local Process* (New York: Routledge, 1997); Benjamin Barber, *Jihad vs. McWorld* (New York: Times Books, 1995); Robert Slater, Barry Schutz and Steven Dorr, *Global Transformation and the Third World* (Boulder: Lynne Rienner, 1993); Jeffrey Freiden, *Global Capitalism: Its Fall and Rise in the Twentieth Century* (New York: W.W. Norton, 2006); Mark Rupert and M. Scott Solomon, *Globalization and the International Political Economy* (Lanham, MD: Rowman & Littlefield, 2006); Stephen Gill (ed.), *Globalization, Democratization and Multilateralism* (New York: St. Martin's Press, 2000), 4; S. Hall, D. Held and T. McGrew (eds.), *Modernity and Its Futures* (Oxford: Polity Press/Open University, 1992); Z. Mlinar (ed.), *Globalization and Territorial Identities* (Aldershot: Avebury, 1992); M. Featherstone (ed.), *Global Culture: Nationalism, Globalization and Modernity*

(London: Sage, 1990); D. Held, *Democracy and the Global Order: From the Modern State to the Cosmopolitan Governance* (Oxford: Polity Press, 1995); Jerry Harris, *The Dialectics of Globalization: Economic and Political Conflict in a Transnational World* (Newcastle: Cambridge Scholars, 2006), especially chapter 4; Introduction, *Regional Perspectives on Globalization,* edited by Paul Bowles, Henry Veltmeyer, Scarlett Cornelissen, Noela Invernizzi and Kwong-leung Tang (New York: Palgrave Macmillan, 2007); Anthony Giddens, *The Consequences of Modernity* (Cambridge: Polity Press, 1990); Roland Robertson, *Globalization: Social Theory and Global Culture* (Newbury Park, CA: Sage, 1992); Johnren Chen (ed.), *Economic Effects of Globalization* (Aldershot: Ashgate, 1992); Gary Gereffi, "The Elusive Last Lap in the Quest for Developed-Country Status" in *Globalization: Critical Reflections,* edited by James Mittelman (Boulder: Lynne Rienner, 1996); Chapter 1 of *The Ends of Globalization.* by Mohammed A. Bamyeh (Minneapolis: University of Minnesota Press, 2000); Patrick Aspers and Sebastian Kohl, "Economic Theories of Globalization" in *The Routledge International Handbook of Globalization Studies,* edited by Bryan S. Turner (New York: Routledge, 2010), 49–50; Arjun Appadurai interestingly describes globalization as the complex disjunctures between economy, culture, and politics as the result of a dysfunctional capitalist global economy and discusses these disjunctures in terms of facets of global cultural flows reflected in "ethhnoscapes, mediascapes, technoscapes, financescapes, and ideoscapes," contending that ideologies of sameness and difference "cannibalize" one another, each claiming the supremacy of the universal and the resilience of the particular, respectively. See his book *Modernity at Large: Cultural Dimensions of Globalization* (Minneapolis: University of Minnesota Press, 1996), 32–43.

3. For example, Martin Wolf, *Why Globalization Works* (New Haven: Yale University Press, 2004); Martin Wolf, "Why This Hatred of the Market?" in *The Globalization Reader, Fourth Edition,* edited by Frank J. Lechner and John Boli (Oxford: Blackwell, 2012; Ian Goldin and Kenneth Reinert, *Globalization for Development: Trade, Finance, Aid, Migration and Policy* (Washington, D.C.: The International Bank for Reconstruction and Development/The World Bank and New York: Palgrave Macmillan, 2006); Dean Baker, Gerald Epstein and Robert Pollin, *Globalization and Progressive Economic Policy* (Cambridge: Cambridge University Press, 1998); Guillermo de la Dehesa, *What Do We Know About Globalization: Issues of Poverty and Income Dis-*

tribution (Malden, MA: Blackwell, 2007); Raphael Kaplinsky, *Globalization, Poverty and Inequality* (Boston, MA: Polity Press, 2005); Gary Burtless, Robert Z. Lawrence, Robert E. Litan and Robert Shapiro, *Globaphobia: Confronting Fears About Open Trade* (Washington, D.C.: Brookings Institution, 1998); Malcolm Waters, *Globalization* (London: Routledge, 1995), 3; Jay Mandle, *Globalization and the Poor* (Cambridge: Cambridge University Press, 2003); and William Greider, *One World, Ready or Not* (New York: Simon & Shuster, 1997).

4. Paul Bowles and Henry Veltmeyer, Introduction, *Regional Perspectives on Globalization,* 1. The quote from Scholte is taken from J. Scholte, *Globalization: A Critical Introduction* (New York: St. Martin's Press, 2000), 40.

5. Immanuel Wallerstein, *World Systems Analysis: An Introduction,* Third Printing (Durham: Duke University Press, 2005).

6. See, for instance, Andre Gunder Frank, *Capitalism and Underdevelopment in Latin America: Historical Studies of Chile and Brazil* (New York: Monthly Review Press, 1967); Walter Rodney, *How Europe Underdeveloped Africa* (Washington, D.C.: Howard University Press, 1982); Manning Marable, *How Capitalism Underdeveloped Black America* (Boston: South End Press, 1983), and Sing Chew and Robert Denemark (eds.), *The Underdevelopment of Development: Essays in Honor of Andre Gunder Frank* (Thousand Oaks, CA: Sage, 1996) for a treatment of the theme of underdevelopment of the peoples of Africa, Asia, and Latin America and of Black people within the U.S. from colonization to recent globalization.

7. World Bank, *Global Economic Prospects and the Developing Countries* (Washington, D. C., 1996), 20.

8. Jeffrey James, *Technology, Globalization and Poverty* (Cheltenham: Edward Elgar, 2002), 54. Owing to a lack of substantive political economic analysis, the author of this book weakly advocates for a more expanded role of underdeveloped countries in the global capitalist economy, particularly in areas of technology as a way of achieving economic "progress," knowing that these impoverished countries are constantly financially disadvantaged and thus will never possess the resources of the West to engage in such globally competitive economic expansion.

9. Felix Moses Edoho (ed.), *Globalization and the New World Order; Promises, Problems, and Prospects for Africa in the Twenty-First Century* (Westport, CT: Praeger, 1997), 11.

10. Fantu Cheru, *African Renaissance: Roadmaps to the Challenge of Globalization* (New

York: Zed Books and Cape Town: David Philip, 2002), 15.

11. Fantu Cheru, *African Renaissance: Road-maps to the Challenge of Globalization*, 15.

12. Reidar Adams and Geoffrey Lawrence, *Globalization, Localization, and Sustainable Livelihoods* (Aldershot: Ashgate, 2001), 8.

13. Annup Shah, "Structural Adjustment: A Major Cause of Poverty" in *Global Issues: Social, Political, Economic and Environmental Issues That Affect Us All*, March 24, 2013, at http://www.globalissues.org/article/3/structural-adjustment-a-major-cause-of-poverty, accessed on April 22, 2014.

14. Asad Ismi, "Impoverishing a Continent: The World Bank and the IMF in Africa," *Halifax Initiative Coalition*, 2004, at http://www.halifax-initiative.org/updir/ImpoverishingAContinent.pdf, accessed on April 22, 2014.

15. Communications Department, Swedish International Development Cooperation Agency (Sida), "Russia: Developments in Russia" (Stockholm: Swedish International Development Cooperation Agency, October 30, 2013) at http://www.sida.se/English/Contact-us/Sida-offices-in-Sweden/, accessed on April 22, 2014. See also N. E. Tikhonova, *Fenomen Gorodskoi Bednosti v Sovremennoi Rossii (The Phenomenon of Urban Poverty in Modern Russia)* (Moscow: Letnii Sad, 2003) and Rob Vos and Malinka Koparanova, *Globalization and Economic Diversification: Policy Changes for Economies in Transition* (London: Bloomsbury Academic, 2011), especially the Introduction and page 9 following.

16. "Gazprom: Russia's wounded giant," *The Economist*, March 23, 2013, at http://www.economist.com/news/business/21573975-worlds-biggest-gas-producer-ailing-it-should-be-broken-up-russias-wounded-giant, accessed on April 22, 2014. For poverty increases in Russia, see Vladamir Shabnov's article "Poverty in Russia grows faster than expected," *Pravda* (English), July 4, 2011, at http://english.pravda.ru/business/finance/04-07-2011/118392-poverty_russia-0/, accessed on April 22, 2014.

17. Robert Schaeffer, "Globalization and Disintegration: Substitutionist Technologies and Disintegration of Global Economic Ties" in *Frontiers of Globalization Research: Theoretical and Methodological Approaches*, edited by Ino Rossi (New York: Springer, 2008), 207–209, at http://www.bloomberg.com/quicktake/chinas-managed-markets/, accessed on May 1, 2009.

18. Eurodad report, "World Bank and IMF Conditionality: A development injustice," Eurodad (European Network on Debt and Development), June 2006, 9, at http://www.eurodad.org/

uploadedfiles/whats_new/reports/eurodad_world_bank_and_imf_conditionality_report.pdf, accessed on April 22, 2014.

19. Eurodad report, "World Bank and IMF Conditionality: A development injustice," Eurodad (European Network on Debt and Development), June 2006, 20, at http://www.eurodad.org/uploadedfiles/whats_new/reports/eurodad_world_bank_and_imf_conditionality_report.pdf, accessed on April 22, 2014.

20. Robert Schaeffer, "Globalization and Disintegration: Substitutionist Technologies and Disintegration of Global Economic Ties" in *Frontiers of Globalization Research: Theoretical and Methodological Approaches*, 205–211.

21. Suttinee Yuvejwattana and Anuchit Nguyen, "Thai Farmers Lose Pickup Trucks as Protests Raise Debt Risk," *Bloomberg News*, February 24, 2014, at http://www.bloomberg.com/news/2014-02-23/thai-farmers-lose-pickup-trucks-as-protests-increase-debt-risk.html, accessed on April 22, 2014.

22. Andrew Malone, "The GM genocide: Thousands of Indian farmers are committing suicide after using genetically modified crops," *Mail Online*, London, November 2, 2008, at http://www.dailymail.co.uk/news/article-1082559/The-GM-genocide-Thousands-Indian-farmers-committing-suicide-using-genetically-modified-crops.html, accessed on April 22, 2014.

23. Muriel Mirak-Weissbach, "Global Food Crisis: Egypt and Sudan Join Forces for Food Security," *Global Research*, May 27, 2008, at http://www.globalresearch.ca/index.php?context=va&aid=9082. The article on misdirected bread subsidy policy in Egypt is "Egypt's Corrupt Bread Policy," *Daily News*, Egypt, April 26, 2008, at http://subalternate.wordpress.com/2008/04/26/egypts-corrupt-bread-policy/.

24. See Peter M. Rosset's book *Food Is Different: Why We Must Get the WTO Out of Agriculture* (Halifax, Nova Scotia: Fernwood; Bangalore: Books for Change; Kuala Lumpur: SIRD; Cape Town: David Philip; and New York: Zed Books, 2006), for an instructive explanation of the manner that impoverished countries are held hostage by the WTO when it comes to food production, food markets, trade barriers, and the control of food trade by large transnational corporations.

25. *The China Post*, April 10, 2008, at http://www.chinapost.com.tw/business/global%20%20markets/2008/04/10/151183/World-food.htm, accessed on April 11, 2008.

26. UNCTAD, "UNCTAD Handbook of Statistics 2012 shows growing Economic influence of developing countries," December 14, 2012, at http://unctad.org/en/pages/newsdetails.aspx?OriginalVersionID=376&Sitemap_x0020_

Taxonomy=Statistics;#20;#UNCTAD%20Home, accessed on January 10, 2014. For the *UNCTAD Handbook of Statistics 2012*, see http://unctad. org/en/PublicationsLibrary/tdstat37_en.pdf, accessed on April 23, 2014.

27. Wendy Kay Olsen, "Liberalization and Financial Exclusion in Sri Lanka" in *Globalization and Identity; Development and Integration in a Changing World*, edited by Alan Carling (New York: I. B. Taurus, 2006), 110–113.

28. Giovanni Arrighi, "Globalization and Uneven Development" in *Frontiers of Globalization Research: Theoretical and Methodological Approaches*, edited by Ino Rossi (New York: Springer Science and Business Media, 2007), 195–198.

29. Roger Moody, "Is Mining Coming to an End—As We Once Knew It?," cited in *Pitfalls and Pipelines: Indigenous Peoples and Extractive Industries*, edited by Andy Whitmore (Baguio City, Philippines: Tebtebba Foundation; Copenhagen: International Work Group for Indigenous Affairs [IWGIA]; and London: Indigenous Peoples Links [PIPLinks], 2012), 48.

30. Giovanni Arrighi, "Globalization and Uneven Development" in *Frontiers of Globalization Research: Theoretical and Methodological Approaches*, edited by Ino Rossi, 195–198.

31. Ian Katz, "China's Treasury Holdings Climb to Record in Government Data," *Bloomberg News*, January 15, 2014, at http://www.bloomberg.com/news/2014–01–15/china-s-treasury-holdings-rose-to-record-in-november-data-show. html, accessed on April 23, 2014. For Chinese offloading of U.S. debt, see Gordon Chang's article "What if China Stops Buying U.S. Government Debt?," *Forbes*, October 6, 2013, at http://www.forbes.com/sites/gordonchang/2013/10/06/what-if-china-stops-buying-u-s-government-debt/, accessed on April 23, 2014. Of course, Chang paints an optimistic picture of the U.S. economy as most globalized capitalism advocates do, without underscoring the point that U.S. debt (including securities debt) was over $33 trillion in 2013 and is fundamentally unsustainable, threatening to implode in the near future. See Damon Vickers' insightful book, *The Day After the Dollar Crushes: A Survival Guide for the Rise of the New World Order* (Hoboken, NJ: John Wiley & Sons, 2011), for elucidation on the inevitable collapse of the artificially inflated U.S. dollar that is the largest "indebted" currency in the world.

32. Cordell Eddings and Daniel Kruger, "China Cuts Treasury Holdings Since 2011 Amid Caper," *Bloomberg News*, February 18, 2014, at http://www.bloomberg.com/news/2014-02-18/china-cuts-treasury-holdings-most-since-2011-amid-taper.html, accessed on April 23, 2014.

33. Roger Moody, "Chinese Syndromes," cited in *Pitfalls and Pipelines: Indigenous Peoples and Extractive Industries*, edited by Andy Whitmore, 55.

34. Roger Moody, "China's Rising," cited in *Pitfalls and Pipelines: Indigenous Peoples and Extractive Industries*, edited by Andy Whitmore, 56.

35. Roger Moody, "China's Rising," cited in *Pitfalls and Pipelines: Indigenous Peoples and Extractive Industries*, edited by Andy Whitmore, 57.

36. Roger Moody, "China's Rising," cited in *Pitfalls and Pipelines: Indigenous Peoples and Extractive Industries*, edited by Andy Whitmore, 57.

37. Roger Moody, "Fast Money," cited in *Pitfalls and Pipelines: Indigenous Peoples and Extractive Industries*, edited by Andy Whitmore, 48.

38. T. Ademola Oyejide, "Globalization and Its Economic Impact: An African Perspective" in *Local Perspectives on Globalisation: The African Case*, edited by Joseph Semboja, Juma Mwapachu and Edward Jansen (Dar es Salaam: Research on Poverty Alleviation, Mkubkina Nyota Publishers, 2000), 24.

39. *City Press*, October 17, 2010.

40. Robert Cummings, "Historical Perspective on the Lagos Plan of Action" in *Beyond Structural Adjustment in Africa: The Political Economy of Sustainable and Democratic Development*, edited by Julius E. Nyang'oro and Timothy Shaw (New York: Praeger, 1992), 35.

41. Cited by Robin Broad and John Cavanagh, "The hijacking of the development debate: How Friedman and Sachs got it wrong" in *World Policy Journal* 23, no. 2 (Summer 2006), p. 21, Expanded Academic ASAP (Gale).

42. Nick Mead, "A developing world of debt," *The Guardian*, London, May 16, 2012, at http://www.theguardian.com/global-development/poverty-matters/2012/may/15/developing-world-of-debt, accessed on April 23, 2014.

43. Robin Broad and John Cavanagh, "The hijacking of the development debate: how Friedman and Sachs got it wrong" in *World Policy Journal* 23, no. 2 (Summer 2006), p. 21, Expanded Academic ASAP (Gale).

44. Robert Cummings, "Historical Perspective on the Lagos Plan of Action" in *Beyond Structural Adjustment in Africa: The Political Economy of Sustainable and Democratic Development*, edited by Julius E. Nyang'oro and Timothy Shaw (New York: Praeger, 1992), 43.

45. South African Reserve Bank, "Gross External Debt-Fourth Quarter 2013," March 31, 2014, at https://www.resbank.co.za/publications/detail-item-view/pages/publications.aspx?sarb web=3b6aa07d-92ab-441f-b7bf-bb7dfb1bedb4 &sarblist=21b5222e-7125-4e55-bb65-56fd33333 71e&sarbitem=6170, accessed on May 7, 2014.

46. Bade Onimode, *Africa in the World of the 21st Century* (Ibadan, Nigeria: Ibadan University Press, 2000), 7.

47. Bade Onimode, *Africa in the World of the 21st Century*, 122.

48. See chapter 2 of "Measuring African Capital Flight" of L. Ndikumana and J. Boyce's book *Africa's Odious Debts: How Foreign Loans and Capital Flight Bled a Continent* (New York: Zed Books, 2011). A significant problem with data compilation on Africa's debt and other financial indicators by most global financial institutions like the World Bank and the IMF and even by many scholars of Africa is the tendency to balkanize Africa into "North Africa and the Middle East" and "sub–Saharan Africa," reproducing the traditional colonial bifurcation of Africa into "Arab Africa" and "Black Africa." Interestingly too, South Africa is removed from the list of heavily indebted countries, even though it is the nation with the largest external debt (accrued from the days of apartheid), because it's considered being outside "Black Africa"! The website of the New African Partnership for African Development (NEPAD) of the African Union, limited in scope as the program depends heavily on foreign investment in Africa as a key solution to Africa's historical and contemporary economic underdevelopment, is one site that provides data on the continent in its entirety. See for instance, Policy Brief No. 3, "External Debt in Africa," October 7, 2010, at http://www.nepad.org/economicand corporategovernance/knowledge/doc/1727/external-debt-africa, accessed on May 7, 2014.

49. Alex MacGillivray, *A Brief History of Globalization: The Untold Story of Our Incredible Shrinking Planet* (New York: Carroll & Graf, 2006), 223.

50. T. Ademola Oyejide, "Globalization and Its Economic Impact: An African Perspective" in *Local Perspectives on Globalisation: The African Case*, 24.

51. Ademola Oyejide, "Globalization and Its Economic Impact: An African Perspective" in *Local Perspectives on Globalisation: The African Case*, 24.

52. http://www.afriqueavenir.org/en/2010/09/06/2010-record-year-for-investments-in-africa/. See also http://africaptv.wordpress.com/2010/08/27/foreign-direct-investment-to-africa-a-force-for-good-or-ill/.

53. http://africaptv.wordpress.com/2010/08/27/foreign-direct-investment-to-africa-a-force-for-good-or-ill/.

54. Yusuf Bangara, "Globalisation and African Development" in *Africa in the New Millennium*, 34–35.

55. *African Development Report 2003: Globalisation and Africa's Development* (Oxford: Oxford University Press, for the African Development Bank, 2003), 12.

56. *African Development Report 2003: Globalisation and Africa's Development*, 8.

57. Sandra Barnes, Presidential Address to the African Studies Association, New Orleans, November 12, 2004.

58. Jedrzej George Frymas and Manuel Paulo, "A new scramble for African oil: historical, political, and business perspectives," *African Affairs* 106, no. 423 (April 2007), 231.

59. Yusuf Bangara, "Globalisation and African Development" in *Africa in the New Millennium*, edited by Raymond Suttner, with Georges Nzongola-Ntalaja, Adebayo Olukoshi, Yusuf Bangara and Steve Kayizzi-Mugerwa (Uppsala: Nordiska Africkainstitutet, 2001), 38.

60. This assertion recalls U.S. Department of Agriculture Earl Butz's statement in 1974 when describing food "aid" to the impoverished nations of the world.

61. See the work of well-known South Asian environmental activist Vandana Shiva, *The Violence of the Green Revolution: Third World Agriculture, Ecology, and Politics* (Penang: Third World Network, 1991).

62. Suresh Raval, "The Role of the Humanities in the Age of Globalization: Reading Mukherjee, Kincaid, and Coetzee," *Western Humanities Review* LXV, no. 3 (Fall 2011), 146.

63. *The Economist, The World in 2010*, December 2009, 93.

64. Jeremy Rifkin, *The Biotech Century: Harnessing the Gene and Remaking the World* (New York: Tarcher/Putnam, 1998), 65.

65. Jeremy Rifkin, "Genetic Blueprints Aren't Mere Utilities," Op-Ed page, *Los Angeles Times*, July 8, 1998.

66. Deborah Barndt, *Tangled Routes: Women, Work and Globalization on the Tomato Trail* (Lanham, MD: Rowman & Littlefield, 2002), 14.

67. Carlos Roco, "Trade liberalization and Economic Development in Mexico: A Case for Globalization" in *Globalization, the Third World State and Poverty Alleviation in the Twenty-First Century*, edited by B. Ikubolajeh Logan (Burlington, VT: Ashgate, 2002), 118.

68. Kat Henrichs (Staff Reports), "Globalization in Mexico, Part 1: Economic and Social Effects," *Borgen Magazine*, April 26, 2013, at http://www.borgenmagazine.com/globalization-in-mexico-part-1-economic-and-social-effects/, accessed on April 24, 2014.

69. Claudia Sadowski-Smith, Reading Across Diaspora" in *Globalization on the Line: Culture,*

Capital, and Citizenship at U.S. Borders, edited by Claudia Sadowski-Smith (New York: Palgrave, 2002), 79.

70. http://www.pbs.org/now/politics/trading democracy.html, February 1, 2002.

71. Ofelia Rivas, a Tohono O'odham spiritual elder, founded an organization called *O'odham Voice Against the Wall*, to challenge the splitting of O'odham ancestral lands at the U.S.–Mexico border. She was detained by Border Patrol agents in 2005 for her resistance to these colonial-border restrictions.

72. Laura Carlsen, "Arizona Border Crosser Rate at Record High," *Americas Program: A New World of Action and Communication For Social Change*, August 8, 2013, at http://www.cipamericas.org/archives/10148, accessed on April 25, 2014.

73. Roque Planas, "Border Patrol Blasted at UN For Killing Mexicans," *The Huffington Post*, October 26, 2012, at http://www.huffingtonpost.com/2012/10/26/border-patrol-killing-un_n_2018731.html.

74. Brenda Norrell, "Mike Wilson: U.S. Border Patrol shot Tohono O'odham at border," *Censored News*, April 8, 2014, accessed on April 9, 2014. *Censored News* is an informative news blog that particularly covers issues pertaining to Indigenous peoples in the Americas.

75. Such accounts of intimidation and violence have been conveyed by traditional elders like Ofelia Rivas and Ray Santiago to the author various times over the past decade.

76. Economic Commission for Latin America and the Caribbean Report, United Nations, November 29, 2011, at http://medicinezine.com/news/latin-american-poverty-levels-fall-lowest-decades-report-finds/, accessed on January 10, 2102.

77. Samuel Moncada, "Isn't it time to respect Venezuela's democracy?" *CNN Opinion*, February 22, 2013, at http://www.cnn.com/2013/02/18/opinion/venezuela-democracy-moncada/, accessed on June 22, 2014.

78. Nicolas Maduro, "Venezuela: A Call for Peace," Op-Ed Contributor, *New York Times*, April 1, 2014, at http://www.nytimes.com/2014/04/02/opinion/venezuela-a-call-for-peace.html?_r=0, accessed on April 2, 2014.

79. Economic Commission for Latin America and the Caribbean Report, United Nations, November 29, 2011, at http://medicinezine.com/news/latin-american-poverty-levels-fall-lowest-decades-report-finds/.

80. The author observed the program in action in rural communities outside Esteli, north of Managua, Nicaragua, on August 29, 2012, with members of the Alliance for Global Justice from the U.S. and Honduras. An educational DVD production on the situation in Nicaragua is currently being undertaken at the Office of Instructional Assessment (OIA) at the University of Arizona, spearheaded by the author and Veronica Rodriguez from the same office.

81. Prior to his performance on September 3, during my Nicaraguan visit, the Indigenous musician and artist, Philip Montalvan, indicated that the Nicaraguan government was being sued by some Indigenous communities over the Monkey Point project that threatened cultural survival and ecological destruction particularly of the San Juan River that runs for 119 miles, drains from Lake Cocibolca to the Caribbean and reflects some of the greatest diversity of birds, caimans, turtles, and monkeys of Central America. A glimpse of the beauty of this Nicaraguan region can be seen at http://visitnicaragua.us/see-do/regions/.

82. See, for instance, Kirkpatrick Sale's instructive work *Conquest of Paradise: Christopher Columbus and the Columbian Legacy* (New York: Plume, 1991) and Ward Churchill, *Indians Are Us* (Monroe, ME: Common Courage Press, 1994) for a treatment of this history of systematic genocide of the Indigenous Taino, Arawak, Caribs, and other Indigenous peoples of the Caribbean. Examples of such scholars of globalized imperialism include Hopeton S. Dunn, *Globalization, Communications, and Caribbean Identity* (New York: St. Martin's Press, 1995); Thomas Klak (ed.), *Globalization and Neoliberalism: The Caribbean Context* (Lanham, MD: Rowman & Littlefield, 1998); Clive Yolande Thomas, *The Poor and the Powerless: Economic Policy and Change in the Caribbean* (New York: Monthly Review Press, 1988); Helen C. Scott, *Caribbean Women Writers and Globalization* (Burlington, VT: Ashgate, 2006); Norman Girvan, "Globalisation, Fragmentation and Integration: A Caribbean Perspective," paper prepared for the International Meeting on Globalisation and Development Problems, Havana, Cuba, January 18–22, 1999, at http://www10.iadb.org/intal/intalcdi/PE/2009/02683.pdf, accessed on May 1, 2014; Norman Girvan, *Cooperation in the Greater Caribbean: The Role of the Association of Caribbean States* (Kingston: Ian Randle, 2006); Linden Lewis (ed.), *Caribbean Sovereignty, Development and Democracy in An Age of Globalization* (New York: Routledge, 2013); Brian Meeks and Folke Lindahl (eds.), *New Caribbean Thought: A Reader* (Kingston: University of West Indies Press, 2001); Kenneth Hall and Denis Benn, *Governance in the Age of Globalisation: Caribbean Perspectives* (Kingston: Ian Randle, 2003); Tennyson S. D. Joseph, *Decolonization*

in St. Lucia: Politics and Global Neoliberalism, 1945–2010 (Jackson: University Press of Mississippi, 2011); and Mimi Sheller, *Consuming the Caribbean: From Arawaks to Zombies* (New York: Psychology Press, c/o of Taylor & Francis Group, 2003).

83. Hilbourne Watson, "Globalization and the Caribbean in the Age of Neo-Mercantilist Imperialism" in *Governance in the Age of Globalisation: Caribbean Perspectives*, edited by Denis Benn and Kenneth O. Hall (Kingston: Ian Randle, 2003), 57–58.

84. Hilbourne Watson, "Globalization and the Caribbean in the Age of Neo-Mercantilist Imperialism" in *Governance in the Age of Globalisation: Caribbean Perspectives*, edited by Denis Benn and Kenneth O. Hall, 57–58.

85. See, for instance, Anthony Payne and Paul Sutton, *Charting Caribbean Development* (London: Macmillan Education, 2001), especially chapter 4, "Liberal Economics vs Electoral Politics in Seaga's Jamaica." For perspectives from Michael Manley, a charismatic Jamaican social change leader and leader of the Peoples' National Party from 1972 to 1980, see Michael Manley, *Jamaica: Struggle in the Periphery* (London: Writers and Readers Publishing Cooperative Society, 1982). Manley's fostering of closer ties with socialist Cuba and promotion of "democratic socialism" earned him the political wrath of the U.S. imperialist system and some pro–U.S. local capitalists. The U.S. has always viewed the island nation as being in its own "backyard" like the rest of the Caribbean countries and thus disallowed from exercising radical self-determination and independence. The classic 2005 film documentary *Life and Debt*, directed by Stephanie Black, provides an accurate portrayal of such imperialist projections of Jamaica.

86. See, for example, Anthony Payne and Paul Sutton, *Charting Caribbean Development*, especially chapter 3, "The Grenadian Revolution," and Anthony Payne, Paul Sutton, and Tony Thorndike, *Grenada: Revolution and Invasion* (New York: St. Martins' Press, 1985); Maurice Bishop and Michael Taber, *Maurice Bishop Speaks, 1979–1983: The Grenada Revolution and Its Overthrow, 1979–1983* (New York: Pathfinder Press, 1983); and *Grenada: The Jewel Despoiled* (Baltimore: Johns Hopkins University Press, 1987).

87. Peter Hallward, *Damming the Flood: Haiti, Aristide, and the Politics of Containment* (New York: Verso, 2007). For more contemporary information on the underdevelopment and recolonization of Haiti, see Justin Joseph Podur and Sasha Liley, *Haiti's New Dictatorship: The Coup, the Earthquake, and the UN Occupation* (To-

ronto: Between the Lines Press, 2012); Randall Robinson, *An Unbroken Agony: Haiti, from Revolution to the Kidnapping of a President* (New York: BasicCivitas Books, 2008); and Jean-Bertrand Aristide, *Eyes of the Heart: Seeking a Path for the Poor in the Age of Globalization* (Monroe, ME: Common Courage Press, 2002). The author was honored to meet and lunch with former Haitian president Jean-Bertrand Aristide following the author's lecture at the University of South Africa in Tshwane (Pretoria), South Africa/Azania in July 2005.

88. Jane Regan and Milo Milfort, "Four years After Haiti's Earthquake, Still Waiting for a Roof," Inter Press Service, January 20, 2014, at http://www.ipsnews.net/2014/01/four-years-haitis-earthquake-tents-homes/, accessed on May 6, 2014.

89. Bryant Harris, "Four Years Later, USAID Funds in Haiti Still Unaccounted For," *Inter Press Service*, January 10, 2014, at http://www.ipsnews.net/2014/01/four-years-later-usaid-funds-haiti-still-unaccounted/, accessed on May 6, 2014.

90. Alex Dupuy, "Class, Power, Sovereignty: Haiti before and after the Earthquake" in *Caribbean Sovereignty, Development and Democracy in An Age of Globalization*, edited by Linden Lewis, 23.

91. Bryant Harris, "Four Years Later, USAID Funds in Haiti Still Unaccounted For," *Inter Press Service*, January 10, 2014, at http://www.ipsnews.net/2014/01/four-years-later-usaid-funds-haiti-still-unaccounted/, accessed on May 6, 2014.

92. Dan Coughlin and Kim Ives, "Newly Released WikiLeaked Cables Reveal Washington Backed Famous Brand-Name Contractors in Fight Against Haiti's Minimum Wage Increase," *Haiti Liberté* 5, no. 45, May 25–30, 2011, at http://www.haiti-liberte.com/archives/volume4-47/Washington%20Backed%20Famous.asp, accessed on May 7, 2014.

93. Kim Ives, "Growing Protests in Haiti: Thousands Demonstrate to Demand the Departure of President Martelly and MINUSTAH," Global Research, April 18, 2014, at http://www.globalresearch.ca/growing-protests-in-haiti-thousands-demonstrate-to-demand-the-departure-of-president-martelly-and-minustah/5378296, accessed on May 7, 2014.

94. Ransford Palmer, *The Caribbean Economy in the Age of Globalization* (New York: Palgrave Macmillan, 2009), especially noted and elaborated upon in chapters 1 and 2.

95. Ransford Palmer, *The Caribbean Economy in the Age of Globalization*, 12.

96. *Latin America and the Caribbean in the World Economy: 2005 Trends* (Santiago: United

Nations Economic Commission for Latin America and the Caribbean, 2005), 134–135.

97. "Nicaragua: Dole settles pesticide case with 4,000 ex-employees" at http://ww4report.com/node/10272.

98. Elizabeth Thomas-Hope and Adonna Jadine-Comrie, "Caribbean Agriculture in the New Global Environment" in *No Island Is an Island: The Impact of Globalization on the Commonwealth Caribbean* edited by Gordon Baker (London: Chatham House, Royal Institute of International Affairs, 2007), 20–21.

99. Elizabeth Thomas-Hope and Adonna Jadine-Comrie, "Caribbean Agriculture in the New Global Environment" in *No Island Is an Island: The Impact of Globalization on the Commonwealth Caribbean*, 24.

100. The 2005 film documentary *Life and Debt*, directed by Stephanie Black, provides an accurate portrayal of such imperialist depictions of Jamaica.

101. See, for instance, Raffaleo Benetti's relatively simple but instructive text, *Survival of Weak Countries in the Face of Globalization: Puerto Rico and the Caribbean* (San Juan: Editorial De La Universidad De Puerto Rico, 2003), 87.

102. Aboushiravan Ehteshami, *Globalization and Geopolitics in the Middle East* (New York: Routledge, 2007), 190.

103. http://www.africaneconomicoutlook.org/en/countries/north-africa/libya/. See also Mary Lynn Cramer's article "Before U.S.–NATO invasion, Libya had the Highest Human Development Index, the Lowest Infant Mortality, the Highest Life Expectancy in Africa," *Countercurrents*, May 4, 2011, at http://www.countercurrents.org/cramer040511.htm.

104. "Libya: The Destruction of a Country: The Bombing of Civilian Targets, Testimony of Russian Doctors in Libya," at http://www.globalresearch.ca/libya-the-destruction-of-a-country-the-bombing-of-civilian-targets/23999, March 28, 2011.

105. Aboushiravan Ehteshami, *Globalization and Geopolitics in the Middle East*, 152.

106. *Business Report*, South Africa, August 20, 2012.

107. "Some truckers suspend strike action," Reuters, October 10, 2012, at http://www.iol.co.za/news/south-africa/some-truckers-suspend-strike-action-1.1399651#UHTlpEKSN_0.

108. "South Africa Platinum Strike 'Over,'" *BBC News-Business*, June 23, 2014, at http://www.bbc.com/news/business-27981977, accessed on June 23, 2014.

109. http://www.southafrica.info/business/economy/econrevenue-010410.htm.

110. Jesse Colombo, "A Guide to South Africa's Economic Bubble and Coming Crisis," *Forbes*, March 19, 2014, at http://www.forbes.com/sites/jessecolombo/2014/03/19/a-guide-to-south-africas-economic-bubble-and-coming-crisis/, accessed on May 22, 2014.

111. Jesse Colombo, "A Guide to South Africa's Economic Bubble and Coming Crisis," *Forbes*, March 19, 2014, at http://www.forbes.com/sites/jessecolombo/2014/03/19/a-guide-to-south-africas-economic-bubble-and-coming-crisis/, accessed on May 22, 2014.

112. The Workers and Socialist Party (WASP) statement "After elections" was communicated to the author via email on May 10, 2014. WASP was founded by the Democratic Socialist Movement and mineworkers in South Africa/Azania on December 18, 2012.

113. http://www.economywatch.com/world_economy/brazil/, July 2010.

114. Michael Klare, *Rising Powers, Shrinking Planet: The New Geopolitics of Energy* (New York: Henry Holt, 2008), 67.

115. Michael Klare, *Rising Powers, Shrinking Planet: The New Geopolitics of Energy*, 79.

116. Trading Economics: Global Economics Research, India GDP Growth Rate, April 3, 2010, http://www.tradingeconomics.com/Economics/GDP-Growth.aspx?Symbol=INR.

117. Michael Klare, *Rising Powers, Shrinking Planet: The New Geopolitics of Energy*, 89.

118. Naercio Menezes-Filho Ligia Vasconcellos, "Has Economic Growth Been Pro-Poor in Brazil? Why?" in http://globetrotter.berkeley.edu/macarthur/inequality/papers/MenezesProPoorEconomicGrowth.pdf, 2000, accessed on October 9, 2010.

119. *The Witness*, Pietermaritzburg, South Africa, October 12, 2010.

120. Naercio Menezes-Filho Ligia Vasconcellos, "Has Economic Growth Been Pro-Poor in Brazil? Why?," 7.

121. Kayako Kitamura and Tsuneo Tanaka, "Examining Asia's Tigers: Nine Economies Challenging Common Structural Problems: Spot Survey, No. 9," Ide-Jetro: Institute of Developing Economies: Japan External Trade Organization, Chiba, Japan, July 1997, at http://www.ide.go.jp/English/Publish/Download/Spot/09.html, accessed on May 7, 2014.

122. Mihir A. Rakshit, "Globalization of capital markets: Some analytical and policy issues" in *Globalization and Economic Development: Essays in Honor of J. George Waardenburg*, edited by Servaas Storm and C.W.M. Naastepad (Cheltenham: Edward Elgar, 2001), 157–158. The five Asian countries experiencing serious financial crises

were Thailand, Malaysia, Indonesia, the Philippines, and South Korea. Britain, Norway, Sweden, and Finland were subject to financial turmoil in the 1990s as the result of the instability of capital movements. Underscoring the point of financial contagion, Rakshit explains that the Russian financial crisis had a direct impact on the Brazilian economy on the other side of the globe, forcing the Brazil real to be floated against the dollar and other currencies.

123. Deepak Nayyar, "Globalization and Development in the Long Twentieth Century" in *Globalization Under Hegemony: The Changing World Economy*, edited by K.S. Jomo, 76.

124. Samir Amin, *Ending the Crisis of Capitalism or Ending Capitalism?* (Cape Town: Pambazuka Press; Dakar: CODESRIA; Bangalore: Books for Change, 2011), 29.

125. *Financial Times*, March 8, 2009.

126. Katy Burne, "Banks Revive Role in Complex Debt," *Wall Street Journal*, May 5, 2014, at http://online.wsj.com/news/articles/SB300014 24052702303948104579537903377231522?mg= reno64-wsj&url=http%3A%2F%2Fonline.wsj. com%2Farticle%2FSB30001424052702303039481 04579537903377231522.html, accessed on May 7, 2014.

127. David McNally, *Global Slump: The Economics and Politics of Crisis and Resistance* (Oakland: PM Press; Halifax, Nova Scotia: Fernwood; and Wales: Merlin Press, 2011), 13.

128. Dee-Ann Durbin, "Chrysler to pay back all but $1.3B of bailout," *USA Today*, June 3, 2011, at http://usatoday30.usatoday.com/money/autos/ 2011-06-03-chrysler-bailout-government_n.htm, accessed on May 8, 2014.

129. Jeff Cobb, "Did the GM and Chrysler Bailouts Do America a Huge Favor?," *HybridCars: Auto Alternatives for the 21st Century*, at http:// www.hybridcars.com/did-the-gm-and-chrysler-bailouts-do-america-a-huge-favor/, accessed on May 7, 2014. See also Jon Rosevear, "Why GM Still Owes Taxpayers," *The Motley Fool*, September 15, 2013, at http://www.fool.com/investing/ general/2013/09/15/why-gm-still-owes-taxpayers. aspx, accessed on May 7, 2014. For a view that articulates a defense of the U.S. government bailout of GM and Chrysler, see Jerri Hirsch, "GM, Chrysler federal bailouts were net economic gain, report argues," *Los Angeles Times*, December 9, 2013, at http://www.latimes.com/business/autos/la-fi-hy-gm-bailout-cost-20131209-story.html, accessed on May 8, 2014.

130. Allie Bidwell, "Obama sidesteps Congress to Expand Student Loan Repayment Program," *US News & World Report*, June 9, 2014, at http:// www.usnews.com/news/articles/2014/06/09/

obama-sidesteps-congress-to-expand-student-loan-repayment-program, accessed on June 9, 2014.

131. Allie Bidwell, "Obama sidesteps Congress to Expand Student Loan Repayment Program," *US News &World Report*, June 9, 2014, at http://www.usnews.com/news/articles/2014/ 06/09/obama-sidesteps-congress-to-expand-student-loan-repayment-program, accessed on June 9, 2014.

132. Erin Carlyle, "Study Finds 6.4 million U.S. Homeowners Still Have Underwater Mortgages," *Forbes*, December 17, 2013, at http://www. forbes.com/sites/erincarlyle/2013/12/17/6-4-million-still-have-underwater-mortgages-as-of-q3-2013-says-corelogic/, accessed on June 11, 2014.

133. Paul A. Eisenstein, "GM's Barra got email in 2011 about steering problems," CNBC, April 11, 2014, at http://www.cnbc.com/id/101574156, accessed on May 8, 2014. See also Laura Lee Baris's article "Guess How Much U.S. Taxpayers Lost on GM Bailout? Hint: More Than They Estimated," *People's Pundit Daily*, April 30, 2014, at http:// www.peoplespunditdaily.com/2014/04/30/ public-policy/guess-much-us-taxpayers-lost-gm-bailout-hint-estimated/, accessed on May 9, 2014.

134. Justin Gillis, "U.S. Climate Has Already Changed, Study Finds, Citing Heat and Floods," *New York Times*, May 6, 2014, at http://www.ny times.com/2014/05/07/science/earth/climate-change-report.html?emc=eta1&_r=0, accessed on May 7, 2014.

135. Jeff Faux, *The Servant Economy: Where America's Elite Is Sending the Middle Class* (Hoboken, NJ: John Wiley & Sons, 2012), 77.

136. Jeff Faux, *The Servant Economy: Where America's Elite Is Sending the Middle Class*, 78.

137. Heidi Shierholz, Jared Bernstein, and Lawrence Mishel, *The State of Working America, 2008/2009* (Washington, D.C.: Economic Policy Institute, 2008).

138. The author observed the financial panic in U.S. markets on CNN International news while in Kampala, Uganda, on May 7, 2010.

139. David McNally, *Global Slump: The Economics and Politics of Crisis and Resistance*, 4.

140. "Spain Recoils as Its Hungry Forage Trash Bins for a Next Meal," *New York Times*, September 24, 2012.

141. "Exclusive: Housing bubble brewing—prices are now unaffordable for middle earners, says Business Secretary Vince Cable," *Independent*, London, April 4, 2014, at http://www.independent. co.uk/news/uk/politics/exclusive-housing-bubble-brewing-as-prices-become-unaffordable-for-middle-earners-says-business-secretary-vince-cable-9236587.html?utm_source=indynewsletter

&utm_medium=email04042014, accessed on April 5, 2014.

142. *The Guardian*, London, October 7, 2011.

143. Joseph Schumpeter, *Capitalism, Socialism and Democracy* (New York: Harper, 1975), 82.

144. Richard Fry and Paul Taylor, "A Rise in Wealth for the Wealthy; Declines for the Lower 93%: An Uneven Recovery, 2009–2011," *Pew Research Social & Demographic Trends*, April 23, 2013 (Washington, D.C.: Pew Research Center) at http://www.pewsocialtrends.org/2013/04/23/a-rise-in-wealth-for-the-wealthydeclines-for-the-lower-93/, accessed on June 7, 2014.

145. Richard Fry and Paul Taylor, "A Rise in Wealth for the Wealthy; Declines for the Lower 93%: An Uneven Recovery, 2009–2011," *Pew Research Social & Demographic Trends*, April 23, 2013 (Washington, D.C.: Pew Research Center) at http://www.pewsocialtrends.org/2013/04/23/a-rise-in-wealth-for-the-wealthydeclines-for-the-lower-93/, accessed on June 7, 2014.

146. Estelle Sommeiller and Mark Price, "The Increasingly Unequal States of America: Income Inequality by State, 1917 to 2011," *Economic Policy Institute*, February 19, 2014, at http://www.epi.org/publication/unequal-states/, accessed on June 9, 2014.

147. Gary Strauss, Matt Krantz, and Barbara Hansen, "The $100 Million Club: CEOs Get Richer; Workers Left Behind," *USA Today*, April 4–6, 2014. The online version by Gary Strauss, Matt Krantz, and Barbara Hansen, "Millions by millions, CEO pay goes up," is at http://www.usatoday.com/story/money/business/2014/04/03/2013-ceo-pay/7200481/, accessed on June 10, 2014.

148. David McNally, *Global Slump: The Economics and Politics of Crisis and Resistance*, 96.

149. David McNally, *Global Slump: The Economics and Politics of Crisis and Resistance*, 98.

150. David McNally, *Global Slump: The Economics and Politics of Crisis and Resistance*, 99.

151. David McNally, *Global Slump: The Economics and Politics of Crisis and Resistance*, 124.

152. http://www.theguardian.com/world/2013/sep/29/us-government-shutdown-services-affected.

153. Damon Vickers, *The Day After the Dollar Crashes: A Survival Guide for the Rise of the New World Order* (New York: John Wiley & Sons, 2011), 58–59, 71.

154. Mihir A. Rakshit, "Globalization of capital markets: Some analytical and policy issues" in *Globalization and Economic Development: Essays in Honor of J. George Waardenburg*, 174.

155. The author was in South Africa/Azania during the 2010 World Cup.

156. Suzanne Craig and Ben Protess, "A Bigger Paycheck on Wall Street," *New York Times*, October 10, 2012.

157. John G. Neihardt, *Black Elk Speaks: Being the Life Story of a Holy Man of the Oglala Sioux* (Albany: Excelsior Editions, State University of New York Press, 2008), 172.

158. Deepak Nayyar, "Globalization and Development in the Long Twentieth Century" in *Globalization Under Hegemony: The Changing World Economy*, edited by K.S. Jomo, 80.

159. Jose Marin, "Globalization, Education, and Cultural Diversity" in *Educational Theories and Practices from the Majority*, edited by Pierre R. Dasen and Abdeljalil Akkari (Thousand Oaks, CA: Sage, 2008), 346.

160. See, for instance, F. A Hayek, *The Road to Serfdom* (Chicago: University of Chicago Press, 1994) and Jose Marin, "Globalization, Education, and Cultural Diversity" in *Educational Theories and Practices from the Majority*, edited by Pierre R. Dasen and Abdeljalil Akkari, 352.

161. See, for instance, *The Economist*, January 15, 2009.

162. *New York Times*, July 29, 2010.

163. Joseph Mensah, "Integrating Culture into Globalization and Development Theory" in *Globalization and the Human Factor*, edited by E. Osei Kwadwo Prempeh, Joseph Mensah and Senyo B-S. K. Adjibolosoo (Aldershot: Ashgate, 2004), 53.

164. *New York Times*, August 8, 2010.

165. Deepak Nayyar, "Globalization and Development in the Long Twentieth Century" in *Globalization Under Hegemony: The Changing World Economy*, edited by K.S. Jomo, 85.

166. Deepak Nayyar, "Globalization and Development in the Long Twentieth Century" in *Globalization Under Hegemony: The Changing World Economy*, edited by K.S. Jomo, 86–87.

167. http://www.theguardian.com/world/2011/apr/03/us-bank-mexico-drug-gangs/print.

168. http://www.alternet.org/economy/whats-wrong-wells-fargo?paging=off&current_page=1#bookmark.

169. Deepak Nayyar, "Globalization and Development in the Long Twentieth Century" in *Globalization Under Hegemony: The Changing World Economy*, edited by K.S. Jomo, 87.

170. Deepak Nayyar, "Globalization and Development in the Long Twentieth Century" in *Globalization Under Hegemony: The Changing World Economy*, edited by K.S. Jomo, 89–90.

171. *New York Times*, August 10, 2010, and *The Independent*, September 16, 2010.

172. "World Economic Situation and Prospects 2012," *United Nations Organization*, New York, 2011, at http://www.un.org/en/development/

desa/policy/wesp/wesp_current/2012wesp_prerel. pdf.

173. Jill Blackmore, "Globalization: A Useful Concept for Feminists Rethinking Theory and Strategies in Education" in *Globalization and Education: Critical Perspectives*, edited by Nicholas C. Burbules and Carlos Alberto Torres, 140.

174. "World Economic Situation and Prospects 2012," *United Nations Organization*, New York, 2011, at http://www.un.org/en/development/desa/policy/wesp/wesp_current/2012wesp_prerel. pdf.

175. D. K. Pithouse, *The West and the Third World: Trade, Colonialism, Dependence and Development*. (Oxford: Blackwell, 1999), 128.

176. D. K. Pithouse, *The West and the Third World: Trade, Colonialism, Dependence and Development*, 128–129.

Chapter 2

1. Deborah McGregor, "Traditional Ecological Knowledge and Sustainable Development Towards Coexistence" in *In the Way of Development: Indigenous Peoples, Life Projects and Globalization*, edited by Mario Blaser, Harvey Feit, and Glenn McRae (New York: Zed Books in association with the International Development Research Centre, Ottawa, Canada, 2004), 73. McGregor is from the Anishinaabeg nation. She cites the reference by J. Mander, *In the Absence of the Sacred: The Failure of Technology and the Survival of the Indian Nations* (San Francisco: Sierra Club Books, 1991).

2. Cited in *The Indigenous Voice: Visions and Realities*, Volume 1, edited by Roger Moody (New York: Zed Books and Copenhagen: International Work Group for Indigenous Affairs, 1988), 355–356.

3. Cited in Anne Marie Todd's article "Environmental Sovereignty Discourse of the Brazilian Amazon: National Politics and the Globalization of Indigenous Resistance," *Journal of Communication Inquiry* 27, No. 4 (October 2003), 364.

4. Konai Helu Thaman, "Decolonizing Pacific Studies: Indigenous Perspectives, Knowledge, and Wisdom in Higher Education," *The Contemporary Pacific*, No. 1 (Spring 2003), 1.

5. Vine Deloria, "Anthros, Indians, and Planetary Reality" in *Indians and Anthropologists*, edited by T. Biolsi and L. Zimmerman (Tucson: University of Arizona Press, 1997), 213–214.

6. Erica-Irene Daes, "Globalization, Intellectual Property and Indigenous Rights" in *Indigenous Peoples: Resource Management and Global Rights*, edited by Svein Jentoft, Henry Minde and Ragnar Nilsen (Delft, The Netherlands: Eburon, 2003), 68.

7. Ragnar Nilsen, "From Norwegianization to Coastal Sami Uprising" in *Indigenous Peoples: Resource Management and Global Rights*, 163.

8. Bjoen Hersoug, "Maori Fishing Rights: Coping with the Aboriginal Challenge" in *Indigenous Peoples: Resource Management and Global Rights*, 125.

9. Cited in Lotta Hughes, *The No-Nonsense Guide to Indigenous Peoples* (Oxford: New Internationalist Publications, in association with Verso, 2003), 38.

10. Robert Yazzie, "Indigenous Peoples and Postcolonial Colonialism" in *Reclaiming Indigenous Voice and Vision*, edited by Marie Battiste (Vancouver: University of British Columbia Press, 2000), 43.

11. Robert Yazzie, "Indigenous Peoples and Postcolonial Colonialism" in *Reclaiming Indigenous Voice and Vision*, edited by Marie Battiste, 43.

12. http://www.nciv.net/milllennium/definitions/some-indigenous-peoples-english. htm, cited in Ken Coates, *A Global History of Indigenous Peoples: Struggle and Survival* (New York: Palgrave Macmillan, 2004), 6.

13. Cited in Marie Battiste and James (Sa'ke'j) Youngblood Henderson, Preface, *Protecting Indigenous Knowledge and Heritage: A Global Challenge* (Saskatoon: Purich, 2002), 63.

14. United Nations Permanent Forum on Indigenous Issues, *Handbook for Participants* (New York: United Nations, 2007), 6, at http://esango.un.org/event/documents/handbook_participants_en.pdf, accessed on May 23, 2014.

15. http://bsnorrell.blogspot.com/2012/09/debra-white-plume-sacred-water.html This is an excellent blog written and maintained by Brenda Norrell, a former journalist with *Indian Country Today*, who provides updated coverage and footage of Indigenous peoples' struggles for cultural and land rights and in defense of Earth in North America especially. Brenda is based in Tucson, Arizona.

16. See, for instance, Etusuko Aoki, Kiyoko Kitahara, Kayano Shigeru, and Koichi Kaizawa, "Voices of Resilience and Resistance: The Ainu Peoples of Hokkaido, Japan" in *Indigenous Peoples' Wisdom and Power: Affirming Our Knowledge Through Narratives* by Julian Kunnie and Nomalungelo Goduka (Farnham: Ashgate, 2006).

17. Lenore A. Stiffarm and Phil Lane, Jr., "The Demography of Native North America: A Question of American Indian Survival" in *The State of Native America: Genocide, Colonization, and Re-*

sistance, edited by M. Annette Guerrero (Boston: South End Press, 1992), 37.

18. Cited by Jorge Calbucura in "Investing in Indigenous People's Territories, a New Form of Ethnocide? The Mapuche Case" in *Walking Towards Justice: Democratization in Rural Life* edited by Michael Bell, Fred Hendricks, with Azril Bacal (Oxford: Elsevier, 2003), 231–232.

19. "Indigenous Mayangna killed in Bosawas confrontation with colonizers," *Nicaraguan Bulletin*, Alliance for Global Justice, April 30, 2013.

20. Margarito Ruiz Hernandez and Aracely Burguete Cal y Mayor, "Indigenous Peoples Without Political Parties: The Dilemma of Indigenous Representation in Latin America" in *Challenging Politics: Indigenous Peoples' Experiences with Political Parties and Elections*, edited by Kathrin Wessendorf (Copenhagen: International Work Group for Indigenous Affairs, Document No. 104, 2001), 48.

21. Anne Marie Todd, "Environmental Sovereignty Discourse of the Brazilian Amazon: National Politics and the Globalization of Indigenous Resistance," *Journal of Communication Inquiry* 27, No. 4 (October 2003), 356.

22. http://www.independent.co.uk/news/science/special-report-catastrophic-drought-in-the-amazon-2203892.html.

23. http://amazonwatch.org/work/belo-monte-dam, June 17, 2011.

24. Ken Coates, *A Global History of Indigenous Peoples: Struggle and Survival*, 224.

25. Simon Romero, "Violence Hits Brazil Tribes in Scramble for Land, "*New York Times*, June 9, 2012, at http://www.nytimes.com/2012/06/10/world/americas/in-brazil-violence-hits-tribes-in-scramble-for-land.html?_r=0, accessed on June 10, 2012.

26. Cited in *Latin America: From Colonization to Globalization*, by Noam Chomsky in conversation with Heinz Dietrich (New York: Ocean Press, 1999), 80.

27. Andy Whitmore (ed.), *Pitfalls and Pipelines: Indigenous Peoples and Extractive Industries* (Baguio City, Philippines: Tebtebba Foundation; Copenhagen: International Work Group for Indigenous Affairs [IWGIA]; and London: Indigenous Peoples Links [PIPLinks], 2012), 18.

28. Makere Stewart-Harawira, *The New Imperial Order: Indigenous Responses to Globalization* (New York: Zed Press, and Wellington, Ao Te Roa/New Zealand: Huia, 2005), 18.

29. Danny Kennedy, "Development or Sustainability at Kutubu, Papua New Guinea?" in *Resources, Nations and Indigenous Peoples: Case Studies from Australasia, Melanesia and Southeast Asia*, edited by Richard Howitt with John Con-

nell and Philip Hirsch (Melbourne: Oxford University Press, 1996), 238.

30. This ancestral land violation of Ramu sacred sites and ancestral lands by Ramu NiCo from China has been graphically captured in the 2013 documentary series *Standing on Sacred Ground: Profit and Loss*, produced by Christopher McLeod and the Earth Island Institute in cooperation with Bullfrog Films. For more information see www.bullfrogfilms.com.

31. "Overview of Impacts of Extractive Industries on Indigenous Peoples" in *Pitfalls and Pipelines: Indigenous Peoples and Extractive Industries*, edited by Andy Whitmore (Baguio City, Philippines: Tebtebba Foundation; Copenhagen: International Work Group for Indigenous Affairs [IWGIA]; and London: Indigenous Peoples Links [PIPLinks], 2012), 19.

32. Dev Nathan and Govind Kelkar, Introduction, *Globalization and Indigenous Peoples in Asia: Changing the Local-Global Interface*, edited by Dev Nathan, Govind Kelkar, and Pierre Walter (New Delhi: Sage, 2004), 29.

33. Pamela Martin, *The Globalization of Contentious Politics: The Amazonian Indigenous Rights Movement* (New York: Routledge, 2003), 103–104.

34. Darrell Addison Posey, "Ethnobiology and Ethnoecology in the Context of National Laws and International Agreements affecting Indigenous and Local Knowledge, Traditional Resources and Intellectual Property Rights" in *Indigenous Environmental Knowledge and Its Transformations: Critical Anthropological Perspectives*, edited by Roy Allen, Peter Parkes, and Alan Bicker (New York: Routledge, 2000), 35.

35. The UN Convention on Biological Diversity was proposed at the UN Conference on Environment and Development in Rio de Janeiro in 1992 and was ratified by 168 nations by June 4, 1993. It became an official UN protocol on December 29, 1993. The convention is at http://www.cbd.int/convention/text/, accessed on May 30, 2014.

36. Darrell Addison Posey, "Ethnobiology and Ethnoecology in the Context of National Laws and International Agreements affecting Indigenous and Local Knowledge, Traditional Resources and Intellectual Property Rights" in *Indigenous Environmental Knowledge and Its Transformations: Critical Anthropological Perspectives*, 38–39.

37. The author participated in the 11th UN Permanent Forum on Indigenous Issues (UNPFII) where Debra Harry, executive director of the Indigenous Peoples' Council on Biocolonialism, read a statement representing 21 Indigenous organizations that denounced the predatory prac-

tices of Permanent Forum on the World Intellectual Property Organization (WIPO) for proclaiming the protection of Indigenous cultural heritage and rights on the one hand, while excluding Indigenous peoples from fundamental decisions made at international forums on such rights, on the other. A joint statement written by Chi Endeh Community Alliance members, Michael Paul Hill and myself, was read by Michael Hill at the same UNPFII forum and simultaneously criticized WIPO for vacillating on questions of "tangible" and "intangible" rights that WIPO representatives at the UN conference described. Essentially, WIPO obscures radical disparities of power wielded by state governments and Indigenous peoples when it comes to protection of Indigenous cultural and property rights and claims to protect Indigenous peoples' rights while working closely in the service of state governments.

38. Makere Stewart-Harawira, *The New Imperial Order: Indigenous Responses to Globalization*, 217. Makere Stewart Harawira cites the following as sources in the discussion of the HUGO project: Sandra Awang, "The Human Genome Diversity Project" in *Indigenous Knowledges in Global Contexts: Multiple Readings of Our World* (Toronto: University of Toronto Press, 2000); Darrell A. Posey and Graham Dutfield, "Human genes for whose humanity" in *Beyond Intellectual Property: Towards Traditional Resource Rights for Indigenous Peoples and Local Communities* (Ottawa: International Development Resource Center, 1996); cited in Meade, Aroha Te Pereake, "Human genetic research and *whakapapa*" in *Mai I Rangiatea: Maori Wellbeing and Development*, edited by Pania Te Whaiti, Marie McCarthy, and Arohia Durie (Auckland: Auckland University Press and Bridget Williams Books, 1997), 132. The work of Turtle Island scholar Mariana Annette Jaimes-Guerrero is very relevant in this regard. See her unpublished paper, "Indigenous Dialectics: Towards an Ecocultural Meta-Science for Biodiversity," which was presented at the Science and Other Knowledge Traditions at James Cook University, Cairns, North Queensland, Australia, August 23–27, 1996.

39. See for instance, Harriet A. Washington, *Medical Apartheid: The Dark History of Medical Experimentation on Black Americans from Colonial Times to the Present* (New York: Harlem Moon, Broadway Books, 2006).

40. Curt Wagner and Kris Karnopp (eds.), "6 sentenced to death for AIDS experiments on children," *Chicago Tribune*, News section, May 7, 2004, at http://articles.chicagotribune.com/2004-05-07/news/0405080129_1_infecting-aids-virus-cia-and-israeli-intelligence, accessed on May 30, 2014.

41. Leo Lucassen, "A Brave New World: The Left, Social Engineering, and Eugenics in Twentieth-Century Europe," *IRSH* 55 (2010), pp. 265–296, doi:10.1017/S0020859010000209, International Instituut voor Sociale Geschiedenis, 2010, 272–277. The point about Myrdal is on page 274 of the article. Gunnar Myrdal, a Nobel Economics Laureate and the well-known author of *An American Dilemma: The Negro Problem and Modern Democracy* (New Brunswick: Transaction, 1995), whose book was highlighted in the movement for civil rights and social justice in the 1960s, in actuality championed eugenic and racist and classist policies that were geared toward "protection" of the Swedish culture from "adulteration" by those from outside the norm of what he viewed as "Swedish culture." Lucassen's article is important in understanding the contradictions within both liberal and radical theoretical circles in many parts of Western Europe that ultimately favored Social Darwinist practices in agreement with Sir Francis Galton, a half-cousin of Charles Darwin who coined the term "eugenics" in 1883. Karl Pearson, the first "Galton Professor of Eugenics" and a self-described socialist, advocated for the elimination of the Indigenous peoples in Australia and North America (267–268) of Lucassen's article.

42. See, for instance, E. Wagner Stearn and Allen E. Stearn, *The Effect of Smallpox on the Destiny of the Amerindian* (Boston: Bruce Humphries, 1945); Elizabeth A. Fenn, *Pox Americana: The Great Smallpox Epidemic of 1775–82* (New York: Hill and Wang, 2001); and the work of historian Francis Parkman, *The Conspiracy of Pontiac and the Indian War After the Conquest of Canada* (Boston: Little, Brown, 1886), which details the correspondence between Colonel Bouquet to General Amherst and vice-versa on July 13 and 16, 1763, affirming the need to distribute blankets with smallpox to "innoculate" the Indians and use every method to "extirpate this execrable race."

43. Helen E. Purkitt and Stephen F. Burgess, *South Africa's Weapons of Mass Destruction* (Bloomington: Indiana University Press, 2005), 90.

44. The shocking disclosure of the U.S. involvement in gonorrhea and syphilis experiments on Guatemalans was reported by Robert Bazzell on MSNBC, "US Apologizes for Guatemala Experiments: Government researchers infected patients with syphilis, gonorrhea without their consent in 1940s," October 1, 2010, at http://www.nbcnews.com/id/39456324/ns/health-sexual_health/t/us-apologizes-guatemala-std-experiments/#.U4kLFhYVvRo, accessed on October 2, 2010.

45. The website http://www.naturalnews.com/
029924_medical_experiments_Guatemala.
html notes that "Guatemalan STD medical experiments were just one crime in a long history of
medical-government collusion to use human beings as guinea pigs," dating back to 1845 when enslaved African women were used in medical experiments and through the 1990s when the U.S.
military used Gulf War soldiers for similar purposes. The U.S. government collaborated with
pharmaceutical corporations like Merck to oversee a biological warfare program in 1942 and used
military personnel as medical guinea pigs at the
Nevada test site that resulted in thousands of citizens around the area contracting thyroid cancer.
See also Winona LaDuke's work, *All Our Relations: Native Struggles for Land and Life* (Boston:
South End Press, 1999) for an illumination of the
effects of mining and toxic waste on the Chey-
enne and Mohawk nation for example. Harriet A.
Washington's book, *Medical Apartheid: The Dark
History of Medical Experimentation on Black
Americans from Colonial Times to the Present*, is
essential further reading on this subject.

46. Cited by Dawn Martin-Hill, "Resistance,
and Perseverance of the Lubicon Cree Women"
in *The Way of Development: Indigenous Peoples,
Life Projects and Globalization*, edited by Mario
Blaser, Harvey A Feit, and Glenn McRae (New
York: Zed Books, 2004), 318–319.

47. This point is made by Malidoma Somé in
his book *Of Water and the Spirit: Ritual, Magic,
and Initiation in the Life of an African Shaman*
(New York: Arkana, Penguin, 1994), 9–10.

48. For a more detailed treatment of the unrealistic character of the Conventions on Biological Diversity and Intellectual Property Rights,
see Darrell Addison Posey's article "Ethnobiology
and Ethnoecology in the Context of National
Laws and International Agreements affecting
Indigenous and Local Knowledge, Traditional
Resources and Intellectual Property Rights" in *Indigenous Environmental Knowledge and Its Transformations: Critical Anthropological Perspectives*,
40.

49. Darrell Addison Posey, "Ethnobiology and
Ethnoecology in the Context of National Laws
and International Agreements affecting Indigenous and Local Knowledge, Traditional Resources and Intellectual Property Rights" in *Indigenous Environmental Knowledge and Its
Transformations: Critical Anthropological Perspectives*, 41.

50. Erica-Irene Daes, "Globalization, Intellectual Property and Indigenous Peoples" in *Indigenous Peoples: Resource Management and Global
Rights*, edited by Svein Jentoft, Henry Minde and

Ragnar Nilsen (Delft, The Netherlands: Eburon
Academic, 2003), 69.

51. Erica-Irene Daes, "Globalization, Intellectual Property and Indigenous Peoples" in *Indigenous Peoples: Resource Management and Global
Rights*, 67.

52. Dev Nathan and Govind Kelkar, Introduction, *Globalization and Indigenous Peoples in Asia:
Changing the Local-Global Interface*, 15.

53. Jorge Calbucura, "Investing in Indigenous
People's Territories, a New Form of Ethnocide?
The Mapuche Case" in *Walking Towards Justice:
Democratization in Rural Life*, 240.

54. Jorge Calbucura, "Investing in Indigenous
People's Territories, a New Form of Ethnocide?
The Mapuche Case" in *Walking Towards Justice:
Democratization in Rural Life*, 239.

55. The pressure on Indigenous peoples' pas-
toralists rights by the forces of globalization and
the responses of local NGOs is described for instance in Greg Cameron's anthropological article
"The globalization of indigenous rights in Tanzanian pastoralist NGOs" in *Development and Local
Knowledge: New Approaches to Issues in Natural
Resources Management, Conservation and Agriculture*, edited by Alan Bicker, Paul Sillitoe, and Johan
Pottier (New York: Routledge, 2004), 135–136.

56. Alison Moodie, "AFRICA: Universities
must halt 'land grab investments,'" *University
World News: The Global Window on Higher Education* 177 (June 26, 2011), http://www.university
worldnews.com/article.php?story=20110625
122929338, accessed on May 30, 2014. See also
the Global Policy Forum, "Land Ownership and
Hunger," at http://www.globalpolicy.org/social-
and-economic-policy/world-hunger/land-
ownership-and-hunger.html, accessed on May 30,
2014.

57. The author attended a panel organized at
the 13th UN Permanent Forum on Indigenous Issues (UNPFII) in New York in May 2014 where
Judy Kipkenda from the Ogiek Peoples Development Program presented a paper on the struggles
of the Ogiek people for autonomy and ancestral
land protection.

58. Andy Whitmore (ed.), *Pitfalls and Pipelines: Indigenous Peoples and Extractive Industries*,
20.

59. Oronto Douglas and Ike Okonta, "Ogoni
People of Nigeria versus Big Oil" in *Paradigm
Wars: Indigenous Peoples Resistance to Globaliza-
tion*, edited by Jerry Mander and Victoria Tauli-
Corpuz (San Francisco: Sierra Club Books,
2006), 153.

60. Dev Nathan and Govind Kelkar, Introduction, *Globalization and Indigenous Peoples in Asia:
Changing the Local-Global Interface*, 21–22.

61. See, for instance, Alexandra Xanthaki's article "Land Rights of Indigenous Peoples in south-east Asia" in *Melbourne Journal of International Law* 4 (2003), 12–13.

62. The author visited the Dayak community of Melikin under the leadership of Indigenous leaders Niloh Ason and Igat Biju in Kuching and documented the resistance of Dayak protesters in August 2012.

63. Andy Whitmore (ed.), *Pitfalls and Pipelines: Indigenous Peoples and Extractive Industries*, 22–23.

64. The author was able to personally document the violations of the rights of Indigenous peoples in Benguet in the Philippines during a research visit there in August 2013, hosted by Ellen Dictaan-Bang-Oa and Mila Singson who represent Tebtebba and the Cordillera Peoples Alliance respectively, both organizations involved in struggles for Indigenous self-determination and cultural and land rights.

65. Andy Whitmore (ed.), *Pitfalls and Pipelines: Indigenous Peoples and Extractive Industries*, 20.

66. See the details of the U.S. Supreme Court ruling, *United States v Dann–470 U.S. 39 (1985)*, which was argued on November 5, 1984, and decided on February 20, 1985, at http://supreme.justia.com/cases/federal/us/470/39/, accessed on June 5, 2014.

67. The details about this case of Indigenous dispossession and perfidy by the U.S. government is described in "Western Shoshone Land and Sovereignty" at http://www.umass.edu/legal/derrico/shoshone/, accessed on May 30, 2014. Shoshone elders Mary and Carrie Dann's struggles to courageously protect their ancestral lands in defiance of invasion by the U.S. Bureau of Land Management is captured in the powerful 2006 film documentary *Our Land, Our Life*, at https://www.youtube.com/watch?v=JJ2N9-n-ka0, accessed on May 30, 2014.

68. See, for instance, Robert D. Bullard, *Dumping in Dixie: Race, Class, and Environmental Quality, Third Edition* (Boulder: Westview Press, 2000), for an exposé of environmental racism that afflicts African Americans in southern states in the U.S. particularly.

69. Andrea Smith, "Ecofeminism through an Anticolonial Framework" in *Ecofeminism: Women, Culture, Nature*, edited by Karen J. Warren with editorial assistance from Nisvan Erkal (Bloomington: Indiana University Press, 1997), 23. The Four Corners region has been dubbed a "National Sacrifice" area because of the genocidal cancerous effects on Indigenous miners and residents living in the area. See Christopher McLeod, Tandy

Hayes, and Glen Switkes, "The Four Corners: A National Sacrifice Guide," reprinted from *The Workbook*, April/June 1985, at http://www.bullfrogfilms.com/guides/4cguideSM.pdf, accessed on May 30, 2014.

70. "Proposed Mt. Taylor uranium mine faces new obstacle," *New Mexico Independent*, May 10, 2010, at http://newmexicoindependent.com/53589/proposed-mt-taylor-uranium-mine-faces-new-obstacle, accessed on May 10, 2010. Cited in Andy Whitmore (ed.), *Pitfalls and Pipelines: Indigenous Peoples and Extractive Industries*, 18.

71. Andrea Smith, "Ecofeminism through an Anticolonial Framework" in *Ecofeminism: Women, Culture, Nature*, 24.

72. National Public Radio report, KQEZ radio, Chicago, September 25, 2006.

73. http://nativeunity.blogspot.com/2010/05/save-san-francisco-peaks-from.html.

74. Marie Battiste and James (Sa'ke'j) Youngblood Henderson, Preface, *Protecting Indigenous Knowledge and Heritage: A Global Challenge*, 110. For the Ninth Circuit Court ruling against San Francisco Peaks and Indian Nations, see Brenda Norell's blog, *Censored News*, August 8, 2008, at http://censored-news.blogspot.com/2008/08/ninth-circuit-court-ruling-against-san.html, accessed on May 30, 2014.

75. This was conveyed by Michael Paul Hill, a relative and Chi Endeh (Chiricahua Apache) spiritual teacher and Indigenous rights activist from the San Carlos community, Arizona, in October 2005.

76. See the U.S. Department of Agriculture (USDA) Forest Service Southwestern Region report, *Environmental Assessment for Integrated Treatment of Noxious or Invasive Plants* (Phoenix: Tonto National Forest and Washington, D.C.: USDA Forest Service, August 2012).

77. This was conveyed by Michael Hill during a conversation with the author on October 7, 2012.

78. See the advertisement in this chapter for the Agent Orange meeting in San Carlos on May 31, 2014.

79. Andrew Pollack, "Coalition Drops Opposition to a Dow Engineered Crop," *New York Times*, September 11, 2012, at http://www.nytimes.com/2012/09/12/business/energy-environment/coalition-drops-opposition-to-dows-genetically-engineered-crops.html, accessed on September 15, 2012.

80. U.S. Department of Veterans Affairs, "Public Health: Facts About Herbicides" at http://www.publichealth.va.gov/exposures/agentorange/basics.asp, accessed on June 5, 2014.

81. Charles M. Benbrook, "Impacts of genet-

ically engineered crops on pesticide use in the U.S.—the first sixteen years," *Environmental Sciences Europe 2012*, 24, no. 24 (September 28, 2012). The abstract of the paper is available at http://www.enveurope.com/content/24/1/24/abstract.

82. "You were wondering: How many people are diagnosed with cancer each year?," at http://archive.delawareonline.com/article/20130924/HEALTH/309240001/You-Were-Wondering-How-many-people-diagnosed-cancer-each-year-, September 23, 2013, accessed on May 30, 2014.

83. World Cancer Day, "Cancer Prevention and Control," Centers for Disease Control and Prevention, February 3, 2014, at http://www.cdc.gov/cancer/dcpc/resources/features/worldcancerday/, accessed on May 30, 2014.

84. This view was conveyed to the author on May 19, 2014.

85. See the letter from Philip W. Grone, Principal Assistant Deputy Under Secretary of Defense, to Congressman Lane Evans, ranking member of the Committee on Veterans Affairs, September 23, 2003, at http://veteransinfo.tripod.com/9-23-03dod1.pdf, a site on Veterans Information, accessed on June 22, 2014.

86. Citizens Commission on Human Rights International: The Mental Health Watchdog, "Behind the Epidemic of Military Suicides," 2014, at http://www.cchrint.org/issues/the-hidden-enemy/, accessed on June 19, 2014.

87. Aaron Cantu, "Apartheid Wall in Arizona: Israeli Company Contracted to Build U.S.–Mexico Border Fence," Alternet, March 7, 2014, at http://www.alternet.org/civil-liberties/apartheid-wall-arizona-israeli-company-contracted-build-us-mexico-border-fence, accessed on May 30, 2014. The sombering fact that TIAA-CREF (Teachers Insurance and Annuity—College Retirement Equities Fund), the large teachers retirement fund in the U.S., has over $1.69 million invested in Elbit Systems underscores how the concatenation of globalized capitalism draws unaware middle-class U.S. citizens inevitably into economic structures of oppression through such avenues as retirement fund investments. For more information and ways to request divestment of one's retirement's funds in Elbit Systems, see the site, http://www.grassrootsonline.org/sites/default/files/fact_sheet-elbit-tiaa-cref-web.pdf, accessed on May 30, 2014.

88. Aaron Cantu, "Apartheid Wall in Arizona: Israeli Company Contracted to Build U.S.–Mexico Border Fence," Alternet, March 7, 2014, at http://www.alternet.org/civil-liberties/apartheid-wall-arizona-israeli-company-contracted-build-us-mexico-border-fence, accessed on May 30, 2014.

89. Sonia Smallacombe, "Fabrication and Aboriginal Cultural Heritage" in *Political Theory and the Rights of Indigenous People*, edited by Duncan Ivison, Paul Patton, and Will Sanders (Cambridge: Cambridge University Press, 2000), 158.

90. Sonia Smallacombe, "Fabrication and Aboriginal Cultural Heritage" in *Political Theory and the Rights of Indigenous People*, 159.

91. N. S. Hill, Jr. (ed.), *Words of Power: Voices from Indian America* (Golden, CO: Fulcrum, 1994), 36. Cited in Marie Battiste and James (Sa'ke'j) Youngblood Henderson, Preface, *Protecting Indigenous Knowledge and Heritage: A Global Challenge*, 105.

92. Makere Stewart-Harawira, *The New Imperial Order: Indigenous Responses to Globalization*, 136.

93. Ward Churchill's *Struggle for the Land: Native North American Resistance to Genocide, Ecocide, and Colonization* (San Francisco: City Lights Press, 2002), is an excellent book that delineates the nature of "internal colonialism" of Indigenous peoples in the Americas, especially North America.

94. Marie Battiste and James (Sa'ke'j) Youngblood Henderson, Preface, *Protecting Indigenous Knowledge and Heritage: A Global Challenge*, 6–7.

95. George Breitman (ed.), *Malcolm X Speaks* (New York: Grove Press, 1965), 35.

96. Dev Nathan and Govind Kelkar, Introduction, *Globalization and Indigenous Peoples in Asia: Changing the Local-Global Interface*, 17. See also the brief summary, "Indigenous peoples of Vietnam" published by the International Working Group for Indigenous Affairs (IWGIA) (Denmark: IWGIA, 2012), at http://www.iwgia.org/regions/asia/vietnam, accessed on June 6, 2014.

97. The author had the opportunity to hear about family economic and educational hardship and rural poverty from some Indigenous Meio women outside Kunming, in southern China, in June 2013. The site http://www.indigenouspeople.net/ChineseLit/chinaindig.htm,l compiled by Glenn Welker from 2009, provides a description of many of China's Indigenous communities, accessed on June 6, 2014.

98. Dev Nathan and Govind Kelkar, Introduction, *Globalization and Indigenous Peoples in Asia: Changing the Local-Global Interface*, 17.

99. Beth Walker (ed.), *State of the Minorities and Indigenous Peoples 2013: Events of 2012: Focus on Health* (London: Minority Rights Group International, 2013), 162.

100. Lester Brown, "China's Water Tables Are Dropping Fast," *Grist: A Beacon in the Smog*, Oc-

tober 26, 2001, at http://grist.org/article/table/, accessed on June 6, 2014.

101. Paul Close and David Askew, *Asian Pacific and Human Rights: A Global Political Economy Perspective* (Aldershot: Ashgate, 2004), 177.

102. For a first-hand account of Ainu land and cultural dispossession, see Etsuko Aoki, Kiyoko Kitahara, Kayano Shigeru, and Koichi Kaizawa, "Voices of Resilience and Resistance: The Ainu People of Hokkaido, Japan" in *Indigenous Peoples' Wisdom and Power: Affirming Our Legacy Through Narratives*, edited by Julian Kunnie and Nomalungelo Goduka (Burlington, VT: Ashgate, 2006).

103. Etsuko Aoki, Kiyoko Kitahara, Kayano Shigeru, and Koichi Kaizawa, "Voices of Resilience and Resistance: The Ainu People of Hokkaido, Japan" in *Indigenous Peoples' Wisdom and Power: Affirming Our Legacy Through Narratives*, edited by Julian Kunnie and Nomalungelo Goduka, 171–172.

104. Paul Close and David Askew, *Asian Pacific and Human Rights: A Global Political Economy Perspective*, 175–176.

105. *Conservation Refugees—Expelled from Paradise*, a video by Steffen Keulig, Just Conservation, at http://www.justconservation.org/conservation-refugees-expelled-from-paradise.

106. "AfricaNews.com: Kenya—Minority Group Decries Forceful Eviction," January 17, 2012, at http://firstpeoples.org/wp/tag/eviction/.

107. *Conservation Refugees—Expelled from Paradise*, a video by Steffen Keulig, Just Conservation, at http://www.justconservation.org/conservation-refugees-expelled-from-paradise.

108. Michael Adams, "Negotiating Nature: Collaboration and Conflict Between Aboriginal and Conservation Interests in New South Wales, Australia," University of Wollongong Online, 2004, 6, at http://ro.uow.edu.au/cgi/viewcontent.cgi?article=1427&context=scipapers&sei-.

109. Alison Johnston, *Is the Sacred for Sale? Tourism and Indigenous Peoples* (London: Earthscan, 2006), 128–130.

110. Alison Johnston, *Is the Sacred for Sale? Tourism and Indigenous Peoples*, 127.

111. Staff reporter, "Maasai Land Protest Ends in Violence," *Mail & Guardian*, August 24, 2004, at http://mg.co.za/article/2004-08-24-maasai-land-protest-ends-in-violence, accessed on May 30, 2014.

112. Alison Johnston, *Is the Sacred for Sale? Tourism and Indigenous Peoples*, 39–40.

113. See the website www.nyakweri.arizona.edu for more information on the Nyakweri Cultural Restoration and Ecological Preservation Project.

114. *Sawubona*, South African Airways in-flight magazine, May 2010.

115. Alison Johnston, *Is the Sacred for Sale? Tourism and Indigenous Peoples*, 125.

116. Alison Johnston, *Is the Sacred for Sale? Tourism and Indigenous Peoples*, 6.

117. Mark Dowie, *Conservation Refugees: The Hundred-Year Conflict Between Global Conservation and Native Peoples* (Cambridge: MIT Press, 2009), 171.

118. Alison Johnston, *Is the Sacred for Sale? Tourism and Indigenous Peoples*, 173.

119. *Financial Times*, September 9, 2006.

120. Felipe S. Molina, "Wa huya Ania Ama Vutti To'Oriwa—The Wilderness World is Respected Greatly: Truth from the Yoeme Communities of the Sonoran Desert" in *On Biocultural Diversity: Linking Language, Knowledge, and the Environment*, edited by Luisa Maffi (Washington, D.C.: Smithsonian Institution Press, 2001), 361.

121. This question was posed to me following a lecture on the Colonization of African Education delivered at the University of South Africa in Tshwane, South Africa, in July 2005. Neville Alexander, the late language academic and political activist, made a similar point at the Towards a National Dialogue: A State of the Nation Truth Conference held in iThekwini on September 24 and 25, 2010. His article, "After Apartheid: The Language Question" at www.yale.edu/macmillan/apartheid/alexanderp2.pdf, is a relevant reading in this regard.

122. Tsitsi Damgerembga, *Nervous Condition* (New York: Seal Press, 2001).

123. Herman M. Batibo, "The Endangered Languages of Africa: A Case Study from Botswana" in *On Biocultural Diversity: Linking Language, Knowledge, and the Environment*, edited by Luisa Maffi (Washington, D.C.: Smithsonian Institution Press), 311–313.

124. Herman M. Batibo, "The Endangered Languages of Africa: A Case Study from Botswana" in *On Biocultural Diversity: Linking Language, Knowledge, and the Environment*, 313.

125. Rachel Carson's book is *Silent Spring* (New York: Houghton Mifflin, 1962). The article by Margaret Atwood, "Rachel Carson's Silent Spring, 50 Years On," *The Guardian*, London, December 7, 2012, is available at http://www.theguardian.com/books/2012/dec/07/why-rachel-carson-is-a-saint, accessed on June 1, 2014.

126. Kirkpatrick Sale, *The Conquest of Paradise: Christopher Columbus and the Columbian Legacy*, 87.

127. Communicated by Philip Smith, A CREDO activist and beekeeper in Eugene, Oregon, and a member of Oregon Sustainable Bee-

keepers via email to the author entitled "Help me protect bees from neonicotinoids," December 9, 2013. "CREDO Action" is a grass-roots environmental and social justice activist and lobbying group and a publication of Working Assets at http://credoaction.com, accessed on June 1, 2014.

128. Email communication to the author from Ricken Patel, avaaz.org, "Before the bees are gone," March 21, 2013.

129. Email communication to the author entitled, "USA: Save the bees," from Iain Keith, avaaz.org, on July 7, 2013.

130. Karen Foster, "37 Million Dead Bees Found in Ontario," at http://www.undergroundhealth.com/37-million-bees-found-dead-in-ontario/, July 13, 2013, accessed on July 21, 2013.

131. Locals Supporting Locals, "Bayer Kills Bees! Neo-nicotinoid pesticides threaten honeybees and other insects worldwide," at http://localssupportinglocals.ca/news/bayer-kills-bees-neo-nicotinoid-pesticides-threaten-honeybees-and-other-insects-worldwide?page=4, accessed on June 1, 2014.

132. Marla Spivak, a bees scholar, provides an instructional presentation on bees, pollination, and the food supply, "Why bees are disappearing," at http://www.ted.com/talks/marla_spivak_why_bees_are_disappearing?source=googleplus#t-816678, June 2013, accessed on June 1, 2014.

133. Karen Foster, "37 Million Dead Bees Found in Ontario," at http://www.undergroundhealth.com/37-million-bees-found-dead-in-ontario/, July 13, 2013, accessed on July 21, 2013.

134. Andrew Kimbrell, "Meet the New Monsanto: Dow Chemical ... and Their New 'Agent Orange' Crops," Huffington Post, February 18, 2014, at http://www.huffingtonpost.com/andrew-kimbrell/dow-chemical-agent-orange-crops_b_4810311.html, accessed on June 1, 2014.

135. Andrew Kimbrell, "Meet the New Monsanto: Dow Chemical ... and Their New 'Agent Orange' Crops," Huffington Post, February 18, 2014, at http://www.huffingtonpost.com/andrew-kimbrell/dow-chemical-agent-orange-crops_b_4810311.html, accessed on June 1, 2014.

136. Eric Post and Jedediah Brodie, "Extinction Risk at High Latitudes" in Saving a Million Species: Extinction Risk from Climate Change, edited by Lee Hannah (Washington, D.C.: Island Press, 2012), 123–124.

137. Ove Hoegh-Guldberg, "Coral Reefs, Climate Change, and Mass Extinction" in Saving a Million Species: Extinction Risk from Climate Change, edited by Lee Hannah, 272–273.

138. National Oceanic and Atmospherica Administration, National Ocean Service, "What Is Coral Bleaching?" at http://oceanservice.noaa.

gov/facts/coral_bleach.html, accessed on June 1, 2014. This brief summary attempts to downplay the effects of global warming on coral reef bleaching probably due to U.S. governmental political dynamics that are reluctant to recognize and address fundamental causes of global warming: toxic greenhouse gases from auto emissions and industrialism.

139. Microdocs: short attention span science video, "Coral Bleaching," April 11, 2012, at http://www.stanford.edu/group/microdocs/coralbleaching.html, accessed on June 1, 2014.

140. Julia Whitty, "Gone: Mass Extinction and the Hazards of Earth's Vanishing Biodiversity" in Mother Jones, May/June 2007, at http://www.motherjones.com/environment/2007/05/gone, accessed on June 1, 2014. For the detailed list of extinct, near extinct, and seriously threatened species, see the IUCN website at www.iucn.org.

141. "New study shows over one fifth of the world's plants are under threat of extinction," The IUCN Red List of Threatened Species, September 29, 2010, at http://www.iucnredlist.org/news/srli-plants-press-release, accessed on June 25, 2014.

142. E. O. Wilson's comments about the incredible virtual countless breadth of biodiversity, "My Wish: Build the Encyclopedia of Life," is found at http://www.ted.com/talks/e_o_wilson_on_saving_life_on_earth, March 2007, accessed on May 1, 2014. For his prediction of species erasure by 2100, see Julia Whitty, "Gone: Mass Extinction and the Hazards of Earth's Vanishing Biodiversity" in Mother Jones, May/June 2007, at http://www.motherjones.com/environment/2007/05/gone, accessed on June 1, 2014.

143. The Independent, London, October 4, 2010.

144. http://www.iol.co.za/news/africa/lions-could-be-extinct-in-20-years-1.683161, October 3, 2010, accessed on October 4, 2010.

145. http://articles.cnn.com/2011–11–10/africa/world_africa_rhino-extinct-species-report_1_white-rhino-black-rhino-extinction?_s=PM:AFRICA, accessed on December 1, 2011.

146. Franz J. Broswimmer, Ecocide: A Short History of the Mass Extinction of Species. (Sterling, VA: Pluto Press, 2002).

147. Rosemary E. Ommer, "Nature and Community in the Global Market" in The Twenty-First Century Confronts Its Gods: Globalization, Technology, and War, edited by David J. Hawkin (Albany: State University of New York Press, 2004), 69.

148. See Lauren Gelfano's article, "Toxic Waste Spill in Ivory Coast Exposes 'Dark Underbelly' of Globalization," World Politics Review, 28 March 2007, at http://www.worldpoliticsreview.com/

articles/665/toxic-waste-spill-in-ivory-coast-exposes-dark-underbelly-of-globalization and "Toxic Shame: Thousands injured in African city," *The Independent*, September 17, 2009.

149. Olurominiyi Ibitayo, "Transboundary Dumping of Hazardous Waste," August 26, 2008, at http://www.eoearth.org.article/Transboundary_dumping_of_hazardous_waste, accessed September 9, 2009.

150. *Financial Times*, October 6, 2006. For the coverage on toxic dispersants in the Gulf of Mexico, including one that is banned in Britain, see the article "BP dispersants 'causing sickness'" at http://english.aljazeera.net/indepth/features/2010/10/20101027132136220370.html, accessed on October 29, 2010.

151. Fidel Castro, *Capitalism in Crisis: Globalization and World Politics Today* (New York: Ocean Press in Association with Editora Politica, Havana, 2000), 52.

152. Claire Roman-Odio, "Transnational Feminism, Globalization, and the Politics of Representation in Chicana Visual Art" in *Transnational Borderlands in Women's Global Networks: The Making of Cultural Resistance*, edited by Clara Roman-Odio and Marta Sierra (New York: Palgrave Macmillan, 2011), 36–37.

153. "Lead from Old U.S. Batteries Sent to Mexico Raises Risks," *New York Times*, December 8, 2011, at http://www.nytimes.com/2011/12/09/science/earth/recycled-battery-lead-puts-me, accessed on December 9, 2011.

154. "Oil Spill Disaster New Zealand's 'Worst in Decades,'" *BBC News*, October 11, 2011, at http://www.bbc.co.uk/news/world-asia-pacific-1525 1319, accessed on October 12, 2011.

155. *New Zealand Herald*, October 7, 2011.

156. Lucy Westcott, "Heavy Cellphone Use Could Actually Cause Brain Cancer (Maybe)," *The Wire: What Matters Now*, May 13, 2014, at http://www.thewire.com/national/2014/05/heavy-cellphone-use-could-actually-cause-brain-cancer-maybe/370818/, accessed on May 30, 2014.

157. Christopher Ketcham, "Radiation from Cell Phones and WiFi Are Making People Sick—Are We All at Risk?," *Earth Island Reporter*, December 2, 2011, at http://www.alternet.org/story/153299/radiation_from_cell_phones_and_wifi_are_making_people_sick_—_are_we_all_at_risk?page=entire, accessed on May 30, 2014.

158. Christopher Ketcham, "Radiation from Cell Phones and WiFi Are Making People Sick—Are We All at Risk?" *Earth Island Reporter*, December 2, 2011, at http://www.alternet.org/story/153299/radiation_from_cell_phones_and_wifi_are_making_people_sick_—_are_we_all_at_risk?page=entire, accessed on May 30, 2014.

159. "No Such Thing as a Safe Dose of Radiation," Nuclear Information and Resource Center, Takoma Park, Maryland, available at www.nirs.org, accessed in November 2011.

160. See Winona LaDuke's *All Our Relations: Native Struggles for Land and Life* (Boston: South End Press, 1999), chapter 7, "Buffalo Nations, Buffalo Peoples," page 140, where the catastrophic near-extermination of 40 million buffalo is discussed, the arduous course of restoring some of the buffalo herd is illuminated, and the struggles of the Oglala Lakota people, closest relatives of the buffalo, are described in detail.

161. "North Atlantic Right Whales," National Oceanic and Atmospheric Administration (NOAA) Fisheries, Office of Protected Resources, December 6, 2013, at http://www.nmfs.noaa.gov/pr/species/mammals/cetaceans/rightwhale_northatlantic.htm, accessed on June 6, 2014.

162. Franz J. Broswimmer, *Ecocide: A Short History of the Mass Extinction of Species*, 88–93.

163. Communicated in the 2011 DVD *Endgame IV* produced by Daniel Lopez.

164. Makere Stewart Harawira, *The New Imperial Order: Indigenous Responses to Globalization* (London: Zed Books, 2005), 182–191.

165. The World People's Conference on Climate Change and the Rights of Mother Earth was covered on May 5, 2010, by the *Vancouver Observer* at ttp://www.vancouverobserver.com/blogs/world/2010/05/05/world-peoples-conference-climate-change-e, accessed on May 30, 2014.

166. Conveyed to the author in Tucson, Arizona, August 2010.

167. Gerardo Rénique, "Strategic Challenges for Latin America's Anti-Neoliberal Insurgency" in *Dispatches from Latin America: On the Frontlines Against Neoliberalism*, edited by Vijay Prashad and Teo Ballvé (Cambridge, MA: South End Press, 2008), 42–44.

168. See, for instance, Eva Golinger's article "Ecuador: A third U.S. sponsored coup d'etat against a member state of the Bolivarian Alliance of the Americas (ALBA)," laying strong grounds for the assertion of a U.S. role in the attempted coup against Correa since many of the U.S. sponsored organizations in the country have repeatedly called for his ouster, at http://www.globalresearch.ca/index.php?context=va&aid=21267 and accessed on May 1, 2011.

169. http://pulitzercenter.org/reporting/ecuador-chinese-mine-indigenous-population-conaie-el-mirador-ecuacorriente-correa. See also http://firstpeoples.org/wp/indigenous-marchers-protest-in-ecuadors-capital-against-mining-project-on-their-lands/ and http://amazonwatch.org/news/2012/0308-ecuador-indigenous-

protesters-march-against-mining, accessed on April 1, 2012.

170. http://www.presstv.ir/detail/2012/07/06/249591/bolivia-police-clash-with-protesters/, accessed on August 1, 2012.

171. Alex MacGillivray, *A Brief History of Globalization: The Untold Story of Our Incredible Shrinking Planet* (New York: Carroll & Graf, 2006), 133.

172. Georgia O. Carvalho, "Environmental Resistance and the Politics of Energy Development in the Brazilian Amazon," *Journal of Environment and Development* 15, no. 3 (September 2006), 257.

173. http://amazonwatch.org/work/belo-monte-dam, accessed on December 22, 2011.

174. Andréa Zhouri, "'Adverse Forces' in the Brazilian Amazon: Developmentalism Versus Environmentalism and Indigenous Rights," *Journal of Environment and Development* 19 (2010), 259–260.

175. The author was able to witness the effective organizing and mobilization of Indigenous people for the protection and restoration of ancestral lands in Manipur, north-east India, of Kavre and Kathmandu, Nepal, and of the Dayak people in Kuching, Sarawak, Malaysia, in July and August 2012. In July 2013, he was able to see Indigenous people organizing educational workshops on land and cultural rights in the hills of Kalinga in the Philippines.

176. "British Columbia: OAS Human Rights Commission Grants Hearing on Hui'qumi'num Treaty Group," at *Hul'qumi'num Treaty Group*, October 11, 2011.

177. Samwel Naikada from the Dupoto Community in Transmara, Kenya, along with the author have initiated an educational and cultural restoration project that involves visitors interested in being in solidarity with the Maasai community in Transmara and in preserving the threatened Nyakweri Forest through educational stays in the forest under the leadership of traditional Maasai practitioners. Information is available at www.nyakweri.arizona.edu.

178. Vine Deloria, *The World We Used to Live In: Remembering the Powers of the Medicine Men* (Boulder: Fulcrum, 2006): 206–207.

179. The author participated in and delivered an address to the UN 13th Permanent Forum on Indigenous Peoples in New York City from May 12 to May 18 as representative of the Chi Endeh Community Alliance based in San Carlos, Arizona. For the UN Declaration on the Rights of Indigenous Peoples, see the UN website at http://www.un.org/esa/socdev/unpfii/documents/DRIPS_en.pdf, accessed on May 11, 2014.

180. La Donna Harris and Jacqueline Wasilewski, "Indigeneity, an Alternative Worldview: Four R's (Relationship, Responsibility, Reciprocity, Redistribution) vs. Two P's (Power and Profit): Sharing the Journey Towards Conscious Evolution" in *Systems Research and Behavioral Science* 21.5 (September–October 2004), Thomson Gale Document Number: A125334902.

Chapter 3

1. Fatou Sow, "Fundamentalisms, Globalization and Women's Human Rights in Senegal" in *Women Inventing Gender*, edited by Joanna Kerr and Caroline Sweetman (Oxford: Oxfam Focus on Gender, 2003), 69.

2. Ken Coates, *A Global History of Indigenous Peoples: Survival and Struggle* (New York: Palgrave Macmillan, 2004), 109.

3. *United Nations Development Program Report*, 2004.

4. *United Nations Development Program Report*, 2005.

5. Cited in the Introduction to Part I, *Rereading Women in Latin America and the Caribbean: The Political Economy of Gender* edited by Jennifer Abbassi and Sheryl Lutjens (Lanham, MD: Rowman & Littlefield, 2002), 19.

6. Marilyn Carr, "Preface: Women's Economic Empowerment: Key to Development" in *Women's Economic Empowerment and Economic Justice: Reflecting on Experience in Latin America and the Caribbean*, edited by Liliana De Pauli (New York: United Nations Development Fund for Women, 2000), 1.

7. "Women and Poverty," Food and Agricultural Organization 2010–2011, at http://www.un.org/womenwatch/directory/women_and_poverty_3001.htm.

8. *Infographic: The Female Face of Farming*, Food and Agricultural Organization, 2010–2011, at http://www.fao.org/gender/infographic/en, accessed on May 17, 2013.

9. *Infographic: The Female Face of Farming*, Food and Agricultural Organization, 2010–2011, at http://www.fao.org/gender/infographic/en/.

10. Nafis Sadik, "A Time to Act: To Save Lives and Promote Gender Equality" in *Building a World Community: Globalisation and the Common Good*, edited by Jacques Badot (Copenhagen: Royal Danish Ministry of Foreign Affairs and Seattle: University of Washington Press, 2001), 222, 223, 225.

11. See, for instance D. Thomas' article "Like Father, Like Son: Gender Differences in Household Resource Allocations," Yale Economic Growth Center Discussion Paper No. 619 (New

Haven: Yale University, 1991), and S. Handa's article "Gender, Headship and Intrahousehold Resource Allocation" in *World Development Bank* 22, no. 10 (1994): 1535–1547.

12. Claudia Piras, "An Overview of the Challenges and Policy Issues Facing Women in the Labor Force" in *Women at Work: Challenges for Latin America*, edited by Claudia Piras (Washington, D.C.: Inter-American Development Bank, 2004), 6.

13. Cited in *Changing Patterns in the World of Work*, International Labor Conference, 95th Session 2006, Report I (C) (Geneva: International Labor Office, 2006), 29.

14. Perry Mars and Alma Young (eds.), Introduction, *Caribbean Labor and Politics: Legacies of Cheddi Jagan and Michael Manley* (Detroit: Wayne State University Press, 2004), xxviii–xxix. The texts cited in this quote are from Susan Christopherson, "Changing Women's Status in a Global Economy," in *Geographies of Global Change: Remapping the World in the Late Twentieth Century*, edited by R. J. Johnston, Peter Taylor, and Michael Watts (London: Blackwell, 1995), and from Saskia Sassen, "Women's Burden: Countergeographies of Globalization and the Feminization of Survival," *Journal of International Affairs* 53, no. 2 (2000): 503–524.

15. "Latin America: 70 Million Women Have Jobs Following Gender Reforms" at http://web.worldbank.org/WBSITE/EXTERNAL/COUNTRIES/LACEXT/0,,contentMDK:22852089~pagePK:146736~piPK:146830~theSitePK:258554,00.html, accessed on April 29, 2011.

16. "Latin America: 70 Million Women Have Jobs Following Gender Reforms" at http://web.worldbank.org/WBSITE/EXTERNAL/COUNTRIES/LACEXT/0,,contentMDK:2852089~pagePK:146736~piPK:146830~theSitePK:258554,00.html, accessed on April 29, 2011.

17. Janet Henshall Momsen, "Caribbean Tourism and Agriculture: New Linkages in the Global Era" in *Globalization and Neoliberalism: The Caribbean Context*, edited by Thomas Klak (Lanham, MD: Rowan & Littlefield, 1998), 119.

18. Nana Oishi, *Women in Motion: Globalization, State Policies, and Labor Migration in Asia* (Stanford: Stanford University Press, 2005), 2.

19. Nana Oishi, *Women in Motion: Globalization, State Policies, and Labor Migration in Asia*, 3.

20. Martha Richards, "A Look at Human Trafficking in South Africa," *Africa Stories*, April 8, 2010, at http://www.africastories.org/human-trafficking/a-look-at-trafficking-in-south-africa/,

accessed on June 2, 2014. See also *Sunday Tribune*, South Africa, July 23, 2006.

21. Kevin Bales, *Disposable People: New Slavery in the Global Economy* (Berkeley: University of California Press, 2004), 57.

22. Nana Oishi, *Women in Motion: Globalization, State Policies, and Labor Migration in Asia*, 35.

23. Nana Oishi, *Women in Motion: Globalization, State Policies, and Labor Migration in Asia*, 37.

24. *Chicago Tribune*, February 12, 2006.

25. Rhacel Salazar Parreñas, *Servants of Globalization: Women, Migration, and Domestic Work* (Stanford: Stanford University Press, 2001), 247–248.

26. Katherine Carter and Judy Aulette, *Cape Verdean Women and Globalization: The Politics of Gender, Culture, and Resistance* (New York: Palgrave Macmillan, 2009), 87.

27. Rhacel Salazar Parreñas, *Servants of Globalization: Women, Migration, and Domestic Work*, 249.

28. Rhacel Salazar Parreñas, *Servants of Globalization: Women, Migration, and Domestic Work*, 249.

29. See Ligya Lindio McGovern's excellent article "Neo-liberal Globalization in the Philippines: Its Impact on Filipino Women and their Forms of Resistance" in *Gender and Globalization: Patterns of Women's Resistance*, edited by Ericka G. Polakoff and Ligaya Lindio-McGovern (Whitby, Ontario: de Sitter, 2011), 45.

30. Ligya Lindio McGovern, "Neo-liberal Globalization in the Philippines: Its Impact on Filipino Women and their Forms of Resistance" in *Gender and Globalization: Patterns of Women's Resistance*, edited by Ericka G. Polakoff and Ligaya Lindio-McGovern, 44.

31. Radhika Balakrishnan, Introduction, *The Hidden Assembly Line: Gender Dynamics of Subcontracted Work in a Global Economy*, edited by Rahika Balakrishnan (Bloomfield, CT: Kumarian Press, 2002), 4–6.

32. Charles Duhigg and David Barboza, "In China, Human Costs Are Built Into an iPad," *New York Times*, January 25, 2012, at http://www.nytimes.com/2012/01/26/business/ieconomy-apples-ipad-and-the-human-costs-for-workers-in-china.html?pagewanted=all&_r=0, accessed on January 26, 2012.

33. David Barboza, "Foxconn Resolves a Dispute with Some Workers in China," *New York Times*, January 12, 2012, at http://www.nytimes.com/2012/01/13/technology/foxconn-resolves-pay-dispute-with-workers.html, accessed on January 13, 2012.

34. David Sarno, "Apple Market Value Hits $500 Billion and Counting," *Los Angeles Times*, February 29, 2012, at http://articles.latimes.com/2012/feb/29/business/la-fi-apple-value-20120301, accessed on March 1, 2012.

35. I cite the case of Anna Zondi who walked four kilometers uphill in Wembley to work each day and then was summarily terminated by her white employer who attempted to find ways of denying Ms. Zondi her last month's pay in September 2010. Such stories were not abnormal in post-apartheid South Africa in 2010.

36. Haifaa A. Jawad, *The Rights of Women in Islam: An Authentic Approach* (New York: St. Martin's Press, 1998), 25–26.

37. Shaddia el Sarraj, "Screaming in Silence" in *Frontline Feminisms: Women, War, and Resistance*, edited by Marguerite Waller and Jennifer Rycenga (New York: Garland, 2000), 20.

38. Salma Galal, "Women and Development in the Maghreb Countries" in *Gender and Development in the Arab World: Women's Economic Participation: Patterns and Policies* (London: Zed Books and Tokyo: United Nations University Press, 1995), 55.

39. Zafiris Tzannatos and Iqbal Kaur, "Women in the MENA Labor Market: An Eclectic Survey" in *Women and Globalization in the Arab Middle East: Gender, Economy, and Society*, 57.

40. UNESCO Institute for Statistics, National literacy rates for youths (15–24) and adults (15+) available from the UIS website, http://www.uis.unesco.org, December 2011, accessed on January 10, 2012.

41. UNESCO Institute for Statistics, National literacy rates for youths (15–24) and adults (15+) available from the UIS website, http://www.uis.unesco.org, December 2011, accessed on January 10, 2012.

42. Salma Galal, "Women and Development in the Maghreb Countries" in *Gender and Development in the Arab World: Women's Economic Participation: Patterns and Policies*, 67.

43. Noha El-Mikawy, "The Informal Sector and the Conservative Consensus: A Case of Fragmentation in Egypt" in *Women, Globalization and Fragmentation in the Developing World*, edited by Haleh Afshar and Stephanie Barrientos (Hampshire: Macmillan and New York: St. Martin's Press, 1999), 88.

44. Noha El-Mikawy, "The Informal Sector and the Conservative Consensus: A Case of Fragmentation in Egypt" in *Women, Globalization and Fragmentation in the Developing World*, edited by Haleh Afshar and Stephanie Barrientos, 88.

45. Heba Nassar, "Egypt: Structural Adjustment and Women's Employment" in *Women and Globalization in the Arab Middle East: Gender, Economy, and Society*, edited by Eleanor Abdella Doumatoi and Marsha P. Posusney (Boulder: Lynne Rienner, 2003), 115.

46. For a glimpse of the massive movement that ushered in the Mubarak regime's downfall see http://www.independent.co.uk/news/world/africa/egyptian-government-offers-concessions-as-street-protests-continue-2206333.html, accessed on January 30, 2012.

47. Philip Marfleet, "Globalization, Islam and the Indigenization of Knowledge" in *Situating Globalization: Views from Egypt*, edited by Cynthia Nelson and Shahnaz Rouse (New Brunswick: Transaction, 2000), 39. "Europe" was an ideological colonial construction from two centuries ago following the consolidation of European imperialist and colonialist military power over much of the rest of the world. Arnold Toynbee's *A Study of World History, Volumes I–VI* (New York: Oxford University Press, 1987), Martin Bernal's *Black Athena: The Afro-Asiatic Roots of Classical Civilizations, Volumes 1, 2, and 3* (New Brunswick: Rutgers University Press, 1987, 1991, and 2006, respectively), and Robert Royal's article "Who Put the West in Western Civilization?," *Intercollegiate Review* (Spring 1998) at http://www.mmisi.org/ir/33_02/royal.pdf, accessed on June 2, 2014, all raise critical questions about the fabrication of a supremacist and exceptionalist "Western European" civilization. Royal was the Vice-President of the Ethics and Public Policy Center in Washington, D.C.

48. Bisi Adeleye-Fayemi, "Creating a New World with New Visions: African Feminism and Trends in the Global Women's Movement" in *The Future of Women's Rights*, edited by Joanna Kerr, Ellen Sprenger, and Alison Symington (New York: Zed Books, published in association with The Association for Women's Rights in Development [AWID], Toronto, and Mama Cash, Amsterdam, 2004), 39.

49. Bisi Adeleye-Fayemi, "Creating a New World with New Visions: African Feminism and Trends in the Global Women's Movement" in *The Future of Women's Rights*, edited by Joanna Kerr, Ellen Sprenger, and Alison Symington, 42.

50. Demba Moussa Dembele, "The Political Economy of Debt, Adjustment and Globalization in Africa" in *Africa: Gender, Globalization and Resistance*, edited by Yassine Fall (Dakar: The African Association of Women for Research and Development, 1999), 51.

51. Demba Moussa Dembele, "The Political Economy of Debt, Adjustment and Globalization in Africa" in *Africa: Gender, Globalization and Resistance*, edited by Yassine Fall, 51.

52. Barbara Frost, Winnie Byanyima, Corinne Woods, and Nick Alipui, "Two Girls Died Look-Ing for a Toilet. This Should Make Us Angry, Not Embarrassed," *The Guardian*, London, May 31, 2014, at http://www.theguardian.com/global-development/2014/jun/01/girls-toilet-rape-murder-anger-embarrassment, accessed on June 1, 2014.

53. "Policy Alternatives" in *Africa: Gender, Globalization and Resistance*, edited by Yassine Fall, 99.

54. Interview with a female member of the South African Clothing and Textile Workers Union (SACTWU), Cape Town, July 2006.

55. Ramola Ramtohul, "Trade Liberalization and the Feminization of Poverty: The Mauritian Scenario" in *Agenda: Empowering Women for Gender Equity* 78 (2008), 63, at www.agenda.org.za, accessed on June 1, 2014.

56. Ramola Ramtohul, "Trade Liberalization and the Feminization of Poverty: The Mauritian Scenario" in *Agenda: Empowering Women for Gender Equity* 78 (2008), 63, at www.agenda.org.za.

57. Yassine Fall, "Globalization, Its Institutions and African Women's Resistance" in *Africa: Gender, Globalization and Resistance*, edited by Yassine Fall, 79, 83.

58. Sisonke Msimang, "HIV/AIDS, Globalization and the International Women's Movement" in *Women Inventing Globalisation*, edited by Joanna Kerr and Caroline Sweetman, 110.

59. Marjorie Mbilinyi, *Budgets, Debt Relief and Globalisation* (Accra: Third World Network-Africa, 2001), 13. Mbilinyi begins her book by exposing the duplicity of the Tanzanian government, which announced in 2000 that Tanzania's "debt" to Western financial institutions of $2 billion would be cancelled as part of the plan to cancel "debt" owed by the world's poorest countries (the Heavily Indebted Poor Countries), while the government failed to acknowledge that the conditionality for cancellation of the "debt" was that it persist in implementing the structural adjustment policies, mass privatization, and liberalization that have severely impoverished the Tanzanian nation, particularly through defunding national education, health, and social welfare programs.

60. Cited by Rosalind P. Petchesky, *Global Prescriptions: Gendering Health and Human Rights* (New York: Zed Books, in association with the United Nations Research Institute for Social Development, 2003), 6.

61. Rosalind P. Petchesky, *Global Prescriptions: Gendering Health and Human Rights*, 86.

62. "HIV/AIDS in the Black Community of Arizona," The Phoenix Birthing Project, Inc., Phoenix, Arizona, February 2006.

63. This issue was detailed in Chapter 2 and substantiated in endnote 39. The unhygienic conditions in Europe, where people from Northern Europe and England rarely bathed, are documented for instance in James Loewen's book, *Lies My Teacher Told Me: Everything Your American History Textbook Got Wrong* (New York: Touchstone, 1996), 79.

64. See the excellent and shocking revelations of U.S. experimentation with people of color from the period of chattel slavery to the late 1990s, in Harriet Washington's *Medical Apartheid: The Dark History of Medical Experimentation on Black Americans from Colonial Times to the Present* (New York: Anchor Books, 2008), especially pages 59–60 describing Thomas Jefferson experimenting on enslaved Africans prior to administering the smallpox vaccine to whites, and the *Natural News* website that documents such governmental atrocities from 1845 at http://www.naturalnews.com/025385_disease_plum_government.html, accessed on January 10, 2011. The infection of Guatemalan prisoners was reported by Robert Bazzell on MSNBC, "US Apologizes for Guatemala Experiments: Government researchers infected patients with syphilis, gonorrhea without their consent in 1940s," October 1, 2010, at http://www.nbcnews.com/id/39456324/ns/health-sexual_health/t/us-apologizes-guatemala-std-experiments/#.U4kLFhYVvRo, accessed on October 2, 2010.

65. David Wahlberg, "UW-Madison Scientists Creates New Flu Virus in Lab," *Wisconsin State Journal*, June 11, 2014, at http://host.madison.com/wsj/news/local/health_med_fit/uw-madison-scientist-creates-new-flu-virus-in-lab/article_4cedeb40-efdc-5d2e-a02d-ffb301a84b53.html, accessed on June 11, 2014.

66. Ian Sample, "Scientists Condemn 'Crazy, Dangerous' Creation of Deadly Airborne Flu Virus," *The Guardian*, London, June 11, 2014, at http://www.theguardian.com/science/2014/jun/11/crazy-dangerous-creation-deadly-airborne-flu-virus, accessed on June 11, 2014.

67. Jon Rappoport, "West Africa: What Are U.S. Biological Warfare Researchers Doing in the Ebola Zone?," Global Research, August 2, 2014, at http://www.globalresearch.ca/what-are-us-biological-warfare-researchers-doing-in-the-ebola-zone/5394582, accessed on October 8, 2014.

68. For an illumination of the effects of globalization on women in Chile, for example, see *Sobre Mujeres Y Globalizacion*, edited by Sonia Yanez and Rosalba Todaro (Santiago: Centro De Estudios De La Mujer, CEM, 1997).

69. Valentine Moghadam, *Globalizing Women:*

Transnational Feminist Networks (Baltimore: Johns Hopkins University Press, 2005), 57.

70. Valentine Moghadam, *Globalizing Women: Transnational Feminist Networks*, 57.

71. Valentine Moghadam, *Globalizing Women: Transnational Feminist Networks*, 58.

72. Andrew Clark, "Ford sees ruthless cost-cutting pay off," *The Guardian*, London, January 24, 2008, at http://www.theguardian.com/business/2008/jan/25/ford.automotive, accessed on January 31, 2008.

73. David Roodman, "Grameen Bank, Which Pioneered Loans for the Poor, Has Hit a Repayment Snag" at http://blogs.cgdev.org/open_book/2010/02/grameen-bank-which-pioneered-loans-for-the-poor-has-hit-a-repayment-snag.php, accessed on April 18, 2012.

74. Tim, "American Household Debt Statistics 2014," *nerdwalletfinance*, April 2014, at http://www.nerdwallet.com/blog/credit-card-data/average-credit-card-debt-household/, accessed on June 3, 2014. For the U.S. student loan debt crisis, see, for instance, Thomas Ferraro, "U.S. Senate Democrats offer student debt refinance bill," Reuters, May 14, 2014, at http://www.reuters.com/article/2014/05/14/us-usa-senate-students-idUSBREA4D0Q220140514, accessed on June 3, 2014.

75. Kavaljit Singh, *Questioning Globalization* (Delhi: Madhyam Books; New York: Zed Books; and Berlin: Asia-Europe Dialogue, 2005), 15.

76. Kavaljit Singh, *Questioning Globalization*, 49.

77. World Bank, *Poverty and Income Distribution in Latin America: The Story of the 1980s*, Report no. 11586-1993-4 (Washington, D.C.: World Bank, 1993).

78. Roberto P. Korzeniewicz, "Rural Poverty, Women and Indigenous Groups in Latin America" in *Rural Poverty in Latin America*, edited by Ramon Lopez and Alberto Valdes (Hampshire: Macmillan and New York: St. Martin's Press, 2000), 51.

79. Report Social Panorama of Latin America, "Poverty Strikes Women and Children Harder in Latin America," UN Economic Commission on Latin America and the Caribbean, November 19, 2009, at http://www.eclac.cl/cgi-bin/getProd.asp?xml=/prensa/noticias/comunicados/6/37836/P37836.xml&xsl=/prensa/tpl-i/p6f.xsl&base=/tpl-i/top-bottom.xslt, acced on June 3, 2014.

80. Report Social Panorama of Latin America, "Poverty Strikes Women and Children Harder in Latin America," UN Economic Commission on Latin America and the Caribbean, November 19, 2009.

81. Roberto P. Korzeniewicz, "Rural Poverty, Women and Indigenous Groups in Latin America" in *Rural Poverty in Latin America*, 50.

82. Helen Safa, "Economic Restructuring and Gender Subordination" in *Rereading Women in Latin America and the Caribbean: The Political Economy of Gender*, edited by Jennifer Abbassi and Sheryl Lutjens (Lanham, MD: Rowman & Littlefield, 2002), 50.

83. *People's Weekly World* 20, no. 33 (February 11–17, 2006).

84. Tiffany Lucienne Scalia, "How Dole Got Away with Poisoning Banana Workers," accessed at http://news.change.org/stories/how-dole-got-away-with-poisoning-banana-workers, on March 28, 2012.

85. Dole's profile in Costa Rica and Latin America is at http://dolecrs.com/press-release-2011/dole-and-standard-fruit-company-recognized-by-costa-rican-american-chamber-of-commerce-for-excellence-in-labor-relations/, accessed on March 28, 2012.

86. This information was documented and videotaped by the author in Managua, Nicaragua on September 1, 2012.

87. Anthony Maingot and Wilfredo Lozano, *The United States and the Caribbean: Transforming Hegemony and Sovereignty* (New York: Routledge, 2005), 76.

88. Joan Browne and Barbara Bailey, "Micro-enterprise Development in Jamaica" in *Women's Empowerment and Economic Justice: Reflecting on Experience in Latin America and the Caribbean*, edited by Liliana De Pauli (New York: United Nations Development Fund for Women, 2000), 55. This research information was conducted by L. Brown and documented in "State of the Art Review: Women and Microenterprise Development in Jamaica," mimeo, Center for Gender and Development Studies, University of the West Indies, Mona, Jamaica, 1995.

89. Joan Browne and Barbara Bailey, "Micro-enterprise Development in Jamaica" in *Women's Empowerment and Economic Justice: Reflecting on Experience in Latin America and the Caribbean*, 53.

90. Joan Browne and Barbara Bailey, "Micro-enterprise Development in Jamaica" in *Women's Empowerment and Economic Justice: Reflecting on Experience in Latin America and the Caribbean*, 60.

91. Anthony Maingot and Wilfredo Lozano express this view on page 80 of *The United States and the Caribbean: forming Hegemony and Sovereignty*, disregarding the colonized status of the Caribbean countries when it comes to advantages that accrue from Economic Processing Zones (EPZ) and the reality of the 1990s enslavement and exploitation of Caribbean workers in this context as I have elaborated.

92. Helen Safa, "Economic Restructuring and Gender Subordination" in *Rereading Women in Latin America and the Caribbean: The Political Economy of Gender*, edited by Jennifer Abbassi and Sheryl Lutjens, 48.

93. J. Delahanty, *A Common Thread: Issues for Women Workers in the Garment Sector*, Women in Informal Employment: Globalizing and Organizing (WIEGO), 1999. Cited in *The gender dimension of globalization: a survey of the literature with a focus on Latin America and the Caribbean* (Santiago: United Nations Division of International Trade and Integration, 2001), 26.

94. Flavia Cherry, "Women's Resistance to the WTO from Small Island Economies," *The Caribbean Gender and Trade Network*, January 2004, at http://www.choike.org/nuevo_eng/informes/1693.html, accessed on June 2, 2014.

95. *Life and Debt* was produced by Stephanie Black in 2001 and is available at http://www.life anddebt.org/.

96. G. Bonder, "Las nuevas tecnologians de informaciona y las mujerees; erfleciones necesarias (Version preliminar)," paper presented at the expert meeting on Globalization, Technological Change and Gender Equality, Sao Paulo, Brazil, November 5–6, 2001, organized by ECLAC, UNIFEM, GTS, Sao Paulo University and Conselho Nacional dos Direitos de la Mulher. Cited in *The gender dimension of globalization: A survey of the literature with a focus on Latin America and the Caribbean*, 26.

97. Vandana Shiva, "WTO, Women and the Environment: An Ecological and Gender Analysis of 'Free Trade'" in *Women in Development: Trade Aspects on Women in the Development Process*, edited by E. Haxton and C. Olsson, 1, 2. See also the link http://www.tkdl.res.in/tkdl/langdefault/common/Biopiracy.asp?GL=Eng for an illumination of issues related to biopiracy and traditional medicinal knowledge, accessed on April 10, 2010.

98. Vandana Shiva, "WTO, Women and the Environment: An Ecological and Gender Analysis of 'Free Trade'" in *Women in Development: Trade Aspects on Women in the Development Process*, edited by E. Haxton and C. Olsson (Uppsala: United Nations Youth and Student Association of Sweden, 1995), 24.

99. Joya Misra, "Latinas and African American Women in the Labor Market: Implications for Policy" in *Latinas and African American Women at Work: Race, Gender and Economic Inequality*, edited by Irene Brown (New York: Russell Sage Foundation, 1999), 408.

100. Bette Wood, *Black Women in the Workplace: Impacts of Structural Change in the Economy* (Westport, CT: Greenwood Press, 1992), 5.

101. Arianna Huffington, *Third World America: How Our Politicians Are Abandoning the Middle Class and Betraying the American Dream* (New York: Crown, 2010), 69.

102. Impacts of Resource Development on Native American Lands, "Environmental and Human Health Impacts at Pine Ridge from Gold Mining" at http://serc.carleton.edu/research_education/nativelands/pineridge/impacts.html, accessed on April 18, 2012.

103. Lys Anzia, "US: Indigenous Lakota Women Face Harsh Winter Wrath Under Climate Change," *Women News Network*, November 2, 2010, at http://womennewsnetwork.net/2010/11/02/lakotaelderwomen-1008/, accessed on June 3, 2014.

104. Mary Hawkesworth, "Women's Struggle for Political Equality in the United States" in *Women, Democracy, and Globalization in North America: A Comparative Study* by Jane Bayers, Patricia Begne, Laura Gonzales, Lois Harder, Mary Hawkesworth, and Laura Macdonald (New York: Palgrave Macmillan, 2006), 103.

105. Mary Hawkesworth, "Women's Struggle for Political Equality in the United States" in *Women, Democracy, and Globalization in North America: A Comparative Study* by Jane Bayers, Patricia Begne, Laura Gonzales, Lois Harder, Mary Hawkesworth, and Laura Macdonald, 103.

106. Mary Hawkesworth, "Women's Struggle for Political Equality in the United States" in *Women, Democracy, and Globalization in North America: A Comparative Study* by Jane Bayers, Patricia Begne, Laura Gonzales, Lois Harder, Mary Hawkesworth, and Laura Macdonald, 103.

107. "Inflation Rears Its Head as Food Prices Rise," NBC News-Reuters, April 11, 2014, at http://www.nbcnews.com/business/economy/inflation-rears-its-head-food-prices-rise-again-n77951, accessed on June 3, 2014.

108. Mary Hawkesworth, "Women's Struggle for Political Equality in the United States" in *Women, Democracy, and Globalization in North America: A Comparative Study*, 103.

109. Elise Gould, Hilary Wething, Natalie Sabadish, and Nicholas Finio, "What Families Need to Get By: The 2013 Update of EPI's Family Budget Calculator," *Economic Policy Institute*, Washington, D.C., July 3, 2013, at http://www.epi.org/publication/ib368-basic-family-budgets/, accessed on June 3, 2014.

110. Elise Gould, Hilary Wething, Natalie Sabadish, and Nicholas Finio, "What Families Need to Get By: The 2013 Update of EPI's Family Budget Calculator," *Economic Policy Institute*, Washington, D.C., July 3, 2013, at http://www.epi.org/publication/ib368-basic-family-budgets/, accessed on June 3, 2014.

111. Joel Handler, "Welfare Reform: Tightening the Screws" in *Women at the Margins: Neglect, Punishment, and Resistance*, edited by Josefina Figueira-McDonough and Rosemary Sarri (New York: Haworth Press, 2003), 45.

112. Jane Bayes, "The Gendered Impact of Globalization on the United States" in *Women, Democracy, and Globalization in North America: A Comparative Study*, 154–155.

113. Anna Celeste, "Triple Jeopardy: Women Marginalized by Substance Abuse, Poverty, and Incarceration" in *Women at the Margins: Neglect, Punishment, and Resistance*, edited by Joesfeina Figueira-McDonoug and Rosemary Sarri, 187.

114. Anna Celeste, "Triple Jeopardy: Women Marginalized by Substance Abuse, Poverty, and Incarceration" in *Women at the Margins: Neglect, Punishment, and Resistance*, edited by Joesfeina Figueira-McDonoug and Rosemary Sarri, 188.

115. Pancho McFarland, "Here Is Something You Can't Understand ... Chicano Rap and the Critique of Globalization" in *Decolonial Voices: Chicana and Chicano Cultural Studies in the 21st Century*, edited by Arturo Aldama and Naomi Quiñonez (Bloomington: Indiana University Press, 2002), 309.

116. Lepa Mladjenovic and Donna Hughes, "Feminist Resistance to War and Violence in Serbia" in *Frontline Feminisms: Women, War, and Resistance*, edited by Marguerite Waller and Jennifer Rycenga (New York: Garland, 2000), 255.

117. Kurt Nimmo, "CIA, FBI and Now Academi Mercenaries on the Ground in Ukraine," Global Research, Center for Research on Globalization, Montreal, May 12, 2014, at http://www.globalresearch.ca/cia-fbi-and-now-academi-mercenaries-on-the-ground-in-ukraine/5381875, accessed on June 4, 2014.

118. Cited by Vesna Goldsworthy, "Intervention and In(ter)vention" in *Balkan as Metaphor: Between Globalization and Fragmentation*, edited by Dusan Bjelic and Obrad Savic (Cambridge: MIT Press, 2002), 26.

119. Vesna Goldsworthy, "Intervention and In(ter)vention" in *Balkan as Metaphor: Between Globalization and Fragmentation*, 29.

120. Arnove, Anthony (ed.), *Iraq Under Siege: The Deadly Impact of Sanctions and War* (Boston: South End Press, 2002), 105.

121. The figures on post–September 11 war expenditures by the U.S. are taken from the *People's Weekly World* 20, no. 33 (February 11–17, 2006). And the figures on the cost of the war against and occupation of Iraq are from Joseph Stiglitz's and Linda Bilmes' work, *The Three Trillion Dollar War: The True Cost of the Iraq Conflict* (New York: W.W. Norton, 2008).

122. Cited in *Globalization or Empire* by Jan Nederveen Pieterse (New York: Routledge, 2004), 57.

123. See Ilja A. Luciak's article "Gender Equality, Democratization, and the Revolutionary Left" in Central America," *Radical Women in Latin America: Left and Right*, edited by Victoria Gonzales and Karen Kampwirth (University Park: Pennsylvania State University Press, 2001) for an illumination of this genocidal history of Guatemala, especially page 189.

124. Ilja A. Luciak, "Gender Equality, Democratization, and the Revolutionary Left" in Central America" in *Radical Women in Latin America: Left and Right* edited by Victoria Gonzales and Karen Kampwirth, 189.

125. Virginia Q. Tilley, *Seeing Indians: A Study of Race, Nation, and Power in El Salvador* (Albuquerque: University of New Mexico Press, 2005), 64.

126. See, for instance, Clara Jimeno's article "Implementation of the Gender Demands Included in the Guatemala Peace Accords: Lessons Learned" in *Women Resist Globalization: Mobilizing for Livelihood and Rights*, edited by Sheila Rowbotham and Stephanie Linkogle (New York: Zed Press, 2001).

127. Clara Jimeno, "Implementation of the Gender Demands Included in the Guatemala Peace Accords: Lessons Learned" in *Women Resist Globalization: Mobilizing for Livelihood and Rights*, edited by Sheila Rowbotham and Stephanie Linkogle, 190.

128. Ilja A. Luciak's article, "Gender Equality, Democratization, and the Revolutionary Left" in Central America," in *Radical Women in Latin America: Left and Right*, elaborates on these critical dimensions of women's struggles in El Salvador, along with Guatemala and Nicaragua.

129. Karen Kampwirth, "The Mother of the Nicaraguans: Doña Violeta and the UNO's Gender Agenda" in *Rereading Women in Latin America and the Caribbean: The Political Economy of Gender*, edited by Jennifer Abbassi and Sheryl Lutjens, 179, 181.

130. The author was part of a Nicaragua delegation of the Alliance for Global Justice, a Central, South American and Caribbean solidarity organization based in Washington, D.C., from August 27 to September 5, 2012.

131. Sylvia Marcos, "The Borders Within: The Indigenous Women's Movement and Feminism in Mexico" in *Dialogue and Difference: Feminisms Challenge Globalization*, edited by Marguerite Waller and Sylvia Marcos (New York: Palgrave Macmillan, 2005), 102.

132. Sylvia Marcos, "The Borders Within:

The Indigenous Women's Movement and Feminism in Mexico" in *Dialogue and Difference: Feminisms Challenge Globalization*, edited by Marguerite Waller and Sylvia Marcos, 102.

133. See, for instance, Irasema Coronado and Kathleen Staudt's illuminating article, "Resistance and *compromiso* at the global frontlines: Gender wars at the U.S.–Mexico border" in *Critical Theories, International Relations and "the Anti-Globalisation Movement": The Politics of Global Resistance*, edited by Catherine Eschle and Bice Maiguashca (New York: Routledge, 2005), 140.

134. See for instance, Keith Harmon Snow's substantive coverage of the role of Western and neighboring surrogate regimes and national corporations in the looting of the Democratic Republic of the Congo (DRC) and in the Great Lakes region of Africa, at his blog, *Black Agenda Report*, at http://blackagendareport.com/?q= blog/144, accessed in June 2014. Snow is an investigative journalist whom the author knows personally through visits to Arizona. Billy Batware's paper, "Resource Conflicts: The Role of Multinational Corporations in the Democratic Republic of the Congo," May 12, 2011, at http://acuns. org/wp-content/uploads/2012/06/Roleof MultinationalCorporations.pdf, accessed on June 4, 2014, provides some information on the range of corporations culpable in the high mortality rate in the DRC stemming from the wars for minerals in the country. The article, "Zimbabwe Accuses De Beers of Looting Diamonds," March 5, 2010, sheds light on De Beers' devious role in illegally extracting diamonds in Zimbabwe, at http:// www.globalpolicy.org/security-council/dark-side-of-natural-resources/diamonds-in-conflict/ debates-and-articles-on-diamonds-in-conflict/ 48826.html, accessed on June 4, 2014.

135. Marjorie Mbilinyi, *Budgets, Debt Relief and Globalisation*, 8.

136. See Eric Elliott's article, "750 Congolese Soldiers Graduate from U.S.–led Military Training, Form Light Infantry Battalion," United States Africa Command, September 20, 2010, at http:// www.africom.mil/Newsroom/Article/7727/750-congolese-soldiers-graduate-from-us-led-milita, accessed on June 4, 2014. In his article "Tomgram: Nick Turse, America's Non-Stop Ops in Africa," March 27, 2014, Nick Turse, Managing Editor at TomDispatchwww, notes that senior military officers from the DRC were implicated by the UN High Commissioner for Human Rights in crimes of rape and violence in Kivu province in 2012. DRC military personnel have been trained by AFRICOM as indicated above. Turse's detailed article on the extensive role of the U.S. in military operations and training in Africa also highlights

that the U.S. mentored the military officer who overthrew the democratically-elected government in Mali in 2012, at http://www.tomdispatch.com/ post/175823/tomgrampercent3A_nick_turse,_ america's_non-stop_ops_in_africa/, accessed on June 4, 2014. The UN Human Rights report, "UN denounces sexual violence, other serious violations in Eastern DRC," May 8, 2013, is at http: //www.ohchr.org/EN/NewsEvents/Pages/ DisplayNews.aspx?NewsID=13308&LangID=E, accessed on June 4, 2014. Eric Schmitt's article "U. S. Training Antiterror Elite Troops in Four African Countries" in the *New York Times* on May 27, 2014, at http://www.nytimes.com/2014/05/27/ world/africa/us-trains-african-commandos-to-fight-terrorism.html?emc=eta1 and accessed on May 27, 2014, elaborates on the expanding U.S. military role in Africa in this globalized era.

137. Noted political science and sociology scholar Samir Amin's excellent article "Rwanda's Proxy's Wars for Imperialist Interest" lucidly explains the colonialist and Western imperialist role in the Rwandan genocide of 1994, *Pambazuka News*, Issue 675, April 24, 2014, at http://www. pambazuka.org/en/category/features/91475, accessed on June 4, 2014. Michel Chossudovsky's instructive book *The Globalization of Poverty and the New World Order* (Montreal: Centre for Research on Globalization, 2003), specifically the section, "Economic Genocide in Rwanda," provides a good background to the economic underpinnings of the Rwanda conflict and globalization being implicated through the radical drop of global coffee prices, where the U.S. intervened in the deliberations of the International Coffee Agreement (ICA) in 1989 on behalf of large coffee producers. Rwanda's economy, which depended on coffee exports, was radically undermined, causing a deep socio-economic crisis in the country. Excerpts from "Economic Genocide in Rwanda" are at http://www.thirdworldtraveler.com/East_ Africa/Rwanda_EconGenocide_GPNWO.html, accessed on June 4, 2012.

138. Fenella Mukangara and Bertha Koda, *Beyond Inequalities: Women in Tanzania*: A Profile of Women in Tanzania produced by the Tanzania Gender Networking Programme (TGNP) and the Women in Development Southern Africa Awareness (WIDSAA) Programme of the Southern Africa Research and Documentation Centre (SARDC) (Dar es Salaam and Harare, 1997), 60.

139. B. A. Jinadu and Andy O. Alali, "Health Communication and Primary Health in Refugee Settings: Lessons and Promises" in *Health Communication in Africa: Contexts, Constraints and Lessons*, edited by Andy O. Alali and B. A. Jinadu (Lanham, MD: University Press of America, 2002), 252.

140. B. A. Jinadu and Andy O. Alali, "Health Communication and Primary Health in Refugee Settings: Lessons and Promises" in *Health Communication in Africa: Contexts, Constraints and Lessons*, 256–257.

141. Lamia Rustum Shehadeh, "Women in the Lebanese Militias" in *Women and the War in Lebanon*, edited by Lamia Rustum Shehadeh (Gainesville: University Press of Florida, 1999), 149.

142. Costs of War, "Growth of Corporate Power and Profiteering," February 2013, at http://costsofwar.org/article/growth-corporate-power-and-profiteering, accessed on June 4, 2014. The American Friends Service Committee has calculated the U.S. defense and security budget that funds all security agencies and war efforts over the past five years at over $1 trillion each year. See American Friends Service Committee, "What would you do with a trillion dollars?" at http://www.afsc.org/story/what-would-you-do-trillion-dollars-3, accessed on June 4, 2014. Information about the Carlyle Group is available in the entry "Carlyle Group" by John Barnhill in the book *Encyclopedia of White-Collar and Corporate Crime*, Volume 2, by Lawrence Salinger (Thousand Oaks, CA: Sage, 2005), 538.

143. Costs of War, "Growth of Corporate Power and Profiteering," February 2013, at http://costsofwar.org/article/growth-corporate-power-and-profiteering, accessed on June 4, 2014.

144. American Friends Service Committee White House Discretionary Budget for 2013, sent in sticker format via mail to the author in March 2012.

145. See, for instance, Chalmers Johnson's book, *The Sorrows of Empire: Militarism, Secrecy, and the End of the Republic* (New York: Metropolitan Books, Henry Holt, 2004), especially page 4 which notes that the U.S. has 725 military bases around the world.

146. It should come as no surprise that a Mass Fatality Planning bill was introduced in Congress on October 6, 2012 (HR 6566), which constitutes an amendment to Section 504 of the Homeland Security Act of 2002 that grants FEMA authority to execute the burial of masses of U.S citizens in the event of a natural disaster or "terrorist" incident. All U.S. citizens need to pay serious attention to the reasons proposed for such a bill and its connection to Homeland Security. Cited from http://www.legitgov.org/FEMA-Ordered-Prepare-Mass-Fatality-Planning-Bill-Introduced-Congress.

147. See the article "100 Professors Question the 9/11 Commission Report," at http://www.weboflove.org/070618professorsquestion911

commissionreport, accessed on June 4, 2013. Skeptics include prominent scholars like David Griffin, *The New Pearl Harbor: Disturbing Questions About the Bush Administration and 9/11* (Northampton, MA: Olive Branch Press, 2004); Michel Chosssudovsky, *War and Globalisation: The Truth Behind September 11* (Shanty Bay, Ontario: Global Outlook, 2002); David Griffin and Peter Dale Scott (co-eds.), *911 and American Empire—Intellectuals Speak Out*, Vol. 1 (Northampton, MA: Olive Branch Press, 2006); John A. Cobb (co-ed.), *9/11 and American Empire: Christians, Muslims, and Jews Speak Out*, Vol. 2 (Northampton, MA: Olive Branch Press, 2006); Steven Jones (founder of *Journal of 9/11 Studies*), Howard Zinn, A. K. Dedwney, Rosemary Radford Ruether, and John McMurtry. French journalist Thierry Meyysan's *l'Effroyable imposture (The Horrifying Fraud)* (Paris: ALPHEE.JEAN-PAUL BERTAND, 2007) is another source of skepticism about official events of September 11, 2001.

148. Karoli, "New Documents Show Bush Administration Planned War in Iraq Well Before 9/11/2001," *Crooks and Liars*, September 24, 2010, at http://crooksandliars.com/karoli/new-documents-show-bush-administration-plan, accessed on June 4, 2014. See also Julian Borger's article "Bush team 'agreed plan to attack the Taliban the day before September 11,'" *The Guardian*, London, March 24, 2004, at http://www.theguardian.com/world/2004/mar/24/september11.usa2, accessed on June 4, 2014.

149. Gerhard Kummel, "A Soldier is a Soldier is a Soldier" in *Handbook of the Sociology of the Military*, edited by Giuseppe Caforio (New York: Kluwer Academic/Plenum, 2003), 432.

150. Samir Amin, *The Liberal Virus* (New York: Monthly Review Press, 2004), 73.

151. Lee Maracle, *Daughters Are Forever* (Vancouver: Polestar, 2002), 15.

Chapter 4

1. Malcolm X, *By Any Means Necessary* (New York: Pathfinder Press, 1980), 116.

2. Cited in Renford Reese, *Prison Race* (Durham: Carolina Academic Press, 2006), 181.

3. *New York Times*, October 8, 2009.

4. Howard Steven Friedman, "7 OECD Countries with the Highest Incarceration Rates: U.S. and Israel Top List," *Huffington Post*, July 7, 2011, at http://www.huffingtonpost.com/howard-steven-friedman/7-oecd-countries-with-the_b_912680.html#s317353&title=7_Mexico_208, accessed on January 2, 2012.

5. *Broken on All Sides: Race, Mass Incarcer-*

ation and New Visions for Criminal Justice in the U.S., Accolade Competition Winner film documentary, 2012.

6. Howard Steven Friedman, "7 OECD Countries with the Highest Incarceration Rates: U.S. and Israel Top List," *Huffington Post*, July 7, 2011, at http://www.huffingtonpost.com/howard-steven-friedman/7-oecd-countries-with-the_b_912680.html#s317353&title=7_Mexico_208, accessed on January 2, 2012.

7. Eduardo Porter, "In the U.S., Punishment Comes Before the Crimes," *New York Times*, April 29, 2014, at http://www.nytimes.com/2014/04/30/business/economy/in-the-us-punishment-comes-before-the-crimes.html accessed on May 3, 2014.

8. Eduardo Porter, "In the U.S., Punishment Comes Before the Crimes," *New York Times*, April 29, 2014, at http://www.nytimes.com/2014/04/30/business/economy/in-the-us-punishment-comes-before-the-crimes.html, accessed on May 3, 2014.

9. Melissa S. Kearney, Benjamin H. Harris, Elisa Jácome, and Lucie Parker, "Ten Economic Facts About Crime and Incarceration in the United States" (Washington, D.C.: The Hamilton Project, May 2014), 13, at http://www.hamiltonproject.org/files/downloads_and_links/v8_THP_10CrimeFacts.pdf, accessed on June 22, 2014.

10. Melissa S. Kearney, Benjamin H. Harris, Elisa Jácome, and Lucie Parker, "Ten Economic Facts About Crime and Incarceration in the United States" (Washington, D.C.: The Hamilton Project, May 2014), 11, at http://www.hamiltonproject.org/files/downloads_and_links/v8_THP_10CrimeFacts.pdf, accessed on June 22, 2014.

11. The Editorial Board, "End Mass Incarceration Now," *New York Times*, May 24, 2014, at http://www.nytimes.com/2014/05/25/opinion/sunday/end-mass-incarceration-now.html?hp&rref=opinion, accessed on June 22, 2014.

12. Eduardo Porter, "In the U.S., Punishment Comes Before the Crimes," *New York Times*, April 29, 2014, at http://www.nytimes.com/2014/04/30/business/economy/in-the-us-punishment-comes-before-the-crimes.html, accessed on May 3, 2014.

13. Dan Berger, with Lars Din, Zein El-Amine, and Kenyon Farrow, "Like Prisons? You'll Love Globalization. Like Globalization? You'll Love Prisons," at http://www.coloursofresistance.org/273/like-prisons-you'll-love-globalization-like-globalization-you'll-love-prisons/, accessed on September 2, 2014.

14. Dan Berger, with Lars Din, Zein El-Amine,

and Kenyon Farrow, "Like Prisons? You'll Love Globalization. Like Globalization? You'll Love Prisons," at http://www.coloursofresistance.org/273/like-prisons-you'll-love-globalization-like-globalization-you'll-love-prisons/, accessed on September 2, 2014.

15. See Alfred W. McCoy, *The Politics of Heroin: CIA Complicity in the Global Drug Trade* (New York: Lawrence Hill, 1991), especially chapters 4–9; Alexander Cockburn and Jeffrey St. Clair, *Whiteout: The CIA, Drugs, and the Press* (New York: Verso, 1998), especially chapters 9–12; Christopher Robbins, *The Invisible Air Force: The Story of the CIA's Secret Airlines* (New York: Macmillan, 1979); and William Blum, *Rogue State: A Guide to the World's Only Superpower* (Monroe, ME: Common Courage Press, 2005), especially chapter 24.

16. Alexander Cockburn and Jeffrey St. Clair, *Whiteout: The CIA, Drugs, and the Press*, chapter 12.

17. See, for instance, Peter Dale Scott and Jonathan Marshall, *Cocaine Politics: Drugs, Armies and the CIA in Central America* (Berkeley: University of California, 1998), especially part II, "Exposure and Cover-Up." There is clear evidence that the CIA intervened to obstruct law enforcement investigations of known drug traffickers in California in 1983 during the San Francisco "Frogman Case" when the largest bust of cocaine occurred in the state's history, resulting in the U.S. Attorney General returning confiscated cash to the contra drug traffickers. See Wes Hill's article "CIA Admitted Guilt in U.S. Citizen's Death and Addictions: CIA Complicity in Cocaine Distribution," *Progress Report*, January 4, 2002, at http://www.progress.org/tpr/cia-admitted-guilt-in-deaths-and-addictions/, accessed on May 3, 2014.

18. This was conveyed to the author by an electrician who worked on prison construction in Indigenous communities in Northern Arizona on September 21, 2014.

19. Thomas P. Bonczar, "Prevalence of Imprisonment in the U.S. Population 1974–2001," U.S. Department of Justice, Office of Justice Programs, *Bureau of Justice Special Report*, at http://www.cbsnews.com/htdocs/pdf/prisontime.pdf, accessed on May 4, 2014.

20. Thomas P. Bonczar, "Prevalence of Imprisonment in the U.S. Population 1974–2001," U.S. Department of Justice, Office of Justice Programs, *Bureau of Justice Special Report*, at http://www.cbsnews.com/htdocs/pdf/prisontime.pdf, accessed on May 4, 2014.

21. Eric E. Sterling and Julie Stewart, "Undo This Legacy of Len Bias's Death," *Washington*

Post, June 24, 2006, at http://www.washington
post.com/wp-dyn/content/article/2006/06/23/
AR2006062301261.html, accessed on May 3,
2014.

22. Conveyed by legal academic Michelle
Alexander in the film documentary *Broken on All
Sides; Mass Incarceration and New Visions for
Criminal Justice in the U.S.*

23. "Incarceration rate for African Americans
now six times the national average," *Russian
Times*, February 19, 2013, at http://rt.com/usa/
incarceration-african-black-prison-606/ For the
statistics on Latino incarceration, see the article,
"Hispanics in Prisons and Jails," *The Sentencing
Project*, Washington, D.C., at http://www.
sentencingproject.org/doc/publications/inc_
hispanicprisoners.pdf, accessed on September 23,
2014.

24. B.W. Burston, B. Jones, and P. Robertson-
Saunders, "Drug Use and African Americans:
Myth Versus Reality," *Journal of Alcohol and Drug
Education* 40, no. 2 (1995): 19–39.

25. Michael Hallett, *Private Prisons in America: A Critical Race Perspective* (Urbana: University of Illinois Press, 2006), 54.

26. Eddy Zheng and the Asian Prisoner Support Committee, *Other: An Asian & Pacific Is-
lander Prisoner Anthology* (Hayward, CA: Asian
Prisoner Support Committee, 2007), vii.

27. John P. May and Khalid R. Pitts (eds.),
*Building Violence: How America's Rush to Incar-
cerate Creates More Violence* (Thousand Oaks,
CA: Sage, 2000), 71. The picture of forcibly
stripped naked Black men in the picture on this
page prior to being processed for incarceration
kindles images of slavery and apartheid South
Africa.

28. The 2012 FilmBuff film documentary *The
House I Live In*, directed by Eugene Jarecki, provides a vivid pictorial depiction of the lethal effects of the "War on Drugs" on working class people, especially Blacks. Available at Netflix.com.

29. W.E.B. Du Bois, *The Souls of Black Folk*
(New York: Fawcett World Library, 1970), 132–
33.

30. John Irwin, *The Warehouse Prison: Disposal of the New Dangerous Class* (Los Angeles:
Roxbury, 2005), 15.

31. W.D. Lewis, *From Newgate to Dannemora:
The Rise of the Penitentiary System in New York,
1796–1848* (Ithaca: Cornell University Press,
1965), 121.

32. John Hope Franklin and Alfred Moss, Jr.,
*From Slavery to Freedom: A History of African
Americans*, Eighth Edition (New York: McGraw-
Hill, 2000), 308.

33. Cited in "The Black Codes" in *Black Pro-

test: 350 Years of History, Documents and Analyses*,
edited by Joanne Grant (New York: Fawcett Columbine, 1968), 139.

34. Cited in "The Black Codes" in *Black Protest: 350 Years of History, Documents and Analyses*,
144.

35. Katheryn Russell, *The Color of Crime:
Racial Hoaxes, White Fear, Black Protectionism,
Police Harassment, and Other Macroaggressions*
(New York: New York University Press, 1998),
22.

36. Jerome Miller, *Search and Destroy: African
American Males in the Criminal Justice System*
(New York: Cambridge University Press, 1996),
52.

37. In a pre-trial hearing involving racial profiling of an African arrested in Tucson in 2004,
the author was told by the judge at the hearing
that he had been informed by a Black expert on
crime that the Black people in jail were rightly incarcerated since they were essentially criminals
and that he (the judge) used that information as
the basis for his own adjudication.

38. Cited in Jerome Miller, *Search and Destroy: African American Males in the Criminal Justice System*, 55, based on data from the U.S. Department of Justice, *Bureau of Justice Statistics*,
National Corrections Reporting Program, 1990,
NCJ-141879 (Washington, D.C.: U.S. Department of Justice, 1993), 15, and from Andrew
Hacker's *Two Nations: Black and White, Separate,
Hostile, Unequal* (New York: Scribner's, 1992),
197.

39. *World Press Review*, November 1992; Bureau of Justice Statistics Bulletin: *Prisoners in
1989* (Washington, D.C.: U.S. Department of
Justice, May 1990).

40. Elizabeth Alexander, "The Care and Feeding of the Correctional Industrial Complex" in
*Building Violence: How America's Rush to Incar-
cerate Creates More Violence*, edited by John P.
May and Khalid R. Pitts (Thousand Oaks: Sage,
2008), 52.

41. See Cornel West's well-known book *Race
Matters* (New York: Vintage, 1994) and his latest
book authored with Tavis Smiley, *The Rich and
the Rest of Us: A Poverty Manifesto* (New York:
SmileyBooks, 2012) in this regard.

42. Manning Marable, *The Great Wells of
Democracy: The Meaning of Race in American Life*
(New York: Basic Books, 2002), 149–50, 162.

43. Manning Marable, *The Great Wells of Democracy: The Meaning of Race in American Life*,
154.

44. Joy James, "Introduction: Democracy and
Captivity" in *The New Abolitionists: (Neo)Slave
Narratives and Contemporary Prison Writings*, ed-

ited by Joy James (Albany: State University of New York Press, 2005), xxii–xxiii, and Angela Davis, *Abolition Democracy: Beyond Empire, Prisons, and Torture* (New York: Seven Stories Press, 2005).

45. For the protection of privacy rights, the identity of the person and the name of the correctional facility need to remain anonymous.

46. Khalil Gibran Muhammed, *The Condemnation of Blackness: Race, Crime, and the Making of Modern America* (Cambridge: Harvard University Press, 2010).

47. See for instance, Derrick Bell, *Faces at the Bottom of the Well: The Permanence of Racism* (New York: Basic Books, 1992) and *And We Are Not Saved: The Elusive Quest for Racial Justice* (New York: Basic Books, 1987).

48. Derrick Bell, *Silent Covenants: Brown V. Board of Education and the Unfulfilled Hopes for Racial Reform* (New York: Oxford University Press, 2004), especially chapter 15, "Moving Beyond Racial Fortuity" and "Conclusion."

49. See Angela Davis, *Women Race & Class* (New York: Vintage, 1983); *Abolition Democracy: Beyond Prison, Torture, and Empire* (New York: Seven Stories Press, 2005); and *The Meaning of Freedom: And Other Difficult Dialogues* (San Francisco: City Lights Books, 2012). *The Meaning of Freedom* discusses the globalization of prison practices in neo-liberal capitalism on pages 144–148.

50. Patricia Hill Collins, *Black Sexual Politics: African Americans, Gender and the New Racism* (New York: Routledge, 2004), 233.

51. Marcellus Andrews, *The Political Economy of Hope and Fear: Capitalism and the Black Condition in America* (New York: New York University Press), 27.

52. A. Leon Higginbotham, Jr., Aderson Belegarde François, and Linda Y. Yueh, "The O. J. Simpson Trial: Who Was Improperly 'Playing the Race Card?'" in *Birth of a Nation'hood: Gaze, Script, and Spectacle in the O. J. Simpson Case*, edited by Toni Morrison and Claudia Brodsky Lacour (New York: Pantheon, 1997).

53. See, for instance, the section "Conceptualizing Race, Class, and Gender," by Margaret Anderson and Patricia Hill Collins, in *Race, Class and Gender: An Anthology*, edited by Margaret Anderson and Patricia Hill Collins (Belmont, CA: Wadsworth, 2004).

54. Howard Winant, "Racial Dualism at Century's End" in *The House That Race Built: Black Americans, U.S. Terrain*, edited and with an introduction by Whaneema Lubiano (New York: Pantheon, 1997), 105. For Frantz Fanon's work on race, see for instance his most acclaimed work

on this subject, *Black Skins, White Masks* (New York: Grove Press, 2008).

55. Howard Winant, "Racial Dualism at Century's End" in *The House That Race Built: Black Americans, U.S. Terrain*, 105.

56. Frantz Fanon, *Black Skins, White Masks* (New York: Grove Press, 1967), 180.

57. In feudal England, over 200 crimes were subject to capital punishment, and this legacy of moral condemnation and lethal punishment was transmitted into the norms of Anglo-Saxon law and order in the early development of U.S. colonial society. The obsession with adjudicating sexual morality and morés is classically illustrated in the December 2012 decision by the British government to prohibit the Church of England from marrying same-sex couples. See the article "Church of England banned from offering same-sex marriages but all other religions can 'opt-in' for gay ceremonies," *The Independent*, London, December 12, 2012, at http://www.independent.co.uk/news/uk/politics/church-of-england-banned-from-offering-samesex-marriages-but-all-other-religious-organisations-can-opt-in-for-gay-ceremonies-8405966.html

58. Benjamin Weiser, "Wall Street: High Pressure, High Powered, Often Just High," *Washington Post*, May 13, 1994. This was also documented in the excellent documentary on the 2008 engineered financial crisis, *Inside Job*.

59. Dylan Murphy, "Money Laundering and the Drug Trade: The Role of the Banks," Global Research, Centre for Research on Globalization, Montreal, Canada, October 20, 2013, at http://www.globalresearch.ca/money-laundering-and-the-drug-trade-the-role-of-the-banks/5334205, accessed on September 24, 2014.

60. Alexander Cockburn and Jeffrey St. Clair, *Whiteout: The CIA, Drugs, and the Press* (New York: Verso, 1998), 319.

61. The chapter "The Arkansas Connection: Mena," especially pages 333–344, of Alexander Cockburn and Jeffrey St. Clair, *Whiteout: The CIA, Drugs, and the Press*, provides an exposé of the Clinton governorship in the cover-up of drug trafficking in Arkansas in the 1980s.

62. The details of this shocking drug smuggling scandal involving the highest-level government officials including presidents and the National Security Council in the 1980s, which inevitably targeted poor Black and Brown communities for social and economic ruin through illegal drug invasion so that more youth would end up in prison for drug-related crimes are disclosed in Catherine Austin Fitt's explosive article on government-illegal drug design and complicity, "Dillon Read & Co., Inc. and the Aristocracy of

Stock Profits," at http://www.dunwalke.com/4_ Narco_Dollars.htm, accessed on September 25, 2014.

63. Alexander Cockburn and Jeffrey St. Clair, *Whiteout: The CIA, Drugs, and the Press*, 336, 334.

64. This is documented from a Congressional Record of May 7, 1998, Page H2970, and is footnoted in Catherine Austin Fitts's article "Dillon Read & Co., Inc. and the Aristocracy of Stock Profits" at http://www.dunwalke.com/4_Narco_ Dollars.htm. The footnote is at http://www. dunwalke.com/resources/footnotes.html#23, accessed on September 25, 2014. See also William Blum, *Rogue State: A Guide to the World's Only Superpower* (Monroe, ME: Common Courage Press, 2005), 297.

65. Dan Feder, "Gary Webb's 'Dark Alliance' Returns to the Internet," June 23, 2005, at http:// www.narconews.com/darkalliance/, accessed on December 12, 2012. For an illumination of the role of the CIA in narco-trafficking under the pretext of fighting "narco-terrorism" in conjunction with right-wing military regimes in Latin America, see Peter Dale Scott and Jonathan Marshall's *Cocaine Politics: Drugs, Armies, and the CIA in Central America* (Berkeley: University of California Press, 1998). Alfred McCoy's *The Politics of Heroin: CIA Complicity in The Global Drug Trade* (Chicago: Lawrence Hill, 2003) describes in excellent detail the role of the CIA in the opium and heroin trade during the height of the U.S. military involvement in south-east Asia.

66. David Carr, "Resurrecting a Disgraced Reporter: 'Killing the Messenger' Recalls a Reporter Wrongly Disgraced," *New York Times*, October 2, 2014, at http://www.nytimes.com/2014/10/05/ movies/kill-the-messenger-recalls-a-reporter-wrongly-disgraced.html?_r=0, accessed on October 3, 2014.

67. See, for example, William Blum's excellent book, *Rogue State: A Guide to the World's Only Superpower* (Monroe, ME: Common Courage Press, 2005), especially chapter 24, "The CIA and Drugs: Just say, "Why not?'

68. Catherine Austin Fitt, "Dillon Read & Co., Inc. and the Aristocracy of Stock Profits," at http://www.dunwalke.com/4_Narco_Dollars. htm, accessed on September 25, 2014.

69. "1 mn Died from Aghan Heroin, Drug Production '40 Times Higher' Since NATO op," *Russian Times*, April 3, 2013, at http://rt.com/ news/afghanistan-heroin-production-increased-266/, accessed on September 1, 2014.

70. Michel Chossudovsky, "The Spoils of War: Afghanistan's Multibillion Dollar Heroin Trade: Washington's Hidden Agenda: Restore the

Drug Trade," Global Research, Centre for Research on Globalization, Montreal, Canada, June 14, 2005, at http://www.globalresearch.ca/the-spoils-of-war-afghanistan-s-multibillion-dollar-heroin-trade/91, accessed on September 24, 2014.

71. Ghanizada, "Annual Value of Afghan Opium Trade Reach $70 Billion," *Khaama Press, Afghan News Agency*, April 29, 2012, at http:// www.khaama.com/annual-value-of-afghan-opium-trade-reach-70-billion-206, accessed on September 24, 2014.

72. Abby Martin, "How Opium Is Keeping U.S. in Afghanistan: CIA's Shady History of Drug Trafficking," *Media Roots*, January 3, 2014, at http://www.mediaroots.org/opium-what-afghanistan-is-really-about/, accessed on September 24, 2014.

73. "Afghan Drug Trafficking Brings U.S. $50 Billion a Year," *Russian Times*, May 29, 2010, at http://rt.com/usa/afghanistan-us-drug-trafficking/, accessed on September 24, 2014.

74. Chris Arsenault, "Mexican Official: CIA 'Manages' Drug Trade," *Al Jazeera*, July 24, 2012, at http://www.aljazeera.com/indepth/features/ 2012/07/2012721152715628181.html, accessed on September 24, 2014.

75. This documentation of U.S. Border Patrol involvement in drug smuggling and the drug economy was communicated to the author in January 2014 by an Indigenous Tohono O'odham elder who had worked with Tohono O'odham local authorities and subsequently lost his job for such exposure of corruption. Rebecca S. Gambler's article "Border Security: Additional Actions Needed to Strengthen CBP Efforts to Mitigate Risk of Employee Corruption and Misconduct" describes the arrests of 144 U.S. Border Patrol agents for drug smuggling, in *GAO: U.S. Government Accountability Office*, December 4, 2012, at http://www.gao.gov/products/GAO-13-59, accessed on September 24, 2014. Widespread practice of U.S. Border Patrol and other national security personnel, including veteran officers involved in the drug trade is well documented, for instance, in Geoffrey Ramsey's article "US Border Patrol Agent Arrested for Smuggling Drugs on the Job," *Insight Crime: Organized Crime in the Americas*, December 6, 2012, at http://www. insightcrime.org/news-briefs/border-patrol-agent-arrested-smuggling-drugs, accessed on September 24, 2014.

76. Michael C. Ruppert, *Crossing the Rubicon: The Decline of the Roman Empire at the End of the Age of Oil* (Gabriola Island, British Columbia: New Society Publishers, 2004), 53.

77. David Macadam, blog on the United Fruit Company, "The Oligarch Kings: Power, Politics, and America's Noble Families," May 27, 2010, at

http://theoligarchkings.wordpress.com/2010/ 05/27/united-fruit-company/, accessed on October 21, 2014. The acknowledgment of the CIA-orchestrated coup in Guatemala in 1954 was documented for instance by Elizabeth Malkin in her article "An Apology for a Guatemalan Coup, 57 years later," *The New York Times*, October 20, 2011, at http://www.nytimes.com/2011/10/21/ world/americas/an-apology-for-a-guatemalan-coup-57-years-later.html, accessed on October 21, 2014. For a detailed history on the role of the United Fruit Company (Chiquita today) in entrenching the establishment of banana plantations, cheap Indigenous labor, and capitalist empire in Latin America from the 19th century, see Peter Chapman's *Bananas: How the United Fruit Company Shaped the World* (New York: Canongate, 2007).

78. Michael C. Ruppert, *Crossing the Rubicon: The Decline of the Roman Empire at the End of the Age of Oil*, 54. Martha Stewart's conviction was reported in Kara Scannell and Matthew Rose's article "Martha Stewart is Found Guilty of All Charges," *The Wall Street Journal*, March 7, 2004, at http://online.wsj.com/articles/SB1078 33235519345426, accessed on September 25, 2014.

79. Michael C. Ruppert, *Crossing the Rubicon: The Decline of the Roman Empire at the End of the Age of Oil*, 53–57.

80. Nancy Turner Banks, *Aids, Opium, Diamonds and Empire: The Deadly Virus of International Greed* (Bloomington: iUniverse, 2010), 203. Banks, who holds an M.D., has written an excellent book that underscores in cogent detail how the globalized capitalist system has pulverized all life on Earth and generated one crisis after another, from the drug epidemic, to the mortgage financial crisis, the eruption and spread of diseases through genetically modified, hormone-injected, and pesticide-laced food, and the AIDS and cancer pandemics, all for greed for money and power.

81. "Filthy Lucre: Afghan Drug Profits Too Juicy to Resist," *Russian Times*, November 22, 2011, at http://rt.com/news/afghan-drug-us-money-893/.

82. Dylan Murphy, "Money Laundering and the Drug Trade: The Role of the Banks," Global Research, Centre for Research on Globalization, Montreal, Canada, October 20, 2013, at http://www.globalresearch.ca/money-laundering-and-the-drug-trade-the-role-of-the-banks/5334205, accessed on September 24, 2014.

83. Dylan Murphy, "Money Laundering and the Drug Trade: The Role of the Banks," Global Research, Centre for Research on Globalization, Montreal, Canada, October 20, 2013, at http://

www.globalresearch.ca/money-laundering-and-the-drug-trade-the-role-of-the-banks/5334205, accessed on September 24, 2014.

84. Steven Donziger (ed.), *The Real War on Crime: The Report of the National Criminal Justice Commission* (New York: HarperCollins, 1996), 74.

85. Steven Donziger (ed.), *The Real War on Crime: The Report of the National Criminal Justice Commission*, 78.

86. Steven Donziger (ed.), *The Real War on Crime: The Report of the National Criminal Justice Commission*, 79.

87. "Sunday Debate: Is DARE Effective? 'Overwhelming Evidence' Shows DARE Has No Lasting Impact," newstimes.com, February 19, 2010, at http://www.newstimes.com/opinion/article/ Sunday-debate-Is-DARE-effective-Overwhelming-372445.php, accessed on June 1, 2014.

88. Stephen Glass, "DON'T YOU D.A.R.E.," *New Republic,* March 3, 1997, at http://druglibrary. net/schaffer/media/txtglass030397.html, accessed on June 1, 2014.

89. For the number of orphans in Iraq through 2007, particularly as a result of UN–imposed sanctions from 1991 and the U.S. invasion and occupation of the country in 2003, see the article by *Alternet* staff, "Occupation Toll: 5 Million Iraqi Children Orphaned," December 18, 2007, at http://www.alternet.org/story/70886/ occupation's_tollpercent3A_5_million_iraqi_ children_orphaned, accessed on December 12, 2012. This number was disclosed by the Iraqi Anti-Corruption Board in December 2007. For the source of the statistic documenting 600,000 orphans living on the streets, see Gilbert Burnham, Shanon Doocy, Elizabeth Dzeng, Riyadh Lafta, and Les Roberts, "Iraq: The Human Cost of the War in Iraq: A Mortality Study, 2002–2006," at http://web.mit.edu/humancostiraq/ reports/human-cost-war-101106.pdf (Baltimore: Bloomberg School of Public Health, John Hopkins University; Baghdad: School of Medicine, Al Mustansiriya University, in cooperation with MIT Center for International Studies, October 2006), accessed on May 26, 2014.

90. *Socio-Economics History Blog: Socio-Economics & History Commentary*, January 21, 2011, at http://socioecohistory.wordpress.com/ 2011/01/21/ex-cia-official-patriot-act-a-nazi-law/, accessed on June 20, 2014.

91. *The Independent*, London, November 9, 2010. George W. Bush's book is *Decision Points* (New York: Broadway, 2011).

92. *The Independent*, London, November 9, 2010.

93. Associated Press, "Bush: 'We do not tor-

ture' terror suspects," November 7, 2005, at http:
//www.nbcnews.com/id/9956644/ns/us_news-
security/t/bush-we-do-not-torture-terror-
suspects/#.VEc3j97beOI, accessed on October
21, 2014.

94. Jo Becker and Scott Shane, "Secret 'Kill
List' Proves a Test of Obama's Principles and
Will," *New York Times*, May 29, 2012, at http://
www.nytimes.com/2012/05/29/world/obamas-
leadership-in-war-on-al-qaeda.html?pagewanted-
=all, accessed on October 21, 2014.

95. Olivier Knox, "Obama: Senate Report
Will Show 'We Tortured Some Folks,'" *Yahoo
News*, August 1, 2014, at http://news.yahoo.com/
obama—senate-report-will-show—we-tortured-
some-folks-204712041.html, accessed on October
21, 2014.

96. Peter Foster, "CIA 'Tortured al-Qaeda Suspects Close to the Point of Death by Drowning
Them in Water-Filled Baths,'" *The Telegraph*, London, September 7, 2014, at http://www.telegraph.
co.uk/news/worldnews/al-qaeda/11080450/
CIA-tortured-al-Qaeda-suspects-close-to-the-
point-of-death-by-drowning-them-in-water-
filled-baths.html, accessed on September 23, 2014.

97. Bureau of Investigative Journalism,
"More Than 2,400 Dead as Obama's Drone Campaign Marks Five Years," Global Research, Centre
for Research on Globalization, Montreal, Canada,
January 23, 2014, at http://www.globalresearch.
ca/more-than-2400-dead-as-obamas-drone-
campaign-marks-five-years/5366037, accessed on
October 21, 2014.

98. Brendan Fischer and Lisa Graves, "International Law and the War on Terror," *Cost of War*,
n.d., at http://costsofwar.org/sites/default/files/
articles/35/attachments/FischerandGraves
InternationalLaw.pdf, accessed on September 23,
2014.

99. Carmen Velasquez, "Obama Broke His
Promise to Latinos (Maybe We Should Sit This
Election Out)," *Common Dreams*, September 9,
2014, at http://www.commondreams.org/views/
2014/09/09/obama-broke-his-promise-latinos-
maybe-we-should-sit-election-out, accessed on
September 9, 2014.

100. Mary Bosworth, "Identity, Citizenship,
and Punishment," in *Race, Gender, and Punishment: From Colonialism to the War on Terror*, edited by Mary Bosworth and Jeanne Flavin (New
Brunswick, NJ: Rutgers University Press), 139.

101. Mary Bosworth, "Identity, Citizenship,
and Punishment," in *Race, Gender, and Punishment: From Colonialism to the War on Terror*, 143.

102. Ian Urbina, "Using Jailed Migrants as a
Pool of Cheap Labor," *New York Times*, May 25,
2014, at http://www.nytimes.com/2014/05/25/

us/using-jailed-migrants-as-a-pool-of-cheap-
labor.html?emc=edit_th_20140525&nl=todays
headlines&nlid=40858187, accessed on May 26,
2014.

103. Ian Urbina, "Using Jailed Migrants as a
Pool of Cheap Labor," *New York Times*, May 25,
2014, at http://www.nytimes.com/2014/05/25/
us/using-jailed-migrants-as-a-pool-of-cheap-
labor.html?emc=edit_th_20140525&nl=todays
headlines&nlid=40858187, accessed on May 26,
2014.

104. Laura Sullivan, "Prison Economics Help
Drive Ariz Immigration Law," *National Public
Radio*, October 28, 2010, at http://www.npr.org/
templates/story/story.php?storyId=130833741,
accessed on October 29, 2010.

105. The Project for the New American Century is a project outlining the role of the United
States in conjunction with NATO to maintain
military and political dominance in the world,
with Iraq, North Africa and the Arab world featuring prominently as an area that warrants total
U.S. control (due to the region's strategic location
and its possession of vital energy resources), at
http://www.rightweb.irc-online.org/profile/
project_for_the_new_american_century, accessed
on May 27, 2014.

106. United States Space Command, *Vision
for 2020* (United States Space Command, Peterson Air Force Base, 1997), 6, at http://fas.org/spp/
military/docops/usspac/visbook.pdf, accessed on
September 23, 2014. This point was highlighted
toward the end of John Pilger's classic 2001 globalization documentary, *The New Rulers of the
World*, available on video at http://johnpilger.
com/videos/the-new-rulers-of-the-world, accessed
on September 23, 2014.

107. The historic release of Marshall Eddie
Conway was covered by *Democracy Now!* on March
5, 2014, at http://www.democracynow.org/2014/
3/5/exclusive_freed_ex_black_panther_marshall,
accessed on March 5, 2014.

108. The case of Hugo Pinell is described at
the Campaign for Hugo Pinell at http://www.
hugopinell.com, accessed on May 3, 2014. A summary of Cinque McGee's arrest and incarceration
is well described by Mumia Abu-Jamal, "Ruchell
Cinque McGee: Sole Survivor Still," at http://
4strugglemag.org/2012/10/04/ruchell-cinque-
magee-sole-survivor-still/, accessed on May 3,
2014. George Jackson was part of the Soledad
Brothers and his prison letters and political insights are documented in *Soledad Brother: The
Prison Letters of George Jackson* (New York: Coward-McCann, 1970) and in *Blood in My Eye* (Baltimore: Black Classic Press, 1990). See Joy James'
edited work *Imprisoned Intellectuals: America's*

Political Prisoners Write on Life, Liberation, and Rebellion (Lanham, MD: Rowman & Littlefield, 2003) for an illumination of radical struggles for liberation in the U.S., especially within the prison system and in the words of those who have been incarcerated for political reasons over excessively long terms. The case of Oscar López Rivera was highlighted on *Democracy Now!* on May 31, 2013, in the program "Oscar López Rivera: After 32 Years in Prison, Calls Grow for Release of Puerto Rican Activist," at http://www.democracynow.org/2013/5/31/oscar_lpez_rivera_after_32_years, accessed on April 16, 2014.

109. Vernetta D. Young and Rebecca Reviere, *Women Behind Bars: Gender and Race in U.S. Prisons* (Boulder: Lyenne Rienner, 2006), 86.

110. Vernetta D. Young and Rebecca Reviere, *Women Behind Bars: Gender and Race in U.S. Prisons*, 9.

111. Monica Lewis, "Most Female Prisoners Are Black," BlackAmericaWeb.com, Black Radical Congress Listserv, March 16, 2005, accessed on March 16, 2005.

112. Paul Harris, *Black Rage Confronts the Law.* (New York: New York University Press, 1997), 265.

113. Vernetta D. Young and Rebecca Reviere, *Women Behind Bars: Gender and Race in U.S. Prisons*, 86.

114. Vernetta D. Young and Rebecca Reviere, *Women Behind Bars: Gender and Race in U.S. Prisons*, 1.

115. Adrien K. Wing, "Black Women and Gangs" in *States of Confinement: Policing, Detention, and Prisons*, edited by Joy James (New York: St. Martin's Press, 2000), 103.

116. Faith E. Lutze, "Ultramasculine Stereotypes and Violence in the Control of Women Inmates" in *Women in Prison: Gender and Social Control*, edited by Barbara H. Zaitzow and Jim Thomas (Boulder: Lynne Rienner, 2003), 187.

117. Zelma Henriques and Evelyn Gilbert, "Sexual Abuse and Sexual Assault of Women in Prison" in *It's a Crime: Women and Justice* (Upper Saddle River, NJ: Prentice Hall, 2000), 253–268.

118. Cited from the National Coalition of Anti-Violence Programs, "Hate Violence Against the Lesbian, Gay, Bisexual, Transgender, and Queer Communities in the United States in 2009" by Lori A. Saffin, "Identities Under Siege: Violence Against Transpersons of Color" in *Captive Genders: Trans Embodiment and the Prison Industrial Complex* (Oakland: AK Press, 2011), 141.

119. Lori A. Saffin, "Identities Under Siege: Violence Against Transpersons of Color" in *Captive Genders: Trans Embodiment and the Prison Industrial Complex*, 157.

120. O.S. Ray, *Drugs, Society and Human Behavior* (St. Louis: C.V. Mosby, 1972), 38.

121. Vijay Prashad, *Keeping Up with the Dow Joneses: Debt, Prison, Workfare* (Cambridge, MA: South End Press, 2003), 80.

122. Donna Selman and Paul Leighton, *Punishment for Sale: Private Prisons, Big Business, and the Incarceration Binge* (Lanham, MD: Rowman & Littlefield, 2010), 21.

123. Michelle Alexander, "The New Jim Crow: How the War on Drugs Gave Birth to a Permanent American Undercaste," *Mother Jones*, March 8, 2010, at http://motherjones.com/politics/2010/03/new-jim-crow-war-on-drugs, accessed on March 20, 2014. Michelle Alexander's book *The New Jim Crow: Mass Incarceration in the Age of Color Blindness* (New York: New Press, 2010) is essential reading for all students of the prison industrial complex and race and class oppression.

124. Michelle Alexander, "The New Jim Crow: How the War on Drugs Gave Birth to a Permanent American Undercaste," *Mother Jones*, March 8, 2010, at http://motherjones.com/politics/2010/03/new-jim-crow-war-on-drugs.

125. Michelle Alexander, "The New Jim Crow: How the War on Drugs Gave Birth to a Permanent American Undercaste," *Mother Jones*, March 8, 2010, at http://motherjones.com/politics/2010/03/new-jim-crow-war-on-drugs.

126. *Human Rights Watch Report*, "Prisons," 2001, 3.

127. Donna Selman and Paul Leighton, *Punishment for Sale: Private Prisons, Big Business, and the Incarceration Binge*, 37.

128. Christopher Windham, "After 20 Years, the Debate Over Mandatory Minimum Sentencing Laws for Cocaine Heats Up," *Human Nature Magazine*, June 20, 2010, at http://www.humannaturemag.com/index.php?option=com_content&view=article&id=131:after-20-years-the-debate-over-mandatory-minimum-sentencing-laws-for-cocaine-heats-up&catid=38:political-science&Itemid=598, accessed on October 24, 2014.

129. Christopher Windham, "After 20 Years, the Debate Over Mandatory Minimum Sentencing Laws for Cocaine Heats Up," *Human Nature Magazine*, June 20, 2010, at http://www.humannaturemag.com/index.php?option=com_content&view=article&id=131:after-20-years-the-debate-over-mandatory-minimum-sentencing-laws-for-cocaine-heats-up&catid=38:political-science&Itemid=598, accessed on October 24, 2014.

130. Christopher Windham, "After 20 Years, the Debate Over Mandatory Minimum Sentencing Laws for Cocaine Heats Up," *Human Nature*

Magazine, June 20, 2010, at http://www.human naturemag.com/index.php?option=com_content &view=article&id=131:after-20-years-the-debate-over-mandatory-minimum-sentencing-laws-for-cocaine-heats-up&catid=38:political-science &Itemid=598, accessed on October 24, 2014.

131. Vivien Miller, "Race, Class, Age and Punitive Segregation: Prisons and Prison Populations in the Contemporary United States" in *America's Americans: Population Issues in U.S. Society and Politics*, edited by Philip Davies and Iwan Morgan (London: Institute for the Study of the Americas, University of London, 2007), 251.

132. Tom Teepen, "U.S. Legal System Fails to Do Justice to Blacks," *Arizona Daily Star*, May 3, 1999.

133. Jeffrey Reiman, *The Rich Get Richer and the Poor Get Prison* (Needham Heights, MA: Allyn and Bacon, 2001), 131. This book is important too in underscoring the class-biased nature of the criminal justice system, reflecting its own criminality in generally shielding White collar crime and crimes of the thefts of billions by corporations from prosecution and punishment, in contradistinction to the law enforcement's and the legal system's aggressive pursuit of justice when it comes to crimes committed by poor people, particularly people of color.

134. Tom Teepen, "U.S. Legal System Fails to Do Justice to Blacks," *Arizona Daily Star*, May 3, 1999.

135. Gregg Barak, Jeanne M. Flavin, and Paul S. Leighton, *Class, Race, Gender, and Crime: Social Realities of Justice in America* (Los Angeles: Roxbury, 2001), 118.

136. Common Sense for Drug Policy, www.csdp.org and www.drugwarfacts.org, accessed on February 18, 2014.

137. Michelle Alexander, "The New Jim Crow: How the War on Drugs Gave Birth to a Permanent American Undercaste," *Mother Jones*, March 8, 2010, at http://motherjones.com/politics/2010/03/new-jim-crow-war-on-drugs.

138. Vijay Prashad, *Keeping Up with the Dow Joneses: Debt, Prison, Workfare*, 81.

139. Manning Marable, "Facing the Demon Head On" in *The Great Wells of Democracy: The Meaning of Race in American Life* (New York: BasicCivitas Books, 2002), 154.

140. Manning Marable, "Facing the Demon Head On" in *The Great Wells of Democracy: The Meaning of Race in American Life*, 154.

141. Manning Marable, "Facing the Demon Head On" in *The Great Wells of Democracy: The Meaning of Race in American Life*, 158.

142. Vijay Prashad, *Keeping Up with the Dow Joneses: Debt, Prison, Workfare*, 81.

143. *Chicago Tribune*, May 30, 2005.

144. See, for instance, David Griffin's *The New Pearl Harbor* (New York: Olive Branch Press, 2004), and Michael Ruppert's *Crossing the Rubicon* (Gabriola Island, British Columbia: New Society, 2004) in addition to Amiri Baraka's poem on *Who Caused September 11?* for which he was stripped of the Poet Laureate award in the state of New Jersey in 2003, and the work of late indigenous Mohawk activist and leader Decajeweiah-Splitting the Sky-John Boncore, echoed in a presentation at a Voices of Opposition to War, Racism, and Oppression lecture at the University of Arizona on March 7, 2005. The group Scholarsfor911truth.org, consisting of well-known science academics in the country, raises troubling and pointed questions about the truthfulness of government narrated accounts of the causes of September 11, 2001. The site is accessible at http://www.scholarsfor911truth.org, accessed on January 20, 2014.

145. Dirk Chase Eldredge, *Ending the War on Drugs: A Solution for America* (Bridgehampton, NY: Bridge Works, 1998), xi.

146. Dirk Chase Eldredge, *Ending the War on Drugs: A Solution for America*, 63.

147. Dirk Chase Eldredge, *Ending the War on Drugs: A Solution for America*, 63.

148. David Cole, *No Equal Justice: Race and Class in the American Criminal Justice System* (New York: New Press, distributed by W. W. Norton, 1999), 4–5.

149. David Cole, *No Equal Justice: Race and Class in the American Criminal Justice System*, 4–5.

150. National Crime Victimization Survey, *Bureau of Justice Statistics,* U.S. Department of Justice, October 2010, at http://bjs.ojp.usdoj.gov/content/pub/pdf/cv09.pdf.

151. Coramae Richey Mann, *Unequal Justice: A Question of Color* (Bloomington: Indiana University Press, 1993), Preface.

152. Christopher Windham, "After 20 Years, the Debate Over Mandatory Minimum Sentencing Laws for Cocaine Heats Up," *Human Nature Magazine*, June 20, 2010, at http://www.human naturemag.com/index.php?option=com_content &view=article&id=131:after-20-years-the-debate-over-mandatory-minimum-sentencing-laws-for-cocaine-heats-up&catid=38:political-science&Itemid=598, accessed on October 24, 2014.

153. Recounted to the author on April 15, 2013.

154. Manning Marable, "Facing the Demon Head On" in *The Great Wells of Democracy: The Meaning of Race in American Life*, 155.

155. Vivien Miller, "Race, Class, Age and Punitive Segregation: Prisons and Prison Populations in the Contemporary United States" in *America's Americans: Population Issues in U.S. Society and Politics*, 246.

156. "Prison and Jail Inmates at Midyear 2004," *Bureau of Justice Statistics*, U.S. Department of Justice, April 24, 2005.

157. *Quick Facts, Federal Bureau of Prisons*, U.S. Department of Justice, March 26, 2005.

158. Manning Marable, "Facing the Demon Head On" in *The Great Wells of Democracy: The Meaning of Race in American Life*, 157.

159. Michelle Alexander, "The New Jim Crow: How the War on drugs Gave Birth to a Permanent American Undercaste," *Mother Jones*, March 8, 2010, at http://motherjones.com/politics/2010/03/new-jim-crow-war-on-drugs

160. Robert Sherrill, "Death Trip: The American Way of Execution," *The Nation*, January 8, 2001.

161. See, for instance, Henry A. Giroux's book *Neoliberalism's War on Higher Education* (Chicago: Haymarket Books, 2014) for an illumination of the crisis within higher education as the result of globalized neo-liberal policies.

162. *Arizona Republic*, October 9, 2011.

163. Bruce Western and Becky Pitt, "Incarceration and Social Inequality," *Daedalus* 139, no. 3 (Summer 2010), 8–10, at http://www.mitpressjournals.org/doi/pdf/10.1162/DAED_a_00019, accessed on October 9, 2011.

164. Bruce Western and Becky Pitt, "Incarceration and Social Inequality," *Daedalus* 139, no. 3 (Summer 2010), 8–10, at http://www.mitpressjournals.org/doi/pdf/10.1162/DAED_a_00019.

165. Angela Davis, "Masked Racism: Reflections on the Prison Industrial Complex" in *Race and Resistance: African Americans in the 21st Century*, edited by Herb Boyd (Boston: South End Press, 2002), 58.

166. Randall Kennedy, *Race, Crime, and the Law* (New York: Pantheon, 1997).

167. Randall Kennedy, *Race, Crime, and the Law*, 107.

168. Randall Kennedy, *Race, Crime, and the Law*, 125.

169. Jimmy Franco, Sr., "The Martyrs of the Chicano Moratorium," *Martyrs of the Movement: Never Forget/Never Again* by Connie Tucker and Faya Rose Touré (Jackson, MS: Imani Press, 2014), 70–71.

170. *Black Radical Congress Listserv*, March 1999.

171. *Arizona Daily Star*, April 15, 2001.

172. Andres Jauregui, "Cleveland Police Shooting: Cops Investigate After Firing 137 Shots (Video)," *Huffington Post*, April 12, 2012, at http://www.huffingtonpost.com/2012/12/04/cleveland-police-shooting-137-shots-timothy-russell-malissa-williams_n_2239675.html#es_share_ended, accessed on April 30, 2013.

173. John Burris, *Blue vs Black: Let's End the Conflict Between Cops and Minorities* (New York: St. Martin's Press, 1999), 77.

174. Mark Berman, "Video Appears to Show Witnesses Reacting to Michael Brown's Death," *Washington Post*, September 11, 2014, at http://www.washingtonpost.com/news/post-nation/wp/2014/09/11/video-appears-to-show-witnesses-reacting-to-michael-browns-death/, accessed on September 23, 2014.

175. Monica Davey and Michael S. Schmidt, "Recording May Capture Shots Fired at Michael Brown," *New York Times*, August 26, 2014, at http://www.nytimes.com/2014/08/27/us/recording-may-capture-shots-fired-at-michael-brown.html, accessed on September 23, 2014.

176. Ed Mazza, "Sean Groubert, South Carolina State Trooper, Fired & Arrested After Shooting Unarmed Man," *Huffington Post*, September 25, 2014, at http://www.huffingtonpost.com/2014/09/25/sean-groubert-fired-arrested_n_5879694.html, accessed on September 26, 2014.

177. National Advisory Commission on Civil Disorders, *The Kerner Report: The 1968 Report of the National Advisory Commission on Civil Disorder* (New York: Pantheon, 1968).

178. *The Observer*, Notre Dame University and St. Mary's College, March 4, 2005.

179. Documented in the 1998 film *The Farm*, produced by Jonathan Stack and Liz Garbus and nominated for an Academy Award for Best Documentary Feature.

180. Andrew Cohen, "Sheriff Joe Arpaio: The Most Lawless Lawman in America," *The Atlantic*, March 26, 2014.

181. Roland Burris, *Blue vs Black: Let's End the Conflict Between Cops and Minorities*, 78.

182. Reuters, January 19, 2005.

183. See *Operate Ghetto Storm: 2012 Annual Report of Extrajudicial Killings of 313 Black People by Police, Security Guards and Vigilantes* published by the Malcolm X Grassroots Movement, April 13, 2013, at http://www.operationghettostorm.org/uploads/1/9/1/1/19110795/operation_ghetto_storm.pdf, accessed on January 30, 2014.

184. "Oakland police move to stop march protesting sentence," *CNN Wires*, November 5, 2010.

185. The author is engaged in an ongoing research project, "A Comparative Study of the Infliction of Incarceration on Persons in United States and South African Prisons," and has interviewed persons in prisons in the U.S. and South

Africa to understand how factors of race, class, social, and educational backgrounds feature in the end-result of persons incarcerated, especially those of color. The harsh sentences from laws like the three-strikes law in some states are often meted out disproportionately to poor persons of color. Many of the men whom I interviewed received exceptionally long sentences for capital crimes while quite young in age. For the sake of privacy rights of individuals interviewed, institutional and personal names cannot be disclosed in this publication.

186. Matt Apuzo, "War Gear Flows to Police Departments," *New York Times*, June 9, 2014, at http://www.nytimes.com/2014/06/09/us/war-gear-flows-to-police-departments.html?src=me&_r=0, accessed on June 9, 2014.

187. Ali Winston, "US Police Get Anti-terror Training in Israel on Privately Funded Trips," *The Center for Investigative Reporting*, Sacramento, CA, September 16, 2014, at https://beta.ciron-line.org/reports/us-police-get-antiterror-training-in-israel-on-privately-funded-trips/, accessed on September 23, 2014.

188. Niraj Chokshi, "School Police Across the Country Receive Excess Military Weapons and Gear," *The Washington Post*, September 16, 2014, at http://www.washingtonpost.com/blogs/gov beat/wp/2014/09/16/school-police-across-the-country-receive-excess-military-weapons-and-gear/ accessed on September 23, 2014.

189. Dan Bauman, "On Campus, Grenade Launchers, M-16s, and Armored Vehicles," *The Chronicle of Higher Education*, September 11, 2014, at http://chronicle.com/article/On-Campus-Grenade-Launchers/148749/, accessed on September 11, 2014.

190. Ali Winston, "US Police Get Anti-terror Training in Israel on Privately Funded Trips," *The Center for Investigative Reporting*, Sacramento, CA, September 16, 2014, at https://beta.ciron-line.org/reports/us-police-get-antiterror-training-in-israel-on-privately-funded-trips/, accessed on September 23, 2014.

191. Paige Williams, "Witnesses to a Botched Execution," *The New Yorker*, April 30, 2014, at http://www.newyorker.com/online/blogs/news desk/2014/04/witnesses-to-a-botched-execution.html, accessed on May 26, 2014.

192. Eric Eckholm and John Schwartz, "Timeline Describes Frantic Scene at Oklahoma Execution," *New York Times*, May 2, 2014, at http://www.nytimes.com/2014/05/02/us/oklahoma-official-calls-for-outside-review-of-botched-execution.html, accessed on May 2, 2014.

193. Matt Pearce, "In Victim's Oklahoma Home Town, No Tears for Inmate in Botched Ex-ecution," *Los Angeles Times*, May 6, 2014, at http://www.latimes.com/nation/la-na-execution-town-20140506-story.html, accessed on May 6, 2014.

194. Kathleen Hennessey, "White House says Oklahoma Execution 'Fell Short' of Humane Standards," *Los Angeles Times*, April 30, 2014, at http://www.latimes.com/nation/politics/politics now/la-pn-white-house-oklahoma-execution-20140430-story.html, accessed on April 30, 2014.

195. Beth McMurtrie, "Botched Execution in Oklahoma is Part of a Pattern, Says Amherst Scholar," *Chronicle of Higher Education*, May 1, 2014, at http://chronicle.com/article/Botched-Execution-in-Oklahoma/146303/, accessed on May 4, 2014.

196. *Your Black World*, "Samuel L. Jackson Warns Black Men That It's 'Open Season,'" Tweet, August 9, 2013, at http://www.yourblackworld. net/2013/08/black-celebrities/samuel-l-jackson-warns-black-men-that-its-open-season/, accessed on May 4, 2013.

197. *Baltimore Sun*, February 25, 2005.

198. Jenifer Warren and Maura Dolen, "Tookie Williams Is Executed," *Los Angeles Times*, December 13, 2005, at http://articles.latimes.com/2005/dec/13/local/me-execution13, accessed on December 14, 2005. Stanley Tookie Williams was the author of the best-selling book *Blue Rage, Black Redemption* (New York: Simon & Shuster, 2007) and five other books written especially for children and youth about ways of avoiding the tragic concatenation of gang violence.

199. The scene of a pro-capital punishment man spilling blood on Barbara Cottman Becnel, who worked industriously to promote Stanley Tookie Williams' defense and save his life on death row, is captured in the 2005 film *Redemption* starring Jamie Foxx.

200. *The Crisis*, January–February 2005, NAACP, Baltimore.

201. Due to confidentiality protocols, the name of the person interviewed and the institution where he was held needs to be withheld.

202. Philadelphia District Attorney General Seth Williams announced on December 7, 2011, that the attorney general's office will not proceed with the case to execute Mumia Abu-Jamal, leading many supporters of justice for Abu-Jamal to declare that the reason was clearly the lack of evidence for Abu-Jamal's conviction and strengthening the cause for his immediate release as called for by Nobel Laureate Desmond Tutu. See the *New York Times*, December 7, 2011.

203. Lawrence Williams, *Executing Justice: An Inside Account of the Case of Mumia Abu Jamal* (New York: St. Martins' Press, 2001), 102. This

book is fundamentally problematic because it's ambiguous on Mumia's innocence and does not adamantly insist that the fundamental issue in the case is the total abrogation of justice in the conviction of Mumia Abu-Jamal for first-degree murder. A more helpful book is David Lindorff's *Killing Time: An Investigation into the Death-row Case of Mumia Abu-Jamal* (Monroe, ME: Common Courage Press, 2003).

204. David Lindorff's *Killing Time: An Investigation into the Death-row Case of Mumia Abu Jamal*, iii.

205. Campaign to End the Death Penalty Communication, November 2, 2010, at http://socialistworker.org/2010/11/02/life-without-possibility, accessed on November 3, 2010.

206. Mumia Abu-Jamal's most well-known books are with Marc Lamont Hill, *The Classroom and the Cell: Conversations on Black Life in America* (Chicago: Third World Press, 2012); *Jailhouse Lawyers* (San Francisco: City Lights, 2009); with John Edgar Wideman, *Live from Death-row* (New York: Harper Perennial, 1996); *Death Blossoms: Reflections from a Prisoner of Conscience* (Boston: South End Press, 2003); Noelle Hanrahan and Alice Walker, *All Things Censored* (New York: Seven Stories Press, 2000); *We Want Freedom: My Life in Black Panther Party* (Boston: South End Press, 2004); and *Faith of Our Fathers: An Examination of the Spiritual Life of African and African American People* (Trenton: Africa World Press, 2003).

207. "Court Turns Down Philly DA in Cop-Killing Case," Associated Press, October 11, 2011, and conveyed to the author via email from Marth Conley.

208. Capital Punishment, 2003, *Bureau of Justice Statistics*, U.S. Department of Justice, November 2004.

209. Equal Justice Initiative, "Racial Bias," November 8, 2011, at www.eji.org accessed on November 9, 2011.

210. Equal Justice Initiative, "Racial Bias," November 8, 2011, at www.eji.org, accessed on November 9, 2011.

211. Fox Butterfield, "Death Sentences Being Overturned in 2 of 3 Appeals," *New York Times*, June 12, 2000, at http://partners.nytimes.com/library/national/061200death-penalty.html, accessed on June 12, 2014.

212. *San Bernardino County Sun*, February 8, 2005.

213. Jeffrey Ian Ross (ed.), *The Globalization of Supermax Prisons* (New Brunswick: Rutgers University Press, 2013), 3.

214. Jeffrey Ian Ross (ed.), *The Globalization of Supermax Prisons*, 2.

215. S. C. Richards, "USP Marion: The First Federal Supermax," *The Prison Journal* 88, no. 1 (March 2008): 6–22.

216. This was conveyed by the son-in-law of a person imprisoned at Pelican Bay during a radio interview with KPFA, Berkeley, CA, on October 5, 2011.

217. Lindsay M. Hayes and Joseph Rowan, *National Study of Jail Suicides: Seven Years Later* (Alexandria, VA: National Center on Institutions and Alternatives, sponsored by the National Institute of Corrections, U.S. Department of Justice, 1988), Chapter 3.

218. Atul Gawande, "Hellhole: The United States Holds Tens of Thousands of Inmates in Long-Term Solitary Confinement. Is This Torture?" *The New Yorker*, March 30, 2009.

219. Vivien Miller, "Tough Men, Tough Prisons, Tough Times: The Globalization of Supermaximum Prisons" in *Race, Gender, and Punishment: From Colonialism to the War on Terror*, 204.

220. "NYCLU Files Suit Challenging Solitary Confinement in New York State Prisons," *Solitary Watch: News from a Nation in Lockdown*, December 6, 2012, by Jean Casella and James Ridgeway at http://solitarywatch.com/2012/12/06/nyclu-files-suit-challenging-solitary-confinement-in-new-york-state-prisons/, accessed on January 15, 2014.

221. J. T. Hallinan, *Going Up the River* (New York: Random House, 2003), 129.

222. Jeffrey Ian Ross (ed.), *The Globalization of Supermax Prisons*, 20.

223. Eric Schlosser, "The Prison Industrial Complex," *The Atlantic Monthly*, December 1998, 54.

224. Jeffrey Ian Ross (ed.), *The Globalization of Supermax Prisons*, 22.

225. Fran Buntman and Lukas Muntingh, "Supermaximum Prisons in South Africa" in *The Globalization of Supermax Prisons*, edited by Jeffrey Ian Ross, 88. Though Mzimela, one of the South African prison officials denied that Ebongweni was modeled on the Marion, Illinois facility, the influence of U.S. supermax prisons on law enforcement and incarceration in South Africa cannot be under-emphasized given the high prison populations historically in both countries.

226. H. Toch, "The Future of Supermax Confinement," *The Prison Journal* 81, no. 3, 376–388. Toch proposes reforms of the supermax prison system as to outright abolition, a feeble liberal criticism as such.

227. David Kaiser and Lovisa Stannow, *The New York Review of Books*, March 24, 2011, at http://www.nybooks.com/articles/archives/

2011/mar/24/prison-rape-and-,government/? pagination=false, accessed on March 31, 2011.

228. Jill Filpovic, "Is the U.S. the Only Country Where More Men Are Raped Than Women?" *The Guardian*, London, 21 February 2012, at http://www.guardian.co.uk/commentisfree/cifamerica/2012/feb/21/us-more-men-raped-than-women, accessed on January 20, 2013.

229. William Pinar, *The Gender of Racial Politics and Violence in America: Lynching, Prison, Rape, and the Crisis of Masculinity* (New York: Peter Lang, 2001), 1031–1046.

230. John M. Sloop, *The Cultural Prison: Discourse, Prisoners, and Punishment* (Tuscaloosa: University of Alabama Press, 1996), 48–49. The riots mentioned describe events at San Quentin prison in California and Michigan State Penitentiary in Jackson.

231. These figures were taken from the American Correctional Association data, 1994, pages 43–46 and were cited by Elizabeth Alexander in her article "The Care and Feeding of the Correctional Industrial Complex" in *Building Violence: How America's Rush to Incarcerate Creates More Violence*, edited by John P. May and Khaild R. Pitts, 52.

232. *National Association for State Budget Offices*, 1996, 77.

233. John Irwin, *The Warehouse Prison: Disposal of the New Dangerous Class*, 247.

234. http://www.pewcenteronthestates.org/uploadedFiles/Statisticspercent20andpercent20Facts.pdf, Pew Charitable Trust, November 2, 2011, accessed on June 1, 2014.

235. Bruce Western and Becky Pitt, "Incarceration and Social Inequality," *Daedalus* 18, no. 3 (Summer 2010) at http://www.mitpressjournals.org/doi/pdf/10.1162/DAED_a_00019

236. Lindsay McCluskey, "Investing in Prisons Over Education Is Not Being Smart on Crime," *Huffington Post: Education*, July 27, 2011, at http://www.huffingtonpost.com/lindsay-mccluskey/investing-in-prisons-over_b_868081.html, accessed on September 23, 2014.

237. Lindsay McCluskey, "Investing in Prisons Over Education Is Not Being Smart on Crime," *Huffington Post: Education*, July 27, 2011, at http://www.huffingtonpost.com/lindsay-mccluskey/investing-in-prisons-over_b_868081.html, accessed on September 23, 2014.

238. Daniel Scarpinato, "Duval's Tuition Hikes Take Center Stage," *Special to Tucson Local Media, Guest Column*, at http://tucsonlocalmedia.com/northwest_chatter/article_e7498348-3858-11e4-b944-0019bb2963f4.html?mode=jqm accessed on September 23, 2014.

239. Anne Ryman, "GOP Ad Blasts Duval for Tuition Hikes," *The Arizona Republic*, August 29, 2014, at http://www.azcentral.com/story/news/arizona/politics/2014/08/29/gop-ad-blasts-duval-tuition-hikes/14782759,/ accessed on September 23, 2014.

240. Derek Quizon, "Defining 'Nearly Free': Students, Experts Debate Meaning of Arizona Constitution Clause," statepress.com, October 8, 2009, at http://www.statepress.com/archive/node/8199, accessed on September 23, 2014.

241. Tara-Jen Ambrosio and Vincent Schiraldi, "From Classrooms to Cell Blocks: A National Perspective," Washington, D.C.: Justice Policy Institute, February 1997, 17, at http://www.justicepolicy.org/images/upload/97–01_REP_ClassroomsCellblocksNational_BB.pdf, accessed on January 10, 1998.

242. California Budget Project, "California Schools Have Experienced Deep Cuts in Funding Since 2007–08," Sacramento, CA, June 7, 2011, at http://www.cbp.org/pdfs/2012/120410_K-12_by_District_Budget_Cuts.pdf, accessed on October 1, 2014.

243. David Brodwin, "How High Prison Costs Slash Education and Hurt the Economy, *U.S. News & World Report*, May 24, 2012, at http://www.usnews.com/opinion/blogs/economic-intelligence/2012/05/24/how-high-prison-costs-slash-education-and-hurt-the-economy, accessed on September 23, 2014.

244. David Brodwin, "How High Prison Costs Slash Education and Hurt the Economy," *U.S. News & World Report*, May 24, 2012, at http://www.usnews.com/opinion/blogs/economic-intelligence/2012/05/24/how-high-prison-costs-slash-education-and-hurt-the-economy, accessed on September 23, 2014.

245. Chelsea Bono, "Too Much Money Spent on State Prisons," *Michigan Policy Network: Criminal Justice*, December 17, 2013, at http://www.michiganpolicy.com/index.php?option=com_content&view=article&id=1274:too-much-money-spent-on-state-prisons&catid=240:criminal-justice-blog&Itemid=361, accessed on September 22, 2014.

246. Elizabeth Prann, "States Spend Almost Four Times More Per Capita on Incarcerating Prisoners Than Educating Students, Studies Say," Fox News: Politics, March 14, 2011, at http://www.foxnews.com/politics/2011/03/14/states-spend-times-incarcerating-educating-studies-say-464156987/, accessed on September 23, 2014.

247. Graeme Wood, " A Boom Behind Bars," *Bloomberg Businessweek Magazine*, March 17, 2011, at http://www.businessweek.com/magazine/content/11_13/b4221076266454.htm, accessed on March 20, 2011.

248. Silja J.A. Talvi, "American Correctional Association: Exposed at Last," *In These Times*, February 28, 2005, available at http://www.capp.50megs.com/aca_part1.html, accessed on January 15, 2006.

249. W. B. Sabol, T. D. Minton and P.M. Harrison, "Prison and Jail Inmates at Midyear 2006," *Bureau of Justice Statistics*, U.S. Department of Justice, 2007.

250. Quick Facts, *Federal Bureau of Prisons*, U.S. Department of Justice, March 26, 2005.

251. Graeme Wood, "A Boom Behind Bars," *Bloomberg Businessweek Magazine*, March 17, 2011, available at http://www.businessweek.com/magazine/content/11_13/b4221076266454.htm.

252. Graeme Wood, " A Boom Behind Bars," *Bloomberg Businessweek Magazine*, March 17, 2011, accessed on March 18, 2011, at http://www.businessweek.com/magazine/content/11_13/b4221076266454.htm.

253. S. Terrell, "Audit: N.M. Private Prison Costs Soar Exit Notice," *New American*, May 24, 2007, cited in Gerry Gaes, "Cost, Performance Studies Look at Prison Privatization," at http://www.ojp.usdoj.gov/nij/journals/259/welcome.htm, accessed on June 15, 2007.

254. Laura Sullivan, "Prison Economics Help Drive Ariz Immigration Law," National Public Radio, October 28, 2010, at http://www.npr.org/templates/story/story.php?storyId=130833741, accessed on October 30, 2010.

255. Meredith Kolodner, "Private Prisons Expect a Boom: Immigrant Enforcement to Benefit Detention Companies," *New York Times*, July 19, 2006, at http://www.nytimes.com/2006/07/19/business/19detain.html?, accessed on July 30, 2007.

256. *Private Prison Fact Sheet 2009*, at www.PrivateCI.org (accessed August 27, 2010).

257. *Private Prison Fact Sheet 2009*, www.PrivateCI.org, accessed August 27, 2010.

258. Van Jones and Matt Haney, "Gov. Brown's misguided private prison plan" in *SF Gate*, August 28, 2013, at http://www.sfgate.com/opinion/openforum/article/Gov-Browns-misguided-private-prison-plan-4769640.php, accessed on August 30, 2013.

259. Donna Selman and Paul Leighton, *Punishment for Sale: Private Prisons, Big Business, and the Incarceration Binge* (Lanham, MD: Rowman & Littlefield, 2010), 2.

260. Michael A. Hallett, *Private Prisons in America: A Critical Race Perspective*, 91.

261. Victor Hassine, *Life Without Parole: Living in Prison Today*, Fourth Edition (New York: Oxford University Press, 2009), 247.

262. Victor Hassine, *Life Without Parole: Living in Prison Today*, Fourth Edition, 247.

263. Victor Hassine, *Life Without Parole: Living in Prison Today*, Fourth Edition, 247.

264. Michael Hallett, *Private Prisons in America: A Critical Race Perspective*, 65.

265. Joel Dyer, *The Perpetual Prisoner Machine: How America Profits from Crime* (Boulder: Westview Press, 2000), 246. Around 2005, Students Against Sweatshops at the University of Arizona, where the author teaches, organized a rally against the prison industrial complex and highlighted the fact that the university financed the expansion of building construction through bonds with Lehman Brothers, which has investments in the private prison sector.

266. Victor Hassine, *Life Without Parole: Living in Prison Today*, Fourth Edition, 251.

267. Angela Davis, "Masked Racism: Reflections on the Prison Industrial Complex" in *Race and Resistance: African Americans in the 21st Century*, edited by Herbert Boyd (Cambridge, MA: South End Press, 2002), 56.

268. Angela Davis, "Masked Racism: Reflections on the Prison Industrial Complex" in *Race and Resistance: African Americans in the 21st Century*, edited by Herbert Boyd, 55–56.

269. Phil Smith, "Private Prisons: Profits of Crime," *Covert Action Quarterly* (Fall 1993).

270. Silja J.A. Talvi, "American Correctional Association: Exposed at Last" in *In These Times*, February 28, 2005, available at http://www.capp.50megs.com/aca_part1.html, accessed on January 29, 2006.

271. Renford Reese, *Prison Race*, 187.

272. http://www.transcor.com/company-overview.php, accessed on May 1, 2013.

273. Renford Reese, *Prison Race*, 189.

274. Meredith Kolodner, "Private Prisons Expect a Boom: Immigrant Enforcement to Benefit Detention Companies," *New York Times*, July 19, 2006, at http://www.nytimes.com/2006/07/19/business/19detain.html?, accessed on July 31, 2007.

275. Phillip Wood, "Globalization and Prison Privatization: Why Are Most of the World's For-Profit Adult Prisons to Be Found in the American South?" *International Political Sociology* 1 (2007), 223.

276. Evening news program interview with Sonwabo Bhangana of the Department of Correctional Services, Radio 2000, South Africa, November 10, 2010.

277. Angela Davis, "Masked Racism: Reflections on the Prison Industrial Complex" in *Race and Resistance: African Americans in the 21st Century*, 56.

278. Angela Davis, "Masked Racism: Reflections on the Prison Industrial Complex" in *Race*

and Resistance: African Americans in the 21st Century, 57.

279. Sarah Flounders, "The Pentagon Slave Labor in U.S. Prisons," at www.workers.org, June 11, 2011, accessed on June 15, 2011.

280. Vijay Prashad, *Keeping Up with the Dow Joneses: Debt, Prison, Workfare*, 108.

281. Eric Schlosser, "The Prison Industrial Complex," *The Atlantic Monthly* (December 1998) at www.theatlantic.com/doc/199812/prisons, accessed on July 10, 2012.

282. "We're Being Robbed but the People Doing It Will Never Go to Prison," *bravenewfoundation*, November 5, 2013, at https://www.youtube.com/watch?v=Zmlta0DYQ1Y and https://www.youtube.com/user/bravenewfoundation, accessed on April 16, 2014. See https://www.aclu.org/cca?sid=2233547 for more information.

283. Jesse Lava and Sarah Solon, "Meet the Company Making $1.4 Billion a Year Off Sick Prisoners," American Civil Liberties Union (ACLU), October 8, 2013, at https://www.aclu.org/blog/prisoners-rights/meet-company-making-14-billion-year-sick-prisoners, accessed on April 16, 2014.

284. Jesse Lava and Sarah Solon, "Meet the Company Making $1.4 Billion a Year Off Sick Prisoners," American Civil Liberties Union (ACLU), October 8, 2013, at https://www.aclu.org/blog/prisoners-rights/meet-company-making-14-billion-year-sick-prisoners, accessed on April 16, 2014.

285. Jalil Abdul Muntaqim (formerly Jalil Bottom), "The Cold War of the '90's," *A Bulldozer Publication, Prison News Service*, no. 2 (September–October 1995).

286. Jalil Abdul Muntaqim (formerly Jalil Bottom), "The Cold War of the '90's" in *A Bulldozer Publication, Prison News Service*, no. 2 (September–October 1995). For more of Jalil Abdul Muntaqim's writing, see "On the Black Liberation Army (abridged)" in Joy James' edited work, *Imprisoned Intellectuals: America's Political Prisoners Write on Life, Liberation, and Rebellion*, 107–113.

287. Phil Smith, "Private Prisons: Profits of Crime" in *Covert Action Quarterly* (Fall 1993).

288. Phil Smith, "Private Prisons: Profits of Crime" in *Covert Action Quarterly* (Fall 1993).

289. Michael B. Marois, "Brown Proposes Record $106.8 Billion California Budget," *Bloomberg News*, January 9, 2014, at http://www.bloomberg.com/news/2014-01-09/brown-proposes-record-california-budget-of-106-8-billion-1-.html, accessed on April 16, 2014.

290. Barbara Lee, Spring Lecture, University of Arizona, April 2002.

291. Nadia Prupis, "Cash-Strapped States Resurrect "Debtors' Prisons," *t r u t h o u t | Report*, 6 October 2010 at http://www.truth-out.org/punishing-poor-being-poor63949, accessed on November 8, 2010.

292. Nadia Prupis, "Cash-Strapped States Resurrect "Debtors' Prisons," *t r u t h o u t | Report*, 6 October 2010 at http://www.truth-out.org/punishing-poor-being-poor63949, accessed on November 8, 2010.

293. Laura Sullivan, "Bail Burden Keeps U.S. Jails Stuffed with Inmates," *NPR: All Things Considered*, January 21, 2010, at http://www.npr.org/2010/01/21/122725771/Bail-Burden-Keeps-U-S-Jails-Stuffed-With-Inmates, accessed on September 15, 2014.

294. Laura Sullivan, "Bail Burden Keeps U.S. Jails Stuffed with Inmates," NPR: All Things Considered, January 21, 2010, at http://www.npr.org/2010/01/21/122725771/Bail-Burden-Keeps-U-S-Jails-Stuffed-With-Inmates, accessed on September 15, 2014.

295. See Joe Davidson's article "African Americans Are Grist for the Fast-Growing Prison Industry's Money Mill," *Emerge*, October 1997.

296. *Mail and Guardian*, South Africa, May 1–7, 1997.

297. Vivien Miller, "Tough Men, Tough Prisons, Tough Times: The Globalization of Supermaximum Prisons" in *Race, Gender, and Punishment: From Colonialism to the War on Terror*, 213.

298. Phillip Wood's skepticism is described in "Globalization and Prison Privatization: Why Are Most of the World's For-Profit Adult Prisons to be Found in the American South?" *International Political Sociology* 1 (2007), 228. Though his article illuminates the diverse terrain and spatial geography of private prisons in the U.S., it is weak in that it underestimates the forces of globalization that are at the heart of the current system of oppression and exploitation from two to three decades ago that is determined to maximize profits by any route possible, including profits from punishment as extant in private prisons.

299. See, for instance, David Garland, *The Culture of Control: Crime and Order in Contemporary Society* (Chicago: University of Chicago Press, 2001).

300. Lukas Muntingh, "Youth Crime and Violence—Some Perspectives from the Prison Reform Sector," *Human Sciences Research Council Roundtable Discussion on Youth Crime and Violence*, 13 May 2008, 2. Muntingh cites L. Lazarus, *Contrasting Prisoners' Rights*, Oxford Monographs on Criminal Law and Justice 44 as a reference here.

301. Complex Mag, "Soul on Ice Beasts: When Rich White People Go to Prison," at http://www.

complex.com/blogs/2010/08/03/soul-on-ice-beasts-when-rich-White-people-go-to-prison/, accessed on October 1, 2011.

302. Roc Morin, "Former Undercover Drug Narc on Why Police Don't Bust White People and How He Turned Against Drug War," *Alternet*, March 14, 2014, at http://www.alternet.org/drugs/former-undercover-drug-narc-why-police-dont-bust-white-people-and-how-he-turned-against-drug?akid=11622.305522.j95WzW&rd=1&src=newsletter972398&t=8, accessed on March 20, 2014.

303. Katherine Skiba, "Settlement Announced Over Countrywide Loans," *Chicago Tribune*, December 21, 2011. Available at http://articles.chicago tribune.com/2011-12-21/news/chi-settlement-announced-over-countrywide-loans-20111221_1_countrywide-loans-dan-frahm-full-spectrum-lending, accessed on October 4, 2014.

304. Nicole Shoener, "Three Strikes Laws in Different States," *Legal Match*, May 23, 2014, at http://www.legalmatch.com/law-library/article/three-strikes-laws-in-different-states.html, accessed on May 26, 2014.

305. Lynne Stewart Parramore, "More Than Half of Black College Graduates Underemployed," AlterNet, May 23, 2014, at http://www.alternet.org/education/more-half-black-college-graduates-underemployed, accessed on May 26, 2014.

306. Steven Raphael and Michael A. Stoll, *Why Are So Many Americans in Prison* (New York: Russell Sage Foundation, 2014), 173.

307. Steven Raphael and Michael A. Stoll, *Why Are So Many Americans in Prison*, 173.

308. Michelle Wallace, *The New Jim Crow: Mass Incarceration in an Age of Color Blindness* (New York: Free Press, 2010), 12.

309. Michelle Wallace, *The New Jim Crow: Mass Incarceration in An Age of Color Blindness*, 7.

310. Randall Kennedy, *Race, Crime, and the Law*, 135. See also Ta-Nehisi Coates' article "Mapping the New Jim Crow: America's entire history is marked by the state imposing unfreedom on a large swath of the African American population," *The Atlantic*, October 17, 2014, at http://www.theatlantic.com/politics/archive/2014/10/mapping-the-new-jim-crow/381617/, accessed on October 25, 2014.

Chapter 5

1. Frances Drake, *Global Warming: The Science of Climate Change* (London: Arnold, co-published in the U.S. by Oxford University Press, New York, 2000), 65.

2. Paul Brown, *Global Warming: Can Civilization Survive?* (London: Blandford, 1996), 4.

3. This is a statement by John Houghton, co-chair of the Intergovernmental Panel on Climate Change, in 2003. Cited by Takehiko Kambayashi in his article "World Weather Prompts New Look at Kyoto," *Washington Times*, September 5, 2003.

4. Gayle Ehrenman, "Billions of People Will Run Out of Fresh Water by 2050" in *Will the World Run Out of Water*, edited by Debra A. Miller (Detroit: Greenhaven Press, an imprint of Thomson Gale, 2007), 12.

5. Teodoro Estrela Montreal and Elisa Vargas Amelin, "Effects of Climate Change on Hydrological Resources in Europe: The Case of Spain" in *Global Warming and Climate Change: Prospects and Policies in Asia and Europe*, edited by Antonio Marquina (Basingstoke: Palgrave Macmillan, 2010), 58–59.

6. Gayle Ehrenman, "Billions of People Will Run Out of Fresh Water by 2050" in *Will the World Run Out of Water*, edited by Debra A. Miller, 11.

7. *Managing Water Under Uncertainty and Risk: The United Nations World Water Development Report 4, Volume 1* (Paris: UNESCO, 2012), 5.

8. Consultative Group on International Agricultural Research, "One-Third of the World Is Already Facing Water Scarcity" in *Will the World Run Out of Water*, edited by Debra A. Miller, 21.

9. Gayle Ehrenman, "Billions of People Will Run Out of Fresh Water by 2050" in *Will the World Run Out of Water*, edited by Debra A. Miller, 13.

10. Damian Carrington, Suzanne Goldberg, and Graham Readfern, "Environment: How El Niño Will Change the World's Weather in 2014," *The Guardian*, London, June 11, 2014, at http://www.theguardian.com/environment/2014/jun/11/-sp-el-nino-weather-2014, accessed on June 11, 2014.

11. Damian Carrington, Suzanne Goldberg, and Graham Readfern, "Environment: How El Niño Will Change the World's Weather in 2014," *The Guardian*, London, June 11, 2014, at http://www.theguardian.com/environment/2014/jun/11/-sp-el-nino-weather-2014, accessed on June 11, 2014.

12. Frances Drake, *Global Warming: The Science of Climate Change*, 1.

13. IPCC, *IPCC Second Assessment: Climate Change 1995: A Report of the Intergovernmental Panel on Climate Change* (Geneva: World Meteorological Organization and Nairobi; United Nations Environment Program, 1995), 3, 5, at https://www.ipcc.ch/pdf/climate-changes-1995/ipcc-

2nd-assessment/2nd-assessment-en.pdf, accessed on February 19, 2014. See also the *IPCC Third Assessment Report—Climate Change 2001:* Working Group 1: The Scientific Basis. GRID-Arendal Publications: A Centre collaborating with UNEP, 2003, at http://www.grida.no/publications/other/ipcc%5Ftar/?src=/climate/ipcc_tar/wg1/index.htm, accessed on February 19, 2014.

14. Bruce E. Johansen, *Global Warming in the 21st Century. Volume 1: Our Evolving Climate Crisis* (Westport, CT: Praeger, 2006), 7.

15. Bruce E. Johansen, *Global Warming in the 21st Century. Volume 1: Our Evolving Climate Crisis,* xxiii.

16. Ben Saul, Steven Sherwood, Jane McAdam, Tim Stephens, and James Slezak, *Climate Change and Australia: Warming to the Global Challenge* (Annandale, Australia: Federation Press, 2012), 3.

17. Hans Baer, *Global Warming, Human Society and Critical Anthropology: A Research Agenda* (Melbourne: University of Melbourne Press, 2007), 6.

18. Paul G. Harris, "Climate Change Priorities for East Asia: Socio-economic Impacts and International Justice" in *Global Warming and East Asia: The Domestic and International Politics of Climate Change,* edited by Paul Harris (London: Routledge, 2003), 21.

19. The chart on Global Annual Burning/Emission of Carbon is taken from Soumya Dutta, "The Basic Science of Global Warming and Climate Change" in *Critical Issues of Justice, Equity and the Climate Crisis: Resisting Destructive "Development": Those Who Pollute/Emit the Most Are Not the Ones Threatened by Impacts* by Meher Engineer, Soumya Dutta, and Asit Dash (Delhi: Vasudhaiva Kutumbakam, South Asian Dialogues on Ecological Democracy [SADED], 2010), 17.

20. Paul G. Harris, "Climate Change Priorities for East Asia: Socio-economic Impacts and International Justice" in *Global Warming and East Asia: The Domestic and International Politics of Climate Change,* edited by Paul Harris, 21. "Natural" gas is placed in quotation marks because there's nothing "natural" about siphoning gas from the Earth, a process that poisons precious water resources, eliminates biodiversity, discharges toxic waste into nearby rivers, and causes serious health problems due to dangerous chemicals like benzene, xylene, methanol, and formaldehyde. More information is available for instance at http://www.catskillmountainkeeper.org/sample-page/the-truth-about-gas-drilling-and-your-health/?doing_wp_cron=1390350082.5928299427703470703125.

21. Ben Saul, Steven Sherwood, Jane McAdam, Tim Stephens, and James Slezak, *Climate Change and Australia: Warming to the Global Challenge,* 13.

22. The chart on biospheric-related carbon dioxide cycle is taken from Soumya Dutta, "The Basic Science of Global Warming and Climate Change" in *Critical Issues of Justice, Equity and the Climate Crisis: Resisting Destructive "Development": Those Who Pollute/Emit the Most Are Not the Ones Threatened by Impacts* by Meher Engineer, Soumya Dutta, and Asit Dash, 16.

23. David A. Archer and Stefan Rahmstorf, *The Climate Crisis: An Introductory Guide to Climate Change* (Cambridge: Cambridge University Press, 2010), 30.

24. Justin Gillis, "Heat-Trapping Gas Passes Milestone, Raising Fears," *New York Times,* May 10, 2013, at http://www.nytimes.com/2013/05/11/science/earth/carbon-dioxide-level-passes-long-feared-milestone.html?pagewanted=all&_r=1&, accessed on March 19, 2014.

25. "Car Emissions and Global Warming," *Union of Concerned Scientists,* http://www.ucsusa.org/clean_vehicles/why-clean-cars/global-warming/, accessed on May 14, 2014.

26. Yuka Kobayashi, "Navigating Between 'Luxury' and 'Survival' Emissions: Tensions in China's Multilateral and Bilateral Climate Change Diplomacy" in *Global Warming and East Asia: The Domestic and International Politics of Climate Change,* edited by Paul Harris, 86.

27. Adam Welz, "In South Africa, Renewables Vie with the Political Power of Coal," in *Environment 360: Opinion, Analysis, Reporting & Debate,* December 13, 2013, at http://e360.yale.edu/feature/in_south_africa_renewables_vie_with_the_political_power_of_coal/2719/, accessed on January 9, 2014.

28. Pravin Gordhan, "Why Coal Is the Best Way to Power South Africa's Growth, *Washington Post,* March 21, 2010, at http://www.washingtonpost.com/wp-dyn/content/article/2010/03/21/AR2010032101711.html, accessed on March 21, 2014.

29. Gerald R. North, Jurgen Schmandt, and Judith Clarkson (eds.), *The Impact of Global Warming in Texas: A Report of the Task Force on Climate Change in Texas* (Austin: University of Texas Press, 1995), 1.

30. Keith Smith, Paul Crutzen, Arvin Mosier, and Wilfried Winiwarter, "The Global Nitrous Oxide Budget: A Reassessment" in *Nitrous Oxide and Climate Change,* edited by Keith Smith (London and Washington: Earthscan), 67.

31. Keith Smith, Paul Crutzen, Arvin Mosier, and Wilfried Winiwarter, "The Global Nitrous Oxide Budget: A Reassessment" in *Nitrous Oxide and Climate Change,* 67.

32. Keith Smith, Paul Crutzen, Arvin Mosier, and Wilfried Winiwarter, "The Global Nitrous Oxide Budget: A Reassessment" in *Nitrous Oxide and Climate Change*, 68.

33. Keith Smith, Paul Crutzen, Arvin Mosier, and Wilfried Winiwarter, "The Global Nitrous Oxide Budget: A Reassessment" in *Nitrous Oxide and Climate Change*, 71, 72.

34. Heather Saul, "Saharan Dust Lands in England as 'Very High' Levels of Air Pollution Warned This Week," *The Independent*, London, April 2, 2014, at http://www.independent.co.uk/environment/climate-change/england-braced-for-very-high-levels-of-air-pollution-this-week-9231449.html?utm_source=indynewsletter&utm_medium=email02042014, accessed on April 2, 2014.

35. M. K. Gajendra Babu and K. A. Subramanian, *Alternative Transportation Fuels Utilization in Combustion Engines* (Boca Raton: Taylor & Francis, 2013), 417.

36. M. K. Gajendra Babu and K. A. Subramanian, *Alternative Transportation Fuels Utilization in Combustion Engines*, 421.

37. M. K. Gajendra Babu and K. A. Subramanian, *Alternative Transportation Fuels Utilization in Combustion Engines*, 423.

38. Ian Roberts with Phil Edwards, *The Energy Glut: Climate Change and the Politics of Fatness* (London: Zed Books, 2010), 2.

39. Ian Roberts with Phil Edwards, *The Energy Glut: Climate Change and the Politics of Fatness*, 2.

40. Ian Roberts with Phil Edwards, *The Energy Glut: Climate Change and the Politics of Fatness*, 3.

41. David A. Archer and Stefan Rahmstorf, *The Climate Crisis: An Introductory Guide to Climate Change*, 96.

42. Paul Voosen, "The Hard Climb to Scientific Consensus: Behind the Scenes of the U.N.'s Latest Climate Change Report," *Chronicle of Higher Education*, October 18, 2013, A36.

43. Brian Fagan, *The Attacking Ocean: The Past, Present, and Future of Rising Sea Levels* (New York: Bloomsbury Press, 2013), 184–186.

44. Brian Fagan, *The Attacking Ocean: The Past, Present, and Future of Rising Sea Levels*, 189.

45. Brian Fagan, *The Attacking Ocean: The Past, Present, and Future of Rising Sea Levels*, 190.

46. Brian Fagan, *The Attacking Ocean: The Past, Present, and Future of Rising Sea Levels*, 202.

47. Winona LaDuke, *All Our Relations: Native Struggles for Land and Life* (Boston: South End Press, 1999), 30.

48. U.S. Geological Survey: Science Information and Library Services, *The Everglades: What You Need to Know*, at http://online.wr.usgs.gov/outreach/landpeople/students/ever_area.html, accessed on March 28, 2014.

49. Winona LaDuke, *All Our Relations: Native Struggles for Land and Life*, 30.

50. Siyi J. Feng, Amy D. Hagerman, Brian H. Hurd, Bruce A. McCarl, Jian H. Mu, and Wei W. Wang, "Climate Change and Its Impact on Agriculture: Challenges for the 21st Century" in *Global Warming in the 21st Century*, edited by Juliann M. Cossia (New York: Nova Science, 2011) 6.

51. Alissa J. Rubin, "High Levels of Pollution Spur Paris to Action," *New York Times*, March 15, 2014, at http://www.nytimes.com/2014/03/15/world/europe/paris-suffers-a-spring-smog-attack.html?emc=eta1, accessed on January 5, 2015.

52. U.S. Nuclear Regulatory Commission, "Backgrounder on Chernobyl Nuclear Power Plant Accident," May 2013, at http://www.nrc.gov/reading-rm/doc-collections/fact-sheets/chernobyl-bg.html, accessed on March 15, 2014.

53. United Nations Environment Program, *Global Outlook for Ice & Snow*, 11. Nairobi: Division of Early Warning & Assessment, United Nations Environment Program, 2007, at http://www.grida.no/publications/geo%2Dice%2Dsnow/ebook.aspx, accessed on January 5, 2015.

54. Justin Gillis, "Ending Its Summer Melt, Arctic Sea Ice Sets a New Low That Leads to Warnings," *New York Times*, September 19, 2012, at http://www.nytimes.com/2012/09/20/science/earth/arctic-sea-ice-stops-melting-but-new-record-low-is-set.html, accessed on September 19, 2012.

55. United Nations Environment Program, *Global Outlook for Ice & Snow*, 11, at http://www.grida.no/publications/geo%2Dice%2Dsnow/ebook.aspx.

56. United Nations Environment Program, *Global Outlook for Ice & Snow*, 103, at http://www.grida.no/publications/geo%2Dice%2Dsnow/ebook.aspx.

57. David A. Archer and Stefan Rahmstorf, *The Climate Crisis: An Introductory Guide to Climate Change*, 73.

58. "Coastal Areas: Climate Impacts on Coastal Areas," *U.S. Environmental Protection Agency*, at http://www.epa.gov/climatechange/impacts-adaptation/coasts.html, accessed on February 13, 2014.

59. This is well described by Alexander Y. Galashev's chapter "Clusterization of Atmospheric Water Vapor, Absorption of Greenhouse Molecules by Water Clusters, and Climatic Change" in *Global Warming in the 21st Century*, edited by Juliann M. Cossia, 41–43.

60. *South African Press Association* report, September 26, 2006, reported in the IOL online newsletter, October 1, 2006.

61. *New York Times*, September 19, 2012.

62. Barbara Demick, "Glaciers in Southern China Receding Rapidly, Scientists Say," *Los Angeles Times*, December 15, 2009, at http://articles.latimes.com/2009/dec/15/world/la-fg-china-glacier15-2009dec15, accessed on March 19, 2014.

63. Geoffrey Mohan, "Climate Change May Be Baring Mt. Everest," *Los Angeles Times*, May 14, 2013, at http://articles.latimes.com/2013/may/14/science/la-sci-sn-everest-climate-20130514, accessed on March 19, 2014.

64. United Nations Environment Programme, *Global Outlook for Ice & Snow* (Nairobi: Division of Early Warning and Assessment, United Nations Environment Programme, 2007), 145, as an e-book at http://www.unep.org/geo/geo_ice/ published by G R I D Arendal: A Center Collaborating with UNEP, accessed on March 19, 2014.

65. United Nations Environment Programme, *Global Outlook for Ice & Snow*, 145.

66. Shardul Agrawala (ed.), *Bridge Over Troubled Waters: Linking Climate Change and Development* (Paris: Organization for Economic Cooperation and Development [OECD], 2005), 96.

67. Shardul Agrawala (ed.), *Bridge Over Troubled Waters: Linking Climate Change and Development*, 95.

68. Shardul Agrawala (ed.), *Bridge Over Troubled Waters: Linking Climate Change and Development*, 96–7.

69. Shardul Agrawala (ed.), *Bridge Over Troubled Waters: Linking Climate Change and Development*, 101.

70. Communicated by Adel Gamal, Professor of Middle Eastern and North African Studies at the University of Arizona, April 11, 2014.

71. Shardul Agrawala (ed.), *Bridge Over Troubled Waters: Linking Climate Change and Development*, 103.

72. George Ward and Juan B. Valdes, "Water Resources" in *The Impact of Global Warming in Texas: A Report of the Task Force on Climate Change in Texas*, 71.

73. Michael Wines, "Colorado River Drought Forces a Painful Reckoning for States," *New York Times*, January 5, 2014, http://www.nytimes.com/2014/01/06/us/colorado-river-drought-forces-a-painful-reckoning-for-states.html?emc=eta1&_r=0, accessed on January 5, 2014.

74. Paul Rogers, "California Drought: State Water Project Will Deliver No Water This Summer," *San Jose Mercury News*, January 31, 2014, http://www.mercurynews.com/science/ci_25036886/california-drought-state-water-

project-will-deliver-no, accessed on January 31, 2014.

75. Peter H. Gleick, "The Costs of California's Bellwether Drought: What Can We Expect?" in *Huffington Post*, February 8, 2014, http://www.huffingtonpost.com/peter-h-gleick/the-costs-of-californias_b_4747043.html.

76. William E. Riebsame and Jeffrey W. Jacobs, *Climate Change and Water Resources in the Sacramento-San Joaquin region of California, Working Paper #64*, Natural Hazards Research and Applications Information Center, University of Colorado, December 1988, 12, 15.

77. William E. Riebsame and Jeffrey W. Jacobs, *Climate Change and Water Resources in the Sacramento-San Joaquin Region of California, Working Paper # 64*, 8.

78. Judith Clarkson, "Greenhouse Gas Emissions" in *The Impact of Global Warming in Texas: A Report of the Task Force on Climate Change in Texas*, 53–4.

79. Machado, S. and R. Piltz, *Reducing the Rate of Global Warming: The State's Role* (Washington, D.C.: Renew America, 1988), 30.

80. Gerald R. North, George Bomar, John Griffiths, James Norwine, and Juan Valdes, "The Changing Climate of Texas" in *The Impact of Global Warming in Texas: A Report of the Task Force on Climate Change in Texas*, 27.

81. George Ward and Juan B. Valdes, "Water Resources" in *The Impact of Global Warming in Texas: A Report of the Task Force on Climate Change in Texas*, 75.

82. Suzanne Goldenberg, "Fracking Is Depleting Water Supplies in America's Driest Areas, Report Shows," *The Guardian*, London, February 5, 2014, at http://www.theguardian.com/environment/2014/feb/05/fracking-water-america-drought-oil-gas, accessed on April 2, 2014.

83. "Climate Change Cuts U.S. Water Supplies," at http://www.presstv.ir/detail/176742.html.

84. S. Whitman, G. Good, E. Donoghue, N. Benbow, W. Shou, and S. Mou, "Mortality in Chicago attributed to the July 1995 heatwave," *American Journal of Health* 87 (1997): 1515–1551.

85. Mohammed H. I. Dore and Peter Simcisko, "Projecting Future Climate Scenarios for Canada Using General Circulation Models: An Integrated View" in *Climate Change and Water Resources*, edited by Tamim Younos and Caitlan A. Grady (Berlin: Springer, 2013), 10.

86. Anne Fienup-Riordan and Alice Rearden, *Ellavut: Our Yup'ik World & Weather: Continuity and Change on the Bering Sea Coast* (Seattle: University of Washington Press in association with Calista Elders Council, Anchorage, 2012), 302.

87. *New York Times*, August 6, 2010.

88. *The Observer*, September 5, 2010.

89. *The Observer*, September 5, 2010.

90. Butz's and Nixon's comments are cited by Susan George in her classic work on the real reasons for global food poverty, *How the Other Half Dies: The Real Reasons for World Hunger* (Montclair, NJ: Allanheld, Osmun, 1977), 179–180.

91. Peter M. Rossett, *Food Is Different: Why We Must Get the WTO Out of Agriculture* (Halifax, Nova Scotia: Fernwood; Bangalore: Books for Change; Kuala Lumpur: SIRD; Cape Town: David Philip; and London: Zed Books, 2006), 46. Rossett's book is excellent for illuminating the manner in which the WTO and globalization has decimated small farmers around the world and forced millions of them into poverty or away from agriculture due to the hegemonic control of food production by large transnational corporations. Marjoleine Hennis' book *Globalization and European Integration: The Changing Role of Farmers in the Common Agricultural Policy* (Lanham, MD: Rowman & Littlefield, 2005) is an instructive text discussing the situation of effects of globalization on European farming.

92. *The Observer*, September 5, 2010.

93. *BBC News report*, South African Broadcasting Corporation news, October 22, 2010.

94. "Special Report: Catastrophic Drought in the Amazon," *The Independent*, February 4, 2011.

95. H.H. Shugart and F.I. Woodward, *Global Change and the Terrestrial Biosphere: Achievements and Challenges* (Hoboken, NJ: Wiley-Blackwell, 2011), 200–202.

96. *Africa: Climate Change and Natural Resources*, Africa Focus Bulletin Oct. 29, 2009 (091029), http://www.africafocus.org/envexp.php.

97. Meghan Rosen, "Online Map Tracks Forest Shots from Space," *Science News* 184, no. 12, December 14, 2013.

98. Meghan Rosen, "Online Map Tracks Forest Shots from Space," *Science News* 184, no. 12, December 14, 2013.

99. Soumya Dutta, "Reclaiming Our Ecological Commons" in *Critical Issues of Justice, Equity and the Climate Crisis; Resisting Destructive "Development": Those Who Pollute/Emit the Most Are Not the Ones Threatened by Impacts* by Meher Engineer, Soumya Dutta, and Asit Dash, 16.

100. "With Deaths of Forests, A Loss of Crucial Climate Protectors," *New York Times*, October 1, 2011, http://www.nytimes.com/2011/10/01/science/earth/01forest.html?_r=1.

101. Mohamed Abdel Raouf Abdel Hamid, "Climate Change in the Arab World: Threats and Responses" in *Troubled Waters: Climate Change,*

Hydropolitics, and Transboundary Resources edited by David Michel and Amit Pandya (Washington, D.C.: The Henry L. Stimson Center, 2009), 49. See also Mamood Mamdani's book *Saviors and Survivors: Darfur, Politics, and the War on Terror* (New York: Pantheon Books, 2009) for an illumination of the effects of climate change and global warming on the eruption of war and social conflict in Darfur where one-third of forest cover in the region was destroyed by climate warming and lack of rainfall from 1973 to 2006, the desert climate steadily moved south over those four decades, and the northern portion of the Sahel belt in North Africa changed from semi-desert vegetation to full-blown desert, forcing people to migrate further south in search of viable pastures. This environmental degradation coupled with the legacy of inter-ethnic conflict institutionalized by British, French, and Belgian colonialism from the 19th century and the political proxy wars from the Cold War era when the U.S. and the Soviet Union vied for political dominance using vulnerable landless and dispossessed Indigenous groups against each other, were the principal reasons for the Darfur crisis that was seized upon by opportunistic organizations in the U.S. to call for U.S. and Western military intervention in Darfur. Chapters 7 and 8 of Mamdani's book are instructive in this regard.

102. Merrill Singer, "Ecosyndemics: Global Warming and the Coming Plagues of the Twenty-First Century" in *Plagues and Epidemics: Infected Spaces Past and Present*, edited by D. Ann Herring and Alan C. Swedlund (Oxford: Berg, 2010), 33.

103. *New York Times*, October 3, 2012, http://www.nytimes.com/2012/10/04/us/widespread-drought-threatens-way-of-life-for-farmers.html?emc=eta1.

104. William B. Meyer, *Human Impact on the Earth* (Cambridge: Cambridge University Press, 1996), 216.

105. "Earth Is Headed for Disaster, Interdisciplinary Team of Scientists Concludes," *Chronicle of Higher Education*, June 6, 2012.

106. Philip Stephens, "The Inconvenient Truth That Threatens to Change Everything," *Financial Times*, October 6, 2006.

107. http://www.cnn.com/2010/WORLD/americas/09/28/mexicao.landslide/index.html, October 2, 2010, accessed on October 2, 2010.

108. See noted Haitian lawyer and activist, Ezili Danto's website for detailed coverage on the U.S. destabilization of Haiti at http//:www.ezilidanto.com and on video at http://open.salon.com/blog/ezili_danto/2010/10/03/cia_operation_in_haiti_before_the_earthquake. Randall Robinson's book *An Unbroken Agony: Haiti,*

from Revolution to the Kidnapping of a President (New York: Basic Civitas Books, 2008) is an instructive text on the struggle for justice in Haiti.

109. http://www.bbc.co.uk/news/world-latin-america-11410639 and *Natal Mercury*, September 27, 2010.

110. Email communication from Friends of the Earth on March 11, 2011, and accessible at http://action.foe.org/t/7221/blastContent.jsp?email_blast_KEY=1294429. See also posting by Liz,"30 months On: Many Young Fukushima Evacuees Unwilling to Return Home," Recovering tohoku, at https://recoveringtohoku.wordpress.com/category/jiji-press/, posted by Liz, September 10, 2013, accessed on October 10, 2012.

111. *Friends of the Earth* email communication at http://action.foe.org/t/7221/blastContent.jsp?email_blast_KEY=1294429, accessed on March 11, 2014.

112. Larry Pynn, "Troubled Waters: Radiation Found in B.C. May Pose Health Concerns," *Vancouver Sun*, March 12, 2014, at http://www.vancouversun.com/news/Troubled+waters+Nuclear+radiation+found+pose+health+concerns/9606269/story.html, accessed on April 18, 2014.

113. Justin McCurry, "Fukushima Operator May Have to Dump Contaminated Water into Pacific," *The Guardian*, London, March 10, 2014, at http://www.theguardian.com/environment/2014/mar/10/fukushima-operator-dump-contaminated-water-pacific, accessed on April 18, 2014.

114. *Radiation Truth*, "The Myth of Low-Level Radiation" at http://www.radiationtruth.org/the-myth-of-low-level-radiation/, accessed on May 1, 2014. See also Dahr Jamil's article "'No safe levels of radiation in Japan: Experts warn that any detectable level of radiation is 'too much,'" April 4, 2011, at http://www.aljazeera.com/indepth/features/2011/04/20114219250664111.html, accessed on March 17, 2014.

115. Agus P. Sari, "Introduction: Climate Change and Sustainable Development in Asia" in *Climate Change in Asia: Perspectives on the Future Climate Change Regime*, edited by Agus P. Sari, Yasuko Kameyama, and Moekti H. Soejahmoen (Tokyo: United Nations University Press, 2008), 3.

116. Gardiner Harris, "Borrowed Time on Disappearing Land: Facing Rising Seas, Bangladesh Confronts the Consequences of Climate Change," *New York Times*, March 28, 2014, at http://www.nytimes.com/2014/03/29/world/asia/facing-rising-seas-bangladesh-confronts-the-consequences-of-climate-change.html?emc=eta1, accessed on March 30, 2014.

117. http://weather.about.com/b/2007/11/20/cyclone-sidr-horrible-but-not-the-worst.htm, accessed on March 19, 2014.

118. Gardiner Harris, "Borrowed Time on Disappearing Land: Facing Rising Seas, Bangladesh Confronts the Consequences of Climate Change," *New York Times*, March 28, 2014, at http://www.nytimes.com/2014/03/29/world/asia/facing-rising-seas-bangladesh-confronts-the-consequences-of-climate-change.html?emc=eta1, accessed on March 30, 2014.

119. Gardiner Harris, "Borrowed Time on Disappearing Land: Facing Rising Seas, Bangladesh Confronts the Consequences of Climate Change," *New York Times*, March 28, 2014, at http://www.nytimes.com/2014/03/29/world/asia/facing-rising-seas-bangladesh-confronts-the-consequences-of-climate-change.html?emc=eta1, accessed on March 30, 2014.

120. Jeff Goodell, "The End of Australia," *Rolling Stone*, October 13, 2011.

121. Jeff Goodell, "The End of Australia," *Rolling Stone*, October 13, 2011.

122. Jayashree Vivekanandan and Sreeja Nair, "Climate Change and Water: Examining the Interlinkages" in *Troubled Waters: Climate Change, Hydropolitics, and Transboundary Resources*, edited by David Michel and Amit Pandya, 3.

123. N. Kurian, "Takes Two to Solve a Water Crisis," *Indian Express*, Delhi, August 17, 2004.

124. Rachel Oblack, "Cyclone Nargis Storm Statistics," About.com: Weather, May 2008, at http://weather.about.com/od/hurricanes/qt/nargisfacts.htm, accessed on April 26, 2014. See also Seth Mydan's article "Myanmar Reels as Cyclone Toll Hits Thousands," *New York Times*, May 8, 2008, at http://query.nytimes.com/gst/fullpage.html?res=9C0CE4D8153AF935A35756C0A96E9C8B63&ref=cyclonenargis, accessed on March 19, 2014.

125. Carolotta Gall, "Pakistan Flood Sets Back Infrastructure by Years," *New York Times*, August 26, 2010, http://www.nytimes.com/2010/08/27/world/asia/27flood.html, accessed on January 17, 2012.

126. Tran Van Minh, "Floods Continue to Punish Asia," *Natal Mercury*, South Africa, October 7, 2010, at http://www.iol.co.za/news/world/floods-continue-to-punish-asia-1.684275#.U5zpZRbbfRo, accessed on October 8, 2010.

127. *Manila Standard Today*, The Philippines, October 7, 2011.

128. Agence France-Press, "New Cyclone Hits Victims of Typhoon Haiyan," *News 24*, South Africa, January 20, 2014, at http://www.news24.com/World/News/New-cyclone-hits-victims-of-Typhoon-Haiyan-20140120, accessed on January 31, 2014.

129. Niniek Karmini, "Indonesia Volcano Erupts: 100,000 Flee Mount Kelud Eruption That Could Be Heard 200km," *The Independent*, London, February 14, 2014, http://www.independent.co.uk/news/world/asia/indonesia-volcano-erupts-100000-flee-mount-kelud-eruption-that-could-be-heard-200km-away-, accessed on April 8, 2014.

130. Kashmira Gander, "UK Weather Gets Even Freakier: After Storms, Floods and Gales—a Bog Fire Raged," *The Independent*, February 14, 2014, http://www.independent.co.uk/news/uk/home-news/weather-gets-even-freakier-after-storms-floods-and-gales—a-bog-fire-raged-9127516.html, accessed on April 18, 2014.

131. U.S. Geological Survey: Science Features, *Landslide in Washington State*, at http://www.usgs.gov/blogs/features/usgs_top_story/landslide-in-washington-state/?from=title, accessed on March 28, 2014.

132. Laura Dattaro, "Washington Mudslide: Survivor Thanks Her Rescuer," Wunderground.com, at http://www.wunderground.com/news/washington-mudslide-survivor-thanks-her-rescuer-20140327, accessed on March 28, 2014.

133. Jonathan Franklin, "Tsunami Warning and Evacuation of Thousands After Earthquake in Chile," *The Guardian*, London, April 2, 2014, at http://www.theguardian.com/world/2014/apr/02/chile-earthquake-sparks-tsunami-warning-and-evacuation-of-thousands, accessed on April 2, 2014.

134. Rob Williams, "Chile Earthquake: Tsunami Warning Triggered, Thousands Evacuated and Six Killed as Area Declared a Disaster Zone," *The Independent*, April 2, 2014, London, at http://www.independent.co.uk/news/world/americas/chile-earthquake-disaster-declared-after-huge-quake-generates-tsunami-kills-five-and-prompts-mass-evacuations-9231484.html, accessed on April 2, 2014.

135. Ashok Jaitly, "South Asian Perspectives on Climate Change and Water Policy" in *Troubled Waters: Climate Change, Hydropolitics, and Transboundary Resources*, edited by David Michel and Amit Pandya, 25.

136. James D. Hansen, D. Johnson, A. Lacis, S. Lebedeff, P. Lee, D. Rind, et al., "Climate Impact of Increasing Atmospheric Carbond Dioxide," *Science* 213, August 28, 1981, 957–966. Hanson's work on global warming was also covered in a South African Press Association report, September 26, 2006, in the IOL online newsletter, October 1, 2006.

137. Personal communication from Andrew Lacis to Bruce Johansen, February 10, 2005. Cited in *Global Warming in the 21st Century. Volume 1:* *Our Evolving Climate Crisis* by Bruce E. Johansen, 16.

138. Foreword, *Human Development Report 2006: Beyond Scarcity: Power, Poverty, and the Global Water Crisis* (New York: United Nations Development Program, 2006), v.

139. Naomi Oreskes, Foreword, *Climate Change Denial: Heads in the Sand* by Haydn Washington and John Cook (London: Earthscan, 2011), xii.

140. Shelley Smithson, "Senate Candidates Weigh In on Climate Change, Uranium Mining," *KNAU and Arizona News*, October 25, 2012, at http://knau.org/post/senate-candidates-weigh-climate-change-uranium-mining, accessed on April 2, 2014.

141. *On the Issues: Every Political Leader on Every Issue* at http://www.ontheissues.org/international/Jeff_Flake_Energy_+_Oil.htm, accessed on April 2, 2014.

142. George Monbiot, "The Denial Industry," *The Guardian*, London, September 18, 2006, at http://www.theguardian.com/environment/2006/sep/19/ethicalliving.g2, accessed on April 2, 2014.

143. George Monbiot, "The Denial Industry," *The Guardian*, London, September 18, 2006, at http://www.theguardian.com/environment/2006/sep/19/ethicalliving.g2, accessed on April 2, 2014.

144. Greenpeace USA, "Koch Industries: Still Fueling Climate Denial" at http://www.greenpeace.org/usa/en/campaigns/global-warming-and-energy/polluterwatch/koch-industries/, accessed on April 2, 2014.

145. Ben Saul, Steven Sherwood, Jane McAdam, Tim Stephens, and James Slezak, *Climate Change and Australia: Warming to the Global Challenge*, 1.

146. Haydn Washington and John Cook, *Climate Change Denial: Heads in the Sand*, 4.

147. Agus P. Sari, "Introduction: Climate Change and Sustainable Development in Asia" in *Climate Change in Asia: Perspectives on the Future Climate Change Regime*, edited by Agus P. Sari, Yasuko Kameyama, and Moekti H. Soejahmoen, 5.

148. Agus P. Sari, "Introduction: Climate Change and Sustainable Development in Asia" in *Climate Change in Asia: Perspectives on the Future Climate Change Regime*, edited by Agus P. Sari, Yasuko Kameyama, and Moekti H. Soejahmoen, 5.

149. Antonio Marquina, "Introduction," *Global Warming and Climate Change: Prospects and Policies in Asia and Europe*, edited by Antonio Marquina, 7.

150. Dianne Rahm, *Climate Change Policy in the U.S.: The Science, Politics, and the Prospects for Change* (Jefferson, NC: McFarland, 2010), 71.

151. Ian Roberts with Phil Edwards, *The Energy Glut: Climate Change and the Politics of Fatness*, 78.

152. Alana Herro, "Plenty of Shale, Plenty of Problems." *Worldwatch Institute: Vision for a Sustainable World*, updated on February 13, 2014, http://www.worldwatch.org/node/5167.

153. Dianne Rahm, *Climate Change Policy in the U.S.: The Science, Politics, and the Prospects for Change*, 64.

154. "Greenhouse Gases," Center for Sustainable Systems, University of Michigan, http://css.snre.umich.edu/css_doc/CSS05-21.pdf, accessed on February 13, 2014.

155. Dianne Rahm, *Climate Change Policy in the U.S.: The Science, Politics, and the Prospects for Change*, 19.

156. Agus P. Sari, "Introduction: Climate Change and Sustainable Development in Asia" in *Climate Change in Asia: Perspectives on the Future Climate Change Regime*, edited by Agus P. Sari, Yasuko Kameyama, and Moekti H. Soejahmoen, 6.

157. Justin Gillis and Michael Wines, "In Some States, Emissions Cuts Defy Skeptics," *New York Times*, June 7, 2014, at http://www.nytimes.com/2014/06/07/science/in-some-states-emissions-cuts-defy-skeptics.html?emc=edit_th_20140607&nl=todaysheadlines&nlid=4085 8187&_r=0, accessed on June 8, 2014.

158. The emissions graph for the states mentioned are found in the article by Justin Gillis and Michael Wines, "In Some States, Emissions Cuts Defy Skeptics," *New York Times*, June 7, 2014, at http://www.nytimes.com/2014/06/07/science/in-some-states-emissions-cuts-defy-skeptics.html?emc=edit_th_20140607&nl=todays headlines&nlid=40858187&_r=0, accessed on June 8, 2014.

159. Lydia Depillis, "Keystone XL's Hired Guns Have John Kerry Connections, But Does It Matter?" *New Republic*, May 8, 2013, at http://www.newrepublic.com/article/113161/keystone-xl-lobbyists-john-kerry-connections, accessed on May 14, 2014.

160. Jacques Leslie, "Is Canada Tarring Itself?" Op-Ed, *New York Times*, March 30, 2014, at http://www.nytimes.com/2014/03/31/opinion/is-canada-tarring-itself.html?emc=eta1&_r=0, accessed on March 30, 2014.

161. Jacques Leslie, "Is Canada Tarring Itself?" Op-Ed, *New York Times*, March 30, 2014, at http://www.nytimes.com/2014/03/31/opinion/is-canada-tarring-itself.html?emc=eta1&_r=0, accessed on March 30, 2014. John O'Connor is featured in an interview in the outstanding 2014 film documentary *Standing on Sacred Ground:*

Profit and Loss, that describes the resistance of the Mikisew Cree people to the toxic and destructive effects of the tar sands project in Alberta and the struggle of the Ramu people in Papua New Guinea against land dispossession, mining for nickel by Chinese corporations, and toxic dumping by Australian companies. *Standing on Sacred Ground* is a four-part series on Indigenous peoples struggling for land and protection of sacred sites produced by Christopher McLeod and Bullfrog Films, accessible at www.bullfrogfilms.com.

162. http://therightsofnature.org/cochabama-rights/, accessed on March 12, 2014.

163. "World Peoples Conference on Climate Change and the Rights of Mother Earth: Building the People's World Movement for Mother Earth" at http://pwccc.wordpress.com/programa/, accessed on March 12, 2014. Ofelia Rivas, a traditional elder from the Tohono O'odham nation in Arizona, was one of the delegates to the Cochabamba conference in 2010 and has shared the power of the experience at Cochabamba with the author on several occasions.

164. "4 Ways Green Groups Say Trans-Pacific Partnership Will Hurt Environment," *National Geographic Daily News*, January 17, 2014, http://news.nationalgeographic.com/news/2014/01/140117-trans-pacific-partnership-free-trade-environment-obama/.

165. Justin Gillis, "Panel's Warming on Climate Risk: Worse Is Yet to Come," *New York Times*, March 31, 2014, at http://www.nytimes.com/2014/04/01/science/earth/climate.html?emc=eta1, accessed on March 31, 2014.

166. Soumya Dutta, "Reclaiming Our Ecological Commons" in *Critical Issues of Justice, Equity and the Climate Crisis; Resisting Destructive "Development": Those Who Pollute/Emit the Most Are Not the Ones Threatened by Impacts* by Meher Engineer, Soumya Dutta, and Asit Dash, 61.

167. Soumya Dutta, "Reclaiming Our Ecological Commons" in *Critical Issues of Justice, Equity and the Climate Crisis: Resisting Destructive "Development": Those Who Pollute/Emit the Most Are Not the Ones Threatened by Impacts* by Meher Engineer, Soumya Dutta, and Asit Dash, 63.

168. Soumya Dutta, "The Basic Science of Global Warming and Climate Change" in *Critical Issues of Justice, Equity and the Climate Crisis/; Resisting Destructive "Development": Those Who Pollute/Emit the Most Are Not the Ones Threatened by Impacts* by Meher Engineer, Soumya Dutta, and Asit Dash, 16.

169. See, for instance, Roger Pielke, *The Climate Fix: What Scientists and Politicians Won't Tell You About Global Warming* (New York: Basic Books, 2010), 219. The problem is that such schol-

ars still adhere to the reform of the discredited, morally incorrigible, and unsustainable globalized industrialized capitalist system as the solution to the crisis of global warming and the extinction of life itself.

170. Trailer, *Standing on Sacred Ground*, a four-part series on Indigenous peoples resisting globalization and annihilation of their ancestral lands and cultures by Christopher McLeod, 2014, available at http://www.bullfrogfilms.com/catalog/ssg.html, accessed on March 28, 2014.

171. See for example Toni Johnson's article "Economic Challenges for Climate Change Policy," *Council for Foreign Relations*, July 7, 2009, at http://www.cfr.org/world/economic-challenges-climate-change-policy/p16009, accessed on June 9, 2014.

172. See the beautiful words of Leon Shenandoah, *To Become a Human Being: The Message of Tadodaho Chief Leon Shenandoah*, by Steve Wall (Charlottesville: Hampton Roads, 2001).

Epilogue

1. The author proposes this term as an accurate description of the peoples of Africa, Asia and the Pacific, and Latin America and the Caribbean, since collectively these regions constitute three-quarters of the world's human beings. The term is proposed as an alternative to the pejorative "third world" coined by Western economists of the 1960s and 1970s to describe the peoples of these regions.

2. See, for instance, the article "Mortgage Meltdown: Interest Rate 'Freeze'—The Real Story Is Fraud," *San Francisco Chronicle*, Insight Section, December 9, 2007, for an analysis of the dynamic of the interwovenness of greed and fraud by the custodians of U.S. financial capital, the banking industry, exposed through the subprime mortgage crisis.

3. Julia Werdigier, "Dutch-Trade Fund Moves Toward Collapse," *New York Times*, March 14, 2008, at http://www.nytimes.com/2008/03/14/business/worldbusiness/14carlyle.html, accessed on March 15, 2008.

4. Don Lee, "Jobless Rate Falls to 8.3%, Cheering a Surprised Wall Street," *Los Angeles Times*, February 6, 2012, at http://articles.latimes.com/2012/feb/04/business/la-fi-jobs-20120204, accessed on February 10, 2012.

5. Allan Greenspan, "Equities Show Us the Way to Recovery," *Financial Times*, March 30, 2009, at http://www.ft.com/intl/cms/s/0/1e955244-1cc3-11de-977c-00144feabdc0.html#axzz34gKmrYAw accessed on April 2, 2009.

6. Allan Rappeport, "Record Falls in Net Worth of U.S. Citizens," *Financial Times*, March 13, 2009, at http://www.ft.com/intl/cms/s/0/6369a6e6-0f70-11de-ba10-0000779fd2ac.html, accessed on March 14, 2009.

7. Michael Gerrity, "Special Report: U.S. Homes Lost $1.7 Trillion in Value in 2010, Total Value Destruction Since Market Peak Now $9 trillion, Cost of 12 Iraq Wars," *World Property Channel*, December 9, 2010, at http://www.worldpropertychannel.com/us-markets/residential-real-estate-1/real-estate-news-home-value-declines-home-value-destruction-zillow-report-lost-home-equity-values-home-foreclosures-bulk-condo-sales-worst-real-estate-markets-3601.php, accessed on June 6, 2014.

8. The stellar documentary *Inside Job* provides a moving dramatic account of the revolving door between the U.S. government, especially the White House, and Wall Street, with former president George W. Bush and current president Barack Obama ensuring that the corporate banking sector and Wall Street bankers have their profits solidly protected by U.S. taxpayer bailouts. This was one of Obama's first major financial policy moves in his first six months in office.

9. *Sunday Independent*, South Africa, February 3, 2008.

10. "'Lungs of the Planet' Under Threat," IOL online news at www.iol.co.za, December 6, 2007.

11. Tony Davis and Tim Steller, "I Baited Jaguar Trap, Research Worker Says," *Arizona Daily Star*, April 2, 2009, at http://azstarnet.com/news/science/environment/i-baited-jaguar-trap-research-worker-says/article_8fa21c82-d1c9-5750-ab9a-fd2744565e01.html, accessed on June 23, 2014.

12. Felix Tongkul, *Traditional Systems of Indigenous Peoples of Sabah, Malaysia: Wisdom Accumulated Through Generations* (Penambang, Sabah, Malaysia: PACOS Trust, 2002), 60–61.

13. John Murungi, "The Academy and the Crisis of African Governance," *African Issues* XXXII, nos. 1 and 2 (Fall 2004), 21, published by the African Studies Association, Rutgers University, 2004.

14. B. A Ogot, *Building on the Indigenous: Selected Essays 1981–1998* (Kisumu, Kenya: Anyange Press, 1999), 17–18.

15. Dev Nathan and Govind Kelkar, Introduction, *Globalization and Indigenous Peoples in Asia: Changing the Local-Global Interface*, edited by Dev Nathan, Govind Kelkar, and Pierre Walter (New Delhi: Sage, 2004), 25.

16. *Sunday Independent*, South Africa, December 30, 2007.

17. Tariq Ali, "Daughter of the West," *London Review of Books*, 13 December 2007.

18. *Blackfire*, an award-winning Native American musical group in Flagstaff, Arizona, has now been replaced by Sihasin, another award-winning musical group constituted by Jeneda and Clayson Benally, daughter and son of Hataali Jones Benally.

19. Ed McGaa, Eagle Man, *Mother Earth Spirituality: Native American Paths to Healing Ourselves and Our World* (San Francisco: HarperCollins, 1990), xi.

20. Ed McGaa, Eagle Man, *Mother Earth Spirituality: Native American Paths to Healing Ourselves and Our World*, xv.

21. Peter Fimrite, "1-Year Ban on Chinook Salmon Fishing Proposed," *San Francisco Gate*, March 17, 2008, at http://www.sfgate.com/green/article/1-year-ban-on-chinook-salmon-fishing-proposed-3291301.php, accessed on June 23, 2014.

22. David Loy, "Can Corporations Become Enlightened? Buddhist Reflections on TNC's" in *Globalisation: The Perspectives and Experiences of the Religious Traditions of Asia Pacific*, edited by Joseph A. Camilleri and Chandra Muzaffa (Selangor, Malaysia: International Movement for a Just World, 1998), 63.

23. David Loy, "Can Corporations Become Enlightened? Buddhist Reflections on TNC's" in *Globalisation: The Perspectives and Experiences of the Religious Traditions of Asia Pacific*, 70.

24. David Loy, "Can Corporations Become Enlightened? Buddhist Reflections on TNC's" in *Globalisation: The Perspectives and Experiences of the Religious Traditions of Asia Pacific*, 71.

25. Samir Amin, *Beyond U.S. Hegemony? Assessing the Prospects for a Multipolar World* (Beirut: World Book; Kuala Lumpur: SIRD; Scottsville, South Africa: University of Kwazulu-Natal Press; London: Zed Press, 2006), 38.

26. Samir Amin, *Beyond U.S. Hegemony? Assessing the Prospects for a Multipolar World*, 151.

27. Samir Amin, *Beyond U.S. Hegemony? Assessing the Prospects for a Multipolar World*, 174.

28. Malidoma Somé, *Of Water and the Spirit: Ritual, Magic, and Initiation in the Life of an African Shaman* (New York: Arkana/Penguin, 1995), 178.

29. Vine Deloria, *For This Land: Writings on Religion in America* (New York: Routledge, 1999), 241.

30. Winona LaDuke, *All Our Relations: Native Struggles for Land and Life* (Boston: South End Press, 1999), 197. LaDuke cites these facts from Lester R. Brown, Christopher Flavin, and Hilary French, *State of the World 1997: A Worldwatch Institute Report on Progress Toward a Sustainable Society* (New York: W.W. Norton, 1997), 13.

31. Mary Graham, "Globalisation: An Indigenous Perspective" in *Globalisation: The Perspectives and Experiences of the Religious Traditions of Asia Pacific*, 130–131.

32. Mary Graham, "Globalisation: An Indigenous Perspective" in *Globalisation: The Perspectives and Experiences of the Religious Traditions of Asia Pacific*, 128–129.

33. Vine Deloria, *The World We Used to Live In* (Boulder: Fulcrum Books, 2006), 199.

34. Vine Deloria, *The World We Used to Live In*, 194.

35. In this regard, the instructive words of Leon Shenandoah, Indigenous Tadodaho spiritual leader from the Six Nations Iroquois Confederacy are captured in *To Become a Human Being: The Message of Tadodaho Chief Leon Shenandoah* by Steve Wall (Charlottesville: Hampton Roads, 2001).

36. This point is made by Anoushiravan Ehteshami in *Globalization and Geopolitics in the Middle East: Old Games, New Rules* (New York: Routledge, 2007), 7. See also the work by John Jackson, *Introduction to African Civilizations* (New York: Citadel, 1980), and W. E. B. Du Bois, *The World and Africa* (New York: International Publishers, 1965) for an illumination of pre-colonial global commercial and trade interactions among the peoples of Africa, Asia, the Pacific, Europe, and the nations of the Western hemisphere.

Bibliography

Books (Print)

Abbassi, Jennifer, and Sheryl Lutjen (eds.). *Rereading Women in Latin America and the Caribbean: The Political Economy of Gender.* Lanham, MD: Rowman & Littlefield, 2002.

Abu-Jamal, Mumia. *Death Blossoms: Reflections from a Prisoner of Conscience.* Boston: South End Press, 2003.

_____. *Faith of Our Fathers: An Examination of the Spiritual Life of African and African American People.* Trenton: Africa World Press, 2003.

_____. *Jailhouse Lawyers.* San Francisco: City Lights, 2009.

_____. *We Want Freedom: My Life in the Black Panther Party.* Boston: South End Press, 2004.

_____, with Noelle Hanrahan and Alice Walker. *All Things Censored.* New York: Seven Stories Press, 2000.

_____, with John Edgar Wideman. *Live from Death-row.* New York: Harper Perennial, 1996.

_____, with Marc Lamont Hill. *The Classroom and the Cell: Conversations on Black Life in America.* Chicago: Third World Press, 2012.

Adams, Reidar, and Geoffrey Lawrence. *Globalization, Localization, and Sustainable Livelihoods.* Aldershot: Ashgate, 2001.

Adjaye, Joseph. *Time in the Black Experience.* Westport, CT: Greenwood Press, 1994.

Adjibolosoo, S. K., et al. (eds.). *Globalization and the Human Factor.* Aldershot: Ashgate, 2004.

Afshar, Haleh, and Stephanie Barrientos (eds.). *Women, Globalization and Fragmentation in the Developing World.* New York: St. Martin's Press, 1999.

Agrawala, Shardul (ed.). *Bridge Over Troubled Waters: Linking Climate Change and Development.* Paris: Organization for Economic Cooperation and Development (OECD), 2005.

Akkari, Abdeljalil, and Pierre R. Dasen (eds.). *Educational Theories and Practices from the Majority.* Thousand Oaks, CA: Sage, 2008.

Alali, Andy O, and B.A. Jinadu (eds.). *Health Communication in Africa: Contexts, Constraints and Lessons.* Lanham, MD: University Press of America, 2002.

Aldama, Arturo, and Naomi Quinonez (eds.). *Decolonial Voices: Chicana and Chicana Cultural Studies in the 21st Century.* Bloomington: Indiana University Press, 2002.

Alexander, Michelle. *The New Jim Crow: Mass Incarceration in the Age of Color Blindness.* New York: New Press, 2010.

Allen, Roy, et al. (eds.). *Indigenous Environmental Knowledge and Its Transformations: Critical Anthropological Perspectives.* New York: Routledge, 2000.

Amin, Samir. *Beyond U.S. Hegemony? Assessing the Prospects for a Multipolar World.* London: Zed Press, 2006.

_____. *Ending the Crisis of Capitalism or Ending Capitalism?* Dakar, Senegal: CODESRIA, 2011.

_____. *The Liberal Virus.* New York: Monthly Review Press, 2004.

Amoroso, Bruno. *Globalization: Capitalism in the 21st Century.* New York: Palgrave, 1998.

Anderson, Margaret, and Patricia Hill Collins (eds.). *Race, Class and Gender: An Anthology.* Belmont, CA: Wadsworth, 2004.

Andrews, Marcellus. *The Political Economy of Hope and Fear: Capitalism and the Black Condition in America.* New York: New York University Press, 2007.

Appadurai, Arjun. *Modernity at Large: Cultural Dimension of Globalization.* Minneapolis: University of Minnesota Press, 1996.

Archer, David A., and Stefan Rahmstorf. *The Climate Crisis: An Introductory Guide to Climate Change.* Cambridge: Cambridge University Press, 2010.

Aristide, Jean-Bertrand. *Eyes of the Heart: Seeking a Path for the Poor in the Age of Globalization*. Monroe, ME: Common Courage Press, 2002.

Arnove, Anthony (ed.). *Iraq Under Siege: The Deadly Impact of Sanctions and War*. Boston: South End Press, 2002.

Babu, Gajendra M.K., and K.A. Subramanian. *Alternative Transportation Fuels Utilization in Combustion Engines*. Boca Raton: Taylor & Francis, 2013.

Bacal, Azril, et al. (eds.). *Walking Towards Justice: Democratization in Rural Life*. Oxford: Elsevier, 2003.

Badot, Jacques (ed.). *Building a World Community: Globalisation and the Common Good*. Seattle: University of Washington Press, 2001.

Baer, Hans. *Global Warming, Human Society and Critical Anthropology: A Research Agenda*. Melbourne: University of Melbourne Press, 2007.

Baker, Dean, Gerald Epstein, and Robert Pollin. *Globalization and Progressive Economic Policy*. Cambridge: Cambridge University Press, 1998.

Baker, Gordon (ed.). *No Island Is an Island: The Impact of Globalization on the Commonwealth Caribbean*. London: Chatham House, Royal Institute of International Affairs, 2007.

Balakrishnan, Radhika. *The Hidden Assembly Line: Gender Dynamics of Subcontracted Work in a Global Economy*. Bloomfield, CT: Kumarian Press, 2002.

Bales, Kevin. *Disposable People: New Slavery in the Global Economy*. Berkeley: University of California Press, 2004.

Bamyeh, Mohammed A. *The Ends of Globalization*. Minneapolis: University of Minnesota Press, 2000.

Bangara, Yusuf, et al. (eds.). *Africa in the New Millennium*. Uppsala: Nordiska Africkainstitutet, 2001.

Banks, Nancy Turner. *Aids, Opium, Diamonds and Empire: The Deadly Virus of International Greed*. Bloomington: iUniverse, 2010.

Barak, Gregg, Jeanne M. Flavin, and Paul S. Leighton. *Class, Race, Gender, and Crime: Social Realities of Justice in America*. Los Angeles: Roxbury, 2001.

Barndt, Deborah. *Tangled Routes: Women, Work and Globalization on the Tomato Trail*. Lanham, MD: Rowman & Littlefield, 2002.

Battiste, Marie (ed.). *Reclaiming Indigenous Voice and Vision*. Vancouver: University of British Columbia Press, 2000.

_____, and James Youngblood Henderson. *Protecting Indigenous Knowledge and Heritage: A Global Challenge*. Saskatoon: Purich, 2002.

Bayers, Jane, et al. *Women, Democracy, and Globalization in North America: A Comparative Study*. New York: Palgrave Macmillan, 2006.

Bell, Derrick. *And We Are Not Saved: The Elusive Quest for Racial Justice*. New York: Basic Books, 1987.

_____. *Faces at the Bottom of the Well: The Permanence of Racism*. New York: Basic Books, 1992.

_____. *Silent Covenants: Brown v. Board of Education and the Unfulfilled Hopes for Racial Reform*. New York: Oxford University Press, 2004.

Bell, Michael, and Fred Hendricks, with Azril Bacal (eds.). *Walking Towards Justice: Democratization in Rural Life*. Oxford: Elsevier, 2003.

Benetti, Raffaleo. *Survival of Weak Countries in the Face of Globalization: Puerto Rico and the Caribbean*. San Juan: Editorial De La Universidad De Puerto Rico, 2003.

Benn, Denis, and Kenneth O. Hall (eds.). *Governance in the Age of Globalisation: Caribbean Perspectives*. Kingston: Ian Randle, 2003.

Bernstein, Jared, et al. *The State of Working America, 2008/2009*. Washington, D.C.: Economic Policy Institute, 2008.

Bicker, Allen, et al. (eds.). *Development and Local Knowledge: New Approaches to Issues in Natural Resources Management, Conservation and Agriculture*. New York: Routledge, 2004.

Bilmes, Linda, and Joseph Stiglitz. *The Three Trillion Dollar War: The True Cost of the Iraq Conflict*. New York: W.W. Norton, 2008.

Bishop, Maurice, and Michael Taber. *Grenada: The Jewel Despoiled*. Baltimore: Johns Hopkins University Press, 1987.

_____, and _____. *Maurice Bishop Speaks, 1979–1983: The Grenada Revolution and Its Overthrow, 1979–1983*. New York: Pathfinder Press, 1983.

Bjelic, Dusan, and Obrad Savic. *Balkan as Metaphor: Between Globalization and Fragmentation*. Cambridge: MIT Press, 2002.

Blaser, Mario, Harvey A. Feit, and Glenn McRae. *In The Way of Development: Indigenous Peoples, Life Projects and Globalization*. New York: Zed Books, 2004.

Blum, William. *Rogue State: A Guide to the World's Only Superpower*. Monroe, ME: Common Courage Press, 2005.

Boli, John, and Frank J. Lechner (eds.). *The Globalization Reader*. Oxford: Blackwell, 2008.

Bosworth, Mary, and Jeanne Flavin (eds.). *Race, Gender, and Punishment: From Colonialism to the War on Terror*. New Brunswick: Rutgers University Press, 2007.

Bowles, Paul, et al. (eds.). *Regional Perspectives on Globalization*. New York: Palgrave Macmillan, 2007.

Boyd, Herbert (ed.). *Race and Resistance in the*

21st Century. Cambridge, MA: South End Press, 2002.

Broswimmer, Franz J. *Ecocide: A Short History of the Mass Extinction of Species.* Sterling, VA: Pluto Press, 2002.

Brown, Irene (ed.). *Latinas and African American Women at Work: Race, Gender and Economic Equality.* New York: Russell Sage Foundation, 1999.

Brown, Lester R., et al. *State of the World 1997: A Worldwatch Institute Report on Progress Toward a Sustainable Society.* New York: W.W. Norton, 1997.

Brown, Paul. *Global Warming: Can Civilization Survive?* London: Blandford, 1996.

Bullard, Robert D. *Dumping in Dixie: Race, Class, and Environmental Quality.* Third Edition. Boulder: Westview Press, 2000.

Burbules, Nicholas C., and Carlos A. Torres (eds.). *Globalization and Education: Critical Perspectives.* New York: Routledge, 2000.

Burgess, Stephen F., and Helen E. Purkitt. *South Africa's Weapons of Mass Destruction.* Bloomington: Indiana University Press, 2005.

Burris, John. *Blue vs. Black: Let's End the Conflict Between Cops and Minorities.* New York: St. Martin's Press, 1999.

Burtless, Gary, Robert Z. Lawrence, Robert E. Litan, and Robert Shapiro. *Globaphobia: Confronting Fears About Open Trade.* Washington, D.C.: Brookings Institution, 1998.

Caforio, Giuseppe (ed.). *Handbook of the Sociology of the Military.* New York: Kluwer Academic/Plenum, 2003.

Camilleri, Joseph A., and Chandra Muzaffar (eds.). *Globalisation: The Perspectives and Experiences of the Religious Traditions of Asia Pacific.* Selangor, Malaysia: International Movement for a Just World, 1998.

Carling, Alan (ed.). *Globalization and Identity: Development and Integration in a Changing World.* New York: I. B. Taurus, 2006.

Carson, Rachel. *Silent Spring.* New York: Houghton Mifflin, 1962.

Carter, Katherine, and Judy Aulette. *Cape Verdean Women and Globalization: The Politics of Gender, Culture, and Resistance.* New York: Palgrave Macmillan, 2009.

Casalis, Georges. *Correct Ideas Don't Fall from the Skies: Elements for an "Inductive Theology."* New York: Orbis Books, 1984.

Castro, Fidel. *Capitalism in Crisis: Globalization and World Politics Today.* New York: Ocean Press, 2000.

Chapman, Peter. *Bananas: How the United Fruit Company Shaped the World.* New York: Canongate, 2007.

Chen, Johnren (ed.). *Economic Effects of Globalization.* Aldershot: Ashgate, 1992.

Cheru, Fantu. *African Renaissance: Roadmaps to the Challenge of Globalization.* New York: Zed Books, and Cape Town: David Phillip, 2002.

Chew, Sing, and Robert Denemark (eds.). *The Underdevelopment of Development: Essays in Honor of Andre Gunder Frank.* Thousand Oaks, CA: Sage, 1996.

Chomsky, Noam. *Latin America: From Colonization to Globalization.* New York: Ocean Press, 1999.

Chossudovsky, Michel. *The Globalization of Poverty and the New World Order.* Montreal: Centre for Research on Globalization, 2003.

_____. *War and Globalisation: The Truth Behind September 11.* Shanty Bay, Ontario: Global Outlook, 2002.

Churchill, Ward. *Indians Are Us.* Monroe, ME: Common Courage Press, 1994.

_____. *Struggle for the Land: Native North American Resistance to Genocide, Ecocide, and Colonization.* San Francisco: City Lights Press, 2002.

Clarkson, Judith, et al. (eds.). *The Impact of Global Warming in Texas: A Report of the Task Force on Climate Change in Texas.* Austin: University of Texas Press, 1995.

Close, Paul, and David Askew. *Asian Pacific and Human Rights: A Global Political Economy Perspective.* Burlington, VT: Ashgate, 2004.

Coates, Ken. *A Global History of Indigenous Peoples: Survival and Struggle.* New York: Palgrave, 2004.

Cobb, John A. (co-ed). *9/11 and American Empire: Christians, Muslims, and Jews Speak Out* (Vol. 2). Northampton, MA: Olive Branch Press, 2006.

Cockburn, Alexander, and Jeffrey St. Clair. *Whiteout: The CIA, Drugs, and the Press.* New York: Verso, 1998.

Cole, David. *No Equal Justice: Race and Class in the American Criminal Justice System.* New York: New Press, 1999.

Collins, Patricia Hill. *Black Sexual Politics: African Americans, Gender and the New Racism.* New York: Routledge, 2004.

Common Sense for Drug Policy. www.csdp.

Connell, John, et al. (eds.). *Resources, Nations, and Indigenous Peoples: Case Studies from Australasia, Melanesia and Southeast Asia.* Melbourne: Oxford University Press, 1996.

Cossia, Juliann M. (ed.). *Global Warming in the 21st Century.* New York: Nova Science, 2011.

Damgeremba, Tsitsi. *Nervous Condition.* New York: Seal Press, 2001.

Davies, Phillip, and Iwan Morgan (eds.). *America's Americans: Population Issues in U.S. Society and*

Politics. London: Institute for the Study of the Americas, University of London, 2007.

Davis, Angela. *Abolition Democracy: Beyond Empire, Prisons, and Torture*. New York: Seven Stories, 2005.

_____. *The Meaning of Freedom: And Other Difficult Dialogues*. San Francisco: City Lights, 2012.

_____. *Women, Race & Class*. New York: Vintage, 1983.

De la Dehesa, Guillermo. *What Do We Know About Globalization: Issues of Poverty and Income Distribution*. Malden, MA: Blackwell, 2007.

Deloria, Vine. *For This Land: Writings on Religion in America*. New York: Routledge, 1999.

_____. *God Is Red: A Native View of Religion*. Golden, CO: Fulcrum, 2003.

_____. *Red Earth, White Lies: Native Americans and the Myth of Scientific Fact*. New York: Scribner, 1995.

De Pauli, Liliana (ed.). *Women's Empowerment and Economic Justice: Reflecting on Experience In Latin America and the Caribbean*. New York: United Nations Development Fund for Women, 2000.

Donziger, Steven (ed.). *The Real War on Crime: The Report of the National Criminal Justice Commission*. New York: HarperCollins, 1996.

Dorr, Steven, Barry Schutz, and Robert Slater. *Global Transformation and the Third World*. Boulder: Lynne Rienner, 1993.

Doumatoi, Eleanor Abdella, and Marsha P. Posusney (eds.). *Women and Globalization in the Arab Middle East: Gender, Economy, and Society*. Boulder: Lynne Rienner, 2003.

Dowie, Mark. *Conservation Refugees: The Hundred Year Conflict Between Global Conservation and Native Peoples*. Cambridge: MIT Press, 2009.

Drake, Frances. *Global Warming: The Science of Climate Change*. London: Arnold, 2000.

Du Bois, W.E.B. *The Souls of Black Folk*. New York: Fawcett World Library, 1970.

_____. *The World and Africa*. New York: International, 1965.

Dunn, Hopeton S. *Globalization, Communication, and the Caribbean Identity*. New York: St. Martin's Press, 1994.

Dyer, Joel. *The Perpetual Prisoner Machine: How America Profits from Crime*. Boulder: Westview Press, 2000.

Eade, John (ed.). *Living the Global City. Globalization as a Local Process*. New York: Routledge, 1997.

Edoho, Felix Moses (ed.). *Globalization and the New World Order: Promises, Problems, and Prospects for Africa in the Twenty-First Century*. Westport, CT: Praeger, 1997.

Ehteshami, Anoushiravan. *Globalization and Geopolitics in the Middle East: Old Games, New Rules*. New York: Routledge, 2007.

Eldredge, Dirk Chase. *Ending the War on Drugs: A Solution for America*. Bridgehampton, NY: BridgeWorks, 1998.

Engineer, Meher, Soumya Dutta, and Asit Dash. *Critical Issues of Justice, Equity and the Climate Crisis; Resisting Destructive "Development": Those Who Pollute/Emit the Most Are Not the Ones Threatened by Impacts*. Delhi: Vasudhaiva Kutumbakam, South Asian Dialogues on Ecological Democracy (SADED), 2010.

Eschle, Catherine, and Bice Maiguashca (eds.). *Critical Theories, International Relations and "the Anti-Globalisation Movement": The Politics of Global Resistance*. New York: Routledge, 2005.

Fagan, Brian. *The Attacking Ocean: The Past, Present, and Future of Rising Sea Levels*. New York: Bloomsbury Press, 2013.

Fall, Yassine (ed). *Africa: Gender, Globalization and Resistance*. Dakar: The African Association of Women for Research and Development, 1999.

Fanon, Frantz. *Black Skins, White Masks*. New York: Grove Press, 1967.

Faux, Jeff. *The Servant Economy: Where America's Elite Is Sending the Middle Class*. Hoboken, NJ: John Wiley & Sons, 2012.

Frank, Andre Gunder. *Capitalism and Underdevelopment in Latin America: Historical Studies of Chile and Brazil*. New York: Monthly Review Press, 1967.

Franklin, John Hope, and Alfred Moss, Jr. *From Slavery to Freedom: A History of African Americans. Eighth Edition*. New York: McGraw-Hill, 2000.

Featherstone, M. (ed.). *Global Culture: Nationalism, Globalization and Modernity*. London: Sage, 1990.

Fenn, Elizabeth A. *Pox Americana: The Great Smallpox Epidemic of 1775–82*. New York: Hill and Wang, 2001.

Fienup-Riordan, Anne, and Alice Rearden. *Ellavut: Our Yup 'ik World & Weather: Continuity and Change on the Bering Sea Coast*. Seattle: University of Washington Press in association with Calista Elders Council, Anchorage, 2012.

Figueira-McDonough, Josefina, and Rosemary Sarri (eds.). *Women at the Margins: Neglect, Punishment, and Resistance*. New York: Haworth Press, 2003.

Freiden, Jeffrey. *Global Capitalism: Its Fall and Rise in the Twentieth Century*. New York: W.W. Norton, 2006.

Freire, Paulo. *Pedagogy of the Oppressed*. New York: Continuum, 1970.

Garland, David. *The Culture of Control: Crime*

and Order in Contemporary Society. Chicago: University of Chicago Press, 2001.

George, Susan. *How the Other Half Dies: The Real Reasons for World Hunger.* Montclair, NJ: Allanheld, Osmun, 1977.

Giddens, Anthony. *The Consequences of Modernity.* Cambridge: Polity Press, 1990.

Gill, Stephen (ed). *Globalization, Democratization and Multilateralism.* New York: St. Martin's Press, 2000.

Giroux, Henry A. *Neoliberalism's War on Higher Education.* Chicago: Haymarket Books, 2014.

Girvan, Norman. *Cooperation in the Greater Caribbean: The Role of the Association of Caribbean States.* Kingston: Ian Randle, 2006.

Goldin, Ian, and Kenneth Reinert, *Globalization for Development: Trade, Finance, Aid, Migration and Policy.* Washington, DC: The International Bank for Reconstruction and Development/The World Bank and New York: Palgrave Macmillan, 2006.

Gonzales, Victoria, and Karen Kampwirth (eds.). *Radical Women in Latin America: Left and Right.* University Park: Pennsylvania State University Press, 2001.

Grady, Caitlan A., and Tamim Younos (eds.). *Climate Change and Water Resources.* Berlin: Springer, 2013.

Grant, Joanne (ed.). *Black Protest: 360 Years of History, Documents and Analyses.* New York: Fawcett Columbine, 1968.

Greider, William. *One World, Ready or Not.* New York: Simon & Shuster, 1997.

Griffin, David. *The New Pearl Harbor.* New York: Olive Branch Press, 2004.

_____, and Peter Dale Scott (eds.). *911 and American Empire—Intellectuals Speak Out (Vol. 1).* Northampton, MA: Olive Branch Press, 2006.

Guerrero, Annette M. (ed.). *The State of Native America: Genocide, Colonization, and Resistance.* Boston: South End Press, 1992.

Hacker, Andrew. *Two Nations: Black and White, Separate, Hostile, Unequal.* New York: Scribner's, 1992.

Hall, Budd L., George Jerry Sefa Dei, and Dorothy Goldin Rosenberg (eds.). *Indigenous Knowledges in Global Contexts: Multiple Readings of Our World.* Toronto: University of Toronto Press, 2000.

Hall, S., D. Held, and T. McGrew (eds.). *Modernity and Its Futures.* Oxford, UK: Polity Press/Open University, 1992.

Hallett, Michael. *Private Prisons in America: A Critical Race Perspective.* Urbana: University of Illinois Press, 2006.

Hallinan, J.T. *Going Up the River.* New York: Random House, 2003.

Hallward, Peter. *Damming the Flood: Haiti, Aristide, and the Politics of Containment.* New York: Verso, 2007.

Hannah, Lee (ed.). *Saving a Million Species: Extinction Risk from Climate Change.* Washington, DC: Island Press, 2012.

Harris, Jerry. *The Dialectics of Globalization: Economic and Political Conflict in a Transformational World.* Newcastle: Cambridge Scholars, 2006.

Harris, Paul. *Black Rage Confronts the Law.* New York: New York University Press, 1997.

Harris, Paul G. *Global Warming and East Asia: The Domestic and International Politics of Climate Change.* New York: Routledge, 2003.

Hassine, Victor. *Life Without Parole: Living in Prison Today.* 4th Edition. New York: Oxford University Press, 2009.

Hawkin, David J. (ed.). *The Twenty-First Century Confronts Its Gods: Globalization, Technology, and War.* Albany: State University of New York Press, 2004.

Haxton, E., and C. Olsson (eds.). *Women in Development: Trade Aspects on Women in the Development Process.* Uppsala, Sweden: United Nations Youth and Student Association of Sweden, 1995.

Hayek, F.A. *The Road to Serfdom.* Chicago: University of Chicago Press, 1994.

Hayes, Lindsay, and Joseph Rowan. *National Study of Jail Suicides: Seven Years Later.* Alexandria, VA: National Center on Institutions and Alternatives, sponsored by the National Institute of Corrections, U.S. Department of Justice, 1988.

Held, D. *Democracy and the Global Order: From the Modern State to the Cosmopolitan Governance.* Oxford, UK: Polity Press, 1995.

Hennis, Marjoleine. *Globalization and European Integration: The Changing Role of Farmers in the Common Agricultural Policy.* Lanham, MD: Rowman & Littlefield, 2005.

Herring, D. Ann, and Alan C. Swedlund. *Plagues and Epidemics: Infected Spaces Past and Present.* Oxford: Berg, 2010.

Hersh, Jacques, and Johannes Dragsbaeck Schmidt. *Globalization and Social Change.* New York: Routledge, 2000.

Hill, C.W.I. *International Business: Competing in the Global Market Place.* New York: Unwin-McGraw-Hill, 2001.

Hill, Jr., N.S. (ed.). *Words of Power: Voices from Indian America.* Golden, CO: Fulcrum, 1994.

Houtart, L.F., and F. Polet. *L'autre Davos: Mondialisation des resistances et des lutes.* Paris: L'Harmattan, 1999.

Howitt, Richard, with John Connell and Philip Hirsch (eds.). *Resources, Nations and Indige-*

nous Peoples: Case Studies from Australasia, Melanesia and Southeast Asia. Melbourne: Oxford University Press, 1996.

Huffington, Arianna. Third World America: How Our Politicians Are Abandoning the Middle Class and Betraying the American Dream. New York: Crown, 2010.

Hughes, Lotta. The No-Nonsense Guide to Indigenous Peoples. Oxford: New Internationalist Publications, 2003.

Irwin, John. The Warehouse Prison: Disposal of the New Dangerous Class. Los Angeles: Roxbury, 2005.

Ivison, Duncan, et al. (eds.). Political Theory and the Rights of Indigenous People. Cambridge: Cambridge University Press, 2000.

Jackson, George. Blood in My Eye. Baltimore: Black Classic Press, 1990.

_____. Soledad Brother: The Prison Letters of George Jackson. New York: Coward-McCann, 1970.

Jackson, John. Introduction to African Civilizations. New York: Citadel, 1980.

James, Jeffrey. Technology, Globalization and Poverty. Northampton, MA: Edward Elgar, 2002.

James, Joy (ed.). The New Abolitionists: (Neo) Slave Narratives and Contemporary Prison Writings. Albany: State University of New York Press, 2005.

_____ (ed.). States of Confinement: Policing, Detention, and Prisons. New York: St. Martin's Press, 2000.

Jansen, Edward, et al. (eds.). Local Perspectives on Globalization: The African Case. Dar es Salam: Mkubkina Nyota, 2000.

Jawad, Haifaa A. The Rights of Women in Islam: An Authentic Approach. New York: St. Martin's Press, 1998.

Jenson, Derrick. Endgame: The Problem of Civilization, Vol. 1 and Vol. 2: Resistance. New York: Seven Stories, 2006.

Jentoft, Svein, et al. (eds.). Indigenous Peoples: Resource Management and Global Rights. Delft, The Netherlands: Eburon, 2003.

Johansen, Bruce. E. Global Warming in the 21st Century. Volume 1: Our Evolving Climate Crisis. Westport, CT: Praeger, 2006.

Johnson, Chalmers. The Sorrows of Empire: Militarism, Secrecy, and the End of the Republic. New York: Henry Holt, 2004.

Johnston, Alison. Is the Sacred for Sale? Tourism and Indigenous Peoples. London: Earthscan, 2006.

Johnston, R.J., et al. (eds.). Geographies of Global Change: Remapping the World in the Late Twentieth Century. London: Blackwell, 1995.

Joseph, Tennyson S. D. Decolonization in St. Lucia: Politics and Global Neoliberalism, 1945–2010. Jackson: University Press of Mississippi, 2011.

Jomo, K.S. Globalization Under Hegemony: The Changing World Economy. New Delhi: Oxford University Press, 2006.

Juhasz, Antonia. The Tyranny of Oil. New York: HarperCollins, 2008.

Kameyama, Yasuko, et al. (eds.). Climate Change in Asia: Perspectives on the Future Climate Change Regime. Tokyo: United Nations University Press, 2008.

Kaplinsky, Raphael. Globalization, Poverty and Inequality. Malden, MA: Polity Press, 2005.

Kelkar, Govind, et al. (eds.). Globalization and Indigenous Peoples in Asia: Changing the Local-Global Interface. New Delhi: Sage, 2004.

Kennedy, Randall. Race, Crime, and the Law. New York: Pantheon, 1997.

Kerr, Joanna, and Caroline Sweetman (eds.). Women Inventing Gender. Oxford: Oxfam Focus on Gender, 2003.

Kerr, Joanna, et al. (eds.). The Future of Women's Rights. New York: Zed Books, 2004.

Klak, Thomas (ed.). Globalization and Neoliberalism: The Caribbean Context. Lanham, MD: Rowman & Littlefield, 1998.

Koparanova, Malinka, and Rob Vos. Globalization and Economic Diversification: Policy Changes for Economies in Transition. London: Bloomsbury Academic, 2011.

Kunnie, Julian, and Nomalungelo Goduka (eds.). Indigenous Peoples' Wisdom and Power: Affirming Our Knowledge Through Narratives. Burlington, VT: Ashgate, 2006.

Lacour, Claudia Brodsky, and Toni Morrison (eds.). Birth of a Nation'hood: Gaze, Script, and Spectacle in the O.J. Simpson Case. New York: Pantheon, 1997.

LaDuke, Winona. All Our Relations: Native Struggles for Land and Life. Boston: South End Press, 1999.

Leighton, Paul, and Donna Selman. Punishment for Sale: Private Prisons, Big Business, and the Incarceration Binge. Lanham, MD: Rowman & Littlefield, 2010.

Levine, Ron, and Michael Wou. Prisoners of Age: The Alcatraz Exhibition. Montreal: Synchronicity Productions, 2000.

Lewis, Linden (ed.). Caribbean Sovereignty, Development and Democracy in an Age of Globalization. New York: Routledge, 2013.

Lindorff, David. Killing Time: An Investigation into the Death-row Case of Mumia Abu-Jamal. Monroe, ME: Common Courage Press, 2003.

Linkogle, Stephanie, and Sheila Rowbotham

(eds.). *Women Resist Globalization: Mobilizing for Livelihood and Rights.* New York: Zed Books, 2001.

Logan, B. Ikubolajeh (ed.). *Globalization, the Third World State and Poverty Alleviation in the Twenty-First Century.* Burlington, VT: Ashgate, 2002.

Loewen, James. *Lies My Teacher Told Me: Everything Your American History Textbook Got Wrong.* New York: Touchstone, 1996.

Lopez, Ramon, and Alberto Valdes (eds.). *Rural Poverty in Latin America.* New York: St. Martin's Press, 2000.

Lozano, Wilfredo, and Anthony Maingot. *The United States and the Caribbean: Transforming Hegemony and Sovereignty.* New York: Routledge, 2005.

Lubiano, Whaneema (ed.). *The House That Race Built: Black Age Americans, U.S. Terrain.* New York: Pantheon, 1997.

MacGillivray, Alex. *A Brief History of Globalization: The Untold Story of Our Incredible Shrinking Planet.* New York: Carroll & Graf, 2006.

Mander, J. *In the Absence of the Sacred: The Failure of Technology and the Survival of the Indian Nations.* San Francisco: Sierra Club Books, 1991.

_____, and Victoria Tauli-Corpuz (eds.). *Paradigm Wars: Indigenous Peoples' Resistance to Globalization.* San Francisco: Sierra Club Books, 2006.

May, John P., and Khalid Pitts (eds.). *Building Violence: How America's Rush to Incarcerate Creates More Violence.* Thousand Oaks, CA: Sage, 2000.

Maffi, Luisa (ed.). *On Biocultural Diversity: Linking Language, Knowledge, and the Environment.* Washington, DC: Smithsonian Institution Press, 2001.

Maingot, Anthony, and Wilfredo Lozano. *The United States and the Caribbean: Transforming Hegemony and Sovereignty.* New York: Routledge, 2005.

Malcolm X. *By Any Means Necessary.* New York: Pathfinder Press, 1980.

Mamdani, Mahmood. *Saviors and Survivors: Darfur, Politics, and the War on Terror.* New York: Pantheon, 2009.

Mandle, Jay. *Globalization and the Poor.* Cambridge: Cambridge University Press, 2003.

Manley, Michael. *Jamaica: Struggle in the Periphery.* London: Writers and Readers Publishing Cooperative Society, 1982.

Mann, Coramae Richey. *Unequal Justice: A Question of Color.* Bloomington: Indiana University Press, 1993.

Marable, Manning. *The Great Wells of Democracy: The Meaning of Race in American Life.* New York: Basic Books, 2002.

_____. *How Capitalism Underdeveloped Black America.* Boston: South End Press, 1983.

Maracle, Lee. *Daughters Are Forever.* Vancouver: Polestar, 2002.

Marcos, Sylvia, and Marguerite Waller (eds.). *Dialogue and Difference: Feminisms Challenge Globalization.* New York: Palgrave Macmillan, 2005.

Marquina, Antonio (ed.). *Global Warming and Climate Change: Prospects and Policies in Asia and Europe.* Basingstoke: Palgrave Macmillan, 2010.

Mars, Perry, and Alma Young (eds.). *Caribbean Labor and Politics: Legacies of Cheddi Jagan and Michael Manley.* Detroit: Wayne State University Press, 2004.

Marshall, Jonathan, and Peter Dale Scott. *Cocaine Politics: Drugs, Armies, and the CIA in Central America.* Berkeley: University of California Press, 1998.

Martin, Pamela. *The Globalization of Contentious Politics: The Amazonian Indigenous Rights Movement.* New York: Routledge, 2003.

May, John P., and Khalid R. Pitts (eds.). *Building Violence: How America's Rush to Incarcerate Creates More Violence.* Thousand Oaks, CA: Sage, 2000.

Mbilinyi, Marjorie. *Budgets, Debt Relief and Globalisation.* Accra, Ghana: Third World Network-Africa, 2001.

Mbiti, John. *Introduction to African Religion.* London: Heinemann, 1991.

McAdam, Jane, et al. *Climate Change and Australia: Warming to the Global Challenge.* Annandale, Australia: Federation Press, 2012.

McCoy, Alfred. *The Politics of Heroin: CIA Complicity in the Global Drug Trade.* Chicago: Lawrence Hill, 2003.

McGaa, Ed, Eagle Man. *Mother Earth Spirituality: Native American Paths to Healing Ourselves and Our World.* San Francisco: HarperCollins, 1990.

McNally, David. *Global Slump: The Economics and Politics of Crisis and Resistance.* Oakland: PM Press, 2011.

Meyer, William B. *Human Impact on the Earth.* Cambridge: Cambridge University Press, 1996.

Meyysan, Thierry. *l'Effroyable imposture.* Paris: Alphee Jean-Paul Bertrand, 2007.

Michel, David, and Amit Pandya (eds.). *Troubled Waters: Climate Change, Hydropolitics, and Transboundary Resources.* Washington, DC: Henry L. Stimson Center, 2009.

Miller, Debra A. (ed.). *Will the World Run Out of Water.* Detroit: Greenhaven Press, 2007.

Miller, Jerome. *Search and Destroy: African American Males in the Criminal Justice System*. New York: Cambridge University Press, 1996.

Minde, Henry, et al. (eds.). *Indigenous Peoples: Resource Management and Global Rights*. Delft, The Netherlands: Eburon, 2003.

Mittelman, James (ed.). *Globalization: Critical Perspectives*. Boulder: Lynne Rienner, 1996.

Mlinar, Z. *Globalization and Territorial Identities*. Aldershot, UK: Avebury, 1992.

Moghadam, Valentine. *Globalizing Women: Transnational Feminist Networks*. Baltimore: Johns Hopkins University Press, 2005.

Muhammed, Khalil Gibran. *The Condemnation of Blackness: Race, Crime, and the Making of Modern America*. Cambridge, MA: Harvard University Press, 2010.

Mukangara, Fenella, and Bertha Koda. *Beyond Inequalities: Women in Tanzania:* A Profile of Women in Tanzania Produced by the Tanzania Gender Networking Programme (TGNP) and the Women in Development Southern Africa Awareness (WIDSAA) program of the Southern Africa Research and Documentation Centre (SARDC). Dar es Salaam and Harare, 1997.

Murove, Felix Munyaradzi (ed). *African Ethics: An Anthology of Comparative and Applied Ethics*. Scottsville, South Africa: University of Kwazulu-Natal Press, 2009.

Myrdal, Gunnar. *An American Dilemma: The Negro Problem and Modern Democracy*. New Jersey: Transaction Publishers, 1995.

Nathan, Dev, Govind Kelkar, and Pierre Walter (eds.). *Globalization and Indigenous Peoples in Asia: Changing the Local-Global Interface*. New Delhi: Sage Publications, 2004.

National Advisory Commission on Civil Disorders, *The Kerner Report: The 1968 Report of the National Advisory Commission on Civil Disorder*. New York: Pantheon Books, 1968.

Ndikumana, L., and J. Boyce. *Africa's Odious Debts: How Foreign Loans and Capital Flight Bled a Continent*. New York: Zed Books, 2011.

Nelson, Cynthia, and Shahnaz Rouse (eds.). *Situating Globalization: Views from Egypt*. New Brunswick, NJ: Transaction Publishers, 2000.

North, Gerald R., Jurgen Schmandt, and Judith Clarkson (eds.). *The Impact of Global Warming in Texas: A Report of the Task Force on Climate Change in Texas*. Austin: University of Texas Press, 1995.

Nyang'oro, Julius E., and Timothy Shaw (eds.). *Beyond Structural Adjustment in Africa: The Political Economy of Sustainable and Democratic Development*. New York: Praeger, 1992.

Ogot, B.A. *Building on the Indigenous: Selected Essays 1981–1998*. Kisumu, Kenya: Anyange Press, 1999.

Onimode, Bade. *Africa in the World of the 21st Century*. Ibadan, Nigeria: Ibadan University Press, 2000.

Oishi, Nana. *Women in Motion: Globalization, State Policies, and Labor Migration in Asia*. Stanford, CA: Stanford University Press, 2005.

Palmer, Ransford. *The Caribbean Economy in the Age of Globalization*. New York: Palgrave Macmillan, 2009.

Parkman, Francis. *The Conspiracy of Pontiac and the Indian War After the Conquest of Canada*. Boston: Little, Brown, 1886.

Parrenas, Rhacel Salazar. *Servants of Globalization: Women, Migration, and Domestic Work*. Stanford, CA: Stanford University Press, 2001.

Payne, Anthony, and Paul Sutton. *Charting Caribbean Development*. London: Macmillan Education, 2001.

_____, Paul Sutton, and Tony Thorndike. *Grenada: Revolution and Invasion*. New York: St. Martin's Press, 1985.

Petchesky, Rosalind P. *Global Prescriptions: Gendering Health and Human Rights*. New York: Zed Books, 2003.

Pielke, Roger. *The Climate Fix: What Scientists and Politicians Won't Tell You About Global Warming*. New York: Basic Books, 2010.

Pieterse, Jan Nederveen. *Globalization or Empire*. New York: Routledge, 2004.

Pinar, William. *The Gender of Racial Politics and Violence in America: Lynching, Prison, Rape, and the Crisis of Masculinity*. New York: Peter Lang, 2001.

Pithouse, D.K. *The West and the Third World: Trade, Colonialism, Dependence and Development*. Oxford, U.K.: Blackwell, 1999.

Podur, Justin Joseph, and Sasha Liley. *Haiti's New Dictatorship: The Coup, the Earthquake, and the UN Occupation*. Toronto: Between the Lines Press, 2012.

Polokoff, Ericka G., and Ligya Lindio-McGovern (eds.). *Gender and Globalization: Patterns of Women's Resistance*. Whitby, Ontario: de Sitter Publications, 2011.

Posey, Darrell A., and Graham Dutfield. *Beyond Intellectual Property: Towards Traditional Resource Rights for Indigenous Peoples and Local Communities*. Ottawa: International Development Resource Center, 1996.

Prashad, Vijay. *Keeping Up with the Dow Joneses: Debt, Prison, Workfare*. Cambridge, MA: South End Press, 2003.

_____, and Teo Ballvé (eds.). *Dispatches from Latin America: On the Frontlines Against Neoliberalism*. Cambridge, MA: South End Press, 2008.

Raphael, Steven, and Michael A. Stoll. *Why Are So Many Americans in Prison.* New York: Russell Sage Foundation, 2014.

Rahm, Dianne. *Climate Change Policy in the United States: The Science, Politics, and the Prospects for Change.* London: McFarland, 2010.

Ray, O.S. *Drugs, Society and Human Behavior.* St. Louis: C.V. Mosby, 1972.

Reese, Renford. *Prison Race.* Durham, NC: Carolina Academic Press, 2006.

Reiman, Jeffrey. *The Rich Get Richer and the Poor Get Prison.* Needham Heights, MA: Allyn and Bacon, 2001.

Reviere, Rebecca, and Vernetta D. Young. *Women Behind Bars: Gender and Race in U.S. Prisons.* Boulder: Lynne Rienner, 2006.

Rifkin, Jeremy. *The Biotech Century: Harnessing the Gene and Remaking the World.* New York: Tarcher/Putnam, 1998.

Robbins, Christopher. *The Invisible Air Force: The Story of the CIA's Secret Airlines.* New York: Macmillan, 1979.

Roberts, Ian, with Phil Edwards. *The Energy Glut: Climate Change and the Politics of Fatness.* New York: Zed Books, 2010.

Robertson, Roland. *Globalization, Social Theory and Global Culture.* Newbury Park, CA: Sage, 1992.

Robinson, Randall. *An Unbroken Agony: Haiti, from Revolution to the Kidnapping of a President.* New York: Basic Civitas Books, 2008.

Rodney, Walter. *How Europe Underdeveloped Africa.* Washington, DC: Howard University Press, 1982.

Ross, Jeffrey Ian (ed.). *The Globalization of Supermax Prisons.* New Brunswick: Rutgers University Press, 2013.

Rossett, Peter M. *Food Is Different: Why We Must Get the WTO Out of Agriculture.* New York, 2006.

Rossi, Ino (ed.). *Frontiers of Globalization Research: Theoretical and Methodical Approaches.* New York: Springer Science and Business Media, 2007.

Rowbotham, Sheila, and Stephanie Linkogle (eds.). *Women Resist Globalization: Mobilizing for Livelihood and Rights.* New York: Zed Press, 2001.

Rupert, Mark, and M. Scott Solomon. *Globalization and the International Political Economy.* Lanham, MD: Rowman & Littlefield, 2006.

Ruppert, Michael. *Crossing the Rubicon.* Gabriola Island, British Columbia: New Society, 2004.

Russell, Katheryn. *The Color of Crime: Racial Hoaxes, White Fear, Black Protectionism, Police Harassment, and Other Macroaggressions.* New York: New York University Press, 1998.

Rycenga, Jennifer, and Marguerite Waller (eds.). *Frontline Feminisms: Women, War, and Resistance.* New York: Garland, 2000.

Sadowski-Smith, Claudia (ed.). *Globalization on the Line: Culture, Capital, and Citizenship at U.S. Borders.* New York: Palgrave, 2002.

Sale, Kirkpatrick. *Conquest of Paradise: Christopher Columbus and the Columbian Legacy.* New York: Plume, 1994.

Salinger, Lawrence. *Encyclopaedia of White-Collar and Corporate Crime. Volume 2.* Thousand Oaks, CA: Sage, 2005.

Saul, Ben, Steven Sherwood, Jane McAdam, Tim Stephens, and James Slezak. *Climate Change and Australia: Warming to the Global Challenge.* Annandale, Australia: Federation Press, 2012.

Scholte, J. *Globalization: A Critical Introduction.* New York: St. Martin's Press, 2000.

Schumpeter, Joseph. *Capitalism, Socialism and Democracy.* New York: Harper, 1975.

Scott, Helen C. *Caribbean Women Writers and Globalization.* Burlington, VT: Ashgate, 2006.

Scott, Peter Dale, and Jonathan Marshall. *Cocaine Politics: Drugs, Armies and the CIA in Central America.* Berkeley: University of California, 1998.

Selman, Donna, and Paul Leighton. *Punishment for Sale: Private Prisons, Big Business, and the Incarceration Binge.* Lanham, MD: Rowman & Littlefield, 2010.

Semboja, Joseph, Juma Mwapachu, and Edward Jansen (eds.). *Local Perspectives on Globalisation: The African Case.* Dar es Salaam: Research on Poverty Alleviation, Mkubkina Nyota, 2000.

Shehadeh, Lamia Rustum. *Women and the War in Lebanon.* Gainesville: University Press of Florida, 1999.

Sheller, Mimi. *Consuming the Caribbean: From Arawaks to Zombies.* New York: Psychology Press, c/o of Taylor & Francis Group, 2003.

Shierholz, Heidi, Jared Bernstein, and Lawrence Mishel. *The State of Working America, 2008/2009.* Washington, DC: Economic Policy Institute, 2008.

Shiva, Vandana. *The Violence of the Green Revolution: Third World Agriculture, Ecology, and Politics.* Penang: Third World Network, 1991.

Shugart, H.H., and F.I. Woodward. *Global Change and Terrestrial Biosphere: Achievements and Challenges.* Hoboken, NJ: Wiley-Blackwell, 2011.

Singh, Kavaljit. *Questioning Globalization.* New York: Zed Books, 2005.

Sloop, John M. *The Cultural Prison: Discourse, Prisoners, and Punishment.* Tuscaloosa: University of Alabama Press, 1996.

Smiley, Tavis, and Cornel West. *The Rich and the Rest of Us: A Poverty Manifesto*. New York: Smiley Books, 2012.

Somé, Malidoma. *Of Water and Spirit: Ritual, Magic, and Initiation in the Life of an African Shaman*. New York: Arkana/Penguin Books, 1995.

Stearn, E. Wagner, and Allen E. Stearn. *The Effect of Smallpox on the Destiny of the Amerindian*. Boston: Bruce Humphries, 1945.

Stewart-Harawira, Makere. *The New Imperial Order: Indigenous Responses to Globalization*. New York: Zed Books, 2005.

Stiglitz, Joseph, and Linda Bilmes. *The Three Trillion Dollar War: The True Cost of the Iraq Conflict*. New York: W.W. Norton, 2008.

Storm, Servaas, and C.W.M. Naastepad (eds.). *Globalization and Economic Development: Essays in Honor of J. George Waardenburg*. Northampton, MA: Edward Elgar, 2001.

Thomas, Clive Yolande. *The Poor and the Powerless: Economic Policy and Change in the Caribbean*. New York: Monthly Review Press, 1988.

Thomas, Jim, and Barbara H. Zaitzow (eds.). *Women in Prison: Gender and Social Control*. Boulder: Lynne Rienner, 2003.

Tikhonova, N.E. *Fenomenon Gorodskoi Bednosti v Sovremennoi Rossi* (*The Phenomenon of Urban Poverty in Modern Russia*). Moscow: Letnii Sad, 2003.

Tilley, Virginia Q. *Seeing Indians: A Study of Race, Nation, and Power in El Salvador*. Albuquerque: University of New Mexico Press, 2005.

Todaro, Rosalba, and Sonia Yanez (eds.). *Sobre Mujeres Y Globalization*. Santiago: Centro De Estudios De La Mujer, CEM, 1997.

Tongkul, Felix. *Traditional Systems of Indigenous Peoples of Sabah, Malaysia: Wisdom Accumulated Through Generations*. Penambang, Malaysia: PACOS Trust, 2002.

Turner, Bryan S. (ed.). *The Routledge International Handbook of Globalization Studies*. New York: Routledge, 2010.

Vickers, Damon. *The Day After the Dollar Crashes: A Survival Guide for the Rise of the New World Order*. New York: John Wiley & Sons, 2011.

Walker, Beth (ed.). *State of the World's Minorities and Indigenous Peoples 2013: Events of 2012: Focus on Health*. London: Minority Rights Group International, 2013.

Wall, Steve. *To Become a Human Being: The Message of Tadodaho Chief Leon Shenandoah*. Charlottesville: Hampton Roads, 2001.

Wallerstein, Immanuel. *World Systems Analysis:* *An Introduction*. Third Printing. Durham: Duke University Press, 2005.

Warren, Karen J. (ed.). *Ecofeminism: Women, Culture, Nature*. Bloomington: Indiana University Press, 1997.

Washington, Harriet. *Medical Apartheid: The Dark History of Medical Experimentation on Black Americans from Colonial Times to the Present*. New York: Anchor Books, 2008.

Washington, Haydn, and John Cook. *Climate Change Denial: Heads in the Sand*. London: Earthscan, 2011.

Waters, M. *Globalization*. London: Routledge, 1995.

Wessendorf, Kathrin (ed.). *Challenging Politics: Indigenous Peoples' Experiences with Political Parties and Elections*. Copenhagen: International Work Group for Indigenous Affairs, Document No. 104, 2001.

West, Cornel. *Race Matters*. New York: Vintage, 1994.

Whaiti, Pania Te, Marie McCarthy, and Arohia Durie (eds.). *Mai I Rangiatea: Maori Wellbeing and Development*. Auckland: Auckland University Press and Bridget Williams Books, 1997.

Whitmore, Andy (ed.). *Pitfalls & Pipelines: Indigenous Peoples and Extractive Industries*. Baguio City, Philippines: Tebtebba Foundation, 2012.

Williams, Lawrence. *Executing Justice: An Inside Account of the Case of Mumia Abu Jamal*. New York: St. Martin's Press, 2001.

Williams, Stanley "Tookie." *Blue Rage, Black Redemption*. New York: Simon & Schuster, 2007.

Wiseman, J. *Global Nation: Australia and the Politics of Globalization*. Cambridge: Cambridge University Press, 1995.

Wolf, Martin. *Why Globalization Works*. New Haven: Yale University Press, 2004.

Wood, Bette. *Black Women in the Workplace: Impacts of Structural Change in the Economy*. Westport, CT: Greenwood Press, 1992.

Yanez, Sonia, and Rosalba Todaro. *Sobre Mujeres Y Globalizacion*. Santiago: Centro De Estudios De La Mujer, CEM, 1997.

Young, Vernetta D., and Rebecca Reviere. *Women Behind Bars: Gender and Race in U.S. Prisons*. Boulder: Lyenne Rienner, 2006.

Younos, Tamim, and Caitlan A. Grady (eds.). *Climate Change and Water Resources*. Berlin: Springer, 2013.

Zaitzow, Barbara H., and Jim Thomas (eds.). *Women in Prison: Gender and Social Control*. Boulder: Lynne Rienner, 2003.

Zinn, Howard. *New Deal Thought*. Indianapolis: Bobbs-Merrill, 1966.

Journal Articles (Print)

Benbow, N., et al. "Mortality in Chicago attributed to the July 1995 heatwave." *American Journal of Health* 87 (1997): 1515–1551.

Broad, Robin, and John Cavanagh. "The hijacking of the development debate: How Friedman and Sachs got it wrong." *World Policy Journal* 23, no. 2 (Summer 2006): 21.

Burston, B.W., et al. "Drug Use and African Americans: Myth Versus Reality." *Journal of Drug and Alcohol Education* 40, no. 2 (1995): 19–39.

Carvalho, Georgia O. "Environmental Resistance and the Politics of Energy Development in the Brazilian Amazon." *Journal of Environment and Development* 15, no. 3 (2006): 257.

Cohen, Andrew. "Sheriff Joe Arpallo: The Most Lawless Lawman in America." *The Atlantic,* March 26, 2014.

Davidson, Joe. "African Americans are grist for the fast-growing prison industry's money mill." *Emerge,* October 1997.

Franco, Jimmy, Sr. "The Martyrs of the Chicano Moratorium." Connie Tucker and Faya Rose Touré (eds.). *Martyrs of the Movement: Never Forget/Never Again.* Jackson, MS: Imani Press, August 2014.

Gawande, Atul. "Hellhole: The United States holds tens of thousands of inmates in long-term solitary confinement. Is this torture?" *New Yorker,* March 30, 2009.

Gelfano, Lauren. "Toxic Waste Spill in Ivory Coast Exposes 'Dark Underbelly' of Globalization." *World Politics Review* 28 (March 2007).

Handa, S. "Gender, Headship and Intrahousehold Resource Allocation." *World Development Bank* 22, no. 10 (1994): 1535–1547.

Hansen, James D., et al. "Climate Impact of Increasing Atmospheric Carbon Dioxide." *Science* 213. (August 28, 1981): 957–966.

Harris, La Donna, and Jacqueline Wasilewski. "Indigeneity, an alternative worldview: Four R's (Relationship, Responsibility, Reciprocity, Redistribution) vs. two P's (Power and Profit): Sharing the journey towards conscious evolution." *Systems Research and Behavioral Science* 21, no. 5 (September–October 2004).

Lee, E. "Globalization and Labour Standards: A Review of Issues." *International Labour Review* 136, no. 2 (1997): 173–189.

Muntaqim, Jalil Abdul. "The Cold War of the '90's." *A Bulldozer Publication, Prison News Service,* no. 2 (September–October 1995).

Murungi, John. "The Academy and the Crisis of African Governance." *African Issues* XXXII, nos. 1 and 2 (Fall 2004): 21.

Pitt, Becky, and Bruce Western. "Incarceration and Social Inequality." *Daedalus.* Vol. 139, No. 3, (Summer 2010): 16–17.

Raval, Suresh. "The Role of the Humanities in the Age of Globalization: Reading Mukherjee, Kincaid, and Coetzee." *Western Humanities Review,* Vol. LXV, No. 3, Fall 2011, 146.

Riebsame, William E., and Jeffrey W. Jacobs, "Climate Change and Water Resources in the Sacramento–San Joaquin Region of California," Working Paper #64, Natural Hazards Research and Applications Information Center, University of Colorado, December 1988.

Rosen, Meghan. "Online map tracks forest shifts from space." *Science News* 184, no. 12 (December 14, 2013).

Sabol, W.B., T. D. Minton, and P.M. Harrison. "Prison and Jail Inmates at Midyear 2006." *Bureau of Justice Statistics,* U.S. Department of Justice, 2007.

Sassen, Saskia. "Women's Burden: Countergeographies of Globalization and the Feminization of Survival." *Journal of International Affairs* 53, no 2 (2000): 503–524.

Sherrill, Robert. "Death trip: The American way of Execution." *The Nation,* January 8, 2001.

Smith, Phil. "Private Prisons: Profits of Crime." *Covert Action Quarterly* (Fall 1993).

Thaman, Konai Helu. "Decolonizing Pacific Studies: Indigenous Perspectives, Knowledge, and Wisdom in Higher Education." *The Contemporary Pacific* 15, no. 1 (Spring 2003).

Todd, Anne Marie. "Environmental Sovereignty Discourse of the Brazilian Amazon: National Politics and the Globalization of Indigenous Resistance." *Journal of Communication Inquiry* 27, no. 4 (October 2003): 364.

U.S. Department of Justice. "Environmental Sovereignty Discourse of the Brazilian Amazon: National Politics and the Globalization of Indigenous Resistance." *Journal of Communication Inquiry* 27, no. 4 (October 2003).

U.S. Department of Justice. "Prison and Jail Inmates at Midyear 2004." Bureau of Justice Statistics, April 24, 2005.

U.S. Department of Justice. *Quick Facts: Federal Bureau of Prisons.* March 26, 2005.

Whitman, S., G. Good, E. Donoghue, N. Benbow, W. Shou, and S. Mou, "Mortality in Chicago attributed to the July 1995 heatwave." *American Journal of Health* 87 (1997): 1515–1551.

Wood, Phillip. "Globalization and Prison Privatization: Why Are Most of the World's For-Profit Adult Prisons to Be Found in the American South?" *International Political Sociology* 1 (2007): 222–239.

Xanthaki, Alexandra. "Land Rights of Indigenous Peoples in South-East Asia." *Melbourne Journal of International Law* 4 (2003): 12–13.

Zhouri, Andrea. "'Adverse Forces' in the Brazilian Amazon: Developmentalism Versus Environmentalism and Indigenous Rights." *Journal of Environment and Development* 19 (2010): 259–260.

Multimedia (Videos)

Broken on All Sides: Race, Mass Incarceration and New Visions for Criminal Justice in the U.S. Accolade Competition Winner Film Documentary, 2012.

Conservation Refugees-Expelled from Paradise. Producer: Steffen Keulig http://www.justconservation.org/conservation-refugees-expelled-from-paradise.

END: CIV: Resist or Die. Producer: Franklin Lopez. Oakland: PM Press, 2011.

The Farm. Producers: Jonathan Stack and Liz Garbus, Documentary, 1998.

The Hidden Enemy. Citizens Commission on Human Rights International: The Mental Health Watchdog. Los Angeles, 2014.

The House I Live In. Director: Eugene Jarecki, FilmBuff Documentary, 2012.

Life and Debt. Producer: Stephanie Black, 2001.

New Rulers of the World. Producer: John Pilger. Available on video at http://johnpilger.com/videos/the-new-rulers-of-the-world (accessed September 23, 2014).

Standing on Sacred Ground: Profit and Loss. Producers: Christopher Mcleod and the Earth Institute with Bullfrog Films, 2013.

Sugar Cane Alley. Director: Euzhan Palcy, 1983.

Unpublished Dissertations

Brown, Shirley Ann Vining. "Race as a Factor in the Intra-Prison Outcomes of Youthful First Offenders." University of Michigan, 1975.

Online Resources (Websites)

Abu-Jamal, Mumia. "Ruchell Cinque McGee: Sole Survivor Still." http://4struggle.org/2012/10/04/ruchell-cinque-magee-sole-survivor-still/ (accessed May 3, 2014).

Adams, Michael. "Negotiating Nature: Collaboration and Conflict Between Aboriginal and Conservation Interests in New South Wales, Australia." *University of Wollongong Online* 6 (2004). http://ro.uow.edu.au/cgi/viewcontent.cgi?/article=1427&content=scipapers&sei (accessed May 1, 2005).

Agence France-Press. "New cyclone hits victims of Typhoon Haiyan." *News 24*, South Africa, January 20, 2014. http://www.news24.com/World/News/News-cyclone-hits-victims-of-Typhoon-Haiyan-20140120 (accessed January 31, 2014).

Alexander, Michelle. "The New Jim Crow: How the War on Drugs Gave Birth to a Permanent American Undercaste." *Mother Jones*, March 8, 2010. http://motherjones.com/politics/2010/03/new-jim-crow-war-on-drugs (accessed March 24, 2014).

Alexander, Neville. "After Apartheid: The Language Question." www.yale.edu/macmillan/apartheid/alexanderp2.pdf (accessed May 5, 2013).

Alternet Staff. "Occupation Toll: 5 Million Iraqi Children Orphaned." December 18, 2007. http://www.alternet.org/story/70886/occupation's_toll%3A_5_million_iraqi_children_orphaned (accessed December 12, 2012).

Ambrosio, Tara-Jen, and Vincent Schiraldi. "From Classrooms to CellBlocks: A National Perspective." Washington, DC: Justice Policy Institute, February 1997. http://www.justicepolicy.org/images/upload/97–01_REP_Classrooms CellblocksNational_BB.pdf (accessed January 10, 1998).

American Friends Service Committee. "What would you do with a trillion dollars?" http://afsc.org/story/what-would-you-do-trillion-dollars-3 (accessed June 4, 2014).

Amin, Samir. "Rwanda's Proxy's Wars for Imperialist Interest." *Pambazuka News* 675, April 24, 2014, http://www.pambazuka.org/en/category/features/91475 (accessed June 4, 2014).

Anzia, Lys. "U.S: Indigenous Lakota women face harsh winter wrath under climate change." *Women News Network*, November 2, 2010. http://womennewsnetwork.net/2010/11/02/lakota-elderwomen-1008/ (accessed June 3, 2014).

Apuzo, Matt. "War Gear Flows to Police Departments." *New York Times*, June 9, 2014. http://www.nytimes.com/2014/06/09/us/war-gear-flows-to-police-departments.html?src=me&_r=0 (accessed June 9, 2014).

Arsenault, Chris. "Mexican official: CIA 'manages' drug trade," *Al Jazeera*, July 24, 2012, at http://www.aljazeera.com/indepth/features/2012/07/2012721152715628181.html (accessed September 24, 2014).

Associated Press. "Bush: 'We do not torture' terror suspects." November 7, 2005. http://www.nbcnews.com/id/9956644/ns/us_news-security/t/bush-we-do-not-torture-terror-suspects/#.VEc3j97beOI (accessed October 21, 2014).

Atwood, Margaret. "Rachel Carson's Silent Spring, 50 Years On." *The Guardian*, London. December 7, 2012. http://www.theguardian.com/books/2012/dec/07/why-rachel-carson-is-a-saint (accessed June 1, 2014).

Barboza, David. "Foxconn Resolves a Dispute with Some Workers in China." *New York Times*, January 12, 2012. http://www.nytimes.com/2012/01/13/technology/foxconn-resolves-pay-dispute-with-workers.html (accessed January 13, 2012).

Barboza, David, and Charles Duhigg. "In China, Human Costs Are Built Into an iPad." *New York Times*, January 25, 2012. http//www.nytimes.com/2012/01/26/business/ieconomy-apples-ipad-and-the-human-costs-for-workers-in-china.html?pagewanted=all&_r=0 (accessed January 26, 2012).

Bastanmehr, Rod. "Prison Shocker: U.S. Imprisons Three Times as Many Black People as South Africa During Apartheid." *Alternet*, September 20, 2013. http://www.alternet.org/civil-liberties/prison-shocker-us-imprisons-three-times-many-black-people-south-africa-during (accessed October 25, 2014).

Batware, Billy. "Resource Conflicts: The Role of Multinational Corporations in the Democratic Republic of the Congo." May 12, 2011. http://acuns.org/wp-content/uploads/2012/06/RoleofMultinationalCorporations.pdf (accessed June 4, 2014).

Bauman, Dan. "On Campus, Grenade Launchers, M-16s, and Armored Vehicles." *The Chronicle of Higher Education*, September 11, 2014. http://chronicle.com/article/On-Campus-Grenade-Launchers/148749/ (accessed September 11, 2014).

Bazzell, Robert. "US Apologizes for Guatemala Experiments: Government Researchers Infected with Syphilis, Gonorrhoea Without Their Consent in 1940s." October 1, 2010. http://www.nbcnews.com/id/39456324/ns/health-sexual_health/t/us-apologizes-guatemala-std-experiments/#.U4LFhYVvRo (accessed October 2, 2010).

Becker, Jo, and Scott Shane. "Secret 'Kill List' Proves a Test of Obama's Principles and Will." *New York Times*, May 29, 2012. http://www.nytimes.com/2012/05/29/world/obamas-leadership-in-war-on-al-qaeda.html?pagewanted=all (accessed October 21, 2014).

Benbrook, Charles M. "Impacts of genetically engineered crops on pesticide use in the U.S.—the first sixteen years." *Environmental Sciences Europe* 24, no. 24 (2012), September 28, 2012, http://www.enveurope.com/content/241/24/abstract (accessed September 28, 2012).

Berman, Mark. "Video appears to show witnesses reacting to Michael Brown's death." *Washington Post*, September 11, 2014. http://www.washingtonpost.com/news/post-nation/wp/2014/09/11/video-appears-to-show-witnesses-reacting-to-michael-browns-death/ (accessed September 23, 2014).

Bonczar, Thomas P. "Prevalence of Imprisonment in the U.S. Population 1974–2001." *Bureau of Justice Special Report*. U.S. Department of Justice, Office of Justice Programs http://www.cbsnews.com/htdocs/pdf/prisontime.pdf (accessed May 4, 2014).

Bono, Chelsea. "Too Much Money Spent on State Prisons." *Michigan Policy Network: Criminal Justice*, December 17, 2013. http://www.michiganpolicy.com/index.php?option=com_content&view=article&id=1274:too-much-money-spent-on-state-prisons&catid=240:criminal-justice-blog&Itemid=361 (accessed September 22, 2014).

Borger, Julian. "Bush team 'agreed plan to attack the Taliban the day before September 11.'" *The Guardian*, London, March 24, 2004. http://www.theguardian.com/world/2004/mar/24/september11.usa2 (accessed June 4, 2014).

Bravenewfoundation. "We're Being Robbed but the People Doing It Will Never Go to Prison." November 5, 2013. http://www.youtube.com/watch?v=Zmlata0DYQ1Y (accessed January 10, 2014).

Brodwin, David. "How High Prison Costs Slash Education and Hurt the Economy." *U.S. News & World Report*, May 24, 2012. http://www.usnews.com/opinion/blogs/economic-intelligence/2012/05/24/how-high-prison-cost-slash-education-and-hurt-the-economy (accessed September 23, 2014).

Bureau of Investigative Journalism. "More Than 2,400 Dead as Obama's Drone Campaign Marks Five Years." Global Research, Centre for Research on Globalization, Montreal, Canada, January 23, 2014. http://www.globalresearch.ca/more-than-2400-dead-as-obamas-drone-campaign-marks-five-years/5366037 (accessed October 21, 2014).

Burnham, Gilbert, et al. "Iraq: The Human Cost of the War in Iraq: A Mortality Study, 2002–2006." http://web.mit.edu/humancostiraq/reports/human-cost-war-101106.pdf Baltimore: Bloomberg School of Public Health, Johns Hopkins University; Baghdad: School of Medicine, Al-Mustansiriya University, in cooperation with MIT Center for International Studies, October 2006 (accessed May 26, 2014).

Butterfield, Fox. "Death Sentences Being Overturned in 2 of 3 Appeals." *New York Times*, June 12, 2000. http://partners.nytimes.com/library/national/061200death-penalty.html (accessed June 12, 2014).

Byanyima, Winnie, et al. "Two Girls Died Looking for a Toilet. This Should Make Us Angry, Not Embarrassed." *The Guardian*, London, May 31, 2014. http://www.theguardian.com/global-development/2014/jun/01/girls-toilet-rape-murder-anger-embarrassment (accessed June 1, 2014).

California Budget Project. "California Schools Have Experienced Deep Cuts in Funding Since 2007-08." Sacramento, CA, June 7, 2011. http://www.cbp.org/pdfs/2012/120410_K-12_by_District_Budget_Cuts.pdf (accessed October 1, 2014).

Campaign for Hugo Pinell. http://www.hugopinell.com (accessed May 3, 2014).

Campaign to End the Death Penalty. November 2, 2010. http://socialistworker.org/2010/11/02/life-without-possibility (accessed November 3, 2010).

"Cancer Prevention and Control." Center for Disease Control and Prevention. February 3, 2014. http://www.cdc.gov/cancer/dcpc/resources/features/worldcancerday/ (accessed May 30, 2014).

Cantu, Aaron. "Apartheid Wall in Arizona: Israel Company Contracted to Build U.S.–Mexico Border Fence." *Alternet,* March 7, 2014. http://www.alternet.org/civil-liberties/apartheid-wall-arizona-israel-company-contracted-build-us-mexico-border-fence (accessed May 30, 2014).

Carr, David. "Resurrecting a Disgraced Reporter: 'Killing the Messenger' Recalls a Reporter Wrongly Disgraced." *New York Times*, October 2, 2014. http://www.nytimes.com/2014/10/05/movies/kill-the-messenger-recalls-a-reporter-wrongly-disgraced.html?_r=0 (accessed October 3, 2014).

Carrington, Damian, et al. "Environment: How El Nino Will Change the World's Weather in 2014." *The Guardian*, London, June 11, 2014. http://www.guardian.com/environment/2014/jun/11-sp-el-nino-weather-2014 (accessed June 11, 2014).

Carlyle, Erin. "Study Finds 6.4 Million U.S. Homeowners Still Have Underwater Mortgages." *Forbes,* December 17, 2013. http://www.forbes.com/erincarlyle/2013/12/17/6-4-million-still-have-underwater-mortgages-as-of-q3-2013-says-corelogic/ (accessed June 11, 2014).

Casella, Jean, and James Ridgeway. "NYCLU Files Suit Challenging Solitary Confinement in New York State Prisons." *Solitary Watch: News from a Nation in Lockdown.* December 6, 2012. http://solitarywatch.com/2012/12/06/nyclu-files-suit-challenging-solitary-confinement-in-new-york-state-prisons/.

Center for Sustainable Systems, University of Michigan. "Greenhouse Gases." http://css.snre.umich.edu/css_doc/CSS05-21.pdf (accessed February 13, 2014).

Cherry, Flavia. "Women's Resistance to the WTO from Small Island Economies." The Caribbean Gender and Trade Network, January 2004. http://www.choike.org/nuevo_eng/informes/1693.html (accessed June 2, 2014).

Chokshi, Niraj. "School Police Across the Country Receive Excess Military Weapons and Gear." *The Washington Post,* September 16, 2014. http://www.washingtonpost.com/blogs/govbeat/wp/2014/09/16/school-police-across-the-country-receive-excess-military-weapons-and-gear/ (accessed September 23, 2014).

Chossudovsky, Michel. "The Spoils of War: Afghanistan's Multibillion Dollar Heroin Trade: Washington's Hidden Agenda: Restore the Drug Trade." Global Research, Centre for Research on Globalization, Montreal, Canada, June 14, 2005. http://www.globalresearch.ca/the-spoils-of-war-afghanistan-s-multibillion-dollar-heroin-trade/91 (accessed September 24, 2014).

Citizens Commission on Human Rights International: The Mental Health Watchdog. "Behind the Epidemic of Military Suicides," 2014. http://www.cchrint.org/issues/the-hidden-enemy/ (accessed June 19, 2014).

Clark, Andrew. "Ford Sees Ruthless Cost-Costing Pay Off." *The Guardian*, London, January 24, 2008. http://www.theguardian.com/business/2008/jan/25/ford.automotive (accessed January 31, 2008).

Coates, Ta-Nehisi. "Mapping the New Jim Crow: America's Entire History Is Marked by the State Imposing Unfreedom on a Large Swath of the African American Population." *The Atlantic*, October 17, 2014. http://www.theatlantic.com/politics/archive/2014/10/mapping-the-new-jim-crow/381617/ (accessed October 25, 2014).

Cobb, Jeff. "Did the GM and Chrysler Bailouts Do America a Huge Favor?" HybridCars: Auto alternatives for the 21st century.

Complex Mag. "Soul on Ice Beasts: When Rich White People Got to Prison." August 3, 2010. http://www.complex.com/blogs/2010/08/03/soul-on-ice-beasts-when-rich-White-people-go-to-prison/ (accessed October 1, 2011).

Common Sense for Drug Policy. www.csdp.org and www.drugwarfacts.org (accessed February 18, 2014).

Dattaro, Laura. "Washington Mudslide: Survivor Thanks Her Rescuer." Wunderground.com, March 27, 2014. http://www.wunderground. com/news/washington-mudslide-survivor-thanks-her-rescuer-20140327 (accessed March 28, 2014).

Davey, Monica, and Michael S. Schmidt. "Recording May Capture Shots Fired at Michael Brown." *New York Times*, August 26, 2014. http://www.nytimes.com/2014/08/27/us/recording-may-capture-shots-fired-at-michael-brown.html (accessed September 23, 2014).

Davis, Tony, and Tim Steller, "I Baited Jaguar Trap, Research Worker Says." *Arizona Daily Star*, April 2, 2009. http://azstarnet.com/news/science/environment/i-baited-jaguar-trap-research-worker-says/article_8fa21c82-d1c9-5750-ab9a-fd2744565e01.html (accessed June 23, 2014).

Demick, Barbara. "Glaciers in Southern China Receding Rapidly, Scientists Say." *Los Angeles Times*, December 15, 2009. http://articles.latimes. com/2009/dec/15/world/la-fg-china-glacier 15-2009dec15 (accessed March 19, 2014).

Democracy Now! "Exclusive: Freed Ex-Black Panther Marshall 'Eddie' Conway on 44 Years in Prison & FBI Surveillance." March 5, 2014. http://www.democracynow.org/2014/3/5/exclusive_freed_ex_black_panther_marshall (accessed March 5, 2014).

_____. "Oscar Lopez Rivera: After 32 Years in Prison, Calls Grow for Release of Puerto Rican Activist." http://www.democracynow.org/2013/05/5/31/oscar_lopez_rivera_after_32_years (accessed April 16, 2014).

Depillis, Lydia. "Keystone XL's Hired Guns Have John Kerry Connections, but Does It Matter?" *New Republic*, May 8, 2013. http://www.newrepublic.com/article/113161/keystone-xl-lobbyists-john-kerry-connections (accessed May 9, 2013).

Durbin, Dee-Ann. "Chrysler to Pay Back All but $1.3B of Bailout." *USA Today*, June 3, 2011. http://www.usatoday30.usatoday.com/money/autos/2011-06-03-chrysler-bailout-government_n. html (accessed May 8, 2014).

Eckholm, Eric, and John Schwartz. "Timeline Describes Frantic Scene at Oklahoma Execution." *New York Times*, May 2, 2014. http://www.nytimes.com/2014/05/02/us/oklahoma-official-calls-for-outside-review-of-botched-execution.html (accessed May 2, 2014).

"Economic Genocide in Rwanda." http://www.thirdworldtraveler.com/East_Africa/Rwanda_ EconGenocide_GPNWO.html (accessed June 4, 2012).

Editorial Board. "End Mass Incarceration Now." *New York Times*, May 24, 2014. http://www.nytimes.com/2014/05/25/opinion/sunday/end-mass-incarceration-now.html?hp&rref= opinion (accessed June 22, 2014).

Elliott, Eric. "750 Congolese Soldiers Graduate from U.S.–led Military Training, Form Light Infantry Battalion." United States Africa Command, September 20, 2010. http://www.africom. mil/Newsroom/Article/7727/750-congolese-soldiers-graduate-from-us-led-milita (accessed June 4, 2014).

Equal Justice Initiative. "Racial Bias." November 8, 2011. www.eji.org (accessed November 9, 2011).

Eurodad Report. "World Bank and IMF Conditionality: A Development Injustice." June 9, 2006.

Feder, Dan. "Gary Webb's 'Dark Alliance' Returns to the Internet." June 23, 2005. http://www.narconews.com/darkalliance/ (accessed December 12, 2012).

Ferraro, Thomas. "U.S. Senate Democrats Offer Student Debt Refinance Bill." Reuters, May 14, 2014. http://www.reuters.com/article/2014/05/14/us-usa-senate-students-idUSBREA4 D0Q220140514 (accessed June 3, 2014).

Filpovic, Jill. "Is the U.S. the Only Country Where More Men Are Raped Than Women?" *The Guardian*, London, 21 February 2012. http://www.guardian.co.uk/commentisfree/cifamerica/2012/feb/21/us-more-men-raped-than-women (accessed January 20, 2013).

Fimrite, Peter. "1-Year Ban on Chinook Salmon Fishing Proposed." *San Francisco Gate*, March 17, 2008. http://www.sfgate.com/green/article/1-year-ban-on-chinook-salmon-fishing-proposed-3291301.php (accessed June 23, 2014).

Finio, Nicholas, et al. "What Families Need to Get By: The 2013 Update of EPI's Family Budget Calculator." Economic Policy Institute, Washington, D.C., July 3, 2013. http://www.epi.org/publication/ib368-basic-family-budgets/ (accessed June 3, 2014).

Fischer, Brendan, and Lisa Graves. "International Law and the War on Terror." Cost of War, n.d. http://costsofwar.org/sites/default/files/articles/35/attachments/FischerandGraves InternationalLaw.pdf (accessed September 23, 2014).

Fitt, Catherine Austin. "Dillon Read & Co., Inc. and the Aristocracy of Stock Profits." http://www.dunwalke.com/4_Narco_Dollars.htm. n.d. (accessed September 25, 2014).

Flounders, Sarah. "The Pentagon Slave Labor in U.S. Prisons." www.workers.org, June 11, 2011 (accessed June 15, 2011).

Foster, Karen. "37 Million Dead Bees Found in Ontario." July 13, 2013. http://www.under groundhealth.com/37-million-bees-found-dead-in-ontario/ (accessed July 21, 2013.)

Foster, Peter. "CIA 'Tortured al-Qaeda Suspects Close to the Point of Death by Drowning Them in Water-filled Baths.'" The Telegraph, London, September 7, 2014. http://www.telegraph.co.uk/news/worldnews/al-qaeda/11080450/CIA-tortured-al-Qaeda-suspects-close-to-the-point-of-death-by-drowning-them-in-water-filled-baths.html (accessed September 23, 2014).

Franklin, Jonathan. "Tsunami Warning and Evacuation of Thousands After Earthquake in Chile." The Guardian, London, April 2, 2014. http://www.theguardian.com/world/2014/apr/02/chile-earthquake-sparks-tsunami-warning-and-evacuation-of-thousands (accessed April 2, 2014).

Friedman, Howard Steven. "7 OECD Countries with the Highest Incarceration Rates: U.S. and Israel Top List." Huffington Post, July 7, 2011. http://www.huffingtonpost.com/howard-steven-friedman/7-oecd-countries-with-the_b_912680.html#s317353&title=7_Mexico_208 (accessed January 2, 2012).

Friends of the Earth. Email communication, March 11, 2011 (accessible at http://action.foe.org/t/7221/blastContent.jsp?email_blast_KEY=1294429).

Gander, Kashmira. "UK Weather Gets Even FreakIer: After Storms, Floods and Gales—A Bog Fire Raged." The Independent, February 14, 2014. http://www.independent.co.uk/news/uk/home-news/weather-gets-even-freakier-after-storms-and-gales-a-bog-fire-raged-9127516.html (accessed February 15, 2014).

Gelfano, Lauren. "Toxic Waste Spill in Ivory Coast Exposes 'Dark Underbelly' of Globalization." World Politics Review 28 (March 2007). http://www.worldpoliticsreview.com/articles/665/toxic-waste-spill-in-ivory-coast-exposes-dark-underbelly-0f-globalization (accessed February 15, 2014).

Gerrity, Michael. "Special Report: U.S. Homes Lost $1.7 Trillion in Value in 2010, Total Value Destruction Since Market Peak Now $9 trillion, Cost of 12 Iraq Wars." World Property Channel, December 9, 2010.

Ghanizada. "Annual Value of Afghan Opium Trade Reach $70 Billion." Khaama Press, Afghan News Agency, April 29, 2012. http://www.khaama.com/annual-value-of-afghan-opium-trade-reach-70-billion-206 (accessed September 24, 2014).

Gillis, Justin. "Ending Its Summer Melt, Artic Sea Ice Sets a New Low That Leads to Warnings." New York Times, September 19, 2012. http://www.nytimes.com/2012/09/20/science/earth/artic-sea-ice-stops-melting-but-new-record-low-is-set.html (accessed September 20, 2012).

_____. "Panel's Warning on Climate Risk: Worse Is Yet to Come." New York Times, March 31, 2014. http://www.nytimes.nytimes.com/2014/04/01/science/earth/climate.html?emc=eta1 (accessed March 31, 2014).

_____, and Michael Wines. "In Some States, Emissions Cuts Defy Skeptics." New York Times, June 7, 2014. http://www.nytimes.com/2014/06/07/science/in-some-states-emissions-cuts-defy-skeptics.html?emc=edit_th_20140607&n1=todaysheadlines&nlid=40858187&_r=0 (accessed June 8, 2014).

Glass, Stephen. "DON'T YOU D.A.R.E.," New Republic, March 3, 1997. http://druglibrary.net/schaffer/media/txtglass030397.html (accessed June 1, 2014).

Global Policy Forum. "Land Ownership and Hunger." http://www.globalpolicy.org/social-and-economic-policy/world-hunger/land-ownership-and-hunger.html (accessed May 30, 2014).

Goldenberg, Suzanne. "Fracking Is Depleting Water Supplies in America's Driest Areas, Report Shows." The Guardian, London, February 5, 2014. http://www.theguardian.com/environment/2014/feb/05/fracking-water-america-drought-oil-gas (accessed April 2, 2014).

Golinger, Eva. "Ecuador: A Third U.S. Sponsored Coup D'etat Against a Member State of the Bolivarian Alliance of the Americas (ALBA)." http://www.globalresearch.ca/index.php?context=va&=21267 (accessed May 1, 2011).

Gordhan, Pravin. "Why Coal Is the Best Way to Power South Africa's Growth." Washington Post, March 21, 2010. http://www.washingtonpost.com/wp-dyn/content/article/201equences-o0/03/21/AR201003210711.html (accessed March 21, 2014).

Greenpeace USA. "Koch Industries: Still Fueling Climate Denial." http://www.greenpeace.org/usa/en/campaigns/global-warming-and-energy/polluterwatch/koch-industries/ (accessed April 2, 2014).

Greenspan, Allan. "Equities Show Us the Way to Recovery." Financial Times, March 30, 2009. http://www.ft.com/intl/cms/s/0/1e955244-1cc3-11de-977c-00144feabdc0.html#axzz34KmrYAw (accessed April 2, 2009).

"Growth of Corporate Power and Profiteering."

February 2013. http://costsofwar.org/article/ growth-corporate-power-and-profiteering (accessed June 4, 2014).

Hansen, Barbara, et al. "The $100 Million Club: CEOs Get Richer; Workers Left Behind." *USA Today*, April 4–6, 2014. http://www.usatoday. com/story/money/business/2014/04/03/ 2013-ceo-pay/7200481/ (accessed June 10, 2014).

Harris, Gardiner. "Borrowed Time on Disappearing Land: Facing Rising Seas, Bangladesh Confronts the Consequences of Climate Change." *New York Times*, March 28, 2014. http://www. nytimes.com/2014/03/29/world/asia/facing-rising-seas-bangladesh-confronts-the-consequences-of-climate-change.html?emc= eta1 (accessed March 30, 2014).

Hayes, Tandy, et al. "The Four Corners: A National Sacrifice Guide." *The Workbook*, April/June 1985. http://www.bullfrogfilms.com/guides/ 4cguidesSM.pdf (accessed May 30, 2014).

Hennessey, Kathleen. "White House Says Oklahoma Execution 'Fell Short' of Humane Standards." *Los Angeles Times*, April 30, 2014. http: //www.latimes.com/nation/politicsnow/la-pn-white-house-oklahoma-execution-2014 0430-story.html (accessed April 30, 2014).

Hill, Wes. "CIA Admitted Guilt in U.S. Citizen's Death and Addictions: CIA Complicity in Cocaine Distribution." *Progress Report*, January 4, 2002. http://www.progress.org/tpr/cia-admitted-guilt-in-deaths-and-addictions/ (accessed May 3, 2014).

Horowitz, L.G. "Polio, Hepatitis B and AIDS: An Integrative Theory on a Possible Vaccine Induced Epidemic." *Medical Hypothesis* 56, no. 5 (May 2001). http://www.medical-hypothesis. com/article/S0306-9877(00)91171-X/abstract.

http://www.aclu.org/cca?sid=2233547 (accessed June 10, 2014).

http://www.democracynow.org/2014/3/5/ exclusive_freed_ex_black_panther_marshall (accessed March 5, 2014).

http://www.hugopinell.com (accessed May 3, 2014).

http://www.pewcenteronthestates.org/uploaded Files/Statisticspercent20andpercent20Facts. pdf. Pew Charitable Trust, November 2, 2011 (accessed June 1, 2014).

http://www.rightweb.irc-online.org/profile/ project_for_the_new_american_century (accessed January 2010).

http://www.scholarsfor911truth.org. (accessed January 15, 2005).

http://www.un.org/en/development/desa/policy/ wesp/wesp_current/2012wesp_prerel.pdf. (accessed April 21, 2014).

http://veteransinfo.tripod.com/9-23-03dod1. pdf (accessed June 22, 2014).

Ibitayo, Olurominiyi. "Transboundary Dumping of Hazardous Waste." August 26, 2008. http:// www.eoearth.org.article/Trarnsboundary_ dumping_of_hazardous_waste. "Inflation Rears Its Head as Food Prices Rise." NBC News-Reuters, April 11, 2014. http://www.nbcnews. com/business/economy/inflation-rears-its-head-food-prices-rise-again-n77951 (accessed June 3, 2014).

IPCC. *IPCC Second Assessment: Climate Change 1995: A Report of the Intergovernmental Panel on Climate Change.* Geneva: World Meteorological Organization, and Nairobi: United Nations Environment Program, 1995. http:// www.ipcc.ch/pdf/climate-chnages-1995/ipcc-2nd-assessment/2nd-assessment-en.pdf (accessed February 19, 2014).

_____. *IPCC Third Assessment Report—Climate Change 2001:* Working Group 1: The Scientific Basis. GRID-Arendal Publications: A Centre collaborating with UNEP, 2003. http://www. grida.no/publications/other/ipcc%5Ftar/? src=/climate/ipcc_tar/wg1/index.html (accessed February 19, 2014).

Ismi, Asad. "Impoverishing a Continent: The World Bank and IMF in Africa." *Halifax Initiative Coalition* (2004). http://www.halifax initiative.org/updir/ImpoverishingAContinent. pdf (accessed April 22, 2014).

Jamil, Dahir. "'No Safe Levels' of Radiation in Japan: Experts Warn That Any Detectable Level of Radiation Is 'Too Much.'" April 4, 2011. http: //www.aljazeera.com/indepth/features/2011/ 04/20114219250664111.html (accessed March 17, 2014).

Jauregui, Andresi. "Cleveland Police Shooting: Cops Investigate After Firing 137 Shots (Video)." *Huffington Post*, April 12, 2012. http://www. huffingtonpost.com/2012/12/04/cleveland-police-shooting-137-shots-timothy-russell-malissa-williams_n_2239675.html#es_share_ ended (accessed April 30, 2013).

Johnson, Toni. "Economic Challenges for Climate Change Policy." *Council for Foreign Relations*, July 7, 2009. http://www.cfr.org/world/ economic-challenges-climate-change-policy/ p16009 (accessed June 9, 2014).

Kaiser, David, and Lovisa Stannow. *New York Review of Books*, March 24, 2011. http://www. nybooks.com/articles/archives/2011/mar/24/ prison-rape-and-government/?pagination= false (accessed March 31, 2011).

Karmini, Niniek. "Indonesia Volcano Erupts: 100,000 Flee Mount Kelud Eruption That Could Be Heard 200km." *The Independent*, London, February 14, 2014. http://www. independent.co.uk/news/world/asia/indonesia-volcano-erupts-100000-flee-mount-kelud-eruption-that-could-be-heard-200km-away (accessed April 8, 2014).

Karnopp, Kris, and Curt Wagner (eds.). "6 Sentenced to Death for AIDS Experiments on Children." *Chicago Tribune.* May 7, 2004. http://articles.chicagotribune.com/2004-05-ducation07/news/0405080129_1_infecting-aids-virus-cia-and-israel-intelligence (accessed May 30, 2014).

Kearney, Melissa S., Benjamin H. Harris, Elisa Jácome, and Lucie Parker, "Ten Economic Facts About Crime and Incarceration in the United States." Washington D.C.: The Hamilton Project, May 2014. http://www.hamiltonproject.org/files/downloads_and_links/v8_THP_10CrimeFacts.pdf (accessed June 22, 2014).

Ketcham, Christopher. "Radiation from Cellphones and WiFi Are Making People Sick—Are We All at Risk?" *Earth Island Reporter*, December 2, 2011. http://www.alternet.org/story/153299/radiation_from_cell_phones_and_wifi_are_making_people_sick_are_we_all_at_risk?page=entire (accessed June 22, 2014).

Kimbrell, Andrew. "Meet the New Monsanto: Dow Chemical...Their New 'Agent Orange' Crops." *Huffington Post*, February 18, 2014. http://www.huffingtonpost.com/andrew-kimbrell/dow-chemical-agent-orange-crops_b_4810311.html (accessed June 1, 2014).

Knox, Olivier. "Obama: Senate Report Will Show 'We Tortured Some Folks.'" Yahoo News, August 1, 2014. http://news.yahoo.com/obama—senate-report-will-show—we-tortured-some-folks-204712041.html (accessed October 21, 2014).

Kolodner, Meredith. "Private Prisons Expect a Boom: Immigrant enforcement to benefit detention companies." *New York Times*, July 19, 2006. http://www.nytimes.com/2006/07/19/business/19detain.html? (accessed July 16, 2007).

Krauss, Clifford, and John M. Broder, "Deepwater Oil Drilling Begins Again as BP Disaster Fades, *New York Times*, March 4, 2012. http://www.nytimes.com/2012/03/05/business/deepwater-oil-drilling-accelerates-as-bp-disaster-fades.html?pagewanted=all (accessed June 22, 2014).

"Latin America: 70 Million Women Have Jobs Following Gender Reforms." http://web.worldbank.org/WBSITE/EXTERNAL/COUNTRIES/LACEXT/0,contentMDK:22852089~pagePK:146736~piPK:146830~theSitePK:258554,00.html (accessed April 29, 2011).

Lava, Jesse, and Sarah Solon. "Meet the Company

Making $1.4 Billion a Year Off Sick Prisoners." American Civil Liberties Union (ACLU), October 8, 2013. https://www.aclu.org/blog/prisoners-rights/meet-company-making-14-billion-year-sick-prisoners (accessed April 16, 2014).

"Lead from Old U.S. Batteries Sent to Mexico Raises Risks." *New York Times,* December 8, 2011. http://www.nytimes.com/2011/12/09/science/earth/recycled-battery-lead-puts-me (accessed December 9, 2011).

Lee, Don. "Jobless Rate Falls to 8.3%, Cheering a Surprised Wall Street." *Los Angeles Times*, February 6, 2012. http://articles.latimes.com/2012/feb/04/business/la-fi-jobs-20120204 (accessed February 10, 2012).

Leslie, Jacques. "Is Canada Tarring Itself?" Op-Ed, *New York Times*, March 30, 2014. http://www.nytimes.com/2014/03/03/31/opinions/is-canada-tarring-itself.html?emc=eta1&_r=0 (accessed March 30, 2014).

"Maasai Land Protest Ends in Violence." *Mail & Guardian*, August 24, 2004. http//mg.co.za/article/2004-08-24-maasai-land-protest-ends-in-violence (accessed May 30, 2014).

Macadam, David. "The Oligarch Kings: Power, Politics, and America's Noble Families." Blog on The United Fruit Company, May 27, 2010. http://theoligarchkings.wordpress.com/2010/05/27/united-fruit-company/ (accessed October 21, 2014).

Malkin, Elizabeth. "An Apology for a Guatemalan Coup, 57 Years Later." *New York Times*, October 20, 2011. http://www.nytimes.com/2011/10/21/world/americas/an-apology-for-a-guatemalan-coup-57-years-later.html (accessed October 21, 2014).

Malone, Andrew. "The GM Genocide: Thousands of Indian Farmers Are Committing Suicide After Using Genetically Modified Crops." *Mail Online*, London, November 2, 2008. http://www.dailymail.co.uk/news/article-1082559/The-GM-genocide-Thousands-Indian-farmers-committing-suicide-using-genetically-modified-crops.html (accessed April 22, 2014).

Marois, Michael B. "Brown Proposes Record $106.8 Billion California Budget." Bloomberg News, January 9, 2014. http://www.bloomberg.com/news/2014-01-09/brown-proposes-record-california-budget-of-106-8-billion-1-html (accessed April 16, 2014).

Martin, Abby. "How Opium Is Keeping U.S. in Afghanistan: CIA's Shady History of Drug Trafficking." Media Roots, January 3, 2014. http://www.mediaroots.org/opium-what-afghanistan-is-really-about/ (accessed September 24, 2014).

Mazza, Ed. "Sean Groubert, South Carolina State Trooper, Fired & Arrested After Shooting Unarmed Man." *Huffington Post*, September 25, 2014. http://www.huffingtonpost.com/2014/09/25/sean-groubert-fired-arrested_n_58796 94.html (accessed September 26, 2014).

McCarthy, Michael. "A Cloud of Nuclear Mistrust Spreads Across the World." *The Independent,* London, March 16, 2011. http://www.independent.co.uk/news/world/asia/four-explosions-two-fires-and-a-cloud-of-nuclear-mistrust-spreads-around-the-world-2242988.html (accessed March 21, 2011).

McCluskey, Lindsay. "Investing in Prisons Over Education Is Not Being Smart on Crime." *Huffington Post: Education*, July 27, 2011. http://www.huffingtonpost.com/lindsay-mccluskey/investing-in-prisons-over_b_868081.html (accessed September 23, 2014).

McMurtrie, Beth. "Botched Execution in Oklahoma Is Part of a Pattern, Says Amherst Scholar." *Chronicle of Higher Education*, May 1, 2014. http://chronicle.com/article/Botched-Execution-in-Oklahoma/146303/ (accessed May 4, 2014).

Minh, Tran Van. "Floods Continue to Punish Asia." *Natal Mercury*, South Africa, October 7, 2010. http://www.iol.co.za/news/world/floods-continue-to-punish-asia-1.684275#.U5zpZR bbfRo (accessed October 8, 2010).

Mirak-Weissbach, Muriel. "Global Food Crisis: Egypt and Sudan Join Forces for Food Security." Global Research, May 27, 2008. http://www.globalresearch.ca/index.php?context=va&aid=9082.

Mohan, Geoffrey. "Climate Change May Be Baring Mt. Everest." *Los Angeles Times*, May 14, 2013. http://articles.latimes.com/2013/may/14/science/la-sci-sn-everest-climate-20130514 (accessed March 19, 2014).

Monbiot, George. "The Denial Industry." *The Guardian*, London, September 18, 2006. http://www.theguardian.com/environment/2006/sep/19/ethicalliving.g2 (accessed April 2, 2014).

Moncada, Samuel. "Isn't It Time to Respect Venezuela's Democracy?" CNN Opinion, February 22, 2013. http://www.cnn.com/2013/02/18/opinion/venezuela-democracy-moncada/ (accessed June 22, 2014).

Moodie, Alison. "AFRICA: Universities Must Halt 'Land Grab Investments.'" *University World News: The Global Window on Higher Education* 177 (June 26, 2011). http://www.universityworldnews.com/article.php?story=20110625122929338 (accessed May 30, 2014).

Morin, Roc. "Former Undercover Drug Narc on Why Police Don't Bust White people and How He Turned Against Drug War." *Alternet*, March 14, 2014. http://www.alternet.org/drugs/former-undercover-drug-narc-why-police-dont-bust-white-people-and-how-he-turned-against-drug?akid=11622.305522.j95WzW&rd=1&src=newsletter972398&t=8 (accessed March 20, 2014).

Murphy, Dylan. "Money Laundering and the Drug Trade: The Role of the Banks." Global Research, Centre for Research on Globalization, Montreal, Canada, October 20, 2013. http://www.globalresearch.ca/money-laundering-and-the-drug-trade-the-role-of-the-banks/5334205 (accessed September 24, 2014).

Mydan, Seth. "Myanmar Reels as Cyclone Tolls Hit Thousands." *New York Times*, May 8, 2008. http://www.nytimes.com/gst/fullpage.html?res=9C0CE48153AF935A35756C0A96E9C8B63&ref=cyclonenargis (accessed March 19, 2014).

National Oceanic and Atmospheric Administration. "What Is Coral Bleaching?" http://oceanservice.noaa.gov/facts/coral_bleach.html (accessed June 1, 2014).

New York State Department of Labor and Empire State Development. "The Offshore Outsourcing of Information Technology Jobs in New York State: A Report to David A. Patterson, Governor, and the Legislature of State of New York." September 2010. http://labor.ny.gov/stats/PDFs/Offshore_Outsourcing_IT Jobs_NYS.pdf (accessed June 10, 2014).

Nguyen, Anuchit, and Suttinee Yuvejwattana. "Thai Farmers Lose Pickup Trucks as Protests Raise Debt Risk." Bloomberg News, February 24, 2014. http//www.bloomberg.com/news/2014-02-23/thai-farmers-lose-pickup-trucks-as-protests-increase-debt-risk.html (accessed April 22, 2014).

Nimmo, Kurt. "CIA, FBI and Now Academic Mercenaries on the Ground in Ukraine." Global Research, Center for Research on Globalization, Montreal, May 12, 2014. http://www.globalresearch.ca/cia-fbi-and-now-academi-mercenaries-on-the-ground-in-ukraine/5381875 (accessed June 4, 2014).

"No Such Thing as a Safe Dose of Radiation." Nuclear Information and Resource Center, Tacoma Park, MD. www.nirs.Org (accessed November 2011).

Norrell, Brenda. http://bsnorrell.blogspot.com/2012/09/debra-white-plume-sacred-water.html (accessed December 2012).

Nyakweri Forest Restoration Project. www.nyakweri.arizona.edu (accessed December 2012).

Oblack, Rachel. "Cyclone Nargis Storm Statistics." About.com: Weather, May 2008. http://weather.about.com/od/hurricanes/qt/nargisfacts.htm (accessed April 26, 2014).

"Oil Spill Disaster New Zealand's 'Worst in Decades.'" *BBC News*, October 11, 2011. http://www.bbc.co.uk/news/world-asia-pacific-15251319 (accessed October 12, 2011).

On the Issues: Every Political Leader on Every Issue. http://www.ontheissues.org/international/Jeff_Flake_Energy_+_Oil.htm (accessed April 2, 2014).

Operate Ghetto Storm: 2012 Annual Report of Extrajudicial Killings of 313 Black People by Police, Security Guards and Vigilantes. Malcolm X Grassroots Movement, April 13, 2013. http://www.operationghettostorm.org/uploads/1/9/1/1/19110795/operation_ghetto_storm.pdf (accessed April 14, 2013).

Parramore, Lynne Stewart. "More Than Half of Black College Graduates Underemployed." *AlterNet*, May 23, 2014. http://www.alternet.org/education/more-half-black-college-graduate-underemployed (accessed May 26, 2014).

Pearce, Matt. "In Victim's Oklahoma Home Town, No Tears for Inmate in Botched Execution." *Los Angeles Times*, May 6, 2014. http://www.latimes.com/nation/la-na-execution-town-20140506-story.html (accessed May 6, 2014).

Pelaez, Vicky. "The Prison Industry in the United States: Big Business or a New Form." *Global Research* 10 (March 2008). Montreal, Center for Research on Globalization. http://www.globalresearch.ca/the-prison-industry-in-the-united-states-big-business-or-a-new-form-of-slavery (accessed December 8, 2013).

Pollack, Andrew. "Coalition Drops Opposition to a Dow Engineered Crop." *New York Times*, September 11, 2012, at http://www.nytimes.com/2012/09/12/business/energy-environment/coalition-drops-opposition-to-dows-genetically-engineered-crops.html (accessed September 15, 2012).

Porter, Eduardo. "In the U.S., Punishment Comes Before the Crimes." *New York Times*, April 29, 2014. http://www.nytimes.com/2014/04/30/business/economy/in-the-us-punishment-comes-before-the-crimes.html (accessed May 3, 2014).

Prann, Elizabeth. "States Spend Almost Four Times More Per Capita on Incarcerating Prisoners than Educating Students, Studies Say." Fox News: Politics, March 14, 2011. http://www.foxnews.com/politics/2011/03/14/states-spend-times-incarcerating-educating-studies-say-464156987/ (accessed September 23, 2014).

Project for a New Century. http://www.rightweb.

irc-online.org/profile/project_for_the_new_american_century (accessed May 3, 2014).

Quizon, Derek. "Defining 'Nearly Free': Students, Experts debate Meaning of Arizona Constitution Clause." statepress.com, October 8, 2009. http://www.statepress.com/archive/node/8199 (accessed September 23, 2014).

Prupis, Nadia. "Cash-Strapped States Resurrect 'Debtors' Prisons." *Truthout Report*, October 6, 2010. http://www.truth-out.org/punishing-poor-being-poor63949 (accessed November 8, 2010).

Radiation Truth. "The Myth of Low-Level Radiation." http://www.radiationtruth.org/the-myth-of-low-level-radiation/ (accessed May 1, 2014).

Ramsey, Geoffrey. "US Border Patrol Agent Arrested for Smuggling Drugs on the Job." *Insight Crime: Organized Crime in the Americas*, December 6, 2012, at http://www.insightcrime.org/news-briefs/border-patrol-agent-arrested-smuggling-drugs (accessed September 24, 2014).

Rappeport, Allan. "Record Falls in Net Worth of U.S. Citizens." *Financial Times*, March 13, 2009. http://www.ft.com/intl/cms/s/0/6369a6e6-0f70-11de-ba10-0000779fd2ac.html (accessed March 14, 2009).

Richards, Martha. "A Look at Human Trafficking in South Africa." Africa Stories, April 8, 2010. http://www.africastories.org/human-trafficking/a-look-at-trafficking-south-africa/ (accessed June 2, 2014).

Richards, Stephen C. "USP Marion: The First Federal Supermax." *The Prison Journal* 88, no. 1 (March 2008): 6–22.

Roodman, David. "Grameen Bank, Which Pioneered Loans for the Poor, Has Hit a Repayment Snag." http://blogs.cgdev.org/open_book/2010/02/grameen-bank-which-pioneered-loans-for-the-poor-has-hit-a-repayment-snag.php (accessed April 18, 2012).

Romero, Simon. "Violence Hits Brazil Tribes in Scramble for Land." *New York Times,* June 9, 2012. http://www.nytimes.com/2012/06/10/world/americas/in-brazil-violence-hits-tribes-in-scramble-for-land.html?r=0 (accessed June 10, 2012).

Royal, Robert. "Who Put the West in Western Civilization?" *Intercollegiate Review*, Spring 1998. http://www.mmisi.org/ir/33_02/royal.pdf (accessed June 2, 2014).

Russian Times. "Afghan Drug Trafficking Brings U.S. $50 Billion a Year." May 29, 2010. http://rt.com/usa/afghanistan-us-drug-trafficking/ (accessed September 24, 2014).

_____. "1 mn Died from Afghan Heroin, Drug Production '40 Times Higher' Since NATO op,"

April 3, 2013. http://rt.com/news/afghanistan-heroin-production-increased-266/ (accessed September 1, 2014).

Ryman, Anne. "GOP Ad Blasts Duval for Tuition Hikes." *The Arizona Republic*, August 29, 2014. http://www.azcentral.com/story/news/arizona/politics/2014/08/29/gop-ad-blasts-duval-tuition-hikes/14782759/ (accessed September 23, 2014).

Sample, Ian. "Scientists Condemn 'Crazy Dangerous' Creation of Deadly Airborne Flu Virus." *The Guardian*, London, June 11, 2014. http://www.theguardian.com/science/2014/jun/11/crazy-dangerous-creation-deadly-airborne-flu-virus (accessed June 11, 2014).

Sarno, David. "Apple Market Value Hits $500 Billion and Counting." *Los Angeles Times*, February 29, 2012. http://articles.latimes.com/2012/feb/29/business/la-fi-apple-value-20120301 (accessed March 1, 2012).

Saul, Heather. "Saharan Dust Lands in England as 'Very High' Levels of Air Pollution Warned This Week." *The Independent*, London, April 2, 2014. http://www.independent.co.uk/environment/climate-change/england-braced-for-very-high-levels-of-air-pollution-this-week-9231449.html?utm_source=indynewsletter&utm_medium=email02042014 (accessed April 2, 2014).

Scalia, Tiffany Lucienne. "How Dole Got Away with Poisoning Banana Workers." http://news.change.org/stories/stories/how-dole-got-away-with-poisoning-banana-workers. March 28, 2012 (accessed April 30, 2014).

Scannell, Kara, and Matthew Rose. "Martha Stewart Is Found Guilty of All Charges" *Wall Street Journal*, March 7, 2004. http://online.wsj.com/articles/SB107833235519345426 (accessed September 25, 2014).

Scarpinato, Daniel. "Duval's Tuition Hikes Take Center Stage." Special to Tucson Local Media, Guest Column. http://tucsonlocalmedia.com/northwest_chatter/article_e7498348-3858-11e4-b944-0019bb2963f4.html?mode=jqm (accessed September 23, 2014).

Schaeffer, Robert. "Globalization and Disintegration: Substitutionist Technologies and Disintegration of Global Economic Ties." *Frontiers of Globalization Research: Theoretical and Methodical Approaches*. Ed. Ino Rossi, New York: Springer, 2008. http://www.bloomberg.com/quicktake/chinas-managed-markets/ (accessed May 1, 2009).

Schlosser, Eric. "The Prison Industrial Complex." *The Atlantic* December 1998. www.theatlantic.com/doc/199812/prisons (accessed July 10, 2012).

Schmitt, Eric. "U.S. Training Antiterror Elite Troops in Four African Countries." *New York Times*, May 27, 2014. http://www.nytimes.com/2014/05/27/world/africa/us-trains-african-commandos-to-fight-terrorism.html?emc=eta_I (accessed May 27, 2014).

Schuessler, Jennifer. "Lessons from Ants to Grasp Humanity." *New York Times*, April 8, 2012. http://www.nytimes.com/2102/04/09/books/edward-o-wilsons-new-book-social-conquest-of-earth.html? (accessed April 18, 2012)

Shabnov, Vladimir. "Poverty in Russia Grows Faster Than Expected." *Pravda* (English), July 4, 2011. english.pravda.ru/business/finance/04-07-2011/118392-poverty_russia-0/ (accessed April 22, 2014).

Shah, Annup. "Structural Adjustment: A Major Cause of Poverty." *Global Issues: Social, Political, Economic and Environmental Issues That Affect Us All*. March 24, 2013. http://www.globalissues.org/article/3/structural-adjustment-a-major-cause-of-poverty (accessed April 22, 2014).

Shoener, Nicole. "Three Strikes Laws in Different States." *Legal Match*, May 23, 2014. http://www.legalmatc.com/law-library/article/three-strikes-laws-in-different-states.html (accessed May 26, 2014).

Skiba, Katherine. "Settlement Announced Over Countrywide Loans." *Chicago Tribune*, December 21, 2011. http://articles.chicagotribune.com/2011-12-21/news/chi-settlement-announced-over-countrywide-loans-20111221_1_country wide-loans-dan-frahm-full-spectrum-lending (accessed October 4, 2014).

Smithson, Shelley. "Senate Candidates Weigh in on Climate Change, Uranium Mining." *KNAU and Arizona News*, October 25, 2012. http://knau.org/post/senate-candidates-weigh-climate-change-uranium-mining (accessed April 2, 2014).

Socio-Economics History Blog: Socio-Economics & History Commentary. January 21, 2011. http://socioecohistory.wordpress.com/2011/01/21/ex-cia-official-patriot-act-a-nazi-law/ (accessed June 20, 2014).

Spivak, Marla. "Why Bees Are Disappearing." June 2013. http://www.ted.com/talks/marla_spivak_why_bees_are_disappearing?source=googleplus#t-816678 (accessed June 1, 2014).

Sterling, Eric E., and Julie Stewart. "Undo This Legacy of Len Bias's Death." *Washington Post*, June 24, 2006. http://www.washingtonpost.com/wp-dyn/content/article/2006/06/23/AR2006230261.html (accessed May 3, 2014).

Sullivan, Laura. "Bail Burden Keeps U.S. Jails Stuffed with Inmates." *NPR: All Things Considered*, January 21, 2010. http://www.npr.org/

2010/01/21/122725771/Bail-Burden-Keeps-U-S-Jails-Stuffed-With-Inmates (accessed September 15, 2014).

_____. "Prison Economics Help Drive Ariz Immigration Law." *National Public Radio*, October 28, 2010. http://www.npr.org/templates/story.php?storyId=130833741 (accessed October 29, 2010).

Talvi, Silja J.A. "American Correctional Association: Exposed at Last." *In These Times*, February 28, 2005. http://www.capp.50megs.com/aca_part1.html (accessed January 26, 2006).

Terrell, S. "Audit: N.M. Private Prison Costs Soar Exit Notice." *New American*, May 24, 2007. Cited in Gerry Gaes. "Cost, Performance Studies Look at Prison Privatization." http://www.ojp.usdoj.gov/nij/journals/259/welcome.htm (accessed June 15, 2007).

Toch, H. "The Future of Supermax Confinement." *The Prison Journal* 81, no. 3, 376–388.

The IUCN Red List of Threatened Species. "New study shows over one fifth of the world's plants are under threat of extinction." September 29, 2010. http://www.iucnredlist.org/news/srli-plants-press-release (accessed June 25, 2014).

UN Declaration on the Rights of Indigenous Peoples. http://www.un.org/esa/socdev/unpfii/documents/DRIPS_en.pdf (accessed May 11, 2014).

UNESCO Institute for Statistics. National literacy rates for youths (15–24) and adults (15+). http://www.uis.unesco.org December 2011 (accessed January 10, 2012).

Union of Concerned Scientists. "Car Emissions and Global Warming." http://www.ucsusa.org/clean_vehicles/why-clean-cars/global-warming/ (accessed May 14, 2014).

Urbina, Ian. "Using Jailed Migrants as a Pool of Cheap Labor." *New York Times*, May 25, 2014. http://www.nytimes.com/2014/05/25/us/using-jailed-migrants-as-a-pool-of-cheap-labor.html (accessed May 26, 2014).

U.S. Geological Survey: Science Information and Library Services. *The Everglades: What You Need to Know*. http://online.wr.usgs.gov/outreach/landpeople/students/ever_area.html (accessed March 28, 2014).

_____. *Science Features, Landslide in Washington State*. March 26, 2014. http://www.usgs.gov/blogs/features/usgs_top_story/landslide-in-washington-state/?from=title (accessed March 28, 2014).

United States Nuclear Regulatory Commission. "Backgrounder on Chernobyl Nuclear Power Plant Accident." May 2013. http://www.nrc.gov/reading-rm/doc-collections/fact-sheets/chernobyl-bg.html (accessed March 15, 2014).

United States Space Command. *Vision for 2020*. United States Space Command, Peterson Air Force Base, 1997. http://fas.org/spp/military/docops/usspac/visbook.pdf (accessed September 23, 2014).

Velasquez, Carmen. "Obama Broke His Promise to Latinos (Maybe We Should Sit This Election Out)." Common Dreams, September 9, 2014. http://www.commondreams.org/views/2014/09/09/obama-broke-his-promise-latinos-maybe-we-should-sit-election-out (accessed September 9, 2014).

Wahlberg, David. "UW-Madison Scientists Creates New Flu Virus in Lab." *Wisconsin State Journal*, June 11, 2014. http://host.madison.com/wsi/news/local/health_med_fit/uw-madison-scientist-creates-new-flu-virus-in-lab/article_4ccdcb40-cfdc-5d2c-a02d-ffb30a84b53.html (accessed June 11, 2014).

Warren, Jenifer, and Maura Dolen. "Tookie Williams Is Executed." *Los Angeles Times*, December 13, 2005. http://articles.latimes.com/2005/dec/13/local/me-execution13 (accessed December 14, 2005).

Werdigier, Julia. "Dutch-Trade Fund Moves Toward Collapse." *New York Times*, March 14, 2008. http://www.nytimes.com/2008/03/14/business/worldbusiness/14carlyle.html (accessed March 15, 2008).

Westcott, Lucy. "Heavy Cellphone Use Could Actually Cause Brain Cancer (Maybe)." *The Wire: what matters now*. May 13, 2014. http://www.thewire.com/national/2014/05/heavy-cell phone-use-could-actually-cause-brain-cancer-maybe/370818/ (accessed May 30, 2014).

Western, Bruce, and Becky Pitt. "Incarceration and Social Inequality." *Daedalus* 139, no. 3 (Summer 2010): 8–10. http://www.mitpressjournals.org/doi/pdf/10.1162/DAED_a_00019 (accessed August 31, 2010).

"Western Shoshone Land and Sovereignty." http://www.umass.edu/legal/derrico/shoshone/ (accessed May 30, 2014).

Whitty, Julia. "Gone: Mass Extinction and the Hazards of Earth's Vanishing Biodiversity." *Mother Jones*, May/June 2007. http://www.motherjones.com/environment/2007/05/gone (accessed June 1, 2014).

Williams, Paige. "Witnesses to a Botched Execution." *The New Yorker*, April 30, 2014. http://www.newyorker.com/online/blogs/newsdesk/2014/04/witnesses-to-a-botched-execution.html (accessed May 26, 2014).

Williams, Rob. "Chile Earthquake: Tsunami Warning Triggered, Thousands Evacuated and Six Killed as Area Declared a Disaster Zone." *The Independent*, London, April 2, 2014. http://

www.independent.co.uk/news/world/ americas/chile-earthquake-disaster-declared- after-huge-quake-generates-tsunami-kills-five- and-prompts-mass-evacuations-9231484html (accessed April 2, 2014).

Wilson, E. O. "My Wish: Build the Encyclopedia of Life." March 2007. http://www.ted.com/ talks/e_o_wilson_on_saving_life_on_earth (accessed May 1, 2014).

Windham, Christopher. "After 20 Years, the De- bate Over Mandatory Minimum Sentencing Laws for Cocaine Heats Up." *Human Nature Magazine*, June 20, 2010. http://www.human naturemag.com/index.php?option=com_ content&view=article&id=131:after-20-years- the-debate-over-mandatory-minimum- sentencing-laws-for-cocaine-heats-up&catid= 38:political-science&Itemid=598 (accessed October 24, 2014).

Winston, Ali. "US Police Get Anti-Terror Train- ing in Israel on Privately Funded Trips." The Center for Investigative Reporting, Sacramento, CA, September 16, 2014. https://beta.ciron line.org/reports/us-police-get-antiterror-train- ing-in-israel-on-privately-funded-trips/ (ac- cessed September 23, 2014).

Wood, Graeme. "A Boom Behind Bars." *Bloom- berg Businessweek Magazine*, March 17, 2011. http://www.businessweek.com/magazine/ content/11_13/b4221076266454.html (ac- cessed March 20, 2011).

"World Economic Situation and Prospects 2012." United Nations Organization, New York, 2011.

Your Black World. "Samuel L. Jackson Warns Black Men That It's 'Open Season.'" Tweet, August 9, 2013. http://www.yourblackworld. net/2013/08/black-celebrities/samuel-L- jackson-warns-black-men-that-its-open- season/ (accessed May 4, 2013).

"Zimbabwe Accuses De Beers of Looting Dia- monds." March 5, 2010. http//www.globalpolicy. org/security-council/dark-side-of-natural- resources/diamonds-in-conflict/debates-and- articles-on-diamonds-in-conflict/48826.html (accessed June 4, 2014).

Newspapers, Periodicals

Arizona Daily Star
Arizona Republic
The Atlantic
Baltimore Sun
Bloomberg Businessweek Magazine
Bloomberg News
Business Report, South Africa
Chicago Tribune
The China Post, Beijing
Chronicle of Higher Education
City Press, Johannesburg, South Africa
The Crisis
The Economist, London
The Guardian, London
Huffington Post
Human Rights Report
Independent, London
Indian Express, Delhi
In These Times
Mail & Guardian, South Africa
Manila Standard Today, Philippines
Natal Mercury, Durban, South Africa
National Geographic Daily News
New Republic
The New York Review of Books
New York Times
The New Yorker
The Observer
Pravda (English), Russia
Progress Report
Russian Times, Moscow
San Bernardino County Sun
Vancouver Sun
Washington Post
The Witness, Pietermaritzburg, South Africa
World Press Review

Index

Numbers in **bold italics** indicate pages with photographs.